T0304782

PRINCIPLES OF CONTEMPORARY CORPORATE GOVERNANCE

Fourth edition

Now in its fourth edition, *Principles of Contemporary Corporate Governance* offers comprehensive coverage of the key topics and emerging themes in private sector corporate governance. It explains both the principles of corporate governance systems and their real-world application in an authoritative and engaging manner.

This fully revised and updated text has four parts: basic concepts, board structures and company officers; corporate governance in Australia; corporate governance in international and global contexts; and shareholder activism and business ethics. The coverage of international contexts, written by specialists, includes sections on the US, the UK, Canada, South Africa, the EU, the OECD, Germany, Japan, China and Indonesia, plus new sections on New Zealand and India. A new chapter on business ethics and corporate governance presents contemporary discussions on the topic and explores some of the broader legal issues.

Principles of Contemporary Corporate Governance is an indispensable resource for business and law students studying corporate governance, and also for academic researchers and practitioners wanting a deeper understanding of its underlying principles.

Jean Jacques du Plessis is Professor (Corporate Law) in the Deakin Law School, Deakin University.

Anil Hargovan is Associate Professor in the School of Taxation and Business Law at the University of New South Wales.

Jason Harris is Associate Professor in the Faculty of Law at the University of Technology Sydney.

PRINCIPLES OF CONTEMPORARY CORPORATE GOVERNANCE

Fourth edition

Jean Jacques du Plessis,
Anil Hargovan and Jason Harris

Contributors

Vivienne Bath, Indrajit Dube, Irene-marié Esser,
Miko Kamal, Souichirou Kozuka,
Suzanne Le Mire, Jeanne Nel de Koker,
Luke Nottage and Susan Watson

CAMBRIDGE
UNIVERSITY PRESS

Shaftesbury Road, Cambridge CB2 8EA, United Kingdom

One Liberty Plaza, 20th Floor, New York, NY 10006, USA

477 Williamstown Road, Port Melbourne, VIC 3207, Australia

314–321, 3rd Floor, Plot 3, Splendor Forum, Jasola District Centre, New Delhi – 110025, India

103 Penang Road, #05–06/07, Visioncrest Commercial, Singapore 238467

Cambridge University Press is part of Cambridge University Press & Assessment,
a department of the University of Cambridge.

We share the University's mission to contribute to society through the pursuit of
education, learning and research at the highest international levels of excellence.

www.cambridge.org
Information on this title: www.cambridge.org/9781108413022

First published 2005
Second edition 2011
Third edition 2015
Fourth edition 2018 (version 3, April 2019)

Cover designed by Cameron McPhail

A catalogue record for this publication is available from the British Library

A Cataloguing-in-Publication entry is available from the catalogue of the National Library of Australia at
www.nla.gov.au

ISBN   978-1-108-41302-2   Paperback

Additional resources for this publication at www.cambridge.edu.au/academic/principles

CONTENTS

PART 4   SHAREHOLDER ACTIVISM AND BUSINESS ETHICS

AUTHORS AND CONTRIBUTORS

Authors

Jean Jacques du Plessis is a Professor (Corporate Law) in the Deakin Law School, Deakin University. He developed and taught a 1-year corporate governance Graduate Diploma in South Africa in 1998 (this was one of the first such courses in the world). He also developed a Corporate Governance Postgraduate Unit (MLM706) for Deakin University in 2004 and redirected the content of that Unit to reflect the content of the first edition of *Principles of Contemporary Corporate Governance*. Jean also publishes actively in the area of corporate governance, with more than 100 articles published in refereed Australian and international journals. He is co-author of 10 books, published in Australia, Germany and South Africa. He is an Alexander von Humboldt Scholar and received the Anneliese Maier Research Award from the Alexander von Humboldt Foundations for a 5-year period (2013–18). He assisted the South African Government with its Corporate Law Reform Program. This resulted in the South African *Companies Act 71 of 2008*, which became law in April 2012. He has been involved in that Reform Program since 2004. He was also the Head of the Deakin Law School (2000–02), President of the Corporate Law Teachers Association (CLTA) (2008–09) and became a graduate of the Australian Institute of Company Directors (AICD) in October 2011. Jean teaches in the areas of corporate governance, corporate law and business law. He was co-editor of the *Deakin Law Review* in 2012 and currently serves on the editorial board of the *European Journal of Economics and Management*.

Anil Hargovan is an Associate Professor in the School of Taxation and Business Law at the University of New South Wales (UNSW). His research interests are in the area of corporate and insolvency law, a discipline in which he has presented many conference papers and published widely in refereed Australian and international law journals. His academic work, which includes over 110 publications, has been cited by the Corporations and Markets Advisory Committee and the judiciary. He has been a guest editor of the *Australian Journal of Corporate Law* and currently serves on the editorial board of the *Insolvency Law Bulletin*. Anil has authored and co-authored several books, including *Australian Corporate Law* (LexisNexis, 2016). He was President of the Corporate Law Teachers Association (CLTA) in 2011–12 and is currently a member of the Executive Committee of the CLTA. Anil currently serves on the Corporate Governance Subject Advisory Committee and on the Applied Corporate Law Subject Advisory Committee at the Governance Institute of Australia. He has conducted the Corporate Governance course in the MBA program at the Australian Graduate School of Management at UNSW.

Jason Harris is an Associate Professor in the Faculty of Law at the University of Technology, Sydney (UTS), where he teaches corporate law, insolvency and commercial law. Jason is the President of the Australian Corporate Law Teachers' Association (CLTA) for 2017. Jason's research interests are primarily in the area of directors' duties, corporate groups and disclosure obligations. Jason has written extensively on these areas. He has published 12 books and over 90 articles in scholarly and professional journals. Jason's research has been cited in the Federal Court of Australia and the Supreme Courts of NSW, South Australia and Western Australia, and by the Corporations and Markets Advisory Committee. Jason is a Fellow of Governance Institute of Australia (and is the Chair of its National Education Committee), a member of the Corporations and Insolvency Committees of the Law Council of Australia, a member of the academic executive committee of the Banking and Financial Services Law Association and an academic member of the Australian Restructuring, Insolvency and Turnaround Association.

Contributors

Vivienne Bath is Professor of Chinese and International Business Law at the University of Sydney. She has first-class honours in Chinese and in Law from the Australian National University (ANU), and a Master of Laws from Harvard University. Prior to joining the Faculty of Law, she was a partner in international firm Coudert Brothers, working in the Hong Kong and Sydney offices and specialising in commercial law, with a focus on foreign investment and commercial transactions in the People's Republic of China. Vivienne is the co-author of Burnett and Bath, *International Business Law in Australasia* (Federation Press, 2009) and has published widely in the area of Chinese law and international business law. She is a frequent participant in conferences and seminars focusing on developments in international economic law and the Chinese legal regime.

Indrajit Dube (PhD) is an Associate Professor at Rajiv Gandhi School of Intellectual Property Law, Indian Institute of Technology Kharagpur, India. His areas of specialisation include corporate laws and corporate governance. He has numerous publications in refereed journals published from India and abroad. His writings are mainly focused on independent directors, directors liability, integrated reporting, corporate social responsibility, and corporate governance in energy sector. He has several books to his credit. His book on corporate governance, published by LexisNexis Butterworths, is widely referred in national and international institutes of eminence. He has conducted about 20 funded projects from agencies both national and international. He has led the team on development of institutional framework of the Indian Institute of Corporate Affairs, New Delhi, India's premier Institute of Corporate Law Governance and Research, set up under the aegis of the Indian Ministry of Corporate Affairs. He has also been a Visiting Faculty member at the University of Western Ontario, Canada (2010), and the University of British Columbia, Canada (2011). He delivered the Kirby Lecture Series at the School of Law, University of New England, Australia (2016). He participated in multi-stakeholder expert consultations in Toronto in support of the mandate of Prof. John G. Ruggie, the Special Representative of the United Nations on Business and Human Rights (2009).

Irene-marié Esser is a Professor *Extraordinarius* at the University of South Africa (UNISA), a Visiting Professor at the Open University, UK and a Senior Lecturer in Commercial Law at the University of Glasgow. She is also an expert panel member of the EU/Africa Chamber of

Commerce. In South Africa she was Professor and Co-Subject Head of Corporate Law at UNISA until March 2013, when she relocated, with her family, to Edinburgh, Scotland. Irene-marié obtained her LLB at Stellenbosch University (2001), her LLM at the University of Aberdeen, Scotland (2003) and her LLD at UNISA (2008). She is also an admitted attorney of the High Court of South Africa. Irene-marié's research interests are primarily in the area of directors' duties, corporate social responsibility and stakeholder protection, and she publishes widely in this field. She was a contributor of the first edition of the leading textbook *Henochsberg on the Companies Act 71 of 2008* and contributes to the company law chapter in the *Annual Survey of South African Law*. She is also the co-editor of the *Corporate Governance Annual Review*. During 2009 Irene-marié received the 'Women in Research: Youngest staff member with a doctorate degree' award at UNISA, as well as the Principal's Prize for Excellence in Research. During 2016 Irene-marié was awarded, as co-winner, the prize for the best article published in the *Journal of Contemporary Roman Dutch Law* for the co-authored work: Esser and Delport, 'Shareholder protection in terms of the Companies Act 71 of 2008'. Irene-marié has also been presenting workshops and seminars for professionals working in the field of corporate governance, and a 4-day workshop on board governance, for eight years, at the University of Johannesburg. She redeveloped this course extensively during 2015. Irene-marié acted as an external advisor to the South African *King IV Report on Corporate Governance*. She currently teaches Corporate Governance, Corporate Social Responsibility and Company Law and supervises postgraduate research students in South Africa and the UK.

Miko Kamal is a legal governance specialist. He is the principal of Miko Kamal & Associates. He completed his Doctor of Philosophy (PhD) at Macquarie University, Sydney, in 2012. His thesis was titled 'The Role of Board of Commissioners in Creating Good Governance of Indonesia's State-owned Enterprises'. Miko also completed a Master of Law (Commercial Law) in 2003 at Deakin University, Australia, and a Bachelor of Law (Constitutional Law) in 1996 at Bung Hatta University, Indonesia. His work has been published in several international and national academic and professional journals and books, and in print media. His main focus is on anti-corruption policies and strategy, governance (private and public sectors) and boards of commissioners in state-owned enterprises. He is a licensed advocate and member of the Indonesian Advocates Association (PERADI) and has been practising since 1996. He teaches at Bung Hatta University in addition to working as a lawyer. At the end of 2016, the Government of Padang appointed him as a chief of commissioner of a municipality-owned enterprise.

Souichirou Kozuka is a Professor at Gakushuin University, Tokyo. He holds a PhD in Law from Tokyo University and taught at Chiba University and Sophia University before starting to teach at Gakushuin University. As well as researching in his field – commercial law and corporate law – he has also been active in comparative law studies, being a correspondent of UNIDROIT and an associate member of the International Academy of Comparative Law (IACL). He has helped establish contacts with Japanese law specialists outside of Japan on many occasions. He is a program convenor (in eastern Japan) of the Australian Network for Japanese Law (ANJeL) and serves on the editorial board of the Journal of Japanese Law (*Zeitschrift für japanisches Recht*), which is published in Germany.

Suzanne Le Mire is an Associate Professor at the Adelaide Law School and Deputy Executive Dean of the Faculty of the Professions, University of Adelaide. Suzanne's research and teaching interests are focused in the areas of corporate law and professional ethics. She is particularly interested in the role and regulation of independence in a number of contexts, including corporate and superannuation boards, judges, regulators and lawyers. As well as holding a number of senior university roles in recent years, including Associate Dean (Learning and Teaching) and Dean of Law, Suzanne has been a distinguished overseas visitor at the Chinese University of Hong Kong and the University of Mannheim, Germany, and visiting scholar at University College London.

Jeanne Nel de Koker is a researcher who teaches corporate and commercial law at an undergraduate and postgraduate level at Deakin University, Australia. Jeanne graduated from the Faculty of Law of the University of the Orange Free State with a B.Iuris, an LLB and an LLM in Constitutional Law. She was admitted as an Advocate of the High Court of South Africa and practised as a member of the Bar. She was a senior lecturer in the Department of Business Law and Taxation at Monash University, Australia, deployed to their new South African campus to develop and present their commercial law courses. She has delivered more than 25 academic papers at national and international conferences and published 13 articles in national and international peer-reviewed journals. Jeanne authored chapters in *Anti Money Laundering Guide* (Thomson Reuters, 2015) and *The Changing Family* (Hart Publishing, 1998). Most recently, Jeanne and Jean du Plessis co-edited *Disqualification of Company Directors* (Routledge, 2017).

Luke Nottage is Professor of Comparative and Transnational Business Law in the Faculty of Law at the University of Sydney, Associate Director (Japan) at its Centre for Asian and Pacific Law, Program Director (Comparative and Global Law) at the Sydney Centre for International Law, and founding Co-Director of the Australian Network for Japanese Law. He specialises in commercial and consumer law, and has published over 100 works, including Nottage, Wolff and Anderson (eds) *Corporate Governance in the 21st Century: Japan's Gradual Transformation* (Elgar, 2008) and Puchniak, Baum and Nottage (eds) *Independent Directors in Asia* (CUP, 2017). Luke is qualified in New South Wales and New Zealand, has worked closely with law firms in Japan since 1990, and is a Director of Japanese Law Links Pty Ltd. He has served as expert witness or consulted for many other law firms worldwide, as well as for ASEAN, the OECD, the European Commission, the Japanese Cabinet Office and the UN Development Programme.

Susan Watson is a Professor of Law at the University of Auckland Faculty of Law, where she is the Deputy Dean. She researches and teaches corporate law and corporate governance. She is the joint editor and author of *Company and Securities Law in New Zealand* (Thomson Reuters), collections *Contemporary Issues in Corporate Governance*, *Corporate Governance After the Financial Crisis* and *Innovations in Corporate Governance* (Edward Elgar). She is also the author of over 60 articles and book chapters. 'How the Company Became an Entity – A New Understanding of Corporate Law', published in the *Journal of Business Law*, won the 2015 Legal Research Foundation Sir Ian Barker Published Article Award. This award is given for the best article, essay or discrete book chapter published by a New Zealand-based author.

PREFACE

The modern corporation knows few bounds – its widespread use in business and the corporatisation of essential services means that it permeates almost every aspect of our daily lives. It is companies, small and large, that drive economies and that can create economic prosperity for countries. However, all is not bright and shining; companies, especially large multinational public companies, have been the cause of considerable harm to the environment and society generally because of pollution, exploitation of employees and not providing safe working environments. There are too many examples in too many countries to name them all, but as this book originated in Australia, the James Hardie case, where many suffered tremendously because of exposure to asbestos, with little or no respect by the company for those who suffered, is a prime example of why it is of considerable importance that companies are governed properly. We discuss the James Hardie case in detail in Part 2.4.2, as well as in Part 14.2.3 from a business ethics perspective. Principles of corporate governance have a vital role to play in protecting consumers, shareholders, creditors, the environment and society, and in ensuring that companies act responsibly as well as legally.

Since the appearance of the first edition of *Principles of Contemporary Corporate Governance* in 2005, developments have gained velocity, and the volume of materials on corporate governance has grown exponentially. This made the appearance of a second edition in 2011 inevitable. The global financial crisis that emerged in about 2008 and global financial uncertainties in the European Union (since 2008) made us predict in 2011 (in the Preface to the second edition of this book) that the discipline of corporate governance would retain its prominence in future. That has indeed been the case, and it was a main motivation for us to bring out the third edition and now this fourth edition of *Principles of Contemporary Corporate Governance*.

Again we looked at the book in its entirely and asked how we could keep it relevant and contemporary. We decided not to simply add more materials to the book and make it a monstrous work. Rather, we decided to stick to our original approach of focusing on the fundamental and contemporary principles of corporate governance. However, we also wanted to include more of the corporate governance themes and issues that have become particularly prominent in recent years. It meant that we had to delete some of the dated discussions to make place for new contemporary corporate governance themes and pressing issues. In this era of globalisation, we expanded the coverage on comparative corporate governance by adding a part on corporate governance in New Zealand (written by Susan Watson) and on India (written by Indrajit Dube) to complement the other jurisdictions we cover in Part Three of this book.

Part One (Chapters 1–4) introduces the reader to basic concepts, different types of board structures and different types of company officers. Chapters 1 and 2 deal with basic corporate governance principles and the all-inclusive stakeholder approach. We aim at stimulating debate on the dominant corporate shareholder primacy model. We contrast some prominent corporate governance theories, such as the shareholder primacy theory, the enlightened shareholder value theory, the stakeholder theory and the director primacy theory. In addition, we discuss disclosure of, and reporting on, non-financial information by way of different forms of voluntary reporting, such as integrated reporting, sustainability reporting and corporate responsibility reporting, which encompasses more than just corporate social responsibility (CSR). We also emphasise the importance of responsible behaviour by corporations and the creating of long-term, sustainable growth for corporations. In Chapter 3 we contrast the unitary and two-tier board systems and point out the virtues of both. In that chapter we draw attention to the fundamentally important difference between the managerial role of management and the supervisory or governance role of the board of directors. In Chapter 4 we deal with directors' and executives' remuneration and the importance of board diversity, with a focus on gender diversity.

Part Two (Chapters 5–10) deals with corporate governance in Australia. We have updated this part with the latest developments and we also discuss some of the most significant new Australian cases on directors' duties and liability.

Part Three (Corporate governance in international and global contexts), in common with earlier editions, offers a concise and updated discussion of the United States (US), the United Kingdom (UK), Canadian, German, Japanese and Chinese corporate governance models. Having added new parts in the third edition on the European Union (EU), Indonesia and South Africa, we added New Zealand and India to the fourth edition. In Chapter 12 we continue to discuss the *OECD Principles of Corporate Governance*, and updated the entire book with references to the 2015 *G20/OECD Principles of Corporate Governance*.

In **Part Four** we focus on 'Shareholder Activism and Business Ethics'. Chapter 13 gives an overview of the role of shareholder activism as one of the checks or balances in ensuring that companies adhere to good corporate governance practices. Chapter 14 has been completely re-written by Suzanne Le Mire, with a renewed focus on 'Business ethics and corporate governance'. The chapter now combines academic discussions with case studies, some broader legal issues and other more general aspects impacting on business ethics.

The fourth edition will again broaden the perspectives and understanding of all people interested in corporate governance and corporate regulation and management, including company secretaries, compliance officers, judicial officers, lawyers, accountants, academics and students of law and business management.

With the third edition we added Jason Harris as author and relied on the specialised expertise of four new contributors, Irene-marié Esser (South Africa), Miko Kamal (Indonesia), Souichirou Kozuka (Japan) and Jeanne Nel de Koker (Australia) – our contributors from the previous editions, Vivienne Bath (corporate governance in China) and Luke Nottage (corporate governance in Japan) updated their parts extensively. The current edition is now enriched further by the contributions of Susan Watson (on New Zealand), Indrajit Dube (on India) and Suzanne Le Mire (on Business ethics and corporate governance). We would like to acknowledge the input of Mirko Bagaric as author of the first three editions of this book and thank him for giving us permission to use some of the parts he wrote in the past.

Jean du Plessis (Deakin University)
Anil Hargovan (University of New South Wales)
Jason Harris (University of Technology Sydney)
May 2017

ACKNOWLEDGEMENTS

The authors and Cambridge University Press would like to thank the following for permission to reproduce material in this book.

Figures 3.1–3.6: Reproduced with permission from Robert Tricker. **Extracts** from ASX Corporate Governance Council material: © Copyright 2017 ASX Corporate Governance Council. Association of Superannuation Funds of Australia Ltd, ACN 002 786 290, Australian Council of Superannuation Investors, Australian Financial Markets Association Limited ACN 119 827 904, Australian Institute of Company Directors ACN 008 484 197, Australian Institute of Superannuation Trustees ACN 123 284 275, Australasian Investor Relations Association Limited ACN 095 554 153, Australian Shareholders' Association Limited ACN 000 625 669, ASX Limited ABN 98 008 624 691 trading as Australian Securities Exchange, Business Council of Australia ACN 008 483 216, Chartered Accountants Australia and New Zealand, CPA Australia Ltd ACN 008 392 452, Financial Services Institute of Australasia ACN 066 027 389, Group of 100 Inc, The Institute of Actuaries of Australia ACN 000 423 656, ABN 50 084 642 571,The Institute of Internal Auditors – Australia ACN 001 797 557, Financial Services Council ACN 080 744 163, Governance Institute of Australia Ltd ACN 008 615 950, Law Council of Australia Limited ACN 005 260 622, National Institute of Accountants ACN 004 130 643, Property Council of Australia Limited ACN 008 474 422, Stockbrokers Association of Australia ACN 089 767 706. All rights reserved 2017. **Extracts** from Supreme Court of Western Australia reproduced with permission. **Extract** from James McConvill, 'Revisiting holding company liability for subsidiary company debts in Australia: A response to the James Hardy controversy' © 2005 Research-Online@ND. **Extract** from *Report of the Special Commission of Inquiry into the Medical Research and Compensation Foundation* © 2017 Department of Premier and Cabinet. Reproduced under Creative Commons Attribution 4.0 International. **Extract** from *Redefining the Corporation: Stakeholder Management and Organizational Wealth* by James E. Post, Lee E. Preston and Sybille Sachs. Copyright © 2002 by the Board of Trustees of the Leland Stanford Jr. University. All rights reserved. Used by permission of the publisher, Stanford University Press, sup.org. **Extract** from *Corporate Governance* 2nd Edition by Christine Mallin (2007) reproduced by permission of Oxford University Press. **Extracts** from the Federal Register of Legislation (www.legislation.gov.au) reproduced under Creative Commons Attribution 4.0 International (CC BY 4.0) (https://creativecommons.org/licenses/by/4.0/). **Extracts** from CLERP (Audit Reform & Corporate Disclosure Bill Commentary on the Draft Provisions – Corporate Law Economic Reform Program No. 9 (October 2003) reproduced under Creative Commons Attribution 3.0 Australia (CC BY 3.0 AUS). **Extracts** from the Report of the HIH Royal Commission (Owen Report), The Failure of HIH Insurance – Volume 1: A Corporate Collapse and its Lessons reproduced under Creative Commons Attribution 3.0 Australia (CC BY 3.0 AUS). **Extracts** from *German Corporate Governance in International and European*

Context 3rd Edition (2017) by J.J. du Plessis, B. Großfeld, C. Luttermann, I. Saenger, O. Sandrock and M. Casper reproduced with permission from Springer-Verlag GmbH. **Extracts** from the *New York Stock Exchange Listed Company Manual* used with permission of the NYSE Group, Inc. © 2017 NYSE Group, Inc. Note that book only contains a summary of the NYSE material created by the authors, and may not contain the most up-to-date information. Readers should refer to wallstreet.cch.com/LCM for the most current information. **Extract** from FMA Corporate Governance in New Zealand: Principles and Guidelines – A handbook for directors, executives and advisers reproduced under Creative Commons Attribution 3.0 New Zealand (CC BY 3.0 NZ). **Extract** from *India Business guide – Start-up to Set-up* (2015) by Vaish Associates Advocates, India (www.vaishlaw.com) and published by Wolters Kluwer India. Reproduced with permission. **Extract** from *Directors' Responsibilities in Canada* by Institute of Corporate Directors reproduced with permission from Ontario Securities Commission. **Extract** from National Policy 58–201 Corporate Governance Guidelines reproduced with permission from Ontario Securities Commission.

Every effort has been made to trace and acknowledge copyright. The publisher apologises for any accidental infringement and welcomes information that would redress this situation.

TABLE OF CASES

Australia

TABLE OF STATUTES

BASIC CONCEPTS, BOARD STRUCTURES AND COMPANY OFFICERS

1

THE CONCEPTS OF 'CORPORATE GOVERNANCE' AND 'ESSENTIAL' PRINCIPLES OF CORPORATE GOVERNANCE

It is necessary only for the good man to do nothing for evil to triumph.

> Attributed to Edmund Burke (18th century English political philosopher) – *The Australian*,
> 6 December 2004, 4, reporting on the most favoured phrase of quotation-lovers,
> as determined by an Oxford University Press poll

Many companies today no longer accept the maxim that the business of business is business. Their premise is simple: Corporations, because they are the dominant institution on the planet, must squarely address social justice and environmental issues that afflict humankind.

> Paul Hawken, *The Ecology of Commerce* (Harper Business, revised edn, 2010), xi

1.1 The meaning of corporate governance

1.1.1 Generally

Corporate governance is as old as the corporate form itself.[1] However, the phrase 'corporate governance' was scarcely used until the 1980s.[2] Issues of corporate governance first gained international prominence in the late 1990s and early 2000s in the wake of a series of corporate accounting scandals, most notably Enron in the US and HIH in Australia.[3] The focus on corporate governance increased after 2008, in the aftermath of the Global Financial Crisis.[4] Inasmuch as a discussion of the principles of contemporary governance requires a closer description of 'corporate governance', the concept remains one that does not lend itself to a single,[5] specific or narrow definition. Corporate governance, by its very nature, is organic and flexible, constantly evolving in response to a changing corporate environment.[6]

---

1   Jean J du Plessis, 'Corporate law and corporate governance lessons from the past: Ebbs and flows, but far from "The end of history . . .: Part 1"' (2009) 30 *Company Lawyer* 43, 44; H Wells, 'The birth of corporate governance' (2010) 33 *Seattle University Law Review* 1247–92.

2   Bob Tricker, *Corporate Governance: Principles, Policies and Practices* (Oxford University Press [OUP], 2nd edn, 2012) 4. See Corina Gavrea and Roxana Stegerean, 'Comparative study on corporate governance' (2011) 20 *Annals of the University of Oradea, Economic Science Series* 674 for a literature review and an analysis of the concept of 'corporate governance'. Note, however, that Cheffins points out that in the US, the term came into vogue during the 1970s. See Brian R Cheffins, 'The History of Corporate Governance' in Mike Wright, Donald S. Siegel, Kevin Keasey and Igor Filatotchev (eds), *The Oxford Handbook of Corporate Governance* (OUP, 2013) <www.oxfordhandbooks.com.ezproxy-f.deakin.edu.au/view/10.1093/oxfordhb/9780199642007.001.0001/oxfordhb-9780199642007-e-3>.

3   Du Plessis, 'Corporate law and corporate governance lessons from the past' 43. See also Gerry H Grant, 'The evolution of corporate governance and its impact on modern corporate America' (2003) 41 *Management Decision* 923–4.

4   Iilia Lupu, 'The indirect relation between corporate governance and financial stability' (2015) 22 *Procedia Economics and Finance* 538.

5   See generally Janet Dine and Marios Koutsias, *The Nature of Corporate Governance: The Significance of National Cultural Identity* (Edward Elgar, 2013) 67–70.

6   The discussion of different corporate governance theories in Section 1.1.2 illustrates how changed perceptions and expectations of corporations impact on the concept and, ultimately, on how we define 'corporate governance'. For an insightful review of the history of corporate governance that underscores the evolutionary nature of corporate governance, see Cheffins, 'The History of Corporate Governance'

A comparison of older definitions or descriptions of corporate governance, such as those used in the South African King Report (King I) in 1994, and more recent definitions, such as those used in the G20/OECD *Principles of Corporate Governance* and the King IV (2016) Report reveals how the focus has shifted from a narrow, inward-looking approach that primarily addresses internal director-related rules within the corporation to an outward-looking, more inclusive and multifaceted approach that recognises that corporate governance is about much more than managing the manner in which directors exercise and control authority in corporations.[7]

Early attempts at a definition focused on 'corporate governance' as a 'system': the UK Cadbury Report (1992)[8] and King I[9] both defined 'corporate governance' as 'the system by which companies are directed and controlled'.

In 2003, the Report of the HIH Royal Commission on the collapse of HIH Insurance Ltd (the Owen Report), one of Australia's largest corporate collapses, emphasised that 'corporate governance' extends beyond mere models and systems and includes the 'practices by which that exercise and control of authority is in fact effected'.[10]

The Australian Securities Exchange's (ASX) Corporate Governance Council continued the trend to define 'corporate governance' more precisely by including references to the setting and achieving of objectives, the monitoring of risk and the optimisation of performance in the 2003 ASX *Principles of Good Corporate Governance and Best Practice Recommendations*.[11] The description used in the 2014 version of the ASX *CG Principles and Recommendations* broadened the concept even further to add another layer: accountability:

> The phrase 'corporate governance' is 'the framework of rules, relationships, systems and processes within and by which authority is exercised and controlled in corporations. It encompasses the mechanisms by which companies, and those in control, *are held to account*' (emphasis added).[12]

(2013). Gilson argues that the manner and degree to which we complicate the inquiry into the (legal) structures that bear on corporate decision-making and performance have informed the manner in which corporate governance has developed. See Ronald J Gilson, 'From Corporate Law to Corporate Governance' (2016) in *Oxford Handbook of Corporate Law and Governance* (forthcoming); European Corporate Governance Institute (ECGI), Law Research Paper No. 324/2016; Stanford Law and Economics, Olin Working Paper No. 497, 5 <https://ssrn.com/abstract=2819128>.

7   King IV defines 'corporate governance' as 'the exercise of ethical and effective leadership by the governing body towards the achievement of the following governance outcomes: ethical culture, good performance, effective control and legitimacy': King IV 11.

8   *Report of the Committee on the Financial Aspects of Corporate Governance* (hereafter Cadbury Report (1992)) (Committee on the Financial Aspects of Corporate Governance, 1992).

9   *The King Report on Corporate Governance* (hereafter King (1994)) (Institute of Directors in Southern Africa, 1994).

10   Report of the HIH Royal Commission (Owen Report), *The Failure of HIH Insurance – Volume I: A Corporate Collapse and its Lessons* (Commonwealth of Australia, 2003) xxxiii.

11   ASX, *Principles of Good Corporate Governance and Best Practice Recommendations* (March 2003) 3 <www.asx.com.au/documents/asx-compliance/principles-and-recommendations-march-2003.pdf>.

12   ASX, *CG Principles and Recommendations* (3rd edn, 2014) 3 <www.asx.com.au/documents/asx-compliance/cgc-principles-and-recommendations-3rd-edn.pdf>.

More recently, the G20/OECD *Principles of Corporate Governance* specifically included a reference to the relationships between the parties involved and described corporate governance as:

> a set of relationships between a company's management, its board, its shareholders and other stakeholders. Corporate governance also provides the structure through which the objectives of the company are set, and the means of attaining those objectives and monitoring performance are determined.[13]

As will be seen below, we attempt to define 'corporate governance' in wide terms. However, in an approach similar to the recent OECD definition, we incorporate some specific aspects – in particular, the interests of all parties involved and the relational nature of corporate governance[14] – to give the definition some substance.

Before we attempt to give our own definition, it is important to consider the origins of both the corporate governance and the stakeholder debates.

1.1.2 Origins of the corporate governance debate and some corporate governance and corporate law theories

It is difficult to determine exactly when the corporate governance debate started.[15] However, there is little doubt that there were many factors that brought the debate to prominence: the separation of ownership and control (so pertinently illustrated in 1932 by Berle and Means in their book, *The Modern Corporation and Private Property*), which resulted in the so-called managerial revolution,[16] or 'managerialism';[17] the pivotal role of the corporate form in

---

13   G20/OECD, *Principles of Corporate Governance* (2015) 9 <http://dx.doi.org/10.1787/9789264236882-en>. The 2015 revision commenced in 2014. In 2013 the OECD launched an inclusive review of the *Principles*, with all G20 countries invited to participate on an equal footing. The review also benefited from extensive public consultations and the participation of key international institutions such as the Basel Committee, the FSB and the World Bank. The updated *Principles* were adopted by the OECD in July 2015, launched at the meeting of G20 Finance Ministers and Central Bank Governors in Ankara on 4–5 September 2015 and subsequently endorsed at the G20 Leaders' Summit in Antalya on 15–16 November 2015. The *Principles* have been adopted as one of the Financial Stability Board's key standards for sound financial systems, and have been used by the World Bank Group in more than 60 country reviews. They also serve as the basis for the guidelines on corporate governance of banks issued by the Basel Committee on Banking Supervision. The OECD *Principles of Corporate Governance* are discussed in more detail in Chapter 12.3.

14   Increasingly, corporate governance discussions reflect a growing consensus that compliance and security best practices should extend beyond directors and senior management. See Brian Stafford, 'The evolution of corporate governance' (2015) *The Corporate Board* 10.

15   See John Farrar, *Corporate Governance: Theories, Principles and Practice* (OUP, 3rd edn, 2008) 8–20. Gilson traces it back to the mid 1970s, when Jensen and Meckling reframed corporate law into something far broader than disputes over statutory language. See Michael C Jensen and William H Meckling, 'Theory of the firm: Managerial behavior, agency costs and the theory of the firm' (1976) 3 *Journal of Financial Economy* 305 in Gilson, 'From Corporate Law to Corporate Governance' (2016) 6 <https://ssrn.com/abstract=2819128>.

16   See, for example, Klaus J Hopt, 'Preface' in Theodor Baums, Richard M Buxbaum and Klaus J Hopt (eds) *Institutional Investors and Corporate Governance* (W de Gruyter, 1994) I; and OECD, *Principles of Corporate Governance* (April 2004) 12 <www.oecd.org/dataoecd/32/18/31557724.pdf>.

17   Stephen M Bainbridge, *The New Corporate Governance in Theory and Practice* (OUP, 2008) 9, 19–20, 155 *et seq.*

generating wealth for nations; the huge powers of corporations,[18] and the effects of these on our daily lives; the enormous consequences that flow from collapses of large public corporations;[19] and the practical reality of the almost unfettered powers of boards of directors, or what Stephen Bainbridge identified as 'the director primacy model of corporate governance' (see discussion below and in Chapter 3). We are, indeed, as Allan Hutchinson describes it so appropriately, living in an age of *corpocracy*.[20]

It is also beyond dispute that the corporate governance debate became particularly prominent when the basic perception of the company changed. At first the only real concern of a company was the maximisation of profits.[21] Profits for whom? – the shareholders.[22] This was confirmed in 1919 in the US case of *Dodge v Ford Motor*,[23] and is a view many commentators adhered to for a considerable period of time; a further confirmation of the Dodge theory occurred in 1986 in another US case, *Katz v Oak Industries*.[24] According to this view, the shareholders are the 'owners of the company',[25] the primary stakeholders and most importantly, the providers of capital to enable the company to conduct business. This is called the shareholder primacy theory,[26] although it was hardly ever mentioned that in fact nobody can 'own' the company, as it is a separate 'legal person' and it is just as unfitting to talk about 'ownership' here as it is to say (after the eradication of slavery) that one or more 'natural persons' can 'own' another 'natural person'.

Gradually the 'shareholder supremacy'[27] view changed, and the company, especially the large public company, came to be seen in a different light. It was observed more pertinently that there were other stakeholders in a company; that if the only purpose of a company was 'the maximisation of profits for the shareholders', society could suffer tremendously – poor

---

18   Kent Greenfield, *The Failure of Corporate Law* (University of Chicago Press, 2006) 4–5.

19   See, generally, Roberta Romano, *The Genius of American Corporate Law* (AEI Press, 1993); and David SR Leighton and Donald H Thain, *Making Boards Work* (McGraw-Hill Ryerson, 1997) 9–10.

20   Allan C Hutchinson, *The Companies We Keep* (Irwin Law, 2005) 8.

21   Adolf A Berle, 'The Impact of the Corporation on Classical Theory' in Thomas Clarke (ed.), *Theories of Corporate Governance: The Philosophical Foundations of Corporate Governance* (Routledge, 2004) 45, 49 *et seq.*

22   Margaret M Blair, 'Ownership and Control: Rethinking Corporate Governance for the Twenty-First Century' in Clarke (ed.), *Theories of Corporate Governance* (2004) 175, 181. See also Bainbridge, *The New Corporate Governance in Theory and Practice* (2008) 53.

23   *Dodge v Ford Motor Company*, 170 N.W. 668 (Mich. 1919) at 684; (1919) 204 Mich. 459 at 507: 'A business corporation is organized and carried on primarily for the profit of the stockholders. The powers of the directors are to be employed for that end. The discretion of directors is to be exercised in the choice of means to attain that end, and does not extend to the change of the end itself, to the reduction of profits, or to the nondistribution of profits among stockholders in order to devote them to other purposes.' For an overview of the *Dodge* case, see Leonard I Rothman, 'Re-evaluating the Basis of Corporate Governance in the Post-Enron Era' in PB Vasudev and Susan Watson (eds), *Corporate Governance after the Financial Crisis* (Edward Elgar, 2012) 101, 110–12.

24   *Katz v Oak Industries Inc.*, 508 A 2d 873, 879 (Del. Ch. 1986).

25   See, generally, Greenfield, *The Failure of Corporate Law* (2006) 43, but also see his arguments dispelling this 'myth' (44–7).

26   See generally, on the theory of 'shareholder primacy', Irene-marié Esser, *Recognition of Various Stakeholder Interests in the Company Management: Corporate Social Responsibility and Directors' Duties* (VDM Verlag Dr Müller, 2009) 19–23.

27   See, generally, Greenfield, *The Failure of Corporate Law* (2006) 2 and 44–6.

working conditions for workers, exploitation of the environment, pollution and so on.[28] Then came the realisation that:

> enterprise, private as well as public, because it both contributes to and benefits from society (local, national and larger), can be said to have rights and duties vis-à-vis that society in somewhat the same way as has an individual;[29]

and

> [t]he limited liability company does not simply represent one interest. It represents an arena in which there is a potential clash of many interests. We may identify the interests underlying it as: (1) investors – share capital/loan capital; (2) outside creditors – commercial finance/trade creditors; (3) employees; (4) consumers; (5) the public.[30]

The concept of 'managing the corporation' then came to be expressed in terms of these other interests:

> The balancing of the company's responsibilities – to workers as members of the company, to consumers of the goods and services it provides, and to the community of which it is a citizen – with its primary one of operating at maximum efficiency and lowest cost, so as to make profits and discharge its obligations to its shareholders, represents the full scope of management.[31]

Thus the concept of 'corporate governance' began to adopt this new articulation of 'managing the corporation', with a central focus on the interrelationship among internal groups and individuals such as the board of directors, the shareholders in general meetings, the employees, the managing directors, the executive directors, the non-executive directors, the managers, the audit committees and other committees of the board. However, the profit motive was still dominant. Furthermore, it should be realised that outside interests are also at stake; for example, those of creditors, potential investors, consumers and the public or community at large (so-called stakeholders).

Other interests started to be recognised judicially. For instance, in *Westpac Banking Corporation v Bell Group Ltd (in liq) (No 3)* Drummond AJA pointed out as follows:

> The impacts of corporate decision-making on a wider range of interests than shareholders are now being given more recognition. The need to ensure protection of those interests also I think serves to explain why modern company courts have become more interventionist, in reviewing the activities of directors, than was traditionally the case.[32]

---

28   See also Kent H Baker and John R Nofsinger, 'Socially Responsible Finance and Investing: An Overview' in Kent H Baker and John R Nofsinger (eds), *Socially Responsible Finance and Investing: Financial Institutions, Corporations, Investors, and Activists – Robert W. Kolb Series in Finance* (John Wiley & Sons, 2010–12) Vol. 612, 2.

29   Charles de Hoghton (ed.), *The Company: Law, Structure and Reform in Eleven Countries* (Allen & Unwin, 1970) 7.

30   John J Farrar et al., *Farrar's Company Law* (Butterworths, 1991) 13.

31   George Goyder, *The Responsible Company* (Blackwell, 1961) 45.

32   *Westpac Banking Corporation v Bell Group Ltd (in liq)* (2012) WAR 1 (*Westpac v Bell No 3*), [2049], [2051]: 'Owen J was correct, in my opinion, when he said at [4438] and [4439] that when a company is in an insolvency context the interests of creditors are not in all circumstances paramount, to the exclusion of other interests including that of the shareholders. His conclusion at [4440] was that

One of the most recent judicial recognitions that there are several interests that can be harmed by the acts or omissions of directors is the case of *Australian Securities and Investments Commission v Cassimatis (No 8)*, where Justice Edelman refers specifically to several interests, including the interest in a company's reputation.[33] There are some commentators now arguing for the recognition of a corporate social responsibility duty for directors, based on 'contemporary community expectations'.[34]

Traditional wisdom regarding shareholder primacy[35] began to be challenged more forcefully from at least the early 1990s, with statements such as 'managerial accountability to shareholders is corporate law's central problem';[36] 'corporate law is currently in the midst of crisis, because of the exhaustion of the shareholder primacy model';[37] 'shareholder dominance should be questioned';[38] 'shareholder primacy theory is suffering a crisis of confidence';[39] and most recently even stronger calls for urgent change to the shareholder primacy model, arguing that shareholder primacy may be 'the main barrier to sustainable companies'.[40] Although there is little doubt that the shareholder primacy theory of corporate law still underpins the corporate law models of many countries, including Australia,[41] calls ring loud for a rethinking of the

directors could not properly commit their company to a transaction if the circumstances were such that "the only reasonable conclusion to draw, once the interests of creditors have been taken into account, is that a contemplated transaction will be so prejudicial to creditors that it could not be in the interests of the company as a whole". I would prefer to say that if the circumstances of the particular case are such that there is a real risk that the creditors of a company in an insolvency context would suffer significant prejudice if the directors undertook a certain course of action, that is sufficient to show that the contemplated course of action is not in the interests of the company.' For a critical analysis of the majority decision of the Court of Appeal, see Jason Harris and Anil Hargovan, 'For whom the bell tolls: Directors' duties to creditors after *Bell*' (2013) 35 *Sydney Law Review* 433.

33   *Australian Securities and Investments Commission v Cassimatis (No 8)* (2016) 336 ALR 209 at [480]–[483].

34   See Jean J du Plessis, 'Corporate social responsibility and "contemporary community expectations"' (2017) 35 *Company & Securities Law Journal (C&SLJ)* 30, 37–9.

35   See again Esser, *Recognition of Various Stakeholder Interests in the Company Management* (2009) 19–23.

36   David Millon, 'New directions in corporate law: communitarians, contractarians, and the crisis in corporate law' (1993) 50 *Washington & Lee Law Review* 1373, 1374.

37   Ibid. 1390.

38   Morten Huse, *Boards, Governance and Value Creation: The Human Side of Corporate Governance* (Cambridge University Press [CUP], 2007) 29.

39   Lynn A Stout, 'The Shareholder Value Myth', *European Financial Review*, 1 April 2013 <http://ssrn.com/abstract=2277141>. Despite these statements, the shareholder primacy model remains prominent in the UK and continues to be supported by a shareholder-centric company law framework. See Marc Moore, 'Shareholder primacy, labour and the historic ambivalence of UK company law' (September 2016) 5 <https://papers.ssrn.com/sol3/papers.cfm?abstract_id=2835990>. However, Moore suggests that although most directors and senior managers of UK companies would likely regard shareholder supremacy as underpinning the current UK company law model, the notion of shareholder supremacy will increasingly be challenged in the future.

40   Beate Sjåfjell, 'Corporate Governance for Sustainability: The Necessary Reform of EU Company Law' in Beate Sjåfjell and Anja Wiesbrock (eds), *The Greening of European Business under EU Law: Taking Article 11 TFEU Seriously* (Routledge, 2015) 97–117.

41   See Jean J du Plessis, 'Shareholder primacy and other stakeholder interests' (2016) 34 *C&SLJ* 238, 241; and Jean J du Plessis 'Corporate social responsibility and "contemporary community expectations"' (2017) 35 *C&SLJ* 30.

traditional Western notion of the company, which still relies on 18th and 19th century principles, concepts and notions.[42]

From all this a slightly different theory has emerged, one moving away from 'shareholder primacy' theory to what is called an 'enlightened shareholder value' theory. We discuss this theory in greater detail in Chapter 2, but will touch upon it briefly here as well. The 'enlightened shareholder value' theory, very generally, holds that productive relationships (with other stakeholders) can be achieved within the framework of existing corporate law and corporate governance concepts, in fact maintaining 'shareholder supremacy', but ensuring that directors pursue shareholders' interests in an enlightened and inclusive way, meaning *having regard* to the interests of other stakeholders, *but no more than that*.[43] The principal manifestation of this theory is found in s 172 of the UK *Companies Act 2006*:

172 Duty to promote the success of the company

(1) A director of a company must act in the way he considers, in good faith, would be most likely to promote the success of the company for the benefit of its members as a whole, and in doing so have regard (amongst other matters) to –

   (a) the likely consequences of any decision in the long term,

   (b) the interests of the company's employees,

   (c) the need to foster the company's business relationships with suppliers, customers and others,

   (d) the impact of the company's operations on the community and the environment,

   (e) the desirability of the company maintaining a reputation for high standards of business conduct, and

   (f) the need to act fairly as between members of the company.

(2) Where or to the extent that the purposes of the company consist of or include purposes other than the benefit of its members, subsection (1) has effect as if the reference to promoting the success of the company for the benefit of its members were to achieving those purposes.

(3) The duty imposed by this section has effect subject to any enactment or rule of law requiring directors, in certain circumstances, to consider or act in the interests of creditors of the company.[44]

There is no space in this book to discuss this in detail, but just reflecting on the approach generally will reveal how difficult it seems to break with the 'shareholder-dominance

---

42   See in particular Tricker, *Corporate Governance* (2012) 164–5 and 488.

43   See, generally, David Millon, 'Enlightened Shareholder Value, Social Responsibility and the Redefinition of Corporate Purpose Without Law' in Vasudev and Watson (eds), *Corporate Governance after the Financial Crisis* (2012) 68 and 79–80; Andrew Keay, 'Tackling the issue of corporate objective: An analysis of the United Kingdom's "enlightened shareholder value approach"' (2007) 29 *Sydney Law Review* 577, 589–90; I Esser and Jean J du Plessis, 'The stakeholder debate and directors' fiduciary duties' (2007) 19 *South African Mercantile Law Journal* 346, 351–2.

44   See Andrew Keay, 'Section 172(1) of the Companies Act 2006: An interpretation and assessment' (2007) 28 *The Company Lawyer* 106; Millon, 'Enlightened shareholder value, social responsibility and the redefinition of corporate purpose without law' (2012) 69 and 79–80.

indoctrination' that has been so strong over so many years.[45] Clinging to the past, and even seeing the interests of other stakeholders in an 'enlightened' way, still makes other non-shareholder interests peripheral – as Janet Dine and Marios Koutsias put it, this approach is simply 'a fig leaf for stakeholders other than shareholders'.[46] The 'enlightened shareholder value' theory could be described as the interim stop, buying more time to reflect further on the flaws in the 'shareholder primacy' theory and the merits of a proper 'all-inclusive stakeholder' theory – one that is emerging fast, as will be seen in the discussion that follows.

That the days of the 'shareholder primacy' theory are numbered is strikingly illustrated by Lynn Stout in her 2012 essay, 'New thinking on "shareholder primacy"'.[47] Note that we briefly discuss a new theory, called the 'director primacy' theory, in Chapter 3, in the context of the powers of boards of directors.

Nowadays, it is fairly generally accepted that 'in future the development of loyal, inclusive stakeholder relationships will become one of the most important determinants of commercial viability and business success';[48] that 'recognition of stakeholder concern is not only good business, but politically expedient and morally and ethically just, even if in the strict legal sense [corporations] remain directly accountable only to shareholders';[49] and that 'the corporation as a legal entity grew out of its ability to protect not only the shareholders but also other stakeholders'.[50]

Before we discuss the 'stakeholder model'[51] in greater detail in Chapter 2 and before we comment on some broader views on what the ultimate aims of corporations, especially large public corporations, should be, we first need to mention a few other issues that dominated corporate governance debates for several years. They are 'corporate social responsibility' (CSR)[52] and the concept of 'corporate citizenship' – we discuss these in greater detail in Chapter 2.[53]

---

45   See Marc Moore's comments on the lasting prominence of shareholder primacy in the UK, in 'Shareholder primacy, labour and the historic ambivalence of UK company law' (September 2016).

46   Janet Dine and Marios Koutsias, *The Nature of Corporate Governance* (Edward Elgar, 2013) viii.

47   Lynn Stout, 'New Thinking on "Shareholder Primacy"' in Vasudev and Watson (eds), *Corporate Governance after the Financial Crisis* (2012) 25.

48   David Wheeler and Maria Sillanpää, *The Stakeholder Corporation* (Pitmann, 1997) ix. See further James E Post, Lee E Preston and Sybille Sach, *Redefining the Corporation: Stakeholder Management and Organizational Wealth* (Stanford Business Books, 2002) 1–3; and Mark J Roe, 'Preface' in Margaret M Blair and Mark J Roe (eds), *Employees & Corporate Governance* (Brookings Institute, 1999) v.

49   Leighton and Thain, *Making Boards Work* (1997) 23.

50   Huse, *Boards, Governance and Value Creation* (2007) 29. Gilson argues that corporate governance models or theories that focus on single elements in the corporate governance mix, i.e. shareholder primacy or director primacy, are too simple to explain the real-world dynamics. He states that there is no one 'right' governance model, that governance models should be contextual and dynamic. See Gilson, 'From Corporate Law to Corporate Governance' (2016) 36.

51   See generally PM Vasudev, 'Corporate Stakeholders in New Zealand – the Present, and Possibilities for the Future' in Vasudev and Watson (eds), *Corporate Governance after the Financial Crisis* (2012) 120.

52   For a good explanation of the relationship between corporate governance and corporate social responsibility (CSR), see Andreas Rühmkorf, 'The promotion of corporate social responsibility in English private law', PhD thesis, University of Sheffield (2013) 58–62.

53   For an informative review of the history of CSR and the meaning of CSR, see Ray Broomhill, 'Corporate social responsibility: Key issues and debates' (2007) 1 *Dunstan Papers* 9; Ina Freeman and Amir Hasnaouvi, 'The meaning of corporate social responsibility: The vision of four nations' (2011) 100 *Journal of Business Ethics* 419.

The continued relevance and importance of companies being 'good corporate citizens' and having corporate social *responsibilities* is highlighted by the sheer number of articles and books dedicated to corporate citizenship and the importance of companies being good corporate citizens[54] as well as corporations' 'corporate social responsibilities', especially since about 1990.[55]

However, it seems that the debate is now getting wider, moving away from narrower corporate *social* responsibilities issues to the issue of *corporate responsibility* generally. As is explained in a 2013 consultation paper by the UK Department for Business Innovation & Skills:

> Corporate responsibility – the increasingly more acknowledged term for corporate social responsibility – is the responsibility of an organisation for the impacts of its decisions and activities on society and the environment through transparent and ethical behaviour above and beyond its statutory requirements.[56]

It seems we have truly – and inevitably – moved away from the view that the primary aim of corporations is 'to make a profit' or 'to make money',[57] and towards a view that corporations, especially large public corporations, should strive 'to build a better society'[58] and that they 'have a responsibility for the public good'.[59] Based on these views, a new trend has developed, namely for corporations, again especially large public corporations, to illustrate, in a practical

---

54   For example, the following books, in their entirety, focus on corporate citizenship: Mervyn King, *The Corporate Citizen: Governance for All Entities* (Penguin, 2008) and Jesús Conill, Christoph Luetge and Tatjana Schönwälder-Kuntze (eds), *Corporate Citizenship, Contractarianism and Ethical Theory: On Philosophical Foundations of Business Ethics* (Ashgate, 2008). See also Ingo Pies and Peter Koslowski (eds), *Corporate Citizenship and New Governance: The Political Role of Corporations* (Springer, 2011); Karin Svedberg Helgesson and Ulrika Mörth (eds), *The Political Role of Corporate Citizens: An Interdisciplinary Approach* (Palgrave Macmillan, 2013); and Dr Christoph Luetge, Tatjana Schönwälder-Kuntze and Jesús Conill (eds), *Corporate Citizenship, Contractarianism and Ethical Theory: On Philosophical Foundations of Business Ethics* (Ashgate, 2013).
55   A few could be mentioned: Güler Aras and David Crowther (eds), *Global Perspectives on Corporate Governance and CSR* (Gower Publishing Ltd, 2009); Frank den Hond, Frank GA de Bakker and Peter Neergaard, *Managing Corporate Social Responsibility in Action: Talking, Doing and Measuring* (Ashgate, 2007); Ana Maria Dávila Gómez and David Crowther (eds), *Ethics, Psyche and Social Responsibility* (Ashgate, 2007); Wim Vandekerckhove, *Whistleblowing and Organizational Social Responsibility: A Global Assessment* (Ashgate, 2006); David Crowther and Lez Rayman-Bacchus (eds), *Perspectives on Corporate Social Responsibility* (Ashgate, 2004). More recently, Baker and Nofsinger, 'Socially Responsible Finance and Investing: An overview' in Baker and Nofsinger (eds), *Socially Responsible Finance and Investing* (2010–12) Vol. 612; Jill Solomon, *Corporate Governance and Accountability* (John Wiley & Sons, 2011); Lorenzo Sacconi, Margaret Blair, R Edward Freeman and Alessandro Vercelli (eds), *Corporate Social Responsibility and Corporate Governance: The Contribution of Economic Theory and Related Disciplines* (Palgrave Macmillan, 2010); and Kathryn Haynes, Alan Murray and Jesse Dillard, *Social Responsibility: A Research Handbook* (Taylor & Francis, 2012). Ironically, despite the wealth of literature on the topic of CSR, confusion and inconsistency as to what it means in practice remain. See David Chandler, *Corporate Social Responsibility: A Strategic Perspective* (Business Expert Press, 2015) xxiv.
56   UK Department for Business Innovation & Skills, 'Corporate Responsibility', Consultation Paper (June 2013) 3 <www.gov.uk/government/uploads/system/uploads/attachment_data/file/209219/bis-13-964-corporate-responsibility-call.pdf>.
57   Paul Hawken, *The Ecology of Commerce* (Harper Business, revised edn, 2010) 1–2 makes this point very clear.
58   Hutchinson, *The Companies We Keep* (2005) 326.
59   Rühmkorf, *The Promotion of Corporate Social Responsibility in English Private Law* (2013) 18, fn 47, referring to M Blowfield and A Murray, *Corporate Responsibility: A Critical Introduction* (OUP, 2008) 13.

way, that they behave in a *responsible* way. Thus the concepts of 'corporate responsibility reporting (CR reporting)', which includes CSR reporting and sustainability reporting,[60] and integrated reporting (<IR>) (again including CSR reporting and sustainability reporting) have become prominent in recent years – we discuss these in greater detail in Chapter 2.

The 8th edition of *KPMG Survey of Corporate Responsibility Reporting 2013* (released in December 2013) illustrates this wider reporting expectation, and that companies are starting to live up to such expectations. That edition of the KMPG Report surveyed 4100 companies across 41 countries and found that CR reporting has evolved into a mainstream business practice over the last two decades. The KPMG survey found that 71 per cent of the companies surveyed undertook CR reporting and, in particular, that there had been a dramatic increase in CR reporting rates in the Asia-Pacific in 2012 and 2013.[61]

Thus several strands form an integral part of the principles of contemporary corporate governance today: considering the interests of all stakeholders; corporations' social responsibility; corporations being good citizens; corporate responsibility beyond CSR; and corporations' responsibility to aim at sustainable growth. These forms of reporting on, and disclosing, non-financial information provide a powerful corporate governance tool in the sense that they compel companies to think beyond the financial bottom line.[62] Investors are indeed insisting on getting reliable information on non-financial issues to enable them to make responsible investments in responsible companies that are focused on more than short-term financial profits.

The focus on corporate *governance* has enabled commentators and researchers to identify new trends and to articulate these trends in the form of new models of governance, reflecting the current reality regarding the governance of, in particular, large public corporations.[63] This has resulted in the possibility of offering a more articulated definition of 'corporate governance'.

1.1.3 Proposed definition of 'corporate governance'

Taking recent developments into consideration, we believe that one way 'corporate governance' could be defined is as follows:

> The system of regulating and overseeing corporate conduct and of balancing the interests
> of all internal stakeholders and other parties (external stakeholders, governments and
> local communities – see Chapter 2) who can be affected by the corporation's conduct, to

---

60   See Global Reporting Initiative (GRI) <www.globalreporting.org/Pages/default.aspx>; GRI,
      Sustainable Reporting Guidelines: Version 3.1 (GRI, 2011) <www.globalreporting.org/resourcelibrary/
      G3.1-Guidelines-Incl-Technical-Protocol.pdf>.

61   KMPG, Corporate Responsibility Reporting Survey 2013 <www.kpmg.com/AU/en/IssuesAndInsights/
      ArticlesPublications/Pages/corporate-responsibility-reporting-survey-2013.aspx>. According to the
      Corporate Responsibility Reporting Survey 2015, the inclusion of Corporate Responsibility information in
      annual reports has risen by 36% since 2011: KPMG, Corporate Responsibility Reporting Survey 2015
      <https://home.kpmg.com/content/dam/kpmg/pdf/2015/11/kpmg-international-survey-of-corporate-
      responsibility-reporting-2015.pdf>.

62   See Jean J du Plessis, 'Disclosure of non-financial information: A powerful corporate governance tool'
      (2016) 34 *C&SLJ* 69.

63   See Esser, *Recognition of Various Stakeholder Interests in the Company Management* (2009) 19–36 for a
      useful summary of these theories.

ensure responsible behaviour by corporations and to create long-term, sustainable growth for the corporation.[64]

The most important elements of this definition are that corporate governance:

- is the system of regulating and overseeing corporate conduct;
- takes into consideration the interests of internal stakeholders and other parties who can be affected by the corporation's conduct;
- aims at ensuring responsible behaviour by corporations; and
- aims at creating long-term, sustainable growth for the corporation.

A comparison with the definition of 'corporate governance' we provided in the first edition (2005) of this work will reveal that we have changed the first element of the definition from 'a process of controlling management' to 'the system of regulating and overseeing corporate conduct'. This adjustment reflects a widening of the corporate governance debate and the prominence that regulating and overseeing corporate conduct has gained since 2005. The Global Financial Crisis, which commenced in 2007, provided further impetus to view corporate governance in an even wider context.[65]

A comparison with the second edition of this book (2011) will reveal that we have replaced 'has the ultimate goal of achieving the maximum level of efficiency and profitability' with 'creating long-term, sustainable growth for the corporation'. This adjustment is based on the very clear trend in recent years away from a simple, single bottom-line, profit-maximisation-for-shareholders approach to an approach focusing more and more on CSR and, most recently, on long-term, sustainable growth, which should be achieved in a responsible way.[66] In other words, we argue for a move away from 'short-termism' – the pressure to deliver quick results to

---

64   For other useful definitions of corporate governance, see Ken Rushton, 'Introduction' in Ken Rushton (ed.), *The Business Case for Corporate Governance* (CUP, 2008) 2–3; Huse, *Boards, Governance and Value Creation* (2007) 15 and 18–24; Bob Garratt, *Thin on Top* (Nicholas Brealey Publishing, 2003) 12; John Farrar, 'Corporate governance and the judges' (2003) 15 *Bond Law Review* 65; and Güler Manisali Darman, *Corporate Governance Worldwide: A Guide to Best Practices and Managers* (ICC Publishing, 2004) 9–11.

65   In particular, the global financial crisis highlighted the importance of regulation and oversight in supporting good governance. See Grant Kirkpatrick, 'The Corporate Governance Lessons from the Financial Crisis' in *Financial Market Trends* (OECD, 2009). The relationship between regulation and governance in restoring public trust and investor confidence remains an important point of discussion. The International Federation of Accountants focused on aspects of governance and regulation at two Roundtables, in Hong Kong and London in February and October 2016. It is important to note the shift to 'smart and effective' values-based regulation as a means to improve confidence in the financial and capital markets, business, and government, rather than complex rules-based regulation. See International Federation of Accountants, *From Crisis to Confidence: A Call for Consistent, High-quality Global Regulation* (IFAC, 2016) <http://html5.epaperflip.com/?docid=7b4bf0af-503f-4294-a0f3-a5a1012a48b3#page=1> and International Federation of Accountants, *From Crisis to Confidence: Good Regulation, Governance, and Culture* (IFAC, 2016) <www.ifac.org/system/files/publications/files/From-Crisis-to-Confidence-Good-Regulation-Governance-and-Culture-Sept-2016.pdf>. The transition to a values-based approach in preference to a rules-based one is also evident in the King IV Report on Corporate Governance for South Africa.

66   Pamela Queen contends that wealth creation for shareholders is best achieved by focusing on long-term value-added financial performance measures and attention to non-financial performance indicators. Pamela E Queen, 'Enlightened shareholder maximization: Is this strategy achievable?' (2015) 127 *Journal of Business Ethics*, 683, 693.

the potential detriment of the longer-term and sustainable development of a company.[67] We discuss this trend in greater detail in Chapter 2. This is, of course, a goal that we would hope all companies would aspire to as a result of this definition of 'corporate governance'. However, it is aspirational, and there are some who doubt that short-termism will *not* remain the dominant focus for corporate management.[68] Thus, if companies do not voluntarily strive to create long-term, sustainable growth, will more radical measures, such as legislation, be required to ensure this? We hope not, but it is not inconceivable that such measures might be needed if self-regulation, soft law and voluntary market-based pressures do not have the desired effect.

Although views differ on this,[69] it is important to note that the Global Financial Crisis was no indication of a total failure of corporate governance. This is explained in the King Report (2009) from a South African and UK perspective, but it rings true much more widely:

> The credit crunch, and the resulting crisis among leading financial institutions, is increasingly presented as a crisis of corporate governance. However, although current problems are to an extent indicative of shortcomings in the global financial architecture, they should not be interpreted as reflecting dysfunction in the broader South African and UK corporate governance models where values-based principles are followed and governance is applied, not only in form but also in substance.[70]

In a report commissioned by the OECD, 'The Corporate Governance Lessons from the Financial Crisis', it was pointed out that the problems with risk management in the Global Financial Crisis context were not so much caused by the models and systems used but had more to do with *governance* of risk, including inadequate board oversight and an increased appetite for risk.[71] In addition, as David Millon explains, reckless behaviour and irresponsible activities of companies, major causes of the Global Financial Crisis, happened as a result of the demands of investors for immediate profits – all short-term driven.[72] What we need to establish

---

67   Sir George Cox, 'Overcoming Short-termism within British Business: The Key to Sustained Economic Growth', independent review commissioned by the Labour Party (March 2013) <www.yourbritain .org.uk/uploads/editor/files/Overcoming_Short-termism.pdf>. In 2015, Angel Gurría, OECD Secretary-General, stated the purpose of corporate governance as helping to build an environment of trust, transparency and accountability necessary for fostering long-term investment, financial stability and business integrity, thereby supporting stronger growth and more inclusive societies: G20/OECD, *Principles of Corporate Governance* (2015) 7.

68   See Millon, 'Enlightened Shareholder Value, Social Responsibility and the Redefinition of Corporate Purpose without Law' (2012) 96–7.

69   See Thomas Clarke and Jean-Francois Chanlat, 'Introduction: A new world disorder?' in Thomas Clarke and Jean-Francois Chanlat (eds), *European Corporate Governance* (Routledge, 2009) 1 and 13–18. See generally, and for a more radical plea for a total overhaul and new perspectives on the state of health of corporate governance, Hutchinson, *The Companies We Keep* (2005) 12–19 and 203 *et seq.* See also Anjan Thakor, 'The Financial Crisis of 2007–09: Why did it happen and what did we learn?', Research Paper (7 January 2014) <http://ssrn.com/abstract=2372449> or <http://dx.doi.org/10.2139/ssrn.2372449>.

70   *King Report on Governance for South Africa 2009* (King Report (2009)) (Institute of Directors (2009) 9 <http://african.ipapercms.dk/IOD/KINGIII/kingiiireport/>.

71   Grant Kirkpatrick, 'The Corporate Governance Lessons from the Financial Crisis' in *Financial Market Trends* (OECD, 2009) 5–6.

72   Millon, 'Enlightened Shareholder Value, Social Responsibility and the Redefinition of Corporate Purpose without Law' (2012) 77–8. See also Dine and Koutsias, *The Nature of Corporate Governance* (2013) ix.

is how the principles of contemporary corporate governance contribute to ensuring better governance of large public companies. This will become clear in the following chapters of this book.

1.2 'Essential' principles of corporate governance

In recent years there have been several attempts to identify and explain the 'essential' principles of corporate governance. Although there are several examples,[73] different principles have been identified as 'essential' and, over time, views have changed. There is nothing wrong or inconsistent with this evolutionary process. As we stated at the beginning of this chapter, corporate governance is a subject area that grows and expands, and it adjusts according to new insights and new challenges. As Mervyn King puts it, 'good governance is a journey and not a destination'[74] or, as Tricker puts it:

> Undoubtedly, corporate governance continues to evolve. The metamorphosis that will determine the bounds and the ultimate structure of the subject has yet to occur. Present practice is still rooted in a 19th century legal concept of the corporation that is totally inadequate in the emerging global business environment.[75]

A good illustration of the evolutionary nature of corporate governance as subject area is provided by the various South African King Reports. In the King Report (2002), seven 'essential' principles of corporate governance were identified, namely:

1. discipline;
2. transparency;
3. independence;
4. accountability;
5. responsibility;
6. fairness; and
7. social responsibility.

In the King Report (2009), the emphasis shifted slightly, towards some 'key aspects of the report', which are explained as follows in the Introduction and Background:

> The philosophy of the Report revolves around leadership, sustainability and corporate citizenship. To facilitate an understanding of the thought process, debate and changes in the Report, the following key principles should be highlighted:

---

73   See, for example, OECD, *Principles of Corporate Governance* (April 2004) and *The Combined Code on Corporate Governance* (UK Combined Code (2008)) <www.ecgi.org/codes/documents/combined_code_june2008_en.pdf>.

74   King Report (2009) 4.

75   Tricker, *Corporate Governance* (2012) 488.

1. Good governance is essentially about effective *leadership*. Leaders should rise to the challenges of modern governance. Such leadership is characterised by the ethical values of responsibility, accountability, fairness and transparency and based on moral duties ... Responsible leaders direct company strategies and operation with a view to achieving sustainable economic, social and environmental performance.

2. *Sustainability* is the primary moral and economic imperative for the 21st century.[76] It is one of the most important sources of both opportunities and risks for businesses. Nature, society, and business are interconnected in complex ways that need to be understood by decision-makers. Most importantly, current, incremental changes towards sustainability are not sufficient – we need a fundamental shift in the way companies and directors act and organise themselves.

3. The concept of *corporate citizenship* which flows from the fact that the company is a person and should operate in a sustainable manner ...

The King IV Report[77] continues to recognise the importance of ethical leadership, sustainability and corporate citizenship. Ethical and effective leadership, in particular, is cited in the Preface as an enduring foundational value. However, the Report strongly focuses on governance in a broader context and lists the organisation as an integral part of society, stakeholder inclusivity, and integrated thinking and integrated reporting as its underpinning philosophies. The Report is drafted against the background of and informed by three interrelated 'paradigm shifts' in the corporate environment: the shift from financial capitalism to inclusive capitalism, from short-term capital market to long-term, sustainable capital markets and from siloed reporting to integrated reporting. The concepts of inclusiveness and integration lie at the heart of King IV.[78]

Another illustration of changing views on 'essential' principles of corporate governance is revealed by comparing the original (2003)[79] version of the ASX *Principles of Good Corporate Governance and Best Practice Recommendations* and the 2014 ASX *CG Principles and Recommendations*. In 2003, 10 essential principles of good corporate governance were identified; these 10 were consolidated to 8 essential principles in 2007 and they are still the 8 principles contained in the ASX *CG Principles and Recommendations* (3rd edn, 2014).[80] They are:

1. Lay solid foundations for management and oversight: A listed entity should establish and disclose the respective roles and responsibilities of its board and management and how their performance is monitored and evaluated.

2. Structure the board to add value: A listed entity should have a board of an appropriate size, composition, skills and commitment to enable it to discharge its duties effectively.

3. Act ethically and responsibly: A listed entity should act ethically and responsibly.

---

76   See also our discussion on sustainable, integrated and responsibility reporting in Chapter 2.

77   The Report was published on 1 November 2016. It is effective in respect of financial years commencing on or after 1 April 2017 and replaces King III in its entirety. The Report contains the first outcomes-based governance code in the world.

78   *The King IV Report on Corporate Governance* (Institute of Directors, 2016).

79   ASX, *Principles of Good Corporate Governance and Best Practice Recommendations* (March 2003).

80   ASX, *CG Principles and Recommendations* (2014) 4.

4. Safeguard integrity in corporate reporting: A listed entity should have formal and rigorous processes that independently verify and safeguard the integrity of its corporate reporting.

5. Make timely and balanced disclosure: A listed entity should make timely and balanced disclosure of all matters concerning it that a reasonable person would expect to have a material effect on the price or value of its securities.

6. Respect the rights of security holders: A listed entity should respect the rights of its security holders by providing them with appropriate information and facilities to allow them to exercise those rights effectively.

7. Recognise and manage risk: A listed entity should establish a sound risk management framework and periodically review the effectiveness of that framework.

8. Remunerate fairly and responsibly: A listed entity should pay director remuneration sufficient to attract and retain high quality directors and design its executive remuneration to attract, retain and motivate high quality senior executives and to align their interests with the creation of value for security holders.[81]

1.3 Is 'good corporate governance' important and does it add value?

When corporate governance was raised in conversation and commentaries a few years ago, there were often references to the need for corporations to implement and maintain 'good governance practices'. However, there has been a continuing debate as to whether a focus on governance practices comes at the expense of what is really important to the company and its stakeholders – creating long-term, sustainable growth for the corporation! Did giving attention to 'conformance', in terms of adhering to corporate governance rules and principles, come at the expense of 'performance'? Was implementing good corporate governance practices a necessary ingredient for corporate success, or merely a distraction from the real business of the company? Naturally, given that there is still debate and uncertainty as to what 'corporate governance' means, there are varying perspectives on what constitutes good practice in corporate governance, and whether good corporate governance is indeed important to the company and actually adds value or 'makes a difference'.[82]

Nowadays, however, these questions seem almost rhetorical, as it is easy to find numerous very good reasons – and even empirical proof – that good corporate governance is important to companies and that it does add value and make a difference. As will be clear from the few sources quoted in the footnote, the need for good corporate governance is still gaining considerable momentum, especially in light of the broader and long-term focus on sustainable and responsible corporations.[83]

81   Ibid.
82   See, generally, Jonathan Charkham, *Keeping Better Company* (OUP, 2nd edn, 2005) 23–4; Sir Geoffrey Owen, 'The Role of the Board' in Rushton (ed.), *The Business Case for Corporate Governance* (2008) 11.
83   See, for example, Owen Report, *The Failure of HIH Insurance – Volume I: A Corporate Collapse and its Lessons* (Commonwealth of Australia, 2003) 104–5 para 6.1.2 and 133 para 6.6; Rushton (ed.),

1.4 Are corporate governance models converging?

Scholars across a range of academic disciplines have debated whether corporate governance systems and practices are indeed converging on the Anglo-American shareholder-value-oriented model since Henry Hansmann and Reinier Kraakman announced 'The End of History for Corporate Law' in 2001.[84] It was to be expected that their proposition – that all corporate governance models in actual fact converged upon the US corporate governance model – would be challenged. Douglas Branson wrote an article titled 'The very uncertain prospect of "global" convergence in corporate governance',[85] and many other articles that challenged Hansmann and Kraakman's hypothesis followed.[86] This debate is still alive, with part of Thomas Clarke and Jean-Francois Chanlat's *European Corporate Governance* dedicated to the question.[87]

Tricker has correctly pointed out that cultural differences will always play a role in the development of the most appropriate corporate governance model for a particular country – such differences will almost guarantee that there will always be differences between the corporate governance principles and corporate governance models of countries and jurisdictions.[88] This is also illustrated well by *The Nature of Corporate Governance: The Significance of National Cultural Identity*, by Janet Dine and Marios Koutsias,[89] and by a large number of essays on several jurisdictions, published under the title *Comparative Corporate Governance: A Functional and International Analysis*.[90] These essays make it very clear how many

The Business Case for Corporate Governance (2008); Donald H Chew and Stuart L Gillan, 'Introduction' in Donald H Chew and Stuart L Gillan (eds), *Global Corporate Governance* (Columbia Business School, 2009) IX; and René M Stulz, 'Globalization, Corporate Finance, and the Cost of Capital' in Chew and Gillan (eds), *Global Corporate Governance* (2009) 108 *et seq*; Henry Bosch, 'The changing face of corporate governance' (2002) 25 *University of New South Wales (UNSW) Law Journal* 270, 271; Rick Sarre, 'Responding to corporate collapses: Is there a role for corporate social responsibility?' (2002) 7 *Deakin Law Review* 1; Sir Bryan Nicholson, 'The Role of the Regulator' in Rushton (ed.), *The Business Case for Corporate Governance* (2008) 100; Scot Miller, 'Assessing the components of effective corporate governance' (2013) 7 *Strategic Management Review* 47.

84   Henry Hansmann and Reinier Kraakman, 'The end of history for corporate law' (2001) 89 *Georgetown Law Journal* 439. Also see Jeffrey N Gordon and Mark J Roe (eds), *Convergence and Persistence in Corporate Governance* (CUP, 2004).

85   Douglas M Branson, 'The very uncertain prospect of "global" convergence in corporate governance' (2001) 34 *Cornell International Law Journal* 321.

86   Clarke refers to 'one of the liveliest debates of the last two decades concerning the globalisation and convergence of corporate governance'. See Thomas Clarke, 'The continuing diversity of corporate governance: Theories of convergence and variety' (2016) 16 *Ephemera Theory and Politics in Organization* 19, 23.

87   Clarke and Chanlat (eds), *European Corporate Governance* (2009) 141–97. Clarke continues to support the divergence approach. He argues that 'shareholder value' is a debilitating ideology that undermines corporations with an oversimplification of complex business reality. It weakens managers, corporations and economies, and ignores the diversity of investment institutions and interests. See Clarke, 'The continuing diversity of corporate governance' (2016) 19, 22.

88   Tricker, *Corporate Governance* (2012) 153. See also Chew and Gillan, 'Introduction' in Chew and Gillan (eds), *Global Corporate Governance* (2009) X; Huse, *Boards, Governance and Value Creation* (2007) 103–4.

89   Dine and Koutsias, *The Nature of Corporate Governance* (2013).

90   Andreas M Fleckner and Klaus J Hopt (eds), *Comparative Corporate Governance: A Functional and International Analysis* (CUP, 2013).

differences there still are as far as company and corporations laws are concerned among the 23 countries covered.[91]

Tricker lists the forces that could lead to convergence of corporate governance principles, and also those that accentuate divergence, or at least cause differentiation among corporate governance principles in different countries and jurisdictions:

Converging forces:[92]

- corporate governance codes of good practice;
- securities regulation;
- international accounting standards;
- global concentration of audit practices;
- globalisation of companies;[93]
- raising capital on overseas stock exchanges;
- international institutional investors;
- private equity funding;
- cross-border mergers of stockmarkets; and
- research publications, international conferences and professional journals.

Diverging forces:

- legal differences;
- standards in the legal process;
- stockmarket differences;
- ownership structures; and
- history, cultural, and ethical groupings.[94]

Although there is some scepticism about whether even strong market forces will lead to the ultimate convergence of corporate governance models,[95] it is very difficult to disprove the convergence of corporate governance principles and practices in an internationalised and globalised world.[96] In this book we deal with core principles, themes and issues such as the

---

91   More recently, Clarke concluded that 'To assume that all countries will adapt to the same corporate governance structures is unrealistic, unfounded and unimaginative.' He contended that 'To the extent [that] countries adopt universal principles they will do so within a culturally diverse set of corporate values, structures, objectives and practices': Clarke, 'The continuing diversity of corporate governance' (2016) 47.

92   Tricker, *Corporate Governance* (2012) 163–4. See also Dine and Koutsias, *The Nature of Corporate Governance* (2013) 313.

93   Globalisation's impact on university governance is well illustrated in Simon Marginson and Mark Considine, *The Enterprise University* (CUP, 2000) 41, 45–51.

94   Tricker, *Corporate Governance* (2012) 164.

95   See Paul L Davies and Klaus J Hopt, 'Boards in Europe – Accountability and Convergence', ECGI – Law Working Paper No. 205/2013; Oxford Legal Studies Research Paper No. 40/2013, 6–8 <http://ssrn.com/abstract=2212272>.

96   See Inaugural ICGL Forum: 4–5 November 2013 Muenster Germany, 'Key Themes and Issues in a Globalised and Internationalised World' <www.icgl.org.au/>. See also Dine and Koutsias, *The Nature of Corporate Governance* (2013) 75. Krenn, however, contends that although the internationalisation and integration of markets made the boundaries of corporate governance systems more permeable for the transfer of ideas, firms' exposure to global market pressures may not always lead to convergence on shareholder-oriented standards: Mario Krenn, 'Convergence and divergence in corporate governance: An integrative institutional theory perspective' (2016) 39 *Management Research Review* 1447, 1457.

recognition of the interests of all stakeholders; responsibility, sustainability or integrated reporting; the distinction between directing, supervising and governing as a board function and managing the business of the corporation as a management function; codes of good corporate governance;[97] measures to prevent excessive executive remuneration; and board diversity and quota legislation to ensure gender diversity, to name but a few issues. All of these carry strong hallmarks of the convergence of contemporary corporate governance principles and illustrate that corporate governance models are converging generally.[98] There will, of course, never be a complete convergence (different forms of convergence are now distinguished: formal, functional, contractual, hybrid, normative and institutional)[99] of all corporate governance models because of the strong diverging forces Tricker lists,[100] the reality of 'path dependency'[101] and unique cultural approaches to certain governance issues,[102] but that there are signs of the convergence of contemporary corporate governance principles is hard to deny. A third alternative is 'converging divergences', an approach that integrates the opposing viewpoints in the convergence–divergence debate.[103] Proponents of this approach suggest that the processes that direct the dynamics of convergence and/or divergence may coexist and lead to increasing diversity in corporate governance systems and in firms' corporate governance arrangements.[104] Chhillar and Lellapalli do not view converging divergences as much as an alternative to convergence or divergence, but rather a hybrid model, the inevitable practical outcome of the interplay between the forces to adapt best governance practices at the firm level and the differences in legal and institutional frameworks at the macro-economic level.[105]

---

97   See Paul L Davies and Klaus J Hopt, 'Corporate boards in Europe – Accountability and convergence' (2013) 61 *The American Journal of Comparative Law* 301 (Abstract), making the following observation: 'More recently, in particular in the wake of the rise of the international corporate governance code movement, there has been a clear tendency towards convergence, at least in terms of the formal provisions of the codes.'

98   See generally Klaus J Hopt, 'Conflict of interest, secrecy and insider information of directors, a comparative analysis' (2013) 2 *European Company and Financial Law Review (ECFR)* 168.

99   Mathias Siems and David Cabrelli, 'Form, Style and Substance in Comparative Company Law' in Mathias Siems and David Cabrelli (eds), *Comparative Company Law: A Case-Based Approach* (Hart Publishing, 2013) 367–9.

100 Tricker, *Corporate Governance* (2012) 164.

101 See David Cabrelli and Mathias Siems, 'A Case-Based Approach to Comparative Company Law' in Siems and Cabrelli (eds), *Comparative Company Law: A Case-Based Approach* (2013) 5; Klaus J Hopt, 'Comparative corporate governance: The state of the art and international regulation' (2011) 59 *The American Journal of Comparative Law* 1; Stephen M Bainbridge, 'Insider trading regulation: The path-dependent choice between property rights and securities fraud' (1999) 52 *Southern Methodist University Law Review* 1589 <http://ssrn.com/abstract=208272> or <http://dx.doi.org/10.2139/ssrn.208272>; Stephen M Bainbridge 'Director primacy and shareholder disempowerment' (2006) 119 *Harvard Law Review* 1735/UCLA School of Law, Law-Econ Research Paper No. 05–25 <http://ssrn.com/abstract=808584>; Lucian Arye Bebchuk and Mark J Roe, 'A theory of path dependency in corporate ownership and governance' (1999) 52 *Stanford Law Review* 127; Mark J Roe, 'Path Dependency, Political Options, and Governance Systems' in Klaus J Hopt and Eddy Wymeersch (eds) *Comparative Corporate Governance* (Walter de Gruyter, 1997), 167–8 and 178.

102 John Farrar, *Corporate Governance in Australia and New Zealand* (OUP, 3rd edn, 2008) 6–7.

103 Mario Krenn, 'Convergence and divergence in corporate governance: An integrative institutional theory perspective' (2016) 39 *Management Research Review* 1447, 1448.

104 Ibid. 1462.

105 See Palka Chhillar and Ramana Venkata Lellapalli, 'Divergence or convergence: Paradoxes in corporate governance?' (2015) 15 *Corporate Governance* 693, 702.

1.5 Conclusion

There are various definitions of 'corporate governance'. We believe, however, that the most realistic approach to corporate governance is the so-called inclusive approach – viewing all stakeholders as part of the corporate governance debate. At the end of the day, corporate governance deals with the system of regulating and overseeing corporate conduct, balancing the interests of all internal stakeholders and other parties who may be affected by the corporation's conduct in order to ensure responsible behaviour by corporations and creating long-term, sustainable growth for the corporation. There is ample evidence that there are real economic benefits in following good practice in corporate governance – by doing so, boards of directors and managers will potentially be able to add significant shareholder value and investors will be prepared to pay a premium for investments in companies in which good corporate governance practices are followed.

There are some powerful forces responsible for the convergence of corporate governance principles and models.[106] However, there are also several forces and factors that will almost guarantee that there will always be differences in the corporate governance models of different countries and jurisdictions.

There are many challenges ahead if we look at the bigger picture, and that is why it is appropriate to have not only an opening quote, but also a concluding quote, from Paul Hawken's excellent visionary book, *The Ecology of Commerce*:

> [B]usiness[es] ... will breathe their own exhaust as long as they can profit by it. This intransigency hasn't changed as much as one would have hoped, but it is more about human nature than it is about commerce – the inability to subordinate short-term monetary gains to the long-term well-being of humanity.[107]

We are still firmly of the opinion that the principles of corporate governance will remain relevant and become of increasing importance in the future.[108]

---

106 Initiatives steered by international and regional agencies such as the Organization for Economic Co-operation and Development (OECD) to integrate corporate governance codes globally are a case in point. See Chhillar and Lellapalli, 'Divergence or convergence: Paradoxes in corporate governance?' (2015) 699.

107 Hawken, *The Ecology of Commerce* (2010) xx.

108 Garratt, *Thin on Top* (2003) 29–64.

2

STAKEHOLDERS IN CORPORATE GOVERNANCE AND CORPORATE SOCIAL RESPONSIBILITY

What we are witnessing is a shift in the content of the shareholder value norm, so that it comes to represent the idea that shareholders exercise their powers not as representatives of the market, but as agents of society as a whole. The corporate governance of the future will be centrally concerned with how this idea is worked out in practice.

Simon Deakin, 'The Coming Transformation of Shareholder Value' (2005) 13
Corporate Governance: An International Review 16

To create an enduring society we need a system of commerce and production where each and every act is inherently sustainable and restorative. Business will need to integrate economic, biologic, and human systems to create a sustainable method of commerce. As hard as we may try to become sustainable on a company-by-company level, we cannot fully succeed until the institutions surrounding commerce are redesigned.

Paul Hawken, *The Ecology of Commerce* (Harper Business, revised edn, 2010) xii

2.1 Introduction

As touched upon in Chapter 1, contemporary commentary on corporate governance can, in general terms, be divided into two main camps: those who consider corporate governance as being about building effective mechanisms and measures to satisfy the expectations of the variety of individuals, groups and entities (collectively, 'stakeholders')[1] that inevitably interact with the corporation,[2] and those who focus on it in relation to the narrower expectations of shareholders (shareholder primacy).[3]

This chapter focuses on the first of these objectives,[4] with attention being given to the stakeholders of the company, how the law influences corporations to recognise and protect the interests of these stakeholders, and the relationship between these stakeholders and the underlying objective of companies of achieving and maintaining good corporate governance.

Steve Letza, Xiuping Sun and James Kirkbride explain the difference between the two corporate governance paradigms, 'shareholding' and 'stakeholding', as follows:

Such a division hinges on the purpose of the corporation and its associated structure of governance arrangements understood and justified in theory. On one side is the trad-itional shareholding perspective, which regards the corporation as a legal instrument for

---

1   For a review of the history and nature of the stakeholder theory, see also Emerson Wagner Mainardes, Helena Alves and Mario Raposo, 'Stakeholder theory: Issues to resolve' (2011) 47 *Management Decision* 229–32 and Corina Gavrea and Roxana Stegerean, 'Comparative study on corporate governance' (2011) 20 *Annals of the University of Oradea, Economic Science Series* 674.

2   EM Dodd, 'For whom are corporate managers trustees?' (1932) 45 *Harvard Law Review* 1145.

3   A Berle, 'Corporate powers as powers in trust' (1931) 44 *Harvard Law Review* 1049; A Berle, 'For whom corporate managers are trustees: A note' (1932) 45 *Harvard Law Review* 1365.

4   For a broader discussion on competing corporate law theories and the public and private dimensions of corporate law, see Stephen Bottomley, *The Constitutional Corporation – Rethinking Corporate Governance* (Ashgate, 2007).

shareholders to maximise their own interests – investment returns. A three-tier hierarch-ical structure, i.e. the shareholder general meeting, the board of directors and executive managers, is given in company law in an attempt to secure shareholders' interests ...

On the other side is the stakeholding perspective newly emerged in the later 20th century, which positions itself on the contrary to the traditional wisdom and views the corporation as a locus in relation to wider external stakeholders' interests rather than merely shareholders' wealth. Employees, creditors, suppliers, customers and the local community are major stakeholders often mentioned and emphasised within a broad definition of stakeholding. [5]

The central place of non-shareholder stakeholders in corporate governance has been explicitly recognised by the Organisation for Economic Co-operation and Development (OECD) in the preamble to the 2015 version of the G20/OECD *Principles of Corporate Governance*:

Corporate governance involves a set of relationships between a company's management, its board, its shareholders *and other stakeholders*. Corporate governance also provides the structure through which the objectives of the company are set, and the means of attaining those objectives and monitoring performance are determined. (emphasis added)[6]

The revised version of the OECD principles in 2015, now called G20/OECD *Principles of Corporate Governance*, maintains and strengthens the core values and principles expressed in the 2004 version. Also contained in the 2004 version of the OECD *Principles of Corporate Governance* is the following statement, recognising three key non-shareholder stakeholders (creditors, employees and government):

Corporate governance is affected by the relationships among participants in the govern-ance system. Controlling shareholders, which may be individuals, family holdings, bloc alliances, or other corporations acting through a holding company or cross shareholdings, can significantly influence corporate behaviour. As owners of equity, institutional invest-ors are increasingly demanding a voice in corporate governance in some markets. Individual shareholders usually do not seek to exercise governance rights but may be highly concerned about obtaining fair treatment from controlling shareholders and management. Creditors play an important role in a number of governance systems and can serve as external monitors over corporate performance. Employees and other stakeholders play an important role in contributing to the long-term success and perform-ance of the corporation, while governments establish the overall institutional and legal framework for corporate governance.[7]

The G20/OECD *Principles of Corporate Governance*, a non-binding statement of what the OECD believes to constitute best practice in corporate governance, is discussed extensively in this book.

---

5   See Steve Letza, Xiuping Sun and James Kirkbride, 'Shareholding versus stakeholding: A critical review of corporate governance' (2004) 12 *Corporate Governance: An International Review* 242, 243.
6   G20/OECD, *Principles of Corporate Governance* (2015) <http://dx.doi.org/10.1787/9789264236882-en>.
7   OECD, *Principles of Corporate Governance* (2004). For reinforcement of this approach, see Part IV of the G20/OECD *Principles of Corporate Governance* (2015), which discusses the role of stakeholders in corporate governance.

The structure of this chapter is as follows. Section 2.2 below commences by acknowledging that there is no fixed definition of what a 'stakeholder' is; however, it provides some useful examples of definitions that have been adopted in mainstream literature, and which can be used for the purposes of this chapter. This section then proceeds to identify, and provide a brief explanation of, the nature and corporate governance role of each 'stakeholder' recognised by the G20/OECD *Principles of Corporate Governance*.

Having provided this general understanding of what is meant by 'stakeholder' and to whom this concept applies, Section 2.3 then explains whether and how the law requires – or at least encourages – companies and their directors and executives to take into account the interests of these stakeholders. The principal focus of this section is the requirement for listed companies to have in place a 'code of conduct' specifying how the company intends to deal with its stakeholders – particularly employees. The section also discusses similar obligations for non-listed companies, as well as legal obligations applying to companies (both listed and non-listed) – outside company law and corporate governance – that require them to protect and respect the interests of stakeholders.

Having considered how the law requires or encourages companies, both listed and non-listed, to take into consideration and protect the interests of a variety of stakeholders, Section 2.4 then discusses why a stakeholder-oriented approach to management (known as the 'stakeholder model') is considered important from the perspective of good corporate governance. This includes discussion (albeit brief) on emerging trends and issues in relation to the role of particular stakeholders in the corporation (particularly employees) in maintaining a sound internal governance framework, from the perspective of good corporate governance.

We also revisit the debate on the interaction between the 'shareholder primacy' approach to corporate decision-making and the 'enlightened self-interest' approach, and use the James Hardie asbestos compensation case to illustrate what devastating consequences can occur if a company ignores its responsibilities towards stakeholders such as employees. Corporate social responsibility (CSR) was touched upon in Chapter 1, but in this chapter we discuss CSR in more detail.

2.2 Stakeholders in the corporation: An overview[8]

2.2.1 What is a stakeholder?

The definition of 'stakeholder' is not set in stone.[9] Indeed, there are almost as many definitions of what a 'stakeholder' is and who can be characterised as a stakeholder as there are individuals who have written about stakeholders in corporate governance.

---

8   For empirical evidence regarding the way in which Australian directors perceive their obligations to various stakeholders, see Shelley Marshall and Ian Ramsay, 'Stakeholders and directors' duties: Law, theory and Evidence' (2012) 35 *University of New South Wales (UNSW) Law Journal* 291.

9   Corporations and Markets Advisory Committee (CAMAC), *The Social Responsibility of Corporations Report* (Australian Government, 2006) [2.4] notes that the notion of 'stakeholders' has no precise or commonly agreed meaning: <www.camac.gov.au/camac/camac.nsf/byHeadline/PDFFinal+Reports +2006/$file/CSR_Report.pdf>. See further B Horrigan, 'Fault lines in the intersection between corporate governance and social responsibility' (2002) 25 *UNSW Law Journal* 515.

Christine Mallin provides the following explanation:

> The term 'stakeholder' can encompass a wide range of interests: it refers to any individual or group on which the activities of the company have an impact.[10]

According to Mallin, apart from shareholders, 'stakeholder' encompasses employees, suppliers, customers, banks and other creditors, the government, and various 'pressure groups'. This is a useful definition, although it fails to include those individuals or entities whose activities have impacts upon the company.

Perhaps a better definition of 'stakeholder', one which does recognise such a mutual relationship between stakeholders and the corporation, is that provided in *Redefining the Corporation: Stakeholder Management and Organizational Wealth* by James E Post, Lee E Preston and Sybille Sachs.[11] They define 'stakeholder' as follows:

> The stakeholders in a corporation are the individuals and constituencies that contribute, either voluntarily or involuntarily, to its wealth-creating capacity and activities, and that are therefore its potential beneficiaries and/or risk bearers.[12]

The authors go on to explain:

> The fundamental idea is that stakeholders have a *stake* in the operation of the firm, in the same sense that business partners have a common stake in their venture or players on a team a common stake in the outcome of a game. Stakeholders share a common risk, a possibility of gaining benefits or experiencing losses or harms, as a result of corporate operations.

In developing a 'stakeholder model' of the corporation, Post et al. posit that there is a series of flows running through the corporation, with stakeholders holding a central position:

> The flows between the firm and its stakeholders run in both directions; each stakeholder is perceived as contributing something and receiving something from the corporation (even involuntary and essentially passive stakeholders contribute by tolerating the existence and operation of the firm, and receive some combination of benefits and harms as a result).[13]

Another important perspective on stakeholders and the corporation is contained in the 1990 article, 'Corporate governance: A stakeholder interpretation', by RE Freeman and WM Reed.[14] Freeman and Reed refer to the organisation as being a 'multiple agreement' between the enterprise and its stakeholders, and suggest that there are 'external' and 'internal' stakeholders. The 'internal' stakeholders include employees, managers and owners. Employees are included because management depends upon employees to fulfil strategic intentions. 'External' stakeholders include customers, suppliers, competitors and 'special interest' groups – with each

---

10   Christine Mallin, *Corporate Governance* (OUP, 2nd edn, 2007) 49.
11   JE Post, LE Preston and S Sachs, *Redefining the Corporation: Stakeholder Management and Organizational Wealth* (Stanford Business Books, 2002).
12   Ibid. 19.
13   Ibid. 22.
14   See RE Freeman and WM Reed, 'Corporate governance: A stakeholder interpretation' (1990) *Journal of Behavioural Economics* 337.

relationship constrained by formal and informal rules. Finally, governments and local communities set the legal and formal rules within which businesses must operate.

Due to the quite broad, and to some degree 'vague', definition of 'stakeholder' that has been put forward in various ways by commentators, the question has been raised – mainly in management and finance literature – about who the stakeholders in the corporation actually are, with this flowing on to further questions about the practice of stakeholder management.

Perhaps the most inclusive definition of stakeholders, as recognised by the Corporations and Markets Advisory Committee (CAMAC) report on *The Social Responsibility of Corporations*,[15] is the following:

> Stakeholders are defined as entities or individuals that can reasonably be expected to be significantly affected by the organization's activities, products, and/or services; and whose actions can reasonably be expected to affect the ability of the organization to successfully implement its strategies and achieve its objectives. This includes entities or individuals whose rights under law or international conventions provide them with legitimate claims vis-à-vis the organization.[16]

This broad definition can therefore include all the constituents discussed earlier, as well as pressure groups or non-government organisations (NGOs), usually characterised as public interest bodies that espouse social goals relevant to the activities of the company.

It is important to note that different attitudes towards the place of stakeholders in corporate governance are evident in different jurisdictions, and that these are influenced by differences in tradition and culture. Mallin, for example, notes that:

> In the UK and the US, the emphasis is on the relationship between the shareholders (owners), and the directors (managers). In contrast, the German and French corporate governance systems, which view companies as more of a partnership between capital and labour, provide for employee representation at board level, whilst banks (providers of finance) may also be represented on the supervisory board.[17]

2.2.2 Discussion of stakeholders

This section provides a general account of the role of some of the key stakeholders in the governance of a company. The explanation provided for each stakeholder draws heavily on Mallin's book, which contains a clear and concise description of the place of stakeholders in contemporary corporate governance.

What is emphasised below in the discussion of the different stakeholders is that, apart from shareholders, discrete areas of legal regulation operating independently of company law and corporate governance principles have a direct and significant impact on the relationship between particular stakeholders and the company.

---

15   CAMAC, *The Social Responsibility of Corporations: Report* (2006) [2.4].
16   Global Reporting Initiative (GRI), *Sustainable Reporting Guidelines: Version 3.1* (GRI, 2011) 10 <www.globalreporting.org/resourcelibrary/G3.1-Guidelines-Incl-Technical-Protocol.pdf>.
17   Mallin, *Corporate Governance* (2007) 57.

2.2.2.1 Shareholders

As stakeholder management is often discussed as an alternative to the traditional shareholder-oriented approach to corporate governance (emphasising wealth maximisation), shareholders are regularly excluded from the definition of 'stakeholder'.

Mallin includes shareholders as part of her concept of 'stakeholder', but deals with shareholders separately from all the other constituents that are also stakeholders. She defines 'shareholder' as 'an individual, institution, firm, or other entity that owns shares in a company'.[18] As Mallin appreciates, however, the reality of shareholding is more complex than this definition suggests, once beneficial ownership and cross-holdings are considered.

Mallin treats shareholders differently from other stakeholders for two reasons: '[F]irst, shareholders invest their money to provide risk capital for the company and, secondly, in many legal jurisdictions, shareholders' rights are enshrined in law whereas those of the wider group of stakeholders are not.'[19] Mallin goes on to say that a rationale for privileging shareholder interests over the interests of other stakeholders is that they are:

> the recipients of the residual free cash flow (being the profits remaining once other stakeholders, such as loan creditors, have been paid). This means that the shareholders have a vested interest in trying to ensure that resources are used to maximum effect, which in turn should be to the benefit of society as a whole.[20]

Justice Owen, in the Report of the HIH Royal Commission (Owen Report), articulates a similar conception of corporate governance when explaining the 'organs of governance':

> [P]rimary governance responsibility lies with the board of directors. In formal terms the directors are appointed by, and are accountable to, the body of shareholders ... The role of the shareholders is to exercise the powers that are reposed in them by the *Corporations Act* and the constitution of the corporation. The perceived wisdom is, I think, that shareholders play a passive role as the objects of corporate governance rather than an active role as part of it.[21]

2.2.2.2 Employees

Following is a summary of the explanation given by Mallin of the role of employees as stakeholders in the corporation:

> The employees of a company have an interest in the company as it provides their livelihood in the present day and at some future point, employees would often also be in receipt of a pension provided by the company's pension scheme. In terms of present day employment, employees will be concerned with their pay and working conditions, and how the company's strategy will impact on these. Of course the long-term growth and prosperity of the company is important for the longer term view of the employees, particularly as concerns pension benefits in the future ...

---

18   Ibid. 49.
19   Ibid.
20   Ibid.
21   Report of the HIH Royal Commission (Owen Report), *The Failure of HIH Insurance – Volume I: A Corporate Collapse and its Lessons* (Commonwealth of Australia, 2003) 103 para 6.1.1.

> Many companies have employee share schemes which give the employees the
> opportunity to own shares in the company, and feel more of a part of it; the theory being
> that the better the company does (through employees' efforts, etc), the more the employ-
> ees themselves will benefit as their shares increase in price . . .
>
> *Companies need to also consider and comply with employee legislation, whether*
> *related to equal opportunities, health and safety at work, or any other aspect.* Companies
> should also have in place appropriate whistle-blowing procedures for helping to ensure
> that if employees feel that there is inappropriate behaviour in the company, they can
> 'blow the whistle' on these activities whilst minimizing the risk of adverse consequences
> for themselves as a result of this action. (emphasis added)[22]

There are several rationales for promoting employee share ownership,[23] but in essence
employee share schemes provide employees an opportunity to have a 'real interest' in the
corporation. Research generally supports the principle that ongoing ownership interests can
lead to greater employee engagement and improved business outcomes.[24]

However, the legal arrangements regarding these schemes are often quite complex and do
not provide employees with any power to have an impact, albeit indirectly, on managerial
decision or the board composition, as is the case in the German system of codetermination.[25]
Subsequent to the release of a 2013 consultation paper on employee incentive schemes by the
Australian Securities and Investments Commission (ASIC), the regulator has issued a Regulatory Guide[26] and Class Orders[27] aimed at cutting the red tape[28] and reducing the administrative
burden associated with these schemes.[29]

It is important to note that Australia also has in place a sophisticated array of legislation and
regulations, at both state/territory and federal levels, which are designed to protect the interests
of employees in relation to their interaction with the employer and the workplace. At the state/
territory level, there is equal opportunity legislation, workplace health and safety legislation

---

22   Mallin, *Corporate Governance* (2007) 51.

23   Ingrid Landau, Ann O'Connell and Ian Ramsay, *Incentivising Employees* (Melbourne University Press,
      2013) 11–13.

24   See <http://asic.gov.au/regulatory-resources/corporate-governance/corporate-governance-articles/
      changes-for-employee-incentive-schemes>.

25   See discussion of the German model in Chapter 12.

26   See ASIC Regulatory Guide 49: Employee Incentive Schemes (November 2015).

27   See Class Orders ([CO 14/1000] *Employee incentive schemes: Listed bodies* and [CO 14/1001] *Employee*
      incentive schemes: Unlisted bodies).

28   See ASIC's website <www.asic.gov.au/asic/asic.nsf/byheadline/Consultation+papers?
      openDocument#cp218> linking to this document <www.asic.gov.au/asic/pdflib.nsf/
      LookupByFileName/cp218-attachment–draft-updated-RG49-published-14-November-2013.pdf/$file/
      cp218-attachment–draft-updated-RG49-published-14-November-2013.pdf>.

29   This development should be seen in the wake of tax laws that have severely affected employee share
      schemes in Australia since 1 July 2009. In April 2013, an expert panel of Employee Ownership Australia
      and New Zealand (EOA) released a report entitled *The Changing ESS Landscape since 1 July 2009*,
      which argues that the introduction of Division 83A of the *Income Tax Assessment Act 1997* (Cth) in
      2009 has reduced participation in employee share schemes (ESSs). See further Ian Ramsay (ed.), *SAI*
      Global Corporate Law Bulletin, Bulletin No. 189 (21 May 2013) Part 1.11 <http://services.exchange
      .deakin.edu.au/owa/?ae=Item&a=Open&t=IPM.Note&id=RgAAAADQkKPZnH8bSK1ZsAOGhKq
      RBwB613auimC2QKc7Qa085vWNAAAKFoP4AADjk0JJRfE1TJWpXqvgv1WaAABldGLGAAAJ&pspid=_
      1389651956669_617557064>.

(the obligations under which operate to preserve the well-being, health and safety of contractors and customers, in addition to employees), as well as general regulations and criminal laws to protect employee rights. At the federal level, the principal legislation designed to uphold and protect the interests of employees is the *Fair Work Act 2009* (Cth), which regulates workplace conditions, wage-setting arrangements and the conciliation and arbitration of workplace disputes over pay and working conditions. The government also provides financial assistance to people owed employee entitlements following the insolvency or bankruptcy of employers, through the Fair Entitlements Guarantee (FEG).[30]

Australia has also introduced new whistleblower protection rules under the *Corporations Act 2001* (Cth) (the Act or Corporations Act) and listed companies are encouraged, as part of the Australian Securities Exchange's (ASX) *CG Principles and Recommendations*,[31] to explain in the company's code of conduct how the company protects 'whistleblowers' (including employees) who report violations in good faith – see Chapter 7 for a more detailed discussion of whistleblowing legislation in Australia. Part 9.4AAA of the Act operates to prohibit employers from victimising whistleblowers when they have acted in good faith and on reasonable grounds, and also provides the whistleblower with qualified privilege when information regarding a suspected breach of the law (the Act or the *Australian Securities and Investments Commission Act 2001* (Cth) or regulations made under either Act) has been reported to ASIC or another person specified in the Act. Principle 3 of the ASX *CG Principles and Recommendations* requires listed companies to have a code of conduct for directors, senior executives and employees that, among other things, encourages the reporting of unlawful/unethical behaviour by employees and others, and identifies measures the company follows to protect whistleblowers who report violations in good faith.[32]

In the 2016–17 Federal Budget the Australian Government announced the introduction of new arrangements to better protect tax whistleblowers as part of its commitment to tackling tax misconduct. In addition, as part of the Open Government National Action Plan, the Government has committed to ensuring that appropriate protections are in place for people who report corruption, fraud, tax evasion or avoidance, and misconduct within the corporate sector.[33]

Another useful explanation of the role of the employee in the corporation, and the significance of this role in terms of contemporary corporate governance, comes from the HIH Royal Commission's final report. In the part of the report discussing 'Organs of governance', Justice Owen states:

----

30   FEG, introduced under the *Fair Entitlements Guarantee Act 2012* (Cth) replaced the previous
      employee entitlement scheme known as the General Employee Entitlements and Redundancy
      Scheme (GEERS).

31   ASX, *CG Principles and Recommendations* (3rd edn, 2014) 20 (Box 3.1(5)) <www.asx.com.au/
      documents/asx-compliance/cgc-principles-and-recommendations-3rd-edn.pdf>. For guidance on the
      provision of a whistleblowing service, ASX recommends the Australian Standard, *Whistleblowing
      Protection Programs for Entities* (AS 8004).

32   Ibid. 30 (Box 3.1(1))). See ASIC Information Sheet 52 (INFO 52) August 2015, which sets out guidance
      for whistleblowers.

33   See <www.treasury.gov.au/ConsultationsandReviews/Consultations/2016/Review-of-whistleblower-
      protections>. For discussion on the need for whistleblower law reform, see <http://aicd
      .companydirectors.com.au/membership/membership-update/why-australia-needs-better-protection-
      for-whistleblowers>.

It is difficult to define with precision the part that employees play in corporate governance. It will depend on the extent to which the employee is involved in or can influence the decision-making process. Senior management is more likely to have such a role. But in large corporations or complex groups it may be that employees further down the corporate hierarchy have a decision-making function that involves elements of control in the process. There is a danger in the current emphasis on the role and responsibilities of boards of directors. It may cause to be overlooked the reality of the necessarily greater part that executives and other employees play in the day-to-day running of many corporate businesses.[34]

As to how employees can become important stakeholders in the corporation, again the G20/OECD *Principles of Corporate Governance* provides a useful discussion:

> The degree to which employees participate in corporate governance depends on national laws and practices, and may vary from company to company as well. In the context of corporate governance, performance-enhancing mechanisms for participation may benefit companies directly as well as indirectly through the readiness by employees to invest in firm-specific skills. Examples of mechanisms for employee participation include: employee representation on boards; and governance processes such as works councils that consider employee viewpoints in certain key decisions. With respect to performance-enhancing mechanisms, employee stock ownership plans or other profit-sharing mechanisms are to be found in many countries.[35]

The topic of employee participation, and more generally the role of employees as stakeholders, has been written about and commented upon a great deal over the past decade, and is still heavily debated and returned to regularly when considering reform options to improve corporate regulation and the governance practices of corporations.[36] In the Anglo-American, or 'outsider' system of corporate governance (which loosely describes Australia's system of corporate governance), neither employees nor shareholders have a particularly prominent role in the day-to-day governance arrangements of the corporation. The prospect for change was flagged in a speech in July 2016 by the British Prime Minister, Theresa May,[37] who envisaged a wider role for employees in corporate governance in the UK through direct participation at board level. Subsequent remarks in a later speech, however, indicate a watering down of the idea and a rejection of the German model of corporate governance for the UK.[38] In some European countries, most notably Germany, employees (as well as shareholders) are central to a company's governance practices through a two-tier board

---

34   Owen Report, *The Failure of HIH Insurance* (2003) Vol. 1, 104, para 6.1.1.

35   G20/OECD, *Principles of Corporate Governance* (2015) 35.

36   See Irene Lynch-Fannon, 'Employees as corporate stakeholders: Theory and reality in a transatlantic context' (2004) 4(1) *Journal of Corporate Law Studies* 155 (which contains a fresh analysis of what is meant by 'ownership' in order to argue for a central relationship between the corporation and employees in the corporate governance mix), and a collection of essays, Howard Gospel and Andrew Pendleton (eds), *Corporate Governance and Labour Management* (OUP, 2005).

37   *The Independent*, 'Theresa May's plan to put workers on boards is borrowed from Germany and France', 12 July 2016 <www.independent.co.uk/news/business/news/theresa-may-board-corporate-plan-germany-france-productivity-economics-a7132221.html>.

38   Prime Minister's Speech at CBI Annual Conference 2016 <www.gov.uk/government/speeches/cbi-annual-conference-2016-prime-ministers-speech>.

structure and a legislated system of 'codetermination' (see Section 12.4 for a discussion of Germany's system of corporate governance).

In the US, in particular, a lot of attention has been given over the past decade to the concept of 'wealth creation', which embodies a view that a long-term focus on wealth, rather than a short-term focus on returns to shareholders, is truly in the best interests of the company. Respect for employees is central to this emerging perspective, as the development of firm-specific skills by loyal and happy employees is considered an integral ingredient of 'wealth creation'. In a leading work on wealth creation, *Ownership and Control: Rethinking Corporate Governance for the 21st Century*, published in 1995, Margaret Blair argues that corporations should not be regarded as 'bundles of assets' that are the sole property of shareholders, but rather as institutional arrangements governing the relationship between all parties and contributing firm-specific assets – embracing not only shareholders, but also employees who develop specialised skills of value to the enterprise.

Blair explains that the idea of 'wealth creation' for the corporation extends beyond short-term profit-taking by shareholders to include the corporation's long-term interests (see further discussion of sustainable growth below), and thus views employees, customers and creditors as integral to the ensuring of the best interests of the corporation. Blair strongly associates achievement of wealth creation with recognition and respect for human capital: that is, employees. According to Blair:

> [I]n the 1990s, fewer and fewer publicly traded corporations actually look like the factory model. Much of the wealth-generating capacity of most modern firms is based on the skills and knowledge of the employees and the ability of the organization as a whole to put those skills to work for customers and clients. Even for manufacturing firms, physical plant and equipment make up a rapidly declining share of the assets, while a growing share consists of intangibles ... such as patent rights, brand reputation, service capabilities, and the ability to innovate and get the next generation product to market in a timely manner.[39]

Another emerging area of discourse that emphasises the importance of employee involvement in the overall governance framework of the corporation is the 'participatory management' philosophy. Commentators have referred to participatory management as the most important industrial relations phenomenon of the past three decades.[40] According to Stephen Bainbridge, there are two basic forms of participatory management – operational participation and strategic participation:

> Operational participation refers to programs in which employee involvement is limited to day-to-day issues of productivity and working conditions at the plant level ...
>
> Strategic participation refers to programs in which employees participate in major policy decisions, such as those traditionally viewed as falling within the realm of corporate governance.[41]

---

39   Margaret Blair, *Ownership and Control: Rethinking Corporate Governance for the 21st Century* (Brookings Institute, 1995) Ch. 1 ('Primer on Corporate Governance').

40   Stephen M Bainbridge, 'Corporate decision-making and the moral rights of employees: Participatory management and natural law' (1998) 43 *Villanova Law Review* 741.

41   Ibid. 742.

2.2.2.3 Creditors

Creditors always rate a mention as one group of key stakeholders in the corporation. Apart from the rapidly increasing literature on corporate governance, over the years many commentators have examined whether company directors can[42] and should owe a duty to act in the best interests of creditors while serving the company.[43]

The majority judgment in the Appellate Court decision in *Westpac Banking Corporation v Bell Group Ltd (in liq) (No 3)*[44] reaffirms that the precise nature and scope of directors' duties to creditors upon corporate insolvency remains an unresolved judicial issue. In particular, following the majority judgment in this case, it is now unclear whether directors must go beyond consideration of creditors' interests and ensure that creditors are protected in conformity with the pari passu principle.[45]

In discussing the place of creditors as company stakeholders, Mallin separates creditors into two categories: 'providers of credit' and 'suppliers'.[46] As to the former:

> Providers of credit include banks and other financial institutions. Providers of credit want to be confident that the companies that they lend to are going to be able to repay their debts ... It is in the company's best interest to maintain the confidence of providers of finance to ensure that no calls are made for repayment of funds, that they are willing to lend to them in the future, and that the company is able to borrow at the best possible rate.

As to the latter:

> Suppliers have an interest in the companies which they supply on two grounds. First, having supplied the company with goods and services, they want to be sure that they will be paid for these and in a timely fashion. Secondly, they will be interested in the continuance of the company as they will wish to have a sustainable outlet for their goods and services.

---

42 Directors have no direct fiduciary duties to creditors: *Spies v The Queen* (2000) 201 CLR 603.

43 For a discussion of the much-vexed issue of directors' fiduciary duties to creditors following the High Court decision in *Spies*, see the scholarly debate, starting with James McConvill, 'Directors' duties towards creditors in Australia after *Spies v The Queen*' (2002) 20 *Company and Securities Law Journal (C&SLJ)* 4; in reply Anil Hargovan, 'Directors' duties to creditors in Australia after *Spies v The Queen* – Is the development of an independent fiduciary duty dead or alive?' (2003) 21 *C&SLJ* 390; James McConvill, 'Geneva finance and the "duty" of directors to creditors: Imperfect obligation and other imperfections' (2003) 11 *Insolvency Law Journal* 7; in reply Anil Hargovan, 'Geneva finance and the "duty" of directors to creditors: Imperfect obligation and critique' (2004) 12 *Insolvency Law Journal* 134. The debate appears to be resolved: Justice Owen in *Bell Group Ltd (in liq) v Westpac Banking Corporation (No 9)* (2008) 70 ACSR 1 at [4398] held that the question was 'determined authoritatively' by the High Court in *Spies*. For comprehensive examination of this topic, see Andrew Keay, *Company Directors' Responsibilities to Creditors* (Routledge-Cavendish, 2006).

44 (2012) WAR 12 Ch 392.

45 For exploration of this issue and the extent to which the judiciary can intervene to adjudicate directors' beliefs and business judgments in an insolvency context, see Anil Hargovan and Jason Harris, 'For whom the bell tolls: Directors' duties to creditors after *Bell*' (2013) 35(2) *Sydney Law Review* 433. The *Bell* case was settled by the parties on the eve of the High Court appeal hearings. For a comparative perspective with the law in the US, see Anil Hargovan and Tim Todd, 'Financial twilight re-appraisal: Ending the judicially created quagmire of fiduciary duties to creditors' (2016) 78(2) *University of Pittsburg Law Review* 135.

46 See Mallin, *Corporate Governance* (2007) 51–2.

The G20/OECD *Principles of Corporate Governance* also discusses the significant place of creditors in contemporary corporate governance, and the various ways in which creditor interests may be, or in fact are, protected by law. Importantly, rather than requiring the internal governance arrangements of corporations to recognise and embrace creditor interests, reference is made to the discrete area of insolvency law (which generally includes directors' duties to creditors) to protect creditors in their relationship with the corporation:

> ... creditors are a key stakeholder and the terms, volume and type of credit extended to firms will depend importantly on their rights and on their enforceability. Companies with a good corporate governance record are often able to borrow larger sums and on more favourable terms than those with poor records or which operate in non-transparent markets. The framework for corporate insolvency varies widely across countries. In some countries, when companies are nearing insolvency, the legislative framework imposes a duty on directors to act in the interests of creditors, who might therefore play a prominent role in the governance of the company. Other countries have mechanisms which encourage the debtor to reveal timely information about the company's difficulties so that a consensual solution can be found between the debtor and its creditors.
>
> Creditors' rights vary, ranging from secured bond holders to unsecured creditors. Insolvency procedures usually require efficient mechanisms for reconciling the interests of different classes of creditors. In many jurisdictions provision is made for special rights, such as through 'debtor in possession' financing, which provides incentives/protection for new funds made available to the enterprise in bankruptcy.[47]

2.2.2.4 Customers

Mallin provides the following very brief explanation of how a company's customers also fit the description of 'stakeholder' from a corporate governance perspective:

> Increasingly customers are also more aware of social, environmental, and ethical aspects of corporate behaviour and will try to ensure that the company supplying them is acting in a corporately socially responsible manner.[48]

Under Chapter 7 of the *Corporations Act* (dealing with financial services and markets), retail clients of a financial product must receive a 'product disclosure statement', which must provide an explanation of, among other things, the extent to which labour standards or environmental, social or ethical considerations are taken into account in the selection, retention or realisation of an investment if the product has an 'investment component' (see s 1013D(1)(l) of the Act).

Australian Consumer Law (ACL), as set out in Schedule 2 of the *Competition and Consumer Act 2010* (Cth), is also important in ensuring that the interests of customers are a central consideration of the corporation in its day-to-day activities. There is an extensive number of rules under Chapter 2 of the ACL, 'Consumer Protection', including the general prohibition on misleading and deceptive conduct and unconscionable conduct, and further aims to protect and uphold the interests of consumers through rules on product recalls, defective goods and anti-competitive conduct.

---

47   G20/OECD, *Principles of Corporate Governance* (2015) 36.
48   Mallin, *Corporate Governance* (2007) 52.

These requirements (as well as a number of others) work together so that, in Australia, the role of customers in corporate governance is neatly aligned with Mallin's description above.

2.2.2.5 The community

A great deal has been written about whether society as a whole is also a specific stakeholder of the modern corporation, and the implications for directors' duties and corporate regulation more generally if society is, indeed, a stakeholder. Referring to 'society' as a whole as being a stakeholder presents some difficulties, as it makes it very difficult to provide any meaningful conception of what obligation this imposes on the corporation. Mallin's approach of examining society at the micro-level of the 'local community' seems useful and workable. According to Mallin:

> Local communities have a number of interests in the companies which operate in their region . . . companies will be employing large numbers of local people and it will be in the interest of sustained employment levels that companies in the locality operate in an efficient way. Should the company's fortunes start to decline then unemployment might rise and could lead to part of the workforce moving away from the area to seek jobs elsewhere . . . [L]ocal communities would also be concerned that companies in the area act in an environmentally friendly way, as the last thing they would want is pollution in local rivers, in the soil or in the atmosphere generally. It is therefore in the local community's interest that companies in their locality continue to thrive but do so in a way that takes account of local and national concerns.[49]

2.2.2.6 The environment

In the first edition of this book, it was noted that:

> just as contentious as the question of whether 'society' is a stakeholder of the corporation is whether 'the environment' can be considered to be a stakeholder. Perhaps this is because the implications of both, in terms of how a company must structure its affairs and do business, are enormous.

The call for environmental change has progressed rapidly since then, with a growing sense of urgency[50] that negates the need for the 'contentious' claim made earlier.[51]

Following the launch of the Kyoto Protocol in 2005,[52] managing greenhouse gas emissions has become a routine part of doing business in key global trading markets, and shareholders and financial analysts increasingly assign value to companies that prepare for and capitalise upon business opportunities posed by climate change – whether from greenhouse gas

---

49   Ibid.

50   For example, see Intergovernmental Panel on Climate Change (IPCC), *Climate Change 2007: The Physical Science Basis – Contribution of Working Group 1 to the Fourth Assessment Report of the Intergovernmental Panel on Climate Change* (Cambridge University Press [CUP], 2007).

51   See generally Janet Dine and Marios Koutsias, *The Nature of Corporate Governance: The Significance of National Cultural Identity* (Edward Elgar, 2013) 56–62.

52   The Kyoto Protocol was adopted at the Third Session of the Conference of the Parties to the UN Framework Convention on Climate Change in 1997, in Japan. Countries signatory to the Protocol undertook legally binding commitments to reduce greenhouse gas emissions in the commitment period 2008 to 2012.

regulations, direct physical impacts or changes in corporate reputation.[53] In a report on climate change and corporate governance, the following observations were made:[54]

> For corporations, climate change is a financial problem that presents significant economic and competitive risks and opportunities. Corporate boards, executives and shareholders simply cannot afford to ignore it[55] ... Given the sweeping global nature of climate change, climate risk has become embedded, to a greater or lesser extent, in every business and investment portfolio.[56]

In *Corporate Governance*, Mallin speaks not just of the 'environment' as being a stakeholder, but also of the various environmental lobby groups, both on the domestic level and the international level, that operate to ensure that companies meet environmental standards. These standards can be either self-imposed standards or standards derived from obligations under environment protection and other legislation (for example, the *Environment Protection Act 1970* (Vic) and the *Environment Protection and Biodiversity Conservation Act 1999* (Cth)).[57]

Tied in with the concept of 'wealth creation' discussed above is the concept of 'sustainability'. That is, growth can only be maintained over the long term if the manner in which resources (both natural and human) are used and treated is sustainable. Thus attention must quickly turn to the environment and the ways in which it is being used and protected,[58] with a view to maintaining long-term growth (recently contrasted with 'short-termism': the pressure to deliver quick results to the potential detriment of the longer-term development of a company).[59] Put simply, if the manner in which resources are being used to achieve growth now cannot be sustained, then long-term growth is not achievable. What is needed is *long-term, sustainable growth*. However, it is one thing to promote long-term, sustainable growth, but how do we measure whether we are on the right track at the right pace, and how do we encourage sustainable growth? This is where the new trend of 'sustainability reporting' comes in. It is reporting not only on the traditional single bottom-line financial reporting, but also on the long-term business success of companies. As is pointed out in the Australian Council of Superannuation Investors' (ACSI's) 2013 research paper, 'Corporate reporting in Australia: Disclosure of sustainability risks among S&P/ASX200 companies', environmental, social and

---

53   This account is drawn from Douglas Cogan, 'Corporate Governance and Climate Change: Making the Connection' (March 2006) 1 – this report was commissioned by Ceres from the Investor Responsibility Center.

54   Ibid. 11. The report is the first comprehensive examination of how 100 of the world's largest corporations are positioning themselves to compete in a carbon-constrained world.

55   For an interesting discourse on the corporate and securities law obligations on US companies in the context of climate change, see Perry Wallace, 'Climate change, fiduciary duty, and corporate disclosure: Are things heating up in the boardroom?' (2008) 26 *Virginia Environmental Law Journal* 293.

56   'Between 1994 and 2002, 62 shareholder resolutions on global warming issues were filed with the SEC in the US and 26 of them came to votes': E Hancock, 'Corporate risk of liability for global climate change and SEC disclosure dilemma' (2005) 17 *Georgetown International Environmental Law Review* 233, 249.

57   The Australian Government's Carbon Pollution Reduction Schemes Bill 2009 was rejected by the Senate in December 2009. See further 'Garnaut Climate Change Review: Emissions Trading Scheme Discussion Paper' (March 2008) <www.garnautreview.org.au/index.htm>.

58   See generally Dine and Koutsias, *The Nature of Corporate Governance* (2013) 56–62.

59   Sir George Cox, *Overcoming Short-termism within British Business: The Key to Sustained Economic Growth*, independent review commissioned by the Labour Party (March 2013) <www.yourbritain.org.uk/uploads/editor/files/Overcoming_Short-termism.pdf>.

governance (ESG) issues will have a profound impact on the ability of companies and their investors to achieve sustainable growth and prosperity into the future.[60] To enable investors to effectively price and manage risk during their analysis of an investment, they need relevant information, and companies need to understand the form that that information should take[61] – that is the ultimate aim with sustainability reporting: investors being able to analyse the information obtained from such reporting to make informed decisions about whether or not they invest in companies. While the sustainability reporting agenda is also promoted actively internationally, there appears to be some reluctance to adopt integrated reporting in some countries.[62] The concept of integrated reporting has been warmly embraced in other countries, such as South Africa.[63] Under the banner 'Integrated Reporting <IR>',[64] the International Integrated Reporting Council (IIRC) [65] explains as follows:

> [Integrated reporting] is a process founded on integrated thinking that results in a periodic integrated report by an organization about value creation over time and related communications regarding aspects of value creation … An integrated report is a concise communication about how an organization's strategy, governance, performance and prospects, in the context of its external environment, lead to the creation of value in the short, medium and long term.[66]

To promote consistency with integrated reporting, the IIRC released an *International <IR> Framework* on 9 December 2013. It followed a three-month global consultation led by the IIRC[67] earlier in 2013,[68] which elicited over 350 responses, coming from every region in the world, the overwhelming majority of which expressed support for integrated reporting.[69] Since

---

60   Australian Council of Superannuation Investors' (ACSI), 'Corporate reporting in Australia: Disclosure of sustainability risks among S&P/ASX200 companies' 2 <www.acsi.org.au/images/stories/ACSIDocuments/generalresearchpublic/Sustainability%20Reporting%20Journey%202013%20-%20public%20version.pdf>.

61   Ibid.

62   For example, see Anna Huggins, Roger Simnett and Anil Hargovan 'Integrated reporting and directors' concerns about personal liability exposure: Law reform options' (2015) 33 *C&SLJ* 176; Jean du Plessis and Andreas Rühmkorf, 'New trends regarding sustainability and integrated reporting for companies: What protection do directors have?' (2015) 36 *Company Lawyer* 49.

63   King IV, 4–5, 13 and 23 <www.iodsa.co.za/?page=KingIV>. See further Mervyn King and Jill Atkins, *Chief Value Officer: Accountants can Save the Planet* (Greenleaf Publishing Ltd, 2016) Chs 8 and 11.

64   See <www.theiirc.org/>.

65   See <www.theiirc.org/the-iirc/structure-of-the-iirc/>.

66   See <www.theiirc.org/>. For a holistic view of the evolution and practice of integrated reporting, see Chiaro Mio (ed.), *Integrated Reporting: A New Accounting Disclosure* (Palgrave Macmillan, 2016).

67   See <www.theiirc.org/the-iirc/structure-of-the-iirc/>.

68   On 26 March 2013, at the request of the International Integrated Reporting Council (IIRC), the International Federation of Accountants (IFAC), together with the Chartered Institute of Management Accountants (CIMA) and PwC, released a background paper, titled 'Business model', which highlights the business model as being at the heart of integrated reporting. The report revealed wide variation in how organisations define their business models and approach to disclosure and highlighted the need for a clear, universally applicable, international definition of a business model – see IFSA, 'Companies lagging on business model reporting; Background paper released to tackle the issue', Press Release (26 March 2013) <www.ifac.org/news-events/2013-03/companies-lagging-business-model-reporting-background-paper-released-tackle-issu>.

69   See <www.theiirc.org/international-ir-framework/>.

then 1500 companies have signed up to use integrated reporting.[70] In April 2013 the European Commission (EC) announced a possible amendment to existing legislation to ensure transparency and require companies with more than 500 employees to report, in a shorter form, information on policies, risks and results as regards:[71]

• environmental matters;
• social and employee-related aspects;
• respect for human rights;
• anti-corruption and bribery issues; and
• diversity on the boards of directors.

Consequently, the European Union (EU) recently adopted a directive that will mandate sustainability reporting starting in 2017.[72] More than 6000 large companies and groups across the EU will be affected by the new directive. The approach taken ensures that the administrative burden is kept to a minimum. Companies will be required to disclose concise, useful information necessary for an understanding of their development, performance, position and the impact of their activity, rather than a fully fledged and detailed report. Furthermore, disclosures may be provided at group level, rather than by each individual affiliate within a group.[73]

On 9 June 2014 the UK Financial Reporting Council (FRC) released its *Guidance on the Strategic Report*.[74] That report and the IIRC's *International <IR> Framework* are now much more closely aligned, ensuring better quality reporting in the UK.[75] Another indication of the dynamic developments in the area of voluntary reporting was the release of the UN Environment Programme's (UNEP's) report, *Integrated Governance: A New Model of Governance for Sustainability*, in June 2014.[76] The report contains useful information on the impact of large corporations on society, how to develop a sustainability strategy and notes that 'integrated governance' is 'a model that combines bringing sustainability oversight into the boardroom together with addressing some of the identified current governance weaknesses that prevent boards from operating in the most efficient way'.[77] In the introductory message it is made very clear that the question of whether or not sustainability could be considered financially material is now irrelevant, as it has been illustrated by more than 200 academic reports that there is a significant relationship between sustainability performance and financial performance.[78]

---

70   See <http://boardagenda.com/2017/03/03/iirc-seeks-global-feedback-integrated-reporting/>.
71   See EC, 'Commission moves to enhance business transparency on social and environmental matters',
      Press Release (16 April 2013) <http://europa.eu/rapid/press-release_IP-13-330_en.htm>.
72   See <http://framework-llc.com/eu-mandates-esg-disclosures/>.
73   EC, 'Disclosure of non-financial information by certain large companies' (26 February 2014).
74   See FRC, *Guidance on the Strategic Report* (June 2014) <https://frc.org.uk/Our-Work/Publications/
      Accounting-and-Reporting-Policy/Guidance-on-the-Strategic-Report.pdf>.
75   See IIRC, 'IIRC welcomes move towards better quality reporting in the UK', Press Release
      (9 June 2014) <www.theiirc.org/2014/06/09/iirc-welcomes-move-towards-better-quality-reporting-in-
      the-uk/>.
76   UNEP, *Integrated Governance: A New Model of Governance for Sustainability* (June 2014)
      <www.unepfi.org/fileadmin/publications/investment/UNEPFI_IntegratedGovernance.pdf>.
77   Ibid. 35.
78   Ibid. 4.

The now revised (3rd edn, 2014) ASX *CG Principles and Recommendations* contains a new Recommendation 7.4 dealing with sustainability reporting:

> A listed entity should disclose whether it has any material exposure to economic, environmental and social sustainability risks and, if it does, how it manages or intends to manage those risks.[79]

The disclosure expectation is explained further:

> How a listed entity conducts its business activities impacts directly on a range of stakeholders, including security holders, employees, customers, suppliers, creditors, consumers, governments and the local communities in which it operates. Whether it does so sustainably can impact in the longer term on society and the environment.
>
> Listed entities will be aware of the increasing calls globally for the business community to address matters of economic, environmental and social sustainability and the increasing demand from investors, especially institutional investors, for greater transparency on these matters so that they can properly assess investment risk.
>
> To meet this recommendation does not require a listed entity to publish a sustainability report. However an entity that does publish a sustainability report may meet this recommendation simply by cross-referring to that report.[80]

Whether under the banner of 'sustainability reporting', 'integrated reporting (IR)' or 'corporate responsibility reporting (CR reporting)', the environment is central. As Mallin explains, for companies to promote sustainability, they must be environmentally responsible. An environmentally responsible company must not subject its workers to potentially hazardous processes without adequate protection, must not pollute the environment and should, where possible, use recyclable materials and engage in a recycling process. Mallin states: 'Ultimately all of these things will benefit society at large and the company itself.'[81]

In an excellent contribution to his 2004 collection of essays, Thomas Clarke emphasises the importance of protecting 'the environment' from a stakeholder–management perspective. According to Clarke:

> It is time for the principal–agent problematic to be reinforced with the environment–trustee problematic in both theory and practice. The competitive struggle to grow business and accumulate capital (whether measured by shareholder value or not) has disturbed the natural balance of the earth and threatened essential life-support systems.[82]

Clarke discusses how, incrementally, management philosophy and practice have embraced the concept of sustainability, rather than remaining focused purely on profit maximisation. The literature stresses that the way in which economic activity has been organised recently is not

---

79   ASX, *CG Principles and Recommendations* (3rd edn, 2014) <www.asx.com.au/documents/asx-compliance/cgc-principles-and-recommendations-3rd-edn.pdf>. For approaches to reporting, see Katherine Ng, 'New guidance on ESG reporting' (2016) 68 *Governance Directions* 439.

80   Ibid. 30. Katherine Ng, 'New guidance on ESG reporting' (2016) 68 *Governance Directions* 439.

81   Mallin, *Corporate Governance* (2007) 53.

82   See Thomas Clarke, 'Theories of Governance – Reconceptualizing Corporate Governance Theory after the Enron Experience' in Thomas Clarke (ed.), *Theories of Corporate Governance – The Philosophical Foundations of Corporate Governance* (Routledge, 2004) 25.

sustainable – which (as explained above) sits uncomfortably with a more long-term perspective on growth. According to Clarke:

> In the past, companies did not recognize or acknowledge the environmental or social effects of their operations ... The environmental context in which business must operate in the future suggests the following imperatives which all corporations will face, and all corporate governance systems will need to resolve: maintaining a licence to operate via transparency and accountability; generating more value with minimum impact; preserving the natural resource base, and doing business in a networked, intelligent multi-stakeholder world.[83]

With a more long-term approach to management, based on a wealth-creation perspective on corporate governance, it is clear that the environment is a central stakeholder of the corporation – in terms both of what the environment offers the corporation (long-term growth) and of the risk to the environment as a result of corporate activities.

From a practical perspective, the place of the environment as a principal stakeholder of the corporation has been emphasised not only in company codes of conduct and ethics that have recently become a feature of Australian corporate governance arrangements (as discussed in greater detail below), but also through discrete environmental policies that companies have adopted. These are designed to ensure that companies fulfil their core environmental obligations, and require employees and managers to act in an environmentally sensitive manner when at work and utilising the company's resources. Indeed, some companies have gone even further and implemented 'environmental procurement policies' requiring that, in order for suppliers to maintain business with the company, they need to maintain certain environmental 'KPIs' (key performance indicators). Some financial institutions take environment risks into account when evaluating business strategies in order to avoid environmental harm and credit risk.

As part of its 2017 sustainability strategy, Westpac Corporation Ltd, one of Australia's largest banks, has committed up to $6 billion to lending and investment in clean technologies and environmental services. Westpac was ranked number one in the 'Global 100 Most Sustainable Corporations in the World' at the World Economic forum in Davos, Switzerland, in January 2014.[84] Such initiatives and accolades suggest that some companies recognise the value of environmental, social and governance (ESG) factors to their long-term performance and view such factors as a business imperative with important outcomes for investors and the company.

2.2.2.7 Government

As noted earlier, Mallin's account of the place of stakeholders in contemporary corporate governance identifies government as a key stakeholder. In discussing the role of government as stakeholder, Mallin states:

> The government has an interest in companies for several diverse reasons.
>
> Firstly, as with the local and environmental groups – although not always with such commitment – it will try to make sure that companies act in a socially responsible way taking account of social, ethical, and environmental considerations. Secondly, it will

---

83   Ibid.
84   George Liondis, 'Westpac named world's most sustainable company at Davos', *Sydney Morning Herald*, 23 January 2014.

analyse corporate trends for various purposes such as employment levels, monetary policy, and market supply and demand of goods and services. Lastly, but not least, it will be looking at various aspects to do with fiscal policy such as capital allowances, incentives for investing in various industries or various parts of the country, and of course the taxation raised from companies![85]

2.2.2.8 All stakeholders have vested interests in the sustainability of corporations

At the end of the day, it is not difficult to conclude that all stakeholders have vested interests in the sustainability of corporations.[86] The *shareholders* want to maximise returns on their investment, not only by receiving good dividends, but also by making profits when they sell securities in a corporation. The *employees* are dependent on the company, not only to support themselves and their families, but in some cases also as holders of employee benefits, including retirement benefits. The *creditors* also have a strong interest in the sustainability of the company, as their expectation is that they are paid in accordance with the conditions agreed upon with the corporation, while supplier–creditors are of necessity dependent upon corporations to continue manufacturing products and services. *Customers* want to continue trading with corporations that provide excellent goods and services, and they will deal with the company to enforce guarantees and warranties against suppliers. The *communities* in which corporations do business, manufacture their goods or deliver their services gain by corporations providing job opportunities and creating wealth that leads to the improvement of living conditions, as long as the corporations adhere to good practice in corporate governance and do business in an environmentally friendly manner. The *environment* is our 'pearl', and is highly dependent on sustainable and environmentally friendly corporations. The *government* has an interest in the sustainability of corporations, as not only do they provide job opportunities to citizens, but they are also responsible for the majority of governmental income through taxes, levies, licences etc, which income is eventually reinvested into a country's infrastructure, health, education etc to ensure prosperity for its citizens.

2.3 Stakeholders' interests and the corporation: The role of the law

A major work (first published in 2004) titled *The Anatomy of Corporate Law: A Comparative and Functional Approach*, produced by seven leading corporate law and corporate governance scholars,[87] emphasises the important role of company law (including rules of corporate governance) in protecting stakeholder interests. Indeed, recognition and protection of stakeholder interests are regarded as two of the key functions of company law. The underlying thesis of this book is that in every jurisdiction, the central issue for corporate law is how to

---

85   Mallin, *Corporate Governance* (2007) 53.
86   Mervyn King, *The Corporate Citizen* (Penguin, 2006) 63.
87   Reinier Kraakman, Henry Hansmann, Edward Rock, Paul Davies, Gerard Hertig, Klaus Hopt and Hideki Kanda all made contributions to *The Anatomy of Corporate Law: A Comparative and Functional Approach* (OUP, 2nd edn, 2009).

mediate three kinds of 'agency conflicts': between managers and shareholders; between majority and minority shareholders; and between the firm *and third parties* (that is, stakeholders).

In this section we move beyond the rules of company law to look at how corporate governance regulation, in general, manages and protects stakeholder interests. We begin by examining a recent development in corporate governance regulation in Australia that has ensured a more prominent place for stakeholders in contemporary corporate governance, particularly in relation to listed companies. We also illustrate issues in corporate social responsibilities (CSR) arising from a September 2004 report of the Special Commission of Inquiry into the James Hardie asbestos compensation case.

A short discussion of the overseas position with respect to the recognition and protection of stakeholder interests is also provided in this section.

2.3.1 The Australian position

Since 1 July 2004, listed companies in Australia have been required, in order to comply with the ASX Corporate Governance Council's *Principles of Good Corporate Governance and Best Practice Recommendations* (as it was originally titled in 2003), to have in place and posted on their websites a code of conduct and ethics indicating how they intend to deal with stakeholder concerns and interests.[88] Unfortunately, this requirement disappeared from all later editions of the ASX's *Corporate Governance Principles and Recommendations*. In fact the entire Principle 10 ('Recognise the legitimate interests of stakeholders') disappeared in 2007 and stakeholders were only mentioned marginally in all later editions. The revised guide (2014)[89] represents Australia's attempt to develop a 'voluntary' regulatory framework that promotes adherence to best practice in corporate governance, in response to a series of corporate collapses in the earlier part of this century. As will be explained in greater detail in Chapter 5, the ASX *CG Principles and Recommendations* operates according to an 'if not, why not' approach[90] (called the 'comply or explain' principle in most other jurisdictions – see discussion of the principle in Chapters 11 and 12). Pursuant to ASX Listing Rule 4.10.3, listed companies must either comply with each recommendation or clearly explain the reasons for their non-compliance in their annual report. The recommendations build upon eight core principles, with each principle explained in detail and with commentary about implementation in the form of Recommendations.

The explanatory text accompanying the original (2003) *Principles of Good Corporate Governance and Best Practice Recommendations*[91] indicated that codes of conduct are intended to state the values and policies of the company, in order to ensure adequate public *or social accountability* by corporations. This broader aim did not form part of any of the later editions of the *Principles of Good Corporate Governance and Best Practice Recommendations*. It is also particularly noteworthy that the term 'corporate social responsibility' (CSR) is not even

---

88   ASX, *Principles of Good Corporate Governance and Best Practice Recommendations* (March 2003) 59 ff.
89   ASX, *CG Principles and Recommendations* (2014).
90   Ibid. 3, 5 and 7.
91   ASX, *Principles of Good Corporate Governance and Best Practice Recommendations* (March 2003) 59 ff.

mentioned in the 2014 edition.[92] 'Stakeholders' other than shareholders are currently only mentioned in passing or to point out who potential stakeholders are.[93]

Commentators, focusing on a range of empirical studies demonstrating that an increasing number of companies since the mid-1990s have adopted policies consistent with the concept of CSR, have made the following observation:

> the studies conducted to date suggest that the 'Australian approach' to CSR is still largely characterized by tentative and short term initiatives of a philanthropic nature. While there are exceptions, most businesses in Australia have not yet sought to integrate the precepts of CSR or corporate citizenship into their strategic approach or corporate culture.[94]

In 2004, the question of whether corporate governance, and more specifically rules concerning the duties of company directors, should be oriented towards protecting the interests of stakeholders, became a heavily debated issue in Australia. This debate resulted from a major scandal involving manufacturer James Hardie and that company's under-funding of an entity set up to compensate claimants with asbestos-related illnesses who had come into contact with James Hardie building products. More details of the James Hardie asbestos compensation affair are discussed later in this chapter. The potential for future asbestos victims to go uncompensated due to the arrangements set up by James Hardie led to calls for company law reform so that directors of the James Hardie parent company, and directors in the future under similar circumstances, could be made personally liable for claimant (that is, stakeholder) debts. In light of this, in March 2005 the Australian Government asked its Corporations and Markets Advisory Committee (CAMAC) to consider and report on whether the statutory duties of directors should be amended to clarify the extent to which directors can take stakeholder interests into account, or to require directors to take stakeholder interests into account.[95] The findings of the report, and its implications for stakeholders, are considered later in this chapter with reference to the debate on the interaction of the 'shareholder primacy' approach to corporate decision-making with the 'enlightened self-interest' approach.

2.3.2 Overseas position: A snapshot

What follows is a brief discussion of the approaches of the OECD, the EU, the US, the UK, Canada and South Africa to recognising and protecting the interests of company stakeholders, through corporate governance principles and/or company law rules.[96]

2.3.2.1 OECD

The G20/OECD *Principles of Corporate Governance* is very useful when considering how the regulation of corporate governance has recognised the importance of companies accommodating stakeholder interests. The G20/OECD Principles state that:

---

92   ASX, *CG Principles and Recommendations* (2014).
93   Ibid. 28 and 30.
94   H Anderson and I Landau, 'Corporate Social Responsibility in Australia: A review', in Corporate Law and Accountability Research Group Working Paper No. 4, Monash University (October 2006).
95   See further CAMAC, *The Social Responsibility of Corporations Report* (2006).
96   For insights into CSR in various European countries, see Andre Habisch, Jan Jonker, Martina Wegner and Rene Schmidpeter (eds), *Corporate Social Responsibility Across Europe* (Springer, 2005).

The corporate governance framework should recognise the rights of stakeholders established by law or through mutual agreements and encourage active co-operation between corporations and stakeholders in creating wealth, jobs, and the sustainability of financially sound enterprises.[97]

More specifically, the G20/OECD Principles recommend that OECD countries adhere to these principles:

(a) Laws and mutual agreements with stakeholders are to be respected.

(b) Where stakeholder interests are protected by law, stakeholders should have the opportunity to obtain effective redress for violation of their rights.

(c) Performance-enhancing mechanisms for employee participation should be permitted to develop.

(d) Where stakeholders participate in the corporate governance process, they should have access to relevant, sufficient and reliable information on a timely and regular basis.

(e) Stakeholders, including individual employees and their representative bodies, should be able to freely communicate to the board their concerns about illegal or unethical practices, and their rights should not be compromised for doing this.

(f) The corporate governance framework should be complemented by an effective, efficient insolvency framework and by effective enforcement of creditor rights. [98]

2.3.2.2 European Union (EU)[99]

The EU Green Paper, *Promoting a European Framework for Corporate Social Responsibility* (2001), described CSR as 'a concept whereby companies integrate social and environmental concerns in their business operations and in their interaction with their stakeholders on a voluntary basis'. Although the emphasis on the voluntary nature of CSR did not find favour with some of the respondents to the Green Paper,[100] this definition was reaffirmed by the European Commission (the executive arm of the EU) in its policy communication in 2006.[101]

The philosophical approach behind a definition of CSR, which integrates social and environmental concerns with business, and which is based on the fact that it should be 'voluntary', was described as follows:[102]

---

97   G20/OECD, *Principles of Corporate Governance* (2015) 90.

98   Ibid. See Part IV.

99   For a description of the development of CSR in the EU, see Sorcha MacLeod, 'Corporate Social Responsibility within the European Union framework' (2005) 23 *Wisconsin International Law Journal* 541. For a broader perspective, see Sorcha MacLeod, 'Reconciling regulatory approaches to Corporate Social Responsibility: The European Union, OECD and United Nations compared' (2007) 13 *European Public Law* 671.

100   For a summary of criticisms directed to this definition in the Green Paper by trade unions and NGOs, see MacLeod, 'Corporate Social Responsibility within the European Union framework' (2005), 545–7.

101   *Implementing the Partnership for Growth and Jobs: Making Europe a Pole of Excellence on CSR*, COM (22 March 2006). Andreas Rühmkorf, 'The promotion of Corporate Social Responsibility in English private law', PhD thesis, University of Sheffield (2013) 15 points out that 'there is no generally accepted definition of CSR and the growing academic and public interest in the concept of CSR has only added to the number of existing definitions'.

102   See EU Corporate Social Responsibility Briefing (16 March 2009) <www.eubusiness.com/topics/social/csr-guide/?searchterm=16%20March%202009%20corporate%20social>.

> It is essentially about companies being prepared to take the lead, and illustrate to the [European] Commission and to their stakeholders voluntarily that they take CSR seriously. CSR is always about going beyond the law. Ideally, CSR is a win–win scenario, whereby companies increase their profitability and society benefits at the same time.

In July 2002, the EC commented on the conflict between maximising short-term profits and achieving shareholder value by noting:[103]

> the growing perception among enterprises that sustainable business success and shareholder value cannot be achieved solely through maximising short-term profits, but instead through market-oriented yet responsible behaviour.

In May 2003, the EU released another communication, titled 'Modernising Company Law and Enhancing Corporate Governance in the European Union: A Plan to Move Forward'. This document again outlined the approach that the Commission intends to follow in the area of company law and corporate governance. Importantly, the Commission's position was that member states of the EU, on a voluntary basis, should take an *inclusive approach* – recognising and protecting the interests of key corporate stakeholders – as they move forward with reforming company law and corporate governance regulation. The document states:

> Ensuring effective and proportionate protection of shareholders *and third parties* must be at the core of any company law policy. A sound framework for protection of members and third parties, which properly achieves a high degree of confidence in business relationships, is a fundamental condition for business efficiency and competitiveness. In particular, an effective regime for the protection of shareholders and their rights, protecting the savings and pensions of millions of people and strengthening the foundations of capital markets for the long term in a context of diversified shareholding within the EU, *is essential if companies are to raise capital at the lowest cost.* (emphasis added)[104]

This general communication followed on from the communication on CSR of 2002. The document addressed the social and environmental aspects of doing business in the global economy, and led to the setting up by the EU of a European Multi-Stakeholder Forum, which aims to promote voluntary social and environmental practices as part of businesses' core activities. Indeed, a stakeholder-oriented approach to corporate governance is heavily emphasised and promoted in EU countries, with the Multi-Stakeholder Forum (formed in 2002) bringing together employers, employees, NGOs, academics and socially responsible investors every two years to discuss further ways for the EU to raise awareness of CSR, to encourage its adoption and to facilitate the exchange of best practices across Europe.[105] In addition, the European Coalition for Corporate Justice (ECCJ) was formed in 2006.

---

103   *The Commission Communication Concerning Corporate Social Responsibility: A Business Contribution to Sustainable Development*, COM (2 July 2002) 5.

104   EC, *Modernising Company Law and Enhancing Corporate Governance in the European Union: A Plan to move Forward* COM (2003) 284 (May 2003) 8 <http://eur-lex.europa.eu/LexUriServ/LexUriServ.do?uri=COM:2003:0284:FIN:EN:PDF>.

105   Other EU initiatives include a High-Level Group of Member States' representatives, which meets every six months to share approaches to CSR and encourage peer learning. A Commission inter-service group on CSR has the task of ensuring a coherent approach across the Commission services concerned. It involves the following policy areas: environment, justice, liberty and security; internal markets; health and consumer affairs; and external affairs.

A renewed EU strategy on CSR within the EU was launched in 2006, leading to the creation of the European Alliance for CSR, which is viewed as an important pillar of European policy on CSR. The Alliance lays the foundation for its partners to promote CSR in the future around the following three areas of activity:[106]

1. raising awareness and improving knowledge of CSR and reporting on its achievements;

2. helping to mainstream and develop open coalitions of cooperation; and

3. ensuring an enabling environment for CSR.

In 2013, Andreas Rühmkorf, focusing on the definition of CSR and whether it should be seen as 'voluntary' or 'mandatory', concluded that that issue is still far from settled.[107] However, there is a definite trend away from seeing CSR as purely voluntary, and that trend is clearly illustrated by the fact that in the 2011 communications on CSR, the EU changed course: CSR is no longer classified as 'voluntary', but is now seen as a definite 'responsibility' of corporations because of their impact on society.[108] It is, therefore, not surprising that there is now more prominent mention of directors' *duties* regarding CSR,[109] and it can be expected that these duties will in future be expanded to other areas on which there is an expectation to report on under 'sustainability reporting', 'integrated reporting <IR>' or 'corporate responsibility reporting (CR reporting)'.

2.3.2.3 United States

In the US,[110] a concept of 'corporate constituency' – through which the interests of stakeholders have been recognised – has been embedded in the takeover laws of the various states (corporate law in the US is predominantly regulated at state level) since the 1980s,[111] in response to strong hostile takeover activity during that decade.[112] By 1998, over 30 state legislatures had introduced 'corporate constituency' laws designed to protect companies from hostile takeovers by enabling or requiring directors to consider the impact of their activities

---

106   EC, 'Launch of "European Alliance for Corporate Social Responsibility"', Press Release, IP/06/358 (22 March 2006) <http://europa.eu/rapid/press-release_IP-06-358_en.htm?locale=en>.

107   Rühmkorf, *The Promotion of Corporate Social Responsibility in English Private Law* (2013) 5, 16 and 18.

108   EC, 'Communication from the Commission to the European Parliament, the Council, the European Economic and Social Committee and the Committee of the Regions: A renewed EU strategy 2011–14 for Corporate Social Responsibility' COM (2011) 681, para 3.1. See also Rühmkorf, 'The promotion of Corporate Social Responsibility in English private law' (2013) 18.

109   See Beate Sjåfjell and Linn Anker-Sørensen, 'Directors' Duties and Corporate Social Responsibility' in Hanne S Birkmose, Mette Neville and Karsten Engsig Sørensen (eds), *Boards of Directors in European Companies* (Wolters Kluwer, 2013) 153.

110   For an overview of the development of CSR in the US, see CA Harwell Wells, 'The cycles of corporate social responsibility: An historical perspective for the twenty-first century' (2002) 51 *Kansas Law Review* 77. For discussion of the operation of the constituency statutes, see Nathan Standley, 'Lessons learned from the capitulation of the constituency statues' (2012) 4 *Elon Law Review* 209.

111   For a summary of the US state statutes, see K Hale, 'Corporate law and stakeholders: Moving beyond stakeholder statutes' (2003) 45 *Arizona Law Review* 823. For criticism of corporate constituency statutes, see S Bainbridge, 'Interpreting nonshareholder constituency statutes' (1992) 19 *Pepperdine Law Review* 971.

112   See, for example, decisions of the Delaware Supreme Court in *Unocal Corporation v Mesa Petroleum Co*, 493 A 2d 946 (Del. 1985); *Revlon, Inc. v McAndrews & Forbes Holdings, Inc.*, 506 A 2d 173 (Del. 1986).

(including decisions on whether to accept or reject a takeover offer) on constituencies other than shareholders – including employees, customers, suppliers and the community. For example, the statute in Illinois provides that:[113]

> in discharging the duties of their respective positions, the board of directors, committees of the board, individual directors and individual officers may, in considering the best interests of the corporation, consider the effects of any action upon employees, suppliers, and customers of the corporation, communities in which offices or other establishments of the corporations are located and all other pertinent factors.

In Australia the notion of directors owing a duty to stakeholders is not stated explicitly in statute law; in the US it is more prominently mentioned, at least in relation to takeovers regulation.

According to Margaret Blair in *Ownership and Control: Rethinking Corporate Governance for the 21st Century*, the constituency statutes make it legal for directors to consider other interests in addition to those of shareholders when making major decisions. Typically, the statutes require directors to consider the 'best interests of the corporation' as a whole, and then to identify a specific set of stakeholders, including employees, creditors, suppliers and the community in general, whose interests are tied to the corporation. However, the exact nature and scope of these provisions is still uncertain.[114]

It is worth noting that Australia considered the pluralist approach in the US and rejected any move to introduce legislation obliging directors to have regard to the interests of groups other than shareholders in making decisions.[115] More recent Australian reports have adopted a similar approach,[116] and are considered later in the chapter.

According to some commentators,[117] 'the US is in the process of moving beyond the traditional conception of society as divided neatly into three sectors – business, non-profit, and government – and is witnessing the emergence of a new fourth sector that encompasses elements of both the business and non-profit sectors'.[118] Some US states have recently introduced a new corporate structure, known as the 'low-profit limited liability company'

---

113   For a listing of the states that have enacted non-shareholder constituency statutes, see Alissa Mickels, 'Beyond corporate social responsibility: Reconciling the ideals of a for-benefit corporation with director fiduciary duties in the US and Europe' (2009) 32 *Hastings International and Comparative Law Review* 271. For an analysis of the corporate constituency statutes, see E Orts, 'Beyond shareholders: Interpreting corporate constituency statutes' (1992) 61 *George Washington Law Review* 14.

114   Bayless Manning, 'Principles of corporate governance: One viewer's perspective on the ALI Project' (1993) 48 *The Business Lawyer* 1319.

115   The Report of the Senate Standing Committee on Legal and Constitutional Affairs, *Company Directors' Duties: Report on the Social and Fiduciary Duties and Obligations of Company Directors* (November 1989).

116   See further CAMAC, *The Social Responsibility of Corporations Report* (2006); Commonwealth of Australia, Parliamentary Joint Committee on Corporations and Financial Services Report, *Corporate Responsibility and Managing Risk and Creating Value* (June 2006).

117   See, for example, Thomas Billitteri, *Mixing Mission and Business: Does Social Enterprise Need a New Legal Approach?* (2007) <www.nonprofitresearch.org/usr_doc/New_Legal_Forms_Report_FINAL.pdf> (Report of an Aspen Institute Round Table Discussion). Google.org is a celebrated example of a for-profit organisation formed largely for the purpose of providing social benefit.

118   Thomas Kelley, 'Law and choice of entity on the social enterprise frontier' (2009) 84 *Tulane Law Review* 337.

(L3C), for business entities whose primary goal is to achieve a socially beneficial objective.[119] This is a new hybrid structure for profit-making ventures that have profits as a secondary goal; hence the name 'low-profit'. The L3C is a variation of the limited liability company (LLC) that currently exists in the US and shares many of its characteristics. The L3C, as a for-profit entity, is treated like an LLC for tax purposes, and its members enjoy limited liability.[120] L3Cs can distribute their profits to shareholders, a major distinction between them and non-profit companies.

In order for an entity to qualify as an L3C, it must be established to significantly further one or more charitable or educational purposes. Furthermore, it must not have as a significant purpose the production of income or the appreciation of property (though it is permissible to earn profits). Additionally, the entity must not be organised to accomplish any political or legislative purposes. These three characteristics of L3Cs mirror the Program-Related Investment (PRI) requirements under US federal tax laws, which allow private foundations to invest in business entities without triggering tax penalties.[121]

This new company structure is designed to make it easier for social enterprises to attract capital by offering investors a financial return. It is envisaged that an L3C could create new jobs by supporting social enterprises that otherwise could not exist; the timing of its introduction has been opportune given the credit crunch and Global Financial Crisis.[122] On 1 January 2010, Illinois became one of five states to recognise such a structure (joining Michigan, Wyoming, Utah and Vermont, the latter of which passed the first law on 30 April 2008). As of July 2014, nine state legislatures have provided for L3Cs, resulting in 1051 L3Cs nationwide.[123]

The US legislatures' creation of this new type of corporate structure demonstrates a movement away from the traditional boundary between for-profit and non-profit organisations, and is in line with the development of the community interest company (CIC) in the UK, discussed below.[124] It remains to be seen whether this development 'holds particular promise for responding to the legal needs of the emerging fourth sector',[125] particularly when at least one US state (North Carolina) abolished L3C in 2014, after its introduction in 2010.[126]

---

119   See further James Austin, Roberto Gutiérrez, Enrique Ogliastri and Ezequiel A Reficco, 'Capitalizing on convergence' (2007) 24 *Stanford Social Innovation Review* 24 <http://ssrn.com/abstract=1011017>.

120   Acumen Law Group, 'The Low-Profit LLC: A New Entity in Illinois' (9 December 2009) <www.acumenlawgroup.com/index.php?s=Low+Profit+LLC>.

121   'Illinois Recognizes New Business Entity that Mixes For-Profit and Nonprofit Elements', Tax Law Centre, Practitioners' Corner, State Taxation (28 August 2009) <http://law.lexisnexis.com/practiceareas/Practitioners-Corner/Tax/Illinois-Recognizes-New-Business-Entity-That-Mixes-For-Profit-and-Nonprofit-Elements>.

122   'New Corporate Structure Could Give Social Entrepreneurs New Funding Stream', *Chicago Tribune*, 10 August 2009.

123   Kate Cooney, Justin Koushyar, Matthew Lee and Haskell Murray, 'Benefit Corporation and L3C Adoption: A Survey' (2014) *Stanford Social Innovation Review* <https://ssir.org/articles/entry/benefit_corporation_and_l3c_adoption_a_survey>.

124   For comparative discussion on the US and UK approach to hybrid entities, see Heather Sertial, 'Hybrid entities: Distributing profits with a purpose' (2012) 17 *Fordham Journal of Corporate and Financial Law* 261.

125   Kelley, 'Law and choice of entity on the social enterprise frontier' (2009) 342.

126   For critical analysis on the operation of L3C, see John Pearce and Jamie Patrick Hopkins, 'Regulation of L3Cs for social entrepreneurship: A prerequisite to increased utilization' (2014) 92(2) *Nebraska Law Review* <https://ssrn.com/abstract=2379482>.

2.3.2.4 United Kingdom

The embodiment of the concept of 'enlightened shareholder value' is a key aspect of the new corporate law regulatory environment in the UK.[127] Section 172 of the *Companies Act 2006* (UK) (quoted in Chapter 1) adopts the 'enlightened shareholder value' approach to directors' duties, which is described under the Act as 'a duty to promote the success of the company'.[128] According to the Department of Trade and Industry, this will ensure that 'regard has to be paid by directors to the long term as well as the short term, and to wider factors where relevant, such as employees, effects on the environment, suppliers and customers'.[129] This is principally achieved through the high-level 'statement of directors' duties' set out in the Act.

The genesis of s 172, discussed below, can be traced to the work of the UK Company Law Steering Group, which viewed the 'enlightened shareholder value' as being different from the pluralist approach (in the US) and explained the concept as follows:[130]

> There will inevitably be situations in which the interests of shareholders and other participants will clash, even when the interests of shareholders are viewed as long-term ones. Examples include a decision whether to close a plant, with associated redundancies, or to terminate a long-term supply relationship, when continuation in either case is expected to make a negative contribution to shareholder returns. In such circumstances, the law must indicate whether shareholder interests are to be regarded as overriding, or some other balance should be struck. This requires a choice . . . between the enlightened shareholder value and pluralist approaches. An appeal to the 'interests of the company' will not resolve the issue, unless it is first decided whether 'the company' is to be equated with its shareholders alone (enlightened shareholder value) or the shareholders plus other participants (pluralism).

In line with the above approach, section 172 of the *Companies Act 2006* (UK) makes it clear that directors owe their fiduciary duty only to the shareholders generally, rather than to a range of interest groups. Section 172 (quoted in Chapter 1) sets out a non-exhaustive list of matters to which directors must have regard.[131] Two principal reasons for the law reform, closely linked with one another, are identified by Paul Davies:[132]

> The first . . . was that the existing common law duty was thought to be insufficiently precise in the guidance it gave to directors about whose interests should be promoted in the exercise of their discretion . . . the [old formulation] that directors must act *in the*

---

127   For critical appraisal, see Andrew Keay, 'Tackling the issue of the corporate objective: An analysis of the United Kingdom's "Enlightened Shareholder Value"' (2007) 29 *Sydney Law Review* 577. See also I Esser and JJ du Plessis, 'The stakeholder debate and directors' fiduciary duties' (2007) 19 *South African Mercantile Law Journal* 346, 355–6.

128   See generally Esser and Du Plessis, ibid. 351–6.

129   'Draft Company Law Reform Bill Puts Small Business First', Press Release (17 March 2005) <www.parliament.uk/documents/commons/lib/research/rp2006/rp06-030.pdf>.

130   UK Company Law Steering Group Consultation Paper, *Modern Company Law for a Competitive Environment: The Strategic Framework* (February 1999) para 5.1.15.

131   See further Andrew Keay, 'Section 172(1) of the Companies Act 2006: An interpretation and assessment' (2007) 28 *Company Lawyer* 106. For some critical views on the UK approach, see Esser and Du Plessis, 'The stakeholder debate and directors' fiduciary duties' (2007) 355–6.

132   Paul L Davies, *Gower and Davies Principles of Modern Company Law* (Sweet & Maxwell, 8th edn, 2008) 507–8.

interests of 'the company' comes close to being meaningless. This is because the company is an artificial legal person and it is impossible to assign interests to it unless one goes further and identifies with the company the interests of one or more groups of human persons. (emphasis added)

[The second was that] ... the statutory formulation clearly rejects the 'pluralist' approach to the law of directors' duties ... however, the rule of shareholder primacy was not intended by the Government to be adopted in an unsophisticated way. Instead, the degree of overlap between the interests of the members and those of other stakeholders is emphasised through the directors' duty to 'have regard' to the interests of other stakeholders ... [giving rise to] adopting a modernised version of shareholder primacy ...

According to the then UK Trade and Industry Secretary, Patricia Hewitt: 'The proposals [now law] are part of a wide programme of action to boost enterprise, encourage investment and promote long-term company performance.'

Express recognition of the importance of stakeholders, and stakeholder interests, within the general business community is also reflected in a major initiative introduced in the UK in 2005. Under the *Companies (Audit, Investigations and Community Enterprise) Act 2004* (UK), a new type of company called the community interest company (CIC) can be established. The CIC is a limited liability business form designed for enterprises that wish to use their profits and assets for the 'public good'.

The CIC is similar to the European Economic Interest Grouping (EEIG), a specialised form of incorporation facilitated by EC law and based on the model of the French *Groupement d'Intérêt Economique*.[133] According to Davies, this form of incorporation is designed to enable existing business undertakings in various EU member states to form an autonomous body to provide services ancillary to the primary activities of its member businesses.[134] The EEIG has not been popular in the UK: only 185 were set up there by 2006.[135]

The reason for the unpopularity of EEIGs, and what distinguishes the new CIC business form from the EEIG, is that members of an EEIG are not protected by limited liability, meaning that members are – personally – jointly and severally liable for its debts.

Under the *Companies (Audit, Investigations and Community Enterprise) Act 2004* (UK), an enterprise that wishes to be a CIC can choose one of three company forms: (1) private company limited by shares; (2) private company limited by guarantee, or (3) public limited company. Social enterprises tackle a wide range of social and environmental issues and operate in all parts of the economy. The introduction of CICs came about because of the UK Government's belief that social enterprises have a distinct and valuable role to play in helping create a strong, sustainable and socially inclusive economy.

While CICs will provide the same certainty and flexibility as a standard company, they will be subject to a unique requirement – a so-called asset lock, limiting the ability of CICs to distribute profits to members in the form of dividends, or to distribute assets to members. This is to ensure that (subject to certain exceptions and exemptions) the assets and profits of CICs will be used for the community interest, rather than for private gain. It is intended that CICs will

---

133   *European Council Regulation 2137/85*, [1985] O.J. L199/1, Art 16.
134   Davies, *Gower and Davies Principles of Modern Company Law* (2008) 27.
135   Ibid. 28.

be subject to less formal legal requirements than charities, but will not enjoy the same tax benefits as charities. An organisation cannot be both a CIC and a charity.

According to the Act, CICs are overseen by an independent regulator. The regulator has responsibility for considering CICs' constitutions (including proposed changes) and for providing 'general guidance' to CICs and their stakeholders, and generally aims to maintain public confidence in CICs.

As an overview, the new regulatory regime has been designed so that CICs are:[136]

- easy to set up, subject to adopting a suitable constitution and satisfying an objective and transparent 'community interest' test (the test is whether a reasonable person would consider the CIC's activities as benefiting the community);
- able to issue shares to raise investment, but the dividends paid on those shares are capped (by the independent regulator, after consultation), to protect the 'asset lock';[137]
- required to produce annual 'community interest' reports (which will be made publicly available) on how they have pursued their social or community objectives and how they have worked with their stakeholders. This requirement is to ensure that the community served by the CIC will have easy access to the key information on its activities; and
- allowed to transfer assets to other suitable organisations, such as other CICs or charities.[138]

It is thought that a CIC may be a suitable vehicle for an enterprise engaging in social purposes, as shareholders, financial backers, customers and other stakeholders will be clear that the enterprise is working principally for the benefit of the community rather than for private gain, thus avoiding potential liability for breaches of directors' duties, oppression or other action for not focusing on commercial objectives and maximising profits and dividends for shareholders. Thus, while the UK common law continues to uphold the traditional principle that directors owe their duty to the company, and that this requires directors to focus on maximising profits, the introduction of the CIC has changed the landscape somewhat by enabling this form of company to give priority to social objectives – with non-shareholder stakeholders being the principal beneficiaries. As of June 2015, there were 10,000 CICs on the public register, covering health and social care, business advice, education and training, and transport.

2.3.2.5 Canada

Until 2012, operators of social or community enterprises have been working creatively with the available patchwork of legal structures in Canada under provincial or federal legislation (partnerships, companies, cooperatives, non-profit organisations, registered charities) with

---

136   The operation of the community interest companies is detailed in the *Community Interest Company Regulations 2005*.

137   For discussion on changes to the dividend cap which are seen to be restrictive and complex, see Department for Business Innovation & Skill, 'Changes to the Dividend and Interest Caps for Community Interest Companies – Response to the CIC Consultation' (10 December 2013) <www.bis.gov.uk/cicregulator>. The Regulator, in consultation with the Secretary of State, has the ability to change the terms of the dividend cap from time to time. In October 2014 the 20% limit on dividends per share (calculable with reference to the paid-up value of a given share) was removed.

138   See 'New corporate governance laws for UK', *Corporate Law Electronic Bulletin*, Lawlex, November 2004, 1.12; Department of Trade and Industry (UK), 'An Introduction to Community Interest Companies' (December 2004) <www.ssec.org.uk/files/cicfactsheet1.pdf>.

'virtually no corresponding legislative or regulatory innovation'[139] comparable to the position in the UK (CICs) and the US (L3Cs).

This has now changed, with the introduction of the UK-style CIC legislation in British Columbia in April 2012 and in Nova Scotia in November 2012.

The Community Contribution Company (C3 or CCC) in British Columbia, the first of its kind in Canada, has now bridged the gap between non-profit businesses and non-profit enterprises and provides for socially focused investment options. This new hybrid entity, which was created through amendment of the *Business Corporations Act* (BC) and came into effect in July 2013, must have a commitment to 'community purpose', which is defined in s 51.91(1) as:

> A purpose beneficial to
>
> (a) society at large, or
> (b) a segment of society that is broader than the group of persons who are related to the community contribution company
>
> and includes, without limitation, a purpose of providing health, social, environment, cultural, educational or other services …

From a comparative perspective, the underlying framework of the C3 is similar to that of the CIC in the UK and the CIC in Nova Scotia. All of these hybrid structures are subject to an 'asset lock', with a cap on dividends, as well as a limit on the assets that shareholders are entitled to receive upon dissolution of the company. The purpose is to ensure that the assets and profits of such hybrid structures are devoted to community purposes.

It is apparent that the UK model of the CIC is beginning to gain traction overseas, providing the impetus for the Canadian approach and consideration of law reform along similar lines in Asia and Europe (Japan, South Korea, France and Italy in particular).[140] The steady growth of the social enterprise sector suggests that hybrid structures, with their emphasis on trading in the market with a social purpose, are becoming more economically significant in the global economy.

2.4 Stakeholder interests, good governance and the interests of the corporation: A mutual relationship

2.4.1 General analysis

How does taking into account, and protecting, the interests of stakeholders contribute to good corporate governance? Can taking into account a broad constituency of interests actually lead

---

139 Richard Bridge and Stacey Corriveau, *Legislative Innovations and Social Enterprise: Structural Lessons for Canada* (BC Centre for Social Enterprise, 2009) 3 <www.centreforsocialenterprise.com/f/ Legislative_Innovations_and_Social_Enterprise_Structural_Lessons_for_Canada_Feb_2009.pdf>. This report provides a useful overview of legal structures available for blended enterprise in North America. See further Centre for Sustainable Community Development (Simon Fraser University) with BC Centre for Social Enterprise, 'Social Enterprise Legal Structure: Options and Prospects for a "Made in Canada" Solution' (June 2011).

140 Regulator of Community Interest Company, *Annual Report 2012–2013* <www.bis.gov.uk/ cicregulator>.

to poor corporate governance? Whether or not an integrated approach to managing the corporation is consistent with good corporate governance, and in the best interests of the corporation, is a question upon which divergent views are held, and upon which – especially recently – there has been a great deal of commentary.

While the virtue of protecting the interests of the collection of stakeholders is generally acknowledged, there are some who believe that any approach to corporate governance that departs from a strict wealth-maximisation view is simply unworkable. For example, Mallin contends:

> Another very important point is that if the directors of a company were held to be responsible to shareholders and the various stakeholders groups alike, then what would be the corporate objective? How could the board function effectively if there were a multiplicity of different objectives, no one of which took priority over the others? . . . This could actually lead to quite a dangerous situation where directors and managers were not really accountable.[141]

In a similar vein, Clarke writes that:

> The difficulty is whether in trying to represent the interests of all stakeholders, company directors simply slip the leash of the only true restraint that regulates their behaviour – their relationship with shareholders. In apparently seeking to become the arbiter of the general interest, all that occurs is that executives become a self-perpetuating group of princes.[142]

In our view, an integrated approach to corporate governance, by which directors and management consider not only the impact that company decisions will have on the bottom line but also the broader social, political and economic impacts of the decision, is desirable and is the most effective way to ensure that a company achieves long-term, sustainable growth. This section of the chapter briefly explores the importance of 'redefining the corporation' by integrating stakeholder interests as a component of managing the corporation. The recent James Hardie asbestos scandal in Australia, in which James Hardie's parent company ultimately agreed to provide compensation to asbestos victims (who could be viewed as employees, creditors or both) even though there was no clear legal obligation to do so, is used as a case study highlighting how the adoption of an integrated approach to management is more in tune with the best interests of the corporation over the long term than a short-term, narrow focus on the company's share price and what is best for shareholders.[143]

In *Redefining the Corporation* – perhaps the most important work so far this decade on the role of stakeholders in corporate governance, and mentioned earlier in this chapter – the authors explain that:

---

141   Mallin, *Corporate Governance* (2007) 58.
142   Thomas Clarke, 'The Stakeholder Corporation: A Business Philosophy for the Information Age' in Clarke (ed.), *Theories of the Corporation* (2004) 189, 193.
143   For discussion on the web of social norms, expectations and sanctions that bear upon corporations, see Paul Redmond, 'Directors duties and corporate social responsiveness' (2012) 35 *UNSW Law Journal* 317.

> The modern corporation is the center of a network of interdependent interests and constituents, each contributing (voluntarily or involuntarily) to its performance, and each anticipating benefits (or at least no uncompensated harms) as a result of the corporation's activities.[144]

Indeed, a field of 'stakeholder management' has emerged as a distinctive component of strategic management, out of recognition of how so-called stakeholder linkages can contribute to organisational wealth and to the overall well-being and success of the corporation. Most of the constituents in the corporation are essential to the operations of the corporation because they contribute inputs, receive outputs, or – whether actively or passively – provide its 'licence to operate' as an institution within the economy and society.[145] Post, Preston and Sachs express the positive relationship between respect for stakeholder interests and the best interests of the corporation as follows:

> Although the ultimate justification for the existence of the corporation is its ability to create wealth, the legitimacy of the contemporary corporation as an institution within society – its social charter, or 'license to operate' – depends on its ability to meet the expectations of an increasingly numerous and diverse array of constituents. The modern, large, professionally managed corporation is expected to create wealth for its constituents in a responsible manner (that is, not by theft or deception). The connection between wealth and responsibility has been stressed by both business leaders and critics for more than a century, and if the corporation can continue to survive and succeed today it must continue to adapt to social change.[146]

In presenting the case for a 'stakeholder model' of the corporation, based on their wider definition of 'stakeholder'[147] (discussed above), Post and colleagues argue that there are two principal reasons to reassess and redefine the large, well-established corporation in a way that accommodates or integrates stakeholder interests:

1. *Size and socioeconomic power* – Leading global corporations have access to vast resources (including specialised knowledge), overwhelming bargaining power with respect to most of their constituents, and extraordinary ability to influence their environments. They are not microscopic economic actors at the mercy of market forces and omnipotent governments.

2. *Inaccuracy of the 'ownership' model and its implications* – Shareowners hold securities, but they do not own the corporation in any meaningful sense, nor are they the only constituents vital to its existence and success. The notion that shareowner interests should dominate those of all other corporate constituents is inconsistent with the observed behaviour of successful firms. Therefore, the conventional shareowner-dominant model of the corporation is unrealistic, as well as normatively unacceptable.[148]

---

144   Post, Preston and Sachs, *Redefining the Corporation* (2002) 8.
145   Ibid. 229.
146   Ibid. 9.
147   Ibid. 10.
148   Ibid. 10–11.

In light of the above reasons, Post, Preston and Sachs then emphasise the commercial imperative of stakeholder management, stating:

> The corporation requires and receives inputs, some of them involuntary, from multiple sources, and has an impact on many constituents, favourable or otherwise. The corporation cannot – and should not – survive if it does not take responsibility for the welfare of all of its constituents, and for the well-being of the larger society within which it operates.[149]

And further:

> In democratic political systems, which are uniquely hospitable to market-oriented economic arrangements, no business activity that causes substantive negative impact on any significant group of people or interests can be expected to survive, unless it offers conspicuous and broadly distributed offsetting benefits.[150]

In addition to the significant work undertaken by the 'Redefining the Corporation' project in alerting interested observers to the important link between recognition of stakeholders and good corporate governance and performance, the G20/OECD *Principles of Corporate Governance* is another excellent source. A particularly good summary of the importance of the stakeholder debate as an integral part of the corporate governance debate appears there:

> A key aspect of corporate governance is concerned with ensuring the flow of external capital to companies both in the form of equity and credit. Corporate governance is also concerned with finding ways to encourage various stakeholders in the firm to undertake economically optimal levels of investment in firm-specific human and physical capital. The competitiveness and ultimate success of a corporation is the result of teamwork that embodies contributions from a range of different resource providers including investors, employees, creditors, and suppliers. Corporations should recognise that the contributions of stakeholders constitute a valuable resource for building competitive and profitable companies. It is, therefore, in the long-term interest of corporations to foster wealth-creating co-operation among stakeholders. The governance framework should recognise that the interests of the corporation are served by recognising the interests of stakeholders and their contribution to the long-term success of the corporation.[151]

The article by Steve Letza, Xiuping Sun and James Kirkbride[152] explains the consequentialist view of stakeholder management, stressing the important connection between protecting stakeholder interests and good corporate governance and performance. This is referred to in the management literature as 'instrumental stakeholder theory' – as distinct from social entity theory (a general theory that the company should serve multiple stakeholder interests).[153] According to Letza and colleagues, rather than justifying stakeholder interests on the basis of moral value and fundamental human rights, the 'instrumental stakeholder theory' legitimises

---

149   Ibid. 16.
150   Ibid. 21.
151   G20/OECD, *Principles of Corporate Governance* (2015) 34.
152   Letza, Sun and Kirkbride, 'Shareholding versus stakeholding' (2004) 242.
153   Ibid. 251.

stakeholder value on the grounds that stakeholder management is an effective means to the improvement of efficiency, profitability, competition and economic success.

2.4.2 Case study of James Hardie's asbestos compensation settlement[154]

The James Hardie asbestos scandal – which filled Australian media and in 2004 was the subject of a Special Commission of Inquiry[155] – is an excellent case study supporting what has been stated above about the positive link between respect for stakeholder interests and good corporate governance and performance. The lessons from the James Hardie experience are not purely legal ones.[156] One salient lesson concerns the need for ethical standards and increased social responsibility.[157] The strategy embarked upon by James Hardie – to divest itself of its asbestos liabilities – has been described by the Australian Council of Trade Unions (ACTU) as 'one of the most morally and legally repugnant acts in Australian corporate history'.[158] Although the actions of James Hardie (discussed below) are not unprecedented,[159] the conscience of the former directors of James Hardie, in relation to its strategic behaviour in the separation plan and the limited funding of claims made by its asbestos victims, has been found to be sorely wanting.[160]

Some background on James Hardie and the 2004 asbestos scandal is required in order to appreciate the significance of the agreement negotiated in December 2004, and its direct relevance to the present discussion of the relationship between stakeholders and corporate governance and performance.[161]

Companies in the James Hardie group were major participants in the manufacture of asbestos products in the 1920s; these were used extensively in Australia during the major part of the past century, particularly in building products and insulation materials. James Hardie had

---

154   The following discussion draws largely on Anil Hargovan, 'Corporate governance lessons from James Hardie' (2009) 33 *Melbourne University Law Review* 984.

155   David Jackson, *Report of the Special Commission of Inquiry into the Medical Research and Compensation Foundation* (Jackson Report) (September 2004). See further Matt Peacock, *Killer Company: James Hardie Exposed* (HarperCollins, 2009).

156   See Chapter 9 ('Directors' duties and liability') for discussion of the legal lessons that emerged from the James Hardie litigation in *Australian Securities and Investments Commission v Macdonald (No 11)* (2009) 256 ALR 199; *Australian Securities and Investments Commission v Hellicar* (2012) 247 CLR 345; *Shafron v Australian Securities and Investments Commission* (2012) 247 CLR 465; and the civil penalty decision in *Gillfillan v Australian Securities and Investments Commission* (2012) 92 ACSR 460.

157   For the views of the leading advocate of corporate goals and social responsibilities, see Dodd, 'For whom are corporate managers trustees?' (1932) 1145.

158   ABC 7.30 Report Transcript, 'James Hardie Executives Accused of Fraud' (29 July 2004) <www.abc.net.au/7.30/content/2004/s1164158.htm>.

159   For a critical and valuable examination of the use of the limited fund strategy by the largest manufacturer and supplier of asbestos products in the US, see Peta Spender, 'Blue asbestos and golden eggs: Evaluating bankruptcy and class actions as just responses to mass tort liability' (2003) 25 *Sydney Law Review* 223.

160   Peta Spender, 'Weapons of mass dispassion: James Hardie and corporate law' (2005) 14 *Griffith Law Review* 280.

161   See Chapter 9 for a discussion of the directors and officers duty of care and diligence in the James Hardie litigation. See further Anil Hargovan, 'Caution against board groupthink – civil penalties in James Hardie' (2013) 65 *Keeping Good Companies* 36.

been responsible for 70 per cent of Australian asbestos consumption.[162] However, asbestos is injurious to health and its fibres can give rise to asbestosis, lung cancer and mesothelioma, all of which are often fatal. Mesothelioma may not manifest itself immediately, and it is not uncommon for this severe medical condition to arise some decades after exposure to the asbestos fibre. Asbestosis was common in the 1920s, and the insidious effect of asbestos and its link to mesothelioma was established in 1960.[163]

James Hardie Industries Ltd (later ABN 60 Pty Ltd) manufactured asbestos products until 1937, whereupon this activity was taken over by its subsidiary, James Hardie & Coy Pty Ltd (now Amaca Pty Ltd), which became a substantial producer until it ceased this business activity in the 1980s. Another business arm of the corporate group manufactured brake-lining products (formerly Jsekarb Pty Ltd, now Amaba Pty Ltd) until its sale to an independent party in 1987. These three companies in the James Hardie Group were the main participants in the manufacture and distribution of asbestos products. These companies, together with Mr Macdonald as its CEO, Mr Shafron as the company secretary and general counsel and Mr Morley as the chief financial officer (CFO), were to form the *dramatis personae* in the corporate reconstruction of James Hardie[164] and the subsequent litigation culminating in the High Court of Australia, discussed in Chapter 9.

2.4.2.1 Impetus for the corporate restructure

A switch in business focus to the US and the development of new, non-asbestos products in the 1980s proved successful for the James Hardie Group and provided the impetus to separate the accruing asbestos liabilities in Australia from the Group's core business in the US. The impetus to divest itself of its asbestos liabilities also came from the desire of the Group to remove what it perceived as an obstacle to its aspirations to access the capital market in the US. An aborted attempt to issue 15 per cent of the shares of a related Dutch company (JHI NV) on the New York Stock Exchange added to the impetus for a corporate restructure to 'fully realise the value of JHIL, and for its growth prospects to be realised'[165] by adopting the US as the Group's base. Without separation of the asbestos-related liabilities on its balance sheet, it was thought that listing in the US was commercially unrealistic.[166]

Three other influential factors impacted on the momentum towards corporate reconstruction and its timing. The first factor included the desire to avoid the impact of a proposed new Australian Accounting Standard, due to come into force in October 2001, which would require disclosure of the Group's total estimated asbestos liabilities.[167] The second was the desire to capitalise on the timing of the announcement of the Group's third-quarter results to the market on 16 February 2001.[168] It was envisaged that simultaneous announcement of the Group's profits and the corporate restructure plan would deflect attention from a controversial issue

---

162   Jackson Report 59.
163   Ibid. 18.
164   There have been many changes in the identity and names of the James Hardie companies over the years. This chapter, however, refers to the three companies relevant for purposes of this discussion as James Hardie Industries Ltd (JHIL), Amaca and Amaba.
165   Jackson Report 24.
166   Ibid. 340.
167   Ibid. 25.
168   Ibid. 26, 351.

that might otherwise attract undesirable publicity. The third factor related to the effluxion of time and the Group's new business and stewardship of the business. Within this context, the James Hardie Group's asbestos liabilities were treated as 'non-core issues',[169] a source of 'management distraction'[170] and 'legacy issues'[171] that formed 'part of the rump'.[172]

Against this backdrop of corporate aspiration and apparent indifference to the fact that the James Hardie Group remained accountable for negligence in the manufacture or distribution of asbestos products over the past century, and notwithstanding the cessation of that business, the Group marched forward with a separation plan that was poorly executed, as illustrated below, and that paid inadequate attention to the interests of the employees and the community.

2.4.2.2 Key features of the separation plan

In the period from 2000 to 15 February 2001, management of JHIL worked on a plan (known as Project Green) to divest the Group of its asbestos liabilities through the use of a trust structure in the following way. Amaca and Amaba were to remain responsible to claimants for asbestos-related liabilities, to the extent of their existing assets, but ownership of both these companies would pass from JHIL to a new company unrelated to JHIL, known as the Medical Research and Compensation Foundation Ltd (the Foundation), which would operate as a trust. The Foundation, a company limited by guarantee, became the trustee of the Foundation trust. New directors were appointed to the trust and to Amaca and Amaba. The structure adopted sought to exploit the benefits of the separate legal entity rule[173] and limited liability ordinarily conferred on companies, and extended to corporate groups, by the corporate veil.[174]

Furthermore, as part of the concerted effort to quarantine JHIL from its asbestos liabilities, the following arrangements were put in place. In return for payments to be made over time by JHIL to each of Amaca and Amaba, JHIL was to be indemnified by both these companies against any asbestos-related liabilities that JHIL might have. Moreover, both these companies agreed to forego any claims against JHIL arising from any past dealings with it, including the

---

169   Ibid. 19.
170   Ibid.
171   Ibid.
172   Ibid.
173   *Salomon v Salomon & Co. Ltd* [1897] AC 22.
174   *Walker v Wimborne* (1976) 137 CLR 1; *Industrial Equity Ltd v Blackburn* (1977) 13 CLR 567. The question whether existing laws concerning the operation of limited liability or the corporate veils within corporate groups require reform is explored in a wealth of literature. See, for example, F Easterbrook and D Fischel, 'Limited liability and the corporation' (1985) 52 *University of Chicago Law Review* 89; P Blumberg, 'Limited liability and corporate groups' (1986) 11 *Journal of Corporation Law* 573; P Blumberg, 'The transformation of modern corporation law: The law of corporate groups' (2005) 37 *Connecticut Law Rev (Conn L Rev)* 605; K Strasser, 'Piercing the veil in corporate groups' (2005) 37 *Conn L Rev* 637; James McConvill, 'Revisiting holding company liability for subsidiary company debts in Australia: A response to the James Hardy [sic] controversy' (2005) 7 *The University of Notre Dame Australia Law Review* 23; Anil Hargovan and Jason Harris, 'Piercing the corporate veil in Canada: A comparative analysis' (2007) 28 *The Company Lawyer* (UK) 58; P Prince, J Davidson and S Dudley, 'In the Shadow of the Corporate Veil: James Hardie and Asbestos Compensation' (2004) <http://parlinfo.aph.gov.au/parlInfo/download/library/prspub/KXED6/upload_binary/kxed65.pdf;fileType=application%2Fpdf#search=%22Prince%20Davidson%20Dudley%22>. The deficiencies in Australian corporate law concerning the operation of limited liability within corporate groups were noted in the Jackson Report (571–3).

payment of dividends or management fees. Recovery of such intra-group payments was barred by a deed of covenant and indemnity (DOCI) entered into by the contracting parties.[175]

2.4.2.3 Public announcement of the separation plan

The events surrounding the public announcement of the separation were germane to the litigation in *Australian Securities and Investments Commission v Macdonald (No 11)*,[176] which culminated in decisions by the High Court of Australia (discussed in Chapter 9). The draft ASX media announcement, which ASIC alleged was before the board on 15 February 2001[177] and which was released to the public on 16 February 2001, was an integral part of the public relations planning in relation to the separation. The theme of certainty of sufficient funding pervaded this, and future, media statements that became the focus of attention in the James Hardie case (see Chapter 9). The final ASX announcement included the following statements, which ASIC alleged to be false or misleading and the basis of the directors' breach of the statutory duty of care and diligence in s 180(1) of the *Corporations Act 2001* (Cth):

> The Foundation has sufficient funds to meet all legitimate compensation claims ... Mr Peter Macdonald said that the establishment of a fully-funded Foundation provided certainty for both claimants and shareholders ... In establishing the Foundation, James Hardie sought expert advice ... James Hardie is satisfied that the Foundation has sufficient funds to meet anticipated future claims ...[178]

2.4.2.4 Scheme of arrangement and relocation to The Netherlands

After the establishment of the Foundation in February 2001, steps were implemented in October pursuant to an arrangement[179] to substitute a new Dutch company (JHI NV) for JHIL as the holding company of the Group – with JHIL becoming a wholly owned subsidiary of JHI NV. The impetus for the move to The Netherlands centred on the prospect of further international growth for the Group, as well as being in the best interests of the shareholders as a whole due to the improvement in the after-tax returns to shareholders.[180]

A brief overview of the mechanics of the scheme is relevant to the legal issues raised in *Australian Securities and Investments Commission v Macdonald (No 11)*.[181] One of the main features of the scheme involved JHI NV subscribing for partly paid shares in JHIL.

---

175   The events surrounding the execution of the separation plan were relevant to the litigation in *Australian Securities and Investments Commission v Macdonald (No 11)* (2009) 256 ALR 199, which was upheld by the High Court of Australia.
176   (2009) 256 ALR 199.
177   This point was contested, unsuccessfully, by the 10 former directors and officers who claimed that they had no recollection of this document being tabled at the board meeting. See *Australian Securities and Investments Commission v Macdonald* (2009) 256 ALR 199, 239–44.
178   Ibid. 229–30.
179   *Corporations Act 2001* (Cth) s 411.
180   Jackson Report 33. James Hardie, ironically, offered a similar reason for its plan to move its corporate domicile from The Netherlands to Ireland following approval by the Federal Treasurer, but subject to approval of a meeting of shareholders anticipated in early 2010: 'James Hardie Cleared for Ireland Move', *Sydney Morning Herald*, 22 September 2009.
181   (2009) 256 ALR 199.

Consequently, JHIL could call on its holding company to pay any or all of the remainder of the issue price of those shares at any time in the future. Significantly, the amount callable under the partly paid shares would be equal to the market value of the James Hardie Group less the subscription monies already paid up. This sum was considerable: it was likely to be in the region of $1.9 billion.[182] The significance of this feature of the scheme was underscored when JHIL assured Justice Santow, during the application for approval of the scheme in the NSW Supreme Court in October 2001, that JHIL had the ability to satisfy any asbestos-related liabilities by calling upon the partly paid shares.[183]

The cancellation of the partly paid shares, and the formation in March 2003 of a new foundation to acquire the shares in JHIL, ensured the complete removal of JHIL from the James Hardie Group. The subsequent failure to inform the public immediately of this development also became the focus of attention in the *Macdonald* litigation.

It is against this background of the very large discrepancy between the initial funding of the Foundation and the actuarial assessments of its liabilities that gave rise to controversy and the appointment of the Commission of Inquiry. Concerns about the adequacy of the arrangements available to the Foundation to meet its liabilities were also underscored by its application to court[184] to seek relief that would permit payments to claimants in full, notwithstanding statutory provisions that prohibit insolvent trading.[185]

2.4.2.5 Jackson Report and its significance

Because of the emerging crisis facing the Foundation and asbestos victims, in February 2004 the NSW Government set up a Special Commission of Inquiry, chaired by David Jackson QC, to put on the record how the crisis had developed, who was responsible, what had gone wrong and why, with a view to determining whether imposing liability on the ultimate holding company of James Hardie was an appropriate and reasonable course of action to take. Specifically, Commissioner Jackson was to report on:

1.1 the current financial position of the Foundation, and whether it was likely to meet its future asbestos-related liabilities in the medium to long term

1.2 the circumstances in which the Foundation was separated from the James Hardie Group, and whether this may have resulted in or contributed to a possible insufficiency of assets to meet its future asbestos-related liabilities

1.3 the circumstances in which any corporate reconstruction or asset transfers occurred within or in relation to the James Hardie Group prior to the separation of the Foundation from the James Hardie Group, to the extent that this may have affected the ability of the Foundation to meet its current and future asbestos-related liabilities

---

182   Jackson Report 34.

183   Management of JHIL did not alert the court to the Foundation's concerns over the inadequacy of the initial funding and the Foundation's fears of being unable to meet the claims of all asbestos victims that were expressed by the Foundation in a director's letter dated 24 September 2001. Justice Santow approved the scheme under these circumstances.

184   *Edwards v Attorney General (NSW)* (2004) 60 NSWLR 667.

185   *Corporations Act 2001* (Cth) s 588G.

1.4   the adequacy of current arrangements available to the Foundation under the Corporations Act to assist the Foundation to manage its liabilities, and whether reform is desirable to those arrangements to assist the Foundation to manage its obligations to current and future claimants.[186]

The first, and most important, term of reference dealt with in the Report related to 'the circumstances in which MRCF [the Foundation] was separated from the James Hardie Group and whether this may have resulted in or contributed to a possible insufficiency of assets to meet its future asbestos-related liabilities'.

Commissioner Jackson explained in his report that the restructuring of the James Hardie Group and the separation of the asbestos-liable subsidiary companies – Amaca and Amaba – from the Group was not illegal, and indeed was a valid arrangement by the company, with a view to elevating its share price and attracting capital from the US. Commissioner Jackson did find, however, that the separation from the Group was a cause of the Foundation's dilemma, and that on the facts the Group did bear some responsibility for this. The Commissioner remarked incredulously:

> I find it difficult to accept that management could really have believed that the funds of the Foundation would have been sufficient ... yet that was the message that JHIL propounded ... the day after separation, to the Australian Stock Exchange (ASX), to government, the media, its shareholders, unions, plaintiffs' solicitors, asbestos victims and anybody else it felt the need to convince.[187]

Later in the Report, Commissioner Jackson stated that:

> *[T]here was no legal obligation* on JHIL to provide Amaca and Amaba, on separation, with any funds in addition to the assets of those companies. Amaca and Amaba were not stripped of assets; they retained them. Indeed they obtained more than those assets by reason of the additional periodic payments ... But in practical terms, separation was, in my opinion, likely to have an effect of that kind. If separation had not taken place in February 2001, it seems likely that, for the indefinite future, the asbestos liabilities would have been treated, as they had been for years, as one of the annual expenses of the Group.[188] (emphasis added)

After the wide-ranging inquiry into the financial position of the Foundation, its likelihood of being able to meet its asbestos-related liabilities into the future and the circumstances of the corporate reconstruction of James Hardie, Commissioner Jackson came to the following conclusions, which are relevant for the purposes of this discussion and the litigation in James Hardie (discussed in Chapter 9):

- As at 30 June 2004, the liabilities of the Foundation were estimated at not less than $1.5 billion. Against that, the value of the total assets acquired by the Foundation was $293 million.[189]

---

186   See Jackson Report Part A, 1.
187   Ibid. [1.1.4].
188   Ibid. [1.23].
189   Ibid. 8.

- There was no prospect of the Foundation meeting the liabilities of Amaca and Amaba in either the medium or long term due to the rapid depletion of the funds used in the payment of current claims,[190] and the life of the Foundation was about three years or a little less.[191]

- The actuarial report produced by Trowbridge (February 2001) provided no satisfactory basis for the assertion that the MRCF [the Foundation] would have sufficient funds to meet all future claims.[192]

- The evidence demonstrated that the February 2001 estimates of future liabilities were 'far too low and that the results of the financial modelling were wildly optimistic'.[193]

- The public announcements made by JHIL at the time of separation (16 February 2001) emphasised that JHIL had provided for a Foundation which had sufficient funds to satisfy all future legitimate asbestos-related claims.[194]

- The media release sent to ASX, conveying the idea of 'certainty' with respect to the Foundation's funding, was seriously misleading and also conveyed the misleading impression that the funding amount JHIL arrived at had been checked by independent experts.[195]

- Contrary to the claims in the media release sent to ASX, the Foundation was not 'fully funded'. It was massively under-funded.[196]

- The JHIL board meeting of 15 February 2001 approved the ASX announcement to be made by JHIL.[197] (This view was unsuccessfully challenged by the board in *Macdonald* despite the absence of direct evidence of board approval.)

The company's patent failure to observe CSR norms was crystallised in the Jackson Report with the following observation:

> The notion that the holding company would make the cheapest provision thought 'marketable' in respect of those [asbestos] liabilities so that it could go off to pursue its other more lucrative interests insulated from these liabilities is singularly unattractive. Why should the victims and the public bear the cost not provided for?[198]

2.4.2.6 Aftermath

Despite the fact that it was made clear in the Special Commissioner's report that James Hardie had no legal obligation to make up for the shortfall of funds in the Foundation, the company was pressured to do so by a sliding share price and the implementation of government bans on the purchase of James Hardie products, as well as by the threat of specific legislation being introduced to, in effect, unwind the company's 2001 restructure so that liability could be imposed on the parent company. Accordingly, over a period of 13 weeks following the handing down of Commissioner Jackson's report, James Hardie entered into negotiations with

---

190   Ibid. 7.
191   Ibid. 63.
192   Ibid. 9.
193   Ibid. 12.
194   Ibid. 8.
195   Ibid. 10.
196   Ibid. 356.
197   Ibid. 351.
198   Ibid. 13.

the NSW Government and the ACTU to find a satisfactory way to resolve the impending funding crisis. The willingness of James Hardie to agree to negotiations was significant, given that the predominant reason for its move to The Netherlands in 2001 was, allegedly, to avoid having to fund the asbestos claims.

On 21 December 2004, an agreement between James Hardie, the ACTU and the NSW Government was announced. The agreement detailed the way in which James Hardie would compensate asbestos victims for at least 40 years.[199] James Hardie agreed to make annual payments to a special-purpose fund, the Asbestos Injuries Compensation Fund (AICF) capped at 35 per cent of its free cash flow. Since the establishment of the AICF in 2007, James Hardie has stated in its 2009 media statement that it contributed $302.2 million to the fund.

The decision by James Hardie to negotiate a settlement was obviously designed with shareholder interests in mind, with the agreement seen as a way to improve the company's economic and share price performance – indeed, on the day of the announcement the company's share price rose by 6 per cent and a number of boycotts on James Hardie products were lifted. It was, in effect, the lesser of two evils (the other option being specific legislation). Nevertheless, commentators emphasised that there was also a moral element to the agreement.

One commentator described the James Hardie episode as 'one of Australia's most pro-tracted and bitter fights for moral justice [by] James Hardie Industries signing the nation's largest compensation settlement, worth up to $4.5 billion'.[200] Indeed, James Hardie's CEO, Meredith Hellicar, described the agreement as a 'compassionate' outcome.[201] Another com-mentator stated:

> This year's Special Commission found there was 'no fundamental legal impediment' to what Hardie did before it moved offshore: divorce itself from subsidiaries that had manufactured building products and brake linings containing the deadly fibre.
>
> Hardie therefore gets some credit for negotiating a new funding deal and not relying on the letter of the law to try to avoid its moral responsibility. Only some, however, because it had next to no choice.[202]

As alluded to above, James Hardie provides a significant recent case study of a large corpor-ation recognising and embracing the importance of stakeholder management from the point of view of corporate performance and good governance. Through the agreement reached in December 2004, the interests of some of the company's stakeholders – the increasing number of claimants who had contracted asbestos-related diseases from James Hardie products – were

---

199   There have been 310 mesothelioma claims, 130 asbestos claims and 32 lung cancer claims reported against James Hardie in 2012/13. There have been 46 claims settled with awards in excess of $1 million in 2006–07 money terms. In aggregate, the claims have been settled for $87.6 million in mid-2012–13 money terms, at an average cost of approximately $1.90 million. There have been claims of more than $4.5 million each in mid-2012–13 money terms: KPMG, 'Valuation of Asbestos-Related Disease Liabilities of Former James Hardie Entities To Be Met By the AICF Trust', Actuaries Report (May 2013).

200   See Roz Alderton, Bianca Wordley and Kaaren Morrissey, 'Hardie Agrees to $4.5bn Payout', *The Age* (Melbourne), 22 December 2004.

201   In response, Spender, 'Weapons of mass dispassion' (2005) 292 makes the following observation: 'I suppose I have a different understanding of compassion as a spontaneous response to the human condition rather than one based on institutional pressure.'

202   Malcolm Maiden, 'Cost of Asbestos Exposure Does Not End Here', *The Age* (Melbourne), 22 December 2004.

placed above the short-term interests of shareholders. Reference to the agreement being a 'moral' development emphasises the point that James Hardie has aligned itself with a stakeholder model of governance; a consistent theme in stakeholder literature is that there is considered to be an 'intrinsic moral value in business operation'.[203]

As a result of the agreement, the company's performance and future prospects have improved.[204] The company's share price gained ground after deteriorating to historic lows during the Special Commission inquiry; the September 2004 bans on the purchase of company products were lifted and representatives of union organisations appear to be prepared to deal with the company.

It is to be hoped that the James Hardie affair will generate a genuine change of culture within organisations.[205] This historic agreement, the largest personal injury settlement in Australian history, could potentially represent, or at least heavily influence, a turning of the tide in the attitude of management towards stakeholder interests, with companies genuinely appreciating the intrinsic value of an integrated approach to management – as opposed to regarding recognition of stakeholder interests (through codes of conduct etc) as a mere compliance burden.

It is an important case study that highlights how the need to embrace a stakeholder-oriented approach to management can ultimately be more beneficial to shareholders than a narrowly focused approach of maximising wealth in the short term.[206] As Robert E Wood, CEO of Sears in the 1980s, once said, in explaining why his company adhered to a stakeholder model of governance, 'shareholders' long-term project [can] be enhanced by satisfying the needs and expectations of other stakeholders'.[207]

The Jackson Report had a direct bearing on ASIC's decision to launch civil penalty proceedings in February 2007 against James Hardie, its directors and officers. The Report was used as a springboard to launch further investigations into the activities of the James Hardie Group. ASIC investigated the conduct of JHIL and that of both executive and non-executive directors, and, ultimately, successfully sought court declarations that a range of directors and officers had breached the duty of care and diligence owed to JHIL.[208] The practical application of the scope and content of directors' and officers' duties, particularly the statutory duty of care and diligence, was one of the essential tasks requiring judicial

203   Letza, Sun and Kirkbride, 'Shareholding versus stakeholding' (2004) 253.
204   Illustrating the company's commitment to making returns to shareholders, James Hardie announced a special dividend of US28.0c per share in recognition of the company's 125-year anniversary: Media Release (28 February 2014).
205   For an exploration of the concept of corporate responsibility and its relationship with international human rights law, see Justine Nolan, 'Corporate responsibility in Australia: Rhetoric or reality?' (2007) *University of New South Wales Faculty of Law Research Series* 47.
206   For research evidence in support of this proposition, see Pamela Queen, 'Enlightened shareholder maximization: Is this strategy achievable?' (2015) 127 *Journal of Business Ethics* 683. Her research shows that firms that embrace an enlightened shareholder maximisation strategy do create long-term value for shareholders.
207   Letza, Sun and Kirkbride, 'Shareholding versus stakeholding' (2004) 252–3.
208   See Chapter 9 for case law discussion on the James Hardie litigation. The investigation spanned three countries (the US, the UK and Australia) and involved about 348 billion documents, 72 examinations and the issuing of 284 notices to obtain evidence: ASIC, 'ASIC Commences Proceedings Relating to James Hardie', Media Release 07–35 (15 February 2007) <www.asic.gov.au/asic/asic.nsf/byheadline/07–35 +ASIC+commences+proceedings+relating+to+James+Hardie?openDocument>.

determination in *Australian Securities and Investments Commission v Macdonald (No 11)*,[209] which has been upheld on appeal by the High Court of Australia.

2.5 CSR and directors' duties

This part of the chapter addresses general concerns when seeking to achieve the correct balance in corporate governance regulation and then focuses, in particular, on the key issue of whether Australian law reform is desirable in order to clearly articulate the duties of company directors.[210] As pointed out in Chapter 1 and earlier in this chapter, the focus has shifted slightly away from corporate social responsibility (CSR) and towards whether companies act in a responsible way more generally, and that is why the concepts of 'corporate responsibility reporting (CR reporting)', including CSR reporting and sustainability reporting, and integrated reporting (again including CSR reporting) have become prominent in recent years.

The Corporations and Markets Advisory Committee (CAMAC) in its May 2005 discussion paper, 'Personal Liability for Corporate Fault', noted that in addition to companies, company directors can be personally liable by virtue of their position as directors under a raft of federal and state/territory legislation (in relation to, *inter alia*, environmental regulation, workplace health and safety, hazardous goods and fair trading). This complex area of the law, concerning 'derivative liability' of directors, is subject to ongoing review.

The repeated call for law reform over the years to extend the duties of company directors has been quickly countered by commentary from some of Australia's leading corporate lawyers. For example, soon after the Special Commission of Inquiry examining the James Hardie affair handed down its report, Bob Baxt wrote in the *Australian Financial Review*:

> ... from time to time we have flirted with allowing wider interests to be taken into account by directors in running the company (for example, in takeovers). But, in fact, those obligations are already imposed on them and their companies in a different form. Directors of companies must obey the laws relating to environmental protection, taxation, occupational health and safety, trade practices and consumer protection as well as many others. Failure to comply with these laws not only exposes companies to potential fines but, in appropriate cases, directors and officers to potential fines or even jail.
>
> Directors who act negligently in such cases run the added risk that they will be liable for a breach of duty to act with appropriate care and diligence and may be sued by the company.[211]

---

209   (2009) 256 ALR 199.
210   The call for law reform in this regard has been made by many commentators. See, for example, Paul Redmond, 'Directors' duties and corporate social responsiveness' (2012) 35 *UNSW Law Journal* 317, who argues that directors should be given explicit discretion to respond to negative social impacts and stakeholder expectations despite profit sacrifice. There is some sympathy for the suggestion of law reform by Robert Austin, writing in a non-judicial capacity in the Foreword to an excellent collection of essays on directors' duties in (2012) 35 *UNSW Law Journal* 248.
211   'Corporations Law a Fragile Structure', *Australian Financial Review*, 19 November 2004, 55. See also Ian Ramsay, 'Pushing the Limits for Directors', *Australian Financial Review*, 5 April 2005, 63; Angus Corbett and Stephen Bottomley, 'Regulating Corporate Governance' in Christine Parker, Colin Scott, Nicola Lacey and John Braithwaite (eds), *Regulating Law* (OUP, 2004) 60, 65: 'There are many different regulatory schemes which affect the conduct of directors and the system of corporate governance adopted by companies.'

The basic point made by Baxt and others is that if (in light of recent developments) corporate governance is to be taken seriously as a sophisticated and discrete area of legal regulation, then what is required is an examination of where corporate governance fits into the overall jigsaw of rules and regulations – rather than continuing to accept the commonly held perception that corporate governance is an intangible, 'airy fairy' (or what Justice Owen in the HIH Royal Commission Final Report referred to as 'hortatory'[212]), amorphous concept that is allowed to overlap and intrude into areas already well and truly covered by discrete, self-contained areas of law.

As alluded to earlier, the James Hardie scandal was the catalyst for the topic of CSR to receive renewed popular and government interest. This is not surprising, as recognised by CAMAC,[213] given the prominence of corporate enterprises in contemporary society, the considerable power and influence of particular companies, the ways in which companies conduct themselves and the extent to which they are perceived to be taking responsibility for the consequences of their actions.[214]

Against this backdrop, in March 2005 CAMAC was requested by the government to consider and report on a range of matters, including:

> Should the Corporations Act be revised to clarify the extent to which directors may take into account, or be required to take into account, the interests of specific classes of stakeholders or the broader community when making corporate decisions?

The G20/OECD *Principles of Corporate Governance* also recognises the need to consider the interests of a range of stakeholders:

> The rights of stakeholders are often established by law (e.g. labour, business, commercial, environmental and insolvency laws) or by contractual relations that companies must respect. Nevertheless, even in areas where stakeholder interests are not legislated, many firms make additional commitments to stakeholders, and concern over corporate reputation and corporate performance often requires the recognition of broader interests.[215]

The traditional position in Australia, as we explore further in Chapter 9, dealing with directors' duties and liability, is that the overriding duty of directors is to act in the best interests of the company – a separate legal entity – to which they have been appointed and which they are meant to be representing. There are very limited circumstances in which Australian courts have held that directors owe a duty to creditors or individual shareholders, but almost always the expression of such a duty is qualified or followed by a statement that the ultimate loyalty of directors is to the company.[216]

Prior to the issuance of the CAMAC Report in December 2006, a parallel inquiry by the Parliamentary Joint Committee on Corporations and Financial Services (PJC) reported in June

---

212   Owen Report, *The Failure of HIH Insurance* (2003) Vol. 1, 102 para 6.1.
213   See further CAMAC, *The Social Responsibility of Corporations Report* (2006) [iii] <www.camac.gov.au/camac/camac.nsf/byHeadline/PDFFinal+Reports+2006/$file/CSR_Report.pdf>.
214   See further Bryan Corrigan, *Corporate Social Responsibility in the 21st Century: Debates, Models and Practices Across Government, Law and Business* (Edward Elgar, 2010).
215   G20/OECD, *Principles of Corporate Governance* (2015) 34.
216   For empirical evidence regarding the way in which Australian directors perceive their obligations to various stakeholders, see Marshall and Ramsay, 'Stakeholders and directors' duties' (2012) 291.

2006 and recommended no changes to the provisions concerning directors' duties.[217] Similarly, the CAMAC Report did not support revision of the Corporations Act to either clarify or increase its width of coverage, for the following reasons:[218]

> The Committee considers that the current common law and statutory requirements on directors and others to act in the interests of their companies . . . are sufficiently broad to enable corporate decision-makers to take into account the environmental and other social impacts of their decisions, including changes in societal expectations about the role of companies and how they should conduct their affairs . . . a non-exhaustive catalogue of interests to be taken into account serves little useful purpose for directors and affords them no guidance on how various interests are to be weighted, prioritised or reconciled.

CAMAC was also of the view that the current legal requirements for directors to act in the 'best interests of the company' can assist in aligning corporate behaviour with changing community expectations.[219] CAMAC supported the view that the courts, through judicial interpretation of the law, can also assist in aligning corporate behaviour with changing community expectations.[220] Given this, CAMAC considered it unnecessary to amend the *Corporations Act 2001* (Cth) to comport with s 172 of the *Companies Act 2006* (UK) (discussed earlier), because 'no worthwhile benefit is to be gained'.[221] In fact, CAMAC thought alignment with the 'enlightened shareholder value' approach in the UK could be 'counterproductive' because in the Committee's view 'there is a real danger that such a provision would blur rather than clarify the purpose that directors are expected to serve. In so doing, it could make directors less accountable to shareholders without significantly enhancing the rights of other parties.'[222]

Justice Austin, writing in a non-judicial capacity, was critical of the findings of both Australian law reform reports.[223] In particular, his Honour was struck by the disparities in the reasoning of both reports when compared with the depth of the analysis carried out by the UK law reform bodies in the lead-up to the passage of s 172 of the *Companies Act 2006* (UK).[224] His Honour queried why the existing approach in Australia (for directors to act in the 'best interests of the company') was preferable to declaring a duty of directors to take stakeholder interests into account in the course of promoting the success of the company for the benefit of its members as a whole (as the UK Act does).[225] According to his Honour:

---

217   Commonwealth of Australia, Parliamentary Joint Committee on Corporations and Financial Services Report, *Corporate Responsibility and Managing Risk and Creating Value* (June 2006).

218   Ibid. 3.12.

219   Ibid.

220   Ibid. Cf Paul Redmond, 'Directors duties and corporate social responsiveness' (2012) 35 *UNSW Law Journal* 317, 329, who views this as an 'excessively benign view of the past influence and future prospects of judicial regulation of corporate social responsiveness through directors' duties'.

221   Ibid.

222   Ibid.

223   Robert Austin, 'Remarks on the Launching of Company Directors and Corporate Social Responsibility: UK and Australian Perspective' (16 March 2007) <www.lawlink.nsw.gov.au/lawlink/Supreme_Court/ll_sc.nsf/pages/SCO_austin160307>.

224   Ibid.

225   Ibid. For exploration of directors' duty to act in the best interests of the company, see Ian Ramsay, 'The Duty to Act in the Best Interests of the Company (Including Creditors)' in RP Austin and AY Bilski (eds), *Directors in Troubled Times: Monograph 7* (Ross Parsons Centre of Commercial, Corporate and Taxation Law, 2009) 24.

The 'flexibility' that [CAMAC] wishes to maintain [in relation to the traditional formulation of directors' duties is really ... a profound lack of clarity; and I see no good reason for giving directors a discretion to do or not to do something which, on any rational public policy basis, they should be duty-bound to do ... [CAMAC] has not given sufficient weight to the argument that a provision like s 172 will clarify the law for the benefit of everyone concerned, including directors themselves, fortifying them to resist the pressures of short-termism.[226]

These contrasting perspectives continue to be debated,[227] and except as regards the interests of creditors,[228] there is no authoritative pronouncement at the appellate level, as noted by Justice Austin.

Section 172 of the UK Act rejects a pluralist approach in favour of the 'enlightened shareholder value' approach, which retains the overall objective of promoting the success of the company for the benefit of its shareholders. To that extent, it is arguably a better approach to the current position in Australia for the reasons proffered by Justice Austin[229] – if it is accepted that the UK approach is devoid of uncertainty.[230] That caveat, however, will only be understood and clarified over time, as the boundaries and operation of s 172 of the UK Act are fully tested.[231]

2.6 Conclusion

The inherent tension between the shareholder primacy theory and the stakeholder theory, famously identified in the public debate in the 1930s in the *Harvard Law Review* between Berle and Dodd, remains.[232] The alignment of CSR concerns with legal duties continues to be a vexed issue, particularly in the aftermath of the Global Financial Crisis and the accompanying credit crunch. According to one commentator, 'in the current market-based economy, directors all over the world are questioning whether corporations should exist solely to maximize shareholder profit' and 'many corporate directors no longer abide by Milton Friedman's famous declaration that a corporation's only social responsibility is to provide a profit for its owners'.[233]

---

226 Ibid.
227 For a wide-ranging discussion on shareholders as the conduit of CSR and the capacity of the board to integrate the interests of stakeholders into corporate decision-making, see the book review essay by Angus Corbett and Peta Spender, 'Corporate constitutionalism' (2009) 31 *Sydney Law Review* 147.
228 *Spies v The Queen* (2000) 201 CLR 603.
229 Cf Particia Dermansky, 'Should Australia Replace Section 181 of the Corporations Act 2001 (Cth) with Wording Similar to Section 172 of the Companies Act 2006 (UK)?' <http://cclsr.law.unimelb.edu.au/go/centre-activities/research/research-reports-and-research-papers/index.cfm>.
230 For identification of some of the uncertainties that may be associated with the construction of s 172, see CAMAC, *The Social Responsibility of Corporations Report* (2006) [3.9.2].
231 See judicial observation in *Coppage v Safety New Security Ltd* [2013] EWCA Civ 1176 [28] on the uncertainty as to how the statutory provisions in the UK and the existing common law principles are intended to bed down together.
232 See, for instance, Esser and Du Plessis, 'The stakeholder debate and directors' fiduciary duties' (2007) 347–51.
233 Alissa Mickels, 'Beyond corporate social responsibility: Reconciling the ideals of a for-benefit corporation with director fiduciary duties in the US and Europe' (2009) 32 *Hastings International and Comparative Law Review* 272.

Despite the sweeping nature of these claims, which are incapable of precise measure, they do, however, reflect clear trends that have been identified in this chapter and Chapter 1.

The stress of the Global Financial Crisis, and the emergence of the 'fourth sector'[234] of the US, UK and other economies (the 'for-benefit' companies that measure profitability by financial and social components), highlights the importance of CSR initiatives as a means to promote economic prosperity via long-term business expectations. The impact of these innovative developments on the existing business landscape (dominated by large, for-profit corporations) in the US and the UK will become clearer over time.

The Global Financial Crisis raised a question as to whether CSR, and the interests of stakeholders, are still relevant during hard economic times. On one view, in line with the shareholder primacy model, the corporate focus should be exclusively on survival and shareholder interests. An alternative view, as espoused by the EC, is that CSR remains relevant during times of economic crisis and should not be jettisoned. According to the Commission:

> overcoming the economic recession and finding solutions to our environmental and social problems must not be a zero sum game. If we make the right decisions, we can show that European leadership on social and environment issues will contribute to our competitiveness.[235]

As noted by the Australian Senate Standing Committee on Legal and Constitutional Affairs, if contemporary public policy requires directors to be obliged to take into account non-shareholder interests, then a rethink of some of the fundamentals of company law would be required.[236] Therein lies the fundamental challenge for any law reform in this area, but we have little doubt that the interests of all stakeholders and how to look after these interests will remain some of the most dominating issues in future in the areas of corporate law and corporate governance.

---

234   For a description of over 20 different names used to describe activity within the fourth sector (such as 'hybrid organisations', 'corporate citizenship', 'social enterprise', 'social business' and 'entrepreneurship'), see Mickels, 'Beyond corporate social responsibility' (2009).

235   VP Verheugen, Speech at CSR Alliance event (4 December 2008). For a similar proposition, where it has been argued that corporate decision-making is not a 'zero sum' game in which the interests of one group can only be advanced at the expense of another group, see E Orts, 'Beyond shareholders: Interpreting corporate constituency statutes' (1992) 61 *George Washington Law Review* 14.

236   Senate Standing Committee on Legal and Constitutional Affairs, *Company Directors' Duties: Report on the Social and Fiduciary Duties and Obligations of Company Directors* (Parliament of Australia, 1989) 12.

3

BOARD FUNCTIONS AND STRUCTURES

There is now overwhelming evidence that the board system is falling well short of adequately performing its assigned duties. Without fundamental improvement by individual boards, the entire board system will continue to be attacked as impotent and irrelevant and the boards of troubled and failing companies will, with good reason, increasingly become the targets of not only aggrieved and angry shareholders but also employees, creditors, suppliers, governments, and the public.

David SR Leighton and Donald H Thain, *Making Boards Work* (1997) 3

Unless they served on a board, people may well imagine that directors behave rationally, that board level discussions are analytical, and that decisions are reached after careful consideration of alternatives. Not often. Experience of board meetings, or of the activities of any governing body for that matter, shows that reality can be quite different. Directors' behaviour is influenced by interpersonal relationships, by perceptions of position and prestige, and by the process of power. In fact, corporate governance is more about human behavior than about structures and strictures, rules and regulations. Corporate governance involves the use of power. It is a political process.

Bob Tricker, *Corporate Governance: Principles, Policies and Practices* (2012) 327

3.1 Higher community expectations of directors

3.1.1 Initially low standards of care, skill and diligence expected of directors

Directors' statutory duties and liability are discussed in greater detail in Chapter 9. It is, however, important to first make a few observations regarding the higher community expectations of directors.

Based on antiquated English precedents, it has been accepted that directors are not liable for a breach in their duty of care, skill and diligence if they merely acted negligently. One of the first indications that more than ordinary negligence was required is found in an English case decided in 1872, where it was held that directors are liable only for a breach of their duty of care, skill and diligence if they acted with *crassa negligentia* (gross negligence).[1] This rule was confirmed in a later case (1899) by Lord Lindley MR, one of the most famous English commercial Lords:

> The inquiry, therefore, is reduced to want of care and bona fides with a view to the interests of the nitrate company. The amount of care to be taken is difficult to define; but it is plain that directors are not liable for all the mistakes they may make, although if they had taken more care they might have avoided them: see *Overend, Gurney & Co. v Gibb*

---

1   *Overend & Gurney Company v Gibb* [1872] LR 5 HL 480 at 487, 488, 489, 493, 496 and 500.

(1872) LR 5 HL 480. Their negligence must be not the omission to take all possible care; it must be much more blameable than that: it must be in a business sense culpable or gross. I do not know how better to describe it.[2]

These sentiments were repeated in several later English cases,[3] and the fact that negligence alone was not enough to hold directors liable for a breach of their common law duties or equitable duties was also referenced in the leading Australian case, *Daniels v Anderson*.[4] In *Daniels v Anderson* the majority (Clark and Sheller JJA) referred to the concept of 'negligence' as used in the context of equitable remedies, and concluded that 'The negligence spoken of was something grosser or more culpable determined by subjective rather than objective tests.'[5] The subjective test referred to by Clark and Sheller JJA was that a director was to exercise only *the care which can reasonably be expected of a person of his (or her) knowledge and experience*.

The combined effect of a higher requirement than ordinary negligence and the fact that subjective elements were used to judge whether a particular director was in breach of her or his duty of care, skill and diligence, ensured that it was very rare to find cases in which directors were held liable for a breach of those duties.

In *Daniels v Anderson*[6] the court referred to the low standards of care, skill and diligence expected of directors in the past and observed that 'However ridiculous and absurd the conduct of the directors, it was the company's misfortune that such unwise directors were chosen.'[7] There were several reasons given by the courts and commentators as to why in the past the courts were reluctant to expect high standards of directors. Or, to put it differently, why the courts were reluctant to scrutinise closely the business decisions taken by directors. Some of the reasons given were that:

• taking up a position as non-executive director on a part-time basis was simply 'an appropriate diversion for gentlemen but should not be coupled with onerous obligations';[8]

• 'directors are not specialists, like lawyers and doctors';[9]

• directors are expected to take risks and they are dealing with uncertainties, which would be compromised if too high standards of care were expected of them;

• courts are ill-equipped to second-guess directors' business decisions;

• the internal management of the company is one that companies can arrange as they wish, and courts should be reluctant to interfere with internal company matters.

---

2   *Lagunas Nitrate Co v Lagunas Syndicate* [1899] 2 Ch 392 at 435.

3   *Re National Bank of Wales Ltd* [1899] 2 Ch 629 at 672; *Re Brazilian Rubber Plantation and Estates Ltd* [1911] 1 Ch 425; *Re City Equitable Fire Insurance Co Ltd* [1925] Ch 407 at 427.

4   (1995) 37 NSWLR 438 at 493.

5   Ibid.

6   (1995) 37 NSWLR 438.

7   Ibid. at 494–5.

8   RBS Macfarlan, 'Directors' duties after the National Safety Council case: Directors' duty of care' (1992) 3 *Australian Bar Review* 269, 270. See also J Dodds, 'New developments in directors duties – the Victorian stance on financial competence' (1991) 17 *Monash University Law Review* 133, 134.

9   P Redmond, 'The reform of directors' duties' (1992) 15 *University of New South Wales (UNSW) Law Journal* 86, 98, quoting from *Barnes v Andrews* 298 Fed 614 (1924) at 618.

As will be seen below, the scene has changed considerably, and there are now much higher expectations of directors to act with due care and diligence, and these higher expectations are reflected in several court cases decided since the early 1990s.[10]

3.1.2 Legal recognition of changed community expectations of directors

That the scene has changed considerably for directors in recent years was strikingly illustrated by the case of *Daniels v Anderson*.[11] Although the court specifically recognised the potential tension between expecting objective professional standards of all directors in all types of companies, the court did not hesitate to conclude that community expectations of the standards of performance of directors have increased since the case of *City Equitable Fire Insurance Co. Ltd* (decided in 1925). Thus the court held that it is the modern law of negligence that should be used to determine whether a director was in breach of his or her duty of care, skill and diligence.[12] In fact, the court held that the modern law of negligence (also called the tort of negligence) has developed sufficiently to cope with expecting objective professional standards of all types of directors (for instance, executive directors and non-executive directors) in all types of companies (from the one-person proprietary company to the multinational listed public company).

The court adopted the general principles of the tort of negligence and the duty of care after drawing attention to three very important things. First, there were historic reasons why directors' duties of care, skill and diligence were viewed in a particular manner by the English courts of the late 1800s and early 1900s. Referring to the article by Jennifer Hill,[13] the court made the following observation:

> The nature and extent of directors' liability for their acts and omissions developed as the body corporate evolved from the unincorporated joint stock company regulated by a deed of settlement and was influenced by the partnership theory of corporation where-under shareholders were ultimately responsible for unwise appointment of directors.[14]

Second, in embracing the tort of negligence as the basis of liability for a breach of a director's duty of care, skill and diligence, the court took into consideration that 'the law about the duty of directors' had developed considerably since the decision in *Re City Equitable Fire Insurance Co.* (1925).[15] The court then, in roughly seven pages,[16] painstakingly quoted from

---

10   *Daniels v Anderson* (1995) 37 NSWLR 438, *Permanent Building Society (in liq) v Wheeler* (1994) 11 WAR 187, *Australian Securities and Investments Commission v Adler* (2002) 41 ACSR 72, *Australian Securities and Investments Commission v Rich* (2003) 44 ACSR 341, *Australian Securities and Investments Commission v Macdonald (No 11)* (2009) 256 ALR 199 and *Australian Securities and Investments Commission v Healey* (2011) 196 FCR 291.

11   (1995) 37 NSWLR 438.

12   Ibid. at 500–2.

13   J Hill, 'The liability of passive directors: *Morley v Statewide Tobacco Services Ltd*' (1992) 14 *Sydney Law Review* 504.

14   *Daniels v Anderson* (1995) 37 NSWLR 438 at 493.

15   Ibid. at 661. See also The Honourable Sir Douglas Menzies 'Company directors' (1959) 33 *The Australian Law Journal* 156, 156–8 and 163–4; Macfarlan, 'Directors' duties after the National Safety Council case' (1992) 272–3.

16   *Daniels v Anderson* (1995) 37 NSWLR 438 at 497–504.

contemporary cases before reaching the conclusion that the tort of negligence and the modern concept of a duty of care now form an acceptable basis for liability of directors for breach of their duty of care.[17] Third, the court mentions that the law of negligence has developed considerably in the 70 years (the *Daniels* case was decided in 1995) since the decision in *Re City Equitable Fire Insurance Co.*[18]

Since *Daniels v Anderson*, it can safely be stated that the standard of care expected of Australian directors under the common law has reached new heights – *Daniels v Anderson* brought an abrupt end to the notion that directors' duty of care, skill and diligence should be judged subjectively and that their negligence 'must be in a business sense culpable or gross'.

Similar developments, and the fact that there are nowadays higher expectations of directors, are neatly summarised by Bob Tricker in the first edition of his book:

> Once upon a time a directorship was a sinecure – an occasional meeting between friends, maybe a few supportive questions, then a fee and probably lunch. Not now. Today more is expected of company directors, indeed the members of all governing bodies, than ever. The work of governing corporate entities has become demanding, often difficult, and open to challenge. Nevertheless, the work and responsibility is often crucial and can be rewarding, both financially and personally.[19]

As will be seen in Chapter 9, directors' liability in Australia is dominated by liability for a breach of their statutory duties. Also, it will be seen that it is the primary corporate regulator (the Australian Securities and Investments Commission (ASIC)) that takes a lead role in instituting actions against directors for a breach of their statutory duties.[20] However, as was illustrated

---

17   Ibid. at 505.

18   Ibid. at 497.

19   Bob Tricker, *Corporate Governance: Principles, Policies and Practices* (OUP, 2009) 17 – the quote from the first edition illustrates the point more succinctly than the second edition (cf Bob Tricker, *Corporate Governance: Principles, Policies and Practices* (OUP, 2nd edn, 2012) 25).

20   See, for example, *Australian Securities and Investments Commission v Adler* (2002) 42 ACSR 80; *Australian Securities and Investments Commission v Rich* (2003) 44 ACSR 341; *Elliott v Australian Securities and Investments Commission* (2004) 10 VR 369; *Australian Securities and Investments Commission v Vines* (2005) 55 ACSR 617; *Australian Securities and Investments Commission v Vizard* (2005) 145 FCR 57; *Australian Securities and Investments Commission v Maxwell* (2006) 59 ACSR 373; James Hardie litigation (*Australian Securities and Investments Commission v Macdonald (No 11)* (2009) 256 ALR 199; *Australian Securities and Investments Commission v Hellicar* (2012) 247 CLR 345 and *Shafron v Australian Securities and Investments Commission* (2012) 247 CLR 465); *Australian Securities and Investments Commission v Healey* (2011) 196 FCR 291. An empirical study of court proceedings brought by ASIC and the CDPP for breach of directors' duties provisions of the *Corporations Act 2001* (Cth) from 2005 to 2014 reflects that ASIC and the CDPP initiated approximately half of all public and private proceedings involving breach of directors' duties. See Jasper Hedges, Helen Bird, George Gilligan, Andrew Godwin and Ian Ramsay, *An Empirical Analysis of Public Enforcement of Directors' Duties in Australia: Preliminary Findings* (Centre for Corporate Law and Securities Regulation, 2015) 1. In a recent article, Ian Ramsay examined ASIC's power to litigate to enforce breaches of directors' duties and evaluated the advantages and disadvantages of enforcement of directors' and officers' duties by ASIC. He found that, as an active litigant, ASIC is setting the standards for directors in the boardroom through such litigation and that in some circumstances, ASIC-instigated litigation is desirable. See Ian Ramsay, 'Increased corporate governance powers of shareholders and regulators and the role of the corporate regulator in enforcing duties owed by corporate directors and managers' (2015) 26 *European Business Law Review* 49–73.

above, the standards of skill, care and diligence expected of directors have risen considerably over the past two decades, and the statutory standards of care found under s 180(1) of the *Corporations Act 2001* (Cth) (the Act) reflect these higher standards.[21]

3.2 The organs of governance[22]

The *Report of the HIH Royal Commission* (Owen Report)[23] summarises very well the concept of organs of a corporation in the context of corporate governance.[24] Justice Owen explained that a corporation is a legal entity separate and apart from its board of directors (one of the primary organs of a corporation) and shareholders (the other primary organ of a corporation), and that the corporation can only 'act through the intervention of the human condition'.[25] The classic statement of this principle is to be found in *Lennard's Carrying Co Ltd v Asiatic Petroleum Co Ltd* per Lord Haldane:

> My Lords, a corporation is an abstraction. It has no mind of its own any more than it has a body of its own; its active and directing will must consequently be sought in the person of somebody who is really the directing mind and will of the corporation, the very ego and centre of the personality of the corporation.[26]

Historically, the power to manage the business of all companies and corporations was conferred upon the board of directors. The fact that it was impossible for a board of directors to manage the day-to-day business *of large public corporations* was realised only quite recently (see discussion under 'Board functions', below). Today, the board of directors is seen as the primary governance or supervisory organ.

The powers conferred upon shareholders are primarily conferred upon them by the Act. The power to appoint directors and to remove directors are some of the most important powers of shareholders, but there are also several other decisions in a company that cannot

---

21   *Vines v Australian Securities and Investments Commission* (2007) 73 NSWLR 451; *Australian Securities and Investments Commission v Macdonald (No 11)* (2009) 256 ALR 199. In the recent case of *Australian Securities and Investments Commission v Cassimatis (No 8)* (2016) 336 ALR 209 the Federal Court of Australia held that 'Directors of a solvent company may breach their duties of care and diligence, even if they are the only shareholders, if their conduct as directors causes the corporation to contravene the law.' See Maxine Tills and Cassandra Wills, 'Australian directors found guilty of breaching duties following corporation's breaches', *Insight & Knowledge*, 14 September 2016 <www.clydeco.com/insight/article/australian-directors-found-guilty-of-breaching-duties-following-corporation?utm_source=Mondaq&utm_medium=syndication&utm_campaign=View-Original>.

22   This section presents and reflects on the prevailing approach in corporate decision-making processes: that is, the board of directors are appointed by, and accountable to, the body of shareholders. Andrew Keay, however, suggests that the board must be accountable to the company entity, either to an accountability council or to the general meeting of shareholders. See Andrew Keay, 'Board accountability and the entity maximization and sustainability approach' (2016) in Barnali Choudhury and Martin Petrin (eds), *Understanding the Company: Corporate Governance and Theory* (CUP, 2017) <https://ssrn.com/abstract=2747398>.

23   Report of the HIH Royal Commission (Owen Report), *The Failure of HIH Insurance – Volume I: A Corporate Collapse and its Lessons* (Commonwealth of Australia 2003).

24   Ibid. 103 (Ch 6, section 6.1.1).

25   Ibid.

26   [1915] AC 705, 713.

be taken without the approval of the shareholders by way of a special resolution (a 75 per cent majority of the shareholders present at a shareholders' meeting in person or by proxy).[27]

In the past the shareholders were considered 'the owners' of the company, based on the fact that they provided the original capital ('share capital'), which would enable a company to get involved in commercial activities. This is, however, only partly true, as proprietary companies are often incorporated with no significant share capital at all: these are the so-called $2 companies, with typically two shareholders each holding a share worth $1. Furthermore,[28] giving shareholders 'ownership' of the company based on the fact that they are the providers of share capital has been exposed as incorrect in terms of the legal nature of a company: a company is a separate legal entity,[29] a legal or juristic person or body corporate, and as natural persons cannot be 'owned', neither can these 'creatures of statute' be 'owned'. In addition, there is a growing trend to recognise other forms of capital apart from financial capital, namely manufactured, intellectual, human, social and relationship, and natural capitals.[30]

The current view, that directors are accountable to the body of shareholders, is partly based on the incorrect assumption that the shareholders 'own' the company, but also on the fact that it is the shareholders who appoint the directors and who normally have the power to remove the directors.[31] The dominance of shareholders is reflected in the 'shareholder primacy' theory of corporate law, which was discussed in greater detail in Chapter 2, but as was explained, that theory is under attack at the moment: it is argued that the board must be accountable to the company as separate legal entity[32] and that there are definitely interests other than those of shareholders in the company as separate legal entity.[33]

3.3 Board functions[34]

AWA Ltd v Daniels (t/as Deloitte Haskins & Sells)[35] is one of the very few cases in which an attempt was made to explain the division of functions between the board of directors and management; non-executive directors and the chief executive officer (CEO) or managing

---

27   One of the most important powers that the shareholders have is to change the company's constitution (if any) by way of a special resolution – see *Corporations Act 2001* (Cth) s 136(2).

28   See Jean J du Plessis, 'Shareholder primacy and other stakeholder interests' (2016) 34 *Company and Securities Law Review (C&SLJ)* 238.

29   Illustrated very well by the classic case of *Salomon v Salomon & Co. Ltd* [1897] AC 22.

30   See International Integrated Reporting Council, The International <IR> Framework (IIRC, 2013) 2, 12–13, <http://integratedreporting.org/wp-content/uploads/2013/12/13-12-08-THE-INTERNATIONAL-IR-FRAMEWORK-2-1.pdf>.

31   *Corporations Act 2001* (Cth) s 203D gives the shareholders an inalienable right to remove directors of public companies by ordinary resolution, following the procedures prescribed in s 203D.

32   See Keay, 'Board accountability and the entity maximization and sustainability approach' (2016).

33   See Jean J du Plessis, 'Corporate social responsibility and "contemporary community expectations"' (2017) 35 *C&SLJ* 30, 33–5.

34   For some interesting reflections on the gap between what directors in fact do and what the business literature professes that they *should* do, see Myles L Mace, 'Directors: Myth and Reality' in Thomas Clarke (ed.), *Theories of Corporate Governance: The Philosophical Foundations of Corporate Governance* (Routledge, 2004) 96 *et seq*, based on his book, Myles L Mace, *Directors: Myth and Reality* (Harvard University Press, 1971). For a more theoretical analysis, distinguishing between 'board tasks' and 'board functions', see Morten Huse, *Boards, Governance and Value Creation* (CUP, 2007) 33 and 38–40.

35   (1992) 7 ACSR 759.

director; and the chairman and the board of directors.[36] Rogers CJ explained that, apart from statutory ones, a board's functions are said to be normally fourfold, namely:

(1)   to set goals for the corporation;

(2)   to appoint the corporation's chief executive;

(3)   to oversee the plans of managers for the acquisition and organisation of financial and human resources towards attainment of the corporation's goals; and

(4)   to review, at reasonable intervals, the corporation's progress towards attaining its goals.[37]

Rogers CJ pointed out the practical limitations on the ability of the board of a large public corporation *to manage the day-to-day business of the corporation*:

> The Board of a large public corporation cannot manage the corporation's day to day business. That function must of necessity be left to the corporation's executives. If the directors of a large public corporation were to be immersed in the details of the day to day operations the directors would be incapable of taking more abstract, important decisions at board level . . .[38]

This distinction is now also widely accepted in legislation. In the past the power 'to manage the business of the company' was invariably conferred upon the board of directors by way of the model set of articles of association (Table A) that accompanied most of the Companies Acts that preceded the Act. The practical reality that in large public corporations the business of the corporation is not done by the board as such, but under the direction of the board, is currently reflected in s 198A(1) (replaceable rule – see Chapter 5 for the meaning of the term 'replaceable rule') of the Act, providing that 'The business of a company is to be managed by or under the direction of the directors.' In proprietary companies, the business of the company will be managed 'by' the board, but in large public corporations it will be managed 'under the direction' of the board.

   With reference to some US perspectives, which are equally relevant for the purposes of the current Australian corporations law, it is necessary to say a few words on 'the director primacy theory'. Stephen Bainbridge refers to §141(a) of the *Delaware General Corporation Act*, which provides that '[t]he business and affairs of every corporation organized under this chapter shall be managed by or under the direction of a board of directors' and mentions that this power conferred upon the board is enshrined in every piece of state legislation, except in Missouri. He then calls the statutory recognition of directors' powers 'the director primacy model'[39] and points out that this model, which he developed, 'has been recognised by several other commentators'.[40] This is, indeed, a new model that can be contrasted to what has been called the 'shareholder primacy model', the 'enlightened shareholder value model' and the 'stakeholder primacy model' (see discussion in Chapters 1 and 2).

---

36   Ibid. at 865–8.
37   Ibid.
38   Ibid. at 866.
39   Stephen M Bainbridge, *The New Corporate Governance in Theory and Practice* (OUP, 2008) ix.
40   Ibid. xi–xii.

Bainbridge's 'director primacy model' is based on the reality that even though it is said (incorrectly) that the shareholders 'own' the corporation, they have virtually no power to control either its day-to-day operation or its long-term policies. Instead, Bainbridge argues, the corporation is controlled by its board of directors.[41] It is the boards of the directors, and not the shareholders, other stakeholders or managers, in large public corporations that actually control the corporation and 'have the ultimate right of fiat'.[42] An excellent illustration of the dominant role boards play is captured in *Corporate Boards in Law and Practice: A Comparative Analysis in Europe*, a collection of essays by leading academics and practitioners from 10 European countries.[43]

The distinction between managing and directing the business of a corporation is also well accepted in managerial circles. As early as 1997, Bob Garratt explained it as follows:

> But there is a vast difference between 'directing' and 'managing' an organisation. Managing is literally, given its Latin root, a hands-on activity thriving on crisis action. On the operations side of an organisation it is a crucial role. Directing is different. Directing is essentially an intellectual activity. It is about showing the way ahead, giving leadership. It is thoughtful and reflective and requires the acquisition by each director of a portfolio of completely different thinking skills.[44]

He repeated these sentiments in 2003:

> We seem to rely excessively on an ill defined and weakly assessed notion called 'experience' to get by. Unfortunately such experience is rarely directoral. It is usually managerial and professional, and so concerned with the day-to-day operations of a business – these are not directoral roles and there is a big difference between managing and directing an organization.[45]

The Australian Securities Exchange's (ASX) *CG Principles and Recommendations* (2014)[46] summarises the responsibilities of the board. Usually the board of a listed entity will be responsible for:

- providing leadership and setting the strategic objectives of the entity;
- appointing the chair and, if the entity has one, the deputy chair and/or the 'senior independent director';
- appointing, and when necessary replacing, the CEO;
- approving the appointment, and when necessary replacement, of other senior executives;

41 Ibid. 3.
42 Ibid. 11.
43 Paul Davies et al. (eds), *Corporate Boards in Law and Practice: A Comparative Analysis in Europe* (OUP, 2013).
44 Bob Garratt, *The Fish Rots from the Head* (HarperCollins Business, 1997) 4. See also Robert AG Monks and Nell Minow, *Corporate Governance* (Blackwell, 3rd edn, 2004) 195 and 202–3; JB Reid, *Commonsense Corporate Governance* (Australian Institute of Company Directors [AICD], 2002) 22; Stephen M Bainbridge, *Corporation Law and Economics* (Foundation Press, 2002) 194–5.
45 Garratt, *The Fish Rots from the Head* (1997) 69.
46 ASX, *CG Principles and Recommendations* (3rd edn, 2014) 8. <www.asx.com.au/documents/asx-compliance/cgc-principles-and-recommendations-3rd-edn.pdf>.

- overseeing management's implementation of the entity's strategic objectives and its performance generally;
- approving operating budgets and major capital expenditure;
- overseeing the integrity of the entity's accounting and corporate reporting systems, including the external audit;
- overseeing the entity's process for making timely and balanced disclosure of all material information concerning the entity that a reasonable person would expect to have a material effect on the price or value of the entity's securities;
- ensuring that the entity has in place an appropriate risk management framework and setting the risk appetite within which the board expects management to operate;
- approving the entity's remuneration framework; and
- monitoring the effectiveness of the entity's governance practices.

Ultimately the board's functions and responsibilities could be summarised as to 'direct, govern, guide, monitor, oversee, supervise and comply'. The literature on management and managerial strategy makes a distinction between two primary roles of the board, namely a 'performance role' and a 'conformance role'. Tricker classifies 'contributing know-how, expertise and external information' and 'networking, representing the company and adding status' as being part of directors' performance role. Under their conformance role he includes 'judging, questioning and supervising executive management' and a 'watchdog, confidant and safety-valve role'.[47] Garratt sees accountability (for quality of thinking, high ethical standards and values, to obey the law and to treat stakeholders in a consistent way) and supervision of management (conformance to key performance indicators, cash flow, budgets and projects) as part of the board's conformance task.[48] Among its performance tasks he lists policy formulation and foresight and strategic thinking.[49] The distinction between the board's 'performance' and 'conformance' tasks seems a realistic explanation of directors' roles and mirrors the primary functions of the board.

Directors need to have some practical guidelines to ensure that they fulfil their duties and responsibilities diligently. Mervyn King, in his book *The Corporate Citizen*, provides some excellent guidelines to directors in taking decisions or making business judgments. He suggests that directors, when making decisions or business judgments, must ask 10 questions:

1. Do I as a director of this board have any conflict in regard to the issue before the board?
2. Do I have all the facts to enable me to make a decision on the issue before the board?
3. Is the decision being made a rational business decision based on all the facts available at the time of the board meeting?
4. Is the decision in the best interests of the company?

---

47   Robert I Tricker, *International Corporate Governance* (Prentice-Hall, 1994) 98–100. See also Bob Tricker, 'From Manager to Director: Developing Corporate Governors' Strategic Thinking' in Bob Garratt (ed.), *Developing Strategic Thought: Rediscovering the Art of Direction-giving* (McGraw-Hill, 1995) 16–18.
48   Bob Garratt, *The Fish Rots from the Head* (P Profile Books, 2003) 109 *et seq* and 131 *et seq*.
49   Ibid. 57 *et seq* and 88 *et seq*.

5. Is the communication of the decision to the stakeholders of the company transparent, with substance over form, and does it contain all the negative and positive features bound up in that decision?

6. Will the company be seen as a good corporate citizen as a result of the decision?

7. Am I acting as a good steward of the company's assets in making this decision?

8. Have I exercised the concepts of intellectual honesty and intellectual naivety in acting on behalf of this incapacitated company?

9. Have I understood the material in the board pack and the discussion at the boardroom table?

10. Will the board be embarrassed if its decision and the process employed in arriving at its decision were to appear on the front page of the national newspaper?[50]

Some may say it is unrealistic to expect of directors, making decisions 'on the run', to ask all these questions. On the other hand, especially as far as Australian directors are concerned, there is very little doubt that if all the directors of James Hardie had asked all these 10 questions and could answer 'no' to questions 1 and 10 and 'yes' to questions 2–9, they would not have been held liable.[51] Also, the names of the directors of Centro Properties Group would not have been mentioned so prominently in the media during October 2009, when ASIC announced that it would institute action against the directors for a breach of their statutory duty of care and diligence[52] if those directors had asked the 10 questions King suggests and could answer 'no' to questions 1 and 10 and 'yes' to questions 2–9.

3.4 Board structures

Generally speaking, there are two types of board structure, namely the unitary board and the two-tier board. It is, however, not easy to make an exact distinction between these two structures, as most developed countries have moved away from the traditional 'unitary board' structure in the case of large public corporations. In most developed countries, board structures for large corporations have some characteristics that are reminiscent of the more traditional two-tier board. A good way to illustrate this point is to start with a very basic distinction drawn by Tricker in his books *International Corporate Governance*[53] and *Corporate Governance: Principles, Policies and Practices*,[54] between a 'managerial pyramid' and a 'governance circle', and to illustrate this by way of five figures (reproduced with Tricker's original numbering in square brackets, Figures 3.1–3.4 from *International Corporate Governance* and Figure 3.5 from *Corporate Governance: Principles, Policies and Practices*).

---

50   Mervyn King, *The Corporate Citizen* (Penguin, 2006) 53–8.
51   See *ASIC v Macdonald (No 11)* [2009] NSWSC 287.
52   See 'ASIC Commences Proceedings Against Current and Former Directors of Centro', ASIC Media Release 09–202 AD (21 October 2009) <www.asic.gov.au/asic/asic.nsf/byheadline/09–202AD+ASIC +commences+proceedings+against+current+and+former+officers+of+Centro?openDocument>. See further *ASIC v Healey* (2011) 196 FCR 291 (liability decision); *ASIC v Healey (No 2)* [2011] FCA 1003 (penalty decision).
53   Tricker, *International Corporate Governance* (1994) 44–5.
54   Tricker, *Corporate Governance: Principles, Policies and Practices* (2012) 49–50 and 52.

Figure 3.1 [2.1]   The board and management differentiated

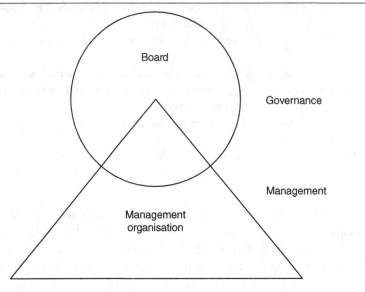

Figure 3.2 [2.2]   All-executive board

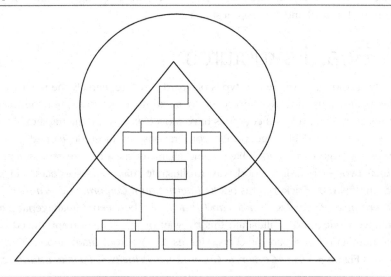

Figure 3.2 illustrates the typical board structure for proprietary companies and the board structure most public corporations used in the past. However, with the drive to have objective checks on management and to bring independence into the board, there has clearly been a move towards the board structure depicted in Figure 3.3. More recently there have been several moves to have a majority of non-executive directors and, in particular, a majority of independent non-executive directors (Figure 3.4). The German system is perhaps best described by Figure 3.5, with the governance circle representing the supervisory board and

Figure 3.3 [2.3]   Majority executive board

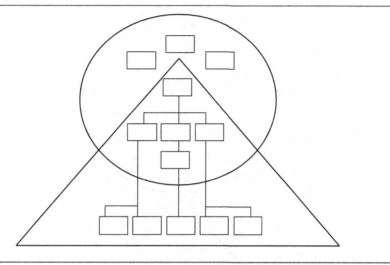

Figure 3.4 [2.4]   Majority outside board

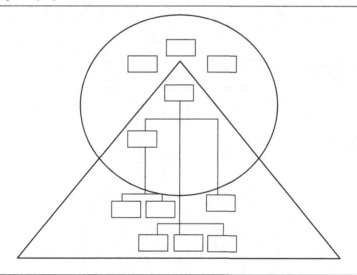

the managerial pyramid representing the management board. The most recent trends, towards independent non-executive directors, will be explained in greater detail in Chapter 4, and the German two-tier board will be discussed in Chapter 12. Figure 3.6 illustrates a board with no executive director. It is rare to find this in listed public companies, but Tricker points out that it is sometimes the board structure for not-for-profit entities such as charitable organisations, arts, health and sports organisations, and 'quangos' (quasi-autonomous non-government organisations)'.[55] Figure 3.7 depicts the South African close corporation, where the statutory presumed

55   Ibid. 51–2.

Figure 3.5 [2.5]   Two-tier board

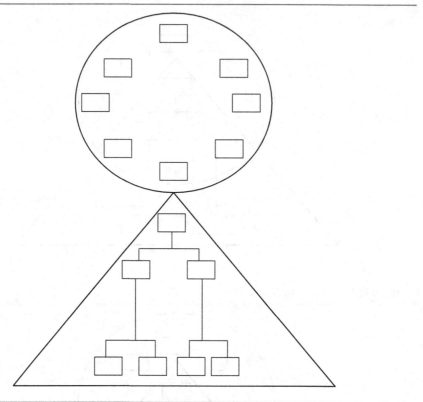

Figure 3.6 [3.4]   The all non-executive director board

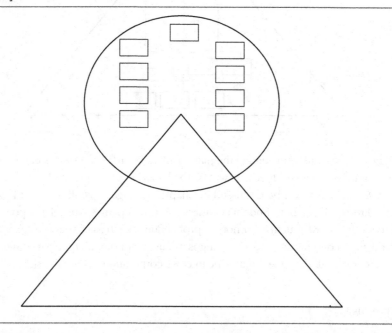

Figure 3.7   The statutory arrangement for South African close corporations

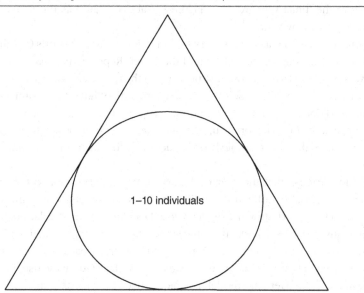

or default arrangement is based on the premise that there is a complete overlap between the governance circle and the managerial triangle in small businesses.[56]

Tricker's basic models could be used to further refine and explain board structures and an effective corporate governance model (see discussion and illustrations). There are several indications that traditional common law jurisdictions recognise the distinctive roles of 'the board' and 'management'. The primary function of 'the board' is to 'direct, govern, guide, monitor, oversee, supervise and comply', and 'management's' function is to 'manage the day-to-day business of the corporation'. This becomes clear if one looks at what is nowadays understood under the 'functions of the board', as explained above. There is no longer a place in large corporations for the board to 'manage the business of the corporation', but there is a place for it to provide strategic direction to the corporation; the development and implementation of risk management policies are also key functions of the board. For these reasons, these days it is misleading to express a preference for 'a unitary board' or 'a two-tier board' without clarifying what is meant by these terms. It is also unwise to make a prediction of a 'convergence towards a unitary board approach' without defining what is meant by a 'unitary board'.[57]

Where the business of the corporation is not managed by the board but is 'under the direction of the directors'[58] – with a majority of independent (or outside) non-executive directors, a senior independent director, an independent non-executive director as chair and

56   See further Jean J du Plessis, 'Reflections and perspectives on the South African close corporation as business vehicle for SMEs' (2009) 15(4) *New Zealand Business Law Quarterly* 252–3 and 257 for some of the reasons for having separate legislation applying to SMEs.

57   Cf Garratt, *The Fish Rots from the Head* (1997) 42–3.

58   See *Corporations Act 2001* (Cth) s 198A(1). See further *AWA Ltd v Daniels (t/a Deloitte Haskins & Sells)* (1992) 10 ACLC 933.

several subcommittees[59] – it can hardly be said that such a corporation has a 'unitary board' comparable to the 'unitary board' (see Figure 3.3 above) that was the focus of attention of many studies over many years.[60]

In various reports, such as the Cadbury Report (UK), the King Reports (South Africa) (1994, 2002 and 2009), the Higgs Report (UK) and the Owen Report (Australia), the 'unitary board' structure was preferred to the 'two-tier structure', but these 'alternative' board structures are not really alternative in the strict sense of the word; rather, they have some similarities and some differences. Additional problems with simply accepting the 'unitary board' as the preferred structure are that it does not open up consideration of other possibilities and it does not stimulate debate on the best possible board structure or the relative merits of alternative board structures.

We do not propose that the 'unitary board' structure is superior to the 'two-tier board' structure or vice versa, but rather that a 'unitary board' structure ought not simply be rejected in favour of a 'two-tier board' structure or vice versa. Deciding on a particular board structure will depend on many variables (for example, the size of the company, the quality of persons sitting as non-executive directors, and the corporate culture within a particular corporation).[61]

As will be seen in Chapter 12, Japan and China, as well as Germany, use the two-tier board system; however, the German model is unique because codetermination[62] is so deeply embedded in its corporate governance model. It is to be expected that – depending on one's understanding and definition of a 'unitary board' or 'two-tier board' – strong support for one or the other will continue to be expressed.[63]

3.5 Conclusion

We started this chapter by focusing on the organs of a company and then discussed the main functions of a board of directors. It was clear that there is an important distinction between managing the business of the company and directing, supervising and overseeing the management of the business of corporations in large public companies. The board is responsible for directing, supervising and overseeing the management of the business of corporations. Managing the business of large public corporations is normally left to management, but under control of the board.

As was pointed out in Chapters 1 and 2, there is now an expectation that corporations should also strive to build a better society and that they should be focused on responsible behaviour and long-term and sustainable growth. The idea that the primary aim of corporations

---

59   See FRC, *The UK Approach to Corporate Governance* (October 2010) <www.frc.org.uk/Our-Work/ Publications/Corporate-Governance/The-UK-Approach-to-Corporate-Governance.aspx>; and ASX, *CG Principles and Recommendations* (2014). See also *Review of the Role and Effectiveness of Non-Executive Directors* (Higgs Report) (January 2003) <www.berr.gov.uk/files/file23012.pdf>.

60   See Tricker, *International Corporate Governance* (1994) 44–5.

61   Se Owen Report, *The Failure of HIH Insurance* (2003) Vol. 1, 105 para 6.12.

62   As will be seen in Chapter 12, the supervisory board in Germany is based on codetermination between shareholders, providers of share capital and employees, representing human capital: up to half of the seats of supervisory boards are filled by employees and the other half are filled by shareholder representatives.

63   See Garratt, *The Fish Rots from the Head* (1997) 42–3 and 210.

is profit maximisation for shareholders and other investors can no longer be taken for granted. We have moved away from the single bottom-line (financial) approach. Boards of directors, as the ultimate control centres of corporations (the organ theory and the board primacy model), need to take serious notice of these trends and of their own ultimate responsibility for sustainability, and for reporting on and disclosing information regarding non-financial matters (see Chapter 2). It is, therefore, important to point out here (as well as in Chapter 9), the responsibilities of directors and the special position in which they are placed. This can hardly be illustrated better than by quoting Justice Middleton in his judgment in *Australian Securities and Investments Commission v Healey*:

> A director is an essential component of corporate governance. Each director is placed at the apex of the structure of direction and management of a company. The higher the office that is held by a person, the greater the responsibility that falls upon him or her. The role of a director is significant as their actions may have a profound effect on the community, and not just shareholders, employees and creditors.[64]

There can be no doubt that in future all investors, especially large institutional investors, will be under tremendous pressure to invest only in corporations that adopt a long-term sustainable and responsible approach to conducting their businesses, and whether or not they adopt such an approach will be measurable, now that reporting on and disclosing information regarding non-financial matters have become so prominent. It is within these parameters that boards will have to fulfil their duties – no longer can the shareholder primacy model, in its pure and traditional form, be justified. The concept of 'profit maximisation' for shareholders will have to be toned down to a 'good return on investment in the long term'. We should strive for law reform that reflects the practical reality of a corporate environment that recognises the interests of multiple stakeholders.[65] In our view, all these developments will ensure that corporate governance as a subject area will remain of considerable importance in future.

---

64   (2011) 196 FCR 291, [14].
65   See Du Plessis, 'Corporate social responsibility and "contemporary community expectations"' (2017) 45–6; and Du Plessis, 'Shareholder primacy and other stakeholder interests' (2016) 242.

4

TYPES OF COMPANY DIRECTORS AND OFFICERS

As the cigar smoke in the boardrooms clears, the comfortably reclining figures are instantly revealed as being of two types: the executive directors who run the business and take the rap, and the non-executive directors who, having read their papers carefully for the pre-lunch board meeting, asked their statutory question, and enjoyed a reasonable rib of beef, are ready to depart blamelessly to their bank, chambers, farm or villa for another two months.

PLR Mitchell, 'Non-executive Directors' (1985) *Business Law Review* 173

The key directors on our board all know what I have done to make our company perform. They made me the CEO because I was the best candidate they could find. I have worked my butt off at great sacrifice to my family and personal life to transform this company and make it perform better than it ever had before. I don't need any of their penetrating questions or second-guessing. Thanks to my own tough bargaining, I am financially secure and set for life. If they can get someone better than me to do the job, then that's what they should do. Until then let them back off and stay out of my way.

David SR Leighton and Donald H Thain, *Making Boards Work* (McGraw-Hill Ryerson, 1997) 6
(quote from an anonymous, sceptical Canadian CEO)

We trained hard – but every time we were beginning to form up into teams, we would be reorganised. I was to learn later in life that we tend to meet any new situation by reorganising, and [what] a wonderful method it can be for creating the illusion of progress while producing confusion, inefficiency and demoralisation.

The famous words of Roman writer Gaius Petronius: Petronii Arbitri Satyricon, 66 CE,
as quoted by Nigel Kendall and Arthur Kendall, *Real-World Corporate Governance*
(Pitman Publishing, 1998) 212

4.1 Overview

Comparing the first two opening quotes of this chapter with current realities illustrates very well how things have changed over a relatively short period of time. In the previous chapter we saw that there are nowadays much higher community expectations that all types of directors fulfil their duties of care and diligence meticulously. No longer may directors hide behind ignorance or inaction; nor are the duties of non-executive directors seen as being of an intermittent nature. All directors have a positive duty to challenge, inquire and investigate when controversial or potentially risky matters are discussed at board level, as was illustrated by the 2009 case of *Australian Securities and Investments Commission v Macdonald (No 11)*,[1] discussed in Chapter 9. In this chapter it will also become clear that the traditional and simplistic distinction between executive and non-executive directors no longer holds true, although as a general rule it can be said that the legal duties of all types of directors are the same.

---

1   (2009) 256 ALR 199; affirmed by the High Court of Australia in *Australian Securities and Investments Commission v Hellicar* (2012) 247 CLR 345.

4.2 Definition of 'director'

Identifying who is a director has practical significance for the law on directors' duties and sanctions for breach under the *Corporations Act 2001* (Cth) (the Act), with particular reference to the civil penalty provisions (pecuniary penalty, compensation and disqualification orders) discussed in Chapter 9. The court in *Murdaca v Australian Securities and Investments Commission*[2] reminds us that a person who is not, strictly speaking, a director may nevertheless be disqualified from managing a company if that person is involved in management in ways that are considered to constitute directing or controlling the affairs of that company, either alone or jointly with others. The expansive definition of 'director' also has significant ramifications for those people who occupy the position of director and cause the company to trade while insolvent. Section 588G of the Act, discussed in greater detail in Chapter 9, imposes personal liability upon those who occupy the office of director or who discharge functions attaching to that office of the kind normally performed by a director.

4.2.1 De jure *and* de facto directors covered

The corporations laws of most common law jurisdictions contain a definition of 'director'. Although there are some differences in these definitions, a common feature is that each aims to define the term quite widely in order to ensure that those who fulfil directorial functions do not escape the provisions of corporations legislation. Thus the definition of 'director' will typically include a reference to the fact that a person could be considered a director irrespective of the fact that the person is not *called* a director,[3] but is known by a name such as 'governor', 'executive', or 'manager'. The definitions of 'director' will also cover, as a general rule, not only those individuals who were validly appointed to the position of 'director' (de jure directors), but also those acting as a 'director' (de facto directors). A recent trend in legislation has also been to include 'shadow directors' under the definition. These are individuals who are neither appointed to the position nor act directly as directors, but who manipulate the board 'from behind the scenes'.

Section 9 of the Act contains a typical definition of 'director', which includes all the features mentioned above:

> 'director' of a company or other body means:
>
> (a) a person who:
>> (i) is appointed to the position of a director; or
>> (ii) is appointed to the position of alternate director and is acting in that capacity,
>>
>> regardless of the name that is given to their position; and
>
> (b) unless the contrary intention appears, a person who is not validly appointed as a director if:
>> (i) they act in the position of a director; or
>> (ii) the directors of the company or body are accustomed to act in accordance with the person's instructions or wishes.

---

2   (2009) 178 FCR 119.

3   See also Bob Tricker, *International Corporate Governance: Text, Readings and Cases* (Prentice Hall, 1994) 42.

Subparagraph (b)(ii) does not apply merely because the directors act on advice given by the person in the proper performance of functions attaching to the person's professional capacity, or the person's business relationship with the directors or the company or body.

The labels accorded to directors, as 'de facto' or 'shadow' directors, are not intended to be prescriptive.[4] In expressing caution on becoming fixated with labels, Justice Gordon in 2008, in *Australian Securities and Investments Commission v Murdaca*,[5] warned:

Such descriptions can, at times, be misleading. Names and labels aside, what is required is a critical assessment of the way in which a corporation is managed and then an assessment as to whether the conduct of the person concerned falls within one or more of the categories identified.

4.2.2 Shadow directors

Subparagraph (b)(ii) covers 'shadow directors', but the proviso to subparagraph (b)(ii) (last paragraph quoted above) was included in order to exclude from its parameters those persons in accordance with whose directions the directors usually act, where that advice is given by the outsider in that person's professional capacity (for example, as solicitor or accountant) or because of their business relationship with the directors or company (for example, as the company's banker).

The expanded definition of 'director' has caused concern among banks, financial institutions and business and professional advisers.[6] These institutions and persons clearly have a strong interest in the company's affairs, especially when companies are in financial difficulty and steps are being taken to send representatives to the board to investigate and make suggestions as to how to overcome the company's financial difficulties. The problem is succinctly stated by Vinelott J in *Re Tasbian (No 3)*:[7]

The dividing line between the position of a watchdog or adviser imposed by an outsider investor and a de facto or shadow director is difficult to draw.

However, in *Buzzle Operations Pty Ltd (in liq) v Apple Computer Australia Pty Ltd*[8] the NSW Court of Appeal held that a secured creditor that imposes conditions on continuing to provide financial support for a debtor company is not a shadow director, even if the debtor's directors felt that they practically had no choice but to agree to the creditor's demands. In such a case the creditor is not acting as part of the governing structure of the debtor company, and hence is making demands or imposing conditions to protect its own independent commercial interest rather than making decisions for the debtor company.

---

4   See *Grimaldi v Chameleon Mining NL (No 2)* (2012) 200 FCR 296 for discussion of legal principles in this area.
5   (2008) 68 ACSR 66 at [11].
6   For example, see *Buzzle Operations Pty Ltd (in liq) v Apple Computer Australia Pty Ltd* (2011) 81 NSWLR 47, which contains a useful collection of the legal principles applicable to shadow directors.
7   *Re Tasbian (No 3)* [1992] BCC 358 at 363.
8   (2011) 81 NSWLR 47.

The use of the plural, 'directors', in subparagraph (b)(ii) suggests that the board, rather than a single director, must be accustomed to acting in accordance with the shadow director's directions or instructions before the subsection is satisfied. This was confirmed in the *Buzzle* case, where it was held that the influence must be exerted over a majority of the board.

That 'accustomed to act' is a tough threshold to satisfy is highlighted further in the case *Natcomp Technology Australia Pty Ltd v Graiche*,[9] in which Stein JA said that in order for directors to be 'accustomed to act' on the instructions or directions of an outsider for the purposes of the Act, it must be established that the outsider is involved in the principal aspects of the company's business. This threshold is, nonetheless, not insurmountable, as evidenced in *Ho v Akai Pty Ltd (in liq)*,[10] where it was found that the directors or officers of Akai Australia (a company in financial difficulty) were accustomed to acting in accordance with the instructions and wishes of Grande Holdings (a Singaporean company) – the latter being held to be a shadow director and therefore exposed to liability under the insolvent trading provisions in s 588G of the Act.

It was held in the British case *Vivendi SA v Richards*[11] that shadow directors owe fiduciary duties to the company; this illustrates the huge potential for their liability towards the company.

4.2.3 Nominee directors

The term 'nominee director' is sometimes loosely used to refer to a director who has been nominated to the board by a majority shareholder or other stakeholder.[12] This practice is common in company groups in which the holding company appoints directors to the boards of its subsidiaries. Conflicts of interest may easily arise for these 'nominee directors', putting them in an unenviable position where they need to consider their duties towards the company upon whose board they serve or the shareholder (another company in the group context) that appointed them, and in groups of companies they will often be senior managers or executives of the holding company. The law is very clear. A director owes his or her duties to the company upon whose board he or she serves, not to the shareholder or stakeholder who nominated the person to be a director.[13] Thus the director will be in breach of his or her statutory, common law and/or equitable duties if he or she does not act in good faith and in the best interests of the company upon whose board he or she serves, but instead in the best interests of the nominator or appointer. There is one exception, and that is provided for in s 187 of the Act. In terms of this section, a director of a corporation that is a wholly owned subsidiary of a body corporate is taken to act in good faith in the best interests of the subsidiary if the following three conditions apply:

1. the constitution of the subsidiary expressly authorises the director to act in the best interests of the holding company; and

2. the director acts in good faith in the best interests of the holding company; and

3. the subsidiary is not insolvent at the time the director acts and does not become insolvent because of the director's act.

---

9   (2001) 19 ACLC 1117.
10   (2006) 24 ACLC 1526.
11   [2013] EWHC 3006 (Ch).
12   See Bob Tricker, *Corporate Governance: Principles, Policies and Practices* (OUP, 2009) 53.
13   *Scottish Co-operative Wholesale Society Ltd v Meyer* [1959] AC 324 at 367 per Lord Denning.

Apart from the obvious dilemma for the 'nominee director' as far as conflicts of interests are concerned, there are also other dangers involved for the nominator or appointer. First, the nominator or appointer could be considered to be a 'shadow director' (see discussion above), thus owing duties similar to other directors towards the company (the holding company in the group context).[14] Second, if the 'nominee directors' are controlled and manipulated by the nominator or appointer, the nominator or appointer could be held liable vicariously for the acts and conduct of the 'nominee directors'.[15]

Although the term 'nominee director' is not used in the Act, there is, in the concluding sentence of s 203D(1), a recognition of the practice of directors being appointed by specific shareholders or debenture holders:

> 203D(1) ... If the director was appointed to represent the interests of particular shareholders or debenture holders, the resolution to remove the director [under s 203D(1)] does not take effect until a replacement to represent their interests has been appointed.

4.3 Definition of 'officer'

4.3.1 Statutory definition

The provisions of the Act often extend beyond directors to any 'officer'. The aim is to ensure that other individuals in the company, not appointed as directors or acting as directors or shadow directors, are also covered by certain provisions of the Act and cannot escape liability if they are in breach of certain provisions.

Under s 9 of the Act:

> *officer* of a corporation means:
>
> (a) a director or secretary of the corporation; or
> (b) a person:
> (i)   who makes, or participates in making, decisions that affect the whole, or a substantial part, of the business of the corporation; or
> (ii) who has the capacity to affect significantly the corporation's financial standing; or
> (iii) in accordance with whose instructions or wishes the directors of the corporation are accustomed to act (excluding advice given by the person in the proper performance of functions attaching to the person's professional capacity or their business relationship with the directors or the corporation); or
> (c) a receiver, or receiver and manager, of the property of the corporation; or
> (d) an administrator of the corporation; or
> (e) an administrator of a deed of company arrangement executed by the corporation; or
> (f) a liquidator of the corporation; or
> (g) a trustee or other person administering a compromise or arrangement made between the corporation and someone else.

---

14   *Standard Chartered Bank of Australia v Antico* (1995) 38 NSWLR 290.
15   *Kuwait Asia Bank v National Mutual Life Nominees Ltd* [1991] AC 187.

Section 201B contains rules about who can be a director of a corporation:

(1) Only an individual who is at least 18 may be appointed as a director of a company.

(2) A person who is disqualified from managing corporations under Part 2D.6 may only be appointed as director of a company if the appointment is made with permission granted by ASIC under section 206F(5) or leave granted by the Court under section 206G.

4.3.2 Senior employees and senior executives as 'officers'

The aim with the broad statutory definition of 'officer' is also to ensure that there is no doubt that certain duties imposed by the corporations law apply to a group of people who will not necessarily fall under the definition of 'director'. It is a well-established principle that senior employees or senior officers of a corporation owe duties similar to those of directors towards the company. The clearest expression of this principle, recognised in most common law jurisdictions, is the case of *Canadian Aero Service Ltd v O'Malley*:[16]

> I do not think it matters whether O'Malley and Zarzycki were properly appointed as directors of Canaero or whether they did or did not act as directors. What is not in doubt is that they acted respectively as president and executive vice-president of Canaero for about two years prior to their resignations. To paraphrase the findings of the trial Judge in this respect, they acted in these positions and their remuneration and responsibilities verified their status as senior officers of Canaero. They were 'top management' and not mere employees whose duty to their employer, unless enlarged by contract, consisted only in respect for trade secrets and for confidentiality of customer lists. Theirs was a larger, more exacting duty which, unless modified by statute or contract (and there is nothing of this sort here), was similar to that owed to a corporate employer by its directors.[17]

4.3.3 Middle management as 'officers'?

In the HIH Royal Commission Report, Justice Owen was struck by the role of middle management as a component of a company's governance systems. He observed that it is customary to focus upon the role of senior or executive-level management when the organs of governance are discussed. However, Justice Owen observed that 'middle management' had played a significant role in HIH and that they were involved in undesirable practices. He was frustrated by the disinclination of those persons to accept responsibility in relation to such practices. Justice Owen then observed as follows regarding middle management:

> I have therefore had occasion to review the current legal regime governing the duties imposed upon persons other than directors. These issues seem to me to be of considerable significance, because it is clear that in larger companies many significant decisions are made by management without reference to the board. It follows that any legal regime

16   (1973) 40 DLR (3d) 371.
17   Ibid. at 381, para 22.

for the enforcement of corporate governance standards which does not extend to the acts or omissions of at least some levels of management is unlikely to be wholly effective.

The evidence I have heard also suggests that it is common for management decisions to be made on a collective or collegiate basis, or at least after interaction with other managers. There is therefore an opportunity for the law significantly to influence the mind-set or culture of those managers, and reinforce their obligations to the company and its shareholders.[18]

As part of the CLERP 9 amendments to the Act in 2004 the term 'employee' was included in several of the provisions of the Act.[19] However, the legislature did not accept Justice Owen's suggestion to make the primary duties imposed upon directors and officers applicable to middle managers. The question of reform in this area was referred to the Corporations and Markets Advisory Committee (CAMAC) for consideration. In May 2005, CAMAC released a discussion paper titled *Corporate Duties Below Board Level*. In that paper, CAMAC put forward preliminary proposals to, *inter alia*, (i) extend the duties in s 180 (due care and diligence), and s 181 (good faith and proper purpose) to apply to 'any other person who takes part in, or is concerned, in the management of that corporation', and (ii) extend the prohibitions in s 182 and s 183 (regarding improper use of company position or information) to apply to 'any other person who performs functions, or otherwise acts, for or on behalf of that corporation'. CAMAC sought comments as to whether 'management' should be defined and, if so, whether it should be defined along the lines of activities that involve policy and decision-making related to the business affairs of a corporation, to the extent that the consequences of the formation of those policies or making of those decisions may have some significant bearing on the financial standing of the corporation or the conduct of its affairs.

These proposals of CAMAC have not, so far, been taken up in the Act, but it should be noted that the duty not to use one's position to gain a personal advantage or to cause the company detriment (s 182) and the duty not to use information to gain a personal advantage or to cause the company detriment (s 183) apply to 'directors', 'officers' and 'employees'. In other words, all employees, including middle and senior management, fall under these provisions and will be liable if they are in breach of these provisions. For example, in *Holyoake Industries (Vic) Pty Ltd v V-Flow Pty Ltd*[20] the court held that a senior manager at an industrial business acted in breach of sections 182 and 183 by participating with the managing director in bidding for a competing business after using confidential information about the business gained from their employer. Another example where an employee was held liable under these provisions is *Hydrocool Pty Ltd v Hepburn (No 4)*.[21] In this case it was found that a senior employee and technical officer (Clarke) contravened s 182 by having had knowledge and having been fully informed by the director (Hepburn), who was held to be in breach of s 182 by using his

---

18   Report of the HIH Royal Commission (Owen Report), *The Failure of HIH Insurance – Volume I: A Corporate Collapse and its Lessons* (Commonwealth of Australia, 2003) 122, para 6.4.

19   See the *Corporate Law Economic Reform Program (Audit Reform and Corporate Disclosure) Act 2004* (the CLERP 9 Act), amending, *inter alia*, the following sections to include 'employees' – ss 411, 418, 422, 436.

20   (2011) 86 ACSR 393.

21   (2011) 83 ACSR 652.

position to gain an advantage for himself or someone else. It was held that Clarke was 'knowingly concerned in Mr Hepburn's contravention of s 182(1) of the Corporations Act'.[22]

4.4 Types of company officer

4.4.1 Executive and non-executive directors

It will be clear from the discussion above that the Act makes no distinction between 'executive' and 'non-executive'[23] directors. All 'directors' fall under the same definition and, *as a general rule*,[24] have the same duties. That this is the correct interpretation of the Act was confirmed in *Daniels v Anderson*.[25]

Although there is, as a general rule, no difference between the duties expected of 'executive' and 'non-executive' directors in the Act, the distinction between 'executive' and 'non-executive' directors is nowadays a very important one in practice.[26] This distinction has become progressively more important with the emphasis on the board's role to 'direct, govern, guide, monitor, oversee, supervise or comply', as explained in greater detail in the previous chapter. The more prominent role of 'independent non-executive directors' has further accentuated this practical distinction.[27]

Executive directors wear two hats. On the one hand, they are executives working full-time in the corporation, and in this capacity they will normally have a contract of service with the corporation.[28] On the other hand, executive directors are also office-bearers of the company, falling under the statutory and common law duties expected of a 'director'. The Australian Securities Exchange's (ASX) *CG Principles and Recommendations* defines 'executive director' as a director of the company 'who is also an executive' of the company or a related entity[29] of the company.[30]

Non-executive directors have the same statutory and common law duties as executive directors, but they do not work in the company on a full-time basis. Their labour is first and foremost directed towards the matters dealt with at board meetings. They serve on the board,

---

22   Ibid. at [417].
23   In the US, the term 'outside director' is used rather than 'non-executive director'.
24   The words, '*as a general rule*' are emphasised because there is a clear recognition in s 180(1) of the Act that although all directors or other officers of a corporation 'must exercise their powers and discharge their duties with the degree of care and diligence that a reasonable person would exercise', the specific type of corporation (for instance, a small proprietary company or a large multinational, listed public company) in which the director fulfilled his or her duties and the specific position the person occupied and the specific responsibilities allocated to the person (for instance, an independent non-executive director or the chief financial officer or CEO, who are also board members) will be taken into consideration in determining whether there was a breach of a particular director's duty of care and diligence under s 180(1) of the *Corporations Act 2001*.
25   (1995) 37 NSWLR 438.
26   *Australian Securities and Investments Commission v Rich* (2009) 75 ACSR 1 [7203].
27   See generally Murray Steele, 'The Role of the Non-executive Director' in Ken Rushton (ed.), *The Business Case for Corporate Governance* (CUP, 2008) 50.
28   See *AWA Ltd v Daniels (t/as Deloitte Haskins & Sells)* (1992) 7 ACSR 759, 867.
29   'Related entity' is defined in detail in s 9 of the Act – it will be noticed that working out which entities are 'related entities' is quite complex.
30   ASX, *CG Principles and Recommendations* (2014) 37 <www.asx.com.au/documents/asx-compliance/cgc-principles-and-recommendations-3rd-edn.pdf>.

and the board's functions and responsibilities are to 'direct, govern, guide, monitor, oversee, supervise and comply'. In this sense their duties and responsibilities are of a continuing nature. The ASX *CG Principles and Recommendations* simply define 'non-executive director' as 'a director who is not an executive director'.[31]

In the past, many non-executives were appointed through and by people they knew (most notably the 'old boys' club') or through their extensive networking. However, especially because of the increasingly demanding and professional nature of the role of non-executive directors, they are nowadays often identified by head-hunter agencies, executive search firms, institutes of company directors or using, for instance, 'Board Direction' (www.boarddirection.com.au) or other board vacancy websites.[32] Non-executive directors will normally be people with considerable previous or current experience as senior managers or directors. Some are also appointed for their particular skills: they may be lawyers, have financial expertise, be bankers, have auditing experience etc.[33] However, these non-executive directors have the same duties as all other directors and would not be able to use their expertise in a particular area to escape liability if they neglected their duties as director in an area not related to their area of expertise.

Getting appointed as non-executive director is not an easy task. David Schwarz, in his booklet, *Board Appointments*,[34] provides some excellent practical advice for finding and gaining experience as non-executive director. He points out that becoming a non-executive director of a not-for-profit organisation involved in an area that the person is passionate about could be a good starting point. However, additional experience and exposure will be required if the aspiration is to become a non-executive director of public listed companies.[35] The booklet also contains very useful guidance regarding the process of applying for board positions, preparing a curriculum vitae, and the 'board-ready' covering letter, and preparing for the interview.[36]

4.4.2 Independent non-executive directors

It has been realised for several years that non-executive directors can play an important role on boards of larger corporations in particular, because they 'bring to bear a broader perspective, more background, a wider range of skills on a particular issue or indeed on the management of the company'.[37] Apart from any expertise they may bring to the company, non-executive

---

31   Ibid. 38.
32   David Schwarz, *Board Appointments: Practical Advice for Finding and Gaining a Non-Executive Director Board Appointment* (Board Direction, 2014) 109.
33   For an illuminating article on the relationship between independence and expertise, see Suzanne Le Mire, 'Independent directors: Partnering expertise with independence' (2016) 16 *Journal of Corporate Law Studies* 1–37.
34   Ibid.
35   Ibid. 20.
36   Ibid. 28 ff.
37   Evidence presented to the Senate Standing Committee on Legal and Constitutional Affairs, *Report on the Social and Fiduciary Duties and Obligations of Company Directors* (1989) 618. Most major Asian jurisdictions have implemented rules for appointing independent directors to their companies' boards since 2016 – see Harald Baum, 'The Rise of the Independent Director: A Historical and Comparative Perspective' in Harald Baum, Luke R Nottage and Dan W Puchniak (eds), *Independent Directors in Asia: A Historical, Contextual and Comparative Approach* (CUP, 2017), Max Planck Private Law Research Paper No. 16/20, 2/34 <https://ssrn.com/abstract=2814978>.

directors often provide a beneficial objective/independent viewpoint and thus a crucial check on self-interest and abuse within corporate management.[38] Thus, the idea of appointing *independent* non-executive directors to boards of listed companies has been promoted in the UK since the 1992 Cadbury Report.

It was, however, the UK Higgs Report (2003) that recommended that at least half of the board (excluding the chair) should be 'independent non-executive directors',[39] and defined 'independence' in great detail.[40] These recommendations were accepted and incorporated into the 2008 UK Combined Code (now called the UK Corporate Governance Code[41] – discussed further in Chapter 11).

In Australia, it is now also expected that listed companies must explain why they do not have at least half of the board (excluding the chair) consisting of 'independent directors'; there are now also extensive guidelines in the ASX *CG Principles and Recommendations* for assessing whether a non-executive director is 'independent'.[42] The current edition (2014) of the ASX *CG Principles and Recommendations* contains detailed provisions to guide companies in determining whether or not a non-executive director is 'independent':[43]

ASX *CG PRINCIPLES AND RECOMMENDATIONS* – INDEPENDENCE

Box 2.3:   Factors relevant to assessing the independence of a director

Examples of interests, positions, associations and relationships that might cause doubts about the independence of a director include if the director:

- is, or has been, employed in an executive capacity by the entity or any of its child entities and there has not been a period of at least three years between ceasing such employment and serving on the board;
- is, or has within the last three years been, a partner, director or senior employee of a provider of material professional services to the entity or any of its child entities;

---

38   Le Mire, 'Independent directors: Partnering expertise with independence' (2016) 1. Tricker suggests that the growing concern that inside directors tend to be self-serving explains the shift away from insider-controlled boards. See Tricker, *International Corporate Governance* (1994) 15. See also Zahid Riaz, Sangeeta Ray and Pradeep Ray, 'The synergistic effect of state regulation and self-regulation on disclosure level of director and executive remuneration in Australia' (2015) 47 *Administration and Society* 623, 627.

39   *Review of the Role and Effectiveness of Non-Executive Directors* (Higgs Report) (January 2003) para 9.5 <www.berr.gov.uk/files/file23012.pdf>.

40   Ibid. para 9.11 and box following para 9.13 on 37. See also Richard Smerdon, *A Practical Guide to Corporate Governance* (Sweet & Maxwell, 2nd edn, 2004) 67 *et seq.*

41   FRC, *The UK Corporate Governance Code* (September 2012) 4 <www.frc.org.uk/Our-Work/Publications/Corporate-Governance/UK-Corporate-Governance-Code-September-2012.aspx>. The new revised and updated Code applies to accounting periods beginning on or after 17 June 2016. FRC, *The UK Corporate Governance Code* (April 2016) <www.frc.org.uk/Our-Work/Publications/Corporate-Governance/UK-Corporate-Governance-Code-April-2016.pdf>.

42   ASX, *CG Principles and Recommendations* (2014) 16.

43   Ibid. 16.

- is, or has been within the last three years, in a material business relationship (eg as a supplier or customer) with the entity or any of its child entities, or an officer of, or otherwise associated with, someone with such a relationship;
- is a substantial security holder of the entity or an officer of, or otherwise associated with, a substantial security holder of the entity;
- has a material contractual relationship with the entity or its child entities other than as a director;
- has close family ties with any person who falls within any of the categories described above; or
- has been a director of the entity for such a period that his or her independence may have been compromised.

In each case, the materiality of the interest, position, association or relationship needs to be assessed to determine whether it might interfere, or might reasonably be seen to interfere, with the director's capacity to bring an independent judgement to bear on issues before the board and to act in the best interests of the entity and its security holders generally.

The shift towards expecting a majority of the directors of listed corporations to be 'independent non-executive directors' has gone hand in hand with a considerable expansion of the role envisaged for independent non-executive directors over recent years. Perceptions of what an 'independent director' is have also changed rapidly over recent times.[44]

In 2014, the Murray Review, an inquiry into the Australian financial system, recommended that there must be a majority of independent directors on the board of corporate trustees of public offer superannuation funds, including an independent chair.[45] The Australian Government responded to this recommendation by proposing legislation that requires a minimum of one-third independent directors, including an independent chair, for superannuation trustee boards.[46] However, the Fraser Review,[47] commissioned by industry groups Industry Super Australia and the Australian Institute of Superannuation Trustees, concluded that setting a quota of independent directors would not necessarily deliver improved governance. The Review found that the focus should be on appointing directors with skills, commitment and values, and recommended that a mandatory code of conduct be introduced instead.[48]

Several factors or barriers may stand in the way of non-executive directors fulfilling their role effectively: the appointment processes for non-executive directors are often inadequate – these may be merely nomination by the board based on close personal relationships with board members, the chief executive officer (CEO) or the chairperson of the board;[49] some are

---

44   See generally Robert AG Monks and Nell Minow, *Corporate Governance* (Blackwell, 3rd edn, 2004) 227 *et seq*.

45   Financial System Inquiry, Final Report (November 2014) xxiii, Recommendation 13 <http://fsi.gov.au/ files/2014/12/FSI_Final_Report_Consolidated20141210.pdf>.

46   Superannuation Legislation Amendment (Trustee Governance) Bill 2015 (16 September 2015) <www.aph.gov.au/Parliamentary_Business/Bills_Legislation/Bills_Search_Results/Result?bId=r5548>.

47   Bernie Fraser, *Board Governance of Not for Profit Superannuation Funds* (16 February 2017).

48   Sally Rose, 'Bernie Fraser Review finds no need for independents', *Investment Magazine*, 16 February 2017 <https://investmentmagazine.com.au/2017/02/bernie-fraser-review-finds-no-need-for-independents/>.

49   See generally Tricker, *Corporate Governance* (2009) 57.

still too closely allied with management; they rely of necessity on information prepared by and received from management to fulfil their monitoring or supervisory functions;[50] there is no guarantee that they will challenge the CEO; they lack detailed knowledge of the company's business; they have limited time to spend on their directorships;[51] 'independence' is a state of mind, rather than something to be determined by ticking a few boxes on a checklist;[52] there are various meanings attached to 'independence';[53] and the more 'involved and engaged' non-executive directors become, the less independent they become.[54] Murray Steele summarises the challenges for non-executive directors very well:

> [A]s a result both of their responsibilities and of the rapidly changing environment in which companies operate, the NED [non-executive director] role today is complex and demanding. It requires skills, experience, integrity, and particular behaviours and personal attributes. NEDs have to deal with interesting dilemmas: they need both to challenge and support the executive directors; be both engaged and non-executive; and [be] both independent and involved.[55]

Recent research on the practical impact of having a majority of independent non-executives on boards is contradictory. On the one hand, Peter Fischer and Marc-Oliver Swan concluded recently that the approach in Australia – expecting (the 'comply or explain' or 'if not, why not' principle) a majority of independent non-executive directors – did not add to firm performance; to the contrary, they concluded that:

> it would appear that the ASX governance recommendation to declare significant share-holders as not independent and have 'independent' directors constitute the board major-ity has destroyed considerable shareholder wealth. This destruction is of no discernible benefit to other than executives and fellow board members. We estimate these losses conservatively at about AUS\$69 billion over the period 2003–2011.[56]

---

50   For some very sceptical, but enlightening, views of the role of boards by young CEOs in Canada, see David Leighton and Donald H Thain, *Making Boards Work* (McGraw-Hill Ryerson, 1997) 6–7. Also see Lawrence Mitchell, 'Structural holes, CEOs and the informational monopolies: The missing link in corporate governance' (2005) 70 *Brook Law Review* 1313.

51   Bonnie Buchanan, Tom Arnold and Lance Nail, 'Beware the Ides of March: The Collapse of HIH Insurance' in Jonathan A Batten and Thomas A Fetherston (eds), *Social Responsibility: Corporate Governance Issues* (JAI, 2003) 199 and 213; John C Shaw, 'The Cadbury Report, Two Years Later' in KJ Hopt et al. (eds), *Comparative Corporate Governance: The State of the Art and Emerging Research* (Clarendon Press, 1998) 21, 27–9; and Tricker, *International Corporate Governance* (1994) 15.

52   See also Tricker, *Corporate Governance* (2009) 51. Bernie Fraser echoed this sentiment when he argued that the values, skills and experience of board members should weigh more than the mere question of independence as such. See Fraser, *Board Governance of Not for Profit Superannuation Funds* (2017) 7.

53   See in particular Donald Clarke, 'Three concepts of the independent director' (2007) 32 *Delaware Journal of Corporate Law* 73.

54   Steele, 'The Role of the Non-executive Director' in Rushton (ed.), *The Business Case for Corporate Governance* (2008) 56–9.

55   Ibid. 65.

56   Peter L Fischer and Marc-Oliver Swan, 'Does board independence improve firm performance? Outcome of a quasi-natural experiment' (2013), 1 <www.researchgate.net/publication/272241996_Does_Board_Independence_Improve_Firm_Performance_Outcome_of_a_Quasi-Natural_Experiment>. See also Peter L Swan and David Forsberg, 'Does board "independence" destroy corporate value?', 26th Australasian Finance and Banking Conference 2013 (15 August 2014); 27th Australasian Finance and Banking Conference 2014, Paper, 18 <https://ssrn.com/abstract=2312325> or <http://dx.doi.org/10.2139/ssrn.2312325>.

This was confirmed by Peter Swan and David Forsberg.[57] In contrast, Kathy Fogel, Liping Ma and Randall Morck found that companies with boards with 'powerful' independent directors have significantly higher firm valuations. They contend that powerful independent directors are better able to monitor CEOs, because they have better access to information and/or greater credibility in challenging errant top managers.[58] Despite such contrasting study results, having independent directors is still regarded as a core governance tool.[59]

There are also widely diverging views on what the actual effect of 'independence'[60] is on directors' perceptions of their role and functions. It has been argued that all directors should have an interest in the corporation through shareholdings;[61] that 'the best boards consist of directors who are also substantial, as opposed to nominal, shareholders';[62] and that it 'has proven hollow at best' to expect outside directors with little or no equity stake in the company to effectively monitor and discipline the managers who selected them.[63]

There is a definite place in the corporate governance picture for independent non-executive directors, as long as expectations of them are realistic and their role is seen as but one part of ensuring good corporate governance. In other words, the role of independent non-executive directors in the complete picture of good corporate governance should not be over-emphasised.

4.4.3 Lead independent directors or senior independent directors

Code Provision A.4.1 of the UK Corporate Governance Code[64] requires the board to appoint one of the independent non-executive directors as 'senior independent director'. The senior independent director is expected to provide a sounding board for the chairman and to serve as an intermediary for the other directors when necessary. The senior independent director should also be available to shareholders if they have concerns that contact through the normal channels of chairperson, CEO or other executive directors has failed, or when such contact is inappropriate.[65] The Code further provides that the annual report should identify 'the senior independent director'.[66] The senior independent director plays a lesser role in the 2016 update

---

57   Swan and Forsberg, 'Does board "independence" destroy corporate value?' (2014).
58   Kathy Fogel, Liping Ma and Randall Morck, 'Powerful independent directors', European Corporate Governance Institute (ECGI) – Finance Working Paper No. 404/2014 (2015) <https://ssrn.com/abstract= 2377106> or <http://dx.doi.org/10.2139/ssrn.2377106>.
59   Baum, 'The Rise of the Independent Director' in Baum, Nottage and Puchniak (eds), *Independent Directors in Asia* (2017) 33, 34.
60   Leighton and Thain, in *Making Boards Work* (1997) 64–5, give good reasons for their belief that 'director independence is a myth'.
61   See further Mirko Bagaric and James McConvill, 'Why all directors should be shareholders in the company: The case against "independence"' (2004) 16 *Bond Law Review* 40.
62   John L Colley (Jr), Jacqueline L Doyle, George W Logan and Wallace Stettinius, *Corporate Governance* (McGraw-Hill, 2003) 78.
63   Jensen, as quoted by Mahmoud Ezzamel and Robert Watson, 'Executive Remuneration and Corporate Performance' in Kevin Keasey and Mike Wright (eds), *Corporate Governance: Responsibility, Risks and Remuneration* (Wiley, 1997) 61, 70.
64   FRC, *The UK Corporate Governance Code* (2016) 9.
65   Ibid. Code Provision A.4.1.
66   Ibid. Code Provision A.1.2.

of the Code. The Code requires that the non-executive directors, led by the senior independent director, should be responsible for performance evaluation of the chairman, taking into account the views of executive directors.[67] Furthermore, the senior independent director should attend sufficient meetings with a range of major shareholders to listen to their views in order to develop a balanced understanding of the issues and concerns of major shareholders.[68]

The 2007 ASX *CG Principles and Recommendations* contained no specific recommendation for a 'senior independent director' to be appointed or identified. However, there was a suggestion that where the chairperson is not an independent director, it may be beneficial to consider the appointment of a 'lead independent director'.[69] Under Principle 1 (Lay solid foundations for management and oversight) it explained that the respective roles of the board and management (senior executives) should be delineated and that the division of responsibilities should be disclosed. In addition, it was suggested that such disclosure should also contain an explanation of the balance of responsibilities between the chair, the lead independent director, if any, and the CEO or equivalent.[70] The lead independent director was also mentioned under Principle 2 (Structure the board to add value). Here it was pointed out that non-executive directors should consider the benefits of conferring regularly without management present, including at scheduled sessions. Their discussions can be facilitated by the chair or lead independent director, if any.[71]

The 2014 ASX *CG Principles and Recommendations*[72] used the UK term, 'senior independent director'. Under commentary on Recommendation 2.5 it suggested that if the chair is not an independent director, a listed entity should consider appointing an independent director as the deputy chair or as the 'senior independent director', the person who can fulfil the role whenever the chair is conflicted.[73] Even where the chair is an independent director, having a deputy chair or 'senior independent director' can also assist the board in reviewing the performance of the chair and in providing a separate channel of communication for security holders (especially where those communications concern the chair).[74] It also suggested that if the board of a listed entity has a deputy chair or a 'senior independent director', the board charter should include a description of that person's roles and responsibilities,[75] and that the non-executive directors, led by the deputy chair or senior independent director (if any), should be responsible for the performance evaluation of the chair, after having canvassed the views of the executive directors.[76]

---

67 Ibid. Code Provision B.6.3. Code Provision B.6.2 drives the concept of independent evaluation even further by determining that the boards of FTSE 350 companies should undergo an externally facilitated evaluation every three years.
68 Ibid. Code Provision E.1.1.
69 ASX, *CG Principles and Recommendations* (2007) 17.
70 Ibid. 13.
71 Ibid. 16.
72 ASX, *CG Principles and Recommendations* (2014) 8, 18 and 38.
73 Ibid. 18.
74 Ibid. 13 and 18.
75 Ibid. 8.
76 Ibid. 13.

4.4.4 The managing director, managing directors, the chief executive officer (CEO), executive directors and senior executives

In terms of s 201J (replaceable rule) of the *Corporations Act 2001* (Cth), the directors of a company may appoint one *or more of themselves* to the office of managing director for such period, and on such terms (including remuneration), as the directors may think fit. Section 198C(1) (replaceable rule) specifically allows the directors to confer on a managing director any of the powers that the directors may exercise, and sections 198C(2) and 203F(2) provide that the directors can revoke or vary such conferral at any time – it seems awkward that two different sections should deal with the revocation or variation of such powers. In addition, s 203F(1) provides that a managing director who ceases to be a director (for example, a director who is removed as a director – which could be done under statutory provisions such as s 203D of the Act, or provisions in a company's constitution) ceases also to be a managing director.

There is, however, no definition of 'managing director' in the Act. The term has also been used, especially in the past, to indicate all those directors involved in managerial functions. Nowadays it is less common to use the terms 'managing directors' or '*the* managing director' in public companies. Under the influence of the US, it is now common to use the terms 'executive directors' or, even if the person is also a director, 'Chief Executive Officer (CEO)'.[77] It is clear that a CEO could be a director, though under the ASX *CG Principles and Recommendations* listed companies will have to explain (under the 'if not, why not' principle) if the CEO is also the chair of the board or if the chair of the board does not meet the independence definition.[78]

There is no reference to 'the managing director' or 'managing directors' in the ASX *CG Principles and Recommendations*: the distinction made throughout is between 'directors', 'senior executives', 'executives' and 'employees'. The term 'senior executive' is defined differently for different types of corporations, but in essence it:

- includes executive directors;
- includes members or executive of the key management personnel of a corporation; and
- excludes non-executive directors.

The acronym 'CEO' is defined in the ASX *CG Principles and Recommendations* as 'the chief executive officer ... (by whatever title called)',[79] which provides a clear indication that it will be the most senior executive and may well be the managing director of the company if the directors have appointed a person with that title.

4.4.5 Chairperson

Section 248E (replaceable rule) of the Act allows the board to appoint one director to chair their meetings. This section further provides that the directors must elect a director present to

---

77   JB Reid, *Commonsense Corporate Governance* (Australian Institute of Company Directors [AICD], 2002) 68.

78   ASX, *CG Principles and Recommendations* (2014) 18 (Recommendation 2.5).

79   Ibid. 37.

chair a meeting, or part of it, if (i) a director has not already been elected to chair the meeting; or (ii) a previously elected chair is not available or declines to act for the meeting or part of the meeting.

If a director is the chairperson of a meeting, he or she is still acting in his or her capacity as a director of the company. If, however, the chairperson is acting as a proxy (an agent for the member), the chairperson owes duties to the individual members who directed their proxies to him or her. Accordingly, in such circumstances a chairperson owes duties distinct from the duties owed by a director – they are not mutually exclusive – and both sets of duties must be complied with: see *Whitlam v Australian Securities and Investments Commission*.[80]

There are good reasons for the ASX *CG Principles and Recommendations* expecting companies to explain if the chair of the board is also the CEO. First, the roles of management and the board are different and it is almost impossible for the same individual to properly fulfil the role of the most senior manager/executive of the company and the role of chairperson of the board. Second, it is also considered to be too much of a concentration of power to combine the roles of CEO and chairperson.[81] However, it should be pointed out that whether or not the CEO is also the chairperson, it is unlikely that other executive directors serving on the board will challenge the CEO on managerial decisions taken by the CEO at board level. The reason for this is simply that such a challenge will probably result in them having to face the wrath of the CEO the next day, when they will again be the subordinates of the CEO, who is their boss as far as line management is concerned. One can also imagine that executive directors will normally not like their internal differences to be displayed at board level, as that can easily get in the way of a harmonious and collegial running of the company by the senior executives. Having someone other than the CEO as chairperson of the board allows sensitive issues related to all executive matters to be discussed with the chairperson.

Mervyn King, in his book, *The Corporate Citizen*, devotes a chapter to the role of the chairperson. Some of the key aspects that chairpersons should keep in mind could be extracted from this chapter:[82]

- A good chairperson will be able to prepare a meeting in such a way that it will finish within two to three hours.
- Because body language is important, members of the board need to be in a place where they can not only hear each other clearly but can see each other as well.
- The chairperson needs to prepare for the meeting by ensuring that he or she has read all the documents carefully, understands them, and has spent time with senior management prior to the meeting.
- The chairman has to ensure that the board does not get involved in management – he or she has to remember that the board's role is a reflective one: strategy rather than activity.
- A good chairman is also a good listener.

80   (2003) 57 NSWLR 559.

81   See generally Rushton, 'The Role of the Chairman' in Rushton (ed.), *The Business Case for Corporate Governance* (2008) 29.

82   Mervyn King, *The Corporate Citizen: Governance for All Entities* (Penguin, 2006) 39–45. For another discussion of the practical importance of the chairperson, see Tricker, *Corporate Governance* (2009) 255–9.

- It is important for the chairperson to liaise with the chairperson of every board committee (especially the audit committee) and have an understanding with them in regard to the presentation of any matter with which the respective subcommittee is concerned.
- While the chairperson has to be collegiate, he or she has to be at arm's length (which is impossible if the role of CEO and chairperson are combined) because at some time the chairperson may to be called upon to arbitrate issues, facilitate the dismissal of a senior executive or call on a colleague to resign.
- The chairperson should try to meet at least twice a year with the non-executive directors so that a discussion without management present can be held about, *inter alia*, issues such as the ability of the management team and succession planning.
- The chairperson must endeavour to find ways in which bad news will reach the top quickly and must become an expert in asking critical questions when he or she does intervene in a debate.
- A chairperson needs to know that the members of the board have done their homework by sometimes asking one of them to summarise an issue and explain why he or she voted in a particular way on an issue.

4.4.6 Alternate director

Section 201K (replaceable rule) of the Act empowers a director to appoint an alternate director to exercise some or all of the director's powers for a specific period. This power is useful when a director is unable to be present at meetings. The appointment of an alternate director must be in writing[83] and must be approved by the other directors.[84] This approval will presumably be by way of a resolution of the board. If so requested by the appointing director, the company must give the alternate director notice of directors' meetings.[85] When an alternate exercises the appointing director's powers, it is just as effective as if the powers were exercised by the appointing director.[86] Although the alternate director may be appointed to act as agent of the appointing director, the alternate is nevertheless a director in the eyes of the law, with all the rights, duties and responsibilities of a director.[87]

The appointing director may terminate the alternate's appointment at any time.[88] The Australian Securities and Investments Commission (ASIC) must be given notice of the appointment and termination of appointment of an alternate director.[89]

4.4.7 Secretary

The Cadbury Report (1992) dealt with the vital role the company secretary should play in ensuring that correct procedures and good corporate governance practices are

---

83   *Corporations Act 2001* (Cth) s 201K(5).
84   Ibid. s 201K(1).
85   Ibid. s 201K(2).
86   Ibid. s 201K(3).
87   Business Council of Australia (BCA), *Corporate Practices and Conduct* (Bosch Report (1993)), (Information Australia, 1993) 18.
88   *Corporations Act 2001* (Cth) s 201K(4).
89   Ibid. s 205B(2) and (5).

followed.[90] This has been confirmed by the Hampel Report (1998).[91] In the Cadbury Report, the role of the company secretary was explained as follows:

> 4.25 The company secretary has a key role to play in ensuring that board procedures are both followed and regularly reviewed. The chairman and the board will *look to the company secretary for guidance on what their responsibilities are under the rules and regulations to which they are subject and on how those responsibilities* should be discharged. All directors should have access to the advice and services of the company secretary and should recognise that the chairman is entitled to the strong and positive support of the company secretary in ensuring the effective functioning of the board. It should be standard practice for the company secretary to administer, attend and prepare minutes of board proceedings. (emphasis in original)[92]

In Australia, a public company must have at least one secretary.[93] A proprietary company is no longer required to appoint a secretary, but if it does have one or more secretaries, at least one must ordinarily reside in Australia.[94] Section 188(2) of the Act serves as an encouragement for even proprietary companies to appoint a secretary, by providing that the directors of such a company will be liable if sections 142, 145, 205B or 345 are contravened.

The power to appoint a company secretary rests with the board[95] and the appointee holds office on the terms and conditions (including remuneration) that the directors determine.[96] The secretary must be a natural person who is at least 18 years old, and no person disqualified from being a director may be a secretary without the approval of ASIC.[97] The secretary, or one of the secretaries, must be ordinarily a resident in Australia.[98] The company secretary may also be a director of the company. Unlike in the UK,[99] there is no requirement in Australia for the company secretary to have any relevant business experience or formal educational qualifications. It is not uncommon, however, for a company secretary to have a legal background and to also serve as the company's general counsel.[100]

---

90   Cadbury Report (1992) paras 4.25–4.27. Joseph Lee points out that the need to ensure investor confidence led the company secretary's role to develop beyond mere administration to that of custodian of transparency and board independence. See Joseph Lee, 'From "housekeeping" to "gatekeeping": The enhanced role of the company secretary in the governance system' (1 October 2015) <http://dx.doi.org/10.2139/ssrn.2733180>.

91   Committee on Corporate Governance (Hampel Report), *Final Report* (1998) para 1.7 <www.econsense.de/_CSR_INFO_POOL/_CORP_GOVERNANCE/images/hampel_report.pdf>.

92   Cadbury Report, *Report of the Committee on the Financial Aspects of Corporate Governance* (1992) para 4.25. See generally Smerdon, *A Practical Guide to Corporate Governance* (2004) 93 *et seq.*

93   *Corporations Act 2001* (Cth) s 204A(2).

94   Ibid. s 204A(1).

95   Ibid. s 204D.

96   Ibid. s 204F (replaceable rule).

97   Ibid. s 204B(2).

98   Ibid. s 204A(2).

99   *Companies Act 2006* (UK) s 273. This section applies to secretaries of public companies.

100   For liabilities issues arising from this dual capacity, see Anil Hargovan, 'Dual role of general counsel and company secretary: Walking the legal tightrope in *Shafron v ASIC*' (2012) 27 *Australian Journal of Corporate Law* 112. Ian Maurice contends that there is a move towards a separation of the roles in the top 100 companies listed on the London Stock Exchange (FTSE). He acknowledges that combining the roles facilitates the presence of general counsel at board meetings and increases the focus on risk management at board level. However, the increasingly onerous responsibilities of general counsel and

4.5 Training and induction of directors

4.5.1 Training

After the collapse of the HIH Insurance company, Trevor Sykes, one of the leading commentators on corporate collapses and the impact they have on society, wrote:

> The whole [HIH] episode underlines the long-established lesson that whatever structures are devised to impose corporate honesty, they won't work unless you have the right people in them.[101]

This is almost stating the obvious as, in practical terms, the real difficulty is to find the right people and, once they have been found, to train them and then to monitor, over time, their performance: they need to be efficient, and to adhere to good corporate governance practices.

The importance of training directors was emphasised in the Cadbury Report. Training was considered to be 'highly desirable' because directors come from a range of backgrounds and their qualifications and experience vary considerably.[102] It was also emphasised that the training of directors is a very important way to ensure that directors adhere to good corporate governance practices.[103] The simple reality is that directors should be trained so that they understand and can discharge their duties as directors.[104] Bob Garratt, however, exposed a serious problem with director training in the past: that is, that the training was based upon managerial training at a higher level, or a type of 'mini-MBA' training. He argues that 'managing' and 'directing' require completely different types of training.[105]

Kendall and Kendall emphasise the need for director training in at least the following areas:[106]

- their statutory and regulatory obligations;
- their ethical obligations; and
- what constitutes good operational practice.

Tricker provides a useful list of types of director training:[107]

- formal external training courses on aspects of the director's work;
- in-house board development programs designed specifically for the entire board;

---

company secretaries and the complexity of both roles point towards diversion. See Ian Maurice, 'General counsel and company secretary: To combine or not to combine' (2011) 3 *Experts* 15. Joseph Lee discusses the question of combining the position of company secretary and general counsel. He points out that in the context of public interest disclosures there is an advantage for companies in appointing a legally qualified person to act as the company secretary. See Lee, 'From "housekeeping" to "gatekeeping"' (2015) 16.

101   Trevor Sykes, 'Cocktail of Greed, Folly and Incompetence', *Australian Financial Review*, 14 January 2003.

102   Cadbury Report (1992) para 4.19.

103   Ibid.

104   Shaw, 'The Cadbury Report, Two Years Later' in Hopt et al. (eds), *Comparative Corporate Governance* (1998) 27.

105   Bob Garratt, *Thin on Top* (Nicholas Brealey Publishing, 2003) 214–15.

106   Kendall and Kendall, *Real-World Corporate Governance* (1998) 9.

107   Tricker, *Corporate Governance* (2009) 295–6.

- updating and briefing sessions for the board, or individual directors;
- relevant higher degree courses in corporate governance, corporate strategy and other board-related topics;
- experiential sponsorship programs;
- mentoring, with a one-to-one personal trainer;
- self-directed learning and continuous self-development; and
- board experience itself, which provides one of the best learning experiences.

4.5.2 Induction

It is worthwhile mentioning that the UK Institute of Chartered Secretaries and Administrators (ICSA) provides some useful practical guidance on what things non-executive directors should consider before they join a board, as well as what first steps they should take once they have been appointed.[108] Once appointed, as part of the training process for directors, they should be properly introduced to the company; this is especially important for independent non-executive directors, because the ways in which companies conduct their business may vary considerably or, to put it differently, 'corporate cultures' may differ hugely among corporations. The appointment of directors will normally be based upon their proven skills, experience, qualifications and past track record, but they may know nothing about the 'corporate culture' of their new corporation or about the other directors and senior executives of the corporation. A good induction process for non-executive directors was considered to be of great importance by a large number of the non-executive directors surveyed two years after the Cadbury Report.[109]

Particularly useful guidelines regarding a proper induction program formed part of the 2003 UK Combined Code. These guidelines were based on recommendations made by the Higgs Committee (2003). It was suggested that the induction process should aim at achieving the following:[110]

1. Building an understanding of the nature of the company, its business and the markets in which it operates. For example, induction should cover:
   - the company's products or services;
   - group structure/subsidiaries/joint ventures;
   - the company's constitution, board procedures and matters reserved for the board;
   - summary details of the company's principal assets, liabilities, significant contracts and major competitors;

---

108 ICSA, *ICSA Guidance on Liability of Non-executive Directors: Care, Skill and Diligence*, Guidance Note 130117 (January 2013).

109 Shaw, 'The Cadbury Report, Two Years Later' in Hopt et al. (eds), *Comparative Corporate Governance* (1998) 30.

110 *The Combined Code on Corporate Governance* (UK Combined Code (2003)) (July 2003) 75–6; *Review of the Role and Effectiveness of Non-Executive Directors* (Higgs Report) (January 2003) 111–12 <www.berr.gov.uk/files/file23012.pdf>. See also Smerdon, *A Practical Guide to Corporate Governance* (2004) 38–40.

- the company's major risks and risk management strategy;
- key performance indicators; and
- regulatory constraints.

2. Building a link with the company's people including;
   - meetings with senior management;
   - visits to company sites other than the headquarters, to learn about production or services and meet employees in an informal setting. It is important not only for the board to get to know the new non-executive director, but also for the non-executive director to build a profile with employees below board level; and
   - participating in board strategy development: 'Away days' enable a new non-executive director to begin to build working relationships away from the formal setting of the boardroom.

3. Building an understanding of the company's main relationships, including meeting with the auditors and developing a knowledge of, in particular:
   - who are the major customers;
   - who are the major suppliers; and
   - who are the major shareholders and what is the shareholder relations policy – participation in meetings with shareholders can help give a first-hand feel as well as letting shareholders know who the non-executive directors are.

The 2016 *UK Corporate Governance Code* addresses induction and training as an aspect of development. The Code states that 'All directors should receive induction on joining the board and should regularly update and refresh their skills and knowledge.'[111] The chairman of the board is responsible for ensuring that 'new directors receive a full, formal and tailored induction on joining the board' and regularly reviewing and agreeing with each director on their training and development needs.[112]

4.6 Ethical behaviour of directors

Ethical behaviour by directors is one of the most important cornerstones of good corporate governance, as it sets the tone for the ethical behaviour of the corporation and that, in turn, goes a long way to ensure that the corporation adheres to good corporate governance practices.

Principle 3 of the 2014 ASX *CG Principles and Recommendations* states that listed companies should act ethically and responsibly and that not acting in such a way is likely to destroy value over the longer term.[113] The expectation that a corporation must have 'ethics, morals and

111 The *UK Corporate Governance Code* (UK Corporate Governance Code (2016)) (April 2016) 13. The Supporting Principles provide that 'The chairman should ensure that the directors continually update their skills and the knowledge and familiarity with the company required to fulfil their role both on the board and on board committees. The company should provide the necessary resources for developing and updating its directors' knowledge and capabilities. To function effectively all directors need appropriate knowledge of the company and access to its operations and staff.'
112 Ibid. B.4.1 and B.4.2, 13.
113 ASX, *CG Principles and Recommendations* (3rd edn, 2014) 19 <www.asx.com.au/documents/asx-compliance/cgc-principles-and-recommendations-3rd-edn.pdf>. Principle 9 of the

values' became prominent with the recognition of the corporation as a person and of the 'social responsibilities of corporations'.[114] As was pointed out in Chapters 1 and 2, there is now an expectation that companies will carry out sustainability, integrated and responsibility reporting to enable investors to, *inter alia*, see whether companies actually adhere to high ethical values. Ultimately it is the responsibility of the board of directors to promote ethical decision-making in the corporation.

The 2003 ASX *Principles of Good Corporate Governance and Best Practice Recommendations* was one of the first corporate governance reports to deal specifically with the ethical behaviour of directors. It recommended that corporations should establish a code of ethical and legal conduct to guide the board and executives as to:[115]

>   (a) the practices necessary to maintain confidence in the company's integrity; and
>   (b) the responsibility and accountability of individuals for reporting and investigating reports of unethical practices.[116]

The expectation in the 2014 ASX *CG Principles and Recommendations* is that these aspects are dealt with in the code of conduct.[117]

The importance of 'ethics, morals and values' was also commented on by Justice Owen in the HIH Royal Commission Report, under the heading 'The Royal Commission: A personal perspective':

> Right and wrong are moral concepts, and morality does not exist in a vacuum. I think all those who participate in the direction and management of public companies, as well as their professional advisers, need to identify and examine what they regard as the basic moral underpinning of their system of values. They must then apply those tenets in the decision-making process.[118]

The Appellate Court in *Australian Securities and Investments Commission v Ingleby*[119] was scathing about the conduct of a company officer involved in the company's 'oil for food' scandal in Iraq. The officer was held to be 'wilfully blind' to the company's corrupt practices, which were later investigated by a Royal Commission and found to be corporate bribes. The court held:

Good Governance Principles and Guidance for Not-for-Profit Organisations (Principles and Guidance) highlights the important role directors play in developing a culture of ethics and integrity in a corporation. It states that the board sets the tone for ethical and responsible decision-making throughout the organisation. AICD, *Good Governance Principles and Guidance for Not-for-Profit Organisations* (2013) 45.

114 Kendall and Kendall, *Real-World Corporate Governance* (1998) 17 and 139 *et seq*. See also Batten and Fetherston (eds), *Social Responsibility: Corporate Governance Issues* (2003) 1, 5–6; Philip TN Koh, 'Responsibilities of Corporate Governance and Control of Corporate Powers' in Philip TN Koh (ed.), *3Rs of Corporate Governance* (Malaysian Institute of Corporate Governance, 2001) 1, 5–6; and Monks and Minow, *Corporate Governance* (2004) 17–18 and 77 *et seq*.

115 ASX, *Principles of Good Corporate Governance and Best Practice Recommendations* (2003) 25 (Recommendation 3.1) <www.asx.com.au/documents/asx-compliance/principles-and-recommendations-march-2003.pdf>.

116 ASX, *Principles of Good Corporate Governance and Best Practice* (2007) 25.

117 ASX, *Principles of Good Corporate Governance and Best Practice Recommendations* (2003) 20.

118 Owen Report, *The Failure of HIH Insurance* (2003) Vol. l, xiii.

119 (2013) 39 VR 554.

It is essential that those who accept the rewards of important offices also accept the responsibilities which go with them. Proper corporate and professional behaviour depends upon that acceptance, and must be supplemented by the knowledge that the courts will play their part in the maintenance of appropriate standards.[120]

'Ethics, morals and values' for corporations will become increasingly important considerations for corporations in the future. 'Ethical behaviour' adds value to the corporation:

[A] highly ethical operation is likely to spend much less on protecting itself against fraud and will probably have to spend much less on industrial relations to maintain morale and common purpose.[121]

It is difficult to define 'business ethics': it is often very closely linked to concepts such as 'business culture' and 'cultural values generally', as well as to perceptions about business in a particular country or community. Some would say that business 'is all about business', and that ethics has little place in the hard business world. Others would simply say that the ways in which people view ethics differ so much that we will never be able to find common ground on what is meant by 'ethical behaviour' – what is seen as a good and sound business deal or a clever business strategy by some would be considered 'unethical behaviour' by others. However, as Kendall and Kendall illustrate, there are certain general guidelines against which 'ethical behaviour' can be judged, and which will assist in detecting 'unethical behaviour'. They list the following aspects:

1. General views on ethics – what and how important the issues are, such as:
   - consideration and protection of the environment;
   - fair trading, especially with poor countries;
   - defending human rights, for example non-exploitation of workers in poor countries;
   - not investing in countries with unacceptable regimes;
   - supporting local communities;
   - fair treatment of staff.
2. Particular stakeholder views/angles, such as:
   - customers' beliefs when purchasing – how much do ethical issues actually affect their buying behaviour?
   - employees' moral values – how important is it for them to work in an ethically sound company?
   - shareholders' feeling of responsibility – to what extent do they feel obliged to enforce ethical behaviour?
   - local community's interest – how much are they interested in the company's active involvement in the community?[122]

---

120   Ibid. at [95].
121   Kendall and Kendall, *Real-World Corporate Governance* (1998) 139. See also Stephen Cohen and Damien Grace, 'Ethics and the Sustainability of Business' in John D Adams et al., *Collapse Incorporated: Tales, Safeguards & Responsibilities of Corporate Australia* (CCH Australia, 2001) 99, 105–6.
122   Kendall and Kendall, *Real-World Corporate Governance* (1998) 142.

The internationalisation and globalisation of business make it imperative that we strive to find common ground on what is meant by 'ethical behaviour' by corporations, and that we promote such behaviour as a core practice in good corporate governance.

4.7 Remuneration of directors and executives

4.7.1 A controversial and politically sensitive issue

The debate on excessive executive remuneration became particularly sensitive politically as a result of the Global Financial Crisis, which commenced in 2007, but it is not a new topic. In 1995, the Greenbury Report in the UK was one of the first corporate governance reports to promote transparency and disclosure of executive remuneration. This was taken further in the 1998 UK Hampel Report, and Australia followed suit, reiterating the call for disclosure of executive remuneration in the Bosch and Hilmer corporate governance reports. As a result, legislation was introduced to ensure disclosure in both jurisdictions.

It is not remuneration of directors and executives as such that causes resentment from the public and politicians, but 'excessive' remuneration. This was illustrated very well in 2017 when it was revealed that the CEO of Australia Post, Ahmed Fahour, was paid $5.6 million in 2016.[123] There were allegations that Australia Post tried to hide this from the public eye, and that caused concerns as Australia Post is a government-controlled entity. Under considerable political and public pressure, Ahmed Fahour resigned less than a month after this 'excessive remuneration'[124] was revealed.[125] The fundamental question is, however, how was such a remuneration package negotiated? Was there benchmarking done against organisations similar to Australia Post? What was the role of the remuneration committee and the board in all of this?

In addition, the huge differences between the remuneration of executives and that of other employees, which has been illustrated by disturbing statistics, has been of concern as well.[126] The average income for the top 20 Australian CEOs in 2008–09 was $6.4 million – almost

---

123   Frank Chung, 'Australia Post CEO paid $5.6 million in 2016', *News.com.au*, 8 February 2017 <www.news.com.au/finance/work/leaders/australia-post-ceo-paid-56-million-in-2016/news-story/7e8b26ed0660abf9c7d60b4ec539017e>.

124   See comments by the Prime Minister, Malcolm Turnbull: Australia Associated Press, 'Australia Post CEO's $5.6 "too high" says Turnbull', *The Guardian*, 8 February 2017 <www.theguardian.com/business/2017/feb/08/turnbull-calls-australia-post-after-ceos-multimillion-salary-revealed>; Michael Koziol, 'Malcolm Turnbull urged to review rules after slamming "cult" of excessive CEO pay', *Sydney Morning Herald*, 10 February 2017 <www.smh.com.au/federal-politics/political-news/malcolm-turnbull-urged-to-review-rules-after-slamming-cult-of-excessive-ceo-pay-20170210-gu9yku.html>.

125   Frank Chung and Liz Burke, 'Australia Post CEO Ahmed Fahour quits and takes dig at Pauline Hanson', *News.com.au*, 23 February 2017 <www.news.com.au/finance/work/leaders/australia-post-ceo-to-quit/news-story/fd19cd2d5ab741286e075a06c77d8ead>.

126   See Carola Frydman, 'Executive compensation: A new view from a long-term perspective, 1936–2005' (2010) 23 *The Review of Financial Studies* 2099 <http://web.mit.edu/frydman/www/trends_rfs2010.pdf>; John Shields, 'Setting the double standard: Chief Executive pay the BCA way' (2005) 56 *Journal of Australian Political Economy* 299, 302. See <http://inequality.is/real> for a basic explanation for the widening gap between top earners and other earners from a US perspective.

100 times that of the average worker.[127] The average earnings of ASX 100 CEOs was $3 million, which was 42 times the average earnings in Australia.[128] Furthermore, in Australia, since 2001, the base pay for executives has risen by 130 per cent, while average weekly earnings for other employees have risen by only 52 per cent.[129]

A very interesting study by Mike Pottenger and Andrew Leigh[130] used BHP Ltd, a company for which data since 1887 is available, to determine director, CEO and executive remuneration trends in BHP. They also compared these with average earnings. Although they point out that there were some variations during certain periods, overall there was a widening gap between the BHP CEOs' remuneration and average earnings.[131] Interestingly, they found that the ratio of the BHP CEOs' earnings to the average Australian earnings fell in the late 19th century, but then rose from around 25 to 45 times the average earnings in 1900; however, it declined to around 30 times by 1930.[132] This ratio rose to about 75 times by 1999 and that was roughly the ratio during the period 1999–2012. However, if non-salary benefits are also taken into consideration, the BHP CEOs' compensation ranged from 150 to 250 times the average earnings from 1999–2012.[133]

The fact that the widening gap between executive and other employee remuneration is a real concern is also illustrated by the fact that on 18 September 2013 the US Securities and Exchange Commission (SEC) voted 3–2 to propose a new rule that would require public companies to disclose the ratio of the compensation of the CEO to the median compensation of its employees. The new rule was required by s 953(b) of the *Dodd-Frank Wall Street Reform and Consumer Protection Act 2010* (the Dodd-Frank Act).[134] It would not prescribe a specific methodology for companies to use in calculating a 'pay ratio'. Instead, companies would have the flexibility to determine the median annual total compensation of its employees in a way that best suited its particular circumstances and still comply with the statutory mandate.[135]

---

127   Productivity Commission, *Executive Remuneration in Australia*, Report No. 49 (19 December 2009) xiv <www.pc.gov.au/__data/assets/pdf_file/0008/93590/executive-remuneration-report.pdf>.

128   See Australian Council of Trade Unions (ACTU), 'Executive Paywatch' <www.actu.org.au/Issues/ExecutivePayWatch/default.aspx>.

129   Productivity Commission, *Executive Remuneration in Australia* (2009) 41.

130   Mike Pottenger and Andrew Leigh, 'Long run trends in Australian executive remuneration: BHP 1887–2012', IZA Discussion Paper No. 7486, <http://ssrn.com/abstract=2293303>.

131   Ibid. Figure 3.

132   Ibid. Figure 2 and text following that figure (there are no page numbers in the discussion paper).

133   Ibid.

134   From 1 January 2017, US companies are required to disclose the ratio of a CEO's annual total remuneration to the median annual total remuneration of all company employees. Similarly, *The Large and Medium-sized Companies and Groups (Accounts and Reports) (Amendment) Regulations 2013* require UK companies to disclose CEOs' remuneration in comparison to their employees from 1 January 2017. See discussion in Chapter 11. Aditi Gupta, Jenny Chu and Xing Ge examined the effect of mandated disclosure on executive remuneration and firm performance since 2013 in a recent article. They found that mandated disclosure in the first year of the post-reform period did not enhance the link between CEO pay and firm performance, and nor did it have any impact on the discrepancy between the average employee's salary and the CEO's salary. See Aditi Gupta, Jenny Chu and Xing Ge, 'Form Over Substance? An Investigation of Recent Remuneration Disclosure Changes in the UK' (21 June 2016) <https://ssrn.com/abstract=2798001>.

135   See SEC Press Release, 'SEC Proposes Rules for Pay Ratio Disclosure' (18 September 2013) <www.sec.gov/News/PressRelease/Detail/PressRelease/1370539817895#.Us8jfiQqEjU> and the related explanatory document <www.sec.gov/rules/proposed/2013/33–9452.pdf>.

The SEC Chair, Mary Jo White, mentioned this flexibility specifically and invited comment on it, indicating that there are some who would probably argue that the arrangement is too flexible. The disclosure requirements will now require companies falling under the Dodd-Frank Act to disclose:

- the median of the annual total compensation of all its employees except the CEO;
- the annual total compensation of its CEO; and
- the ratio of the two amounts.

One of the arguments used to justify the high levels of payments to CEOs is international competitiveness – if CEOs in some countries are not paid competitively in an international sense, they will be poached by companies in other countries. This is probably true of most developed countries, but is this just a self-serving argument, like several others used in the past, to justify the extraordinarily high compensation of CEOs and senior executives? A very interesting report (*Global CEO Appointments – A Very Domestic Issue*) by the UK High Pay Centre found that a very small percentage (less than 1 per cent – 4 CEOs out of 489 companies) of top chief executives are poached from overseas. In the executive summary the following interesting facts were also revealed:[136]

- Only one CEO was poached while CEO of another company in another continent.
- In North America, Japan, Latin America and Eastern Europe *not one* CEO was appointed from outside the country where the company is based.
- 80 per cent of CEO appointments in the world's largest companies are internal promotions.
- Just 6.5 per cent (32) of CEOs who formed part of the survey were poached from another company while serving as a CEO.

Turning specifically to developments in Australia, in 2004 the Business Council of Australia (BCA) warned against additional regulation of executive remuneration,[137] but it was clear by 2009 that the BCA had conceded that steps needed to be taken to curb excessive executive remuneration.[138] In early 2009, the Australian Institute of Company Directors (AICD) issued some new guidelines for boards on executive remuneration as a result of the Global Financial Crisis.[139] In short, the Global Financial Crisis drew the attention of the public, politicians and business to excessive executive remuneration. The topic of directors' and executives' remuneration remains a concern all over the world, and all sorts of ways to ensure that directors and executives are compensated fairly and that compensation is linked to performance, skills and

136   High Pay Centre, *Global CEO Appointments – A Very Domestic Issue* 5 <http://highpaycentre.org/files/CEO_mobility_final.pdf>. See also High Pay Centre, *Paid to Perform? What do we want our business leaders to achieve?* (January 2013) <http://highpaycentre.org/files/HPC_11_Paid_to_perform_06.pdf>.
137   BCA, *Executive Remuneration: A Position Paper Prepared by the Business Council of Australia* (June 2004) <www.bca.com.au/Content/101416.aspx>.
138   For example, the BCA's submission of 2 September 2009 to the Australian Parliamentary Senate Economics Legislation Committee re the *Corporations Amendment (Improving Accountability Termination Payments Bill) 2009* <www.bca.com.au/publications/submission-on-the-corporations-amendment-improving-accountability-on-termination-payments-bill-2009>.
139   AICD, *AICD Issues New Guidelines for Boards on Executive Remuneration*, Media Release, 12 February 2009 <http://www.companydirectors.com.au/General/Search?q=AICD%20Issues%20New%20Guidelines%20for%20Boards%20on%20Executive%20Remuneration>.

experience are being considered. [140] There are also some serious efforts being made inter-nationally to publicly report on the relationship between CEO and executive remuneration and the actual financial performance of companies.[141]

The 2015 edition of the Australian Council of Superannuation Investors Report on CEO pay found that fixed pay for CEOs in Australia's top companies was at its lowest in nearly a decade and that realised and reported pay of ASX 100 CEOs declined by 3.1 per cent and 2 per cent, respectively, from 2014. In contrast, more bonuses were awarded in 2015 than at any time since 2008: 93 per cent of the ASX 100 sample CEOs were awarded a bonus for their year's work:[142]

Fixed pay:

- in 2012 the average and median fixed pay for Top 100 CEOs was again steady, with the median Top 100 CEO receiving fixed pay of $1.914 million in 2011; and
- average fixed pay declined by 2.4 per cent to $973,576, almost 5 per cent higher than average fixed pay in 2011.

Bonuses paid:

- average bonuses for Top 100 CEOs increased by 4.8 per cent in 2012, compared with a 20 per cent decline in the size of bonuses in 2011;
- the average bonus in 2012 rose to $1.060 million;
- the overwhelming majority of sample CEOs received a bonus in 2012 – 82 per cent – although the proportion of CEOs who did not receive a bonus was the highest since 2003; and bonuses for the ASX 101–200 cohort were lower in 2012, with the average bonus falling by 4.6 per cent to $402,025, with just over a quarter receiving no bonus.

Cash pay:

- high levels of cash pay remain a feature of the Top 100 CEO sample. In 2012, average and median cash pay remained close to $3 million despite both declining slightly from 2011; and

---

140   See FRC, *Directors' Remuneration: Consultation Document* (October 2013) <www.frc.org.uk/Our-Work/Publications/Corporate-Governance/Directors-Remuneration-Consultation-Document-File.pdf>; High Pay Centre, *Leading or Lagging: Where does the UK stand in the international debate about top pay?* <http://highpaycentre.org/pubs/leading-or-lagging-where-does-the-uk-stand-in-the-international-debate-abou>; Association of British Insurers (ABI), *ABI Principles of Remuneration* (November 2012) <www.ivis.co.uk/PDF/ABI%20Principles%20of%20Remuneration-%20Nov2012.pdf> – for a summary, see <www.ivis.co.uk/ExecutiveRemuneration.aspx>.

141   See, for example, the FRC, *Lab Project Report: Reporting of Pay and Performance* (March 2013) <www.frc.org.uk/Our-Work/Publications/Financial-Reporting-Lab/Lab-project-report-Reporting-of-pay-and-performanc.aspx>; and High Pay Centre, *Paid to Perform? What do we want our business leaders to achieve?* (2013).

142   Australian Council of Superannuation Investors (ACSI), *CEO Pay in ASX 200 Companies*, Research Report (August 2016); 5; Ian Ramsay (ed.), *SAI Global Corporate Law Bulletin*, Bulletin No. 194 (21 October 2013) Part 1.14. Similarly, the annual Equilar 200 study with *The New York Times* reflects that average pay for the Equilar 200 Highest-Paid CEOs in the US in 2015 was $19.3 million, compared to $22.6 million for the 200 CEOs on the list in 2014 <www.equilar.com/press-releases/47-200-highest-paid-ceo-rankings.html>. Reports on the position in the UK, however, reflect a different trend: an annual survey of FTSE 100 CEO pay packages revealed that the average FTSE 100 CEO package increased more than 10% in 2015. High Pay Centre, *The State of Pay: High Pay Centre briefing on executive pay* (August 2016) <http://highpaycentre.org/files/The_State_of_Pay_2015.pdf>.

- average cash pay in the ASX 101–200 rose slightly, with most of the increase attributable to explorers, whose CEOs received a 10 per cent increase in cash pay in 2012.

4.7.2 Disclosure of remuneration and emoluments in Australia

Australia has one of the most extensive disclosure regimes in the world in relation to the remuneration of directors and key management personnel.[143] The *Corporate Law Economic Reform Program (Audit Reform and Corporate Disclosure) Act 2004* (Cth) introduced s 300A into the *Corporations Act 2001* (Cth), which requires enhanced disclosures, either in the directors' remuneration report or the financial report, both of which are audited. These disclosures include:

(1) the board's remuneration policy [s 300A(1)(a)];

(2) the relationship between remuneration policy and company performance [s 300A(1)(ba)];

(3) details of remuneration of key personnel [s 300A(1)(c)];

(4) reasons for failing to subject to performance conditions any remuneration made via shares or options [s 300A(1)(d)];

(5) the relative proportion of remuneration related to performance, value of options granted and aggregate and percentage values of remuneration via options [s 300A(1)(e)].

Further major reforms to both disclosure of and accounting for share-based payments have occurred since 2004. In particular, Accounting Standard AASB 2 *Share-based Payment* requires calculation of the 'fair value' of options granted under remuneration packages and expensing of this value, along with disclosures around the method and assumptions involved in calculating the fair value. Alissa Irgang, however, provides evidence that 'disclosure' does not necessarily ensure that companies will not remunerate executives above averages in the industry. Companies may see above-average pay as making them more attractive for top and high-performing executives; this phenomenon has been described as an example of the 'Lake Wobegon effect'.[144] As will be seen below, there have been several further developments regarding executive remuneration in Australia.

---

143   Kym Sheehan explains the regulatory framework for executive remuneration in Australia in Kym Sheehan, 'The regulatory framework for executive remuneration in Australia' (2009) 31 *Sydney Law Review* 273. See also Zahid Riaz, Sangeeta Ray and Pradeep Ray, 'The synergistic effect of state regulation and self-regulation on disclosure level of director and executive remuneration in Australia' (2015) 47 *Administration and Society* 623, 629 for an excellent exposition of the Australian context.

144   Irgang, 'Capping and Corporate Governance' (2013) 149–51. See also <http://en.wikipedia.org/wiki/Lake_Wobegon>. See Zahid Riaz, Sangeeta Ray, Pradeep Kanta Ray and Vikas Kumar, 'Disclosure practices of foreign and domestic firms in Australia' (2015) 50 *Journal of World Business* 781, 789.

4.7.3 Some provisions of the ASX *CG Principles and Recommendations* dealing with remuneration

It is to be expected that the ASX *CG Principles and Recommendations*, like most voluntary corporate governance codes, would contain provisions regarding the remuneration of directors, executives and employees. The board of directors is ultimately responsible for approving a company's remuneration framework[145] and listed companies should have a formal and transparent process for developing their remuneration policy and for fixing the remuneration packages of directors and senior executives.[146] Apart from suggesting that the remuneration of executive and non-executive directors and senior executives should be agreed contractually, there are several provisions dealing specifically with the determination of remuneration and the disclosure of remuneration. The overall aim is to remunerate 'fairly and responsibly'.[147]

The ASX *CG Principles and Recommendations* provides that all Australian listed companies must have a remuneration committee and that the remuneration committee must have at least three members, a majority of whom must be independent; the chair should also be an independent director. The remuneration committee must disclose its charter and, for every reporting period, the number of times it met.[148] The overall aim of having a remuneration committee becomes clear when one looks at the ASX *CG Principles and Recommendations*: it explains that the remuneration committee is usually tasked with reviewing and making recommendations to the board in relation to:

- the entity's remuneration framework for directors, including the process by which any pool of directors' fees approved by security holders is allocated to directors;
- the remuneration packages to be awarded to senior executives;
- equity-based remuneration plans for senior executives and other employees;
- superannuation arrangements for directors, senior executives and other employees; and
- whether there is any gender or other inappropriate bias in remuneration for directors, senior executives or other employees.[149]

There is a strong suggestion that key performance indicators should be developed and that part of senior executives' remuneration should be linked to achieving them.[150] In addition, the relationship between remuneration and performance and how that is aligned to the creation of value for security holders should be clearly articulated to investors.[151] Recommendation 8.2 expects listed companies to disclose their policies and practices regarding the remuneration of non-executive directors and their policies and practices regarding the remuneration of executive directors and other senior executives. It is also expected that the roles and responsibilities of non-executive directors, executive directors and other senior executives are reflected in the level and composition of their remuneration. [152]

---

145   ASX, *CG Principles and Recommendations* (2014) 8.
146   Ibid. 31.
147   Ibid. 31, Principle 8.
148   Ibid. 31.
149   Ibid. 32.
150   Ibid. 13, Box 1.5(8).
151   Ibid.
152   Ibid. 32.

4.7.4 Further measures to counter excessive remuneration of directors and executives

In Australia, the Federal Government requested the Australian Prudential Regulation Authority (APRA), which regulates entities in the insurance, superannuation and authorised deposit-taking industries, to produce best practice guidelines for both the design and the disclosure of executive remuneration. On 28 May 2009, APRA released a consultation paper,[153] with draft proposals released on 7 September 2009.[154] On 30 November 2009, APRA released Prudential Practice Guide PPG 511 – *Remuneration*.

Briefly, the governance standards require the establishment of remuneration committees and the design of remuneration policy that, in rewarding individual performance, is designed to encourage behaviour that supports the risk management framework of the regulated institution (para 43). Further, in designing remuneration arrangements, the board remuneration committee will need to consider, among other matters:

- the balance between fixed (salary) and variable (performance-based) components of remuneration. Performance-based components include all short-term and longer-term incentive remuneration, payable with or without deferral; and
- whether cash or equity-related payments are used and, in each case, the terms of the entitlements, including vesting and deferral arrangements (para 44).

In March 2009 the Federal Government initiated a Productivity Commission review into the regulation of director and executive remuneration in Australia. The Productivity Commission's final report[155] was released publicly in January 2010. Perhaps the most noteworthy[156] recommendation was the introduction of the 'two-strikes and spill' approach.[157] This approach entails that if 25 per cent or more of shareholders at two successive annual general meetings vote negatively on the board's pay report there should be an immediate vote on whether the entire board should face re-election. If that vote is carried by a majority of those voting at the meeting, all board positions would be up for election, one by one, at a special meeting (the spill meeting) held within three months. This approach became law on 1 July 2011 with the passing of the *Corporations Amendment (Improving Accountability on Director and Executive Remuneration) Act 2011* (Cth). These provisions are currently contained in sections 250U–250Y of the *Corporations Act 2001* (Cth). An interesting summary of an *Australian Financial Review* (AFR) survey of how effective the two-strikes rule had been since its introduction was published by Guerdon Associates.[158] The survey revealed the following:

- A 'strike' (that is, an against vote of more than 25 per cent) has been recorded at approximately 6 per cent of meetings over the three years since the rule's introduction.

---

153   APRA, *Remuneration – Proposed extensions to governance requirements for APRA-regulated institutions*, Discussion Paper (28 May 2009).

154   Ibid. Response to Submissions (7 September 2009).

155   Productivity Commission, *Executive Remuneration in Australia* (2009).

156   See, for instance, Allan Fels, 'Shareholders Can Turn Up the Heat on Executive Pay', *Sydney Morning Herald*, 5 January 2010, 20.

157   See Productivity Commission, *Executive Remuneration in Australia* (2009) xxxii and 296–301.

158   Guerdon Associates, 'Two strikes rule on remuneration report voting – a three-year stock-take' (5 February 2014) <www.guerdonassociates.com/News-Detail.asp?cid=69&navID=120&NewsID=621>.

- In total, 40 companies have recorded two strikes – 18 companies in 2013 and 22 in 2012.
- 17 of the 18 companies that recorded a second strike were outside the ASX 200 (Cash Converters being the exception).
- In 2013, a spill resolution was carried at only 2 of the 18 companies that were required to put up this resolution.
- Only 6 ASX-listed companies in total have been required to hold a spill meeting since the rule was introduced.
- No incumbent directors have lost their board seat at a spill meeting. Any directors who have been 'voted down' at a spill meeting have been new directors seeking election (more often than not, having been put forward by a substantial shareholder).
- 8 companies have technically recorded three consecutive strikes (although the strike rate resets after the second).

It is, however, impossible to determine how many companies' remuneration practices for executives were adjusted or influenced by the fact that the rule exists.[159]

The latest development in Australia came on 12 December 2012, when the then government released an Exposure Draft of the Corporations Legislation Amendment (Remuneration Disclosures and Other Measures) Bill 2012. This legislation deals, *inter alia*, with some further recommendations made by the CAMAC in its *Executive Remuneration Report* of April 2011.[160] The Exposure Draft proposes new requirements for the disclosure of clawbacks based on a discussion paper, 'The Clawback of Executive Remuneration where Financial Statements are Materially Misstated', released in December 2010. The proposed reforms in the Exposure Draft include requiring listed companies to disclose in the remuneration report whether any over-paid remuneration has been 'clawed back', and if not, an explanation, and requiring more transparent disclosure of termination payments or 'golden handshake' payments.[161] Since these proposals there has been a change of government in Australia (in 2013, and maintained in 2016) and it remains to be seen whether the current Coalition Government will proceed with legislation proposed under a Labor Government, especially as the intended legislation was met with considerable resistance – expressed in more than 40 submissions from very influential firms, organisations and institutes.[162] The fact that a considerable period of time has elapsed since the Exposure Draft was released is perhaps an indication that the current government is unlikely to proceed with

---

159 John Egan highlights an unintended consequence of the two-strike rule: that the board of a company, although supported by more than 85% of shareholders, could be forced to stand for re-election if a significant minority of shareholders choose to vote against the remuneration report. He cites UGL Limited as an example where less than 12% of shareholders pushed a negative vote of 30% against its remuneration report. John Egan in Tony Featherstone, 'Two strikes round one', *Morningstar*, 24 February 2017 <www.morningstar.com.au/funds/article/two-strikes/4311?q=printme>.

160 CAMAC, *Executive Remuneration Report* (April 2011) <www.camac.gov.au/camac/camac.nsf/ byHeadline/PDFFinal+Reports+2011/$file/Executive_remuneration_report_April11.pdf>.

161 See further AICD, 'New Executive Pay Worries', *Company Director Magazine*, 1 April 2013 <www.companydirectors.com.au/Director-Resource-Centre/Publications/Company-Director-magazine/2013-back-editions/April/Feature-New-executive-pay-worries>.

162 See <http://agencysearch.australia.gov.au/search/search.cgi?collection=agencies&profile=treasury& query=Corporations%20Legislation%20Amendment%20%28Remuneration%20Disclosures%20and% 20Other%20Measures%29%20Bill%202012&scope_disable=off>. See also Savo Kovacevic, 'Executive remuneration developments in Australia: Responses and reactions' (2012) 23 *Economic and Labour Relations Review* 99, 105–7.

the legislation. However, the market has already responded to it, with the ASX *CG Principles and Recommendations* suggesting that the remuneration contract of executive directors or other senior executives should specify the circumstances in which remuneration may be clawed back (for example, in the event of serious misconduct or if there was a material misstatement in the entity's financial statements).[163]

There is, internationally, considerable pressure from shareholders, especially minority shareholders, to have a bigger say on directors' compensation. Under the banner 'Say on Pay', law reforms that would ensure that shareholders have some say on directors' pay were propagated internationally. In 2002 the UK adopted legislation that compels public companies to give shareholders a vote on the compensation of their top executives. This vote is not binding, but a significant vote by the shareholders against the compensation of their top executives sends a strong message to the directors. Since that time there has been a wave of such legislation enacted in countries around the world, including the US, Belgium, The Netherlands and Sweden; Switzerland, Germany and France appear to be moving rapidly in the same direction.[164] Research that examined the impact of 'Say on Pay' legislation on actual CEO and other executive compensation revealed significant changes in executive compensation policies and firm valuations following the passage of these laws.[165]

It is interesting to note that while such a non-binding vote was also adopted in Australia (previously s 250R of the *Corporations Act 2001* (Cth)),[166] Australia has now taken the lead in going one step further with the 'two-strikes and spill' approach. It is reasonably clear that this approach will capture the imagination of many shareholders in many other countries, and it is to be expected that shareholder lobby groups will put pressure on the legislatures of other countries to adopt comparable provisions with actual – not only non-binding – consequences for directors if the shareholders are not satisfied with directors' and executives' compensation.[167] In the UK there is already a move towards a binding 'Say on Pay' vote. [168]

---

163   ASX, *CG Principles and Recommendations* (2014) 33.

164   Randall S Thomas and Christoph Van der Elst, 'The International Scope of Say on Pay', ECGI Law Working Paper No. 227 (September 2013); Vanderbilt Law and Economics Research Paper No. 13–22 <http://papers.ssrn.com/sol3/papers.cfm?abstract_id=2307510>. See also Marinilka Barros Kimbro and Danielle Xu, 'Shareholders Have a Say on Executive Compensation: Evidence from Say-on-Pay in the United States' (April 2013) <http://papers.ssrn.com/sol3/papers.cfm?abstract_id=2209936>.

165   Ricardo Correa and Ugur Lel, *Say on Pay Laws, Executive Compensation, CEO Pay Slice, and Firm Value around the World*, Board of Governors of the Federal Reserve System, International Discussion Paper No. 1084 (July 2013) <www.federalreserve.gov/pubs/ifdp/2013/1084/ifdp1084.pdf>.

166   For some background on the initial 'say on pay' provision in Australia see Larelle Chapple and Blake Christensen, 'The non-binding vote on executive pay: A review of the CLERP 9 reform' (2005) 18 *Australian Journal of Corporate Law (AJCL)* 263; and Thomas and Van der Elst, 'The International Scope of Say on Pay' (2013) 18–20.

167   For a more comprehensive explanation of the current approach in Australia – see Thomas and Van der Elst, 'The International Scope of Say on Pay' (2013) 20–3. Recent research on the impact on corporate accountability of Australia's unique 'two strikes' rule found that it has been effective in reining in abnormally high CEO pay. It curbs excessive CEO pay, reduces the growth rate of pay and changes the pay mix. It also found that negative 'say on pay' votes are associated with negative market reaction, a lower share price, long-run underperformance, and an increase in CEO turnover. However, directors do not appear to suffer reputational costs, as evidenced by the loss of outside directorships. Martin Bugeja et al., 'Life after a Shareholder Pay "Strike": Consequences for ASX-Listed Firms', CIFR Paper No. 130/2016 (28 November 2016) <https://ssrn.com/abstract=2876925 or http://dx.doi.org/10.2139/ssrn.2876925>.

168   Ibid. 17–18 and 66.

4.8 Board diversity[169]

4.8.1 Another controversial and politically sensitive issue

Board diversity has been a hot topic for several years. However, it is only in recent years that pertinent questions have been asked about what is actually meant by the term 'board diversity' and what would constitute ideal diversity. In the past the debate on board diversity has always been dominated by questions about the very low numbers of women on boards. This has been a fact in most countries with sophisticated corporate law and corporate governance systems. The issue of the percentage of women on boards still dominates the board diversity debate, but other forms of diversity, including age, cultural, nationality and race, have also become part of the debate.[170] Diversity Council Australia published research on the cultural diversity in ASX boards over the past decade in March 2015.[171] The findings reveal that while cultural diversity on ASX boards has increased, boardrooms do not yet reflect the cultural diversity in the Australian community. The key findings of the report were:

- Cultural diversity at board level was increasing over several years before 2015
  - there has been a 22% increase in directors from culturally diverse (non Anglo-Celtic) backgrounds; a 16% increase in chairs; and a 28% increase in the number of ASX companies that have achieved a critical mass of directors from culturally diverse backgrounds
- The number of directors from Asian backgrounds is higher
  - there has been a 74% increase in chairs (from 3.5% to 6.1%); a 61% increase in directors (from 5.9% to 9.5%); and a 14% increase in CEOs (from 4.4% to 5.0%)
- The percentage of directors from Southern, Eastern and Central European backgrounds is increasing
  - there has been a 20% increase in ASX directors and a 63% increase in ASX 200 directors
- Progress in terms of cultural diversity is slower in larger companies and among CEOs
  - there has been a 10% increase in ASX 100 directors from culturally diverse backgrounds versus a 22% increase among all ASX directors; a 5% increase in ASX 100 directors from Asian backgrounds versus a 61% increase among all ASX directors;

---

169   This section is partly based on Jean J du Plessis, Ingo Saenger and Richard Foster, 'Board diversity or gender diversity? Perspectives from Europe, Australia and South Africa' (2012) 17 *Deakin Law Review* 207; and Jean du Plessis, James O'Sullivan and Ruth Rentschler, 'Multiple layers of gender diversity on corporate boards: To force or not to force diversity' (2014) 19 *Deakin Law Review* 1–50.

170   See Global Network of Director Institutes (GNDI), *Board Diversity: GNDI Perspectives* (February 2013) <www.gndi.org/papers>; FRC, *Developments in Corporate Governance 2013* (December 2012) 11–12 <www.frc.org.uk/Our-Work/Publications/Corporate-Governance/Developments-in-Corporate-Governance-2013.pdf>. Michael Adams points out that diversity based on race and cultural heritage (expressed as 'ethnicity'), education, professional background and age, are critical factors in a board's composition. See Michael Adams, 'Board diversity: More than a gender issue? (2015) 20 *Deakin Law Review* 123, 124.

171   Diversity Council Australia, *Capitalising on Culture Over Time: A Study of the Cultural Origins of ASX Directors 2004–2013* (16 March 2015) <www.dca.org.au/dca-research/capitalising-on-culture–asx-directors-2004–2013.html>.

and a 4% increase in CEOs from culturally diverse backgrounds versus a 22% increase in directors

- Anglo-Celtic names dominate CEO positions
  - 21% of ASX CEOs in 2013 had 1 of 5 Anglo-Celtic names (in order of frequency): David (68), Peter (53), John (48), Andrew (47), Michael (46)
- Boardrooms do not yet reflect the cultural diversity in the wider community
  - in ASX 100–500, 24% of directors are now (in 2015) from culturally diverse backgrounds compared to 33% of the Australian community; and 5% of directors are from Asian backgrounds compared to 8.5% of the Australian community.

The question is whether a diversified board would be better, and whether diversified boards will ensure a better return for investors: in other words, whether there is a 'business case' to be made out for diversity on boards. Many studies have been done, but the answer is still not clear. This is not totally unexpected, as the criteria used for these studies differ and the circumstances and complexities of business are such that a final conclusion will probably never be reached.

4.8.2 Gender diversity and quota legislation

There is ample evidence all over the world that in the past, women were under-represented on boards, and there is not a single country in the world without quota legislation where this is still not the case.[172] In countries such as Norway, Spain, Switzerland, France, Israel and The Netherlands,[173] where mandatory quotas for females on boards are set through legislation, the percentages have changed in recent times and there will surely be further improvements in the gender balance on boards. However, as far as we know, there is not a single country in the world where women form more than 50 per cent of the boards of listed companies. Norway leads the way: 36.7 per cent of board seats were held by women in 2012.[174] At 1 January 2016

---

172   See Deloitte, *Women in the Boardroom: A Global Perspective* (November 2011) <www.corpgov.deloitte.com/binary/com.epicentric.contentmanagement.servlet.ContentDelivery Servlet/USEng/Documents/Nominating-Corporate%20Governance%20Committee/Board% 20Composition%20and%20Recruitment/Women%20in%20the%20Boardroom_Deloitte_111511.pdf>; and Jennifer Whelan and Robert Wood, 'Targets and Quotas for Women in Leadership: A Global Review of Policy, Practice, and Psychological Research', Gender Equality Project, Centre for Ethical Leadership, Melbourne Business School, University of Melbourne (May 2012) 5 and 6. See, generally, Boris Groysberg, *2011 Board of Directors Survey* (sponsored by Heidrick & Struggles) (2011) 3–4 <www .corpgov.deloitte.com/binary/com.epicentric.contentmanagement.servlet.ContentDeliveryServlet/ USEng/Documents/Nominating-Corporate Governance Committee/Board Composition and Recruitment/2011BoardSurvey_HeidrickStrugglesWCDGroysb>.

173   Jo Armstrong and Sylvia Walby, Directorate-General for Internal Policies – Policy Department C: Citizens' Rights and Constitutional Affairs, European Parliament, *Gender Quotas in Management Boards* (2012) 4. See Du Plessis, O'Sullivan and Rentschler, 'Multiple layers of gender diversity on corporate boards' (2014) for a short discussion of the legislation in these companies.

174   See comparative data provided by Whelan and Wood, *Targets and Quotas for Women in Leadership* (2012) 17. Deloitte, *Women in the Boardroom: A Global Perspective* (October 2014) <www2.deloitte.com/content/dam/Deloitte/global/Documents/Risk/gx-ccg-women-in-the-boardroom-a-global-perspective4.pdf>. More specifically, in 2014 35.5% of the seats on Norwegian stock index companies were held by women: '2014 Catalyst census: Women board directors', in Cathrine Seierstad, Morten Huse and Silvija Seres, 'Lessons from Norway in getting women onto corporate boards', *The Conversation*, 7 March 2015 <http://theconversation.com/lessons-from-norway-in-getting-women-onto-corporate-boards-38338>.

the share of women serving on all Norwegian public companies stood at 42 per cent. [175] In most countries, especially Western countries, where there are no mandatory quotas, there are serious attempts through voluntary codes of good governance to increase female representation on company boards. It has been shown in Australia, in several European companies and in South Africa that the process of appointing more women as employees, executives and directors is taken seriously.[176] Also, there is considerable investor pressure on companies – especially listed companies – to appoint more women to their boards.[177] There is, indeed, solid research showing that if a country stops short of setting mandatory gender quotas, there should at least be very specific targets set by work units within companies, particularly at top executive levels, to achieve gender equality.[178]

Ensuring qualitative as well as quantitative gender equality at board level requires that the number of women and the remuneration of women on boards must be addressed. A 2013 study found that, on average, women in the EU earn 16.3 per cent less per hour than men.[179]

The reasons for the under-representation of women on boards are somewhat perplexing.[180] In essence, there are those who argue that senior executive positions and board positions were (and still are) filled by men who are the gatekeepers, and who make it almost impossible for more women to be appointed to those positions. There is then a vicious circle: because women are not given the opportunity to fill the positions, the pool of competent and experienced women remains small, providing another excuse for not appointing more women to these positions. There are many who argue that this cycle should be broken, and some argue strongly that it can only be broken through mandatory gender quota legislation. Others argue that a 'one-size-fits-all' approach is not desirable and that board diversity and gender diversity on boards will be achieved through voluntary codes of corporate governance.

4.8.3 Quota legislation

The first corporate board gender quota law in the world was introduced by Norway (not an EU member) through amendments to the *Norwegian Public Limited Liability Companies Act*.[181] In February 2012 it remained 'the only example of fully implemented legislation

175   Deloitte, *Women in the Boardroom: A Global Perspective* (5th edn, 2017) 63 <www2.deloitte.com/content/dam/Deloitte/global/Documents/Risk/Women%20in%20the%20boardroom%20a%20global%20perspective%20fifth%20edition.pdf>.

176   Du Plessis, Saenger and Foster, 'Board diversity or gender diversity?' (2012) 207.

177   Yi Wang and Bob Clift, 'Is there a "business case" for board diversity?' (2009) 21 *Pacific Accounting Review* 88, 89; Nicole Sandford, 'Board diversity: Are we on the eve of real change?' (2011) *Directors & Boards Annual 2011* <www.directorsandboards.com/html/DBAR11contents.html>.

178   Whelan and Wood, *Targets and Quotas for Women in Leadership* (2012) 5 and 24–7.

179   Eurostat, 'Gender pay gap in unadjusted form' <http://ec.europa.eu/eurostat/tgm/table.do?tab=table&init=1&language=en&pcode=tsdsc340&plugin=1> in European Women on Boards, *Gender Diversity on European Boards, Realizing Europe's Potential: Progress and Challenges* (April 2016) 47.

180   See Du Plessis, Saenger and Foster, 'Board diversity or gender diversity?' (2012) 240–2.

181   Aagoth Storvik and Mari Teigen, 'Women on Board: The Norwegian Experience' (June 2010) *Friedrich Ebert Stiftung* 3 <http://library.fes.de/pdf-files/id/ipa/07309.pdf>, cited in Armstrong and Walby, *Gender Quotas in Management Boards* (2012) 4, 6.

(in the sense that the date for meeting the target has passed)'.[182] Norway's model was successful due to the strictness of the sanctions supporting it: the ultimate sanction for a company not achieving the mandatory gender quotas is the dissolution or deregistering of the company.[183]

The 500 largest Norwegian company boards had averaged 7 per cent female representation in 2003, which had caused political embarrassment.[184] Australia reported comparable statistics.[185] By October 2014 women held 36.7 per cent of board seats in Norway whereas women in Australia only held 15.1 per cent.[186] In Australia the *Equal Gender Equality Act 2012* (Cth) requires reporting on the number of male and female employees and board members. There is, however, no specific gender quota specified for the boards of listed companies. Section 18 of the *Equal Gender Equality Act 2012* (Cth), however, provides that employers (defined widely and including companies) failing to comply with the Act may not be eligible to compete for contracts under the Commonwealth procurement framework and may not be eligible for Commonwealth grants or other assistance. Minimum standards in relation to gender equality indicators were mandated to be set before 1 April 2014.[187] On 27 March 2014, however, the Australian Government announced that there would be no change to reporting during the 2014–15 reporting period, and that no minimum standards would be set, but at that stage the then government hoped that from 1 October 2014 all employers with 500 or more staff would have had in place a policy or strategy in at least one of the following areas:[188]

1. gender composition of the workforce;

2. equal remuneration between women and men;

3. availability and utility of employment terms, conditions and practices relating to flexible working arrangements for employees and to working arrangements supporting employees with family or caring responsibilities;

4. sex-based harassment and discrimination.

Australia's 2015–2016 Gender Equality Scorecard revealed that women make up half of the nation's workforce but earn only 77 per cent of men's average full-time income.[189] There is

182   Armstrong and Walby, *Gender Quotas in Management Boards* (2012) 4, 6.

183   Ibid. 4; Deloitte, *Board Effectiveness Corporate Australia: Bridging the Gender Divide* (2010) 3, 21 <www.deloitte.com/assets/Dcom-Tanzania/Local%20Assets/Documents/Deloitte%20Article_Women%20in%20the%20boardroom.pdf>.

184   Arni Hole, *Diversity Deployed, the Norwegian Experiences*, Speech delivered to the 2nd Diversity on Boards Forum, Sydney, 2–3 September 2009.

185   Elizabeth Broderick, *Getting on Board: Quotas and Gender Equality*, Speech delivered at the Gender Matters – 3rd Women on Boards Conference, Sydney, 29 April 2011 <www.hreoc.gov.au/about/media/speeches/sex_discrim/2011/20110429_women_boards.html>.

186   Deloitte, *Women in the Boardroom: A Global Perspective* (October 2014).

187   Catalyst, *Legislative Board Diversity* <www.catalyst.org/legislative-board-diversity#footnote1_7dtzcot>.

188   Workplace Gender Equality Agency, 'WGEA welcomes government's decision on gender reporting', Press Release (27 March 2014) <www.wgea.gov.au/news-and-media/wgea-welcomes-government%E2%80%99s-decision-gender-reporting>.

189   Workplace Gender Equality Agency, 'Australia's gender equality scorecard' (November 2016) 5.

currently no indication from the Australian Government that it will consider gender quota legislation in the near future.[190]

4.8.4 Developments regarding gender quotas at the European Union (EU) level

In Europe, Commissioner and Vice President of the EU Viviane Reding (Justice, Fundamental Rights and Citizenship) has driven reforms to achieve at least 40 per cent women on boards very forcefully in recent years. She has repeatedly stressed the economic advantages of women's participation in boardrooms.[191] In March 2011, following a meeting with business leaders, she announced that she would give 'self-regulation a last chance'.[192] She called on all publicly listed companies in Europe to sign a pledge to increase women's presence on corporate boards to 30 per cent by 2015, and to 40 per cent by 2020. Barely concealed was her threat to use her 'regulatory creativity'[193] as *ultima ratio*[194] if significant progress should not become visible within a year. Commissioner Reding's approach was welcomed by the European Parliament (EP). In a resolution of 6 July 2011[195] the EP urged companies to reach said thresholds by the proposed dates, and strongly supported the idea of mandatory gender quota legislation for the EU if voluntary measures should prove to be insufficient to accomplish these goals.

The EP proposed quotas, while recognising the need to take into account the economic, structural, legal and regional specificities of EU member states. Company size was given as an example of such a factor. On 5 March 2012 Commissioner Reding offered an evaluation of developments in the previous year. She expressed her disappointment about the 'stubbornly slow' change and the 'persistent lack of gender diversity in boardrooms', revealing that only 24 companies across Europe had signed the aforementioned pledge.[196] In reaction to this, she announced the launch of public consultations (they ran until the end of May 2012) seeking views on possible (legislative) action at EU level.[197] At the same time, the Commissioner released data on the progress to date. The share of women on the boards of the largest publicly listed companies in the EU rose from 11.8 per cent in October 2010 to 13.7 per cent in January 2012 – France accounted for around half the increase.[198] It is striking that all Scandinavian EU members find themselves among the top group of countries when it comes to board diversity, while fellow Nordic nations Iceland (25 per cent) and Norway (42 per cent)

---

190 Peta Spender contends that the time is ripe for Australia to legislate for mandatory gender quotas for corporate boards. See Peta Spender, Gender quotas on boards – is it time for Australia to lean in? (2015) 20 *Deakin Law Review* <https://ssrn.com/abstract=2686955>.

191 For example, European Commission (EC), 'EU Justice Commissioner Reding challenges business leaders to increase women's presence on corporate boards with "Women on the Board Pledge for Europe"', MEMO/11/124 (1 March 2011) 1.

192 Ibid.

193 Ibid.

194 Viviane Reding, 'Gesetzliche Frauenquote?' (2011) 44 *Zeitschrift für Rechtspolitik (ZRP)* 127.

195 EP resolution of 6 July 2011 on women and business leadership (2010/2115 (INI)).

196 EC, 'European Commission weighs options to break the "glass ceiling" for women on company boards', Press Release IP/12/213 (5 March 2012) 1, 2.

197 Ibid. 1.

198 Ibid. 2–5.

top the list of non-EU countries.[199] The Commissioner also pointed out that a survey conducted in all EU countries found that 75 per cent of Europeans are in favour of gender balance legislation related to company boards.[200]

The next development was probably to be expected. In October 2012 the European Commission (EC) presented a draft EU directive that aims at a mandatory quota of 30 per cent by 2015, and 40 per cent by 2020.[201] The proposal was presented jointly by Commissioner Reding and several other Vice-Presidents of significant EU portfolios.[202] The consequences of this development are summarised well in the *SAI Global Corporate Law Bulletin*:

> On 20 November 2013, the European Parliament voted by a large majority (459 for, 148 against and 81 abstentions) to back the European Commission's proposed law to improve the gender balance in Europe's company boardrooms. The strong endorsement by the Members of the European Parliament means the Commission's proposal has now been approved by one of the European Union's two co-legislators. Member states in the Council now need to reach agreement on the draft law, among themselves and with the European Parliament, in order for it to enter the EU statute book.[203]

The proposed Directive has several specific aims and objectives:[204]

- It sets an objective of a 40 per cent presence of the under-represented gender among *non-executive directors* (including members serving on supervisory boards) of companies listed on stock exchanges, but excludes small and medium-size enterprises (companies with fewer than 250 employees and an annual worldwide turnover not exceeding €50 million) and non-listed companies.

- Companies which have a lower share (less than 40 per cent) of the under-represented gender among the non-executive directors will be required to make appointments to those positions on the basis of a comparative analysis of the qualifications of each candidate, by applying clear, gender-neutral and unambiguous criteria.

- Given equal qualifications, priority shall be given to the under-represented gender.

- The objective of attaining at least 40 per cent membership of the under-represented gender for the non-executive positions should thus be met by 2020 while public undertakings – over which public authorities exercise a dominant influence – will have two years less, until 2018.

- The proposal is expected to apply to around 5000 listed companies in the EU.

---

199   Ibid. 4. See, however, Deloitte, *Women in the Boardroom: A Global Perspective* (November 2011) 21 for slightly different statistics.

200   EC, 'European Commission weighs options to break the "glass ceiling" for women on company boards' (5 March 2012) 1, 7.

201   'Reding will europaweite Frauenquote durchdrücken', *Financial Times Deutschland*, 14 June 2012 <www.ftd.de/karriere-management/karriere/:gleichberechtigung-reding-will-europaweite-frauenquote-durchdruecken/70050363.html>.

202   See <http://europa.eu/rapid/press-release_IP-12–1205_en.htm>.

203   Ian Ramsay (ed.), *Corporate Law Bulletin*, Bulletin No. 196 (17 December 2013).

204   See EU, Press Release (14 November 2012) <http://europa.eu/rapid/press-release_IP-12–1205_en.htm>.

The directive approved on 20 November 2013 by the EP was road-blocked when the European Council announced that it could not reach agreement on its final adoption.[205] As there is still slight hope that progress will be made in future it is worth quoting the summary of the outcome on the issue of 'Women on boards', specifically noting the part about what is in the best interests of EU economies. Minister Poletti explained as follows:

> Enhancing women's participation in economic decision-making is essential to promote equality between women and men in our societies and would be beneficial to our economies. We have been working hard during these six months to unlock negotiations on the proposed directive for improving the gender balance on company boards and we are now closer to an agreement. Building on our progress I am confident that the Council will be able to move forward with this important dossier.[206]

It is noteworthy that if the directive were adopted in the form approved by the EP and considered by the EU, it would have been expected that EU member states would implement measures to achieve the goal of at least 40 per cent females and 40 per cent males appointed to the boards of larger companies. However, it is important to also note that there is flexibility regarding the legal instruments EU members could use to implement directives. Some countries, such as Germany, have already opted for mandatory gender quota legislation – the 'hard law' approach. Other countries would probably use voluntary Corporate Governance Codes to reach these quotas – the 'soft law' approach: they would probably continue only to expect companies to explain if the quotas are not reached. It would then be left to the market to respond to that. Would investors put pressure on boards to reach the quotas? Would there be expectations in the market that large institutional investors should only invest in companies where 40 per cent of the board members are women? All of this is now just speculation, as the EC could not agree on a general approach.[207]

If one looks at all these developments it is not difficult to predict that more women will be appointed to company boards in future and that more countries will adopt some form of gender quota legislation. This prediction is partly based on recent developments in Germany, Europe's largest economy.

Over many years there has been an argument in Germany that board appointments should be based purely on merit and that the number of women available and willing to serve on boards was just too small to meet a quota of, say, 40 per cent. The issue of gender diversity generally, but mandatory quota legislation in particular, has divided the German business community, academic commentators and politicians – even within political parties.[208] This was

---

205   This part is based on Jean du Plessis and Ingo Saenger, 'Corporate governance in the EU, the OECD Principles of Corporate Governance and corporate governance in selected other jurisdictions' in Jean J du Plessis et al., *German Corporate Governance in International and European Context* (Springer Verlag, 3rd ed, 2017) Part 11.2.8. See also Jean J du Plessis, 'The case for and against mandatory gender quota legislation for company boards' (2015) 20 *Deakin Law Review* 1, 8.

206   3357th EC meeting, Employment, Social Policy, Health and Consumer Affairs, Brussels, Press Release (11 December 2014) 9–10 <www.consilium.europa.eu/uedocs/cms_data/docs/pressdata/en/lsa/146172.pdf>.

207   Ibid.

208   See Du Plessis, Saenger and Foster, 'Board diversity or gender diversity?' (2012) 215–16. See also Patrick Velte, 'Förderung der Gender Diversity bei der Zusammensetzung des Aufsichtsrat' (2012) 10 *Der Konzern* 1, 5–7.

seen clearly with the rejection by the German Parliament in April 2013 of legislation that would have required 40 per cent of the board members of all listed companies to be women. The legislation was rejected by 320 votes to 277.[209] Even a compromise proposal for a gradual introduction of a 20 per cent quota (starting in 2018) was rejected.[210]

That was, however, before the German federal election held on 22 September 2013. Soon after that election, namely on 18 November 2013, Chancellor Angela Merkel's Christian Democratic Union (CDU) and the Social Democrats (SPD) agreed on legislation that now requires 30 per cent of the seats of supervisory boards of listed companies to be filled by women.[211]

The law regarding the equal participation of women and men in leading positions[212] entered into force on 1 May 2015.[213] According to s 96(2) *Aktiengesetz*, 1965 (*AktG*), from the beginning of 2016 the fixed quota legislation of 30 per cent of each gender applies to all supervisory boards of listed companies (s 3(2) *AktG*) which are subjected to codetermination.[214] It is expected that this regulation will cover approximately 100 companies in Germany. The legal binding quota was motivated, *inter alia*, by the fact that the previous regulation of the German Corporate Governance Code (GCGC) had not affected the percentage of women in leading positions.[215] Contrary to the considerations noted in the draft bill,[216] compliance with the quota of 30 per cent is based on the principle of 'total fulfilment'.[217] This means that the quota can generally be fulfilled by an addition of representatives of either shareholders or employees:[218] if all female representatives from both these groups make up 30 per cent of the overall number of representatives, the target quota is met. It is interesting to note that currently the proportion of women representing employees is much higher than the proportion of

---

209   *Spiegel Online International*, 'Gender Gap: Germany Rejects Requiring Board Quotas' <www.spiegel.de/international/germany/germany-rejects-law-requiring-board-quotas-a-895238.html>.

210   Nestor's Quarterly Advisor (Q2 2013).

211   See the Coalition Treaty, 102 ff <www.bundesregierung.de/Content/DE/_Anlagen/2013/2013-12-17-koalitionsvertrag.pdf;jsessionid=399A4657C216C00EDA9A5A5BFE9CD84E.s3t1?__blob=publicationFile&v=2>. See also Susanne Amann, Dinah Deckstein and Ann-Katrin Muller, 'The Slow Pace of Gender Equality in Corporate Germany', *Spiegel Online*, 6 January 2016 <www.spiegel.de/international/germany/german-firms-slowly-adjust-to-new-boardroom-quota-law-a-1070622.html>.

212   This part is based on Du Plessis and Saenger, 'Corporate governance in the EU, the OECD Principles of Corporate Governance and corporate governance in selected other jurisdictions' in Du Plessis et al., *German Corporate Governance in International and European Context* (2017) Part 4.3.5.

213   Law regarding the equal participation of women and men in leading positions in the private sector and in public services (24 April 2015, BGBl I 2015, 642) <www.bgbl.de/xaver/bgbl/start.xav?start=%2F%2F*[%40attr_id=%27bgbl115s0642.pdf%27] - __bgbl__%2F%2F*[%40attr_id=%27bgbl115s0642.pdf%27]__1436521818915>; see also Michael Winter, Eric Marx and Nadine de Decker, 'Zielgrößen für den Frauenanteil in Führungspositionen bei mitbestimmten Unternehmen' (2015) 23 *Der Betrieb (Zeitschrift) (DB)* 1331.

214   Daniel Rubner and Dieter Leuering, 'Die Frauenquote im Unternehmen' (2015) 7 *Neue Juristische Zeitschrift (NJW)* – *Spezial* 207.

215   Tony Grobe, 'Die Geschlechterquote für Aufsichtsrat und Vorstand' (2015) 9 *Die Aktiengesellschaft (Zeitschrift) (AG)* 289.

216   Christian Mense and Marcus Klie, 'Die Quote kommt – aber wie? Konturen der geplanten Neuregelung zur Frauenquote' (2015) 1 *Gesellschafts- und Wirtschaftsrecht (GWR)* 1.

217   Christoph H Seibt, 'Geschlechterquote im Aufsichtsrat und Zielgrößen für die Frauenbeteiligung in Organen und Führungsebenen in der Privatwirtschaft' (2015) 25–26 *Zeitschrift für Wirtschaftsrecht (ZIP)* 1193, 1195

218   Grobe, 'Die Geschlechterquote für Aufsichtsrat und Vorstand' (2015) 289.

shareholders representatives.[219] However, either the shareholder or employee representatives may decide by a majority to suspend the general rule of 'total fulfilment'.[220] In that case both the employee side and the shareholder side of the representatives have to comply with the quota of 30 per cent: the target quota has to be fulfilled for both groups independently. According to s 96(2)6 *AktG* the election of the supervisory board is invalid if the supervisory board does not include 30 per cent women.

Companies which are listed *or* fall under codetermination legislation must establish concrete objectives regarding the percentage of women in leading positions.[221] This regulation applies not only to the management board and the supervisory board but also to the first and second subordinated management level. In addition to stock companies (*Aktiengesellschaft*), companies that have other legal forms, such as limited liability companies (*GmbH*), are also obliged to set specific targets.[222] Since 5 May 2015 this quota has also been included in Art 5.4.1 GCGC.

4.8.5 Impact of women in the corporate world

What the actual effect of more women sitting on company boards will be from a business point of view is impossible to predict, but most studies show that gender-diverse corporate boards enhance corporate governance.[223] The fact that women will have a bigger say in the corporate world in future is beyond dispute even though the pace at which change is happening is still very slow.[224] The problem of under-representation of women on boards can be addressed through mandatory gender quota legislation, [225] through targets and through requirements for more women on boards in voluntary codes of corporate governance. Although the 'business case' for having more women on boards is probably still inconclusive, a number of studies have found significant correlations between the presence of women on corporate boards and strong corporate performance.[226] A meta-analysis of the relationship between women on

---

219   Seibt, 'Geschlechterquote im Aufsichtsrat und Zielgrößen für die Frauenbeteiligung in Organen und Führungsebenen in der Privatwirtschaft' (2015) 1197.

220   Section 96(2)3 *AktG*.

221   Section 111(5) *AktG*.

222   With regard to limited liability companies, see s 36 *GmbHG* and s 52(2) *GmbHG*. Similar obligations also apply to partnerships limited by shares (*KGaA*), European companies (*SE*) and registered cooperative companies (*eG*); see also Michael Winter, Eric Marx and Nadine de Decker, 'Zielgrößen für den Frauenanteil in Führungspositionen bei mitbestimmten Unternehmen' (2015) 23 *DB* 1331; with regard to the international applicability of the quota see also Marc-Philippe Weller, Charlotte Harms, Bettina Rentsch and Chris Thomale, 'Der internationale Anwendungsbereich der Geschlechterquote für Großunternehmen' (2015) 3 *Zeitschrift für Unternehmens und Gesellschaftsrecht (ZGR)* 361, 369 *et seq*.

223   See Mary Jane Lenard, Bing Yu, E Anne York and Shengxiong Wu, 'Female business leaders and the incidence of fraud litigation' (2017) 43 *Managerial Finance* 59, 72; Meggin Thwing Eastman, Damion Rallis and Gaia Mazzucchelli, 'The tipping point: Women on boards and financial performance', Women on Boards Report (December 2016) 6; Linda Peach, 'We need women on boards for many reasons: Ethics isn't one' (2015) *The Conversation* <http://theconversation.com/we-need-women-on-boards-for-many-reasons-ethics-isnt-one-37472>.

224   See Fei He, 'Gender quota on boards in Germany' (2016) 10 *Journal of International Scientific Publications* 77.

225   Kate Stary, 'Gender diversity quotas on Australian boards: Is it in the best interests of the company?', Corporate Governance and Directors' Duties Paper 2, Law School, University of Melbourne, 2015.

226   See Thwing Eastman, Rallis and Mazzucchelli, 'The tipping point: Women on boards and financial performance' (December 2016).

boards and firm financial performance by Corinne Post and Kris Byron found that board diversity is 'neither wholly detrimental nor wholly beneficial to firm financial performance'. Their findings suggest that deriving optimal benefit from having more females on boards requires a better understanding of the particular firm and industry, and of the socio-cultural context in which the board gender diversification occurs.[227]

4.9 Conclusion

There is no doubt that there are much higher community expectations of company directors and company officers now than there were in the past. These higher expectations do not apply only to the exercise of directors' and other officers' general duties, but also to the ethics of their behaviour – company directors' and company officers' conduct is under constant scrutiny, not only from the media and the general public, but also from the regulators. As a corollary, there is constant pressure on politicians to ensure that the law is able to enforce these higher community expectations of company directors and company officers.

In this chapter we have seen that there are various types of company directors and officers, although the basic position is that the law will expect the same duties of all directors and that senior employees and senior executives owe duties to the company comparable to those of directors. The discussion in this chapter has also revealed that the practical distinction between, and expectations of, the various types of directors (for example, independent non-executive directors, executive directors, and senior or lead independent directors) are becoming increasingly important. Also, the roles, functions and expectations of CEOs and chairpersons have become more easily identifiable over time. This is the case not only because various corporate governance reports have begun to accentuate the various responsibilities associated with these positions, but also because the courts have started to focus on the higher responsibilities associated with, and higher standards expected of, persons occupying certain key positions in large public corporations.

Several themes and issues of emerging importance have also been identified in this chapter. They include the training and induction of directors; the ethical behaviour of directors; the remuneration of directors and executives; and board diversity, in particular measures aimed at achieving gender balance. In the 2nd edition (2011) we identified some of these issues and predicted that they would become of increasing importance. That prediction was correct, and we would once again suggest that they will stay core areas of focus in the process of developing principles of contemporary corporate governance.

---

227   See Corinne Post and Kris Byron, 'Women on boards and firm financial performance: A meta-analysis' (2015) 58 *Academy of Management Journal* 1546, 1563.

PART **2**

CORPORATE GOVERNANCE IN AUSTRALIA

5

REGULATION OF CORPORATE GOVERNANCE

The impetus for considering the impact of regulation on law is the growing importance of regulation. There is a broad and general move in the community to manage or regulate risk. This focus on regulation and risk management is, in turn, part of a broader interest in using a range of governance mechanisms to directly and indirectly 'influence the flow of events'.

> Angus Corbett and Stephen Bottomley, 'Regulating Corporate Governance' in
> Christine Parker, Colin Scott, Nicola Lacey and John Braithwaite (eds),
> *Regulating Law* (OUP, 2004) 60

5.1 Overview

It will be clear from Chapter 3 that we consider regulation of corporate governance to be prominent in a good corporate governance model. This chapter builds upon that model by focusing on the regulation of corporate governance in particular. It deals specifically with the various mechanisms, legislative and non-legislative, which regulate the corporation and which set in place, collectively, a framework by which good governance can be achieved. Overall, this collective body of mechanisms forms part of what has recently been described as an emerging 'law of corporate governance'.

The regulation of corporate governance in Australia is achieved through binding and non-binding rules, international recommendations and industry-specific standards, the commentaries of scholars and practitioners, and the decisions of judges. The legislature acts to facilitate the achievement of good corporate governance directly by refining corporate law, and indirectly through the entire panoply of rules and regulations which have an impact on the corporation and its activities. There are other agencies that also assume a role in the regulation of corporate governance.

Section 5.2 of this chapter provides a working definition of 'regulation', to clarify what is meant by references to the 'regulation' of corporate governance throughout this chapter. It also introduces the influential 'pyramid' of regulatory compliance developed by Ian Ayres and John Braithwaite. Section 5.3 explores the common and unifying aims and objectives of regulation, with reference in particular to the Organization for Economic Co-operation and Development's (OECD's) *Principles of Corporate Governance* (2004),[1] and similar statements made when corporate governance reforms were introduced in Australia: namely the CLERP 9 Act (2004), and the Australian Securities Exchange's (ASX) *CG Principles and Recommendations*.[2] These sources emphasise the strong financial objectives underpinning the recent formalisation of corporate governance regulation. Section 5.4 explains the mechanisms (or 'sources'), both

---

1   Note that the revised G20/OECD *Principles of Corporate Governance* was released in 2015 – see Chapter 12.

2   ASX, *CG Principles and Recommendations* (3rd edn, 2014) <www.asx.com.au/documents/asx-compliance/cgc-principles-and-recommendations-3rd-edn.pdf>. The first edition was called *Principles of Good Corporate Governance and Best Practice Recommendations* and was published in March 2003. The second edition was published in 2007, and there were some important amendments made to this edition in 2010. The name was changed in 2007: since then the document has been called *Corporate Governance Principles and Recommendations*.

traditional and more recent, which regulate corporate governance in Australia. These mechanisms are categorised as being examples of 'hard law', 'hybrids' or 'soft law'.[3]

Finally, Section 5.5 assesses whether, in general terms, there is effective corporate governance with reference to the financial markets regulatory framework in Australia. This assessment is based on the guidelines contained in the G20/OECD *Principles of Corporate Governance* (2015).

5.2 Regulation generally

Regulation is a topic of significant and increasing interest in a wide range of disciplines, from politics and economics to sociology, psychology and history. There is, therefore, a variety of definitions of 'regulation' used in the literature, with some commentators referring to a 'definitional free-for-all'.[4]

One of the best and most useful definitions of 'regulation' is provided by Simon Deakin and Jacqueline Cook, of Cambridge University, in an August 1999 research paper prepared by the UK's Company Law Review Steering Group. The paper, 'Regulation and the Boundaries of the Law', offers some general considerations relating to the debate about the appropriate form of corporate regulation, and usefully explores the present structure of company law and corporate governance in the UK. Deakin and Cook state:

> In the present context the term 'regulation' may be taken to refer to the control of corporate and commercial activities through a system of norms and rules which may be promulgated either by governmental agencies (including legislatures and courts) or by private actors, or by a combination of the two. The direct involvement of the state is not a necessary condition for the existence of regulation in this sense, since rules may be derived from the activities of industry associations, professional bodies or similarly independent entities.
>
> This is because the rules of contract, property and tort are seen as empowering commercial actors to enter into and enforce transactions, whereas regulatory interventions are seen as more often controlling the terms of contracts and imposing obligations of various kinds regardless of the intentions of the parties.[5]

A similarly broad working definition of 'regulation' is used in the recent research report of the Centre for Corporate Law and Securities Regulation at the University of Melbourne, *ASIC*

---

3   For scholarly discussion on the strengths and weakness of soft law, see Dimity Kingsford Smith, 'Governing the corporation: The role of "soft regulation"' (2012) 35 *University of New South Wales (UNSW) Law Journal* 378.

4   See Helen Bird, David Chow, Jarrod Lenne and Ian Ramsay, *ASIC Enforcement Patterns*, Research Report (Centre for Corporate Law and Securities Regulation, 2004) 5 referring to Julia Black, 'Decentring regulation: Understanding the role of regulation and self regulation in a "post-regulatory" world' (2001) 54 *Current Legal Problems* 103, 129. For a general discussion of regulation in a legal context, see Christine Parker, Colin Scott, Nicola Lacey and John Braithwaite (eds), *Regulating Law* (Oxford University Press [OUP], 2004), and see Angus Corbett and Stephen Bottomley's chapter, 'Regulating Corporate Governance', 60.

5   Paper prepared in 1999 by the ERSC Centre for Business Research, Cambridge University, for the Department of Trade and Industry's Review of Company Law.

Enforcement Patterns. The authors of the report, Helen Bird, David Chow, Jarrod Lenne and Ian Ramsay, state that:

> Three broad 'textbook' definitions or approaches to regulation are commonly identified, ranging from the narrowest to the widest sense of the term. First, regulation as (government-determined) legal rules backed by mechanisms for monitoring and enforcement. Secondly, in a more encompassing variation of the first, regulation includes any form of deliberate state intervention in the economy or other fields of social activity. Thirdly, regulation, in its widest reading, includes all mechanisms of social control or influence, from whatever source and whether intentional or not.[6]

The report goes on to discuss the 'pyramid' of regulatory compliance developed by Ayres and Braithwaite in their influential book, *Responsive Regulation* (1992). The report's authors argue, by highlighting the purposes and limits of self-regulation, that the 'pyramid' aligns itself with a self-regulatory approach to regulation (as opposed to enforced, mandatory regulation). The report details the findings of an empirical study of court-based enforcement activities undertaken by ASIC during the period 1997–99. One of the key aims of the study was to determine whether ASIC's enforcement activities during this time were consistent with the findings of past sociological studies of legal regulation and enforcement. According to the report, sociological theories contend that the effectiveness of laws as forms of regulation depends on the process by which those laws are received, interpreted and responded to by the participants in the regulatory process: 'Those participants include ASIC, the Commonwealth Director of Public Prosecutions (DPP), and the pool of persons and companies influenced and controlled by company and financial services laws.'[7] The report describes the operation of the pyramid as follows:

> Sanctions are structured in such a way as to combine persuasion in the majority of cases with direct enforcement in a smaller number. At the base of the pyramid, most actors are persuaded to comply through indirect intervention; full sanctions, such as criminal penalties or the withdrawal of a licence to operate, are reserved for the few cases at the top.[8]

In terms of the purpose of the pyramid in Ayres and Braithwaite's theory, the authors of the report explain:

> The purpose of the pyramid is to provide regulatees with maximum incentives for early compliance. This is an acknowledgement that, where 'persuasive' strategies are used, the regulator and the regulatee are, in effect, engaged in bargaining over the terms and timing of compliance, and that without the threat of escalating sanctions, the regulatee may have incentives to hold out in the expectation of being able to negotiate a better deal.[9]

---

6   Bird et al., *ASIC Enforcement Patterns* (2004) 4.
7   Ibid.
8   Ibid. In *Responsive Regulation* (OUP, 1992), Ian Ayres and John Braithwaite explain (39) that: 'Firms that resist initial compliance will be pushed up the enforcement pyramid. Not only escalating penalties, but also escalating frequency of inspection and tripartite monitoring by trade unions … can then negate the returns to delayed compliance.'
9   Ibid. 5. See also John Braithwaite, *Restorative Justice and Responsive Regulation* (OUP, 2002).

Ayres and Braithwaite's pyramid of regulatory compliance has received widespread support – and indeed was endorsed by the authors of *ASIC Enforcement Patterns* – and provides an important context within which to understand the extensive and exciting recent developments in the regulation of corporate governance,[10] enabling us to engage in an informed assessment of why corporate governance regulation has reached the point that it has, and where things may head in the future.

5.3 Objectives in regulating corporate governance

The impetus for corporate governance regulatory reform, both domestically and internationally (such as Sarbanes-Oxley and Dodd-Frank Acts in the US and CLERP 9 in Australia), has been a series of corporate collapses and the perceived need to restore confidence in the market. As a result, financial objectives appear to be the driving factor for most contemporary corporate governance regulation. Most, if not all, contemporary corporate governance reports, guidelines, commentaries and legislative packages strongly emphasise the link between sound corporate governance practices and success within the corporation and throughout the economy. For example, the G20/OECD *Principles of Corporate Governance* (2015) states that:

> The Principles are developed with an understanding that corporate governance policies have an important role to play in achieving broader economic objectives with respect to investor confidence, capital formation and allocation. The quality of corporate governance affects the cost for corporations to access capital for growth and the confidence with which those that provide capital – directly or indirectly – can participate and share in their value-creation on fair and equitable terms. Together, the body of corporate governance rules and practices therefore provides a framework that helps to bridge the gap between household savings and investment in the real economy. As a consequence, good corporate governance will reassure shareholders and other stakeholders that their rights are protected and make it possible for corporations to decrease the cost of capital and to facilitate their access to the capital market.[11]

In discussing the earlier version of the OECD *Principles of Corporate Governance*, Janis Sarra has usefully described the link between effective corporate governance and healthy global capital markets as follows:

> Corporate governance is only one aspect of the larger framework of macro-economic policies, competition and tax policy, global capital, products and labour markets, cultural norms and ethics, and diverse state regulatory systems. The growth of global capital markets has created the potential for greater access to a larger investor pool. Key to the attraction of long-term 'patient capital', whether it is domestic or international, is the ability

---

10   For application of the pyramid in the enforcement of directors' duties, see Commonwealth of Australia, *Review of Sanctions in Corporate Law* (2007).

11   G20/OECD, *Principles of Corporate Governance* (2015) 10 <www.oecd-ilibrary.org/governance/g20-oecd-principles-of-corporate-governance-2015_9789264236882-en>.

to offer corporate governance systems that are clearly articulated and adhered to, within regulatory and legal frameworks that support contractual and ownership rights.[12]

At the domestic level, in Australia, important sources of corporate governance reform – the CLERP 9 amendments to the *Corporations Act 2001* (Cth) (the Act), the ASX *CG Principles and Recommendations* and the revised IFSA Blue Book on corporate governance[13] – all emphasise the financial objectives underlying contemporary regulation of corporate governance.

5.4 Sources of regulation in Australia

The key definitions of 'regulation', as quoted above, highlight some of the main sources of regulation. We now apply this background discussion to the specific context of corporate governance in Australia, and provide an account of the mechanisms, both traditional and more recent, which regulate corporate governance in Australia.

John Farrar has engaged in a very useful task of categorising the various sources of corporate governance regulation in Australia – into 'hard law', 'hybrids' and 'soft law'.[14] Although Farrar does not provide a working definition of any of these categories, it could be said that 'hard law' means 'traditional black-letter law'; 'soft law' includes voluntary sources of corporate governance standards that companies have the freedom to adopt or not; and 'hybrids' fall somewhere between the two, being neither mandatory nor purely voluntary. Below we identify the main sources of corporate governance regulation under the category headings provided by Farrar. We also detail our perspective on each of these sources and add to Farrar's analysis our own viewpoint on corporate governance regulation.

5.4.1 'Hard law'

5.4.1.1 Statutory regulation – corporate law

Australia's primary companies legislation, the *Corporations Act 2001* (Cth), contains a number of provisions that influence, both directly and indirectly, all aspects of a company's governance arrangements. The provisions range from directors' duties and liabilities[15] and shareholder rights and remedies,[16] which influence the relationship between directors, management and shareholders, to the financial reporting provisions under Chapter 2M,[17] which are intended to ensure that the financial aspects of a company's governance practices are characterised by transparency and accountability, and to the provisions under Chapter 2G governing company meetings (both directors' meetings and meetings of members). Many of these provisions are mandatory, with sanctions imposed for non-compliance.

---

12   See Janis Sarra, 'Convergence versus divergence: Global corporate governance at the crossroads' (2001) 33 *Ottawa Law Review* 177, 186–7.
13   See <www.fsc.org.au/resources/guidance-notes/2gn_2_corporate_governance_2009.pdf>.
14   John H Farrar, 'Corporate governance and the judges' (2003) 15 *Bond Law Review* 65.
15   For discussion, see Jason Harris, Anil Hargovan and Michael Adams, *Australian Corporate Law* (LexisNexis, 5th edn, 2016) Chs 15–18.
16   Ibid. Ch 19.
17   Ibid. Ch 21.

While there are many important corporate governance 'mandates' under the Act, this does not mean that all the corporate governance rules that stem from the Act are prescriptive in nature. Indeed, the opposite is the case. The Act provides companies with a great deal of say on the internal arrangements and management of their company. Most of the rules governing a company's internal arrangements and management may be contained in the company's constitution (if the company has one); this is specifically drafted by each company to meet its particular needs and therefore in essence may contain whatever rules the company desires (subject to a special majority of the company's shareholders approving the changes). Instead of a constitution, a company's internal management may be governed by a set of 'replaceable rules' (that is, rules that the company may abide by or 'opt out of' by adopting alternative arrangements in its constitution – see discussion below) contained in the Act (see the list in s 141 of the Act). A company may also use a combination of constitution and replaceable rules.

Most companies, and probably all larger companies, have a constitution. The main reason, in practice, for adopting a constitution is to displace one or more of the 'replaceable rules' under the Act that would otherwise apply to the company. This is implied in s 135(2) of the Act – replaceable rules are so named because they can be modified or displaced by adopting a constitution with alternative procedures.

The replaceable rules regime was introduced in 1998. The key objective of this move was to provide a simplified procedure for setting up and running a company. It is explained in the Explanatory Memorandum to the Company Law Reform Bill 1997:

> The concept of memorandum of association will be abolished (the memorandum of existing companies will be treated as part of their constitution). Also, the adoption of a constitution will be optional. The basic rules that are available to the internal management of companies (Table A of the Law) will be updated and moved into the main body of the Law as replaceable rules. Companies will be able to adopt a constitution displaying some or all of these rules. These reforms will reduce the cost of registering a company for the approximately 80,000 new companies that are registered each year.[18]

Robert Austin and Ian Ramsay explain that while it is possible for a company's internal arrangements and management to be governed entirely according to the replaceable rules contained in the Act, in practice, companies – especially larger companies with more complex internal governance arrangements – find some replaceable rules inappropriate or inadequate, and will therefore adopt a constitution to supplement, or entirely replace, the replaceable rules. Commonly, therefore, companies will be governed by a constitution, or a mix of constitutional provisions and replaceable rules.[19] However, for smaller proprietary companies where there are only a few shareholders with no specific reason to adopt complex internal governance arrangements, the replaceable rules will cover all internal governance needs. The advantage is that the replaceable rules might be amended by the legislature to address shortcomings or to keep up with new developments, and these new

18   Explanatory Memorandum, Company Law Reform Bill 1997, para 10.
19   RP Austin and IM Ramsay, *Ford's Principles of Corporations Law* (LexisNexis Butterworths, 15th edn, 2013) para 6.011.

replaceable rules will then apply to the company without its needing to amend the constitution by way of a special resolution.

5.4.1.2 Statutory regulation – other than corporate law

As already explained in Chapter 2, the manner in which the internal arrangements and management of companies is achieved, and the relationship between the company and its various stakeholders, are also influenced by legal rules operating outside of company law. These rules derive from areas of law such as industrial relations, tax, environmental law, and banking and finance law.

5.4.1.3 'Corporate governance and the judges' – the place of judge-made law

> Regulation encompasses the making of laws, *the interpretation of laws to determine what is required to comply with them* and . . . the actions taken to enforce these laws in cases of non-compliance. (emphasis added)[20]

In Australia, 'company law' (including the rules of corporate governance) as a collective body of rules has traditionally been statute-based, unlike in the UK, where much of company law – including directors' duties and shareholder rights – has principally been governed by common law and equitable principles (although this is progressively changing as a result of company law reform). Within this statute-based regulatory framework, as the above statement suggests, judges have an important role in developing and applying the principles of the law as interpreters (particularly when provisions are vaguely expressed or overly complex). Thus, while the common perception is that regulation of corporate governance comes in the form of black-letter rules – legislative or quasi-mandatory codes and principles – it is important to understand that judges continue to play significant role.[21]

Probably the best recent account of this important role in Australia comes from Farrar. He states:

> If we turn to corporate governance consisting of statutory rules and case law rules and principles, [they have] traditionally been regarded as justiciable [that is, capable of being determined by a court acting judicially]. Indeed, it was left to the courts to fill in the substantial gaps left by the legislation in terms of directors' fiduciary and other duties, and shareholder remedies . . . Court proceedings of any sort are expensive and occasion delay. ASIC prefers to avoid them if possible for these reasons and uses its administrative powers wherever possible and is seeking to impose its own penalties . . . This needs to be considered, as does the question whether the courts have a role in respect of self-regulation.[22]

---

20   From Bird et al., *ASIC Enforcement Patterns* (2004) 2, citing Robert Baldwin and Martin Cave, *Understanding Regulation* (OUP, 1992) 1–2.

21   Paul L Davies, *Gower and Davies' Principles of Modern Company Law* (Sweet & Maxwell, 2008) 61. See also Corbett and Bottomley, 'Regulating Corporate Governance' in Parker et al. (eds), *Regulating Law* (2004) 60.

22   John Farrar, *Corporate Governance: Theories, Principles and Practice* (OUP, 2008).

Farrar also discusses in detail three high-profile recent cases in Australia (relating to the HIH and One.Tel collapses, and the ongoing saga associated with NRMA) to highlight the importance of the continuing role of the courts in corporate governance where self-regulation fails. He gives the following explanation:

> What these situations demonstrate is that self-regulation sometimes fails and there is no alternative to court involvement. Self-regulation lacks an effective system of sanctions, which can only be provided by the courts. In the case of HIH, retribution has been swift. There was not time and perhaps inclination for minority shareholders to seek redress. ASIC took prompt action.[23]

5.4.2 'Hybrids'

'Hybrid' mechanisms of corporate governance regulation have been described in the literature from a broader theoretical context as constituting a strategy of 'enforced self-regulation'. According to Ayres and Braithwaite in *Responsive Regulation*, enforced self-regulation occurs where the law delegates to private-sector bodies (such as self-regulatory organisations, which loosely describes the ASX) the task of formulating substantive rules, to which certain legal sanctions are then attached.

5.4.2.1 ASX Listing Rules

The ASX provides a market for trading in securities. The ASX engages in market surveillance in relation to securities issued by entities that are accepted onto the official list of the ASX ('listed entities'). One way that the ASX does this is through setting the standards of behaviour for listed entities; these are contained in ASX Listing Rules.

According to the ASX, the Listing Rules:

> govern the admission of entities to the official list, quotation of securities, suspension of securities from quotation and removal of entities from the official list. They also govern disclosure and some aspects of a listed entity's conduct.

Compliance with the Listing Rules is a requirement for admission to the official list. Non-compliance is a ground for removal from the official list. The corporate governance rules in the Listing Rules typically require a listed entity to disclose to the market and/or shareholders certain information, or to obtain shareholder approval for a particular transaction or arrangement. Some of the corporate governance-related Listing Rules include:

- LR 3.1 (dealing with continuous disclosure of information upon discovering the information's 'materiality');
- LR 7.1 (requiring shareholder approval if a company issues more than 15 per cent's worth of its securities over a 12 month period);
- LR 10.1 (requiring shareholder approval for, among other things, certain related party transactions);
- LR 11.1 (requiring provision of details to the ASX if an entity proposes to make a significant change, either directly or indirectly, to the nature and scale of its activities);

---

23   Ibid. 80.

- LR 11.2 (requiring shareholder approval if the significant change involves the entity disposing of its main undertaking).

5.4.2.2 ASX *CG Principles and Recommendations*

Farrar includes the ASX *CG Principles and Recommendations* under the category of 'soft law'.[24] The rationale for this is that they differ from the Listing Rules in that they are not strictly mandatory rules backed up by statutory force; rather, as was explained in greater detail in Chapter 4, the ASX *CG Principles and Recommendations* operate under a 'comply or explain' ('if not, why not') regime: ASX-listed companies must either comply with each of the recommendations or, if they do not comply, clearly explain why they do not comply. This must be done in their annual report.

5.4.2.3 Accounting standards

The importance of having in place within a company proper procedures and policies to ensure accurate and transparent financial reporting (which involves complying with standards of accounting and auditing practice) has been highlighted by the collapses of large companies such as Enron and WorldCom in the US and HIH in Australia.

Farrar distinguishes accounting standards from the Corporations Act, categorising accounting standards as 'hybrids' rather than 'hard law', for similar reasons as those given for his position on the ASX Listing Rules.

5.4.2.4 Auditing standards

Since the implementation of the CLERP 9 reforms in 2004, we can now similarly refer to auditing standards (standards of proper auditing practice which, if adhered to, assist auditors in satisfying their duty to use reasonable care and skill) as 'hard law'. Section 307A of the Act, introduced by CLERP 9, provides that if an individual auditor, audit firm or an audit company conducts:

    (a)   an audit of the financial report for a financial year; or

    (b)   an audit or review of the financial report for a half year;

    the individual auditor or audit company must conduct the audit or review in accordance with the auditing standards.

5.4.3 'Soft law'[25]

Corporate governance objectives are also formulated in voluntary codes and standards that do not have the status of law or regulation. While such codes play an important role in improving corporate governance arrangements, they might leave shareholders and other stakeholders with uncertainty concerning their status and implementation. When codes and principles are used as a national standard or as an explicit substitute for legal or regulatory provisions, market

---

24   Ibid. 384 *et seq.*

25   For a very interesting discussion of the impact of 'soft law', see Kent Greenfield, 'No Law?' in Jean J du Plessis and Chee Keong Low (eds), *Corporate Governance Codes for the 21st Century: International Perspectives an Critical Analyses* (Springer Verlag, (2017) 57–73.

credibility requires that their status in terms of coverage, implementation, compliance and sanctions is clearly specified.[26] 'Soft law' involves the purely voluntary (that is, no formal sanctions arise from non-compliance) codes and guidelines articulating benchmarks for what is considered best practice in corporate governance, as well as scholarly[27] and trade writings (books, reports and articles) that have had some role in influencing how companies shape their internal arrangements and management to achieve best practice. Recent examples of these codes/guidelines include the IFSA Blue Book on corporate governance for fund managers and Standards Australia's series of corporate governance standards (released in 2003), which contain benchmarks for a number of governance matters – these are similar to those in the ASX *CG Principles and Recommendations* but are used mostly by public sector bodies, non-listed entities and non-profit organisations.

In terms of reports and other writings, a plethora of such material has been produced and published in Australia (mainly since the early 1990s) – as in other jurisdictions – creating a rich and valuable collection of corporate governance 'soft law'.

A fourth category of regulation that Farrar refers to is 'business ethics'. In this book, we deal with business ethics separately, in Chapter 14.

5.4.4 The role of market forces

Another important source of influence, and perhaps control, over the internal arrangements and management of a company, but one that does not sit comfortably under any of the categories of regulation above,[28] is 'market forces'.

In their 1997 book, *Making Boards Work*, David SR Leighton and Donald H Thain referred to common examples of market forces acting as 'alternatives to self-motivated board improvement'. This lends support to our decision to include market forces as a form of regulation in this chapter. It is perhaps difficult for some to envisage how market forces, which are the natural forces of an intangible entity, could actually be said to be a form of regulation; however, the label 'alternatives to self-motivated board improvement' could be useful in easing 'market forces' into the dialogue on corporate governance regulation.[29]

The significant role of market forces in contributing towards good corporate governance and strong corporate performance has for some time been emphasised in economic literature

---

26   OECD, *Principles of Corporate Governance* (2004) 30.
27   For an excellent analysis on the role of soft regulation in corporate governance, see Kingsford Smith, 'Governing the corporation' (2012).
28   In reference to 'hard law', 'hybrids' and 'soft law', it could perhaps be argued that market forces are 'hybrids', in that they cannot be described either as traditional black-letter law or as purely voluntary – market forces have an important influence on governance practices regardless of the wishes of the company and its management.
29   In their book, Leighton and Thain discuss five such 'alternatives' (some of which are often discussed as market forces, some of which are not): (1) takeovers (ineffective boards leave companies wide open for takeovers); (2) proxy contests (using voting powers to remove inefficient directors and appoint more effective directors); (3) 'power investing' (investment bankers who pool their money with pension funds and other institutional investors to take control of major corporations); (4) shareholder activism (self-explanatory); and (5) legal action (for example, class action; oppressive remedy etc). See David SR Leighton and Donald H Thain, *Making Boards Work* (McGraw-Hill Ryerson, 1997) 10–12.

on the corporation and corporate law.[30] In fact, many consider market forces an effective substitute for formal legal regulation.[31]

Ford's Principles of Corporations Law gives an excellent summary of how market forces, as regulatory mechanism, are presented in the economic literature on corporate law and governance – or 'law and economics', which underlies the 'contractarian' view of the corporation (that the corporation is an abstract entity consisting of a 'nexus of contracts', rather than as having a separate legal personality).[32]

The G20/OECD *Principles of Corporate Governance* also recognise the role of market forces in the decisions of directors and managers in relation to the internal arrangements of companies.

It explains that, in order to achieve the most efficient deployment of resources, policy-makers need to undertake analyses of the impact of key variables that affect the functioning of markets, such as incentive structures, the efficiency of self-regulatory systems and dealing with conflicts of interest. According to the G20/OECD *Principles*:

> The corporate governance framework should be developed with a view to its impact on overall economic performance, market integrity and the incentives it creates for market participants and the promotion of transparent and efficient markets.[33]

5.5 Towards a regulatory framework for the effective supervision of financial markets in Australia – analysis

5.5.1 G20/OECD guidelines for achieving an effective governance framework

We explained in Chapter 1 and above in this chapter why, in order to maintain international money market confidence in the domestic economy and local companies, it is important that Australian companies are perceived to be operating according to best practice corporate

---

30   See Frank H Easterbrook and Daniel R Fischel, *The Economic Structure of Corporate Law* (Harvard University Press, 1991); more recently, consider, for example, Larry E Ribstein, 'Market vs regulatory responses to corporate fraud: A critique of the Sarbanes-Oxley Act of 2002' (2002) 28 *Journal of Corporation Law* 1.

31   The classic article on the role of market forces as an alternative regulatory mechanism to traditional legal regulation is LA Bebchuk, 'Federalism and the corporation: The desirable limits on state competition in corporate law' (1992) 105 *Harvard Law Review* 1437 (which examines the operation of the various markets that may affect the decisions of managers); another significant contribution is JC Coffee, 'Regulating the market for corporate control: A critical assessment of the tender offer's role in corporate governance' (1984) 84 *Columbia Law Review* 1145. Bebchuk's article ultimately contends that there are limits to the effectiveness of market forces and that, at least in the US, there remains a strong place for traditional legal rules in corporate law, if corporate law is truly to maximise shareholder value.

32   The alternative view of the corporation discussed in *Ford* is the 'managerialist' view, which places greater weight on hard law, hybrids and soft law as regulatory mechanisms by which to achieve positive outcomes than on the role of market forces.

33   G20/OECD, *Principles of Corporate Governance* (2015) 14.

governance standards – 'good corporate governance' is important and it does add value. For our companies to meet best practice in corporate governance, our corporate governance regulatory framework needs to be effective. In this section, we discuss the criteria for an effective corporate governance regulatory framework set out in the G20/OECD *Principles*, and assess whether Australia's regulatory framework meets these criteria.

As previously mentioned, the G20/OECD *Principles* are intended to assist OECD (and non-OECD) governments to evaluate and improve the legal, institutional and regulatory frameworks for corporate governance in their countries, and to provide guidance for stock exchanges, investors, corporations and other parties having a role in developing good corporate governance. For a regulatory framework to be effective, according to the G20/OECD *Principles*, the legal and regulatory requirements that affect corporate governance practices should be consistent with the rule of law, transparent and enforceable.[34]

In our view, Australia's regulatory framework for corporate governance satisfies these criteria. Most developed economies with strong democracies do so as a matter of course. That is why Australia is considered an attractive place for international investment and why it has enjoyed a long period of strong economic growth. It is also perhaps why some countries in Asia – with regulatory frameworks that traditionally have not been consistent with Western democratic principles, and generally do not allow markets to operate free of unnecessary controls – have struggled at times, as became apparent with the 1997 East Asian financial crisis.

Achieving a corporate governance regulatory framework that is effective by international standards is not merely an exercise of adding more red tape to an already burdensome framework of regulation; it is also about ensuring (as already emphasised in this chapter) that Australia maintains a positive reputation in the international money markets, thereby providing strong benefits for the economy. In order to ensure that Australia does satisfy the requirement of being seen to have an effective corporate governance regulatory framework it is essential to address potential shortcomings in the current regulatory structures (as the Federal Government has done in a 2009 Consultation Paper)[35] and to avoid a lack of confidence in the market due to perceived conflicts of interest arising from having a private-sector entity (the ASX) with supervisory powers over brokers.[36]

5.5.2 Division of responsibilities between the ASX and ASIC

There is a memorandum of understanding (MOU) between ASIC and the ASX, which seeks to minimise overlap and to increase cooperation in relation to market supervision. On 1 August 2010 ASIC took over responsibility for supervision of real-time trading on Australia's domestic

---

34   Ibid. 14.

35   For background to reforms, see the ASX submission to Treasury Consultation Paper 'Reforms to the Supervision of Australia's Financial Markets Framework' (22 December 2009).

36   For example, see Adele Ferguson, 'Query on ASX's Supervisory Power', *The Australian*, 17 September 2007; Danny John, 'ASX Cited for Conflict of Interest', *Sydney Morning Herald*, Business Day, 5 April 2008.

licensed markets,[37] which includes supervision of Chi-X Australia, which commenced operations on 31 October 2011.

Traditionally, the role of the ASX has been limited to market surveillance and supervision, with ASIC also having some responsibility in this area as part of its general role of enforcing the Corporations Act. The subsequent privatisation of the ASX and its retention of supervisory powers over the financial market have long given rise to accusations of conflicts of interest. In an interview, the then Minister for Financial Services, Chris Bowen, made the following concessions when explaining the reasons for the important structural change to market supervision:

> ... we don't believe it's appropriate any longer for a private-sector entity (the ASX) to have supervisory powers over brokers. So this is important in terms of the perception of conflict of interest, to ensure there's no perception that there's a conflict of interest ... I think it's more appropriate going forward that [supervision] be done by a single, unified supervisor. I think there are issues wherever there's a perception of a conflict of interest. I think that's a real problem ... there are concerns about things falling through the cracks; about grey areas.[38]

A common theme in the recent corporate governance reform movement has been the desire to instil a culture of transparency and accountability into the governance practices of Australian companies. We believe that the parameters should be extended so that the regulators themselves set in place guidelines for the transparency and accountability of their regulation of corporate governance. There is no reason for the regulators to be able to operate outside the more intense regulatory arena – indeed, they should set the lead. The G20/OECD *Principles* make this point very strongly, emphasising that a 'clearly defined' division of responsibilities between corporate governance regulators constitutes one of the three key criteria underpinning an effective corporate governance regulatory framework.

Effective enforcement also requires that the allocation of responsibilities for supervision, implementation and enforcement among authorities is clearly defined so that the competencies of complementary bodies and agencies are respected and used most effectively. Potentially conflicting objectives – for example, where the same institution is charged with attracting business and sanctioning violations – should be avoided or managed through clear governance provisions.

Overlapping and perhaps contradictory regulations between jurisdictions is also an issue that should be monitored so that no regulatory vacuum is allowed to develop (i.e. issues for which no authority has explicit responsibility slipping through) and to minimise the cost for corporations of compliance with multiple systems.[39]

As a consequence of regulatory reforms, brokers and other trading participants in those markets are subject to the direct supervision and enforcement powers of ASIC in relation to

---

37   The memorandum was signed in October 2011. ASIC also has entered into MOUs with a number of other regulators and organisations, including the Australian Competition and Consumer Commission (ACCC). In December 2004, ASIC and the ACCC revised their MOU – believing this was necessary due to the closer relationship that had developed in their respective actions in addressing wealth-creation and get-rich-quick schemes, and misconduct in debt collection.

38   Australian Broadcasting Corporation (ABC), Interview with Minister for Financial Services on *Lateline Business*, Transcript (24 August 2009) <www.abc.net.au/lateline/business/items/200908/s2665567.htm>.

39   G20/OECD, *Principles of Corporate Governance* (2015) 15.

market misconduct. However, market operators retain responsibility for supervising the entities listed on those markets.

The Federal Government, at the time of the introduction of the reforms (2009), noted that the reforms would:

- enhance the integrity of Australia's financial markets;
- support other initiatives implemented by the Federal Government that were aimed at reinforcing Australia's position as a credible and significant financial services hub in this region; and
- bring Australian markets into line with other leading jurisdictions that have moved, or are in the process of moving, to centralised or independent regulation.

5.6 Conclusion

We have seen in this chapter that there has been a recent formalisation in the regulation of corporate governance. Increasingly, where companies once had complete freedom (from a regulatory perspective) to adopt benchmarks of corporate governance best practice, or to choose alternative arrangements, they now have to abide by formal rules (such as those introduced under CLERP 9 in Australia) or provide a clear explanation in their annual report of why they are departing from them (the 'if not, why not?' regime underpinning the ASX *CG Principles and Recommendations*).

The formalisation of corporate governance regulation has been considered a necessary response to high-profile corporate collapses and poor stockmarket performance, which were perceived as being attributable to less-than-desirable corporate governance practices. While corporate governance practices may have been a cause of the problems we have recently witnessed, this does not mean that formalising the regulation of corporate governance is the appropriate – or only – solution. Indeed, many commentators stress that a focus on conformance rather than performance will not resolve the recent problems.

6

THE ROLE OF THE REGULATORS: ASIC AND THE ASX

[HIH Insurance Ltd's collapse] is a tale of scoundrels – crooks even, who jockey and grasp and concoct the most ingenious ways to pocket HIH's cash while they still can. Well-placed mates help well-placed mates ... Mortgages are forgiven, bonuses awarded, dodgy invoices are fast-tracked and cheques are somehow cleared after the banks have closed. But policy-holders get nothing because that is the new policy, and shareholders might as well not exist.[1]

The Australian, 15 January 2003

The regulators failed in their duty to protect the interests of investors in *Forrest v ASIC* (2012). The ASX failed to enforce timely compliance with the continuous disclosure regime to ensure that the market was properly informed ... ASIC failed to succeed in the High Court because of the way it pleaded its case ... From the perspective of investor protection, the combined effect of the approaches taken by the regulators, ASX and ASIC, and the High Court [in this case] ... has resulted in a 'perfect storm'.

John Humphrey and Stephen Corones '*Forrest v ASIC*: "A Perfect Storm"' (2014) 88
Australian Law Journal 26, 37

6.1 Introduction

This chapter highlights the roles of and relationship between the twin regulators, the Australian Securities and Investments Commission (ASIC) and the Australian Securities Exchange (ASX) in the Australian corporate governance regime. The exercise of ASIC's powers is reviewed and enforcement patterns are commented upon. The chapter sketches the role of the ASX in corporate governance and concludes with remarks addressing the broad philosophical debate on the role of the regulator in light of the carnage (the widespread corporate collapses or near collapses)[2] arising from the Global Financial Crisis, and the pressure on ASIC to be more proactive and to perform to a higher standard.[3] The reasons for the parliamentary inquiry into ASIC's performance are captured in the following passage:[4]

> The emerging revelations about the misconduct of financial advisers in Commonwealth
> Financial Planning Limited (CFPL), part of the Commonwealth Bank of Australia Group
> and ASIC's failure to provide satisfactory answers in relation to this matter to the

---

1   See further, Jean J du Plessis, 'Reverberations after the HIH and other recent Australian Corporate collapses: The role of ASIC' (2003) 15 *Australian Journal of Corporate Law* 225, 230.

2   Opes Prime Stockbroking Ltd, Tricom Equities Ltd, Chimaera Capital Ltd, Allco Finance Group Ltd, Babcock & Brown Ltd, Storm Financial Ltd, ABC Learning Ltd, Timbercorp Ltd, Great Southern Ltd, to name a few.

3   On 20 June 2013, the Senate referred the performance of ASIC to the Economics References Committee for inquiry. Based on 578 public submissions, and 5 days of public hearings, a critical report on ASIC's performance was tabled in June 2014, making sweeping recommendations for improvements in ASIC's enforcement reputation and for law reform. See further Commonwealth Government of Australia, *Final Report – Performance of the Australian Securities and Investments Commission* (June 2014) <www.aph.gov.au/Parliamentary_Business/Committees/Senate/Economics/ASIC/Final_Report/index>.

4   Ibid. 4 <www.aph.gov.au/Parliamentary_Business/Committees/Senate/Economics/ASIC/Final_Report/c01>.

Economics Legislation Committee was the main catalyst for the inquiry. But it was not the only driver. A number of previous inquiries and other information in the public domain had exposed serious shortcomings in corporate conduct in Australia and ASIC's response to them. Thus, the committee's terms of reference reflect this broader context and, indeed, the submissions traverse a wide range of concerns about ASIC's performance.

The recommendations of the Report (2014) aimed at encouraging the fulfilment of ASIC's responsibilities and obligations more effectively, and the Report made these trenchant remarks:

However, many of the issues with ASIC's performance cannot be addressed by anyone other than ASIC. In the committee's opinion, ASIC has been in the spotlight far too frequently for the wrong reasons. It is acknowledged that not all of the criticisms levelled at ASIC are justified; ASIC is required to perform much of its work confidentially and in a way that ensures natural justice. It is also constrained by the legislation it administers and the resources given to it for this purpose. Nevertheless, the credibility of the regulator is important for encouraging a culture of compliance. That ASIC is consistently described as being slow to act or as a watchdog with no teeth is troubling. The committee knows, however, that ASIC has dedicated and talented employees that want to rectify the agency's reputation.

This inquiry has been a wake-up call for ASIC. The committee looks forward to seeing how ASIC changes as a result.[5]

In October 2016, the Minister for Revenue and Financial Services announced a taskforce to review the enforcement regime of ASIC, with its report anticipated for 2017.[6] The taskforce will assess the suitability of the existing regulatory tools available to ASIC.

6.2 The Australian Securities and Investments Commission (ASIC)

6.2.1 Overview

ASIC was first called the National Companies and Securities Commission (NCSC) and later the Australian Securities Commission (ASC).[7] The Wallis Report (released in April 1997) recommended several regulatory changes, including the establishment of ASIC, which occurred on 1 July 1998.[8]

---

5   Ibid. xxii <www.aph.gov.au/Parliamentary_Business/Committees/Senate/Economics/ASIC/Final_Report/b02>.

6   See <www.treasury.gov.au/ConsultationsandReviews/Reviews/2016/ASIC-Enforcement-Review>.

7   This chapter focuses on contemporary developments following the rebadging of ASC to ASIC. For an excellent study of the many complexities (political, legal, social and institutional) that have influenced, motivated and constrained the development of the present system of Australian companies and securities regulation, see Bernard Mees and Ian Ramsay, *Corporate Regulators in Australia (1961–2000): From Companies' Registrars to the Australian Securities and Investments Commission*, Research Report (Centre for Corporate Law and Securities Regulation, University of Melbourne, 2008); Bernard Mees and Ian Ramsay, 'Corporate regulators in Australia (1961–2000): From Companies' Registrars to ASIC' (2008) 22 *Australian Journal of Corporate Law* 212.

8   A Cameron, 'Not Another Regulator!!!', 1998 Suncorp-Metway Bob Nicol Memorial Lecture, Brisbane (10 November 1998).

ASIC is Australia's corporate, markets and financial services regulator. It regulates companies, financial markets, financial services organisations and professionals who deal in and advise on investments, superannuation, insurance, deposit-taking and credit. ASIC's work covers consumers, investors and creditors of corporations and other businesses.

As the market regulator, ASIC assesses how effectively authorised financial markets are complying with their legal obligations to operate fair, orderly and transparent markets.[9] As the financial services regulator, ASIC licenses and monitors financial service businesses to ensure that they operate efficiently, honestly and fairly.[10] As the corporate regulator, ASIC is responsible for ensuring that company directors and officers carry out their duties honestly, diligently and in the best interests of the company.[11] This chapter focuses on ASIC's role as corporate watchdog.[12]

6.2.2 Statutory powers under the ASIC Act[13]

ASIC is a Federal Government body, currently (2017) led by Chair Greg Medcraft, with the assistance of commissioners, who is accountable to the Minister for Financial Services, Superannuation and Corporate Law and the Parliament under the *Australian Securities and Investments Commission Act 2001* (Cth) (ASIC Act).

The objects of the ASIC Act are described in general terms in s 1 of the Act. Section 1(2) of the ASIC Act provides, in part, that in performing its functions and exercising its powers, ASIC must take whatever action it can take, and is necessary, in order to enforce and give effect to the laws of the Commonwealth that confer functions and powers upon it.[14]

In order to ensure compliance with the law, ASIC is vested with special powers of investigation and information-gathering. These powers are set out in Part 3 of the ASIC Act. Where ASIC decides to undertake an investigation, it can require any person to render to it all necessary assistance in connection with the investigation.

ASIC is authorised to initiate an investigation if it suspects, on reasonable grounds, that:

- a contravention of the corporations legislation (other than the excluded provisions)[15] may have been committed (s 13(1)(a));

---

9 ASIC, 'Our Role' <http://asic.gov.au/about-asic/what-we-do/our-role/>.

10 Ibid.

11 Ibid.

12 For an interesting perspective of ASIC's role as a regulator, see Farid Assaf, 'What will trigger ASIC's strategies?' (2002) 40 *Law Society Journal* 60–1. For insight into the gatekeeping role expected of directors by the regulator, see Belinda Gibson and Diane Brown, 'ASIC's expectations of directors' (2012) 35 *University of New South Wales (UNSW) Law Journal* 254. For perspective on ASIC's unique role as law-maker, see Stephen Bottomley, 'The notional legislator: The Australian Securities and Investments Commission's role as law-maker' (2011) 39 *Federal Law Review* 1.

13 For a fuller discussion, see Jason Harris, Anil Hargovan and Michael Adams, *Australian Corporate Law* (LexisNexis, 5th edn, 2015) Ch. 2 (ASIC: Role and Powers).

14 See also George Gilligan, Helen Bird and Ian Ramsay, 'Civil penalties and the enforcement of directors' duties' (1999) 22 *UNSW Law Journal* 417, 433–6; George Gilligan, Helen Bird and Ian Ramsay, 'The efficiency of civil penalty sanctions under the Australian Corporations Law' (1999) 136 *Trends and Issues in Crime and Criminal Justice* 1.

15 The excluded provisions are s 12A, which deals with ASIC's other functions and powers, and Div 2 of Pt 2, which deals with unconscionable conduct and consumer protection in relation to financial products: ASIC Act s 5.

- a contravention of a law of the Commonwealth, a state or territory concerning the management of the affairs of a body corporate or managed investment scheme may have been committed (s 13(1)(b)(i));
- a contravention of a law of the Commonwealth, a state or territory which involves fraud or dishonesty in relation to a body corporate, managed investment scheme or financial products may have been committed (s 13(1)(b)(ii));
- unacceptable circumstances within the meaning of the provisions of the Corporations Act dealing with takeovers may have occurred (s 13(2)); and
- a contravention of the consumer protection provisions (Division 2 of Part 2) of the ASIC Act may have been committed (s 13(6)).

Following an investigation or examination, ASIC may, if it is in the public interest to do so, commence proceedings under s 50 of the ASIC Act seeking civil remedies from the court, may take such legal action in the name of a company without the company's consent, and may seek damages for fraud, negligence, default, breach of duty, or other misconduct committed in connection with a matter to which the investigation or examination related. It may also seek to recover property on behalf of individuals. Section 50 has not, it seems, been used to great effect to date.[16]

6.2.3 The role of ASIC in corporate governance[17]

Jillian Segal (a former Deputy Chair of ASIC), in addressing the role of the regulator, captures the complex and multifaceted role that ASIC plays in Australia with the following observation: 'the regulator's role is a continuum of responses. It is bounded by enforcement at one end and education at the other, with policy guidance, industry support and disclosure guidelines in between.'[18]

ASIC has clearly recognised that it has a key and active role to play in corporate governance in Australia. Berna Collier (a former commissioner of ASIC) outlined the role of ASIC in corporate governance as follows:

> So what exactly is our role in corporate governance? What do we do on a daily basis to improve corporate governance in Australia? Essentially, ASIC's role in corporate governance is threefold:
>
> 1. monitors, enforces and administers compliance with the broad range of corporate governance provisions in the Corporations Act;
> 2. has a public education or advocacy role; and
> 3. contributes to law reform in relation to corporate governance.[19]

---

16   'ASIC to Pursue Compensation for Westpoint Investors', ASIC Media Release 07–291 (8 November 2007). For the major reported instances of s 50 actions taken by ASIC, see Janet Austin, 'Does the Westpoint litigation signal a revival of the ASIC s 50 class action?' (2008) 22 *Australian Journal of Corporate Law* 8.

17   For some comparative perspectives and the role and functions of ASIC, see Jean J du Plessis and Niklas Cordes, 'Claiming damages from members of management boards in Germany: Time for a radical rethink and possible lessons from down under?' (2015) 36 *Company Lawyer* 335, 344–52.

18   Jillian Segal, 'Corporate governance: Substance over form' (2002) 25 *UNSW Law Journal* 1, 5.

19   Berna Collier, 'The Role of ASIC in Corporate Governance', Corporate Governance Summit (27 November 2002) 5.

The first of these roles, in particular enforcing compliance, was prominent in ASIC's dealings with the corporate collapses in Australia in 2001 and 2002[20] and the more recent failures of corporate governance.[21]

There is no doubt that in the aftermath of the massive corporate collapses in 2001–02, ASIC fulfilled its role with assiduousness, and it has remained highly active since then, with several actions instituted against directors, albeit with a mixed record of success (discussed below). It should be noted that ASIC's role as regulator, also instituting action against directors to enforce the duties they owe toward the company, is one of the most distinctive aspects of the Australian corporate law and corporate governance model. In other jurisdictions the task of enforcing directors' duties is left to the shareholders, and it has been shown in several jurisdictions that even with such statutory derivative actions available, legal actions against directors for a breach of their fiduciary duties and duty of care and diligence are few.[22] This is not so in Australia because of ASIC's active role enforcing these duties on behalf of companies.[23]

ASIC's successful civil penalty proceedings in *Gillfillan v Australian Securities and Investments Commission*,[24] against the seven former non-executive directors and former officers of James Hardie, was hailed by ASIC as a landmark decision in Australia as far as corporate governance is concerned. The aims of ASIC with this litigation were explained by ASIC's Chair (at the time of the original litigation in 2009), Tony D'Aloisio:

> I encourage Boards to carefully consider this decision and assess what improvements they can make to their decision making processes, the way they convey decisions to the market and the way they conduct investor briefings and so called road shows ... The decision is another important step in improving corporate governance in Australia and that improvement will add confidence to the integrity of our markets. This confidence will be particularly important as we emerge from the financial crisis and companies come to the market to raise funds for new investments, much needed for the recovery of the real economy.[25]

ASIC's reputation for law enforcement has suffered somewhat in recent years,[26] when it lost some high-profile civil cases: against the directors of One.Tel Ltd (Jodee Rich and Mark

---

20   For discussion of enforcement actions against officers of GIO Insurance Ltd, HIH Insurance Ltd, One.Tel Ltd, Water Wheel Holdings Ltd, Centro Ltd and James Hardie Ltd, see Harris, Hargovan and Adams, *Australian Corporate Law* (2015) Chs 15–18 (on directors' and officers' duties).

21   For example, see *Australian Securities and Investments Commission v Macdonald (No 11)* (2009) 256 ALR 199 – discussed in Anil Hargovan, 'Corporate governance lessons from James Hardie' (2009) 33 *Melbourne University Law Review* 984.

22   See Andrew Keay, 'The Public Enforcement of Directors' Duties', Working Paper (16 January 2013) <http://ssrn.com/abstract=2201598> or <http://dx.doi.org/10.2139/ssrn.2201598>; Renee M Jones and Michelle Welsh, 'Towards a public enforcement model for directors' duty of oversight' (2012) 25 *Vanderbilt Journal of Transnational Law* 343. As far as other unique statutory powers of ASIC are concerned, see Bottomley, 'The notional legislator: The Australian Securities and Investments Commission's role as a law-maker' (2011) 1.

23   See Chapter 9.

24   (2012) 92 ACSR 460.

25   'James Hardie Proceedings', ASIC Media Release 09–69 (23 April 2009) <www.asic.gov.au/asic/asic.nsf/byheadline/09–69+James+Hardie+proceedings>.

26   See Vicki Comino *Company Law Watchdog – ASIC and Corporate Regulation* (Thomson Reuters Australia, 2015); Ben Woodhead, 'ASIC Hits and Misses', *Australian Financial Review*, 3 May 2012; Adele Ferguson, Ben Butler and Ruth Williams, 'Scrutinising ASIC: Is it a watchdog or a dog with no teeth?', *Sydney Morning Herald*, 23 November 2013.

Silbermann),[27] and against Fortescue Metals Group Ltd's chairman and chief executive officer, Andrew Forrest .[28] Critical comments on ASIC's litigation strategy made by each of the judges, independently and in different jurisdictions, painted a disturbing picture. A hostile media humiliated ASIC, questioning its ability to carry out complex litigation and its judgment.[29] Ian Ramsay, director of the Centre for Corporate Law at the University of Melbourne, commented on the need for a review of the manner in which ASIC conducts complex litigation.[30]

There was some speculation that, because of the active role ASIC plays in bringing civil penalty actions against directors, Australian directors are becoming risk-averse. This, in turn, led to Treasury commencing a review of criminal and civil sanctions, with a view to possibly widening the protection of directors against civil sanctions.[31]

There are, however, strong views – expressed in the media and by investor groups – that there is no real need to protect directors further because there is no evidence that directors are over-exposed to liability. Also, there was no evidence that directors who were held liable following ASIC's enforcement actions since 2000 should not have been held liable. Finally, it was shown that there are no facts backing the claim that Australian directors are risk-averse because of the wide range of legal sanctions available in Australia. This was established by a survey conducted by the Treasury in conjunction with the Australian Institute of Company Directors (AICD) in 2008.[32] This survey, which was sent to 600 directors of ASX 200 companies, found that only 27.7 per cent (of 101 respondents to this question) said they felt a high degree of risk of being found personally liable (under any law) for decisions they or their boards have made in good faith; 65.3 per cent of the respondents said that they only 'occasionally' take an overly cautious approach to business decision-making because of the risk of personal liability (under any law). The areas of law indicated as the areas most likely to lead to an overly cautious approach to business decisions seem to be 'derivative liability' laws: laws under which the director may be found liable for the misconduct of his or her company because he or she was a director. The examples given of such laws were 'occupational health and safety laws, environmental laws and/or building laws', and of the 94 respondents to this question, 35.1 per cent indicated that these laws lead to overly cautious business decisions.

---

27   *Australian Securities and Investments Commission v Rich* (2009) 75 ACSR 1: Justice Austin of the NSW Supreme Court held that ASIC failed to prove any facet of its pleaded case against either defendant.

28   *Forrest v Australian Securities and Investments Commission* (2012) 247 CLR 486. For stinging judicial criticism by the High Court of Australia of ASIC's poor pleading in its litigation strategy, see *Forrest v Australian Securities and Investments Commission* (2012) 247 CLR 486. See further Anil Hargovan, 'Sharp Message to ASIC as Forrest wins High Court Appeal', *The Conversation*, 3 October 2012 <http://theconversation.com/sharp-message-to-asic-as-forrest-wins-high-court-appeal-9934>.

29   For example, see Matthew Stevens, 'Laughter and Jeers over ASIC Failure', *The Australian*, 31 December 2009; Jennifer Hewett, 'Three Strikes Prove Regulator is out of Touch', *The Australian*, 24 December 2009.

30   Stuart Washington, 'Academics Question ASIC's Ability', *Brisbane Times*, 25 December 2009. For the complexities involved in litigation concerning civil penalty proceedings, see the judgment of Justice Austin in *ASIC v Rich*. See further Tom Middleton, 'The privilege against self-incrimination, the penalty privilege and legal professional privilege under the laws governing ASIC, APRA, the ACCC and the ATO: Suggested reforms' (2008) 30 *Australian Bar Review* 282.

31   Commonwealth of Australia, *Review of Sanctions in Corporate Law* (2007).

32   See <www.treasury.gov.au/PublicationsAndMedia/Publications/2009/Treasury-Working-Paper-2009-02>.

6.2.4 ASIC enforcement patterns

The ground-breaking research on ASIC's enforcement patterns undertaken in 2003[33] by the Centre for Corporate Law and Securities Regulation at the University of Melbourne continues.[34] The 2003 research revealed that ASIC was more likely to pursue court-based enforcement against individuals than against companies. This illustrated the point that actions by ASIC are aimed at deterrence: it hopes that making individuals aware of the possibility of liability influences the behaviour of directors. It was also discovered that more actions are instituted against directors of private companies than against directors of public companies. This is perhaps understandable, as there are far more private companies than public companies and directors of public companies will often also be directors of subsidiary private companies of the public company – see the case study on the HIH Insurance Ltd collapse (*Australian Securities and Investments Commission v Adler*) in Chapter 9.

The research examined 1438 court-based ASIC enforcement actions, all occurring between January 1997 and December 1999. It found that these actions were predominantly penal enforcement actions rather than civil enforcement actions. ASIC would predominantly use settlements – rather than the court processes – as outcomes for civil enforcement. ASIC was more likely to pursue penal enforcement in relation to laws that were mandatory (rather than enabling) in nature, and in relation to laws oriented towards social (rather than economic) regulation, preferring to focus on laws with an ethical foundation, and address conduct that is widely condemned because it exploits and defrauds shareholders and creditors.

Significantly, the preliminary findings of an empirical analysis of sanctions imposed in proceedings brought by ASIC and the Commonwealth Director of Public Prosecutions (CDPP) for contraventions of the directors' duties provisions of the *Corporations Act 2001* (Cth) and its predecessor, the *Corporations Act 1989* (Cth), from 1 January 2005 to 31 December 2014, reaffirm aspects of the findings of the 2003 research.[35]

The key findings of the preliminary research findings on ASIC's enforcement patterns (2016) are noteworthy:[36]

* Most previous commentary on enforcement of directors' duties in Australia has focused on civil penalty proceedings brought by ASIC, yet the research shows that criminal enforcement of directors' duties by the CDPP has been significantly more prevalent than civil enforcement by ASIC. Comparing directors' duties that attract both civil and criminal liability, criminal enforcement by the CDPP was responsible for about 81 per cent of all matters in which liability was established and about 61 per cent of all defendants were found liable.

33 Helen Bird, Davin Chow, Jarrod Lenne and Ian Ramsay, *ASIC Enforcement Patterns*, Research Paper No. 71 (Centre for Corporate Law and Securities Regulation, University of Melbourne, 2003). See also Helen Bird, Davin Chow, Jarrod Lenne and Ian Ramsay, 'Strategic regulation and ASIC enforcement patterms: Results of an empirical study' (2005) 5 *Journal of Corporate Law Studies* 191.
34 Jasper Hedges et al., 'An Empirical Analysis of Public Enforcement of Directors' Duties in Australia: Preliminary Findings', CIFR Paper No. 105/2016 (2016) <https://ssrn.com/abstract=2766132>;
35 Ibid.
36 See <https://corpgov.law.harvard.edu/2016/06/09/an-empirical-analysis-of-public-enforcement-of-directors-duties-in-australia/>.

- Much of the debate surrounding penalties for corporate wrongdoing in Australia has centred on the maximum pecuniary penalty of A$200,000 for contravening a civil penalty provision of the *Corporations Act 2001* (Cth). However, our research reveals that incapacitative sanctions, such as custodial sentences and civil management disqualification orders, were much more frequently imposed than pecuniary penalties. Prison sentences and disqualification orders each accounted for about 33.5 per cent of the total number of sanctions imposed (67 per cent collectively), while about 18 per cent of the sanctions were civil pecuniary penalties and only about 2 per cent were criminal fines.

- While the statutory maximum civil pecuniary penalty is $200,000, our research reveals that the penalties imposed by courts were typically much lower than the maximum. The median civil pecuniary penalty imposed on defendants who had engaged in a single contravention of a directors' duties provision was $25,000 – only 12.5 per cent of the statutory maximum. The median penalty imposed on all defendants, including defendants who had engaged in multiple contraventions, was $50,000.

- The average civil management disqualification order was about 5.2 years. The average maximum prison sentence was about 2.25 years, while the average minimum (i.e. minimum amount of time that must be served) was about 1.4 years. However, a significant proportion of prison sentences, about 46 per cent, involved immediate release subject to a good behaviour bond (i.e. fully suspended sentences).

- Both ASIC and the CDPP enjoyed high litigation success rates. Despite the higher standard of proof applicable to criminal proceedings for breaches of directors' duties, the CDPP's success rates were not significantly lower than ASIC's. The CDPP and ASIC established liability in about 88 per cent and 89 per cent of matters respectively. In terms of individual defendants, the CDPP and ASIC established liability in relation to about 84 per cent and 92 per cent of defendants respectively.

Contrary to a commonly held view that civil enforcement is more efficient than criminal enforcement, the duration of both the civil and criminal enforcement processes was lengthy. From the first detected contravention to the final judgment, the average duration of civil matters was about 6.9 years, while the average duration of criminal matters was about 7.9 years. The Chair of ASIC, Greg Medcraft, has expressed frustration at the low level of penalties for breaches of corporate law and has called for Parliament to increase penalties to deter corporate misconduct.[37] In addition, a call was made for a more graduated set of penalties, to provide an effective response in a wider range of cases. According to the ASIC Chair, 'If the thinking of law-breakers is a tussle between fear versus greed, then we need penalties that amplify the fear and smother the greed. We need penalties that create a fear that overcomes any desire to take risks and break the law.'[38]

Concerns expressed that Australia could become a haven for white-collar criminals led to a Senate Report in which the Senate considered the matter of inconsistencies and inadequacies of current criminal, civil and administrative penalties for corporate and financial misconduct for

37   <www.asic.gov.au/asic/pdflib.nsf/LookupByFileName/Senate-Inquiry–Opening-statement-19-February-2014.pdf/$file/Senate-Inquiry–Opening-statement-19-February-2014.pdf>.

38   Ibid.

white-collar crime.[39] Key recommendations include a substantial increase in civil penalties and, significantly, the introduction of disgorgement powers to be exercised by ASIC. These recommendations await the government's response.

6.3 The Australian Securities Exchange Ltd (ASX)

6.3.1 Slow to get out of the blocks

The ASX was slow in developing and promoting good corporate governance through a code of corporate governance practices and promoting compliance with such a code by including a provision in its Listing Rules that companies that did not comply with such provisions should explain non-compliance in their annual reports. By the early 1990s, both the London Stock Exchange and the Johannesburg Stock Exchange had included a Listing Rule to ensure compliance or an explanation of non-compliance with a code of best practice. Until early 2003, the ASX chose to be 'less prescriptive',[40] and resisted any change in its approach, despite being criticised by ASIC for not following the example of several other securities exchanges.[41]

In 1997, there was vigorous debate between the Australian Investment Managers' Association (AIMA) (or IFSA, as it is now known) and the ASX as to whether listed companies were actually complying with the rule. The ASX alleged that every one of the largest 150 companies listed complied with Listing Rule 4.10.3, while AIMA showed that very few of the listed companies had a clear understanding of what really should be disclosed.[42]

Whether the ASX or the AIMA was right is to a large extent irrelevant today, but it required several huge corporate collapses between 2000 and 2003 to cause the ASX to realise that its 'less prescriptive' approach was probably not the right one. Under the 'less prescriptive' arrangement – in place until March 2003 – listed companies had to rely on the 'indicative list' in Appendix 4A (originally Appendix 33) to the Listing Rules to guide them as to the types of matters considered to be corporate governance practices upon which they had to report.

6.3.2 Rapid change in attitude since the end of 2002

The entire face of corporate governance in Australia changed rapidly with the collapses of HIH, Harris Scarfe, One.Tel, Pasminco, Centaur and Ansett from 2000 to 2003 and the

---

39   Commonwealth Government of Australia, Senate Report, '"Lifting the fear and suppressing the greed": Penalties for white-collar crime and corporate and financial misconduct in Australia' (2017) <www.aph.gov.au/Parliamentary_Business/Committees/Senate/Economics/WhiteCollarCrime45th/Report>.

40   See Paul Redmond, *Companies and Securities Law* (LBC Information Services, 3rd edn, 2000) 268.

41   Phillip Lipton and Abe Herzberg, *Understanding Company Law* (Law Book, 11th edn, 2003) 296.

42   Ian Ramsay and Richard Hoad, 'Disclosure of corporate governance practices by Australian Companies', Research Paper, Centre for Corporate Law and Securities Regulation, University of Melbourne (1997) 1–2 <http://cclsr.law.unimelb.edu.au/go/centre-activities/research/research-reports-and-research-papers/>; also published as Ian M Ramsay and Richard Hoad, 'Disclosure of corporate governance practices by Australian companies' (1997) 15 *Company and Securities Law Journal (C&SLJ)* 454.

establishment by the ASX of the Corporate Governance Council (CGC) on 15 August 2002.[43] The CGC is composed of representatives of the most important players in the financial markets.[44] Its first task was to produce a set of consolidated and up-to-date standards of best practice. The CGC developed these guidelines with great speed, approving the *Principles of Good Corporate Governance and Best Practice Recommendations* in March 2003.

6.3.3 ASX *CG Principles and Recommendations*
6.3.3.1 Changes

As mentioned in Chapter 1, the 2003 ASX *Principles of Good Corporate Governance and Best Practice Recommendations* were amended in 2007 and 2010 (known as the ASX *CG Principles and Recommendations* with 2010 amendments), and a third edition was introduced in 2014.[45] Many of the principles in the original ASX document (2003) have been streamlined, and more substantial changes were introduced in 2014, including new or additional provisions regarding:

* the independence of directors;
* gender diversity;
* the disclosure of environmental and social sustainability risks;
* risk management; and
* corporate governance disclosures.

6.3.3.2 Structure

In addition to the Foreword, the 2014 ASX *CG Principles and Recommendations* consists of the following parts:

* a description of the meaning of 'corporate governance' in Australia;
* the purpose of the Principles and Recommendations;
* the basis of the Principles and Recommendations – the 'if not, why not' approach;
* the application of the Principles and Recommendations;
* the structure of the Principles and Recommendations;
* the linkage with the ASX's Listing Rules;
* where to make corporate governance disclosures;

---

43   The CGC had its fifth meeting on 20 February 2003 – Alan Kohler, 'Directors Face D-day as Old Rules go by the Board', *Australian Financial Review*, 20 February 2003.
44   The Council consists of representatives of 21 business and investor groups: Association of Superannuation Funds of Australia Ltd; Australasian Investor Relations Association; Australian Council of Superannuation Investors; Australian Financial Markets Association; Australian Institute of Company Directors; Australian Institute of Superannuation Trustees; Australian Securities Exchange; Australian Shareholders' Association; Business Council of Australia; CPA Australia Ltd; Financial Services Institute of Australasia; Governance Institute of Australia; Group of 100; Institute of Actuaries of Australia; The Institute of Chartered Accountants in Australia; Institute of Internal Auditors Australia; Investment and Financial Services Association; Law Council of Australia; National Institute of Accountants; Property Council of Australia; and Securities & Derivatives Industry Association.
45   ASX, *CG Principles and Recommendations* (2014) <www.asx.com.au/documents/asx-compliance/cgc-principles-and-recommendations-3rd-edn.pdf>.

- disclosing the fact that a recommendation is followed;
- disclosing the reasons for not following a recommendation; and
- the actual Principles and Recommendations.

The part dealing with the actual Principles and Recommendations contains them plus specific Recommendations, the latter followed generally by a Commentary that serves as general explanation. In addition, there are three Boxes: suggestions for the content of a diversity policy [Box 1.5]; factors relevant to assessing the independence of a director [Box 2.3]; and suggestions for the content of a code of conduct [Box 3.1].

6.3.3.3 Recommendations

There are 29 specific recommendations in the 2014 ASX *CG Principles and Recommendations.*[46]

In contrast to the 'comply or explain' formulation adopted in the UK Corporate Governance Code, the ASX's enforcement is based on an 'if not, why not?' approach. It would appear to be an identical approach; however, Alan Cameron argues that there is a subtle difference between the two, based on the following considerations:[47]

> 'Comply or explain' connotes an assumption, a presumption, that you should be doing it and you have to explain if you are not doing it.
> 'If not, why not?' ... is, and ought to be, morally neutral. It simply says, in effect, 'If you are not doing this, tell us why you are not doing it', but there is no presumption. Despite the use of the word 'recommendation' in the Corporate Governance Guidelines, it is clear that there is not a presumption in favour of compliance in the Australian rules.

6.3.3.4 The roles of and relationship between the ASX and ASIC

Since 1998 there has been an MOU between ASIC and the ASX regarding their respective supervisory roles.[48] This MOU was refined in 2004.[49] In 2011 some of the supervisory responsibilities of the ASX were transferred to ASIC, as the 'front line' regulator of the securities exchange. The aim of this reform was to ensure that Australia has only one 'whole-of-market supervisor', and to thus eliminate any potential conflicts of interest arising from the ASX being both a regulator and a player on the securities market.[50] Before these reforms, the ASX was one of only a few major exchanges with such dual functions[51] and had been continually dogged by allegations of inherent conflicts of interest.

---

46 Ibid.
47 Alan Cameron, 'How Do Directors Sleep at Night?' in RP Austin and AY Bilski (eds), *Directors in Troubled Times*, Ross Parsons Centre of Commercial, Corporate and Taxation Law Monograph 7 (2009) 118.
48 See <www.asic.gov.au/asic/pdflib.nsf/LookupByFileName/98-292.pdf/$file/98-292.pdf>.
49 See <www.asic.gov.au/asic/asic.nsf/byheadline/04–211+ASIC+and+ASX+sign+supervisory+MOU>.
50 Gill North, 'The corporate disclosure co-regulatory model: Dysfunctional and rules in limbo' (2009) 37 *Australian Business Law Review* 75, 80–1. For concerns arising around conflicts of interest under the old regulatory system, see Adele Ferguson, 'Query on ASX's Supervisory Power', *The Australian*, 17 September 2007; Danny John, 'ASX Cited for Conflict of Interest', *Sydney Morning Herald*, Business Day, 5 April 2008.
51 *The Australian*, 'Securities Exchange had Conflicting Roles', 25 August 2009.

As was pointed out in the 2nd edition (2011) of this book, transferring all the regulatory powers to ASIC is a development that should be welcomed as one that is in line with good regulatory corporate governance principles. However, as Ramsay writes:

> The big question now is will ASIC put in sufficient resources? Will it receive sufficient resources from the Government to do an adequate job? Also, there's a second major question, will ASIC have the required expertise? The argument in favour of ASX doing it is that it's close to the market, close to the brokers, knows what the brokers are doing.[52]

ASIC is obliged, under the Corporations Act, to annually assess the extent to which the ASX group licensees have complied with their obligations, to the extent that it is reasonably practicable to do so, and to do all things necessary to ensure that the markets operated by the ASX group licensees are fair, orderly and transparent.[53] In the Market Assessment Report released by ASIC in June 2016, the regulator assessed the ASX listing standards (Listing Rules and administration) for equities to see if they are fit for purpose.[54] ASX is responsible for the listing standards of 99.9 per cent (by market capitalisation) and 96.2 per cent (by number) of entities whose equities are listed in Australia. Listing standards are particularly important in Australia because:[55]

- Australians have one of the highest rates of share ownership in the world (around a third of all adult Australians);
- an enormous proportion of Australians' retirement savings are invested in ASX equities (approximately $500 billion of self-managed and other superannuation fund investments);
- the ASX has one of the highest numbers of publicly listed entities in the world (approximately 2200, only around 200 fewer than New York Stock Exchange or London Stock Exchange); and
- equity funding is a major source of funding for Australian business.

The assessment by ASIC was also undertaken because of significant changes taking place in financial markets, in Australia and overseas, which are being driven by ongoing developments in globalisation, competition and technology and information management.[56] In forming the view that the ASX has met its statutory obligations, ASIC looked at the following features of ASX's listing standards:[57]

(a) ASX's commercial and regulatory strategy for its listing functions;

(b) ASX's relevant governance and internal structure;

(c) ASX's resourcing of its listing standards;

(d) ASX's culture and approach to its listing standards; and

(e) ASX's listing rules and the extent to which they remain fit for purpose.

---

52   Australian Broadcasting Corporation (ABC), 'ASX Stripped of Key Supervisory Powers', *Lateline Business*, Transcript, 24 August 2009. For similar queries, see Allens Arthur Robinson, 'ASIC Market Regulation', 24 August 2009 <www.aar.com.au/pubs/fsr/cufsraug09.htm>.
53   *Corporations Act 2001* (Cth) ss 792A, 794C and 821A.
54   ASIC Report 480, 'Assessment of ASX Limited's Listing Standards for Equities' (June 2016).
55   Ibid.
56   Ibid.
57   Ibid.

6.4 Conclusion

Corporate governance is again high on the corporate law agenda in Australia. Challenging economic times, associated with the Global Financial Crisis, have laid bare some of the shortcomings of the Australian regulators (ASIC and the ASX) in protecting investors: millions of dollars were lost in the collapse of managed investment schemes such as Timbercorp Ltd and Great Southern Ltd, financial planners such as Storm Financial Ltd and Opes Prime Ltd, and other companies, such as Babcock & Brown Ltd and Allco Finance Group Ltd.

These events raise a fundamental question: should the regulators in Australia be acting as an early warning system? Former ASIC Chairman Tony D'Aloisio addressed the regulatory framework in reply to this question (when put by the media) and, in turn, posed a number of challenging questions in a reply that is worth reproducing:[58]

> [A]s a community, is the regulatory framework one where the role of an ASIC is to actually prevent collapses of companies, or is it as it's been traditionally: that you really oversight the markets and you come in and you deal with issues as they unfold? ... what you're seeing is we're not having clear debate about that. I mean, traditionally a regulator such as ASIC has had roles of enforcement, compliance ... investigations ... it's never extended to the fact that ASIC is the guarantor of last resort, or that it actually has the resources to be able to go into every boardroom and every chief executive to make sure that things are being done properly. If that's where the community wants to go, then clearly there would be a need for quite substantial resources. Philosophically, in a free enterprise system I think the community also has to take into account the fact that failures in companies are part of the free enterprise system, as well as success ... you need to ... have a debate on whether ASIC should be preventative or ... should remain in its traditional role ...

The quote raises rich questions about policy settings and about whether the time is ripe for a review of the philosophical considerations underpinning the current regulatory system. It is reasonable to presume that, given a choice, the community would prefer the regulatory framework to be amended to facilitate ASIC's monitoring role becoming more prominent in future, as a way of detecting the signs of potential huge corporate collapses as soon as possible, rather than cleaning up after such collapses.[59] It is interesting to note that the proportion of the adult population of Australia that owns shares is one of the highest in the world:[60] approximately 36 per cent of adult Australians owned shares in 2014.[61] Many of these shareholders, as well as the thousands of creditors and those who lost their insurance cover in the HIH collapse, are likely to support any extension of ASIC's powers that may prevent future spectacular corporate failures.

If this occurs, it will probably mean a much greater focus for ASIC on monitoring companies, rather than strictly on regulating and enforcing. Fulfilling this role will likely be a far greater challenge than the current role, which could be described as primarily picking up the

---

58 ABC, 'ASIC Chairman Defends Role as Corporate Regulator' *Lateline*, Transcript, 22 May 2008.
59 See generally regarding the role of governments in risk minimisation: Rick Sarre, 'Risk Management and Regulatory Weakness', in John D Adams et al. (eds), *Collapse Incorporated* (CCH, 2001) 319–21.
60 ASIC Report 480, 'Assessment of ASX Limited's Listing Standards for Equities' (June 2016).
61 See ASX, 'Australian Share Ownership Study' (2015) <www.asx.com.au/documents/resources/australian-share-ownership-study-2014.pdf>.

leftovers on behalf of affected corporations and individuals after the 'corporate cowboys' and 'bold riders' have left the corporations they have ruined financially. Only time will tell whether ASIC will be allowed to take up this challenge and live up to public expectations in this regard.

Greg Medcraft has repeatedly pointed out that the key areas of focus for improving the implementation of corporate governance are in the areas of culture and risk. The need for companies to pay greater attention to corporate culture has been a recurring theme in public addresses made by the ASIC Chair, as illustrated here:[62]

> Effective corporate governance relies on both: 'hard' structural elements, such as specific legal obligations, and 'soft' behavioural factors driven by directors and management faithfully performing their duty of care to the company. Directors should also ensure that their stewardship drives the right compliance culture in their organisation. They should also go beyond what the law requires.

The call for greater emphasis on setting the tone at the top to guide corporate behaviour has had a mixed response, with critics fearful of a push towards regulation to hold directors accountable for wayward culture.[63] Supporters, however, point to Division 12.3 of the Commonwealth Criminal Code which allows for reliance on corporate culture to establish the 'fault element' of criminal conduct. This debate raises interesting issues around the limits of the law and the tension between 'hard law' and 'soft law' in corporate governance.[64]

---

62   Greg Medcraft, 'What ASIC Expects of Directors', AICD Speech (June 2014) <http://asic.gov.au/about-asic/media-centre/speeches/what-asic-expects-of-directors-speech/>. See <http://asic.gov.au/regulatory-resources/corporate-governance/directors-and-corporate-culture/>; <http://asic.gov.au/about-asic/media-centre/speeches/corporate-culture-and-corporate-regulation/>.

63   See <www.afr.com/business/banking-and-finance/asic-chair-hits-back-at-culture-rule-claims-20160406-gnzgdf>.

64   For several thought-provoking papers grappling with this tension, see See Jean J du Plessis and Chee Keong Low (eds), *Corporate Governance Codes for the 21st Century – International Perspectives and Critical Analyses* (Springer Verlag, 2017) <www.springer.com/br/book/9783319518671>.

7

ACCOUNTING
GOVERNANCE

The effect of taking the design of the accounting ecosystem away from the accounting profession and placing it in the hands of regulators has been to lose the flexibility and market alignment that has been such a key element of having an accounting ecosystem that is consistently fit for purpose. The role of the accounting profession as the designers of the accounting ecosystem brought a degree of innovation, insuring the system itself remained fit for today and tomorrow.

Mervyn King and Jill Atkins, *Chief Value Officer: Accountants Can Save the Planet*
(Greenleaf Publishing Ltd, 2016) 34

7.1 Overview

No matter which corporate code of conduct or corporate governance framework is used, the issue of 'transparency' is referred to, either directly or by implication. The application of 'transparency' to the reporting to the public by companies of their financial and non-financial conduct and performance for a period has come under increasing scrutiny from corporate stakeholders. The single most significant reform in this area in Australia came in response to the high-profile corporate collapses of the early 2000s. On 1 July 2004, the *Corporate Law Economic Reform Program (Audit Reform and Corporate Disclosure) Act 2004* (Cth) came into effect. This Act is commonly referred to as 'CLERP 9', as it was the ninth instalment under the government's Corporate Law Economic Reform Program (CLERP).

The CLERP 9 Act, together with the amendments made to the Australian Securities Exchange (ASX) Listing Rules and the ASX Corporate Governance Council's first edition (2003) of the *Principles of Good Corporate Governance and Best Practice Recommendations* (now called *CG Principles and Recommendations*) represent the most significant reforms regarding regulating corporate governance practices of companies in Australian since the first Companies Acts were introduced here. Since 2003 other important reforms in Australia have been the adoption of International Financial Reporting Standards and International Standards on Auditing, based on those promulgated by the International Accounting Standards Board (IASB) and the International Auditing and Assurance Standards Board (IAASB) respectively.

No book on corporate governance in Australia could do justice to its topic without devoting at least some discussion to accounting governance in terms of CLERP 9, and accounting and auditing reforms and their place in the broader context of corporate governance, and in the regulation of corporate governance in particular.

Considerable parts of the *Corporations Act 2001* (Cth) are now devoted to mandatory corporate governance rules (especially in relation to the financial aspects of corporate governance, with substantial reforms in the area of audit and financial reporting). Prior to CLERP 9, many of the best-practice requirements that are now prescriptive rules forming part of the Corporations Act (dealing with, for example, executive remuneration, shareholder participation and financial reporting) were either part of a self-regulatory approach to corporate governance and standard-setting overseen by professional bodies (for example, the Australian Auditing and Assurance Standards Board), or merely aspirational standards. CLERP 9 helped change the way that corporate governance operates, and the role of the regulators and quasi-regulators such as the ASX.

The CLERP 9 Act was designed, with some minor exceptions, to be consistent with and to complement the ASX *Principles of Good Corporate Governance and Best Practice Recommendations*. The aim was for the two documents together to promote good corporate governance practices within Australian listed companies and achieve effective regulation. Some of the initiatives introduced under CLERP 9, however, go further than the ASX *Principles* (which, as we know, operate under an 'if not, why not?' ['comply or explain'] approach):[1] they apply also to non-listed companies, and deal with non-compliance, which can attract formal penalties.

The establishment of CLERP is said to have been a consequence of the decision to transfer responsibility for legislation on corporations and securities from the Office of the Attorney-General to the Department of Treasury. The perception was that this transfer of responsibility would generate a shift from an emphasis on legal regulation to an emphasis on economic regulation, and would result in a focus on the economic impact of corporations law.

7.2 Impetus for CLERP 9: Responding to corporate collapses

As is discussed in various parts of this book, renewed international attention to corporate governance resulted from the collapse of two of the US's largest companies, Enron and WorldCom, in 2001. The collapse of HIH Insurance Ltd – Australia's largest-ever corporate collapse – followed soon thereafter.

Regulators were quick to focus their attention on any role those companies' auditors may have played in the collapses: through poor audit oversight, lack of transparency and accountability, or the relevant audit firms being too close to their audited clients.

In the US, it was discovered that the global accounting firm Arthur Andersen & Co. (Andersen), which subsequently also collapsed under the weight of the scandal, had signed off on Enron financial reports which overstated the company's earnings by US$586 million over five years, and had allegedly shredded a large volume of Enron's documents (this was found on appeal not to have been the case). It was argued that Andersen's negligence and, indeed, dishonest practices, were due to its dependence upon fees paid to the firm by Enron for non-audit services (such as consultancy and legal services). As other audit firms similarly depended on non-audit fees, lack of 'auditor independence' was considered a major problem that required attention.[2] Unfortunately, these scandals were not isolated events, with subsequent accounting irregularities generating scandals for:

* *Satyam Computer Services* – This large Indian IT company reported falsified accounts in 2009 involving amounts of more than US$1.5 billion. Its auditors (PwC) were fined several million dollars by the Securities and Exchange Commission for failing to fulfil their duties diligently, which would have led to their detecting the exaggerated financial performance of Satyam Computer Services.

---

1   See Chapters 4, 5 and 11.
2   See generally Melissa Fogarty and Alison Lansley, 'Sleepers awake! Future directions for auditing in Australia' (2002) 25 *University of New South Wales (UNSW) Law Journal* 408.

- *Lehman Brothers* – Auditors Ernst and Young paid US$99 million in a settlement for an investor lawsuit that alleged that the accounting firm assisted Lehman Brothers to misreport billions of dollars in repurchase agreements. A lawsuit by the NY State Attorney General over the scandal was settled for $10 million.
- *Tesco Supermarkets* – The large UK-based supermarket chain overstated its accounts by more than £263 million over several years, until 2014, in order to boost apparent profits in FY 13–14. This was done by recognising revenue too early through the use of rebates from suppliers. One of the issues involved the materiality thresholds in the audit report, with several years of overstatements and profit inflation still falling below the materiality threshold, which was stated by the auditor as more than £150 million a year. Tesco was eventually forced to pay more than £235 in fines and compensation to investors following the scandal. Australia has had similar issues (albeit on a smaller scale) in Dick Smith (which subsequently collapsed due to profits being made up largely of supplier rebates) and Target.

Auditor dependence is a problem from a corporate governance perspective because if a company involves the same firm in the provision of both audit services and non-audit services, such as consulting or legal services, the auditor will possibly be reluctant to provide an unfavourable audit report to management, as the result could be a loss of the audit engagement, and/or the non-audit services. Despite the limited role that auditors actually play and their very narrow obligations under law, the renewed focus on corporate governance and the importance of the auditor's role in ensuring the reliability of a company's half-year and full-year accounts warranted serious attention being paid to the regulation of auditors.

In Australia, the same problem – potential auditor dependence on audit clients – was found to be rife, which is discussed further in Chapter 8.

It is not difficult to see why the problems that were believed to be behind these high-profile corporate collapses became the focus of CLERP. Corporate law reform – particularly in the area of corporate disclosure – was seen as a possible way to restore market confidence, by addressing the cause of those collapses and preventing further collapses.

7.3 Key CLERP 9 reforms

In this section, we identify each of the key CLERP 9 reforms implemented. The explanation is divided into three parts: (1) audit reform, (2) corporate disclosure, and (3) miscellaneous reforms. Note that ASIC has released a number of policy statements, practice notes and other documents indicating its intentions in administering different aspects of CLERP 9. Where relevant, we include reference to these documents, but readers are encouraged to visit the CLERP 9 section of ASIC's website.

7.3.1 Audit reform

As noted earlier, Chapter 8 of this book is devoted to explaining the role of auditors in corporate governance, and the reforms to auditing and audit regulation introduced under CLERP 9. This section merely identifies the main initiatives relating to audit reform that were made as part of CLERP 9.

A key area for reform under CLERP 9 was auditor independence. CLERP 9 enhanced auditor independence through a number of reforms, including general and specific independence rules embedded into the Corporations Act, new audit–partner rotation rules (requiring listed companies to essentially replace their external audit partner every five years), the imposition of 'cooling off' periods for ex-auditors before they are able to take up a position with a former audit client, and requirements for auditor disclosure of the dollar value of non-audit services by category (the value of auditor-provided non-audit services purchased had long been a required disclosure under accounting standards), with an explanation in the directors' report of how the provision of these services did not compromise independence.

Other changes increased auditor accountability by requiring that auditors of listed company clients attend the clients' annual general meeting to answer shareholder questions; extended the duty of auditors to report unlawful conduct occurring within an audited body; gave auditing standards the force of law similar to accounting standards, which had long had this requirement; reconstituted the previous professional body that sponsored the Auditing and Assurance Standards Board (AUASB) as a statutory authority under the guidance of the Australian Financial Reporting Council (FRC); allowed registration of audit companies (previously only sole practitioners or partnerships were permitted); formalised auditor competence requirements; and provided jurisdiction to the FRC to supervise and guide auditors regarding independence requirements. ASIC set out its policy in relation to audit reform in Policy Statement (now Regulatory Guide) 180, 'Auditor Registration'.

In 2010 the Commonwealth Treasury conducted a review of audit practices and standards in Australia, which culminated in a report, 'Audit Quality in Australia: A Strategic Review' (5 March 2010). This review found that Australia's audit regulatory framework is robust and in line with international practice, but did recommend a number of amendments to help improve the operation of the CLERP 9 reforms for both auditors and audit clients. These changes were introduced into law by the *Corporations Legislation Amendment (Audit Enhancement) Act 2012* (Cth) and are discussed in Chapter 8.

7.3.2 Corporate disclosure

7.3.2.1 Remuneration of directors and executives

CLERP 9 introduced enhanced disclosure requirements for listed companies in relation to the disclosure of rates of director and executive remuneration and, in particular, of the link between levels of executive pay and company performance.

The major changes to s 300A of the Corporations Act required much greater disclosure by listed companies of director and executive remuneration (both the level of remuneration and the company's policy in determining remuneration) – including the preparation of a specific 'remuneration report' to be included as a section in the directors' report (which is intended to clearly explain board policy in relation to remuneration and demonstrate to shareholders that levels of executive pay are based on company performance, and how this is determined), and disclosure of the remuneration of each director and the five highest-paid managerial personnel in the company and in the group (if applicable).[3] Other CLERP 9 initiatives in relation to remuneration included:

---

3   See also AASB 2 (accounting standard), 'Share-based Payment' for other required disclosures and accounting treatments.

- a requirement (under s 250R) for listed companies to provide shareholders with a non-binding 'advisory' vote on the designated 'remuneration report' prepared by the directors;[4] and

- a tightening of the termination payment rules, with shareholder approval generally being required for all termination payments (including payments arranged pursuant to pre-employment contracts, and damages for breach of contract due to early termination of contract) that are greater than the relevant person's average remuneration for the last three years multiplied by the number of years the person has held an office in relation to the company (up to a maximum seven years) or the person's remuneration for the last 12 months (see s 200F).

Under the Act, a 'company executive' is defined as a company secretary or senior manager of the company (s 300A(1B)). A 'senior manager' is defined under s 9 as 'a person, other than a director or company secretary, who makes, or participates in making, decisions that affect the whole, or a substantial part, of the business of the corporation; or has the capacity to affect significantly the corporation's financial standing'.

7.3.2.2 Financial reporting

CLERP 9 introduced some significant financial reporting reforms requiring further information to be provided in the directors' report or the financial report (which is included in the annual or half-yearly report of the company). Another important financial reporting initiative introduced under CLERP 9 was the Financial Reporting Panel (FRP), which had jurisdiction to hear and determine disputes between ASIC and companies (or other entities) regarding accounting treatments in annual reports.[5] However, the FRP did not work as planned, with less than 10 matters referred to it. It was closed down in 2012.[6]

In terms of the compliance-based reforms, the three key changes made under CLERP 9 were:

1. that listed companies must include in the directors' report a declaration by the directors that they had received a chief executive officer (CEO) and chief financial officer (CFO) joint declaration that the company's financial records have been properly maintained, that the financial statements and accompanying notes have been prepared in accordance with accounting standards, and that the financial statements and notes for the financial year provide a 'true and fair' view of the company's position (sections 295(4)(e) and 295A);

2. that the directors' report for a listed company must include a 'management discussion and analysis' (an MD&A), which contains the information that investors would

---

4   Changes to the Corporations Act in 2011 required that a vote of more than 25% against the remuneration report in two consecutive years gives rise to a board spill motion that could then lead to all of the directors being forced to stand for re-election at a special members' meeting: see *Corporations Act 2001* (Cth) Pt 2G.2 Div 9, and more detailed discussion in Chapter 4.

5   See *Australian Securities and Investments Commission Act 2001* (Cth) (ASIC Act) Pt 13, which established the Panel; also *Corporations Act 2001* (Cth) Pt 2M.3 Div 9.

6   See Explanatory Memorandum to the Corporations Legislation Amendment (Financial Reporting Panel) Bill 2012 (Cth). The Bill was passed in 2012: *Corporations Legislation Amendment (Financial Reporting Panel) Act 2012* (Cth).

reasonably require to make an informed assessment of the company's operations and financial position, as well as business strategies and prospects for future financial years (s 299A); and

3. that if additional information is included in an entity's full year or half-year financial report to ensure a 'true and fair' view (of the financial performance and position of the company, satisfying the existing requirement under the Act (sections 297 and 305)), then the directors' report must set out the reasons for the directors forming the view that the inclusion of this information was necessary and the location of this additional information in the financial report (s 298(1A)), and the auditor's report must include a statement as to whether the auditor believes the inclusion of this additional information was necessary to provide a 'true and fair' view (s 306(2)).

7.3.2.3 Continuous disclosure

One of the most controversial areas of reform under CLERP 9 concerned changes made to the continuous disclosure regime. This regime (under the Corporations Act and the ASX Listing Rules) requires that listed companies (and non-listed 'disclosing entities') immediately release to the market information that could have a material effect on the price or value of affected companies' securities.

There were two key changes relating to continuous disclosure under CLERP 9:

1. the introduction of personal liability for individuals who are deemed to be 'involved' in an entity's contravention of the continuous disclosure provisions (which essentially 'pick up' the continuous disclosure rules under the ASX Listing Rules). This personal liability provision is subject to a 'due diligence' defence;[7] and

2. providing ASIC with the power to issue 'infringement notices' against an entity (but not against an individual 'involved' in a contravention) if ASIC considers that the entity has not met its continuous disclosure obligations. The infringement notice power was introduced with a view to enabling ASIC to take action in relation to less serious contraventions of the continuous disclosure provisions, where court action would not be justified. An infringement notice may only be issued within 12 months of an alleged contravention. The size of the monetary penalty awarded in the infringement notice depends on the offending entity's market capitalisation and whether or not it has previously been convicted of contravening the continuous disclosure provisions. The maximum possible penalty for each offence (at the time of writing) was $100,000. Complying with an infringement notice by paying the specified monetary penalty within the specified time period is not an admission of guilt, but it bars ASIC from commencing civil or criminal proceedings in relation to the alleged contravention.

Importantly, in relation to publicity, ASIC may not issue any press release relating to an infringement notice being issued against a company. ASIC may only publish a statement when

---

7   See *Corporations Act 2001* (Cth) s 674(2A). See also *Australian Securities and Investments Commission v Sino Australia Oil and Gas Ltd (in liq)* (2016) 118 ACSR 43.

an entity complies with an infringement notice, and this statement must include a note clearly stating that compliance is not an admission of the entity's guilt, and that the entity is not regarded as having contravened the continuous disclosure provisions.[8]

7.3.2.4 Shareholder participation

CLERP 9 introduced some important amendments to the Corporations Act designed to facilitate and promote the exercise by shareholders of important governance rights: being informed of company activities, and participation in and voting at general meetings of the company.

The key amendments in this area were designed to:

- encourage companies to embrace technology (particularly the internet and email) and forms of electronic communication (such as web-casting) to improve communication with shareholders, particularly in terms of facilitating the distribution of notices of meeting and annual reports;[9]

- encourage shorter and more comprehensible notices of company meetings so that shareholders can fully understand the contents of the notices (s 249L(3), which introduced a requirement that notices are worded and presented in a 'clear, concise and effective manner');

- improve shareholder access to general meetings by facilitating proxy voting – in particular, to facilitate electronic proxy voting (by permitting regulations to prescribe 'authentication mechanisms', which authenticate proxy appointments made electronically);[10]

- better inform shareholders by requiring that listed company directors disclose other directorships held in the three years prior to the end of the financial year to which the report relates,[11] and by including the qualifications and experience of the company secretary in the directors' report.[12]

7.3.3 Miscellaneous reforms

7.3.3.1 Officers, senior managers and employees

Prior to CLERP 9, the Corporations Act contained two different definitions of 'officer' – one in s 82A, which included employees within the definition, and one in s 9. This anomaly was discussed in detail by Justice Owen in the HIH Royal Commission final report and was eventually addressed in the CLERP 9 Act, which repealed s 82A.

CLERP 9 also introduced a new definition of 'senior manager' in s 9 of the Corporations Act (see above). The concept of 'senior manager' is mainly used in the sections of the Corporations Act introduced by CLERP 9 on executive and director remuneration and audit services.

---

8 See *Corporations Act 2001* (Cth) Pt 9.4AA, and ASIC's policy document, RG 73 'Continuous Disclosure Obligations: Infringement Notices' (June 2012), which sets out ASIC's processes for administering the infringement notice regime, including how hearings are to be conducted and notices issued.

9 *Corporations Act 2001* (Cth) ss 249J and 314.

10 Ibid. s 250A(1A) and *Corporations Regulations 2001* reg 2G.2.01.

11 *Corporations Act 2001* (Cth) s 300(11)(e).

12 Ibid. s 300(10)(d).

7.3.3.2 Enforcement

The CLERP 9 Act introduced a number of important measures to strengthen the enforcement provisions of the Corporations Act, such as increased penalties,[13] and providing courts with the power to extend the period of 'automatic disqualification' of directors managing a corporation, upon application by ASIC, for a further 15 years.[14]

7.3.3.3 Proportionate liability

The CLERP 9 Act introduced a proportionate liability approach in relation to claims for misleading conduct regarding economic loss or property damage, under three provisions: s 1041H of the Corporations Act, s 12DA of the ASIC Act and s 18 of the Australian Consumer Law (which is Schedule 2 of the *Competition and Consumer Act 2010* (Cth)) – formerly s 52 of the *Trade Practices Act 1974* (Cth)).[15] This change in approach facilitated apportionment between a plaintiff and a defendant according to their respective level of blame (similar to the rules of 'contributory negligence' in torts), and between two or more defendants based on their respective levels of blame.

The change to proportionate liability was principally designed to protect auditors, but applies to all professional advisers. Prior to the CLERP 9 reforms, audit partners in firms were jointly and severally liable for professional default within the firm, thus exposing each partner to unlimited liability. Auditors had traditionally protected themselves from unlimited liability through professional indemnity insurance, but the cost of insurance premiums had skyrocketed as a result of the collapse of HIH Insurance.

7.4 Accounting standards

The Australian Financial Reporting Council directed the Australian Accounting Standards Board (AASB) to adopt international financial reporting standards (IFRS) issued in July 2003 by the International Accounting Standards Board. Previously there had been a policy of harmonisation with IFRS, but not outright adoption. The AASB issued the suite of Australian Equivalents to International Financial Reporting Standards (AIFRS) in May 2004 for implementation by all reporting entities for periods beginning on or after 1 January 2005. For 31 December balancers, this gave little time for implementation. Further, since financial statements had to provide comparative numbers from the previous year, these numbers needed to be re-worked according to IFRS too, and certain reconciliations between the previous and new treatments were required. Many other countries (for example, in Europe) that adopted IFRS did so only for the consolidated financial reports required from certain groups of companies. Hence the transition in Australia was a monumental task, and not without cost.

As justification for the reform, the then government argued that 'in a globalised economy with large and growing cross-border capital movements, high quality, internationally accepted accounting standards will facilitate cross-border comparisons by investors and enable

---

13   Ibid. ss 1308 and 1309.
14   Ibid. ss 206BA and 206B(1).
15   See further *Selig v Wealthsure Pty Ltd* (2015) 255 CLR 66.

Australian companies to access international capital markets at lower cost'.[16] However, the initial policy of amending the wording of the original IFRS meant there was still uncertainty internationally over compliance with IFRS, and in 2007 the AASB was given a strategic direction by the Australian Financial Reporting Council to the effect that auditors should attest to compliance with IFRS where companies in their annual reports made this claim.[17]

One important difference between IFRS and the previous accounting standards is the emphasis on the use of 'fair value' to value assets, particularly investments in securities. In the illiquid market for many securities in the aftermath of the Global Financial Crisis, this valuation method has come under enormous scrutiny, even blame.[18] The IASB was forced to compromise on its standard on financial instruments when European banks found themselves at a disadvantage with US banks on recognition of losses on poorly performing loans. Indeed, the struggle for supremacy between accounting standards issued by the IASB and the US standard setter, the American Financial Accounting Standards Board (FASB), was highlighted by the financial crisis. The US had laid out a roadmap itself to adopt IFRS by 2014, but this was subsequently abandoned.

7.5 Conclusion

We have witnessed a major change in the mode of corporate governance regulation in Australia in recent years: from a disclosure-based approach, which preferred companies to disclose the corporate governance policies and practices they implemented in accordance with their particular needs, to an interventionist approach – with CLERP 9 contributing to the formalisation of best-practice governance benchmarks by introducing (or significantly enhancing) substantive corporate governance requirements under the Corporations Act.

There is still considerable debate as to whether many of the compliance-related requirements under CLERP 9 (particularly in relation to audit reform, financial reporting – for example, CEO/CFO declarations and the MD&A discussion in the directors' report – and executive remuneration) were necessary to improve the governance practices and general performance of companies, and therefore to 'fireproof' companies from collapse, or whether they have merely imposed additional burdens on companies. We believe that returning to one of the 'key principles' of the CLERP program, 'cost effectiveness', is an important element in properly assessing the efficacy of the post-CLERP 9 regulatory framework. That key principle (3.4) states:

> The benefits of business regulation must outweigh its associated costs. The regulatory framework should take into account the direct and indirect costs imposed by regulation on business and the community as a whole. What Australia must avoid is outmoded business laws which impose unnecessary costs through reducing the range of products or services, impeding the development of new products or imposing system-wide costs.
>
> The regulatory framework for business needs to be well targeted to ensure that the benefits clearly exceed the costs. A flexible and transparent framework will be more

16   CLERP 9 Proposal 6.2.
17   For detail see CA Jubb and KA Houghton, 'The Australian Auditing and Assurance Standards Board after the implementation of CLERP 9' (2007) 22 *Australian Accounting Review* 688.
18   See, for instance, Tim McCollum, 'Fair value under fire' (2008) 65(6) *The Internal Auditor* 13.

conducive to innovation and risk taking, which are fundamental elements of a thriving market economy, while providing necessary investor and consumer protection.[19]

Do the benefits of moving towards more substantive corporate governance mandates outweigh the additional costs (both time-based and financial) of compliance? Is the post-CLERP 9 regulatory landscape a flexible and transparent framework that is conducive to innovation and risk-taking, or is the overriding objective of contemporary corporate regulation in Australia now 'conformance' rather than 'performance'? We leave you to come to your own conclusion, with the assistance of the overview of the CLERP 9 and other reforms provided in this chapter. It is important to note, however, that many of the key elements of CLERP 9 have been amended in subsequent years (discussed further in Chapter 8).

The Global Financial Crisis raised concerns about the efficacy of disclosure as the bedrock of corporate regulation. Companies, particularly publicly listed companies, are required to produce reams of often technical information that few find useful or intelligible. In a speech to the ASIC Annual Forum in June 2014,[20] ASIC Chair Greg Medcraft noted that future regulatory approaches may need to be better informed by developments in behavioural science and behavioural finance that provide valuable insights into how investors gather and interpret information about their investments.[21] It seems that the debate concerning prescriptive regulation and mandatory disclosure has a long way to run.

---

19   See Australian Government, 'CLERP – Policy Framework' <http://archive.treasury.gov.au/documents/
      267/HTML/docshell.asp?URL=index.asp>.
20   Greg Medcraft, 'Regulating for Real People, Markets and Globalization', Opening Speech to the ASIC
      Annual Forum 2014 (June 2014) <www.asic.gov.au>.
21   This was echoed in the Financial System Inquiry's *Final Report* (November 2014).

8

AUDITORS AND AUDITS

Audited financial statements are an important part of the financial information that
is available to the capital markets and an important part of effective corporate
governance.

> Ian M Ramsay, *Independence of Australian Company Auditors: Review of Current Australian*
> *Requirements and Proposals for Reform*, Report to the Minister for Financial Services and
> Regulation, Department of Treasury (October 2001) [4.01]

8.1   Introduction: The audit role and where it fits into corporate governance

8.1.1   Overview of the audit role

Auditing is defined as an assurance service that objectively gathers evidence and communi-
cates it to third parties.[1] Companies that are required to prepare a financial report for a financial
year must have their financial report audited and obtain an auditor's report.[2] Thus all large
proprietary companies and public companies must appoint an auditor. Small proprietary
companies, and small companies limited by guarantee, are not required to prepare a financial
report in normal circumstances and hence need not appoint an auditor. However, they must
do so in a limited range of circumstances, namely where members holding at least 5 per cent of
the votes in a general meeting require preparation of accounts and ask for an auditor.[3]

Broadly, the function of an auditor is to conduct a review and verification of the financial
affairs of the company and to ascertain whether the financial report provided by the company
complies with relevant legal requirements and accounting principles, and gives a true and fair
account in all material respects of the company's financial affairs. The audit role has several
objectives. The main one is to provide reasonable assurance that the financial information
reported by the company is free from material misstatement. In the process, auditors provide a
barrier of protection against careless or dishonest company officers. In order to fulfil this role,
the auditor must have suitable skills and expertise, and must be independent of the company.

The main auditing requirement is to provide a report to the members, within the financial
report, for a financial year.[4] This is laid before the annual general meeting and lodged with the
Australian Securities and Investments Commission (ASIC).[5]

It is important to note that the auditor's role is essentially procedural, not substantive, in
nature. More particularly, pursuant to sections 307 and 308 of the *Corporations Act 2001* (Cth),
the auditor's report to members must set out a number of matters in relation to the financial
report for a financial year.[6] These include:

---

1   C Jubb, S Topple, P Schelluch, L Rittenberg and B Schwieger, *Assurance and Auditing: Concepts for a*
     Changing Environment (Thomson, 2nd edn, 2008) 4.
2   *Corporations Act 2001* (Cth) s 301.
3   Ibid. ss 293, 294A.
4   Disclosing entities may have their half-year financial report audited or reviewed (*Corporations Act 2001*
     (Cth) s 309).
5   Ibid. ss 308, 317, 319.
6   See also Auditing and Asurance Standards Board, ASA 701 *Communicating Key Audit Matters in the*
     Independent Auditor's Report (2015).

- whether the financial report is in accordance with the Corporations Act, including compliance with accounting standards, and whether the report provides a true and fair view of the financial position and performance of the company;[7]
- if the auditor is of the opinion that the financial report does not comply with an accounting standard, to the extent that it is practicable to do so, quantify the effect that non-compliance has on the financial report. If it is not practicable to quantify the effect fully, the report must state why;
- whether the auditor has been given all information and assistance for the conduct of the audit;
- any defect or irregularity in the financial report;
- whether the company has kept financial records sufficient to enable the conduct of the audit; and
- whether the company has kept other records required by the Corporations Act.

In addition to this, the auditor's report must describe any defect or irregularity in the financial report and any other relevant deficiencies or shortcomings regarding the record-keeping of the company.[8]

The auditor's role does not extend to commenting or passing judgment on the soundness of the business or on the financial decisions of the directors and other officers.[9]

8.1.2 The link between the audit role and corporate governance

The audit role in the context of corporate governance needs some explanation, as the role is largely external to that of company decision-makers.[10] Auditors do not prepare company reports. Their role is one of 'checking', or verifying. In this respect, it has been noted that an auditor is 'a watch dog, but not a bloodhound'.[11] This audit function is, however, integral to the activities and affairs of a company. Although the audit role can be defined relatively easily, it is a role that at various junctures has been perceived not to have been adequately performed. Indeed, doubts about audit quality in the context of high-profile corporate collapses led to the CLERP 9 reforms of the audit function – the *Corporate Law Economic Reform Program (Audit Reform and Corporate Disclosure) Act 2004* (Cth) – so far as it relates to public companies.

The audit role is now regarded as being so central to the activities of a company that, despite the fact that it is in essence a monitoring role performed by parties outside the corporate structure, it is considered by some commentators to be a definitional and cardinal aspect of corporate governance.

In looking at the nexus between external audit and corporate governance, the *Report of the HIH Royal Commission* (the Owen Report) notes that:

---

7   See also *Corporations Act 2001* (Cth) ss 296 and 297.
8   Ibid. s 308.
9   *BGJ Holdings Pty Ltd v Touche Ross & Co* (1987) 12 ACLR 481.
10   For a history of the audit requirement in corporate law see *Australian Securities and Investments Commission v Healey* (2011) 196 FCR 291, [104] ff.
11   See Lopes LJ in *Re Kingston Cotton Mill (No 2)* [1896] 2 Ch 270. For a more expansive view of the duty of an auditor, see, for example, *Pacific Acceptance Corporation v Forsyth* (1970) 92 WN (NSW) 29.

Auditors play a significant role in corporate governance. This is not surprising given the emphasis placed on integrity and on the need for financial reporting that is honest and that presents a balanced picture of the state of the company's affairs. Again, I refer to the Cadbury report:

> The annual audit is one of the cornerstones of corporate governance ... the audit provides an external and objective check on the way in which the financial statements have been prepared and presented, and it is an essential part of the checks and balances required. The question is not whether there should be an audit, but how to ensure its objectivity and effectiveness.

Whether the audit function is viewed as being internal or external to corporate governance, there is no doubt that it is crucial. This, too, is a point emphasised by Justice Owen in the HIH Report:

> The point of an audit is to provide independent assurance of the integrity of the way in which the company has reported. It follows that shareholders in particular have an interest in the proper functioning of the audit process, as it provides them with comfort in making investment decisions. This element of assurance is of course also relevant to the directors themselves, so far as they rely on management in the preparation of the accounts, as well as to others with an interest.[12]

Similar comments were made by Treasury in its Explanatory Memorandum at [4.8] outlining the CLERP 9 proposals:[13]

> Audited financial statements are an important part of the financial information that is available to the capital markets and an essential element of effective corporate governance. Auditor independence is fundamental to the credibility and reliability of auditors' reports and in turn independent audits perform an important function in terms of capital market efficiency. There has been widespread concern about the efficacy of the audit function, including the independence of auditors, as a result of major corporate collapses in Australia and overseas, including HIH.

Over recent years there have been a number of corporate collapses which have called into question the degree of independence of auditors. These cases have demonstrated that while a company's actual financial position may have been poor, the financial statements and the audit report did not reflect the true condition of the company. This has impaired the ability of shareholders and the market more generally to adequately assess the financial health of their investment. While the Global Financial Crisis did not immediately result in major criticisms of auditors,[14] ASIC has undertaken regulatory action against auditors in connection with several corporate failures, including ABC Learning, Babcock and Brown, Centro Properties and Allco

---

12   Report of the HIH Royal Commission (Owen Report), *The Failure of HIH Insurance – Volume I: A Corporate Collapse and its Lessons* (Commonwealth of Australia, 2003) 162 para 7.2.

13   Explanatory Memorandum to the Corporate Law Economic Reform Program (Audit Reform and Corporate Disclosure) Bill 2003 [4.8].

14   See the concluding chapter in KC Houghton, C Jubb, M Kend and J Ng, *The Future of Audit: Towards a National Strategy in Keeping Markets Efficient* (ANU E-Press, 2009) <http://ancaar.fec.anu.edu.au/documents/FutureOfAuditReport.pdf>.

Finance Group. For example, ASIC entered into an enforceable undertaking with the lead PwC auditor for Centro Properties Group. The undertaking prevents the auditor from practising as an auditor for three years (until mid-2015). The former auditor of ABC Learning also entered into an enforceable undertaking, involving a five-year ban on working as an auditor.

8.2 CLERP 9 changes to the audit role

The role and regulation of auditors underwent significant changes following the CLERP 9 reforms. As pointed out in Chapter 7, it was generally acknowledged that the absence of 'auditor independence' within the accounting firm Arthur Andersen & Co. (Andersen) was a significant factor in the collapse of Enron.

In Australia, the lack of independence of auditors was also common. An ASIC study – conducted in January 2002 – of Australia's 100 largest companies revealed that a large majority of these companies retained their audit firms to provide non-audit services, and that non-audit fees accounted for nearly 50 per cent of the total fees paid to the audit firm.[15]

Given the circumstances leading to these high-profile collapses, the principal CLERP 9 audit reforms related to enhanced auditor oversight and independence. They included:

1.   introducing a general requirement for auditors to be independent;
2.   incorporating the best-practice position regarding the employment of auditors and the financial relationships between the audit firm and the firm's clients to ensure independence;
3.   enhancing the disclosure requirement for non-audit services (for example, consulting, legal) performed by the audit firm (so that the type of service and the monetary amount paid is evident);
4.   prohibiting audit firm partners who were directly involved in an audit from becoming directors of the audited client within two years of the auditor resigning from the audit firm; and
5.   establishing an auditor independence 'supervisory board'.

It had been proposed initially that CLERP 9 introduce a requirement that all listed companies have an audit committee. This requirement was subsequently taken up by the Australian Securities Exchange (ASX), which mandated audit committees for the top 500 companies only, on the basis of disproportionate cost for smaller companies. The ASX *CG Principles and Recommendations* (3rd ed, 2014) also recommend (Recommendation 4.1) that listed entities have an audit committee.

In the remainder of the chapter we analyse the audit role insofar as it relates to companies, and focus particularly on some of the above reforms. As noted in Chapter 7, the role and operation of auditors was drastically reformed by CLERP 9.

---

15   See 'ASIC Announces Findings of Audit Independence Survey', ASIC Press Release 02/13 (16 January 2002) <www.asic.gov.au/asic/asic.nsf/byheadline/02%2F13+ASIC+announces+findings+of+auditor+independence+survey?openDocument>.

8.3 Auditor independence

8.3.1 Overview of rationale behind independence requirement

A central aim of the CLERP 9 audit reforms was to ensure greater auditor independence. Prior to those changes, the Corporations Act dealt with auditor independence in only a piecemeal fashion.

The importance of auditor independence was underlined in the HIH Report, where Justice Owen stated:

> Auditor independence is a critical element going to the credibility and reliability of an auditor's reports. Audited financial statements play a key role promoting the efficiency of capital markets and the independent auditor constitutes the principal external check on the integrity of financial statements. The Ramsay Report recognised the following four functions of an independent audit in relation to capital market efficiency:
>
> - adding value to financial statements
> - adding value to the capital markets by enhancing the credibility of financial statements
> - enhancing the effectiveness of the capital markets in allocating valuable resources by improving the decisions of users of financial statements
> - assisting to lower the cost of capital to those using audited financial statements by reducing information risk.[16]

In addition to the above functions, an independent audit contributes to capital market efficiency by enhancing the consistency and comparability of reported financial information.

It is widely accepted that the auditor must be, and be seen to be, free of any interest that is incompatible with objectivity: for an audit to fulfil its functions, there must be public confidence in the auditor. The responsibility of auditors to maintain independence in the carrying out of their function was stated by the US Supreme Court:

> The independent public accountant performing this special function owes allegiance to the corporation's creditors and stockholders, as well as the investing public. This public watchdog function demands that the accountant maintain total independence from the client at all times and requires complete fidelity to the public trust.[17]

It seems striking that an 'independent' auditor could, in relation to another aspect of its business, be 'dependent' upon the fees paid by the company being audited. Human nature dictates that an auditor is likely to be less impartial in assessing a corporation's financial reporting if an unfavourable audit report may jeopardise substantial fees arising from the provision of non-audit services.

CLERP 9 attempted to address this issue by introducing a range of reforms, which aimed to improve both actual and perceived independence, and to lead to greater confidence in the credibility and reliability of audited financial statements – as noted in discussion of the Ramsay Report in Chapter 7, Section 7.4.

---

16   Owen Report, *The Failure of HIH Insurance – Volume 1: A Corporate Collapse and its Lessons* (2003), para 7.2.1.
17   *United States v Arthur Young*, 465 US 805, 817–18 (1984).

8.3.2 General requirement for auditor independence

The CLERP 9 amendment to include s 324CA of the Corporations Act established a general requirement for auditor independence. Section 324CA(1) applies to auditors and audit companies[18] and prohibits an individual auditor or audit company from engaging in 'audit activity'[19] in relation to an audited body at a particular time if:

- a 'conflict of interest situation' exists in relation to the audited body at that time;
- the individual auditor or the audit company is aware that the conflict of interest situation exists;
- the individual auditor or the audit company does not take all reasonable steps to ensure that the conflict of interest situation ceases to exist as soon as possible after becoming aware that the conflict of interest situation exists.

8.3.3 Meaning of 'conflict of interest situation'

The CLERP 9 amendment to s 324CD(1) provided that a 'conflict of interest situation' exists in relation to an audited body at a particular time, if circumstances exist at the time which:

- renders the auditor, or a professional member of the audit team, incapable of exercising objective and impartial judgment in relation to the conduct of an audit of the audited body (s 324CD(1)(a));
- would give a person, with full knowledge of the facts and circumstances, reasonable grounds for concern that the auditor, or a professional member of the audit team, is not capable of exercising objective and impartial judgment in relation to the conduct of an audit of the audited body (s 324CD(1)(b)).

In determining whether a conflict of interest situation exists, s 324CD(2) goes on to provide that regard is to be had to circumstances arising from any relationship (that either exists, has existed, or is likely to exist) between:

- the individual auditor;
- the audit firm or any current or former member of the firm;
- the audit company, any current or former director of the audit company or any person currently or formerly involved in the management of the audit company and any of the following persons and bodies:
  - a company (including a person currently or formerly involved in the management of the company);
  - a disclosing entity (including a person currently or formerly involved in the management of the entity);
  - a registered scheme (including a person currently or formerly involved in the management of the responsible scheme or the entity).

---

18   A general independence requirement for members of audit firms and directors of audit companies, mirroring s 324CA, is contained in *Corporations Act 2001* (Cth) ss 324CB and 324CC, respectively.

19   See the definition of 'engage in audit activity' in *Corporations Act 2001* (Cth) s 9.

8.3.4 Disclosing and resolving conflicts

Section 324CA(1A) provides that if a 'conflict of interest situation' exists in relation to an audited body while an individual auditor or audit company is the auditor of that audited body, the individual auditor or audit company must notify ASIC in writing of the conflict of interest within seven days of the day they became aware of the conflict of interest. If the auditor or audit company does not then notify ASIC within 21 days of the notification (or such other period as ASIC determines) that the conflict has been removed, then the audit appointment will terminate pursuant to s 327B(2A) if the audit is of a public company.[20]

8.3.5 Specific independence requirements – minimising conflicts of interest through employment and financial restrictions

Prior to the CLERP 9 reforms, s 324 of the Corporations Act included a limited number of specific restrictions on auditors to ensure independence. There are now specific independence requirements applying to:

- individual auditors: s 324CE;
- audit firms: s 324CF; and
- audit companies: s 324CG.

For example, s 324CE(1) provides that an individual auditor must not engage in audit activity at a particular time if a 'relevant relationship' outlined in the table in s 324CH(1) (which applies to each of sections 324CE, 324CF and 324CG) applies at that time to a person or entity specified in the table in s 324CE(5). This means, for example, that an individual auditor (subsection 324CE(1) – table item 1) cannot engage in 'audit activity' (as defined in s 9) if the individual is an officer of the audited body (subsection 324CH(1) – table item 1). There are separate but similar tables in the legislation outlining specific independence requirements for members of audit firms (see s 324CF) and authorised audit companies (see s 324CG).

If a relevant item of the table in subsection 324CH(1) applies to a person or entity listed in the table of persons in any of sections 324CE, 324CF or 324CG, then the individual auditor, audit firm or audit company must notify ASIC of this specific conflict within seven days: see sections 324CE(1A), 324CF(1A), or 324CG(1A) (there is also a provision applying to directors of audit companies under s 324CG(5A)). If this initial notification is not followed up within 21 days (or in such other period as ASIC decides) by another notice to ASIC, indicating that the

---

20   *Corporations Act 2001* (Cth) s 324CA(2) deals with circumstances in which a 'conflict of interest situation' exists in relation to the audited body but the individual auditor, or the audit company, is *not* aware that the conflict of interest exists. An audit in such circumstances is prohibited where the individual auditor or audit company would have been aware of the existence of the conflict of interest situation if they had in place a quality control system reasonably capable of making them aware of such a conflict of interest. An individual auditor is not in breach of s 324CA(6) if they have reasonable grounds to believe that they have in place a quality control system providing reasonable assurance that the audit company and the company's employees complied with the general independence requirements. A similar 'quality control' defence is provided for audit companies under s 324CA(5).

conflict of interest is removed, then pursuant to s 327B(2A) (individual auditors), (2B) (audit firms) or (2C) (audit companies), the audit appointment terminates.[21]

CLERP 9 also introduced a cooling-off period concerning the involvement of auditors with firms they have audited. Under the Act, a person is prohibited from becoming an officer of an audited body for two years if the person:

- ceases to be a member of an audit firm or director of an audit company and was a professional member of the audit team[22] engaged in an audit of the audited body (s 324CI); or
- ceases to be a professional employee[23] of the auditor if the person was a 'lead auditor' or 'review auditor' for an audit of the audited body (s 324CJ). Under the Act, a 'lead auditor' is the registered company auditor who is primarily responsible to the audit firm or audit company that is conducting the audit. A 'review auditor' is the registered company auditor (if any) who is primarily responsible to the individual auditor, the audit firm, or audit company for reviewing the conduct of the audit (s 324AF).

Additionally, CLERP 9 requires that a person who has been a member of an audit firm or director of an audit company cannot become an officer of an audited body if another person who is, or was, a member or director of the audit firm or company at a time when the auditor undertook an audit of the audited body is also an officer of the audited body (s 324CK).

8.3.6 Auditor rotation

Prior to the CLERP 9 changes, there was no legislative requirement for audit partner rotation. The requirement for audit partner rotation instead formed part of the self-regulatory Joint Code of Professional Conduct of the ICAA and the CPAA[24] (which recommended rotation after seven years). While these two professional bodies cover most auditors, it was considered necessary to set this rotation requirement into legislation so that it applied to the entire auditing profession and was enforceable.

---

21   It should also be noted that similar to the general independence provisions discussed above, for each of ss 324CE, CF and CG there is a 'quality control' defence, so that the individual auditor, member of an audit firm or audit company is not taken to have contravened the relevant section if they had reasonable grounds to believe that a quality control system was in place to provide reasonable assurance that the auditor, firm or company was complying with its specific independence requirements.

22   *Corporations Act 2001* (Cth) s 324AE defines 'professional members of the audit team' as any registered company auditor who participates in the conduct of the audit, any other person who in the course of doing so exercises professional judgment regarding the application of or compliance with accounting or auditing standards and legal requirements, and any other person who is in a position to directly influence the audit outcome.

23   *Corporations Act 2001* (Cth) s 9 provides that a 'professional employee' of an auditor participates in the conduct of audits and in the course of doing so exercises professional judgment regarding the application or compliance with accounting or auditing standards or legal requirements.

24   These two professional bodies subsequently set up a more independent body for the setting of ethical standards, the Accounting Professional Ethical Standards Board (APESB), and were later joined by a third professional body – the National Institute of Accountants (NIA, subsequently renamed the Institute of Public Accountants or IPA). APES 110 *Code of Ethics for Professional Accountants* superseded the Joint Code of Professional Conduct.

The legislative framework for auditor rotation applies where an individual auditor, an audit firm or an authorised audit company has been appointed as auditor of a listed company or registered scheme. The provisions rely on the concept of an auditor having 'played a significant role', which is defined in s 9. Where an individual plays a significant role in the audit of a listed company for five successive financial years, the individual cannot play a significant role in the audit of that company for at least another two successive financial years (s 324DA). However, amendments in 2012 introduced a procedure that can allow the company to permit the auditor to serve another two successive financial years (s 324DAA). This change was introduced following the Treasury's report, *Audit Quality in Australia: A Strategic Review* (March 2010), which found that audit clients were losing valuable expertise because of the five-year rule. As some other jurisdictions allow for longer periods prior to mandatory rotation, the report recommended a further two years be allowed in certain circumstances. This was introduced by the *Corporations Legislation Amendment (Audit Enhancement) Act 2012* (Cth), via new sections 324DAA–DAD.

Section 324DA(2) goes on to provide that a person may not play a significant role as auditor for more than five out of any seven successive financial years, although this too is subject to the exception outlined above (s 324DA(3)). According to the Explanatory Memorandum to the CLERP 9 Bill:

> This approach recognises that auditors may not necessarily audit a body in consecutive years; however, the relationship between the auditor and the audited body can still give rise to a threat to independence.

8.3.7 Disclosure of non-audit services

The HIH Report noted that non-audit services by auditors to audited bodies raised two threats to audit independence:

1. self-review threats – when the auditor may need to review work performed either by the auditor or the auditor's firm; and

2. the sacrifice of audit integrity in order to procure more lucrative non-audit work.

In response to this, following CLERP 9, the board of directors of a listed company must provide a statement in the company's annual report identifying non-audit services[25] that have been provided by the auditor, audit firm or audit company, and a declaration that the provision of these services does not compromise the auditor's independence (see s 300(11B)). Where the company has an audit committee, this statement must be made in accordance with advice provided by that committee (s 300(11D)).

The *Corporations Legislation Amendment (Audit Enhancement) Act 2012* (Cth) has added to the disclosure obligations of audit firms by introducing a new requirement: the annual transparency report (in the new Part 2M.4A). This requirement applies to auditors, audit firms and audit companies that audit 10 or more listed companies or listed schemes or certain

---

25   The Act does not include a definition of 'non-audit services'; however, it is intended that non-audit services will include any services that are provided by an auditor but not included in the terms of the audit engagement.

APRA-regulated bodies in a given reporting year (s 332A). The content of the annual transparency report is set out in Schedule 7A of the *Corporations Regulations 2001* (Cth).

8.4 Auditors and the AGM

A good way to look beyond the often superficial nature of audit reports is to ask questions of the auditors. Shareholders have traditionally had little meaningful opportunity to probe audit reports. Since the *Company Law Review Act 1998* (Cth) came into effect, company shareholders have been entitled to ask questions of the auditor concerning the conduct of the audit and the contents of the audit report. However, this right was somewhat limited, as it depended on shareholders actually attending the annual general meeting (AGM), which most do not, and on the company's auditor attending the meeting.

CLERP 9 introduced s 250PA, which allows a shareholder of a listed company to submit questions to the auditor about the contents of the audit report or the conduct of the audit. Importantly, s 250PA(5) allows auditors to 'filter' questions according to their relevance to the audit report or conduct of the audit. While the filtering exercise is the task of the auditor, the company can express its opinion to the auditor regarding the relevance of individual questions. Section 250PA(7) requires the company to make the list of questions provided by the auditor reasonably available to members attending the AGM. The list could be provided through distribution of printed copies to shareholders or by other means.

Section 250RA of the Act requires auditors of a listed company to attend the company's AGM. Where the auditor is an individual auditor and is unable to attend the AGM, the auditor can instead be represented by a member of the audit team who is 'suitably qualified', and is in a position to answer questions regarding the audit (s 250RA(1)(b)).[26]

8.5 Auditors' duties

Another change introduced by the CLERP 9 package of reforms involved expanding auditors' reporting obligations to ASIC to include a much wider range of suspected or actual malfeasance. Section 311 requires individual auditors conducting an audit[27] to notify ASIC in writing within 28 days of becoming aware of any circumstances that:

- they have reasonable grounds to suspect amount to a contravention (either a *significant* contravention, or a contravention that the auditor believes has not been or will not be adequately dealt with by commenting on it in the auditor's report or bringing it to the attention of the directors) of the Act;
- amount to an attempt, in relation to the audit, by any person to unduly influence, coerce, manipulate or mislead a person involved in the conduct of the audit; or

---

26   As auditors of listed companies are now required to attend company AGMs, s 1289(3) makes it clear that qualified privilege applies to answers to questions asked before or during a company AGM. *Corporations Act 2001* (Cth) s 1289(4) also extends qualified privilege to a person representing the auditor at the AGM in cases where the auditor is not present.

27   Defined under *Corporations Act 2001* (Cth) s 9 to include a review of a half-year financial report.

- amount to an attempt, by any person, to otherwise interfere with the proper conduct of the audit: s 311(1).

Section 311(4) provides that in determining whether a contravention of the Act is a 'significant' one, regard is to be had to:

    (a)   the level of penalty provided for in relation to the contravention; and

    (b)   the effect that the contravention has, or may have, on:

        (i)   the overall financial position of the company, registered scheme or disclosing entity; or

        (ii)   the adequacy of the information available about the overall financial position of the company, registered scheme or disclosing entity; and

    (c)   any other relevant matter.

Section 311(7) defines 'a person involved in the conduct of the audit' to mean the auditor, the 'lead auditor'[28] for the audit, the 'review auditor'[29] for the audit, a professional member of the audit team[30] or any other person involved in the conduct of the audit.

Where an audit firm or audit company is conducting an audit, s 311(2) imposes an obligation equivalent to that under s 311(1) on the lead auditor. If there is a failure to comply with s 311(2), the lead auditor of either the firm or the company will have contravened s 311(3). The audit company is also taken to have contravened s 311(2) if the lead auditor fails to adhere to his or her obligations.

Section 601HG, which contains similar obligations for auditors of managed investment schemes, was amended to reflect the extended reporting obligations placed on auditors under s 311. CLERP 9 also amended s 990K(2) of the Corporations Act through the addition of a requirement that an auditor must give a report to ASIC in relation to any matter that, in the opinion of the auditor, constitutes an attempt to unduly influence, coerce, manipulate or mislead the auditor in the conduct of the audit (s 990K(2)(c)).

8.6 Reducing the legal exposure of auditors

8.6.1 Overview of auditors' liability

Like all parties, professional or otherwise, auditors may be legally liable where they do not properly discharge their legal duties.[31] This liability can arise in three main ways. First, the auditor is engaged by a company to perform an audit pursuant to a contract (which is normally in writing). The auditor can be liable for breach of contract if the audit function is not performed adequately. Parties to a contract are always free to agree to any express terms in the contract; however, in relation to audit services, the implied duties of an auditor include an undertaking by the auditor to use reasonable skill and care in the conduct of the audit.[32]

---

28   Ibid. s 324AF.
29   Ibid.
30   Ibid. s 324AE.
31   For a detailed discussion regarding the legal liability of auditors, see RP Austin and IM Ramsay, *Ford Austin and Ramsay's Principles of Corporations Law* (LexisNexis, 16th edn, 2015) [11.530]–[11.580].
32   *Shire of Frankston and Hastings Corporation v Cohen* (1960) 102 CLR 607.

As result of the operation of the 'privity' doctrine, only the company may sue the auditor for breach of contractual promise. Other potentially affected parties, such as shareholders, are not a party to the contract and hence have no standing to sue under the contract.

Second, the law on negligence provides that the auditor will be liable to parties to whom they owe a duty of care if they do not complete the audit to the standard required of a professional auditor and the other party suffers loss as a result of the negligent audit.[33] To this end, it is noteworthy that existing case law has held that not only do auditors owe a duty of care to the company, but in some cases the duty may extend to shareholders[34] and potentially also to other third parties, such as financiers of the company, where the financiers made the auditors aware of the fact that the information received from the auditors will be used to determine whether or not finance should be provided to the audited person or entity.[35]

Finally, auditors can be held liable for breach of statutory duties. Where an auditor breaches duties imposed on the auditor by statute (such as s 311), the company may sue for damages for breach of this duty.[36] In these circumstances, only the company may sue, given that the statutory duties are enacted in order to protect the company.[37] There is a range of other statutory actions that might also be available to a company. The main one is the misleading and deceptive conduct cause of action pursuant to s 18 of the Australian Consumer Law (formerly section 52 of the *Trade Practices Act 1974* (Cth)).[38]

Often, the causes of action will be overlapping. Thus it will be open to a company to pursue all the causes of action listed above against an auditor who has not competently audited the company's records. The ways in which damages are assessed will often differ. In relation to proceedings based in contract, the general rule is that damages are assessed on the basis of one's 'expectation loss'. This means that the successful party may recover the amount that is necessary to put it in the same position as if the audit had been conducted properly. Damages in the tort of negligence are assessed on the basis of the amount that it takes to put the plaintiff in the position they were in prior to the negligent conduct. The quantum of damages for breach of statutory duty is often similar to that for breach of contractual duty.[39]

As a result of the operation of normal contract – and, particularly, negligence – principles, auditors might be burdened with a legal liability beyond their level of fault. A moment of inattention in checking company records can result in an auditor failing to observe a significant problem or defect in a company's finances. If the defect had been detected by the auditor it may have enabled the company to, say, stave off insolvency and thereby save many millions of dollars. In order to deal with this possibility, changes introduced as part of CLERP 9 reduced the potential liability of auditors.

---

33   For example, see *Alexander v Cambridge Credit Corporation Ltd* (1987) 9 NSWLR 310; *Northumberland Insurance Co Ltd (in liq) v Alexander* (1988) 13 ACLR 170.

34   *Columbia Coffee & Tea Pty Ltd v Churchill* (1992) 29 NSWLR 141; *Strategic Minerals Corporation NL v Basham* (1996) 15 ACLC 1155; but cf *Esanda Finance Corporation Ltd v Peat Marwick Hungerfords* (1997) 188 CLR 241.

35   See *Esanda Finance Corporation Ltd v Peat Marwick Hungerfords* (1997) 188 CLR 241.

36   *AWA Ltd v Daniels (t/as Deloitte Haskins & Sells) (No 2)* (1992) 9 ACSR 983.

37   Ibid.

38   *Competition and Consumer Act 2010* (Cth) Sch 2, s 18. (The full text of the Australian Consumer Law (ACL) is set out in Schedule 2 of the *Competition and Consumer Act 2010* (Cth), formerly the *Trade Practices Act 1974* (Cth)).

39   Ibid.

Two key changes that were introduced were (i) to enable audit firms to incorporate (so that liability is restricted to the auditor(s) actually responsible); and (ii) to introduce a system of 'proportionate liability' in relation to damages actions involving (but not limited to) auditors concerning economic loss or property damage stemming from misleading or deceptive conduct.

8.6.2 Registration of audit companies

Before the CLERP 9 changes, only a natural person could be registered as an auditor under the Corporations Act; companies could not be registered as auditors. Because of this, partnerships were the main business structure employed by auditing firms. The consequence of this, given that audit partners were subject to unlimited joint and several liability for professional default, was that all partners in an audit firm could be liable for losses caused by another partner in the firm, even if they had no involvement in the particular conduct causing loss. Giving audit firms the option to incorporate was considered the best way to overcome this liability issue.

Section 1299A requires companies to apply to ASIC for registration as an 'authorised audit company'. Section 1299B states that a company may only be registered as an authorised audit company if all of the following conditions are met:

- Each of the directors of the company is a registered company auditor and is not disqualified from managing a corporation under Part 2D.6;
- Each share in the company is held and beneficially owned by a person who is an individual or the legal representative of an individual;
- A majority of the votes that may be cast at a general meeting of the company attach to shares in the company that are held and beneficially owned by individuals who are registered company auditors;
- ASIC is satisfied that the company has adequate and appropriate professional indemnity insurance; and
- The company is not an externally administered body corporate.

8.6.3 Proportionate liability

Prior to the CLERP 9 reforms, audit partners in firms were jointly and severally liable for professional default within the firm, thus exposing each partner to unlimited liability. Auditors had traditionally protected themselves from unlimited liability through professional indemnity insurance. However, as a result of the collapse of HIH, insurers in Australia adopted much tougher risk-selection protocols, which meant that many auditors found it extremely difficult to obtain adequate insurance, or were paying much higher premiums to get the level of professional indemnity insurance they wanted. As a consequence, many auditing firms reduced the scope of the audit and other services provided to their clients, in order to be able to obtain insurance, or obtain it at a reasonable rate.

In response to these problems, the CLERP 9 legislation implemented a regime of 'proportionate' liability to all professional advisers, including auditors. The basic thrust of the provisions is that for claims not involving dishonesty or deliberate breaches, the liability of financial advisers would be commensurate with their degree of wrongdoing.

8.7 Qualifications of auditors

The audit role can only be fulfilled properly if auditors have high-level skills and expertise. Before the CLERP 9 reforms, the law required prospective auditors to have completed a three-year degree course in accountancy from an Australian university, or to have other qualifications and experience that, in the opinion of ASIC, were equivalent to such a degree. In addition to this, professional accounting bodies required completion of an advanced training course in auditing; however, this was not mandatory.

CLERP 9 introduced minimum competency requirements, and standards-based practical experience requirements for all auditors in order to enhance public confidence in auditors. The specific amendments to the Corporations Act in this regard include:

- providing that the practical experience requirements for registration may be satisfied by completion of all the components of a competency standard in auditing;[40]
- revising the education requirements for registration to include completion of a specialist course in auditing;[41]
- making an auditor's continued registration subject to compliance with any conditions that may be imposed by ASIC in accordance with the regulations (with new Corporations Regulations introduced to deal with this);
- replacing the requirement for auditors to lodge a triennial statement with a new requirement to lodge an annual statement;[42] and
- revising the types of matters that may be referred to the Companies Auditors and Liquidators Disciplinary Board (CALDB, now known as CADB after the disciplining of liquidators was removed in 2017) in light of the above.[43]

8.8 Uniform auditing standards

CLERP 9 amended the Corporations Act to give auditing standards the force of law, a status long enjoyed by accounting standards. All registered company auditors, not just professional accounting members (as had been the case previously), are required to use auditing standards when performing auditing work. Division 2A in Part 12 of the ASIC Act, inserted into the legislation through CLERP 9, relates to:

---

40   See *Corporations Act 2001* (Cth) ss 1280A and 1280(2)(b). *Corporations Regulations 2001* (Cth) reg 9.2.01 sets out the practical experience that is prescribed for the purposes of subparagraph 1280(2)(b)(ii). Regulation 9.2.01 provides that the applicant will have had at least 3000 hours' work in auditing, including at least 750 hours spent supervising the audits of companies, during the five years immediately before the date of the application. The expression 'work in auditing' means work under the direction of a registered company auditor, which includes appraising the operations of companies and forming opinions on the matters specified in *Corporations Act 2001* (Cth) ss 307 (Audit), 308 (Auditor's report on annual financial report) and 309 (Auditor's report on half-year financial report). See further ASIC Regulatory Guide (RG) 180 *Auditor Registration* (June 2016).

41   See *Corporations Act 2001* (Cth) ss 1280(2A) and 1280(2B).

42   Ibid. s 1287A. (It should be noted that auditors of public companies and schemes may also need to lodge an annual transparency report under Pt 2M.4A.)

43   Ibid. s 1292(1). Liquidator regulation is no longer included, so the L no longer appears in the name ('CADB').

- the interpretation of auditing standards;[44]
- the powers of the AUASB to make auditing standards;[45]
- the requirements that the AUASB must comply with when making standards; and
- the giving of directions to the AUASB by the Financial Reporting Council (FRC) (see below) and the Minister.

Section 307A of the Corporations Act requires audits of a financial report for a financial year and audits or reviews of a financial report for a half-year period to be conducted in accordance with auditing standards. Sections 308 (Auditor's report on annual financial report) and 309 (Auditor's report on half-year financial report) have been amended to require auditors to include in their reports any statements or disclosures required by the auditing standards: sections 308(3A) and 309(5A).

8.9 Audit oversight

Prior to CLERP 9, there was little genuine oversight of the auditing profession. The oversight that existed was largely self-regulatory, undertaken largely by the professional accounting bodies. This obviously carried a serious risk: that professional bodies would champion the interests of their members rather than broader community interests, thereby potentially under-mining the quality and independence of the audit process.

Following CLERP 9, the role of the FRC, a statutory body created to oversee the accounting standard-setting process, was expanded to include responsibility for overseeing auditor-independence requirements and audit standard-setting. As part of this change, a reconstituted Auditing and Assurance Standards Board was established,[46] under the aegis of the FRC, with an expanded, more representative membership and government-appointed chairperson (to over-come criticisms that the body lacked independence). These arrangements bring together, under a single oversight body – the FRC – policy advice and oversight functions for the key elements of the financial reporting framework. It is assumed that having policy direction coming from a single overarching body will lead to better oversight and protect the independence of the two technical boards within the structure.

In order to allow it to fulfil its role, the FRC was given sweeping powers. Section 225 of the ASIC Act was amended to state that the FRC is formally responsible for overseeing both the AASB and the AUASB.

---

44   See ASIC Act s 234A.

45   *Corporations Act 2001* (Cth) s 336 provides AUASB with the authority to make auditing standards for the purposes of the Act. An auditing standard must be in writing and must not be inconsistent with the Corporations Act or the Corporations Regulations. See also *Corporations Act 2001* (Cth) s 1455.

46   ASIC Act ss 227A and 227B establish the AUASB as a statutory body, and set out its functions and powers: these include the power to make an Australian auditing standard by issuing the text of an international standard with any minimum modification to ensure that the standard operates effectively, having regard to the existing Australian legislative framework and institutional regulatory arrangements. The AUASB, when performing its functions, *must* follow the broad strategic direction determined by the FRC under ASIC Act ss 225(2A)(c), 225(7) and 234C. In relation to auditing standards, see also, especially, s 234D(3).

The FRC's functions in relation to auditor independence are set out in section 225(2B) of the ASIC Act. These include:

- monitoring and assessing the nature and overall adequacy of:
  - ◦ the systems and processes used by auditors to ensure compliance with auditor independence requirements;
  - ◦ professional accounting bodies for planning and performing quality assurance reviews of audit work;
  - ◦ the investigation and disciplinary procedures of the professional accounting bodies;
- monitoring overall compliance by companies and other entities with audit-related disclosure requirements;
- giving the Minister and professional accounting bodies reports and advice about the above matters; and
- promoting the teaching of professional and business ethics by the professional accounting bodies, universities and other tertiary institutions.

Despite the FRC's extensive role in ensuring auditor independence, enforcement of auditor-independence requirements is the responsibility of either ASIC or the professional accounting bodies (depending on whether the independence requirement is contained in the Corporations Act or in APES 110 *Code of Ethics for Professional Accountants*), rather than of the FRC.

8.10 Audit committees

An effective audit committee, which is a committee of the board of directors, can play a critical role in financial reporting by overseeing and monitoring the management's and the auditor's participation in the financial reporting process. They can increase the credibility of the financial reporting process by monitoring the selection of financial accounting policies, and meeting regularly with internal and external auditors, at least occasionally in the absence of management.

A requirement for all listed companies to establish an audit committee was originally proposed to be part of CLERP 9. However, the ASX took charge of this proposal, coinciding with its taking charge of corporate governance best-practice recommendations, originally also proposed to be part of CLERP 9. The ASX introduced a Listing Rule (effective 1 January 2003) mandating audit committees for the top 500 companies. A subsequent review reduced the requirement for compliance with the 2003 ASX *Principles of Good Corporate Governance and Best Practice Recommendations* on committee composition and other matters to only the top 300. Before this, although many listed companies had audit committees, their formation was entirely voluntary. Currently, ASX Listing Rule 12.7 requires that an entity included in the S&P All Ordinaries Index at the beginning of its financial year have an audit committee during that year. If an entity is in the top 300 of that Index, the composition, operation and responsibilities of the audit committee must comply with the relevant recommendations found in the 2014 ASX *CG Principles and Recommendations*.[47]

----

47   ASX, *CG Principles and Recommendations* (2014) <www.asx.com.au/documents/asx-compliance/cgc-principles-and-recommendations-3rd-edn.pdf>.

For an audit committee to be effective and not merely a cosmetic construct, research has shown that it should be composed entirely of independent or non-executive directors, at least some of whom have financial expertise; should have an audit committee charter; and should meet frequently.[48] Recommendation 4.1(a)(1) and (2) of the 2014 ASX *CG Principles and Recommendations* thus state that:

> The board of a listed entity should ... have an audit committee which ... has at least three members, all of whom are non-executive directors and a majority of whom are independent directors ... and ... is chaired by an independent director, who is not the chair of the board.

In terms of expertise, the Commentary to this Recommendation states that:

> The audit committee should be of sufficient size and independence, and its members between them should have the accounting and financial expertise and a sufficient understanding of the industry in which the entity operates, to be able to discharge the committee's mandate effectively.

Recommendation 4.1(a)(3) expects that the charter of the audit committee should be disclosed. The Commentary states that the charter should clearly set out the audit committee's role and confer on it all necessary powers to perform that role. This will usually include the right to obtain information, interview management and internal and external auditors (with or without management present), and seek advice from external consultants or specialists where the committee considers that necessary or appropriate.

Research has provided evidence of increased financial reporting and/or audit quality in association with effective audit committees: reduced manipulation of accounting numbers,[49] greater willingness to issue appropriately modified auditor's reports,[50] a lower incidence of fraudulent financial reporting and financial restatements,[51] a lower incidence of auditor switching following an unfavourable auditor's report,[52] a lower incidence of auditor resignation[53] and a higher frequency of engagement of industry specialist auditors.[54]

---

48   For a review of this research see FT DeZoort, DR Hermanson, D Archambeault and SA Reed, 'Audit committee effectiveness: A synthesis of the empirical audit committee literature' (2002) 21 *Journal of Accounting Literature* 38–75; C Ghafran and N Sullivan, 'The governance role of audit committees: Reviewing a decade of evidence' (2013) 15 *International Journal of Management Reviews* 381.

49   A Klein, 'Audit committee, board of director characteristics, and earnings management' (2002) 33 *Journal of Accounting and Economics* 375; Q Yasser and A Mamun, 'Audit committee structure and earnings management in Asia Pacific' (2016) 2 *Economics and Business Review* 66.

50   JV Carcello and TL Neal, 'Audit committee composition and auditor reporting' (2000) 75 *Accounting Review* 453–67.

51   LJ Abbott, S Parker and GF Peters, 'Audit committee characteristics and restatements' (2004) 23 *Auditing: A Journal of Practice and Theory* 69–87.

52   JV Carcello and TL Neal, 'Audit committee characteristics and auditor dismissal following "new" going concern reports' (2003) 78 *The Accounting Review* 95–117.

53   HY Lee, V Mande and R Ortman, 'The effect of audit committee and board of director independence on auditor resignation' (2004) 23 *Auditing: A Journal of Practice and Theory* 131–46.

54   YM Chen, R Moroney and K Houghton, 'Audit committee composition and the use of an industry specialist audit firm' (2005) 45 *Accounting and Finance* 217–39.

8.11 Conclusion

It will be clear from this chapter not only that auditors and audits are nowadays pivotal to corporate governance, but also that the threshold of what is expected of auditors and audits has been raised considerably in recent times. There is now an expectation that auditors should be independent, that they should report breaches of the law and that if they do not do so, action will be taken against them – either by private suit or by the corporate regulator. The ultimate objective of the CLERP 9 reforms and the audit committee ASX Listing Rules change, as it is of similar reforms in several other countries, is to ensure that financial statements better reflect the true financial position of corporations. This will enable investors to make sound investment decisions. These reforms will not ensure that corporations do not collapse in future, but they should, it is hoped, ensure that the signs of a possible collapse are detected early.

9
DIRECTORS' DUTIES AND LIABILITY

A director is an essential component of corporate governance. Each director is placed at the apex of the structure of direction and management of a company. The higher the office that is held by a person, the greater the responsibility that falls upon him or her. The role of a director is significant as their actions may have a profound effect on the community, and not just shareholders, employees and creditors.

Justice Middleton in *Australian Securities and Investments Commission (ASIC) v Healey* [2011] FCA 717 at [14]

Those responsible for the stewardship of HIH ignored the warning signs at their own, the group's and the public's peril. The culture of apparent indifference or deliberate disregard on the part of those responsible for the well-being of the company set in train a series of events that culminated in a calamity of monumental proportions.

Report of the HIH Royal Commission (Owen Report) (Department of the Treasury, 2003) Vol.1, xiii–xiv

9.1 Introduction

As a general rule, directors owe their duties to the company as a whole, not to individual shareholders.[1] Historically, directors' duties and liability were discussed under general law duties (duties at common law or in equity); more recently,[2] they were added to under statutory duties. Under general law duties, most courts and commentators usually draw a distinction between equitable duties based on loyalty and good faith, with a particular focus on fiduciary duties, and the duty to act with due care and diligence (the duty of care). The duty of care may arise under principles of equity and at common law. Fiduciary duties in Australian law are proscriptive, not prescriptive.[3] That is, the duties prohibit the fiduciary from engaging in particular conduct rather than prescribing what the fiduciary must do in particular situations. The failure to act in a reasonable manner has traditionally fallen within the domain of the duty of care, rather than fiduciary duties in equity. The range of equitable duties that are owed by company directors are generally recognised as follows:

1. the duty to act honestly and in the company's best interests;

2. the duty to act for a proper purpose;

3. the duty not to fetter their discretions;

4. the duty to avoid a conflict of interest; and

5. the duty not to act so as to obtain a private profit.

---

1   *Percival v Wright* [1902] 2 Ch 421. For an example of recognised exception, see *Brunninghausen v Glavanics* (1999) 46 NSWLR 538 (which deals with closely held family companies).

2   For discussion on the rationale and development of directors' statutory duties in Australia, see Jason Harris, Anil Hargovan and Janet Austin, 'Shareholder primacy revisited: Does the public interest have any role in statutory duties?' (2008) 26 *Company and Securities Law Journal (C&SLJ)* 355.

3   *Breen v Williams* (1996) 186 CLR 71.

Duties 4 and 5 are accepted as being fiduciary duties. Duty number 3 is not considered fiduciary in nature. As to duties 1 and 2, there is considerable debate as to whether these duties are fiduciary or not. The majority of the WA Court of Appeal, in the long-running Bell case, has held that the duties are fiduciary in nature,[4] but this decision has been strongly criticised.[5] Those arguing against duties 1 and 2 being fiduciary note that these duties seem to impose positive obligations on directors (to act honestly and to act properly) rather than to prohibit conduct.

These duties are considered strict duties by the courts, which have held on numerous occasions that directors can be in breach of these duties irrespective of the fact that they acted without fault, in terms of either negligence or intent. It has also been held that, as a general rule, the fact that directors acted in what they believed to be the best interests of the company as a whole will not serve as a general defence for a breach of these duties. It also does not matter whether the company suffered any loss.[6] The remedies available will depend upon the nature of the breach. A breach of the duty of care will usually allow for a claim for damages by the company. A breach of the duty not to fetter discretion may give rise to a right to seek compensation or to specifically enforce a contract (depending on what the effect of the unlawful fetter is). Where directors act for an improper purpose, their conduct may be overturned and they may be liable to pay compensation for causing the company to engage in improper conduct. The most common example of this is the improper issue of shares by company directors, which may be challenged by existing members who can seek court orders to overturn the share issue. Similarly, a failure to act in the best interests of the company may lead to the transaction being overturned in equity. This may also overlap with breaches of the duty of care and may give rise to damages payable to the company. The equitable remedy of an injunction may also be available for breaches of both fiduciary and non-fiduciary duties in equity.

The broadest remedies are available for breaches of fiduciary duties (duties 4 and 5, and possibly 1 and 2).[7] Remedies for breaches of fiduciary duties can include an account of profits (stripping away improper benefits from the defaulting fiduciary),[8] equitable compensation or a constructive trust over property held by a defaulting fiduciary or their associate. Where a director has acted under a conflict of interest (for example by entering into a transaction with the company) and the company wishes to reverse the transaction, the remedy of rescission

---

4   *Westpac Banking Corporation v Bell Group Ltd (in liq)* (2012) WAR 1. For a discussion of the issues in this case see Anil Hargovan and Jason Harris, 'For whom the bell tolls: Directors' duties to creditors after *Bell*' (2013) 35 *Sydney Law Review* 433; Rosemary Langford, *Directors' Duties* (Federation Press, 2014); Dyson Heydon, Mark Leeming and Peter Turner, *Meagher Gummow and Lehane's Equity Doctrines and Remedies* (LexisNexis Butterworths, 5th ed, 2014) Ch 2.

5   See, for example, TF Bathurst and Sienna Merope, 'It tolls for thee: Accessorial liability after *Bell v Westpac*' (2013) 87 *Australian Law Journal* 831; William Gummow, 'The equitable duties of company directors' (2013) 87 *Australian Law Journal* 753; Matthew Conaglen, 'Interaction between statutory and general law duties concerning company director conflicts' (2013) 31 *C&SLJ* 403.

6   *Regal (Hastings) Ltd v Gulliver* [1967] 2 AC 134.

7   For a useful discussion on the remedies available for breach of fiduciary duty, see *Western Areas Exploration Pty Ltd v Streeter (No 3)* (2009) 73 ACSR 494.

8   *Regal (Hastings) Ltd v Gulliver* [1967] 2 AC 134; *Furs Ltd v Tomkies* (1936) 54 CLR 583.

may be available. However, the ability of the company to rescind the transaction is limited by a number of exceptions.[9]

In contrast with the judicial approach to directors' fiduciary duties, in the case of the directors' duty to act with due care and diligence the courts originally insisted that directors would only be in breach of this duty if they acted with gross negligence and only if the company suffered damages because the directors acted negligently.[10] In more recent times the courts have grappled with the overlapping nature of the duty as it arises in both equity and common law, and how these duties interact with the statutory duty recognised in s 180(1) of the *Corporations Act 2001* (Cth) (the Act).[11] In addition, under the statutory duty of care, damages suffered by the company need not be proven; only a foreseeable risk of harm to the company needs to be proven.[12]

Directors' duty of care and diligence was, for many years, considered to impose remarkably low standards on directors as the courts used gross negligence[13] as the yardstick for liability and judged a breach of these duties against subjective standards – '[a] director need not exhibit in the performance of his duties a greater degree of skill than may reasonably be expected from a person of his knowledge and experience'.[14] The idea was that the shareholders were ultimately responsible for the unwise appointments of directors that had led to the standards of care, skill and diligence being so low.[15] Historically, directors were viewed as country gentlemen, and not expected to realise the significance of certain information in the financial accounts[16] or to even be aware of the company's affairs.[17]

This laidback approach changed after the landmark 1995 decision in *Daniels v Anderson*,[18] which indicated that the Australian courts were in fact prepared to expect high standards of care and diligence of directors, including non-executive directors.[19]

---

9   The exceptions were if the company affirmed the transaction with knowledge of its right to avoid it; innocent third parties would be prejudiced by the election to avoid the transaction; the company unduly delayed acting to exercise its right to avoid the transaction (a form of estoppel); or it became impossible for the parties' rights to be restored to the position obtaining before (*restitutio in integrum*) the transaction was entered into.

10   *Australian Securities and Investments Commission v Rich* (2009) 75 ACSR 1, [7193].

11   See, in particular, *Daniels v Anderson* (1995) 37 NSWLR 438; 16 ACSR 607 at 652 *et seq*; *Australian Securities and Investments Commission v Rich* (2009) 75 ACSR 1 [7193]; *Vines v Australian Securities and Investments Commission* (2007) 73 NSWLR 451.

12   *Australian Securities and Investments Commission v Rich* (2009) 75 ACSR 1 [7193].

13   Lindley MR in *Lagunas Nitrate Co v Lagunas Syndicate* [1899] 2 Ch 392 at 435.

14   *Re City Equitable Fire Insurance Co Ltd* [1925] Ch 407.

15   For example, see *Turquand v Marshall* (1869) LR 4 Ch App 376.

16   For example, see *Re Denham and Co* (1883) 25 Ch D 752.

17   In *Re Cardiff Savings Bank* [1892] 2 Ch 100 (Marquis of Bute's case), in dismissing a claim of negligence against the Marquis, who had become the president of the board of the bank at the age of six months and held that position for over 40 years (during which time he attended only one board meeting), the court said that the Marquis was entitled to rely on the bank's managers to perform their duties properly and could not be liable for their neglect.

18   (1995) 37 NSWLR 438.

19   For discussion on the development of the modern law in this area, see Anil Hargovan, 'Corporate law's new love: Section 232(4) and the director's duty of care' (1994) 3 *Asia Pacific Law Review* 20; Sally Sievers, 'Farewell to the sleeping director – the modern judicial and legislative approach to directors' duties of care, skill and diligence – further developments' (1993) 21 *Australian Business Law Review* 111 and 'Directors' duty of care: What is the new standard?' (1997) 15 *C&SLJ* 392. See generally, as far as the UK is concerned, ICSA, *ICSA Guidance and Reports: Directors' Duty to Exercise Care, Skill and Diligence* (January 2013).

Nowadays in Australia, the courts more often use the statutory duties of directors (rather than their duties at common law or in equity) to hold directors liable.[20] Under contemporary law, a discussion of directors' duties and liability can be adequately based on provisions in the *Corporations Act 2001* (Cth), notwithstanding the fact that most of the primary statutory duties imposed upon directors 'have effect in addition to, and not in derogation of, any rule of law relating to the duty or liability of a person because of their office or employment in relation to a corporation'.[21] In other words, directors' statutory duties are most important, irrespective of the fact that the legislature did not intend to codify directors' duties at common law and in equity.

We have thus adopted the approach of explaining directors' duties and liability primarily by way of the statutory provisions. Not only are these provisions comprehensive, but in more recent times they have formed the basis of most of the litigation in this area, due largely to the introduction in 1993 of the civil penalty provisions and the lower standard of proof (balance of probabilities) under those provisions.

The enforcement of directors' duties is of particular importance. Enforcement of the civil penalty provisions, with reference to case studies (HIH Insurance Ltd, James Hardie Ltd and One.Tel Ltd), is discussed below. The first part of this chapter will demonstrate that enforcement by the Australian Securities and Investments Commission (ASIC) of civil penalty provisions has been its most common enforcement action in recent years. However, in Chapter 10 we also touch upon the enforcement of directors' duties by the corporation under the statutory derivative action (Part 2F.1A) and the rights of minority shareholders to apply for various remedies in the case of unfairly prejudicial or unfairly discriminatory or oppressive conduct by the corporation or its directors (Part 2F.1). Finally, we deal with injunctions under s 1324 of the *Corporations Act 2001* (Cth), which allow ASIC or 'a person whose interests have been affected' by a contravention of the Act to stop such conduct and to obtain damages for loss suffered because of such conduct.

9.2 Part 9.4B: Civil penalty provisions or pecuniary penalty provisions

9.2.1 Overview

As far as directors' duties and liabilities are concerned, the Corporations Act deals with the most important duties of directors, and breaches of them, under the 'civil penalty provisions'.[22] This basically means that if a breach of any of these provisions is proven, the court will make a declaration of contravention, which is then considered to be conclusive evidence of the following matters:

20   This was not always the case. Prior to the insolvent trading cases in the late 1980s and early 1990s (such as *Statewide Tobacco Services Ltd v Morley* (1990) 2 ACSR 405 and *Commonwealth Bank of Australia v Friedrich* (1991) 5 ACSR 115), which articulated higher standards of care, there was a dearth of reported cases on the directors' statutory duty of care and diligence. See further, Hargovan, 'Corporate law's new love' (1994).
21   *Corporations Act 2001* (Cth) s 185(a).
22   This is confirmed in para 5.3 of Part 1.5 (Small Business Guide) of the Act, listing most of the civil penalty provisions as 'some of the most important duties' of directors of proprietary companies.

- the court that made the declaration;
- the civil penalty provision that was contravened;
- the person who contravened the provision;
- the conduct that constituted the contravention; and
- if the contravention is of a corporation/scheme civil penalty provision[23] – the corporation or registered scheme to which the conduct related.

Once such an order of contravention is made, there are primarily three further orders that ASIC may seek: disqualification orders (for breaches of corporation/scheme civil penalty provisions), pecuniary penalty orders, and/or compensation orders. In recent years it has been common for ASIC to pursue disqualification orders and penalty orders rather than compensation. The relevant corporation (or responsible entity of a registered scheme) may also apply for a compensation order,[24] and the corporation/scheme is also entitled to intervene in any proceedings for a disqualification order or pecuniary penalty (which may only be initiated by ASIC) and is entitled to be heard on all matters other than whether the declaration or order should be made.[25] It is important to emphasise that a declaration order must be made before a pecuniary penalty or disqualification order can be sought by ASIC. A declaration of contravention is not, however, a necessary prerequisite to a compensation order being sought. We deal with disqualification orders, pecuniary penalty orders and compensation orders in some detail later in this chapter.

As far as pecuniary penalty orders are concerned, a court may order a person to pay the Commonwealth up to $200,000 as a pecuniary penalty or a civil penalty – except for 'financial services civil penalty provisions' (including, for example, continuous disclosure, false trading, market manipulation and insider trading)[26] – where the maximum penalty is $1 million. It should be noted that civil penalty orders have nothing to do with orders to cover damages suffered by the company because of a breach of the civil penalty provisions. Civil penalties are statutory penalties paid to the Commonwealth simply for a breach of what are considered to be some of the most important provisions of the Act, namely those in s 1317E. The main aim of these pecuniary penalty or civil penalty provisions is to highlight some of the core provisions of the Act relating to directors' duties and to serve as a serious warning to all directors and officers not to contravene these provisions. This was explained as follows in *Australian Securities and Investments Commission v Adler*:[27]

> It is well established that the principal purpose of a pecuniary penalty is to act as a personal deterrent and a deterrent to the general public against a repetition of like conduct.

---

23   *Corporations Act 2001* (Cth) ss 1317F and 1317E(2).
24   Ibid. s 1317H(2). See further, *V-Flow Pty Ltd v Holyoake Industries (Vic) Pty Ltd* (2013) 93 ACSR 76.
25   See *Corporations Act 2001* (Cth) s 1317J(3). In relation to 'financial services civil penalty provisions', any person who suffers damage in relation to a contravention, or alleged contravention, of such a provision can also apply for a compensation order: s 1317J(3A).
26   There are separate penalty amounts in s 1317G for other penalty provisions dealing with market integrity rules, derivative transaction rules and the best interests duties for providers of financial services.
27   (2002) 42 ACSR 80.

9.2.2 The civil penalty provisions

9.2.2.1 Section 180: Duty of care and diligence – civil obligation[28]

Directors' duty of due care and diligence are captured in s 180 of the Act. This section provides that directors or other officers of a corporation must exercise their powers and discharge their duties with the degree of care and diligence that a reasonable person would exercise if they:

- were a director or officer of a corporation in the corporation's circumstances; and
- occupied the office held by, and had the same responsibilities within the corporation as, the director or officer.

The fact that this duty is judged against objective standards ('a reasonable person') means that the standards of this duty have been raised considerably; this is consistent with its common law counterpart, established in *Daniels v Anderson*.[29] No longer can directors escape a breach of this duty by relying on the fact that they lacked the knowledge or experience to take a certain decision. In other words, they would not be able to rely on the notion that in the performance of their duties they did not exhibit 'a greater degree of skill than may reasonably be expected from a person of [their] knowledge and experience'.[30] In order to ensure consistency in the application of this duty, several provisos have been included: first, the duty is to act as a reasonable *person* would act, not as a reasonable *director* would act. There is no applicable standard for what a reasonable director would do, because directors are not like lawyers or doctors, who apply industry-accepted professional standards. Every director and every company is different. Second, the duty of care and diligence is to be judged against the standards expected of directors or officers in corporations comparable to the corporation in which the accused director or officer held office. Third, the reasonable person benchmark is to be assessed by reference to the office and responsibilities that the director or other officer had within the corporation.[31] The duty posits a reasonable person in a similar position in a similar company and assesses what they would have done against what the director actually did or failed to do.

The expression 'same responsibilities' in s 180(1)(b) requires a consideration of all the work in fact undertaken by the relevant director or officer. So if a director or officer has dual roles – as, for example, a company secretary and in-house counsel – both roles are to be taken into account.[32]

The courts adopt the following test to determine a breach of s 180(1):

> In determining whether a director has exercised reasonable care and diligence one must ask what an ordinary person, with the knowledge and experience of the defendant, might

---

28   For a fuller discussion, see Jason Harris, Anil Hargovan and Michael Adams, *Australian Corporate Law* (LexisNexis, 5th edn, 2016) Ch 17. See also Jean J du Plessis, 'A comparative analysis of directors' duty of care, skill and diligence in South Africa and in Australia' (2010) *Acta Juridica* 263; *Australian Securities and Investments Commission v Cassimatis (No 8)* (2016) 336 ALR 209.

29   (1995) 37 NSWLR 438.

30   *Re City Equitable Fire Insurance Co Ltd* [1925] Ch 407. See further *Australian Securities and Investments Commission v Rich* (2009) 75 ACSR 1, [7207].

31   See further *Australian Securities and Investments Commission v Flugge* (2016) 119 ACSR 1 for a detailed discussion of the role of expert evidence.

32   *Shafron v Australian Securities and Investments Commission* (2012) 247 CLR 465.

have been expected to have done in the circumstances if he or she was acting on their own behalf.[33]

The precise degree or standard of care and diligence required is to be determined with reference to the particular circumstances of the company. These include:[34]

- the type of company;
- the size and nature of the company's business;
- the composition of the board;
- the director's and officer's position and responsibilities within the company;
- the particular function the director or officer is performing;
- the experience or skills of the particular director or officer; and
- the circumstances of the specific case.

The application of s 180(1) to directors (executive and non-executive) and officers (company's general counsel and chief financial officer (CFO)) is demonstrated in Section 9.3.3 (below) with reference to the decision in *Australian Securities and Investments Commission v Macdonald (No 11)*.[35] The content of the directors' duty of care, skill and diligence is also discussed in Section 9.3.4 with reference to the collection of the contemporary case authorities and legal principles in *Australian Securities and Investments Commission v Rich*.[36]

BUSINESS JUDGMENT RULE

There is, however, some protection for directors against a breach of duty of care claim in a safe-haven provision called the 'business judgment' rule[37] – 'business judgment' refers to any decision to take or not take action in respect of a matter relevant to the business operations of the corporation.[38] It is assumed that directors and other officers acted with the required degree of care and diligence if, in exercising a business judgment, they met four standards (s 180(2)):

1. They must have made the judgment in good faith for a proper purpose.

2. They must not have had a material personal interest in the subject matter of the judgment.

3. They must have informed themselves about the subject matter of the judgment to the extent they reasonably believed to be appropriate.

4. They must have rationally believed that the judgment was in the best interests of the corporation.

---

33 *Australian Securities and Investments Commission v Adler* (2002) 41 ACSR 72.
34 *Australian Securities and Investments Commission v Rich* (2009) 75 ACSR 1, Ch 23.
35 (2009) 256 ALR 199.
36 (2009) 75 ACSR 1.
37 For discussion on the origins of the business judgment rule and its operation at common law, see Paul Redmond, 'Safe Harbours or Sleepy Hollows: Does Australia Need a Statutory Business Judgment Rule? in I Ramsay (ed.), *Corporate Governance and the Duties of Company Directors* (Melbourne University Centre for Corporate Law and Securities Regulation, 1997).
38 *Corporations Act 2001* (Cth) s 180(3).

As far as the last requirement is concerned, it is provided that the director's or officer's belief that the judgment is in the best interests of the corporation is a rational one unless the belief is one that no reasonable person in their position would hold. It should be noted that this provides considerable protection to directors, as the requirement is not the ordinary objective requirement that 'a reasonable person in their position will hold', but that 'no reasonable person in their position will hold'. This ensures that only in extreme circumstances, where a director or officer blindly believed something that 'no other person in their position' would believe, will a court withhold the protection of the business judgment rule based on the fact that it was not a rational belief that their business judgment was in the best interests of the corporation. The operation of the business judgment rule is discussed further below with reference to its application in *Australian Securities and Investments Commission v Adler*[39] and to the judicial views on its meaning expressed by Austin J in *Australian Securities and Investments Commission v Rich.*[40]

It is of considerable importance to note that the business judgment rule will only provide protection to directors when the courts must consider whether or not they acted with the required care and diligence. It does not operate in relation to duties under any other provision of the Act – for example, the duty to act in good faith (s 181); the duty not to use their position to gain personally or cause detriment to the corporation (s 182); the duty not to use information to gain personally or cause detriment to the corporation (s 183); and the duty to prevent insolvent trading (s 588G).

There have been suggestions that the business judgment rule be broadened to include other potential liabilities that may be incurred by directors, with both the Australian Institute of Company Directors and leading legal adviser, and former corporate law judge, the Hon Robert Austin (who decided the *Australian Securities and Investments Commission v Rich* case, among many others),[41] proposing potential models. It seems that the operation of the rule will continue to be a matter of keen public interest for the foreseeable future.[42]

DELEGATION AND RELIANCE

The ability to delegate responsibilities and rely on subordinates to carry out tasks is an essential part of effective management. The general law (*Australian Securities and Investments Commission v Adler*[43]) and sections 198D and 189 of the Act permit directors to delegate powers and to reasonably rely on others for information or advice.

In order to obtain the benefit of the reliance defence, the director's reliance on others must be reasonable, which is to be determined on the facts of each case. Justice Santow, in *ASIC v*

---

39   (2002) 41 ACSR 72.

40   (2009) 75 ACSR 1.

41   Robert Austin, 'Time to Lift the Grey Cloud of Litigation', *Australian Financial Review*, 21 March 2014, 33.

42   See Jean J du Plessis and Jim A Mathiopoulos, 'Wider protection for company directors' (2016) 31 *Australian Journal of Company Law (AJCL)* 287; Jason Harris and Anil Hargovan, 'Still a sleepy hollow? Directors' liability and the business judgment rule' (2016) 31 *AJCL* 319. See also Jean J du Plessis, 'Open sea or safe harbour? American, Australian and South African business judgment rules compared' (2011) 32 *Company Lawyer* 377, 380–2.

43   (2002) 41 ACSR 72.

Adler,[44] collated the judicial authorities on this issue and offered the following general legal principles in determining reasonableness:

- The function that has been delegated is such that it is proper to leave it to the delegate.
- The extent to which the director is put on inquiry or, given the facts of a case, should have been put on inquiry.
- The relationship between the director and the delegate must be such that the director honestly holds the belief that the delegate is trustworthy, competent and someone upon whom reliance can be placed. Knowledge that the delegate is dishonest and incompetent will make reliance unreasonable.
- The risk involved in the transaction and the nature of the transaction.
- The extent of steps taken by the director: for example, inquiries made or other circumstances engendering trust.
- Whether the position of the director is executive or non-executive (although, as noted by Santow J, the majority judges in *Daniels v Anderson* (1995) 37 NSWLR 438 moved away from this distinction).

The reliance defence is unavailable when management specifically brings a matter before the board for attention and the task for consideration is not an onerous one, as illustrated in *Australian Securities and Investments Commission v Macdonald (No 11)*, discussed further below.

9.2.2.2 Section 181: Duty of good faith – civil obligation[45]

A director or other officer of a corporation is also expected to exercise their powers and discharge their duties:

(a)   in good faith in the best interests of the corporation; and

(b)   for a proper purpose.

This duty is a slight extension of the equitable duty of directors – that they must always act bona fide in the best interests of the corporation. The part that has been added is that they must also act for a 'proper purpose'. This part was included because of several court cases in which it was held that if directors based their decisions primarily or substantially on the purpose for which a particular power was conferred upon them, a court would not set such decisions aside irrespective of the fact that partially or incidentally the power might have been exercised for an improper or impermissible purpose. On the other hand, if the decision was primarily or substantially taken for an improper or impermissible purpose (for example, issuing shares with a view to defending a hostile takeover of the company), a court will set such a decision aside irrespective of the fact that partially or incidentally the power might have been exercised for a proper purpose. Once the court has determined that primarily or substantially the power was misused, it will not help the directors to allege that they had not gained personally, that the company had benefited from the conduct or that they had acted honestly – the conduct of the

---

44   Ibid.
45   For a fuller discussion, see Harris, Hargovan and Adams, *Australian Corporate Law* (2016) Ch 15. See further *Australian Securities and Investments Commission v Flugge* (2016) 119 ACSR 1 from [1965].

directors under attack will then be set aside because of the breach of their strict fiduciary duty to exercise their powers for the purpose for which the power was conferred upon them.[46]

9.2.2.3 Sections 182 and 183: Duty not to use position or information to gain personally or cause detriment to the corporation[47]

These two duties are discussed together because they deal with basically the same situation. They cover typical conflict of interest situations. Directors occupy a unique position and have access to lots of information about the corporation's business, but they may not use their position or the information they obtain as directors to gain personally; or to gain an advantage for someone else; or to the detriment of the corporation. This duty will also cover situations in which directors use a corporate opportunity to make a secret profit or to allow someone else to gain from a corporate opportunity. It originates from the strict fiduciary duty on directors to act in the best interests of the corporation and to prevent a conflict between their duty to the corporation and their own self-interest.

The following rationale for the no-conflict rule and its codification was offered by Finkelstein J in *Australian Securities and Investments Commission v Vizard:*[48]

> [Sections 182 and 183] bear the stamp of 'regulatory offences'. On a daily basis, a director of a large public company will come across information that is not available to the public or even to the company's shareholders. According to the common law a director is denied the ability to use such information for his or her own purposes. It does not matter that the director's action causes no harm to the company or does not rob it of an opportunity which it might have exercised for its own advantage: *Regal (Hastings) Ltd v Gulliver.*[49] This rule admits of few exceptions. Parliament realised that the common law was too often ignored. The temptation to make an improper profit was too great. So Parliament decided to act. The Companies Acts were amended to create an offence if a director misused information obtained by reason of his fiduciary position. It is in this sense that the sections are regulatory in character, directed to avoiding the potential harmful consequences of a particular type of conduct.
>
> [Section 183 has] another equally important purpose. [It] seek[s] to establish a norm of behaviour that is necessary for the proper conduct of commercial life and so that people will have confidence that the running of the marketplace is in safe hands. For this reason a contravention of ... s 183 carries with it a significant degree of moral blameworthiness. There is moral blameworthiness because a contravention involves a serious breach of trust.

It should be noted that the duties in sections 182 and 183 also apply to the company's employees.[50]

---

46 See Jean J du Plessis, 'Directors' duty to use their powers for proper or permissible purposes' (2004) 16 *South African Mercantile Law Journal* 308, 320.

47 For a fuller discussion, see Harris, Hargovan and Adams, *Australian Corporate Law* (2016) Ch 16.

48 (2005) 145 FCR 57 at [28]–[29].

49 [1967] 2 AC 134.

50 For an example where senior employees were found to have contravened these duties see *Holyoake Industries (Vic) Pty Ltd v V-Flow Pty Ltd (No 2)* (2012) 88 ACSR 679 (the appeal in this decision did not overturn the findings relating to breach of fiduciary duty).

9.2.2.4 Part 2E: Duty relating to related-party transactions

Part 2E stems from the recommendations made by the Companies and Securities Advisory Committee (CSAC) in its *Report on Reform of the Law Governing Corporate Financial Transactions* in 1991. The Committee's draft legislation was intended to introduce 'detailed procedures to monitor and control those matters which [are] otherwise vulnerable to abuse by corporate controllers', including loans to directors, inter-corporate loans, asset transfers and excessive remuneration.[51]

The underlying principle introduced by the legislation was that financial benefits given to persons who are in a position to significantly influence the decision to give the benefit should be subject to shareholder approval unless they are on commercial terms. The legislation is based on the notion that 'uncommercial' transactions with related parties should be referred to disinterested shareholders before the transactions take place. These sentiments are currently echoed in s 207, which states the object of Part 2E as being to protect the interests of a public company's members as a whole by requiring member approval for giving financial benefits to related parties that could endanger those interests.

Part 2E prohibits a company from giving a financial benefit to a related party of the company unless:

- the giving of the financial benefit falls within one of several exceptions to the provision; or
- prior approval is obtained from shareholders to the giving of the financial benefit.[52]

For the purposes of Part 2E, each director of a public company is considered to be a related party of the public company. 'Financial benefit' is given a very wide meaning. In order to determine whether a transaction is a 'financial benefit', the economic and commercial substance of the transaction will be considered, and it is as a general rule irrelevant whether the related party delivered services or paid something (consideration given) to receive the financial benefit. 'Giving a financial benefit' includes things like making an informal agreement, oral agreement or agreement that has no binding force. It can be considered to be giving a financial benefit even if it does not involve paying money, but only confers a financial advantage on the related party. The following examples are given of financial benefits:

(a)   giving or providing the related party finance or property;

(b)   buying an asset from or selling an asset to the related party;

(c)   leasing an asset from or to the related party;

(d)   supplying services to or receiving services from the related party;

(e)   issuing securities or granting an option to the related party; and

(f)   taking up or releasing an obligation of the related party.[53]

---

51   CSAC, *Report on Reform of the Law Governing Corporate Financial Transactions* (The Committee) (1991) 11–12.

52   *Corporations Act 2001* (Cth) ss 208–229.

53   Ibid. s 229.

Two of the main exceptions, where members' approval is not required when a financial benefit is given to a related party, are arm's-length transactions[54] and reasonable remuneration and reimbursement of expenses incurred by directors and other officers.[55]

The civil penalty provisions will be contravened if a financial benefit is given to a related party without prior approval of the general meeting or without it falling under one of the statutory exceptions.[56] The operation of these provisions is illustrated below with reference to the decision in *Australian Securities and Investments Commission v Adler*.[57]

9.2.2.5 Parts 2M.2 and 2M.3: Duty relating to requirements for financial reports

Parts 2M.2 and 2M.3 contain detailed provisions regarding the keeping of financial records, financial reporting and directors' reports. As part of the CLERP 9 amendments, discussed in greater detail in Chapter 7, several of these provisions were refined, and new obligations were added to ensure that sound financial and other information is available to the public regarding the corporation's financial performance and financial practices. These provisions require directors to take all reasonable steps to comply with or to secure compliance with Parts 2M.2 and 2M.3. These provisions were raised for consideration in the Centro decision (*Australian Securities and Investments Commission v Healey*),[58] where the directors of a large public company were found to have failed to take all reasonable steps to ensure that the company complied with its reporting obligations under Part 2M.3 and to keep adequate financial records under Part 2M.2. The directors were all experienced business professionals who acted with qualified professional advisers. The board established an audit committee, which reviewed the draft financial reports, but in approving the final accounts the board failed to read all of the relevant information and hence could not be satisfied that the company was complying with its obligations.[59]

9.2.2.6 Part 5.7B: Duty to prevent insolvent trading[60]

Section 588G of the Act imposes a positive duty on directors to prevent insolvent trading by the corporation.[61] The statutory purpose of this section was considered by the NSW Court of Appeal in *Edwards v Australian Securities and Investments Commission*:

> [Its aim] is to discourage and provide a remedy for a particular type of commercial dishonesty or irresponsibility ... [which] occurs when a company that is at or approaching insolvency obtains a loan, or obtains property or services on credit, and either there is a

54 Ibid. s 210.
55 Ibid. s 211.
56 Ibid. s 1317E(1).
57 (2002) 41 ACSR 72.
58 (2011) 196 FCR 291.
59 See further Jean J du Plessis and Iain Meaney, 'Directors' liability for approving financial statements containing blatant incorrect items: Lessons from Australia for all directors in all jurisdictions' (2012) 33 *Company Lawyer* 273; and Philip Crutchfield and Catherine Button, 'Men over board: The burden of directors' duties in the wake of the Centro case' (2012) 30 *C&SLJ* 33.
60 For a fuller discussion, see Harris, Hargovan and Adams, *Australian Corporate Law* (2016) Ch 18.
61 For a comparative analysis of insolvent trading law see Jason Harris, 'Director liability for insolvent trading: Is the cure worse than the disease?' (2009) 23 *AJCL* 266.

director who knows or suspects the insolvency or approaching insolvency, or a reasonable person in the director's position would know or suspect it. In that situation, any
director ... can be made personally liable ... The section aims to encourage directors to
carry out their duties properly if the company is at or approaching insolvency, and
provides a sanction if they do not.[62]

This section applies to a person who is a director of a company at the time when the company
incurs a debt and the company is insolvent at that time, or becomes insolvent by incurring that
debt, or by incurring at that time debts including that debt; and at that time there are reasonable
grounds for suspecting that the company is insolvent, or would so become insolvent.[63] It is
important to note that the extended definition of director under s 9 of the Act discussed in
Chapter 4, which includes de facto and shadow directors, applies to this provision.

Section 95A of the Act provides that a company is insolvent if, and only if, the company is
unable to pay all the company's debts as and when they become due and payable.
A temporary lack of liquidity does not mean there is insolvency.[64] The practical difficulties in
assessing insolvent trading, and some of the indicia of insolvency, are recognised by Palmer
J in the following passage in *Hall v Poolman*:

> The law recognises that there is sometimes no clear dividing line between solvency and
> insolvency from the perspective of the directors of a trading company which is in
> difficulties. There is a difference between temporary illiquidity and "*an endemic shortage
> of working capital whereby liquidity can only restored by a successful outcome of
> business ventures in which the existing working capital has been deployed*" ... The first
> is an embarrassment, the second is a disaster. It is easy enough to tell the difference in
> hindsight, when the company has either weathered the storm or foundered with all hands;
> sometimes it is not so easy when the company is still contending with the waves. Lack of
> liquidity is not conclusive of insolvency, neither is availability of assets conclusive of
> solvency.[65]

Section 588E assists in proving insolvency under s 588G by allowing for the following rebut-
table presumptions to be made:

- continuing insolvency – if it can be proved that a company was insolvent at a particular
  time during the 12 months ending on the 'relation-back day' (as defined in s 9 of the Act:
  the date of filing the application for a compulsory winding up), it is presumed that the
  company remained insolvent thereafter; and

- absence of accounting records – if the company has contravened either s 286(1) or (2) by failing
  to keep or retain adequate financial records for seven years (except for a minor or technical
  breach), it is presumed that the company is insolvent during the period of contravention.

62   (2009) 76 ACSR 369 at [3] per Campbell JA.
63   For a list of relevant factors that may be used to determine whether or not there are reasonable grounds
      to suspect insolvency, see *Australian Securities and Investments Commission v Plymin (No 1)* (2003)
      46 ACSR 126.
64   *Sandell v Porter* (1966) 115 CLR 666. The authorities in relation to determining whether or not a
      company is insolvent are exhaustively analysed by Mandie J in *Australian Securities and Investments
      Commission v Plymin (No 1)* (2003) 46 ACSR 126 at [370]–[380].
65   (2007) 65 ACSR 123 at [266].

The Act does not contain a definition of 'debt'. What, then, is a debt for purposes of the insolvent trading provisions? Section 588G captures trading debts[66] (including contingent debts such as guarantees)[67] and a range of 'deemed debts' under s 588G(1A) linked to certain share capital transactions undertaken by the company. For example, when the directors make a decision to pay dividends, the debt so incurred will be considered to be incurred when the dividend is paid or, if the company has a constitution that provides for the declaration of dividends, when the dividend is declared.

It is by failing to prevent the company from incurring the debt that the person contravenes this civil penalty provision: s 588G(2). There are certain further requirements for a contravention:

(a) the person was aware at that time that there were grounds for suspecting that the debt would render the company insolvent; or

(b) a reasonable person in a like position in a company in the company's circumstances would be so aware.

Directors need to be vigilant about this duty as it has the potential to make them liable for huge amounts.[68] A non-executive, honorary director of a company limited by guarantee, in *Commonwealth Bank of Australia v Friedrich*,[69] was found personally liable (under the predecessor provisions to s 588G) for a substantial corporate debt of $97 million (owed to the bank). Apart from civil liability, where insolvent trading is accompanied by a dishonest intent there is a separate criminal offence that may result in a fine and/or imprisonment (up to five years).

A director is entitled to rely on any one or more of the following statutory defences, listed in s 588H.

REASONABLE EXPECTATION OF SOLVENCY (SECTION 588H(2))[70]

The courts require evidence greater than a mere hope or possibility that the company will be solvent. In explaining the concept of 'expectation', Austin J in *Tourprint International Pty Ltd v Bott*[71] held:

> Expectation ... means a higher degree of certainty than 'mere hope or possibility' or 'suspecting' ... The defence requires an actual expectation that the company was and would continue to be solvent, and that the grounds for so expecting are reasonable. A director cannot rely on complete ignorance of or neglect of duty ... and cannot hide behind ignorance of the company's affairs which is of their own making or, if not ... has been contributed to by their own failure to make further necessary inquiries.[72]

---

66 For consideration of the question 'when does a company incur a debt?', see the collection of authorities discussed in *Playspace Playground Pty Ltd v Osborn* [2009] FCA 1486.

67 *Hawkins v Bank of China* (1992) 7 ACSR 349.

68 Insolvent trading is made a civil penalty under *Corporations Act 2001* (Cth), ss 588G(2) and 1317E(1).

69 (1991) 5 ACSR 115.

70 For case examples on the operation of this defence, see *Statewide Tobacco Services Ltd v Morley* (1990) 2 ACSR 405; *Metropolitan Fire Systems v Miller* (1997) 23 ACSR 699; *Tourprint International Pty Ltd v Bott* (1999) 32 ACSR 201; *Hall v Poolman* (2007) 65 ACSR 123; *Re McLellan; Stake Man Pty Ltd v Carroll* (2009) 76 ACSR 67.

71 (1999) 32 ACSR 201. See also *Treloar Constructions Pty Ltd v McMillan* (2017) 120 ACSR 130.

72 Ibid. at [67].

Palmer J, in *Hall v Poolman*,[73] offers guidance on the approach required to discharge the defence in s 588H(2):

> There comes a point where the reasonable director must inform himself or herself as fully as possible of all relevant facts and then ask himself or herself and the other directors: 'How sure are we that this asset can be turned into cash to pay all our debts, present and to be incurred, within three months? Is that outcome certain, probable, more likely than not, possible, possible with a bit of luck, possible with a lot of luck, remote, or is there is no real way of knowing?' If the honest and reasonable answer is 'certain' or 'probable', the director can have a reasonable expectation of solvency. If the honest and reasonable answer is anywhere from 'possible' to 'no way of knowing', the director can have no reasonable expectation of solvency.

REASONABLE RELIANCE ON OTHERS PROVIDING THE INFORMATION ON THE SOLVENCY OF THE COMPANY (SECTION 588H(3))[74]

Directors will not be able to rely on s 588H(3) where they are put on inquiry as to whether the delegate was fulfilling their responsibilities and they do not make inquiries and receive reasonable assurances that the duties are being performed.[75] Distrust of the person relied upon for financial information will also negate the defence.[76]

ILLNESS OR SOME OTHER GOOD REASON RESULTING IN ABSENCE FROM MANAGEMENT (SECTION 588H(4))[77]

The law's intolerance of 'sleeping, or passive, directors or a director who is absent from management because of their total reliance on their spousal director due to their love and faith' is captured in the following passage by Chief Justice Spigelman in *Deputy Commissioner of Taxation v Clarke*:[78]

> [Sections 588G and 588H were] based on the assumption that a director would participate in the management of the company. This assumption strongly suggests that a total failure to participate, for whatever reason, should not be regarded as a 'good reason' for failing to participate at a particular time ... it is a basal structural feature of corporations legislation in Australia that directors are expected to participate in the management of the corporation.

---

73   *Hall v Poolman* (2007) 65 ACSR 123 at [269].
74   For case examples on the operation of this defence, see *Manpac Industries Pty Ltd v Ceccattini* (2002) 20 ACLC 1304; *Williams v Scholz* [2007] QSC 266; *Re McLellan; Stake Man Pty Ltd v Carroll* (2009) 76 ACSR 67; *Re Forgione Family Group Pty Ltd (in liq) v Forgione* (2015) 239 FCR 285. See further, Anil Hargovan, 'Relevance of directors' unsecured borrowings, guarantees and honesty in determining liability for insolvent trading' (2009) 17 *Insolvency Law Journal* 36.
75   *Australian Securities and Investments Commission v Plymin (No 1)* (2003) 46 ACSR 126; affirmed in *Elliott v Australian Securities and Investments Commission* (2004) 10 VR 369.
76   *Williams v Scholz* [2007] QSC 266; affirmed in [2008] QCA 94.
77   For case examples on the operation of this defence, see *DCT v Clarke* (2003) 57 NSWLR 113; *Williams v Scholz* [2007] QSC 266.
78   (2003) 57 NSWLR 113 at [114] and [116].

REASONABLE STEPS TO PREVENT THE COMPANY FROM INCURRING ANY DEBTS (SECTION 588H(5))

This defence may be established if the director has acted swiftly in their decision to appoint a voluntary administrator to take over the management of the company: s 588H(6). If the director is unable to persuade the board to pass a written resolution to appoint a voluntary administrator, the director should either seek to wind up the company or resign to protect themselves from personal liability.[79]

9.2.2.7 Reform of insolvent trading[80]

In early 2017 the Federal Government released a draft set of changes that aim to give directors greater confidence to engage in efforts to rescue a business in financial distress by providing a new safe harbour carve-out to s 588G(2).[81] This carve-out would apply where directors took action that was reasonably likely to lead to a better outcome for the company and for its creditors as a whole. Concerns have been raised by various bodies, including the Productivity Commission and the Financial System Inquiry, that Australia's insolvent trading laws are too inflexible and may discourage directors from trying to save the business. The proposed carve-out would require directors to point to steps that they took that were reasonably likely to lead to a better outcome (such as relying on restructuring advice from a competent and qualified adviser). The onus would then shift to a liquidator to disprove the carve-out (in proposed new s 588GA).

9.2.2.8 Chapter 5C: Duties relating to managed investment schemes

Chapter 5C of the Act contains provisions regarding the registration of a managed investment scheme; the corporate form it must use; its constitution; and how it must be administered.[82] This Chapter contains several duties for directors of these schemes. There is also a special requirement that if less than half of the directors of the responsible entity (a public company) are external directors, the responsible entity must establish a compliance committee.[83] Section 601JD(1) imposes duties, similar to the duties of directors, on the members of the compliance committee, who are expected:

    (a)   to act honestly; and

    (b)   to exercise the degree of care and diligence that a reasonable person would exercise if they were in the member's position; and

    (c)   not to make use of information acquired through being a member of the committee in order to:

---

79   *Statewide Tobacco Services Ltd v Morley* (1990) 2 ACSR 405; affirmed [1993] 1 VR 423.

80   See further <www.treasury.gov.au/ConsultationsandReviews/Consultations/2016/Improving-bankruptcy-and-insolvency-laws>.

81   See further Jason Harris, 'Reforming insolvent trading to encourage restructuring: Safe harbour or sleepy hollows? (2016) 27 *Journal of Banking Law and Financial Practice (JBFLP)* 294; Anil Hargovan, 'Governance in financially troubled companies: Australian law reform proposals' (2016) 34 *C&SLJ* 483.

82   CAMAC is currently reviewing the operation of Ch 5C and the regulation of managed investment schemes: see 'The establishment and operation of managed investment schemes' (March 2014); 'Managed Investment Schemes' (July 2012) <www.camac.gov.au>.

83   *Corporations Act 2001* (Cth) s 601JA(2).

> (i) gain an improper advantage for the member or another person; or
>
> (ii) cause detriment to the members of the scheme; and
>
> (d) not make improper use of their position as a member of the committee to gain, directly or indirectly, an advantage for themselves or for any other person or to cause detriment to the members of the scheme.

A breach of any of these duties will expose the members of the compliance committee or the directors to any of the orders a court may make under the civil penalty provisions.[84]

9.2.2.9 Chapter 6CA: Duty relating to continuous disclosure

We deal with the introduction of the continuous disclosure provisions in Chapter 7 as part of the CLERP 9 amendments. Suffice it here to point out that non-compliance with the continuous disclosure provisions is considered a contravention of a 'financial services civil penalty provision', to which a higher maximum penalty applies (as mentioned above).[85]

9.2.2.10 Insider trading[86]

Part 7.10 – Division 3 contains the general prohibition on a person trading in financial products (defined in Division 3: for instance, securities, derivatives and debentures) when that person is in possession of inside information. 'Inside information' is defined as information that is not generally available or information that, if it were generally available, a reasonable person would expect to have a material effect on the price or value of a particular financial product.[87]

A person with inside information (the insider) may not apply for, acquire or dispose of any of the defined financial products, or enter into an agreement to apply for, acquire or dispose of such financial products or procure another person to apply for, acquire, or dispose of such financial products, or enter into an agreement to apply for, acquire, or dispose of such financial products.[88] 'Procuring' is defined as inciting, inducing or encouraging an act or omission of another person by a person in possession of inside information.[89]

The insider must also not, directly or indirectly, communicate the inside information ('tipping'), or cause the information to be communicated, to another person if the insider knows, or ought reasonably to know, that the other person would or would be likely to apply for, acquire or dispose of the defined financial products, or enter into an agreement to apply for, acquire or dispose of such financial products or procure another person to apply for, acquire or dispose of such financial products, or enter into an agreement to apply for, acquire or dispose of such financial products.[90]

Any contravention of the insider trading provisions is a contravention of a 'financial services civil penalty provision'.[91]

---

84   Ibid. ss 588G(2) and 1317E(1): the duty relating to managed investment schemes is made a civil penalty.

85   Ibid. s 1317E(1): the continuous disclosure provisions are made civil penalty provisions.

86   See Gregory Lyon and Jean J du Plessis, *The Law of Insider Trading in Australia* (Federation Press, 2005) for a comprehensive analysis of all legal aspects of insider trading.

87   *Corporations Act 2001* (Cth) s 1042A.

88   Ibid. s 1043A(1).

89   Ibid. s 1042A.

90   Ibid. s 1043A(2).

91   Ibid. s 1317E(1).

9.2.2.11 Relief from civil liability[92]

Section 1317S gives the court discretion to relieve from liability, either wholly or partly, persons held liable to pay compensation if it appears that the person acted honestly and, having regard to all the circumstances of the case, ought fairly to be excused. Section 1318 provides similar relief against breaches of civil penalty provisions. As was pointed out in *Daniels v Anderson*,[93] the purpose of these sections is 'to excuse company officers from liability in situations where it would be unjust and oppressive not to do so, recognising that such officers are businessmen and women who act in an environment involving risk in commercial decision-making'.[94] Acting honestly, which underpins both sections, means to act 'without moral turpitude'.[95] In *Hall v Poolman*,[96] Palmer J considered the following factors as relevant in assessing honesty:

> whether the person has acted without deceit or conscious impropriety, without intent to gain improper benefit or advantage for himself, herself or another, and without carelessness or imprudence to such a degree as to demonstrate that no genuine attempt at all has been made to carry out the duties and obligations of his or her office imposed by the Corporations Act or the general law.

There have not been many cases in which the directors have benefited from the operation of these discretionary provisions. The decisions in *Hall v Poolman* and in *Re McLellan; Stake Man Pty Ltd v Carroll*[97] are notable exceptions to the trend of judicial reluctance in this regard. In the former case, a director was partially absolved from liability for debts incurred during insolvent trading (in breach of s 588G, discussed above). Significantly, the latter case is the first in which a director has been fully exonerated from personal liability through the exercise of judicial discretion.

The court in *Hall v Poolman* was influenced by the commercial conduct of the director, who was found to have acted in a reasonable manner, for a limited time, when attempting to save the business while negotiating over a large debt with the Australian Taxation Office. In adopting an approach widely regarded by commentators as commercially realistic, Palmer J, in *Hall v Poolman*,[98] made the following observations:

> Experienced company directors ... would appreciate that, in some cases, it is not commercially sensible to summon the administrators or to abandon a substantial trading enterprise to the liquidators as soon as any liquidity shortage occurs. In some cases a reasonable time must be allowed to a director to assess whether the company's difficulty is temporary and remediable or endemic and fatal. The commercial reality is that creditors

---

92   This discussion draws upon Michael Adams, Jason Harris and Anil Hargovan, '*Officers' in Australian Corporation Practice* (LexisNexis Loose-leaf Service, 2014) Ch 13. See also Du Plessis and Mathiopoulos, 'Wider protection for company directors' (2016) 316–17.
93   (1995) 37 NSWLR 438.
94   Ibid. 525.
95   *Commonwealth Bank of Australia v Friedrich* (1991) 5 ACSR 115 at 198; *Australian Securities and Investments Commission v Vines* (2005) 56 ACSR 528, affirmed in *Vines v Australian Securities and Investments Commission* (2007) 73 NSWLR 451 at [568] per Ipp JA and at [797], [800] per Santow JA.
96   (2007) 65 ACSR 123 at [325].
97   (2009) 76 ACSR 67. For commentary, see Anil Hargovan, 'Director's liability for insolvent trading, statutory forgiveness and law reform' (2010) 18 *Insolvency Law Journal* 96.
98   (2007) 65 ACSR 123 at [331].

will usually allow some time for payment beyond normal trading terms, if there are worthwhile prospects of an improvement in the company's position.

Honesty, by itself, is insufficient to justify relief.[99] In *Williams v Scholz*,[100] the Court of Appeal in Queensland declined to exercise judicial discretion under s 1318 and excuse the directors from liability for insolvent trading on the basis of their knowledge of deteriorating financial conditions, their suspicions of mismanagement and their failure to take remedial steps. Under these circumstances, despite the honest conduct of the directors, it was held that the function of s 1318 is not to subvert the operation of the insolvent trading laws.

It is an irrelevant consideration, for the exercise of judicial discretion for relief, that directors do not have directors and officers' liability insurance to meet any judgment debt and have to rely on their own resources. In *Hall v Poolman*,[101] Palmer J considered this issue and held:

> The fact that a director has no insurance to meet a judgment debt arising from an insolvent trading claim cannot, without more, play a part in the consideration of discretionary defences under s.1317S and s.1318. Most creditors are not insured against the insolvency of their debtors. The Court should not, in the exercise of discretion under s.1317S or s.1318, hold accountable only a director whose insurer will absorb the pain of a judgment.

9.3 Case studies regarding civil penalty provisions or pecuniary penalty provisions

9.3.1 Overview

Australian Securities and Investments Commission v Adler[102] remains one of the best cases to illustrate how the civil penalty provisions or pecuniary penalty provisions are used by ASIC in practice, because of both the lucid judgment of Santow J and the fact that the case involved multiple breaches of statutory duties and civil penalty provisions. However, there were several other significant cases that ASIC brought against directors and officers that either clarified or demonstrated the operation of the statutory duties of directors. We now provide brief overviews of the key legal issues in *Australian Securities and Investments Commission v Adler*,[103] *Australian Securities and Investments Commission v Macdonald (No 11)*[104] and *Australian Securities and Investments Commission v Rich*.[105]

----

99   *Kenna & Brown Pty Ltd v Kenna* (1999) 32 ACSR 430.
100   [2008] QCA 94.
101   (2007) 65 ACSR 123 at [342].
102   (2002) 41 ACSR 72.
103   Ibid.
104   (2009) 256 ALR 199.
105   (2009) 75 ACSR 1.

9.3.2 *ASIC v Adler* (2002) 41 ACSR 72

9.3.2.1 Summary of the facts

This case basically deals with four different sets of transactions in the lead-up to the collapse of HIH Insurance Ltd. The main defendants were Rodney Adler (director and shareholder in HIH), Ray Williams (CEO, shareholder and founder of HIH) and Dominic Fodera (director and CFO of HIH).

1. *Transfer of funds* – The first transaction took place on 15 June 2000, when an amount of $10 million was transferred from one of HIH's subsidiaries, Casualty & General Insurance Company Limited (HIHC), to a company, Pacific Eagle Equity Pty Limited (PEE), controlled by Rodney Adler. This payment followed correspondence, commencing 9 June 2000, between Rodney Adler and Ray Williams and later steps involving various officers of HIH and HIHC. This transfer was executed by Dominic Fodera, the CFO of HIH and HIHC and also a director of both companies, after Rodney Adler requested such a transfer and the CEO of HIH, Ray Williams, concurred with it and also directed the transfer.

2. *Purchase of HIH shares* – The second set of transactions took place between 16 and 30 June 2000, when PEE began to purchase shares in HIH to the extent of $3,991,856.21. All these purchases were instigated by Rodney Adler. This was in circumstances in which, according to ASIC – but disputed – the stockmarket was led to believe by Rodney Adler that the purchases were made by Rodney Adler or family interests associated with Rodney Adler in order to shore up the HIH share price. On 7 July 2000, the Australian Equities Unit Trust (AEUT) was established, by execution of a Trust Deed, with PEE as trustee. Units of different classes were issued to HIHC and Adler Corporation, a company controlled by Adler. The $10 million investment by HIHC, including the HIH shares purchased with it, then became part of this trust (AEUT).[106] The HIH shares were subsequently sold by AEUT at a loss of $2,121,261.11 on 26 September 2000 – barely three months after they had been purchased.

3. *Purchase of unlisted investments* – The third set of transactions relates to AEUT buying three unlisted investments (unlisted technology and internet companies), from Adler Corporation Pty Ltd (Adler Corp). Adler Corp was a company in which Rodney Adler was the sole director and he and his wife the only shareholders. AEUT bought dstore Limited (dstore) on 25 August 2000 for $50,002, Planet Soccer International Limited (Planet Soccer) on 25 August 2000 for $820,748 and Nomad Telecommunications Limited (Nomad) on 26 September 2000 for $2,539,000 – collectively called 'the unlisted investments'. These sales were all financed with the funds still available (after the purchase of the HIH shares) from the original $10 million payment by HIHC, which became AEUT's after the execution of the Trust Deed. AEUT suffered a loss on all three transactions totalling $3,859,750 (without interest taken into consideration).

---

106   Jason Lang and Giselle McHugh, *Corporate Law Electronic Bulletin*, Mallesons Stephen Jacques Bulletin No. 55 (March 2002) <http://cclsr.law.unimelb.edu.au/bulletins/archive/Bulletin0055.htm>.

4. *Making of unsecured loans* – The fourth set of transactions deals with unsecured loans. Between 26 July 2000 and 30 November 2000, Rodney Adler caused three unsecured loans totalling $2,084,345 to be made by AEUT, without adequate documentation, to companies or funds associated with him and/or Adler Corp, to the latter's advantage and allegedly to the disadvantage of AEUT.

9.3.2.2 Contraventions of civil penalty provisions[107]

RELATED PARTY TRANSACTIONS (CHAPTER 2E)

It was held that the payment of $10 million by HIHC to PEE on 15 June 2000 amounted to the 'giving of a financial benefit' to PEE, Adler Corp and Adler within the meaning of s 229 of the Act. Thus, HIH and HIHC had contravened s 208 of the Act. The transaction was not an 'arm's length' transaction under s 210. The subsequent entering into of the trust deed was also not held to fall within the 'arm's length' exception in s 210 because the trust deed lacked proper safeguards in circumstances in which Adler had a potential conflict of interest, and was significantly one-sided against HIHC.

It was also held that the transaction was carried out at Adler's request and with Williams' concurrence and direction. Both of them were 'involved' in the giving of a financial benefit within the meaning of s 79. Both contravened s 209(2) by being 'involved' in the contravention of s 208 by HIH and HIHC. Fodera was also in breach of s 209(2). He had sufficient knowledge of the essential elements of the contravention, and his attempts to subsequently distance himself from the transaction by referring matters to others did not alter this.

FINANCIAL ASSISTANCE (PART 2J.3)

HIHC suffered material prejudice as a result of financially assisting PEE to acquire shares in HIH and, in so doing, contravened s 260A of the Act. The material prejudice arose from the fact that the rights that HIHC obtained from PEE were of a materially lesser value than the cash handed over. In other words, HIHC was 'impoverished' by this transaction. The court relied on *Charterhouse Investment Trust Ltd v Tempest Diesels Ltd* [1986] BCLC 1, looking 'at all interlocking elements in a commercial transaction as a whole'.

The material prejudice for HIHC resulted from the fact that there was no security or documentation and no control over the disposition of the funds. The AEUT Trust Deed was also one-sided and did not include safeguards to protect against Adler's potential conflict of interest. A loss on the HIH shares traded by PEE was inherently likely from the start, and did in fact occur.

It was held that Rodney Adler and Ray Williams were sufficiently involved in the contravention of s 260A to have breached s 260D(2). They knew that HIHC was providing assistance for the purchase of HIH shares, but it was not necessary for them to have actual knowledge of material prejudice. Dominic Fodera's involvement was more remote and, on the facts, Santow J was not able to conclude that Fodera, while having knowledge that financial assistance was given, also had knowledge that it would materially prejudice HIHC. However, as the onus lay

---

107   Ibid.: this part is based on this excellent summary of the findings of Santow J and on the headnote to the Australian Corporations and Securities Reports – *Australian Securities and Investments Commission v Adler* (2002) 41 ACSR 72 at 72–7.

on the defendants to prove that giving the financial assistance was not materially prejudicial, this element of s 260A was essentially a defence, and proof of knowledge of material prejudice was therefore not necessary for s 260D(2). Accordingly, Fodera was also found to have breached s 260D(2).[108] In making these findings, Santow J stated that 'a combination of suspicious circumstances and the failure to make appropriate enquiry when confronted with the obvious, makes it possible to infer knowledge of the relevant essential matters'.[109]

DUTY OF CARE AND DILIGENCE (SECTION 180)

It was held that a reasonably careful and diligent director or officer in the position of Adler would not have caused the payment of $10 million by HIHC to PEE to be applied in part to purchasing HIH shares. Adler failed to follow authorised practices relating to investments made by HIH/HIHC and to ensure that safeguards were in place to protect HIH or HIHC. In fact, Adler's object was to support the HIH share price (doing so for his own substantial sharehold-ing in HIH), rather than to enable HIH to obtain, through its interests in AEUT, the benefit of a quick profit on the resale of the HIH shares.

Ray Williams was aware the $10 million was to be used in whole or in part to pay for shares in HIH, and permitted that amount to be paid in advance of any documentation and with no stipulation of any necessary safeguards to deal with Adler's potential conflicts of interest, which is a circumstance requiring special vigilance. While the primary responsibility will fall on the director proposing to enter into the transaction, this does not excuse other directors or officers who become aware of the transaction. It was only common sense that a reasonably careful and diligent director would have brought the issue of a $10 million payment being made to a director, to be used at his or her discretion, before the board or at least the HIH Investment Committee.[110]

The directors' attempt to rely on the protection of the business judgment rule (see s 180(2)) failed. In Adler's case, there was no 'business judgment'; moreover, Adler clearly had a material personal interest in the 'subject matter of the judgment'. Williams failed to establish that he had made the decision in good faith for a proper purpose, and that he had informed himself to the extent that he could reasonably believe that the decision was a proper business decision.

DUTY OF GOOD FAITH (SECTION 181)

Rodney Adler was the only director found to be in breach of s 181. This was because Adler, quite apart from failing to make proper disclosure, promoted his personal interest by making or pursuing a gain (of maintaining or supporting the HIH share price) when there was a substantial possibility of a conflict between his personal interests and those of the company in pursuing a profit. The interests of HIH and HIHC were put at risk by illegality under sections 208 and 260A, and by concealing from the market that HIHC, not Adler or his interests, was funding the purchase of HIH shares.[111]

---

108   Lang and McHugh, *Corporate Law Electronic Bulletin* (2002).
109   *Australian Securities and Investments Commission v Adler* (2002) 41 ACSR 72, 163.
110   Lang and McHugh, *Corporate Law Electronic Bulletin* (2002).
111   Ibid.

USE OF POSITION TO GAIN ADVANTAGE FOR ONESELF OR ANOTHER OR TO CAUSE DETRIMENT TO THE CORPORATION (SECTION 182)

Santow J concluded that both Adler and Williams were in breach of s 182. Adler's conduct evinced his improper purpose in supporting the share price in HIH. This included passing up an early opportunity for AEUT to make a profit on the sale of HIH shares, as well as maximising the ultimate loss for AEUT by selling his own interests in HIH ahead of AEUT's when the market was falling. Williams likewise breached s 182 in authorising the $10 million payment without proper safeguards and without the knowledge or approval of the HIH Investment Committee. More generally, Adler was also found to have breached his duties under sections 180 to 182 in relation to PEE's acquisition of the three unlisted technology and internet investments from Adler Corp. No reasonable director in Adler's position and possessing his knowledge would have committed PEE to acquire investments in Nomad, dstore and Planet Soccer at the prices Adler Corp paid for them. The known radical change in market conditions relating to technology stocks, the lack of any due diligence and the misleading statements and omissions made by Adler in relation to the on-sale of these investments all supported this conclusion. Despite being clearly aware of the financial dire straits of these investments, Adler and Adler Corp extricated Adler Corp from its position, at no loss to Adler Corp, but to the disadvantage of PEE, HIH and HIHC.

Adler was in further breach of sections 180 to 182 in relation to the three unsecured loans from AEUT to entities associated with Adler. These loans were not adequately documented and not one of them was even within the scope of the vaguely sketched mandate for AEUT, as discussed by Adler and Williams, to pursue investment in 'venture capital' or 'share trading'.[112]

IMPROPER USE OF INFORMATION (SECTION 183)

Adler was also found by Santow J to have breached his obligations under s 183, in relation to both the acquisition of the three unlisted investments from Adler Corp and the loans to Adler-associated entities. Adler had improperly used information obtained by him to gain an advantage for himself.[113] It must be noted, however, that this part of Santow J's judgment was overturned on appeal. The NSW Court of Appeal held that neither Adler's disregard of HIH's investment guidelines and procedures, nor his knowledge of Williams' susceptibility, amounted to an improper 'use' of information for the purposes of s 183.[114]

9.3.2.3 Court orders

Santow J ordered that Rodney Adler should be disqualified for a period of 20 years and that he and Adler Corp should pay pecuniary penalties of $450,000 each (totalling $900,000). Ray Williams was disqualified for a period of 10 years and was ordered to pay pecuniary penalties of $250,000. Dominic Fodera was not disqualified, but was ordered to pay pecuniary penalties of $5000. In addition, Rodney Adler, Ray Williams and Adler Corp were ordered to pay aggregate compensation of $7,958,112 to HIH Casualty and General Insurance Limited (subject to verification of the calculation of interest).[115]

---

112   Ibid.
113   Ibid.
114   See *Adler v Australian Securities and Investments Commission* (2003) 46 ACSR 504.
115   Lang and McHugh, *Corporate Law Electronic Bulletin* (2002); Jillian Segal, 'Corporate governance: Substance over form' (2002) 25 *University of New South Wales (UNSW) Law Journal* 320, 328.

Criminal proceedings were later brought against Rodney Adler and Ray Williams in relation to their activities.

9.3.3 *ASIC v Macdonald (No 11) (2009) 256 ALR 199* – James Hardie litigation[116]

9.3.3.1 Background and summary of the facts

This case sheds light on the practical application of the scope and content of directors' and officers' duties in a large, publicly listed company. The case illustrates the standard of care expected by management and the board when considering strategic company decisions and market-sensitive information. It offers guidance on the standards expected under s 180(1), with particular reference to non-executive directors, executive directors, CFOs, company secretaries and in-house counsel.

In Chapter 2 we used the James Hardie litigation as a case study in the context of the importance of stakeholders and how stakeholders and pressure groups are able to influence corporate behaviour and corporate governance practices. The irony is that the agreement by James Hardie to establish a fund to cover future medical claims led to further litigation, resulting in the reported cases *Australian Securities and Investmens Commission v Macdonald (No 11)*[117] and *Australian Securities and Investments Commission v Macdonald (No 12)*.[118] Most of the defendants (with the exception of Macdonald, the CEO), and ASIC, appealed these decisions, which led to two Court of Appeal decisions,[119] and two High Court decisions.[120] After the High Court appeals, the penalties were then determined by the NSW Court of Appeal.[121]

As will be recalled, James Hardie Industries Limited (JHIL) faced significant liability for damages claims for asbestos-related conditions resulting from the use of its products since 1920. JHIL was the holding company of the James Hardie group. In order to separate JHIL from this liability, the board decided to establish the Medical Research and Compensation Foundation (MRCF) which would manage and pay out asbestos claims against JHIL.

At a board meeting of JHIL held on 15 February 2001, the board decided to constitute JHIL as trustee of the MRCF. At the same meeting, a draft announcement to the Australian Securities Exchange (ASX) was approved. Although this event was disputed by the 10 defendants (directors and officers), the judge rejected the chorus of non-recollection. This draft announcement explained that MRCF would be 'fully funded' (to meet the outstanding liability). At the same meeting, the board also agreed to execute the Deed of Covenant and Indemnity (DOCI),

---

116   Part of this discussion is based on Anil Hargovan, 'Corporate governance lessons from James Hardie' (2009) 33 *Melbourne University Law Review* 984.

117   (2009) 256 ALR 199.

118   (2009) 259 ALR 116.

119   *Morley v Australian Securities and Investments Commission* (2010) 81 ACSR 285 (which dealt with appeals by ASIC and the individual defendants relating to the breaches of directors and officers' duties); *James Hardie Industries NV v Australian Securities and Investments Commission* (2010) 81 ACSR 1 (which dealt with the company's appeal relating to disclosure contraventions).

120   *Shafron v Australian Securities and Investments Commission* (2012) 247 CLR 465 (which dealt with the company secretary and general counsel's appeal); *Australian Securities and Investments Commission v Hellicar* (2012) 247 CLR 345 (which dealt with ASIC's appeal from the NSWCA and the non-executive directors' appeal from the NSWCA).

121   *Gillfillan v Australian Securities and Investments Commission* (2012) 92 ACSR 460.

which dealt with liability between JHIL and MRCF. The seven non-executive directors attended this meeting (two by phone from the US), as did the CEO (Peter Macdonald), the board secretary and general counsel (Peter Shafron) and the CFO (Phillip Morley).

The minutes of the board meeting contained an entry to the effect that the company had explained the impact of the resolution passed at the meeting to approve an ASX announcement and to execute the ASX announcement and send it to the ASX. The minutes of the meeting were signed by the chairman at the following board meeting, held on 4 April 2001. On 7 April 2001, the minutes of the meeting of 15 February 2001 were sent to the secretary of the company. The evidentiary value of the minutes, however, was negated by the company's non-compliance with the relevant statutory provisions governing minutes, which thereby precluded the court from relying on the minutes to establish the events that transpired at the board meeting.

ASIC alleged that the draft ASX announcement was approved at the board meeting of 15 February 2001 and that it stated that the MRCF would commence operations with assets of $284 million. The draft ASX announcement also contained a number of statements to the effect that MRCF would have sufficient funds to meet all legitimate asbestos claims; that it was fully funded; and that it provided certainty for people with legitimate asbestos claims.

The final ASX announcement included, *inter alia*, the following statements:

> The Foundation has sufficient funds to meet all legitimate compensation claims ... Mr Peter Macdonald said that the establishment of a fully-funded Foundation provided certainty for both claimants and shareholders ... In establishing the Foundation, James Hardie sought expert advice ... James Hardie is satisfied that the Foundation has sufficient funds to meet anticipated future claims ...

9.3.3.2 Legal issues

Based on the facts discussed above, ASIC alleged in Supreme Court hearings in September 2008 that JHIL, its officers and the board breached several civil penalty provisions of the previous Corporations Law and the current *Corporations Act 2001* (Cth), which attracted civil penalties.[122] In particular, ASIC argued that:

1. The draft ASX announcement approved at the board meeting on 15 February 2001 was false or misleading. The approval by the non-executive directors,[123] the CEO (Macdonald), the company secretary and general counsel (Shafron), and CFO (Morley) was in breach of the duty of care in s 180(1).

2. JHIL's failure to disclose information in relation to the DOCI to the ASX was in breach of s 1001A(2).[124]

3. The failure by the CEO and company secretary and general counsel to advise the board that the DOCI information should be disclosed to the ASX was in breach of s 180(1).

---

122   ASIC concluded that there was insufficient evidence to refer any matter to the Commonwealth Director of Public Prosecution for criminal prosecution of the company's officers: 'James Hardie Group Civil Action', ASIC Media Release 08–201 (5 September 2008) <www.asic.gov.au/asic/asic.nsf/byheadline/ 08–201+James+Hardie+Group+civil+action?openDocument>.

123   Mr Brown, Ms Hellicar, Mr Wilcox, Mr O'Brien, Mr Terry, Messrs Gillfillan and Koffel.

124   *Corporations Act 2001* (Cth) s 1001A(2), carried over into the Corporations Act until its repeal in 2002, dealt with breach of continuous disclosure obligations.

4. The CEO had breached s 180(1) by failing to advise that the final ASX announcement on 16 February 2001 should not be released or that it should be amended to cure the defect.

5. Statements made by the CEO at a press conference concerning the adequacy of funding for asbestos claims were false or misleading and involved a breach of s 180(1).

6. A 'continuous disclosure' announcement to the ASX on 23 February 2001 by the CEO, which contained false or misleading statements, was in breach of s 180(1); the approval of an announcement released to the ASX on 21 March 2001 by the same officer, which contained false or misleading statements, was also in breach of s 180(1) and the good faith provisions in s 181(1).[125]

7. In the publication of the final ASX announcement, the press conference statements and the further ASX announcements, referred to in (6) above, JHIL contravened sections 995(2)[126] and 999.[127]

8. The representations made by the CEO with respect to JHI NV at roadshows in Edinburgh and London and in slides for these UK presentations, lodged with the ASX, were false and misleading and in breach of sections 180(1) and 181. On the same facts, it was argued that JHI NV was in breach of s 1041E[128] and, in making ASX representations, breached s 1041H.[129]

9. JHI NV failed to notify the ASX of JHIL information in accordance with Listing Rule 3.1 and thereby contravened disclosure obligations in s 674(2).[130]

9.3.3.3 Judicial decisions and the significance of the litigation[131]

The following discussion centres on the findings made against the directors and officers of JHIL. We focus on the significance of the case for different types of directors and officers.

NON-EXECUTIVE DIRECTORS

The court addressed the question of whether the law differentiated, in the standard of performance expected, between executive and non-executive directors. Justice Gzell referred to the divergent judicial views expressed by Rogers CJ in *AWA Ltd v Daniels (t/as Deloitte*

---

125   Ibid. s 181 requires directors and officers of a corporation to exercise their power and discharge their duties in good faith in the best interests of the corporation and for a proper purpose.

126   Ibid. s 995(2), carried over into the Act until its repeal in 2002, was modelled on the *Trade Practices Act 1974* (Cth) s 52) (now *Competition and Consumer Act 2010* (Cth) s 18). The full text of the Australian Consumer Law (ACL) is set out in Schedule 2 of the *Competition and Consumer Act 2010* (Cth) and prohibits misleading or deceptive conduct in connection with securities. There is a similar provision to s 995 in *Corporations Act 2001* (Cth) s 1041H(1).

127   *Corporations Act 2001* (Cth) s 999, carried over into the Act until repealed in 2002, prohibited false or misleading statements in relation to securities.

128   Ibid. s 1041E prohibits false or misleading statements that induce persons to, *inter alia*, apply for or dispose of financial products.

129   Ibid. s 1041H prohibits misleading or deceptive conduct in relation to a financial product.

130   Ibid. s 674(2) deals with a listed disclosing entity's continuous disclosure obligations.

131   This part is based on Hargovan, 'Corporate governance lessons from James Hardie' (2009); Anil Hargovan, 'Directors' and officers' statutory duty of care following *James Hardie*' (2009) 61 *Keeping Good Companies* 590.

Haskins & Sells)[132] – Rogers CJ appeared to show a readiness to accept a lower standard of care for non-executive directors[133] – and the Court of Appeal in *Daniels v Anderson*,[134] wherein Clarke and Sheller JJA held that the approach of Rogers CJ on this issue did not represent contemporary company law[135] and that all directors are required to take reasonable steps to guide and monitor the management of the company.[136] After reviewing the case law on this point,[137] Gzell J reiterated the analysis of Santow J in *Australian Securities and Investments Commission v Adler*[138] and held that a director should become familiar with the fundamentals of the company's business and is under a continuing obligation to keep informed about the company's activities.

Satisfied that the same standards of care are imposed on all directors, Gzell J focused on the test to determine breach of s 180(1) and relied on *Australian Securities and Investments Commission v Adler*[139] to adopt the following test:

> In determining whether a director has exercised reasonable care and diligence one must ask what an ordinary person, with the knowledge and experience of the defendant, might have expected to have done in the circumstances if he or she was acting on their own behalf.[140]

Justice Gzell commented on the failure of the non-executive directors to discharge their monitoring role as part of the statutory duty of care and diligence:[141]

> ... it was part of the function of the directors in monitoring the management of the company to settle the terms of the Draft ASX Announcement to ensure that it did not assert that the Foundation had sufficient funds to meet all legitimate compensation claims.

The court held that the directors' conduct thereafter, in releasing the defective ASX announcement, fell short of the standards expected to discharge obligations under s 180(1) for the following reasons:

> The *formation of the foundation* and the [restructure of the relevant entities described earlier] from JHIL *were potentially explosive steps*. Market reaction to the announcement of them was critical. This was a matter within the purview of the board's responsibility: what should be stated publicly about the way in which Asbestos Claims would be handled by the James Hardie group for the future. (emphasis added)[142]

---

132   (1992) 7 ACSR 759.
133   Ibid. at 867.
134   (1995) 37 NSWLR 438; 16 ACSR 607.
135   Ibid. at 668.
136   Ibid. at 664.
137   *Statewide Tobacco Services Ltd v Morley* (1990) 2 ACSR 405; *Group Four Industries Pty Ltd v Brosnan* (1992) 59 SASR 22; *Vrisakis v Australian Securities Commission* (1993) 9 WAR 395; *Permanent Building Society (in liq) v Wheeler* (1994) 11 WAR 187; *Australian Securities and Investments Commission v Adler* (2002) 41 ACSR 72; *Australian Securities and Investments Commission v Maxwell* (2006) 59 ACSR 373; *Vines v Australian Securities and Investments Commission* (2007) 73 NSWLR 451.
138   (2002) 41 ACSR 72.
139   (2002) 41 ACSR 72.
140   *Australian Securities and Investments Commission v Macdonald (No 11)* (2009) 256 ALR 199 at [239].
141   Ibid. at [332].
142   Ibid. at [333].

Although two of the non-executive directors attended the relevant board meeting by telephone, and claimed that the draft ASX announcement was neither provided nor read to them, the court held that both directors had breached s 180(1) by voting in favour of the resolution. Justice Gzell, unimpressed by the conduct of both directors in such circumstances, found liability on the following basis:[143]

> Neither [non-executive directors] raised an objection that [they] did not have a copy of the Draft ASX Announcement at the ... meeting. Nor did they ask that a copy be provided to them. Nor did they abstain from approving the ... Announcement.

The entire board's reliance upon, and delegation to, management and experts was held to be inappropriate on the facts of this case for these key reasons:

> This was not a matter in which a director was entitled to rely upon those of his co-directors more concerned with communications strategy to consider the Draft ASX Announcement. *This was a key statement in relation to a highly significant restructure of the James Hardie group.* Management having brought the matter to the board, none of them was entitled to abdicate responsibility by delegating his or her duty to a fellow director. (emphasis added)[144]

The NSW Court of Appeal overturned Gzell J's decision based on a different view of the evidence. The Court of Appeal did not accept that the evidence demonstrated that the board had been asked to approve the ASX release. This was based on a number of factors, including ASIC's failure to call a key witness, which the court held was in breach of ASIC's duty of fairness as a litigant. If the directors were not asked to approve the release, then they could not be in breach of their duties for releasing the misleading document. However, the court also held that if its finding on the evidence was not correct the decision of the trial judge regarding breach of duties was upheld.

ASIC successfully appealed this decision to the High Court of Australia (*Australian Securities and Investments Commission v Hellicar*),[145] which held that the directors did approve the ASX release, and that ASIC's role as a litigant did not give rise to a duty of fairness that would undermine the cogency of evidence. This meant that the decision of the trial judge regarding the directors' breach of duty was reinstated. The High Court appeal did not consider directors' duties, but only matters relating to admissible evidence and the role of ASIC as a model litigant. The other High Court appeal was *Shafron v Australian Securities and Investments Commission*,[146] which did consider the duties of executives and is discussed below.

CHIEF EXECUTIVE OFFICER

The court found that Mr Macdonald, as a director and CEO of JHIL with reporting duties directly to the board, had ultimate responsibility for planning the separation proposals and was the driving force. Furthermore, he was appointed to make public statements on behalf of JHIL

---

143   Ibid. at [233].
144   Ibid. at [260].
145   *Australian Securities and Investments Commission v Hellicar* (2012) 247 CLR 345.
146   (2012) 247 CLR 465.

on these matters and, in keeping with his position, was responsible for dealing with the board on this issue.

As a result of these responsibilities, Gzell J concluded that the CEO bore a high duty of care. In voting in favour of the resolution to approve the draft ASX announcement, the court applied an objective test and found liability under s 180(1) based on reasons similar to those considered applicable to the non-executive directors.

The court also found that the negligent conduct of the CEO resulted in multiple breaches of the statutory duty of care and diligence under s 180(1). These included the failure of the CEO to:

- advise the board of the limited nature of the reviews on the cash-flow model undertaken by external consultants. The review was restricted to issues concerning logical soundness and technical correctness. According to Justice Gzell,[147] a reasonable person with the same responsibilities would have informed the board that the external consultant had been specifically instructed not to consider the key assumptions adopted by the cash-flow model – namely, the fixed investment earnings rates, litigation and management costs and future claim costs;
- advise the board that the draft ASX announcement was expressed in too emphatic terms and, in relation to the adequacy of funding, was misleading and deceptive;
- correct the misleading statements on the adequacy of funding when making representations during international roadshows in Edinburgh and London to promote the company; and
- advise the board of the company's continuous disclosure obligations to release price-sensitive information in a timely manner.

The court, however, rejected ASIC's allegation that the CEO had breached s 180(1) through failure to inquire of each director as to whether they had formed an opinion on the adequacy of the quantum expressed to meet all present and future asbestos claims. The imposition of such a duty, according to Gzell J, was unwarranted because a director is not obliged to analyse the basis upon which fellow directors intend to vote before determining his or her own course.[148]

The CEO failed to offer oral evidence to substantiate all of the statutory criteria under the business judgment rule in s 180(2) (discussed above). This strategic decision proved to be fatal to his defence. It is not easy, as recognised by the court, to rely on documentation alone to discern, for example, if the director had a rational belief that the business judgment was in the best interests of the company.

Macdonald was the only defendant who did not appeal the trial decision and was not involved in either the Court of Appeal or High Court decision.

GENERAL COUNSEL

Mr Shafron, the company secretary and in-house counsel, was held to be a company officer due to his expansive role in the affairs of JHIL and, significantly, attracted the stringent statutory

---

147   *Australian Securities and Investments Commission v Macdonald (No 11)* (2009) 256 ALR 199 at [363].
148   Ibid. at [351].

duties applicable to officers under sections 180–183 of the Act, which include the duty of care and diligence.

Mr Shafron's failure to advise the board of the limited nature of the reviews on the cash-flow model undertaken by external consultants also constituted a breach of s 180(1), for the same reasons discussed above with respect to the conduct of the CEO. Similarly, Shafron's failure to advise the CEO and the board of the company's continuous disclosure obligations, in relation to the failure to release price-sensitive information to the market in a timely manner, constituted a breach of s 180(1).

The Court rejected Shafron's argument that he had no duty to warn the board of the emphatic statements in the draft ASX announcement because a reasonable director would be capable of assessing the statement as false and misleading. On the contrary, according to the Court, there was a compelling duty to speak in such circumstances:[149]

> ... [general counsel] had a duty to protect JHIL from legal risk and if the directors were minded to approve the release of the Draft ASX Announcement in its false and misleading form, there was the danger that JHIL would be in breach ... [of the statute]. Against that harm it was [the] duty [of Mr Shafron] to warn the directors that [such an] announcement should not be released in its too emphatic form.

The High Court upheld the contraventions by Shafron relating to his failure to advise the company regarding the need to disclose the entry into the deed of covenant and indemnity to the market, and his failure to advise the board regarding the limited assumptions upon which the actuarial modelling was based and how this might adversely affect the validity of the modelling. Importantly, Shafron's argument that he had separate roles and responsibilities as company secretary (which was an officer position) and as general counsel (which was not specifically designated an officer position) and that his duties should be divided accordingly was rejected by the High Court. The Court held that his role could not be easily and cleanly divided into the two roles. Shafron worked as a lawyer for the company and his roles and responsibilities covered a number of areas. Shafron's duties arose from the work he did for the company, not simply from the titles of the roles he held. The Court stated (at [16]):

> All of the tasks Mr Shafron performed were undertaken in fulfilment of his responsibilities as general counsel and company secretary. More particularly, because of his qualifications and the position in which he was employed, his responsibilities as general counsel and company secretary extended to proffering advice about how duties of disclosure should be met. And when he procured advice of others and put that advice before the board for its use, his responsibilities could, and in this case did, extend to identifying the limits of the advice that the third party gave.

Another important determination by the High Court was that Shafron's role did involve participation in the decision-making process, despite the fact that Shafron rarely had final authority over decisions. Shafron had argued that his role as general counsel was similar to the position of an external lawyer, and that this should not render him an officer. The Court held (at [30]):

The fact that Mr Shafron was an employee of the company, and not an external adviser, is important. What he did was not confined to proffering advice and information in response to particular requirements made by the company. And what he did went well beyond his proffering advice and information to the board of the company. He played a large and active part in formulating the proposal that he and others chose to put to the board as one that should be approved. It was the board that ultimately had to decide whether to adopt the proposal but what Mr Shafron did, as a senior executive employee of the company, was properly described as his participating in the decision to adopt the separation proposal that he had helped to devise.

CHIEF FINANCIAL OFFICER

Mr Morley, the CFO of JHIL, was also held to be an officer due to his participation in far-reaching decisions of the board. The CFO was responsible for all of the finance, audit, tax and treasury aspects of the James Hardie Group of companies.

Engaging in a similar analysis on this issue with respect to the conduct of the CEO and general counsel described earlier, it was held that s 180(1) was breached by Morley for identical reasons concerning the failure to address the limitations of the cash-flow model and its key assumptions and to communicate this to the board.[150] As CFO, Morley was responsible for verifying the sufficiency of financial information. The court held that a reasonable CFO would have known that the range of limited assumptions meant that the press release could not state with certainty that the Foundation was fully funded. This was upheld by the NSW Court of Appeal. After the Court of Appeal reduced his penalty, Morley did not pursue an appeal to the High Court.

9.3.3.4 Court orders

Justice Gzell (the trial judge) rejected the defendants' submissions relating to the exoneration provisions in sections 1317S and 1318.[151] His Honour held that the contraventions were both serious and flagrant, and that despite the lack of findings of intentional dishonesty, the conduct could not be exonerated by the court. The CEO, Macdonald, was ordered to pay a pecuniary penalty of $350,000 and was disqualified from taking part in the management of corporations for 15 years. As Macdonald did not appeal, this penalty remains unchanged by the later court decisions.

Morley was disqualified by the trial judge for 5 years and ordered to pay a pecuniary penalty of $35,000. Morley appealed and the NSW Court of Appeal reduced his penalty to $20,000 and his period of disqualification to 2 years. Following this reduction in penalties Morley decided not to pursue his High Court appeal.

The trial judge imposed a pecuniary penalty on Shafron for $75,000 and disqualified him for a period of seven years. This penalty was upheld by the NSW Court of Appeal. Shafron's appeal to the High Court was unsuccessful but the High Court remitted the determination of penalties. The NSW Court of Appeal reaffirmed Shafron's original penalty and period of disqualification; Shafron continues to work, as a corporate lawyer, in the US.

150   *Australian Securities and Investments Commission v Macdonald (No 11)* (2009) 256 ALR 199 at [454].
151   *Australian Securities and Investments Commission v Macdonald (No 12)* (2009) 259 ALR 116.

With respect to the non-executive directors, the trial judge imposed penalties of $30,000 and disqualification periods of five years each. As noted above, the Court of Appeal allowed the appeal of the non-executive directors based on a point of evidence regarding whether it had been proved that they were asked to approve the ASX release; thus there were no penalties imposed on them by the Court of Appeal as there was no breach proved. After the High Court allowed ASIC's appeal the Court of Appeal was asked to determine penalties. In *Gillfillan v ASIC*, the court reduced the period of disqualification for the Australian-based directors from five years to two years and three months, and the penalty from $30,000 to $25,000.[152] The overseas-based directors had their period of disqualification reduced to one year and 11 months and their penalty was reduced to $20,000.

9.3.4 *ASIC v Rich* (2009) 75 ACSR 1[153]
9.3.4.1 Background and basic facts

ASIC launched civil penalty proceedings against some directors and officers of One.Tel Ltd (One.Tel) for breach of the statutory duty of care and diligence under s 180(1) of the Act. The proceedings initially brought by ASIC were against four defendants, arising out of the collapse in May 2001 of One.Tel and its local subsidiaries, and the collapse or on-sale of overseas subsidiaries. After a settlement was reached with Bradley Keeling and John Greaves and disqualification orders were made against them, they were not included in the further litigation against Jodee Rich and Mark Silbermann. ASIC sought relief against the defendants, Jodee Rich and Mark Silbermann. Jodee Rich was a director and joint chief executive of One.Tel at all relevant times up to 17 May 2001, and Mark Silbermann was finance director of One.Tel at all relevant times.

ASIC alleged that the defendants did not disclose the true financial position of the company to the board, and that they knew or should have known the true financial position of their company. The central allegation was that the financial position of the Group and the Australian and international businesses within it, in terms of cash, cash flow, creditors, debtors, earnings and liquidity, was much worse during the months of approximately January to March 2001 than the information provided to the board of directors revealed. It was also alleged by ASIC that forecasts of those matters provided to the board, particularly for the period to June 2001, had no proper basis. In addition, ASIC contended that the defendants were aware of the poor financial position of the Group, or ought to have been, and failed to make proper disclosure to the board.

9.3.4.2 Legal issue

In essence, ASIC's case was based on a breach by Jodee Rich and Mark Silbermann of their duty of care and diligence under s 180(1) of the Act. In other words, in not disclosing the true

---

152   (2012) 92 ACSR 460.
153   See further Andrew Lumsden, 'Directors' duties and corporate governance: The business judgment rule: *ASIC v Rich* and the reasonable–rational divide' (2010) 28 *C&SLJ* 423; Du Plessis and Mathiopoulos, 'Wider protection for company directors' (2016); Harris and Hargovan, 'Still a sleepy hollow? Directors' liability and the business judgment rule' (2016); Wesley Bainbridge and Tim Connor, 'Another way forward? The scope for an appellate court to reinterpret the statutory business judgment rule' (2016) 36 *C&SLJ* 415.

financial position of the company to the board, while they knew or should have known the true financial position of their company, they did not act with the required care and diligence expected of directors under s 180(1).

9.3.4.3 The decision and its significance

On 18 November 2009, in a decision of more than 3000 pages, Austin J held that the defendants were not in breach of their duty of care and diligence as required under s 180(1). In short, ASIC had failed to prove its case against either Jodee Rich or Mark Silbermann.

The case is particularly significant because of the observation Austin J made on directors' duty of care and diligence and the business judgment rule as contained in s 180(2) and (3) of the Act. However, almost as significant as these aspects is the fact that this is one of very few prominent and high-profile cases lost by ASIC. Justice Austin's criticism of the way in which ASIC conducted its case is particularly interesting and will probably change the way ASIC handles similar cases in future.

DIRECTORS' DUTY OF CARE AND DILIGENCE AND THE BUSINESS JUDGMENT RULE

Since this part of the case alone stretches over 55 pages, it is hardly possible to discuss it in detail here, but a few of the most important points made will be highlighted. Justice Austin confirmed that the statutory duty of care and diligence under s 180(1) of the Act is essentially the same as the duty of care and diligence of a director under general law. Directors will only be held in breach of this duty if the risk or potential harm was reasonably foreseeable. This basically means that directors will only be in breach of this duty if *they* did not foresee, but objectively other directors in a similar situation would have foreseen, the risk or harm and would have taken steps to prevent it. In judging a breach of directors' duty of care and diligence, a 'forward-looking' approach should be adopted by the courts, and that requires the defendants' conduct to be assessed with close regard to the circumstances existing at the relevant time, without the benefit of hindsight.[154]

Justice Austin pointed out that s 180(1) incorporates a minimum standard of diligence, requiring every director or officer, including a non-executive director:

(i) to become familiar with the fundamentals of the business or businesses of the company;

(ii) to keep informed about the company's activities;

(iii) to monitor, generally, the company's affairs;

(iv) to maintain familiarity with the financial status of the company by appropriate means, including (in the case of a director) reviewing the company's financial statements and board papers, and making further inquiries into matters revealed by those documents where it is appropriate to do so; and

(v) in the case of a director, and at least some officers, to have a reasonably informed opinion of the company's financial capacity.[155]

Although it was pointed out that they have somewhat different consequences for executive and non-executive directors, Austin J accepted the following submissions of ASIC:

---

154   *Australian Securities and Investments Commission v Rich* (2009) 75 ACSR 1 [7242].
155   Ibid. at [7203].

(i)   the statutory duty in terms of s 180(1) encompasses a duty of competence, measured objectively;

(ii) compliance with the duty is determined by reference to what a reasonable person of ordinary prudence would do; a duty is enhanced, where the directorial appointment is based on special skill, by an objective standard of skill referable to the circumstances;

(iii) the statutory standard of skill includes a standard of competence in reading and understanding financial material which is not dependent on the director's subjective inexperience or lack of skill;

(iv) it follows that directors and officers cannot escape liability on the basis that they did not read financial material made available to them for the purposes of their office, and at least to that extent, the statutory duty of care and diligence imports an objective standard of skill irrespective of the directors' or officers' subjective inexperience or lack of skills;

(v)   the legislative history of s 180 confirms that the provision was intended to impose an objective standard of skill; and

(vi) whatever particular skills an individual director or officer actually possesses, or inexperience the individual may suffer from, the director or officer is accountable to a core irreducible requirement of skill, measured objectively.

An interesting, and possibly controversial, point made by Justice Austin is that there are in actual fact two layers of protection for directors against liability:

> If the impugned conduct is found to be a mere error of judgment, then the statutory standard under s 180(1) is not contravened and it is unnecessary to advert to the special business judgment rule in s 180(2). In the view that I have taken of it ... s 180(2) provides a defence in a case where the impugned conduct goes beyond a mere error of judgment, and would contravene the statutory standard but for the defence.[156]

The reason the distinction is perhaps controversial is that there is little guidance for when a matter will be considered to be a mere error of judgment. Can a director simply aver that whatever went wrong was simply an error of judgment and would the plaintiff (in this case ASIC, but it could also be the shareholders – see discussion below regarding statutory derivative actions) then have to provide evidence that it was not merely an error of judgment? Or is the onus from the beginning on the plaintiff to make out a prima facie case that the alleged breach of the duty of care was not a mere error of judgment? Also, there has been a general understanding that there is a presumption that directors will be protected against liability if they have made proper business judgments, even if the judgments are proven, in hindsight, to be wrong. In short, there seems to be confusion between the protection that Austin J describes for mere errors of judgment and the protection provided by the business judgment rule.

Closely linked to this controversial distinction is Justice Austin's finding on who carries the burden of proof to establish that the criteria listed under s 180(2)(a)–(d) of the Act were met.

---

156   Ibid. at [7242].

In order to rely on the protection of the statutory business judgment rule, it has to be shown that a 'business judgment'[157] was made and that, in respect of such a 'business judgment', a director or office:

(a) made the judgment in good faith for a proper purpose; and

(b) did not have a material personal interest in the subject matter of the judgment; and

(c) informed themselves about the subject matter of the judgment to the extent they reasonably believe to be appropriate; and

(d) rationally believed that the judgment was in the best interests of the corporation.

An unresolved issue was whether there is a presumption that directors exercise business judgment by following these four criteria, and thus that the plaintiff carries the burden of proof to rebut these presumptions. In other words, should a court accept that directors exercised their business decision in such a manner unless it is proven not to be the case by the plaintiff? The alternative approach would be that these criteria are not presumptions, but that the defendants (directors or officers) need to prove each one of these aspects in order to be protected by the statutory business judgment rule under s 180(2) and (3) of the Act.

The statutory business judgment rule was supposed to create a presumption in favour of directors, and the way in which the presumption in favour of directors was supposed to work was explained as follows in the Explanatory Memorandum before s 180(2) was introduced:

> Provided directors or other officers fulfil the requirements of proposed subsection 180(2) paragraphs (a) to (d):
>
> • such directors have an explicit safe-harbour, being effectively shielded from liability for any breach of their duty of care and diligence; and
>
> • the merits of directors' business judgments are not subject to review by the Courts.[158]
>
> Proposed subsection 180(2) acts as *a rebuttable presumption in favour of directors* which, if rebutted by a plaintiff, would mean the plaintiff would then still have to establish that the officer had breached their duty of care and diligence.[159]

Whether this has, in fact, been achieved with the way the statutory business rule is currently worded in the Act has been questioned by at least one commentator.[160] A leading commercial law judge, Justice Santow, has also pointed out that it was uncertain[161] whether or not the directors carried the burden of proof to at least establish that they have met the standards set out in s 180(2)(a)–(d). Justice Austin has now determined that the matter will have to be revisited ('at the appellate level') as the language is 'profoundly ambiguous', but for the

---

157 Under *Corporations Act 2001* (Cth) s 180(3), a 'business judgment' is defined as follows: '*business judgment* means any decision to take or not take action in respect of a matter relevant to the business operations of the corporation'.

158 The Parliament of the Commonwealth of Australia – House of Representatives, 'Explanatory Memorandum to the Corporate Law Economic Reform (CLERP) Bill 1998' (ISBN 0642 37879 7) para 6.9.

159 Ibid. para 6.10.

160 See D DeMott, 'Legislating business judgment – a comment from the United States' (1998) 16 *C&SLJ* 575, commented on by RP Austin and IM Ramsay *Ford's Principles of Corporations Law* (LexisNexis Butterworths, 14th edn, 2010) 438 para 8.310.

161 GFK Santow, 'Codification of directors' duties' (1999) 73 *The Australian Law Journal* 336, 348–9 and 350.

moment, and as the provision is currently worded, it will be the defendants (directors and officers) who will carry the burden of proof:

> The question whether the plaintiff or the defendant bears the onus of proving the ingredients of s 180(2) is an important one that will eventually need to be resolved at the appellate level. With some hesitation in light of the US approach, I have reached the conclusion that the Australian statute casts the onus of proving the four criteria in s 180(2) on the defendants [director or officers against whom it is alleged that they have breached their statutory duty of care and diligence under s 180(1)] ... As revealed in the Explanatory Memorandum, paras 6.1–6.10, the purpose of the introduction of a business judgment rule was (generally speaking) to ensure that directors and officers are not discouraged from taking advantage of opportunities that involve responsible risk-taking. Casting the onus of proof of the elements of the defence on the director or officer is not necessarily incompatible with that purpose, because it may happen in practice that the evidential burden can be shifted to the plaintiff relatively easily, if the defendant addresses the statutory elements in his or her affidavit, though the price to be paid is that the defendant is exposed to cross-examination on those matters.[162]

JUDICIAL CRITICISM OF ASIC'S CASE MANAGEMENT

Justice Austin was quite critical of the way ASIC had conducted the case. For instance, he observed that ASICs contentions had 'a superficial appeal, but time and again they were shown to be unpersuasive when the underlying financial detail was investigated'.[163] He observed that a very large number of documents were presented to the court, and that ASIC's case was primarily based upon documentary evidence. However, when those documents were scrutinised in detail, they were found to be, wholly or in part, too unreliable to form the basis for financial findings. Also, there were 'unexplained problems' with the documents, adding to 'a serious flaw in ASIC's case'.[164]

Perhaps the most serious indication that Justice Austin was not impressed with the way ASIC ran the case is the fact that in addition to ordering ASIC to pay the defendants' costs of the proceedings as agreed or assessed, he gave close consideration to the question of whether this was not an appropriate case for ordering costs assessed on an indemnity basis: in other words, not only the actual legal costs, but also additional costs associated with a long, drawn-out court case. It was with some hesitation and unassertiveness that Austin J eventually concluded that it was not warranted to impose indemnity costs.[165] ASIC, and other Australian regulators, should take serious note of his observations, especially stark criticism like this:

> According to my observation, ASIC *doggedly* pursued an extremely large case because of its conviction, erroneously in my view but not reckless or *totally* groundless, that the evidence would support its contentions. (emphasis added)[166]

---

162   *Australian Securities and Investments Commission v Rich* (2009) 75 ACSR 1 at [7269]–[7270].
163   Ibid. at [7319].
164   Ibid.
165   Ibid. at [7325]–[7330].
166   Ibid. at [7330].

9.4 Conclusion

This chapter confirms the view of Lord Hoffman that it is far from easy to succinctly extract the duties expected of directors.[167] For two reasons we have chosen to use the statutory duties, and in particular the civil penalty provisions in the Australian *Corporations Act 2001* (Cth), as the starting point for explaining directors' duties and their potential liability. First, the Corporations Act covers directors' general law duties (duties at common law and in equity) very comprehensively, and provides a neat extraction of most of these. Second, the litigation in recent years, dealing with breaches of directors' duties, has almost exclusively been based on breaches of the statutory duties, not on breaches of the duties at common law and in equity.

167   Lord Hoffman, 'Duties of company directors' (1999) 10 *European Business Law Review* 78.

10

ENFORCEMENT OF DIRECTORS' DUTIES

There are no qualifications for being a company director. Even directors of listed companies do not have to take any examinations . . . In principle, anyone can become a director. One might therefore think that the duties of an office so unexacting in its qualifications would be simple and easy to ascertain. In fact, this is far from the case. In fact, the duties of directors can be discovered only by examining at least three different sources which lie like strata one above the other. The bedrock is the duties which directors owe at common law, or more precisely in equity, simply because they are managing other people's property. Over that layer has been imposed a number of specific statutory duties intended to reinforce the duties at common law. And over that layer has been imposed still further duties under various self-regulatory codes, which are also intended to reinforce the common law duties in areas not thought suitable for legislation.

> Lord Hoffman, 'Duties of Company Directors' (1999) 10
> *European Business Law Review* 78

The governance of a public company should be about stewardship. Those in control have a duty to act in the best interests of the company. They must use the company's resources productively. They must understand that those resources are not personal property. The last years of HIH were marked by poor leadership and inept management. Indeed, an attitude of apparent indifference to, or deliberate disregard of, the company's underlying problems pervades the affairs of the group.

> Report of the HIH Royal Commission (Owen Report), *The Failure
> of HIH Insurance – Volume I: A Corporate Collapse and its Lessons*
> (Commonwealth of Australia, 2003) xiii–xiv

10.1 Introduction

The Australian Securities and Investments Commission (ASIC), as the primary corporate regulator, has had some spectacular successes,[1] as well as failures,[2] in enforcing the civil penalty provisions underpinning breach of directors' duties under the *Corporations Act 2001* (Cth) (Corporations Act). ASIC has played an active role in enforcing civil penalty provisions

---

1   For some of ASIC's successes, see Jean J du Plessis, 'Reverberations after the HIH and other recent Australian corporate collapses: The role of ASIC' (2003) 15 *Australian Journal of Corporate Law* 225, 240–3; Anil Hargovan, 'Corporate governance lessons from James Hardie' (2009) 33 *Melbourne University Law Review* 984, 'Dual role of general counsel and company secretary: Walking the legal tightrope in *Shafron v Australian Securities and Investments Commission*' (2012) 27 *Australian Journal of Corporate Law* 112, and 'Caution against board groupthink – Civil penalties in James Hardie' (2013) 65 *Keeping Good Companies* 36.

2   *Australian Securities and Investments Commission v Rich* (2009) 75 ACSR 1; *Forrest v Australian Securities and Investments Commission* (2012) 247 CLR 486. See John Humphrey and Stephen Corones, '*Forrest v ASIC*: "A perfect storm"' (2014) 88 *Australian Law Journal* 26.

against directors and officers.[3] However, as noted by one commentator, ASIC has shown a marked reluctance in recent years to use its power under s 50 of the *Australian Securities and Investment Commission Act 2001* (Cth) (ASIC Act) to bring civil action in the name of the company, or a class action for shareholders or investors for the recovery of damages for corporate misconduct.[4] The purpose of s 50 has been captured by Justice Lockhart in *Somerville v Australian Securities and Investments Commission*:

> An evident function of s 50 is to permit the commission, acting in the public interest, to cause proceedings to be taken where persons or corporations have suffered loss or harm arising from fraud, negligence or misconduct, but do not have the resources to maintain expensive and complicated litigation ... In the case of a company, the commission may cause the proceedings to be begun and carried on the company's name whether it consents or not.[5]

This reluctance can be attributed, in part, to the rise and rise of class actions,[6] which are discussed further in Chapter 13.

The aim of this chapter, however, is to provide an overview of the enforcement actions available to shareholders and some other parties. It deals briefly with the statutory derivative action (Part 2F.1A); actions aimed at unfairly prejudicial, discriminatory or oppressive conduct by the corporation or its directors (Part 2F.1); and injunctions under s 1324 of the Corporations Act.[7] The chapter also canvasses the criminal liability of directors and selected types of criminal offences under the Corporations Act.

10.2 The statutory derivative action: Part 2F.1A

10.2.1 The case for introducing a statutory derivative action

> These provisions [statutory derivative action] basically make it easier for shareholders and others to institute proceedings (including proceedings against directors) where the directors refuse to do so. These provisions obviously increase the exposure of directors,

---

3   For some of the literature on the growth of civil penalties and its use Andrew Keay and Michelle Welsh, 'Enforcing breaches of directors' duties by a public body and Antipodean experiences' (2015) 15 *Journal of Corporate Law Studies* 255; Michelle Welsh, 'Civil penalties and responsive regulation: The gap between theory and practice' (2009) 33(3) *Melbourne University Law Review* 908; Vicky Comino, 'The enforcement record of ASIC since the introduction of the civil penalty regime' (2007) 20 *Australian Journal of Corporate Law* 183.

4   Janet Austin, 'Does the Westpoint litigation signal a revival of the ASIC s 50 class action?' (2008) 22 *Australian Journal of Corporate Law* 8.

5   (1995) 60 FCR 319; 131 ALR 517 at 523.

6   Michael Legg, 'Shareholder class actions in Australia – The perfect storm' (2008) 31 *University of New South Wales (UNSW) Law Journal* 669, and 'Public and Private Enforcement – ASIC and the Shareholder Class Action' in Michael Legg (ed.), *Regulation, Litigation and Enforcement* (Thomson Reuters, 2011).

7   For a fuller discussion, see Jason Harris, Anil Hargovan and Michael Adams, *Australian Corporate Law* (LexisNexis, 5th edn, 2016) Ch 19.

as there is now greater potential for actions to be brought against directors in the name of the company.[8]

The derivative action allows an individual to bring an action that belongs to another (it should be remembered that directors owe their duty to the corporation and that the corporation is thus the proper plaintiff in the case of any breach of these duties). Furthermore, the benefit of this action, brought by the shareholder, will not directly advantage that member; rather, it will accrue to the corporation which has, for whatever reason, decided not to pursue the matter. Thus it allows the shareholder to usurp the authority that the corporate entity has vested in the board of directors. Significantly, it also allows the minority shareholders of the corporation to act as some sort of corporate watchdog over the majority, and to set the company in motion to establish their rights in situations in which the majority shareholders oppose the company doing so.[9]

The main difficulties associated with the common law derivative action, which preceded the introduction of the statutory derivative action under Part 2F.1A, were summarised as follows in the Explanatory Memorandum to the CLERP Bill 1998 (which became the CLERP Act 1999):

- the effect of ratification of the impugned conduct by the general meeting of shareholders (if effective, the purported ratification by a majority of shareholders could deny the company as a whole, and hence minority shareholders, any right of action against the directors);
- the lack of access to company funds by shareholders to finance the proceedings (where a shareholder seeks to enforce a right on behalf of a company, they are likely to be disinclined to risk having costs awarded against them in a case which will ultimately benefit the company as a whole, not just individual shareholders);[10] and
- the strict criteria that need to be established before a court may grant leave.[11] The statutory derivative action allows an eligible applicant, which includes shareholders and directors, to commence proceedings on behalf of a company, including for breaches of directors' duties under sections 180–184, where the company is unwilling or unable to do so. Proceedings may be commenced in respect of wrongs done to the company, with the company thereby benefiting from successful actions.[12]

10.2.2 Eligible applicants

Section 236(1) of the Act, outlining who is entitled to apply to bring a statutory derivative action, provides as follows:

---

8   Emilios Kyrou, 'Directors' duties, defences, indemnities, access to board papers and D&O insurance post CLERPA' (2000) 18 *Company and Securities Law Journal (C&SLJ)* 555, 561.

9   See *Metyor Inc v Queensland Electronic Switching Pty Ltd* [2003] 1 Qd R 186. For insight into the operation of the derivative action in Asia, see Félix E Mezzanotte, 'The unconvincing rise of the statutory derivative action in Hong Kong: Evidence from its first 10 years of enforcement' (2017) *Journal of Corporate Law Studies* DOI: 10.1080/14735970.2017.1285548; Dan Puchniak, 'The derivative action in Asia' (2013) 9 *Berkeley Business Law Journal* 1. For insight into the UK experience, see Andrew Keay, 'Assessing and rethinking the statutory scheme for derivative actions under the *Companies Act 2006*' (2016) 1 *Journal of Corporate Law Studies* 39–68 DOI: 10.1080/14735970.2015.1090140.

10   For a discussion of costs in derivative actions see: Albert Monichino, 'Costs in statutory derivative actions: The lingering ghost of Wallersteiner' (2015) 33 *C&SLJ* 104.

11   Explanatory Memorandum to the CLERP Bill 1998, para 6.15.

12   Ibid. para 6.17.

(1) A person may bring proceedings on behalf of a company, or intervene in any proceedings to which the company is a party for the purpose of taking responsibility on behalf of the company for those proceedings, or for a particular step in those proceedings (for example, compromising or settling them), if:

    (a) the person is:

        (i) a member, former member, or person entitled to be registered as a member, of the company or of a related body corporate; or

        (ii) an officer or former officer of the company; and

    (b) the person is acting with leave granted under section 237.

Under the common law, only members may institute derivative proceedings on behalf of a company. Former members are included under the statutory provision because they may have been compelled to leave the company in view of the dispute giving rise to the litigation on behalf of the company. Members and former members of a related body corporate are also included as they may be adversely affected by the failure of the company to take action and therefore may have a legitimate interest in applying to commence a derivative action. This will be particularly relevant in a corporate group scenario where subsidiary companies wish to take action against the directors of the holding company; for example, the NSW Supreme Court decision in *Goozee v Graphic World Group Holdings Pty Ltd*.[13] In this case, however, leave to institute a derivative action was refused, as the court held that the applicant was not acting in good faith, and the derivative action would not be in the best interests of each immediate holding company. The conferral of standing on officers recognises that they are most likely to be the first to become aware of a right of action that is not being pursued by the company.[14]

ASIC is not included as an eligible applicant, as one of the purposes of the procedure is to relieve some of the regulatory burden from ASIC.[15]

10.2.3 Cause of action

The statutory derivative action may be used in respect of a cause of action that a company has against either:

- a director of the company for breach of duties owed to the company; or
- a third party for a breach of contract or in respect of a tortious act committed by that third party (it will, however, be presumed that where proceedings involve a third party, granting leave is not in the best interests of the company unless the contrary is proved (proposed section 237(3))).[16]

The provisions allow a person to intervene in proceedings to which a company is a party, on behalf of the company, for the purpose of taking responsibility on behalf of the company for those proceedings, or for a particular step in those proceedings. This includes continuing, defending, discontinuing, compromising or settling the proceedings on behalf of the company.[17]

---

13   (2002) 42 ACSR 534.

14   Explanatory Memorandum to the CLERP Bill 1998, paras 6.26–6.28.

15   Ibid. para 6.30.

16   Ibid. para 6.20.

17   Ibid. para 6.21.

10.2.4 Leave of court required to institute the action

It was realised that appropriate checks and balances should be provided in the legislation to prevent abuse of the proceedings and to ensure that company managements are not undermined by vexatious litigation and that company funds are not expended unnecessarily. This is done by requiring, in s 237, that a court should only grant leave to proceed with the action if:[18]

- there is inaction by the company;
- the applicant is acting in good faith;
- the action appears to be in the best interests of the company;[19]
- there is a serious question to be tried; and
- the applicant gave written notice to the company of the intention to apply for leave, and of the reasons for applying, at least 14 days before making the application, or circumstances are such that it is appropriate to grant leave in any case.

Upon the applicant establishing each of these five elements of s 237(2) to the court's satisfaction, the court is required to grant the application for leave under s 237(1). There is no residual discretion.[20]

Empirical evidence suggests that it is a moot point whether the introduction of the statutory derivative action, as framed in Part 2F.1A,[21] has served as an effective watchdog by empowering shareholders to litigate on behalf of the company to redress wrongs done to the company that the company itself declines to pursue.[22]

10.3 Oppressive conduct of affairs: Part 2F.1

10.3.1 Types of conduct covered

Section 232 of the Corporations Act specifies the grounds for a court order under Part 2F.1. It provides that a court can make any order under s 233 (see discussion below) if certain specified conduct by the corporation is either contrary to the interests of the members as a whole, or oppressive to, unfairly prejudicial to, or unfairly discriminatory against, a member or members whether in that capacity or in any other capacity. Three specified forms of conduct are listed:

---

18   For discussion of the legal principles surrounding the operation of s 237, see *Swansson v RA Pratt Properties Pty Ltd* (2002) 42 ACSR 313; *Chahwan v Euphoric Pty Ltd* (2008) 65 ACSR 661; *Oates v Consolidated Capital Services Ltd* (2009) 76 NSWLR 69.

19   For relevant factors under this section, see *Re Gladstone Pacific Nickel Ltd* (2011) 86 ACSR 432.

20   *Chahwan v Euphoric Pty Ltd* (2008) 65 ACSR 661.

21   For criticisms of law reform proposals leading up to the introduction of Part 2F.1A, see Anil Hargovan, 'Under judicial and legislative attack: The rule in *Foss v Harbottle*' (1996) 113 *South African Law Journal* 631.

22   See further I Ramsay and B Saunders, *Litigation by Shareholders and Directors: An Empirical Study of the Statutory Derivative Action* (Centre for Corporate Law and Securities Regulation, University of Melbourne, 2005).

1. the conduct of a company's affairs; or
2. an actual or proposed act or omission by or on behalf of a company; or
3. a resolution, or a proposed resolution, of members or a class of members of a company.

The oppression remedy is frequently relied upon, especially by members in proprietary companies whose commercial interests may be exploited and who may be unable to sell their shares to exit the company. The Corporations Act does not define 'oppression'. The courts have defined it widely, to mean conduct that is 'burdensome, harsh and wrongful'.[23] In the leading decision on the operation of s 232, the High Court in *Wayde v New South Wales Rugby League Ltd*[24] held that there is no need to establish any irregularity or breach of legal rights to succeed. Thus conduct that is legal may still be oppressive. Furthermore, mere prejudice or discrimination is insufficient to establish a breach of s 232, as the wording in that section requires the prejudice or discrimination to be unfair. Oppression may occur even though all members of a company are treated equally.[25] There is no requirement to prove that the company or its officers intended to cause harm to the members.[26] The broad nature of this provision, together with the wide nature of relief available (identified below), makes it an important remedy for minority shareholders.[27]

10.3.2 Who may apply for relief

Section 234 allows the following parties to bring an application under Part 2F.1:

(a) a member of the company, even if the application relates to an act or omission that is against:
  (i) the member in a capacity other than as a member; or
  (ii) another member in their capacity as a member; or
(b) a person who has been removed from the register of members because of a selective reduction; or
(c) a person who has ceased to be a member of the company if the application relates to the circumstances in which they ceased to be a member; or
(d) a person to whom a share in the company has been transmitted by will or by operation of law; or
(e) a person whom ASIC thinks appropriate having regard to investigations it is conducting or has conducted into:
  (i) the company's affairs; or
  (ii) matters connected with the company's affairs.

The discretion of ASIC under s 234(e) is now wide enough to allow any person to have standing if ASIC thinks it to be appropriate.

---

23 *Scottish Co-operative Wholesale Society Ltd v Meyer* [1959] AC 324.
24 (1985) 180 CLR 459.
25 *John J Starr (Real Estate) Pty Ltd v Robert R Andrew (Australasia) Pty Ltd* (1991) 6 ACSR 63.
26 *Campbell v Backoffice Investments Pty Ltd* (2009) 238 CLR 304.
27 See further Ian Ramsay, 'An empirical study of the use of the oppression remedy' (1999) 27 *Australian Business Law Review* 23.

10.3.3 Nature of relief available

Section 233(1) confers upon a court a broad discretion to make 'any order under this section that it considers appropriate in relation to the company'. Apart from this very wide discretion, s 233(1) lists 10 specific orders the court could consider, namely:

(a)   that the company be wound up;

(b)   that the company's existing constitution be modified or repealed;

(c)   that conduct of the company's affairs be regulated in future;

(d)   for the purchase of any shares by any member or person to whom a share in the company has been transmitted by will or by operation of law;

(e)   for the purchase of shares with an appropriate reduction of the company's share capital;

(f)   for the company to institute, prosecute, defend or discontinue specified proceedings;

(g)   authorising a member, or a person to whom a share in the company has been transmitted by will or by operation of law, to institute, prosecute, defend or discontinue specified proceedings in the name and on behalf of the company;

(h)   appointing a receiver or a receiver and manager of any or all of the company's property;

(i)   restraining a person from engaging in specified conduct or from doing a specified act; and

(j)   requiring a person to do a specified act.

It is clear that the judicial discretion afforded under s 233 may be exercised to mould a remedy appropriate to each particular case. Section 233(2) ensures that the general law applying to winding up will apply if the court orders that the company be wound up.

Where a court's order effects a change to the company's constitution the company cannot, without leave of the court, alter the constitution in a manner that is inconsistent with the order, unless the order states that the company does have the power to make such a change (s 232 (3)(a)) or the company obtains the leave of the court (s 232(3)(b)).

10.4 Section 1324 injunctions

10.4.1 Introduction

The injunctive relief provided for under s 1324 has not been used as often as originally expected. Subsection 1324(1) allows ASIC or a person 'whose interests have been, are or would be affected by the conduct' to apply for an injunction or interim injunction (s 1324(4)) restraining a person who engages in conduct which, in essence, directly or indirectly involves a contravention of the Corporations Act. Under s 1324(2), the court may require a person who fails or refuses to do an act required by the Act to do such an act. We emphasise that s 1324 applies to the contravention of any provision in the entire Act.

10.4.2 Section 1324(1)

In essence, s 1324(1) provides that where a person has engaged, is engaging or is proposing to engage in conduct that constituted, constitutes or would constitute a contravention of the Act, the court may, on the application of ASIC or of 'a person whose interests have been, are or would be affected by the conduct', grant an injunction, on such terms as the court thinks appropriate, restraining the first-mentioned person from engaging in the conduct and, if in the opinion of the court it is desirable to do so, requiring that person to do any act or thing.

Importantly, the phrase 'a person whose interests have been, are or would be affected', has been interpreted broadly to apply to creditors, employees, shareholders and other stakeholders[28] – even though, as discussed earlier, directors owe their duties first and foremost to the company. Accordingly, while the general duties of directors (for example, due care and diligence, good faith, proper purpose) under Chapter 2D of the Act are owed to the company, and only ASIC or the company (if seeking a compensation order – see s 1317(2)) has standing to initiate action for breach as the duties are civil penalty provisions, if a shareholder or a creditor, for example, suffers some loss or damage due to a breach or potential breach of a Chapter 2D duty, he or she may utilise s 1324 to have the particular conduct stopped, and/or to obtain damages (under s 1324(10), discussed below). Without s 1324, stakeholders affected by corporate misconduct, but without standing, would be dependent on ASIC to take action. This highlights the power of s 1324 as a remedial tool for stakeholders, and explains why commentators are frustrated by the fact that it has to date been under-utilised.[29]

10.4.3 The court's discretion

Section 1324 provides the court with a broad discretion to make orders on such terms as it thinks appropriate and to discharge and vary such at any time (s 1324(1), (2) and (5)). The court may also order the person to pay damages to any other person in lieu of or in addition to an order under s 1324(1) and (2): s 1324(10). Moreover, the court may order relief under s 1324 (1) or (2) whether or not it appears that:

- the person will continue to engage, or refuse/fail to engage, in that conduct;
- the person has previously engaged, or refused/failed to engage, in that conduct; and
- there is an imminent danger of substantial damage to any person if that person engages, or refuses/fails to engage, in that conduct (s 1324(6) and (7)).

10.4.4 Remedies in particular

The main force of s 1324 is to provide restraining and mandatory injunctive relief. However, s 1324(9) widens the relief available to include the Mareva-type relief provided for under s 1323 of the Corporations Act. Section 1323 gives power to the court to prohibit payment or transfer of money, securities, futures contracts or property.

---

28   See, for example, *Airpeak Pty Ltd v Jetstream Aircraft* (1997) 73 FCR 161; *Allen v Atalay* (1993) 11 ACSR 753. Cf *Mesenberg v Cord Industrial Recruiters Pty Ltd* (1996) 39 NSWLR 128 for a restrictive interpretation.

29   See James McConvill, 'Part 2F.1A of the Corporations Act: Insert a new s 242(2) or give it the boot?' (2002) 30 *Australian Business Law Review* 309, and 'Australian Securities and Investments Commission's proposed power to issue infringement notices: Another slap in the face to s 1324 of the Corporations Act or an undermining of corporate civil liberties?' (2003) 31 *Australian Business Law Review* 36; Robert Baxt, 'A body blow to section 1324 of the Corporations Law?' (1996) 14 *C&SLJ* 312.

Section 1324(10) provides that:

> Where the Court has power under this section to grant an injunction restraining a person
> from engaging in particular conduct, or requiring a person to do a particular act or thing,
> the Court may, either in addition to or in substitution for the grant of the injunction, order
> that person to pay damages to any other person.

The Queensland Court of Appeal, in *McCracken v Phoenix Constructions (Qld) Pty Ltd*,[30] held
that a creditor cannot obtain an award of damages under s 1324(10) against a director for
breach of director's duties. It was held that an award of damages could only be given where an
injunction could be sought, and the award of damages was therefore ancillary to the power to
grant an injunction.

Moreover, the court reasoned that a construction of s 1324(10) that allowed any person
adversely affected by a contravention to claim damages cannot be reconciled with the specific
civil remedy provisions in Part 9.4B of the Act. Thus,[31] after *McCracken v Phoenix Constructions (Qld)Pty Ltd*, it is unlikely that courts will allow creditors to claim damages directly from
directors under s 1324(10) based on a breach of directors' core duties under sections 180–182
of the Act. By the same token, as the company is the proper plaintiff, it is unlikely that s 1324
will in future be seen as an exception to the statutory derivative action.[32]

10.5 Criminal liability of directors

10.5.1 The importance of the criminal sanction in corporations law

The sanctions explained above could be described as civil sanctions based on statutory
provisions. We have chosen not to deal with non-statutory civil sanctions (for example,
action against directors or other personnel for common law negligence or breach of trust in
equity) because of limited space and because the statutory sanctions are so prominent
nowadays. The criminal sanction is, however, also very prominent in Australian corporations
law and some mention should be made of potential offences directors and officers can
commit under the Act. A comprehensive discussion of possible offences for corporations,
directors and other officers falls outside the scope of this work. Appendix G to the *Report of
the HIH Royal Commission* provides a very useful summary of the offence provisions of
several Acts. It also contains an excellent explanation of the differences between the corporations law before and after 13 March 2000: significant amendments were made to the Act
with effect from that date.[33]

---

30   [2013] 2 Qd R 27.
31   See Jean J du Plessis, 'Company law developments in South Africa: Modernisation and some salient
      features of the Companies Act 71 of 2008' (2012) 27 *Australian Journal of Corporate Law* 46, 62–3. See
      also Nishad Kulkarni, 'In defence of McCracken: A response to "Why do courts cut back on statutory
      remedies provided by Parliament under corporate law?"' (2015) 89 *Australian Law Journal* 175.
32   See *Corporations Act 2001* (Cth) Pt 2F.1A. See the discussion of the relationship between s 1324 and the
      derivative action by RP Austin and IM Ramsay, *Ford's Principles of Corporations Law* (LexisNexis,
      15th edn, 2013) 695–7, para 10.310.
33   Owen Report, *The Failure of HIH Insurance* (2003) Vol 1, 321–30.

We deal here only with some of the most important criminal offences that directors and officers can commit, and only with those mentioned in the Act. There are numerous other offences, in particular in the areas of workplace health and safety and environmental law, and, of course, under general criminal law (for example, theft, complicity and a range of deception offences)[34] that could be committed by directors and officers.

Subject to the provisions of the Act, the *Criminal Code Act 1995* (Code) applies to all offences against the Act.[35] The Code clarifies the operation of general principles of criminal liability by setting in place the 'physical' element (what traditionally was the *actus reus* or physical act of the offence) and the 'fault' element of an offence (traditionally the *mens rea*). To briefly explain, the Code provides that the physical elements of an offence are:

- conduct; or
- the circumstances in which conduct occurs; or
- a result of conduct.

Under the Code, the prosecution has the onus of proving each physical element of the offence. Along with the physical element(s), the prosecution is also required to prove the fault element of the offence. The Code sets down four 'default' fault elements: intention, knowledge, recklessness and negligence. The Code operates such that an offence can have its own fault element specific to the physical element of the offence; however, where there is no specified fault element, the Code expressly states that a default fault element will apply to determine liability. The Code provides that for the 'conduct' part of an offence (for example, improper use of company information), the default element is 'intention'; for 'circumstances' or 'result' (for example, causing detriment to the corporation) the default element is 'recklessness'.

Part 2.5 of the Code is particularly significant, in that it explains how the principles of criminal responsibility in the Code apply to bodies corporate in relation to offences against Commonwealth laws (including the Corporations Act). Thus, to determine whether the company will be criminally liable for intentional offences of directors or other officers under the Act, Part 2.5 needs to be consulted (unless the relevant provision states that the principles of criminal responsibility under the Code do not apply). Part 2.5 provides that the physical element of an offence will be attributed to a body corporate where it is committed by an agent or officer of the body corporate acting within the actual or apparent scope of their authority. This is, in essence, a codification of the traditional common law principle attributing criminal liability to the company when a criminal act is committed by the 'directing mind' of the company.[36] In relation to the fault element, Division 12.3(1) provides that where 'intention, knowledge or recklessness' is a fault element of an offence, that element can be attributed to the company if the company 'expressly, tacitly or impliedly authorised or permitted the commission of the offence'.

Division 12.3(2) of the Code is crucial here, as it provides that 'authorisation or permission' may be established by a number of means, including:

---

34   See, for example, James McConvill and Mirko Bagaric, 'Criminal responsibility based on complicity among corporate officers' (2004) 16 *Australian Journal of Corporate Law* 172.

35   *Corporations Act 2001* (Cth) s 1308A.

36   See *Tesco Supermarkets v Nattrass* [1971] 2 All ER 127.

(c)   proving that a corporate culture existed within the body corporate that directed, encouraged, tolerated or led to non-compliance with the relevant provision; or

(d)   proving that the body corporate failed to create and maintain a corporate culture that required compliance with the relevant provision.

'Corporate culture' is defined under Part 2.5 (div 12.3(6)) of the Code as an 'attitude, policy, rule, course of conduct or practice existing within the body corporate generally or in the part of the body corporate in which the relevant activities take place'. The effect of Part 2.5, therefore, is that the intention of a company will be equated with its 'corporate culture'. It is generally accepted that Part 2.5 of the Code, by embedding the concept of corporate culture, will have a significant impact on the approach to determining criminal liability of companies for the actions of their directors as well as their employees and agents.[37] Part 2.5 may, indeed, impose a direct duty on companies to implement a compliance system to avoid systematic contravention of federal legislation, including the Act.[38]

It is pertinent to note that there is often very little, if any, substantive difference between conduct that is a criminal and conduct that constitutes a civil wrong. As a result of the huge expansion over the past few decades in the types of conduct that are now proscribed by the criminal law, it is not tenable to provide a coherent rationale to distinguish between criminal and civil wrongs. It is certainly not the case, for example, that criminal liability is now reserved for the most heinous or harmful types of conduct. A large amount of very trifling conduct – such as littering and incorrectly parking a motor vehicle, and in some jurisdictions even flying a kite to the annoyance of others – is a criminal offence.[39] Thus, as a general rule, few inferences, in terms of the seriousness of the proscribed conduct, can be drawn merely from whether a director or officer is guilty of a civil or a criminal penalty.

Whether conduct is made a criminal or civil offence often turns on matters such as the (actual or perceived) public sentiment, at the time the offence was created, in relation to the relevant conduct. Given the increasing amount of public disillusionment in recent years regarding corporate behaviour and collapses, it is not surprising that we are seeing a range of new corporate criminal offences being enacted. This, however, does not necessarily mean that the conduct prohibited by these provisions is objectively particularly serious or damaging.

Despite the fact that there is no coherent distinction between civil and criminal wrongs, there are significant differences in the manner in which the respective breaches are treated. Criminal offences tend to result in stigmatisation and subject the agent to a range of coercive measures, including imprisonment. Civil wrongs do not generally involve moral censure, and the harshest measure generally comes in the form of a monetary extraction.

Thus, whether conduct is dealt with by means of civil or criminal liability often seems arbitrary. In addition, the conduct covered by the civil and criminal wrongs is often very similar, and in fact can often be dealt with under either regime. In such circumstances, prosecution authorities may in effect elect to pursue the director or officer in either the civil

---

37   See James McConvill and John Bingham, 'Comply or comply: The illusion of voluntary corporate governance' (2004) 22 *C&SLJ* 208, 213–14.

38   See Christine Parker and Olivia Conolly, 'Is there a duty to implement a corporate compliance system in Australian law?' (2002) 30 *Australian Business Law Review* 273, 282–3.

39   For further discussion regarding the convergence between criminal and civil offences, see Mirko Bagaric, 'The "civil-isation" of the criminal law' (2001) 25 *Criminal Law Journal* 197.

or the criminal jurisdiction. Faced with such a choice, it might seem most appropriate to go down the criminal stream in order that the defendant is held fully accountable for their conduct. However, there are often compelling reasons for pursuing a civil remedy instead.

First, it is generally easier to establish civil wrongdoing, where the burden of proof is 'on the balance of probabilities' rather than 'beyond reasonable doubt'. The rules of evidence in relation to civil proceedings are also far more liberal, and hence prosecution authorities (including the Commonwealth Department of Public Prosecutions in relation to the Act) can normally tender a greater amount of evidence in support of a civil case.[40]

Second, people charged with criminal offences are likely to more fiercely contest such allegations than allegations that have only a civil dimension. This is because criminal offences carry a greater stigma and often involve a risk of imprisonment – which is the harshest penalty in our system of law. Thus the prospect of reaching an agreed settlement with a director or officer is diminished if criminal proceedings are pursued.

Prosecution authorities should not be unduly influenced by seeking to finalise matters as expeditiously as possible. Ultimately, the most important objective is to ensure that all people are held fully responsible for their transgressions. However, it would be remiss of prosecution authorities not to give considerable weight to the likely cost to the public of a long criminal trial – which can easily blow out into millions of dollars – in deciding whether they should launch civil or criminal proceedings against a director or officer.

In some cases, where the evidence is particularly strong, even the most powerful and well-resourced directors or officers may plead guilty to criminal offences. The advantage to them in doing so is that a plea of guilty spares the community significant costs in the form of legal costs and is viewed as evidence of contrition by the accused person, thus entitling the accused to a significant penalty reduction.

10.5.2 Selected criminal offences directors and other officers can commit under the Corporations Act

10.5.2.1 General

Schedule 3 to the Act contains all the penalties (criminal as well as civil) and maximum periods of imprisonment for each of the criminal offences created by the Act. These offences can be committed by a wide variety of persons, but they are primarily offences that can be committed by the directors and officers and employees of the company.

Since we have concentrated on the civil penalty provisions as far as directors' duties are concerned, we will also give only an overview of the offences directors can commit in relation to those provisions. Apart from s 180 (duty of care and diligence) and sections 674(2A) and 675(2A) (continuous disclosure), all the other civil penalty provisions are also made offences under the Act.

10.5.2.2 Specific offences for breaches of duties

Whereas sections 181 to 183 reflect directors' civil obligations, s 184 lays down the requirements for when directors will commit criminal offences in contravening their duties of good

---

40   For a discussion of evidence law and the different rules that apply in the criminal and civil jurisdictions, see Ken Arenson and Mirko Bagaric, *Understanding Evidence Law* (LexisNexis Butterworths, 2002).

faith, use of position and use of information. Under s 184(1) a director or other officer of a corporation commits an offence if they are reckless, or are intentionally dishonest, and fail to exercise their powers and discharge their duties in good faith in the best interests of the corporation, or for a proper purpose.

A director who fails to perform his or her duties under these sections may be guilty of a criminal offence, with a penalty of $360,000 or imprisonment for up to five years, or both.

Schedule 3 imposes a range of pecuniary penalties through 'penalty units' (currently $180 but indexed each year) ranging from 5 to 2000 penalty units.

10.6 Conclusion

In this chapter we have shown that there are several ways of enforcing the provisions of the *Corporations Act 2001* (Cth) and have highlighted the public and private enforcement dichotomy in Australia. Although ASIC has a prominent role to play in the enforcement of the law against corporate misconduct, shareholders, directors and officers, and creditors[41] are also given standing to enforce directors' duties either on behalf of the company or on their own behalf. The statutory derivative actions (Part 2F.1A) and oppressive remedies actions (Part 2F.1) are the most important actions available to shareholders, with the latter often used in unlisted private companies or in closely held quasi-partnership companies. Section 1324 injunctions and damages provide powerful remedies to any person affected by conduct of the company in contravention of provisions of the Act, but its actual use is limited, disappointingly, and constrained by judicial interpretation. There are numerous criminal sanctions for contraventions of the Act, with research showing that criminal enforcement of directors' duties by the Commonwealth Director of Public Prosection is significantly more prevalent than civil enforcement by ASIC.[42]

---

41   Creditors, of course, have limited standing under the *Corporations Act 2001* (Cth).
42   J Hedges et al., 'An Empirical Analysis of Public Enforcement of Directors' Duties in Australia: Preliminary Findings', CIFR Paper No. 105/2016 (4 March 2016) <https://ssrn.com/abstract=2766132>.

PART **3**

CORPORATE GOVERNANCE IN INTERNATIONAL AND GLOBAL CONTEXTS

11

CORPORATE GOVERNANCE IN THE UNITED STATES, THE UNITED KINGDOM, NEW ZEALAND, CANADA, SOUTH AFRICA AND INDIA

Two features can be considered to describe the modern world – globalization and the free market. It is widely accepted – almost unquestioningly – that free markets will lead to greater economic growth and that we will all benefit from this economic growth.

> Güler Aras and David Crowther, 'Convergence: A Prognosis' in Güler
> Aras and David Crowther (eds), *Global Perspectives on Corporate
> Governance and CSR* (Farnham, Gower Publishing Ltd, 2009) 314–15

11.1 Introduction

In this chapter we give a brief overview of corporate governance in the US, the UK, New Zealand, Canada, South Africa and India, some of the major Anglo-American corporate governance jurisdictions that are based on the unitary (one-tier) board model. In Chapter 12 we deal with corporate governance developments in the European Union (EU), the OECD principles of corporate governance, and corporate governance in Germany, China, Japan and Indonesia. The OECD principles include traditional Anglo-American corporate governance principles, but go wider – including principles applying to a traditional unitary board structure and principles applying to a typical two-tier board structure.

11.2 United States (US)

11.2.1 Background to the corporate governance debate in the US

Corporate governance has been a topic for discussion in the US for a very long time, and the materials written on corporate governance in the US are extensive. As such a dominant world economy, US debates on corporate governance will almost invariably influence corporate governance debates in other jurisdictions. It is, therefore, important to deal with corporate governance debates in the US in order to understand corporate governance models in other parts of the world.

The debate on corporate governance in the US started as early as 1932, when Adolf Berle and Gardiner Means published their book, *The Modern Corporation and Private Property*.[1] The importance of this debate was emphasised by Myles Mace's book, *Directors: Myth and Reality*, published in 1971, but the discussion became really heated in 1982 with the publication by the American Law Institute (ALI) of its *Principles of Corporate Governance and Structure: Restatement and Recommendations*. The project was designed as a restatement of the law, but as corporate law (and hence corporate governance law) in the US is based on state law developments, the exact applications of these broad principles vary from state to state. This project, which had started off quite modestly, resulted in a stream of publications on the topic of corporate governance in the US. The Proposed Final Draft (later termed *Principles of Corporate Governance and Structure: Analysis and Recommendations*) was only approved in

---

1   See Klaus J Hopt, 'Preface' in *Institutional Investors and Corporate Governance* (Walter de Gruyter, 1994) i.

May 1992. However, publications on this topic did not stop there. In 1993 alone, 73 articles published in US law review journals dealt directly with the topic of corporate governance.[2] One commentator justly alluded to 'The Emergence of Corporate Governance as a New Legal Discipline';[3] another remarked that between 1990 and 1993 'events have moved at lightning speed for the world of corporate governance'.[4] Things continue to happen at a dazzling pace since the huge corporate collapses of Enron,[5] WorldCom, and others, and the developments since the Global Financial Crisis that began in 2007.

In the US, the theories of shareholder primacy and profit maximisation are still dominant in expressions of 'the objective and conduct of the corporation'. This is clearly set out in the ALI's *Principles of Corporate Governance*:

§2.01 The Objective and Conduct of the Corporation

(a) Subject to the provisions of Subsection (b) ... a corporation should have as its objective the conduct of business activities with a view to enhance corporate profit and shareholder gain.

(b) Even if corporate profit and shareholder gain are not thereby enhanced, the corporation, in the conduct of its business:

(1) Is obliged, to the same extent as a natural person, to act within the boundaries set by law;

(2) May take into account ethical considerations that are reasonably regarded as appropriate to the responsible conduct of business; and

(3) May devote a reasonable amount of resources to public welfare, humanitarian, educational, and philanthropic purposes.

11.2.2 The American Law Institute's involvement in the corporate governance debate

11.2.2.1 Basic aims of the project

In its project, *Principles of Corporate Governance and Structure: Restatement and Recommendations*, the ALI aspired to extract from the body of US corporations law a set of generalised propositions that would instruct managers and directors about their duties, and to provide criteria for judgment by courts in cases involving allegations of improper conduct by managements and directors.[6] It was hoped to extract the basic corporate governance principles applicable in the US from court cases and other sources and to restate the law.[7]

---

2   A search of the large SSRN database, which is dominated by articles with a US focus, listed 580 articles with the term 'corporate governance' in the title for the period April 2015–April 2017: <www.ssrn.com>. It also lists dozens of e-journals with corporate governance in their title.

3   E Norman Veasey, 'The emergence of corporate governance as a new legal discipline' (1993) 48 *The Business Lawyer* 1267.

4   Irna M Millstein, 'The evolution of the certifying board' (1993) 48 *The Business Lawyer* 1485, 1489.

5   For a summary of the circumstances that led to the collapse of Enron, see K Fred Skousen, Steven M Glover and Douglas F Prawitt, *An Introduction to Corporate Governance and the SEC* (Thomson South-West, 2005) 3–5.

6   Bayless Manning, 'Principles of corporate governance: One viewer's perspective on the ALI project' (1993) 48 *The Business Lawyer* 1319, 1320.

7   Ibid. 1324.

11.2.2.2 Impact and importance of the project

The project was supposed to be finished within two years, but eventually took 15 years because of the sensitivities involved and the business interests involved.[8] One commentator observes that 'it is fair to say that the successive drafts of the *Principles* received more intensive review, by a greater number and wider variety of persons and over a longer period of time, than any other project in the history of corporate law',[9] while another states that 'the Project's work ... has occupied the time and effort of leaders of the corporate bar and respected academicians for over a decade of intense work, debate, and drafting'.[10] One thing is certain: the ALI project shaped views on corporate governance and laid the foundations for many of the current discussions and debates on the topic in the rest of the world. This area is complex, and many issues discussed by the ALI are still quite controversial.[11]

11.2.2.3 Some of the key aspects addressed

The key topics addressed by the ALI were:

- the objectives and conduct of the corporation;
- the structure of the corporation;
- the duty of care;
- the duty of fair dealing;
- tender offers; and
- remedies.

The topic of the objectives and conduct of the corporation has been dealt with above. It is, however, necessary to emphasise that the stakeholder debate was to a large extent ignored by the ALI. This is because the theories of shareholder primacy and profit maximisation were adopted by the ALI as its point of departure. There are certain statutes in some US states that allow corporations specifically to consider the interests of other stakeholders such as employees, suppliers and customers, but the exact nature and scope of these provisions are still uncertain.[12]

It is very interesting to study the part of the ALI report dealing with the structure of the corporation, as it illustrates clearly how the corporate governance debate in the US has indeed shaped corporate governance debates in several other jurisdictions.

§3.01 covers 'Management of the corporation's business'. It provides that:

> the management of the business of a publicly held corporation should be conducted by or under the supervision of such principal senior executives as are designated by the board

---

8   Ibid. 1325.
9   Melvin Aron Eisenberg, 'An overview of the principles of corporate governance' (1993) 48 *The Business Lawyer* 1271, 1295.
10   Veasey, 'The emergence of corporate governance as a new legal discipline' (1993).
11   See in particular Stephen M Bainbridge, *Corporation Law and Economics* (Foundation Press, 2002) 218; Eisenberg, 'An overview of the principles of corporate governance' (1993) 1273–4; Manning, 'Principles of corporate governance: One viewer's perspective on the ALI project' (1993) 1328–9.
12   Manning, 'Principles of corporate governance: One viewer's perspective on the ALI project' (1993).

of directors, and by those other officers and employees to whom the management function is delegated by the board or those executives, subject to the functions and powers of the board in §3.02 [see below].[13]

This description clearly provides for a differentiation between the 'governance circle' and the 'managerial pyramid' we described in Chapter 3. In fact, it provides for dual 'managerial circles', namely 'principal senior executives' and 'other officers and employees'. The last-mentioned group receives its managerial powers either from the board or from the principal senior executives.

This description also clearly recognises the 'supervisory role' of the board and is in accordance with the principle (explained in Chapter 3) that the board's function is primarily to 'direct, govern, guide, monitor, oversee, supervise and comply'. It differs from the traditional formulation of the board's function, namely that the business of the corporation 'shall be managed by [its] board'.[14] The new description of the board's functions provides another indication that it is impossible for the board of a large corporation to manage the day-to-day business of the corporation. That task must of necessity be left to senior executives and other employees of the corporation.

§3.02 deals with 'Functions and powers of the board of directors'; §3.02(a) allocates five primary functions to the board:

(1) Select, regularly evaluate, fix the compensation of, and, where appropriate, replace the senior executives.

(2) Oversee the conduct of the corporation's business to evaluate whether the business is being properly managed.

(3) Review and, where appropriate, approve the corporation's financial objectives and major corporate plans and actions.

(4) Review and, where appropriate, approve major changes in, and determinations of other major questions of choice respecting the appropriate auditing and accounting principles and practices to be used in the preparation of the corporation's financial statements.

(5) Perform such other functions as are prescribed by law, or assigned to the board under a standard of the corporation.

It is once again clear that the board's functions of 'directing, governing, guiding, monitoring, overseeing, supervising and complying' are foremost.

11.2.3 The Securities Exchange Commission (SEC)

The SEC is the primary securities markets regulator in the US. It was formed in 1934 after the passing of federal legislation: the *Securities Exchange Act of 1934*. This legislation followed the passing of the *Securities Act of 1933*. The intent of Congress in establishing the SEC is summarised in the following SEC statement:

---

13   §8.01(b) of the *Model Business Corporations Act* (1984 and Supplement) reads as follows: 'All corporate powers shall be exercised by or under the authority of, and the business affairs of the corporation managed by or under the direction of, its board of directors.'

14   Bainbridge, *Corporation Law and Economics* (2002) 195.

> Congress, in establishing the securities laws, created a continuous disclosure system
> designed to protect investors and to assure the maintenance of fair and honest securities
> markets. The Commission, in administering and implementing these laws, has sought to
> coordinate and integrate this disclosure . . .

This *Securities Act of 1933* and the *Securities Exchange Act of 1934* aimed to restore the integrity and reliability of information provided to investors. The stockmarket crash of 1929 and the fraud, deceit and excesses of the 1920s were arguably major factors leading to the Great Depression.[15] The *Securities Exchange Act of 1934* gave the SEC extensive powers to police, oversee and regulate the financial markets, considerable powers to investigate contraventions of the law, and civil as well as criminal sanctions to enforce the law. The SEC experienced slow growth until 1945, but there were rapid expansions in its powers after almost every market crash or market break, in particular in 1962 and 1977.[16]

As will be seen in the next part, the expansion in the powers and overseeing role of the SEC were not enough to prevent several abuses, as became apparent in the early 2000s with the scandals associated with Enron and other corporate giants (Tyco, WorldCom, Xerox, Adelphia etc), brokerage firms (for example, Merrill Lynch), stock exchanges (for example, the New York Stock Exchange), large public accounting firms (Arthur Andersen and others) and managers of mutual funds (for example, Piper Jaffray). The reaction to this was another piece of draconian legislation, the *Sarbanes-Oxley Act of 2002* (SOX).[17]

The organisational structure of the SEC is impressive. It consists of five commissioners and five divisions (Corporation Finance; Enforcement; Investment Management; Trading and Markets; and Economic and Risk Analysis), an executive director and general counsel. The principal Acts defining the SEC's mandate and legal framework are the *Securities Act of 1933*, the *Securities Exchange Act of 1934* and SOX.[18]

11.2.4 The *Sarbanes-Oxley Act of 2002* – the US response to collapses such as Enron and WorldCom

11.2.4.1 Backdrop

The passing of SOX should be seen against the backdrop of several huge corporate failures in the US. These collapses, in particular Enron and WorldCom, caused serious concern and became such a political issue that the US Government of the day (at that stage the George W Bush Administration) saw no option but to act quickly and radically. It was thought by the Bush Administration to be the best way to deal with the issue, but there are those who saw it as a knee-jerk reaction to an immediate crisis rather than a carefully considered and integrated set of responses to wider and underlying corporate governance problems.[19]

---

15   Ibid. 2–3 and 31–2.
16   Ibid. 35–6.
17   Ibid. 5.
18   Ibid. 39, 40–4 and 49 *et seq.*
19   Bob Garratt, *Thin on Top* (Nicholas Brealey Publishing, 2003) 20.

11.2.4.2 Aims and objectives

The SEC's summary of SOX[20] very clearly set out the aims and objectives of the Act soon after it became law:

- restoring confidence in the accounting profession;
- improving the 'tone at the top';
- improving disclosure and financial reporting;
- improving the performance of 'gatekeepers'; and
- enhancing enforcement tools.

SOX is indeed a blunt statutory instrument, with heavy civil and criminal sanctions for contraventions.

Under s 101 a five-member Public Company Accounting Oversight Board, with extensive powers, was established. This Board has regulatory and enforcement powers comparable to those of the SEC itself. Indeed, a breach of the SOX Act is treated in the same manner as a breach of the SEC Act: see s 3(b).

The tentacles of SOX stretch all over the world, as no distinction is made between US and non-US 'Issuers' (s 106). Foreign companies issuing securities on US markets are brought under the umbrella of SOX through the definition of 'Issuer' in s 2 – basically, companies that issue securities on US markets.

Paul von Nessen explains:

> The passage of the Sarbanes-Oxley Act itself would have had minimal impact upon corporations outside the United States were it not for the fact that a number of Australian and other foreign corporations have sought to raise capital on the stock exchanges of the United States. As a result of this, the US legislation and the rules for corporate governance implemented by the US exchanges in response to the requirement of Sarbanes-Oxley Act necessitate that Australian corporations which are listed on US exchanges comply with the listing rules requirements, including requirements relating both to corporate governance generally and to accounting and auditing standards specifically.[21]

Title II of SOX attempts to ensure 'auditor independence' by prohibiting auditors from delivering certain non-audit activities to entities they audit, including (s 201(a)):

> (1) book-keeping or other services related to the accounting records or financial statements of the audit client
>
> . . .
>
> (6) management functions or human resources
>
> . . .
>
> (8) legal services and expert services unrelated to the audit.

Section 303 of SOX aims to prevent improper influence on the audit process by making it 'unlawful . . . to fraudulently influence, coerce, manipulate, or mislead any auditor engaged in

---

20   See <www.sec.gov/news/press/2003–89a.htm>.
21   Paul von Nessen, 'Corporate governance in Australia: Converging with international developments' (2003) 15 *Australian Journal of Corporate Law* 189, 194–5.

the performance of an audit for the purpose of rendering the financial statements materially misleading'.

This overview provides more than enough evidence of the evils SOX aims to prevent,[22] or, to put it differently, the misuses and abuses related to audits that occurred in the past. These misuses and abuses were the main reasons for many of the recent corporate collapses and for the actual (poor!) financial position of these corporations not being detectable by investors.

11.2.4.3 Some perspectives on SOX and its effects

In the first edition of this work it was pointed out that whether SOX was an over-reaction or not was open to debate, and depended on one's personal political views on how far a regulatory system of corporate governance should go, and on whether or not one favoured a self-regulatory corporate governance model.[23] However, as Bob Tricker observed, SOX will go down in history as an important turning point, as SOX made it clear that US and UK corporate governance no longer share similar foundations. The US approach has been, from SOX onwards, prescriptive, rule-based and legal, whereas the UK approach is still non-prescriptive, principles-based and self-regulatory.[24]

Since 2002, several additional perspectives began to emerge regarding the regulatory or hard-law approach of SOX. The principle underlying SOX is 'comply or else'. In other words, there are legal sanctions for non-compliance that could lead to people being convicted of crimes and being sent to jail for long periods, or to huge fines being imposed. The irony is that despite such a draconian piece of legislation being in place, several poor corporate governance practices related to risk management and excessive executive remuneration continued to lurk beneath the surface. As far as executive remuneration is concerned, it is somewhat perplexing that the abuses were well known and commented upon within the United States before the global financial crisis, which commenced in 2008.[25] However, it seems that greed and a highly competitive corporate environment ensured that these poor corporate governance practices were perpetuated, and even flourished, even amid severe criticism of excessive executive remuneration. These practices were, to a large extent, responsible for the Global Financial Crisis – sparked by a meltdown of the US housing market that spread to the broader economy through securitisation markets in 2008 and early 2009.

The ripple effect this caused is well known and has been discussed extensively by academic commentators and in the media.[26] It was, therefore, to be expected that the

---

22   See also Robert AG Monks and Nell Minow, *Corporate Governance* (Blackwell, 3rd edn, 2004) 248–9: Richard Smerdon, *A Practical Guide to Corporate Governance* (Sweet & Maxwell, 2nd edn, 2004) 364–6.

23   For a similar view expressed later, see Sir Bryan Nicholson, 'The Role of the Regulator' in Ken Rushton (ed.), *The Business Case for Corporate Governance* (Cambridge University Press [CUP], 2008) 103–6 and 118: Keith Johnstone and Will Chalk, 'What Sanctions are Necessary?' in ibid. 154.

24   Bob Tricker, *Corporate Governance: Principles, Policies and Practices* (Oxford University Press [OUP], 2012) 154. See also Nicholson, 'The Role of the Regulator' in Rushton (ed.), *The Business Case for Corporate Governance* (2008) 107–8.

25   Commentators such as Skousen, Glover and Prawitt, in *An Introduction to Corporate Governance and the SEC* (2005) 6 provide a very clear picture of unacceptable compensation practices in the US, especially as far as compensation by way of overvalued stock was concerned.

26   See further Michael Legg and Jason Harris, 'How the American dream became a global nightmare: An analysis of the causes of the Global Financial Crisis' (2009) 32 *University of New South Wales (UNSW) Law Journal* 350.

proponents of a self-regulatory corporate governance model, who criticised the hard-law approach of SOX, would say that the global financial crisis illustrates that such an approach does not work.[27] In addition, it has been argued that compliance or agency costs related to SOX may outweigh its efficiency, even though these costs may decrease over time. It has, for instance, been said that the 'total cost to the American economy of complying with SOX is considered to amount to more than the total write-off of Enron, WorldCom and Tyco combined'.[28] Some academic studies have shown that SOX has made US corporate managers more defensive and reduced risk taking.[29] On the other hand, some US companies report benefits from SOX compliance, including better accountability of individuals, reduced risk of fraud and improved accuracy of financial reports.[30]

The causes of the Global Financial Crisis are complex and wide-ranging, and it would be preposterous to state that it was caused by SOX or even that it proves that SOX did not ensure better corporate governance practices, or that SOX was ineffective in preventing corporate collapses – it should be remembered that if several banks had not been bailed out by the US Government, they would surely have collapsed in a similar fashion to Enron, WorldCom and Tyco. What is, however, reasonably safe to conclude is that a one-size-fits-all corporate governance model does not work. Also, the most sensible approach to corporate governance is still to tackle problems along a broad front and in a flexible way. In fact, aspiring to strike a balance between sensible self-regulatory arrangements and a rigid regulatory corporate governance model is still the best approach to corporate governance.

11.2.5 NYSE: Sections 303 and 303A – corporate governance rules

11.2.5.1 Background

The SEC approved the New York Stock Exchange (NYSE) rules on corporate governance on 4 November 2003; they have been amended several times in subsequent years. Almost all listed companies (there are a few exceptions) must comply with certain standards regarding corporate governance as codified in s 303A.[31] The most important exception is that foreign private issuers (defined in Rule 3b-4 under the Exchange Act) are permitted to follow home country practice in lieu of the provisions of s 303A, except that such companies must comply with the following rules:

---

27   *King Report on Governance for South Africa 2009* (King Report (2009)) (Institute of Directors, 2009) 6 and 9 <http://african.ipapercms.dk/IOD/KINGIII/kingiiireport/>.

28   King Report (2009) 6.

29   Kate Livak, 'Defensive management: Does the Sarbanes-Oxley Act discourage corporate risk-taking' [2014] *University of Illinois Law Review* 1663.

30   Bob Tricker, *Corporate Governance: Principles, Policies and Practices* (OUP, 2nd edn, 2012) 112. See also the detailed literature review relating to the SOX Act undertaken by Harvard academics Professor John Coates and Associate Professor Suraj Srinivasan, 'SOX after ten years: A multidisciplinary review' (2014) *Accounting Horizons* (available on ssrn.com).

31   NYSE *Listed Company Manual, Corporate Governance Standards* (31 December 2009) <http://nysemanual.nyse.com/LCMTools/PlatformViewer.asp?selectednode=chp%5F1%5F4%5F3&manual=%2Flcm%2Fsections%2Flcm%2Dsections%2F>.

- Listed companies must have an audit committee that satisfies the requirements of Rule 10A-3 under the Exchange Act.[32]
- Listed foreign issuers must disclose any significant ways in which their corporate governance practices differ from those followed by domestic [US] companies under the NYSE listing standards.[33]
- Each listed company CEO must promptly notify the NYSE in writing after any executive officer of the listed company becomes aware of any material non-compliance with any applicable provisions of s 303A.[34]
- Each such company must submit an executed Written Affirmation annually to the NYSE. In addition, each listed company must submit an interim Written Affirmation as and when required by the interim Written Affirmation form specified by the NYSE.[35]

11.2.5.2 Summary of the most important NYSE corporate governance rules[36]

- Listed companies must have a majority of independent directors ('independence' is defined in detail in s 303A.02 of the NYSE *Listed Company Manual*).
- To empower non-management directors to serve as a more effective check on management, the non-management directors of each listed company must meet at regularly scheduled executive sessions without management.
- Listed companies must have a nominating/corporate governance committee composed entirely of independent directors.
- Listed companies must have a compensation committee, with a minimum of three members, composed entirely of independent directors (as defined in s 303A.02).
- Each listed company must have an internal audit function.
- Listed companies must adopt and disclose[37] corporate governance guidelines, addressing the following subjects:
  - director qualification standards;
  - director responsibilities;
  - director access to management and, as necessary and appropriate, independent advisers;
  - director compensation;
  - director orientation and continuing education;
  - management succession; and
  - annual performance evaluation of the board.

---

32   Ibid. s 303A.06.
33   Ibid. s 303A.11.
34   Ibid. s 303A.12(b).
35   Ibid. s 303A.12(c).
36   Used with permission of NYSE Group, Inc. This summary has been prepared by the author and may not contain the most up-to-date information. Refer to <http://wallstreet.cch.com/LCMTools/ PlatformViewer.asp?selectednode=chp%5F1%5F4%5F3&manual=%2Flcm%2Fsections%2Flcm% 2Dsections%2F> and <http://nysemanual.nyse.com> for the most current full text. See also NYSE Corporate Governance Guide (2014) <www.nyse.com/publicdocs/nyse/.../NYSE_Corporate_ Governance_Guide.pdf>.
37   The code must be available on the company's website: NYSE *Listed Company Manual*, s 303A.10.

- Listed companies must adopt and disclose a code of business conduct and ethics for directors, officers and employees, and promptly disclose any waivers of the code for directors or executive officers. Each listed company may determine its own policies, but all listed companies should address the most important topics, including the following:
  - conflicts of interest;
  - corporate opportunities;
  - confidentiality;
  - fair dealing;
  - protection and proper use of company assets;
  - compliance with laws, rules and regulations (including insider trading laws); and
  - encouraging the reporting of any illegal or unethical behaviour.
- Listed foreign private issuers must disclose any significant ways in which their corporate governance practices differ from those followed by domestic companies under NYSE listing standards.
- Each listed company CEO must certify to the NYSE each year that he or she is not aware of any violation by the company of NYSE corporate governance listing standards, qualifying the certification to the extent necessary.
- Each listed company CEO must promptly notify the NYSE in writing after any executive officer of the listed company becomes aware of any material non-compliance with any applicable provisions of s 303A.
- Each listed company must submit an executed Written Affirmation annually to the NYSE. In addition, each listed company must submit an interim Written Affirmation as and when required by the interim Written Affirmation form specified by the NYSE.
- The NYSE may issue a public reprimand letter to any listed company that violates a NYSE listing standard.

NASDAQ and the American Stock Exchange (AMEX) have also amended their corporate governance listing requirements by including, *inter alia*, the following:[38]

- requiring that a majority of the members of the board of directors of most listed companies be independent of management;
- defining 'independence' using precise rules;
- expanding the duties and powers of the independent directors; and
- expanding the duties and powers of the audit committee of the board of directors.

11.2.6 The *Dodd-Frank Wall Street Reform and Consumer Protection Act 2010* (the Dodd-Frank Act)

The *Dodd-Frank Wall Street Reform and Consumer Protection Act 2010* (Dodd-Frank Act)[39] is a federal statute that was signed into law by President Barack Obama on 21 July 2010.

---

38   Stephen M Bainbridge, *The New Corporate Governance in Theory and in Practice* (OUP, 2008) 177.
39   For an economic assessment of the Dodd-Frank Act, see Viral V Acharya and Matthew Richardson, 'Implications of the Dodd-Frank Act' (2012) 4 *Annual Review of Financial Economics* 1–38 <http://ssrn.com/abstract=2170916 or http://dx.doi.org/10.1146/annurev-financial-030912-140516>.

The Act forms part of the financial regulatory reform agenda in the US and was passed as a response to the late-2000s recession. The President considered it the most far-reaching Wall Street reform in history, as it made substantial changes to the financial system and its regulation,[40] including provisions to increase the accountability of public companies in the context of executive remuneration.[41] The Dodd-Frank Act affects several pieces of legislation, but in particular the *Securities Exchange Act of 1934*. A few of these changes are listed below:[42]

- Compensation of the CEO and other executive officers is required to be submitted to a non-binding shareholder vote at least once every three years ('Say-on-Pay'). At the first meeting where such a Say-on-Pay vote is required (and then at least once every six years), shareholders will vote to decide whether future Say-on-Pay votes will occur every one, two or three years ('Say-when-on-Pay').[43]

- Each time an issuer seeks shareholder approval of an acquisition, merger, consolidation, proposed sale or other disposition of all of the issuer's assets, the company must disclose in a 'clear and simple' form and in accordance with regulations to be established by the SEC, any agreements, understandings and arrangements affecting the compensation of a named officer of the company that are based upon or relate to such corporate events. Such arrangements must be submitted to a separate non-binding shareholder vote ('Say-on-Golden Parachutes').

- A listed company is required to develop and implement a 'clawback' policy, or be prohibited from listing on a national securities exchange or association. The clawback policy will require companies to:
  - develop policies relating to the disclosure of incentive-based compensation that is based on financial information required to be reported under the securities laws; and
  - provide that in the event of an accounting restatement due to material non-compliance with financial reporting requirements under applicable securities laws, the company will recover from any current or former executive officer any excess incentive-based compensation (including stock options) paid during the three-year period preceding the restatement that was based on erroneous data.

---

40   See <www.whitehouse.gov/economy/middle-class/dodd-frank-wall-street-reform>. For opposing views on the utility of the Dodd-Frank reforms, see Stephen Bainbridge, 'Dodd-Frank: Quack federal corporate governance round II' (2010–11) *Minnesota Law Review* 1779; Joseph Coffee, 'Political economy of Dodd-Frank: Why financial reform tends to be frustrated and systemic risk perpetuated' (2012) 97 *Cornell Law Review* 1019. See also Dale Thompson, 'The Dodd-Frank Act and too-big-to-fail: What's missing? A survey of the current literature' (2015) 10 *University of St Thomas Journal of Law & Public Policy* 53.

41   *Bericht der Regierungskommission Deutscher Corporate Governance Kodex an die Bundesregierung* (November 2010) 96 <www.corporate-governance-code.de/ger/download/16122010/Governance_Bericht_Nov_2010.pdf>.

42   Some of the bullet points were extracted from *Bericht der Regierungskommission Deutscher Corporate Governance Kodex an die Bundesregierung* (November 2010) 102–03. For a critical appraisal, see Jill Fisch, 'Leave it to Delaware: Why Congress should stay out of corporate governance' (2013) 37 *Delaware Journal of Corporate Law* 731.

43   See <http://sec.gov/rules/final/2011/33–9178.pdf> for provisions adopted on 4 April 2011.

- The SEC will adopt rules requiring the disclosure of the following executive compensation-related information:[44]
  - the relationship between executive compensation that was actually paid (and which is required to be disclosed) and the financial performance of the company over a five-year period, taking into account any change in the value of the shares of stock and dividends of the company and any distributions;
  - the median annual total compensation of all employees of the company (except the CEO);
  - the annual total compensation of the CEO; and
  - the ratio of the median employee annual total compensation to that of the CEO.
- A new s 10C has been added to the *Securities Exchange Act 1934* to ensure the independence of compensation committees and the independence of compensation consultants and other compensation advisers.

It was observed by the US Department of the Treasury that the Dodd-Frank Act was aimed specifically at addressing the underlying causes of the US financial crisis of 2007–08, but that the Act in fact modernised the US regulatory framework and put powerful consumer financial protections in place. The Dodd-Frank Act means that Americans now have a dedicated consumer financial protection watchdog, financial markets are more transparent, and the government has more tools – to monitor risk, and to prohibit firms whose failure could threaten the entire financial system from continuing to do business.[45]

11.2.7 Future reforms of financial regulation

The election of President Donald Trump has brought widespread conjecture about the future scope of Dodd-Frank Act and other financial regulations. At the time of writing, the President had announced a review of Dodd-Frank legislation, saying at a public town hall meeting that Dodd-Frank would receive 'a very major haircut'.[46] The review is due to report by mid 2017.

11.3 United Kingdom (UK)[47]

11.3.1 The development of corporate governance in the UK

Corporate governance came to prominence in the UK after the Cadbury Committee released the *Report on the Financial Aspects of Corporate Governance* (the Cadbury Report) in 1992.[48] The Financial Reporting Council, the London Stock Exchange (LSE) and the accountancy

---

44   <www.sec.gov/news/pressrelease/2015–78.html>.
45   Anthony Reyes (US Department of the Treasury), 'The Financial Crisis Five Years Later: Response, Reform, and Progress in Charts', Treasury Notes (9 November 2013) <www.treasury.gov/connect/blog/Pages/The-Financial-Crisis-Five-Years-Later.aspx>.
46   See further Presidential Executive Order 3.2.17 'Core principles for regulating the financial system' <www.whitehouse.gov>.
47   This is a new discussion of corporate governance in the UK, retaining elements of the overview in the 3rd edition.
48   For an illuminating introduction and background information to the Cadbury Committee, see Laura F Spira and Judy Slinn, *The Cadbury Committee: A History* (Oxford Scholarship Online, 2013) DOI: 10.1093/acprof:oso/9780199592197.001.0001.

profession established the Cadbury Committee in May 1991 to focus particularly on the control and reporting functions of boards of directors and the role of auditors.[49] The purpose of the inquiry was two-fold: first, to address growing concerns about the country's competitiveness in an international business environment, and second, to restore trust in financial reporting in the wake of the British and Commonwealth Holdings collapse and the Coloroll, Polly Peck, Maxwell and BCCI scandals.[50] The final Report, containing Recommendations and what is widely accepted as the first 'comply or explain' governance code, was published in December 1992. It laid the foundation for the system of corporate governance that has developed in the UK since then and significantly influenced corporate governance developments throughout the world.[51] In line with the Cadbury Committee's approach that best practice is an ever-evolving concept,[52] several corporate governance reports followed the Cadbury Report, including the Greenbury Report (1995), the Hampel Report (1998), the Smith Report (2003) and the Higgs Report (2003).[53] In contrast to the ALI's comprehensive investigation of corporate governance within the context of corporate law generally, all the UK reports addressed specific aspects of corporate governance – including the disclosure of the remuneration of directors and executive officers, audit committees and the role and effectiveness of non-executive directors.

11.3.2 The Cadbury Report and codes of best practice

At the heart of the Cadbury Report was a code of best practice designed to achieve high standards of corporate behaviour.[54] The committee believed that a code of best practice could have prevented a number of the unexpected company failures and frauds which had occurred in the UK. The Code was based on principles of openness, integrity and accountability and set out 19 best practice principles for corporate governance, covering the role and structure of the

---

49   *The Financial Aspects of Corporate Governance* (Cadbury Report (1992)) (Committee on the Financial Aspects of Corporate Governance, 1992) 61; Cally Jordan, 'Cadbury twenty years on' (2013) 58 *Villanova Law Review* 1, 2: Charlotte Villiers, 'Draft report by the Cadbury Committee on the financial aspects of corporate governance' (1992) 13 *Company Lawyer* 214.

50   John C Shaw, 'The Cadbury Report, Two Years Later' in KJ Hopt, H Kanda, MJ Roe, E Wymeersch and S Prigge (eds), *Comparative Corporate Governance: The State of the Art and Emerging Research* (Clarendon Press, 1998) 21, 23: Stanley Christopher, 'Corporate Accountability: Cadbury Committee: Part 1' (1993) 11 *International Banking and Financial Law* 104. See also Peter Montagnon, 'The Role of the Shareholder' in Rushton (ed.), *The Business Case for Corporate Governance* (2008) 81; Spira and Slinn, *The Cadbury Committee: A History* (2013) 32; and BR Cheffins, 'The History of Corporate Governance', ECGI Law Working Paper 184/2012 (2011) 19.

51   Anna Zalewska, 'Challenges of corporate governance: Twenty years after Cadbury, ten years after Sarbanes-Oxley' (2014) 27 *Journal of Empirical Finance* 1, 4; Cheffins, 'The History of Corporate Governance' (2011) 19. The Report highlighted a board's freedom to discharge responsibilities 'within a framework of effective accountability' as the essence of a good corporate governance system: Cadbury Report (Final) (1992) 11, para 1.1. This approach remains relevant and supported internationally.

52   Spira and Slinn, *The Cadbury Committee: A History* (2013) 179.

53   For an excellent overview of the development of Codes of Conduct in the UK corporate environment, see Ilir Haxhi, Hans van Ees and Arndt Sorge, 'A political perspective on business elites and institutional embeddedness in the UK Code-issuing process' (2013) 21 *Corporate Governance* 536–9. See also Susanne Lütz, Dagmar Eberle and Dorothee Lauter, 'Varieties of private self-regulation in European capitalism: Corporate governance codes in the UK and Germany' (2011) 9 *Socio-Economic Review* 319–25.

54   Cadbury Report (1992) 11, para 1.3.

board, and audit and reporting on the company's position, including going concern, board remuneration and internal control.[55]

It was, from its inception, aimed at all listed companies,[56] with compliance to be ensured by the LSE, thus making acceptance of the Code one of its listing requirements.[57] However, the committee specifically encouraged as many other companies as possible to aim at meeting the Code's requirements.[58]

Not only did the Cadbury Code of Best Practice pioneer and set the benchmark for governance codes in the UK; it laid the groundwork and led to the adoption of governance codes across the world.[59] In the UK, the Code formed the basis for the current UK Corporate Governance Code,[60] overseen by the Financial Reporting Council (FRC). To ensure that it remains current and responds to the changing corporate landscape, the Code is reviewed regularly. Consequently, it has gone through several iterations since 1992. The different Best Practice Codes that followed the Cadbury Code are discussed below at Section 11.3.5.

11.3.3 The role of the Financial Reporting Council (FRC)

The Financial Reporting Council (FRC) is the UK's independent regulator, responsible for promoting high-quality corporate governance and reporting to foster investment.[61] The FRC sets the UK Corporate Governance and Stewardship Codes as well as UK standards for accounting, auditing and actuarial work,[62] monitors and acts to promote the quality of corporate reporting and operates independent enforcement arrangements for accountants and actuaries. As the Competent Authority for audit in the UK, the FRC sets auditing and ethical standards and monitors and enforces audit quality.[63] Since its inception in 1992, the Council has amended the UK Governance Code in response to key investigations and reports by specialised committees in 1995 (the Greenbury Report), 1998 (the Hampel Report) and 2003 (the Smith Report and the Higgs Report).[64] The FRC Board is supported by three governance committees (Audit Committee, Nominations Committee and Remuneration Committee) and by two business committees (Codes & Standards Committee and Conduct

---

55   Ibid. 58 *et seq.*
56   Ibid. 16, para 3.1.
57   Ibid. 17, paras 3.7–3.9.
58   Ibid. 16, para 3.1.
59   Jeroen Veldman and Hugh Willmott, 'The cultural grammar of governance: The UK Code of Corporate Governance, reflexivity, and the limits of "soft" regulation' (2016) 69 *Human Relations* 581, 582, DOI: 10.1177/0018726715593160; Ghulam Abid and Alia Ahmed, 'Failing in corporate governance and warning signs of a corporate collapse' (2014) 8 *Pakistan Journal of Commerce and Social Sciences* 846, 851; Anthony, Hilton, '20 years of Cadbury' (2013) 65 *Keeping Good Companies* 153.
60   See <www.frc.org.uk/Our-Work/Publications/Corporate-Governance/UK-Corporate-Governance-Code-April-2016.pdf>.
61   See FRC, *Developments in Corporate Governance and Stewardship 2016* (January 2017).
62   See FRC, *FRC's Strategy for 2016/19* (October 2016).
63   See FRC, *Governance Bible* (February 2017) and *The FRC and its Regulatory Approach* (October 2015). Annexure A contains a table of the FRC's functions and powers.
64   The Walker Review led to the release of the Stewardship Code. See Section 11.3.5 below. Donald Nordberg and Terry McNulty trace the codification of UK corporate governance between 1992 and 2010 and provide some background on the Cadbury and Higgs reports: Donald Nordberg and Terry McNulty, 'Creating better boards through codification: Possibilities and limitations in UK corporate governance, 1992–2010' (2013) 55 *Business History* 350–2 and the table on 354–5.

Committee).[65] The Codes and Standards Committee is responsible for advising the FRC Board on maintaining an effective framework of UK codes and standards for corporate governance, stewardship, accounting, auditing and assurance, and actuarial technical standards.

11.3.4 The UK approach to corporate governance

The key aspects of corporate governance in the UK, as explained in the FRC's 2010 policy statement, *The UK Approach to Corporate Governance*,[66] can be summarised as follows:

- a single (unitary) board that is collectively responsible for the sustainable success of the company;
- the separation of the roles of the Chair and the Chief Executive (CEO);
- a balance of executive and independent non-executive directors, but not prescribing a majority of independent non-executive directors;
- strong, independent audit and remuneration committees;
- the annual evaluation by the board of its performance;
- transparency on appointments and remuneration of directors and executives, including the Chief Executive (CEO);
- effective rights for shareholders, who are encouraged to engage with the companies in which they invest;
- reliance on the UK Corporate Governance Code, which finds application through the 'comply or explain' principle (see below) and which is regularly reviewed in consultation with companies and investors.

11.3.4.1 The 'comply or explain' principle

Since 1992, the Cadbury Code and later amended UK Corporate Governance Codes have formed part of the LSE Listing Rules, requiring listed public companies either *to comply* with the provisions of the Code *or explain* why they have failed to do so – the principle of 'comply or explain'.[67] The principle facilitates flexibility as compliance with a governance code is not mandatory.[68] The significance of this principle is emphasised by the fact that the 2010, 2012, 2014 and 2016 versions of the *Corporate Governance Code* all describe it as the 'trademark of corporate governance in the UK'.[69]

The 2012 UK Corporate Governance Code provided additional explanations of the 'comply and explain' principle.[70] The paper reiterated that non-compliance with a particular provision could be acceptable if it is accompanied by a meaningful explanation that sets the context,

---

65   See <www.frc.org.uk/About-the-FRC/FRC-structure.aspx>.
66   See FRC, *The UK Approach to Corporate Governance* (October 2010).
67   LSE Listing Rule 12.43A. See also Cheffins, 'The History of Corporate Governance' (2011) 19 <http://ssrn.com.ezproxy-b.deakin.edu.au/abstract=1975404>.
68   Andrew Keay, 'Comply or explain in corporate governance codes: In need of greater regulatory oversight?' (2014) 34 *Legal Studies* 279, 281.
69   FRC, *The UK Corporate Governance Code* (June 2010) 4; *The UK Corporate Governance Code* (September 2012) 4; *The UK Corporate Governance Code* (September 2014) 4; *The UK Corporate Governance Code* (April 2016) 4.
70   See also FRC, *What Constitutes an Explanation under 'Comply or Explain'* (February 2012).

gives a convincing rationale and describes mitigating action to address any additional risk.[71] The effect of the 'comply or explain' approach, although it is classified as 'soft law', is not insignificant, as there are powerful market forces at work to ensure compliance rather than tolerating listed public companies explaining why they are not complying.[72]

However, in recent years, the continued efficacy of the 'comply or explain' approach has been questioned, citing lack of shareholder engagement and brief and uninformative explanations of non-compliance.[73] However, full compliance (without explanation) with the Code reached a new high of 62 per cent in 2016, returning to the longer-term trend of increasing compliance.[74] Clearly, the impact of this 'soft law' approach has been significant and the principle continues to enjoy strong support and remains an important tenet of corporate governance in the UK.[75] Internationally, the effectiveness of the 'soft law' approach and voluntary codes of corporate governance have come under fire and there are more and more calls for a 'hard law' approach to ensure adherence to good corporate governance principles.[76]

11.3.5 Corporate Governance Codes in the UK from 1992 to 2016

As mentioned earlier, the Cadbury Code has been revised, refined and renamed since its inception in 1992. The first official Combined Code, published in 1998, was updated in 2003 to include the recommendations of the Higgs Report on non-executive directors and the Smith Report on audit committees. Further small amendments were made to the Combined Code in 2006 and 2008. The Code was revised and renamed the UK Corporate Governance Code in June 2010 following an extensive review carried out by the FRC in parallel with the Walker review of corporate governance in the financial sector.[77] The changes made to the 2008 UK Combined Code included:[78]

- a new principle on the roles of the chairman and non-executive directors; the need for the board to have an appropriate mix of skills, experience and independence; the commitment levels expected of directors; and the board's responsibility for defining the company's risk appetite and tolerance;
- a new 'comply or explain' provision including board evaluation reviews to be externally facilitated at least every three years; the chairman to hold regular development reviews

---

71   Ibid.
72   NAPF, *Corporate Governance Policy and Voting Guidelines* (November 2012) <www.napf .co.uk/PolicyandResearch/DocumentLibrary/~/media/Policy/Documents/0277_Corporate_ governance_policy_and_voting_guidelines_an_NAPF_document.ashx>.
73   Keay, 'Comply or explain in corporate governance codes' (2014) 303.
74   FRC, *Developments in Corporate Governance and Stewardship 2016* (January 2017) 9.
75   Ibid. 4 and Keay, 'Comply or explain in corporate governance codes' (2014) 303.
76   See in particular the majority of papers published in Jean J du Plessis and Chee Keong Low (eds), *Corporate Governance Codes for the 21st Century: International Perspectives and Critical Analyses* (Springer Verlag, 2017).
77   FRC, *Developments in Corporate Governance 2011 – The Impact and Implementation of the UK Corporate Governance and Stewardship Codes* (December 2011) 3.
78   FRC, *2009 Review of the Combined Code: Final Report* (December 2009) 3.

with all directors; and companies to report on their business model and overall financial strategy; and

• changes to the section of the Code dealing with remuneration to emphasise the need for performance-related pay to be aligned with the long-term interests of the company and with the company's risk policies and systems, and to enable variable components to be reclaimed in certain circumstances.

The main changes to the 2012 Code included that boards should confirm that the annual report and accounts are fair, balanced and understandable, that audit committees should report more fully on their activities, and that FTSE 350 companies should put the external audit contract out to tender at least every ten years. In addition, the requirement for companies to report on their boardroom diversity policies came into effect.[79] These changes were designed to give investors greater insight into what company boards and audit committees were doing to promote their interests, and to provide them with a better basis for engagement. It introduced new regulations, including diversity disclosures, to support the recommendations arising from the Lord Davies report.[80] The 2014 update of the Code significantly enhanced the quality of information investors receive by introducing reporting of a longer-term view of a company's prospects in the form of a viability statement. In addition, the 2014 Code introduced new requirements in relation to directors' remuneration and changes to risk management.[81] As part of its ongoing work to improve justifiable confidence in audit, in September 2015 the FRC published a consultation paper related to three areas: revisions to Ethical and Auditing Standards, the UK Corporate Governance Code, and Guidance on Audit Committees. Following this consultation, the FRC issued an updated UK Corporate Governance Code and associated Guidance on Audit Committees in April 2016.[82] In line with the FRC's commitment to help companies embed the requirements that were introduced in earlier Codes,[83] the changes made to the 2014 Code were minor, designed to comply with new EU regulations on statutory audit, and focused on matters related to audit committees.[84] In February 2017 the FRC announced a fundamental review of the UK Corporate Governance Code and plans to commence consultation on its proposals later in 2017.[85] The FRC highlighted the importance of boards taking better account of stakeholder views, of linking executive remuneration with performance and of extending the FRC's enforcement powers to ensure that disciplinary action can be taken against directors where there have been financial reporting breaches. The press release indicated that the review will also consider the FRC's work on corporate culture and succession

---

79   FRC, *Developments in Corporate Governance in 2012* (December 2012) 7.
80   FRC, *Developments in Corporate Governance and Stewardship 2015* (January 2016) 7.
81   Ibid. 10. For a detailed discussion of the 2014 changes, see FRC, *Feedback Statement – Revisions to the UK Corporate Governance Code* (September 2014).
82   See <www.frc.org.uk/Our-Work/Publications/Corporate-Governance/UK-Corporate-Governance-Code-April-2016.pdf>.
83   FRC, *FRC's Strategy for 2016/19* (October 2016) 1.
84   FRC, *Feedback Statement and Impact Assessment: Consultation – Enhancing Confidence in Audit* (April 2016) 27.
85   FRC, *FRC to review the UK Corporate Governance Code* PN8/17 (16 February 2017) <www .frc.org.uk/News-and-Events/FRC-Press/Press/2017/February/FRC-to-review-the-UK-Corporate-Governance-Code.aspx>.

planning[86] and the issues raised in the Government's Green Paper[87] and the Business, Energy and Industrial Strategy (BEIS) Select Committee inquiry.[88]

The UK Corporate Governance Code consists of five Sections, dealing with: Leadership; Effectiveness; Accountability; Remuneration; and Relations with shareholders. In addition, there are two Schedules, dealing with 'The design of performance-related remuneration for executive directors' and 'Disclosure of corporate governance arrangements'. Each Section is divided into three Parts, with the first Part containing the 'Main Principle', the second Part with 'Supporting Principles', and the third Part providing additional explanations under the heading 'Code Provisions'.

11.3.6 The Stewardship Code

In December 2009 the FRC accepted responsibility for a Stewardship Code for institutional investors, following the Walker review of corporate governance in the financial sector.[89] First published in July 2010 and revised in September 2012, the Code was developed to help build a critical mass of investors willing and able to engage with the companies in which they invest, to increase the quantity and quality of engagement, and to increase accountability down the investment chain to clients and beneficiaries.[90] The FRC sees the UK Stewardship Code as complementary to the UK Corporate Governance Code for listed companies and believes that it should also be applied on a 'comply or explain' basis.[91] Membership of the Code is voluntary. At the end of 2016 there were nearly 300 signatories to the Code, including most major institutional investors.[92] Since December 2010 all UK-authorised Asset Managers are required, under the FCA's Conduct of Business Rules, to produce a statement of commitment to the Stewardship Code or explain why it is not appropriate to their business model.[93]

---

86   The FRC's discussion paper, *UK Board Succession Planning* (October 2015), sought views on issues surrounding board succession for both executives and non-executives. The Council released a feedback statement in May 2016 and indicated that guidance in this area will be considered as part of the revision of the Guidance on Board Effectiveness, commencing towards the end of 2016. See FRC, *Feedback Statement: UK Board Succession Planning Discussion Paper* (May 2016).

87   The government published a Corporate Governance Reform Green Paper in November 2016. In the main, the Green Paper covers directors' remuneration, the governance of large private companies and how best to include a wider stakeholder view in company decision-making. See Department of Business, Energy and Industrial Strategy, *Corporate Governance Reform – Green paper* (November 2016).

88   The BEIS Select Committee announced an Inquiry into Corporate Governance in September 2016. The Inquiry addressed a broad range of issues, including how to align directors' duties and executive pay with a company's long-term success and the benefits of diversity on boards and wider employee representation. See FRC, *Developments in Corporate Governance and Stewardship 2016* (January 2017) 20.

89   FRC, *Implementation of the UK Stewardship Code* (July 2010) 1.

90   FRC, *Developments in Corporate Governance and Stewardship 2016* (January 2017) 24.

91   FRC, *The UK Stewardship Code* (September 2012) 2.

92   See FRC, 'Tiering of Signatories to the Stewardship Code', PN 66/16 (14 November 2016) <www.frc.org.uk/News-and-Events/FRC-Press/Press/2016/November/Tiering-of-signatories-to-the-Stewardship-Code.aspx>. In 2012 there were nearly 250 signatories to the Code – see FRC, *Developments in Corporate Governance 2012* (December 2012) 1.

93   FCA, *FCA Handbook* COBS 2.2.3.

The UK Stewardship Code sets out seven principles of effective stewardship by investors. They are as follows:

So as to protect and enhance the value that accrues to the ultimate beneficiary, institutional investors should:

1. publicly disclose their policy on how they will discharge their stewardship responsibilities.
2. have a robust policy on managing conflicts of interest in relation to stewardship which should be publicly disclosed.
3. monitor their investee companies.
4. establish clear guidelines on when and how they will escalate their stewardship activities.
5. be willing to act collectively with other investors where appropriate.
6. have a clear policy on voting and disclosure of voting activity.
7. report periodically on their stewardship and voting activities.[94]

In 2016, the FRC assessed signatories to the Stewardship Code based on the quality of the statements and categorised them into tiers. The exercise was undertaken to improve the transparency of reporting. It has also improved the quality of reporting against the Code and promoted best practice.[95] Several signatories made suggestions for Code amendments in consequence of the tiering exercise. The FRC indicated that as part of its wider corporate governance work it will consider how to achieve further improvements in reporting and possible revisions to the UK Stewardship Code in the future.[96]

11.3.7 The Corporate Governance Code for SMEs

The Quoted Companies Alliance (QCA) is an independent membership organisation that champions the interests of small to mid-size quoted companies (SMEs) in the UK. There are nearly 2000 SMEs in the UK, representing 85 per cent of all quoted companies. They employ approximately 4.6 million people, representing nearly 17 per cent of private sector employment in the UK.[97]

On 1 May 2013, the QCA published an updated edition of its Corporate Governance Code for SMEs.[98] The QCA Code adopts key elements of the UK Corporate Governance Code, current policy initiatives and other relevant guidance and then applies these to the needs and particular circumstances of small and mid-size quoted companies on a public market.[99] Focusing on 12 principles and a set of minimum disclosures, the QCA Code encourages companies to consider how or whether they should apply each principle to achieve good governance and provide quality explanations to their shareholders about what they have done.[100] The QCA

---

94   See FRC, *The UK Stewardship Code* (September 2012) 3.
95   FRC, *Tiering of signatories to the Stewardship Code* PN 66/16 (14 November 2016).
96   FRC, *Developments in Corporate Governance and Stewardship 2016* (January 2017) 26.
97   See <www.theqca.com/about-us/>.
98   See <www.theqca.com/shop/guides/70717/corporate-governance-code-for-small-and-midsize-quoted-companies-2013-downloadable-pdf.thtml>.
99   Ibid.
100   Ibid.

Code is widely recognised as an industry standard for those companies to which the UK Corporate Governance Code is not applicable.[101]

The areas of focus in the 2013 edition are revealing, as they reflect some of the new trends and areas in corporate governance that caused concern over recent years. Some key changes include:

- emphasising the benefits of good governance to a public company, including how it can build trust between the company, its shareholders and potential shareholders;
- focusing on the prime importance of companies delivering good-quality explanations of their approach, actions and behaviour;
- emphasising the central role of the chairman in delivering good governance;
- further embedding the principle of constructive engagement between companies and shareholders in light of the UK Stewardship Code;
- including greater detail on the characteristics of an effective board; and
- reordering the QCA's 12 principles of corporate governance to place greater emphasis on the delivery of growth in long-term shareholder value.[102]

Unfortunately, the Code has not been updated since 2013 and the status of stakeholders other than shareholders remains inadequately addressed in the Code.[103] However, the QCA and UHY Hacker Young have released annual reports on the corporate governance behaviour of SMEs since 2013. The report reviews corporate governance disclosures made by small and mid-size quoted companies against the 2013 QCA Code.[104] It is encouraging to note that the 2016 Review mentions stakeholders other than shareholders several times.[105]

11.3.8 Corporate culture

In July 2016, the FRC published *Corporate Culture and the Role of Boards: A report of observations*, in response to continuing low levels of public trust. The Report is the culmination of the FRC's Culture Coalition, a collaboration with CIMA, the City Values Forum, IBE, IIA and CIPD, as well as interviews with more than 250 chairmen, CEOs and leading industry experts from the UK's largest companies. It explores the importance of culture to long-term value and how corporate cultures are being defined, embedded and monitored, and reflects the results of an 18 month study exploring the relationship between corporate culture and long-term business success in the UK.[106]

---

101   Ibid.
102   QCA, 'The Quoted Companies Alliance's Revised Corporate Governance Code Emphasises How Good Governance Helps to Deliver Growth', Press Release (1 May 2013) <www.theqca.com/news/press-releases/70702/the-quoted-companies-alliances-revised-corporate-governance-code-emphasises-how-good-governance-helps-to-deliver-growth.thtml>.
103   Marc Moore highlights the tension between shareholder primacy and socio-political sentiment in modern Britain in an illuminating exposition of the UK's shareholder-centric company law framework. Marc Moore, 'Shareholder primacy, labour and the historic ambivalence of UK company law', *Legal Studies Research Paper Series* (University of Cambridge, September 2016) <http://ssrn.com/abstract= 2835990>.
104   The QCA-UHY Corporate Governance Reports from 2013 to 2016 are available on the UHY website <www.uhy-uk.com/resources-publications/publications/corporate-governance/>.
105   QCA and UHY Hacker Young, *Corporate Governance Behaviour Review 2016* (December 2016).
106   FRC, *Corporate culture key to sustainable growth* PN41/16 (20 July 2016).

Key findings of the study address the following aspects:[107]

- Recognising a healthy corporate culture as a valuable asset;
- Demonstrating a desired culture in leadership;
- The importance of openness and accountability at every level;
- The values of the company need to be embedded and integrated so as to inform the behaviours which are expected of all employees and suppliers;
- Indicators and measures should be aligned to desired outcomes and material to the business;
- The performance management and reward system should support and encourage behaviours consistent with the company's purpose, values, strategy and business model; and
- Effective stewardship should include engagement about culture and encourage better reporting.

The report raised awareness of and debate on the role of boards in shaping, embedding and assessing company culture, the value of culture in creating sustainable companies and the way companies conduct themselves and interact with a broad range of stakeholders. It is a valuable contribution to a broadening debate about the governance of companies and the scope of governance.

11.4 New Zealand

11.4.1 Background and history of corporate governance in New Zealand

Despite a chequered boom and bust history, New Zealand was slow to introduce corporate governance guidelines. It was only in 2004 that the Securities Commission produced a statement on corporate governance in New Zealand.[108] New Zealand has, however, now jumped enthusiastically onto the corporate governance bandwagon, with the Institute of Directors recently asserting that the 'fragmentation, duplication and inconsistencies in the various corporate governance codes' makes corporate governance reporting challenging for listed companies.[109]

As it did in other jurisdictions, the Global Financial Crisis highlighted flaws in New Zealand's corporate governance regime. Although the direct impact on New Zealand was minimal (largely because its Australian-owned banks were not affected), a knock-on effect was the failure of finance companies, with the Securities Commission, fairly or unfairly, widely considered to be an under-resourced and ineffective regulator and a weak enforcer. The 2009 Prada-Walter report, focusing in part on the role and effectiveness of the Securities Commission, influenced the reform in New Zealand which led to the enactment of the *Financial*

---

107   FRC, *Corporate Culture and the Role of Boards: A report of observations* (July 2016) 6–7.
108   Securities Commission, *Corporate Governance in New Zealand: Principles and Guidelines* (16 February 2004).
109   Felicity Caird et al., 'Corporate Governance Codes Compared', Institute of Directors, 3 <www.iod.org.nz/Portals/0/Governance%20resources/IoD_Corporate_governance_codes_compared.pdf>.

Markets Conduct Act 2013 (FMCA) and the establishment of the Financial Markets Authority (FMA).[110] The FMA has wide oversight and enforcement powers.

The FMA initially adopted the *Corporate Governance in New Zealand: Principles and Guidelines* produced by the Securities Commission, but in 2014 produced new guidelines, also called *Corporate Governance in New Zealand: Principles and Guidelines*.[111] In the new guidelines the FMA acknowledges that the principles listed in the original 2004 handbook and guidelines are still highly relevant for boards and that the new principles refresh and update the existing principles.[112]

Changes relate to:[113]

- reporting against the principles, including publishing information on company websites;
- some ethical standards that align with recent Australian Securities Exchange (ASX) ethical standards, some factors on diversity 'includ[ing] considerations of gender, ethnicity, cultural background, age and specific relevant skills';
- highlighting the importance of audit committees and the inclusion of commentary on other sorts of committees (such as risk committees) that boards may consider forming depending on their size and needs;
- changes in audit and accounting standards and the changes to continuous disclosure requirements for issuers;
- increased focus on transparent remuneration arrangements, including incentive pay;
- ensuring boards have appropriate risk frameworks and strategies in place with oversight over these and ensuring boards report to investors on these matters; and
- changes in practices and legislation relating to auditors.

The New Zealand Stock Exchange (NZX) is currently the only licensed market operator in New Zealand. Under the FMCA, the NZX must have a set of contractually binding listing rules that all issuers must comply with if they trade on the market.[114] Because both the FMA and the NZX have a role in regulating issuers, they have memoranda of understanding, with the most recent of these signed in 2015.[115] The NZX has a corporate governance code (NZX Code) that applies to entities that have equity securities quoted on the NZX.[116] The NZX Code is currently being reviewed, with the intention of aligning the NZX Code more closely with the FMA Code.[117] The

---

110   Michel Prada and Neil Walter, *Report on the Effectiveness of New Zealand's Securities Commission* (September 2009).

111   Financial Markets Authority (FMA), *Corporate Governance in New Zealand: Principles and Guidelines* (December 2014) 3 <https://fma.govt.nz/assets/Reports/141201-FMA-Corporate-Governance-Handbook-Principles-and-Guidelines2014.pdf>.

112   Ibid. 3.

113   Ibid. 4.

114   *Financial Markets Conduct Act 2013* (NZ) ss 327–329.

115   NZX and FMA, 'Memorandum of Understanding: Between the Financial Markets Authority And NZX Limited' (January 2015) <https://fma.govt.nz/assets/MOU/150128-FMA-NZX-MoU-2015.pdf>.

116   NZX Limited, 'Main Board/Debt Market Listing Rules' (7 March 2016), Appendix 16: Corporate Governance Best Practice Code <https://nzx.com/files/static/cms-documents//NZX%20Main%20Board%20&%20Debt%20Market%20Listing%20Rules%20-%20Appendices%20-%20Clean.pdf>.

117   NZX Limited, 'NZX Regulation/NZX Regulation/Announcements: NZX consults on corporate governance best practice codes' (31 August 2016) <www.nzx.com/regulators/NZXR/announcements/288188>.

NZX Listing Rules and current Code require entities to disclose in their annual reports the extent to which their corporate governance processes materially differ from the principles set out in the NZX Code.[118]

Other sets of guidelines also exist. The NZ Corporate Governance Forum (NZCGF) Guidelines expand on the FMA principles and guidelines.[119] These guidelines are intended for use by listed companies and institutional investors. The Institute of Directors (IOD) is the leading industry body for directors of listed companies. Members of the IOD are required to sign up to its code.[120] The New Zealand *Companies Act 1993* sets out the duties of directors in sections 131–149 and (arguably) codifies those duties. Most New Zealand companies are small or medium enterprises and are therefore not required to comply with many of the corporate governance guidelines. For that reason the statutory duties in the Companies Act are significant.

11.4.2 Financial Markets Authority corporate governance in New Zealand: principles and guidelines (FMA Guidelines)

The FMA Guidelines are intended to apply to the governance of entities that either have economic impact on New Zealand or are accountable to the public.[121] The FMA Guidelines will, therefore, apply to issuers and to public sector entities, state-owned enterprises and community trusts, and may even apply to companies that are not listed and do not issue securities. The FMA acknowledges that not all principles and guidelines will apply to all entities; for example, public sector entities do not have shareholders.[122] Listed issuers are required to adopt and report on certain practices by virtue of the NZX Listing Rules (discussed below). The principles in the FMA Guidelines are intended to complement these listing rules requirements.[123] The FMA states that it 'will comment on, or take appropriate and proportionate action, where [it] find[s] examples of poor governance'.[124]

It should be noted at the outset that the UK 'comply or explain' principle has not been adopted by the FMA. In the Introduction to the FMA Guidelines it is explained that the focus is 'on principles, rather than taking a prescriptive approach', and the FMA 'ask(s) boards to explain how they comply with each principle, rather than "comply or explain why not"'.[125] It is explained that this approach provides flexibility, especially as some entities covered by the FMA Guidelines must also comply with the principles published by the NZX and the ASX.

118   NZX Limited, 'Main Board/Debt Market Listing Rules' (2016), Rule 10.4.5(i) and Appendix 16, cl A.
119   New Zealand Corporate Governance Forum (NZCGF), 'Guidelines' (Forum Guidelines) (July 2015) <www.nzcgf.org.nz/assets/Uploads/guidelines/nzcgf-guidelines-july-2015.pdf>.
120   Institute of Directors, 'Code of Practice for Directors' (IOD Code) (2014) cl 1.9 <www.iod.org.nz/Portals/0/Publications/Founding%20Docs/Code%20of%20Practice.pdf>.
121   FMA, *Corporate Governance in New Zealand: Principles and Guidelines* (December 2014) 5.
122   Ibid. 5.
123   Ibid. 7.
124   Ibid. 5.
125   Ibid. 3.

Although listed issuers are required to have a code of ethics, the FMA points out that '[m]ore widespread adoption and implementation' of ethics codes will not only bring New Zealand into line with international best practice, but also 'promote public confidence in governance structures and behaviour'.[126] Boards are asked to consider convening ethics committees and to obtain regular independent verification of the implementation and effectiveness of their ethics codes.[127] The FMA Guidelines require the board of each entity to adopt a written code of ethics that is 'a meaningful statement of its core values'.[128] The code should include expectations for ethical decision-making in respect of:[129]

- acting honestly and with high standards of personal and professional integrity;
- conflicts of interest, including any circumstances where a director may participate in board discussion of, and voting on, matters in which he or she has a personal interest;
- proper use of an entity's property and/or information, including not taking advantage of the entity's property or information for personal gain, except as permitted by law;
- not participating in any illegal or unethical activity, including safeguards against insider trading in the entity's securities;
- fair dealing with customers, shareholders, clients, employees, suppliers, competitors and other stakeholders;
- giving and receiving gifts, koha (a Maori custom of giving gifts, donations, presents – often by visitors to hosts), facilitation payments and bribes;
- compliance with laws and regulations that apply to the entity and its operations;
- reporting of unethical decision-making and/or behaviour; and
- conduct expected of management and the board in responding to and supporting instances of whistleblowing.

Codes of ethics need to include processes for recording and evaluating compliance. Ethics codes have to be communicated to employees, and training has to be provided. The board is charged with putting a system in place to implement and review the code of ethics, and information about steps taken to implement it should be published.[130]

Principle 2 addresses board composition and effectiveness.[131] The size of boards is expected to be 'appropriate to meet the needs of the entity', with each director having skills, knowledge and experience relevant to the needs of the entity and complementary to each other.[132] The range and balance includes 'consideration of gender, ethnicity, cultural background, age and specific relevant skills' as well as a willingness 'to commit the time and effort needed for the position'.[133] External reviews of performance are encouraged.[134]

---

126   Ibid. 10.
127   Ibid. 10.
128   Ibid. 9.
129   Ibid. 9.
130   Ibid. 9.
131   Ibid. 11.
132   Ibid. 13.
133   Ibid. 13.
134   Ibid. 13.

In carrying out their roles directors are required to have independence of mind and to endeavour to have an independent perspective when making judgments. This means putting the interests of the entity ahead of other interests. Boards are encouraged to put criteria together for defining independent directors, but it is recognised that:[135]

> Board effectiveness is not always enhanced by directors' formal independence if it outweighs the independence of mind, and the skills, knowledge, experience and time that a director can contribute. Independent representation is an important contributor to board effectiveness, but only when considered along with the other attributes sought in a non-executive director.

It is also recognised that achieving too high a level of formal independence may be difficult in New Zealand, with its relatively small pool of qualified and experienced directors.

The FMA considers that 'the underlying issues relating to director independence can be addressed by':[136]

- directors having an independent perspective when making decisions;
- a non-executive director being formally classified as independent only where he or she does not represent a substantial shareholder or other key stakeholder, and where the board is satisfied that he or she has no other direct or indirect interest or relationship that could reasonably influence their judgment and decision-making as a director;
- the chairperson of a publicly owned entity being independent;
- every issuer's board including independent director representation;
- boards of publicly owned entities comprising:
  - a majority of non-executive directors
  - a minimum one-third of independent directors; and
- boards taking care to meet all disclosure obligations concerning directors and their interests, and reports including information about the directors, identifying which directors are independent, and describing the criteria used to assess independence.

Boards are encouraged to consider issues around director tenure and to have a board charter.[137] The role of the chairperson is considered critical and pivotal; in particular, the relationship between the board and the CEO. It is desirable that the chairperson be an independent director, not someone who has previously been CEO; and only under special circumstances should the roles of chairperson and CEO be combined.[138] It is explained that this may, for example, occur 'where an individual has skills, knowledge and experience not otherwise available' and there is a strong suggestion that these special circumstances 'are fully explained to investors'.[139] Boards are encouraged to consider nomination committees and non-executive directors are encouraged to make themselves familiar with the activities of the entity.[140]

---

135   Ibid. 13.
136   Ibid. 13–14.
137   Ibid. 14.
138   Ibid.
139   Ibid.
140   Ibid. 15.

The principles are listed as follows:[141]

- Every issuer's board should have an appropriate balance of executive and non-executive directors, and should include directors who meet formal criteria for 'independent directors'.
- All directors should, except as permitted by law and disclosed to shareholders, act in the best interests of the entity.
- Every board should have a formal charter that sets out the responsibilities and roles of the board and directors, including any formal delegations to management.
- The chairperson should be formally responsible for fostering a constructive governance culture and applying appropriate governance principles among directors and with management.
- The chairperson of a publicly owned entity should be independent. No director of a publicly owned entity should simultaneously hold the roles of board chairperson and chief executive (or equivalent). Only in exceptional circumstances should the chief executive go on to become the chairperson.
- Directors should be selected and appointed through rigorous formal processes designed to give the board a range of relevant skills and experience.
- The board should be satisfied that a director will commit the time needed to be fully effective in their role.
- The board should set out in writing its specific expectations of non-executive directors (including those who are independent).
- The board should allocate time and resources to encouraging directors to acquire and retain a sound understanding of their responsibilities, and this should include appropriate induction training for new appointees and ongoing training for all directors.
- The board should have rigorous formal processes for evaluating its performance, along with that of board committees and individual directors, including the chairperson. This could extend to formally reviewing the position of chairperson on a regular basis.
- Reporting should include information about each director, including a profile of experience, length of service, independence and ownership interests in the company. Information on the board's appointment, training and evaluation processes should also be included.

Principle 3 addresses board committees.[142] Boards should use committees where it enhances effectiveness, while at the same time retaining board responsibility.[143] The FMA acknowledges that board committees may not be appropriate or practical for every entity, but in larger or more complex businesses they can enhance effectiveness.[144] Audit committees are encouraged for all issuers, and remuneration committees are encouraged for listed entities and entities with larger boards.[145] Risk committees, nomination committees and workplace health and safety committees are also suggested.[146]

---

141   Ibid. 12.
142   Ibid. 16.
143   Ibid. 18.
144   Ibid.
145   Ibid.
146   Ibid. 19.

The guidelines state:[147]

- Every board committee should have a clear, formal charter that sets out its role and delegated responsibilities while safeguarding the ultimate decision-making authority of the entire board.
- Where boards have board committees, the charter and membership of each should be published on their website and be easily accessible.
- Proceedings of committees should be reported back to the board to allow other directors to question committee members.
- Each publicly owned company should establish an audit committee of the board with responsibilities to: recommend the appointment of external auditors; oversee all aspects of the entity-audit firm relationship; and promote integrity and transparency in financial reporting.
- Audit committees should comprise:
  - all non-executive directors, a majority of whom are independent;
  - at least one director who is a qualified accountant or has another recognised form of financial expertise; and
  - a chairperson who is independent and who is not the chairperson of the board.

Principle 4 addresses reporting and disclosure, highlighting its importance for proper accountability between an entity and its investors and stakeholders, and as an incentive for good corporate governance.[148] The commentary suggests that not just public sector entities and issuers and listed entities, but other entities too, could adopt similar standards:[149] '[E]ntities that have raised money from the public should report to investors on the entity's goals, strategies, position and performance'.[150]

For listed issuers, compliance with continuous disclosure is a board responsibility, with boards 'balanc[ing] their oversight of continuous disclosure compliance with the requirement to disclose material information "immediately"'.[151] The commentary recommends that boards have 'appropriate policies and procedures, including appropriate delegations, in place'.[152]

The guidelines require that:[153]

- All boards should have a rigorous process for ensuring the quality and integrity of financial statements, including their relevance, faithful representation, verifiability, comparability and timeliness.
- Financial reporting and annual reports of all entities should, in addition to all information required by law, include sufficient, meaningful information to enable investors and stakeholders to be well informed. Financial statements are complex and can be challenging for readers. We encourage boards to aim for financial reports that are clear, concise and effective, while meeting the requirements of financial reporting standards.

---

147   Ibid. 17.
148   Ibid. 22.
149   Ibid. 23.
150   Ibid.
151   Ibid.
152   Ibid.
153   Ibid. 21.

- All boards must maintain an effective system of internal control for reliable financial reporting and accounting records.
- The directors should explain in the annual report their responsibility for preparing the annual report, including the financial statements that comply with generally accepted accounting practice.
- Each listed entity should have a clear and robust written internal process for compliance with the continuous disclosure regime. This process should include board examination, at each meeting at least, of continuous disclosure issues and should be published on the issuer's website.
- Every entity should make its code of ethics, board committee charters, and other governance documents readily available to interested investors and stakeholders. This information should be available on the entity's corporate website.

Principle 5 provides that remuneration should be fair and transparent.[154] While acknowledging that 'adequate remuneration is necessary to attract, retain and motivate high quality directors and executives', in the commentary it is suggested that performance should match remuneration.[155] To allow shareholders to assess its quality, the commentary recommends that 'the policy for determining remuneration and how it is set should be disclosed, as well as the total remuneration and a full breakdown of any other benefits and incentives paid to directors'.[156] A clear distinction between 'the remuneration packages of executive directors and non-executive directors' should also be drawn, with performance incentives for executive directors recommended in the form of shares or options.[157]

The guidelines state:[158]

- The board should have a clear policy for setting remuneration of executives (including executive directors) and non-executive directors at levels that are fair and reasonable in a competitive market for the skills, knowledge and experience required.
- Publicly owned entities should publish their remuneration policies on their websites.
- Executive (including executive director) remuneration should be clearly differentiated from non-executive director remuneration.
- Executive (including executive director) remuneration packages should include an element that is dependent on entity and individual performance.
- No non-executive director should receive a retirement payment unless eligibility for such payment has been agreed by shareholders and publicly disclosed during his or her term of board service.

Principle 6 addresses risk management.[159] The commentary states that boards can only be effective in risk management 'if they know of, and can properly assess, the nature and magnitude of risks faced by the entity. Effective risk management can enable an entity to take appropriate risks.'[160] Enterprise-wide risk management processes are recommended, including

---

154   Ibid. 24.
155   Ibid. 26.
156   Ibid.
157   Ibid.
158   Ibid. 25.
159   Ibid. 27.
160   Ibid. 29.

a separate risk management function or committee, 'depending on the nature, size and complexity of the business'.[161] Annual reporting is also recommended.[162]

The guidelines state:[163]

- The board should require the entity to have rigorous processes for risk management and internal controls.
- The board should receive and review regular reports on the operation of the risk management framework and internal control processes, including any developments in relation to key risks. Reports should include oversight of the company's risk register and highlight the main risks to the company's performance and the steps being taken to manage these.
- Boards of issuers should report at least annually to investors and stakeholders on risk identification, risk management and relevant internal controls.

Principle 7 provides that 'the board should ensure the quality and independence' of the audit process.[164] The commentary states that:[165]

> Good governance requires structures that promote auditors' independence from the board and executives, protect auditors' professional objectivity in the face of other potential pressures and facilitates access to information and personnel.

When selecting auditors, boards should ask whether the auditors have been quality reviewed by the FMA, and if any identified issues have been addressed.[166] While rotation of auditors is desirable, this needs to be balanced against the costs when a new auditor is engaged: 'Professional and ethical standards for auditors require seven-yearly partner rotation (for most NZX listed issuers, five-yearly rotation).'[167]

The commentary states that 'Limiting non-audit work from an accounting firm will help maintain independence and objectivity.'[168] The committee should:[169]

> ... have a defined process for dealing with complaints from auditors ... [and] should also be open to the views of employees or others who believe auditor independence and objectivity is, or might be, compromised. This includes whistleblowing actions by individuals who act in good faith with respect to external and internal audit processes.
>
> ...
>
> Boards should engage with auditors to ensure there is a common understanding and expectation around the scope of audit engagements and the evidence that auditors will expect to be able to find when testing judgments applied to financial statements.

---

161   Ibid.
162   Ibid.
163   Ibid. 28.
164   Ibid. 30.
165   Ibid. 32.
166   Ibid.
167   Ibid.
168   Ibid.
169   Ibid. 33.

The guidelines state:[170]

- The board should inform itself fully on the responsibilities of external auditors and be rigorous in its selection of auditors on professional merit.
- The board should satisfy itself there is no relationship between the auditor and the entity, or any related person, that could compromise the auditor's independence. The board should require confirmation of this from the auditor.
- The board should facilitate regular and full dialogue among its audit committee, the external auditors and management.
- No issuer's audit should be led by the same audit partner for more than seven consecutive years. For listed issuers, NZX rules require most listed entities' audit partners to be rotated from the engagement after a maximum of five years.
- Boards of issuers and entities that are obliged to prepare and file financial reports under the FMC Act should report annually to shareholders and stakeholders on the fees paid to auditors, and should differentiate between audit fees and fees for individually identified non-audit work (for example, separating each category of non-audit work undertaken by the auditors, and disclosing the fees for this).
- Boards of issuers should explain in the annual report what non-audit work was undertaken and why this did not compromise auditor objectivity and independence. They should also explain the following:
  - how they satisfy themselves on auditor quality and effectiveness
  - the boards' approach to tenure and reappointment of auditors
  - any identified threats to auditor independence
  - how the threat has been mitigated.

Principle 8 deals with shareholder relations, with boards encouraged to foster good relations with shareholders.[171]

The guidelines encourage widely held entities to:[172]

- Have clear published policies for shareholder relations and regularly review practices, aiming to clearly communicate the goals, strategies and performance of the entity.
- Maintain an up-to-date website, providing:
  - a comprehensive description of its business and structure
  - a commentary on goals, strategies and performance
  - key corporate governance documents and, if not included in its annual report, a separate section which reports against the entity's adherence to these principles
  - all information released to the stock exchange (for listed entities), including reports to shareholders.
- Encourage shareholders to take part in annual and special meetings by holding these in locations, and at times, that are convenient to shareholders and by providing clear and meaningful information about the business to be conducted at these meetings.
- The board should facilitate questioning of external auditors by shareholders during the annual meeting.

---

170   Ibid. 31.
171   Ibid. 34.
172   Ibid. 35.

Principle 9 states that 'The board should respect the interests of stakeholders within the context of the entity's ownership type and its fundamental purpose.' Although purporting to prioritise the interests of stakeholders, the guidelines qualify the requirement by the inclusion of the word 'respect' and by the qualifying of the requirement to consider stakeholder interests as being generally subject to the interests of shareholders.

The stakeholder principle is qualified within the guidelines as follows:[173]

- The board should have clear policies for the entity's relationships with significant stakeholders, bearing in mind distinctions between public, private and Crown ownership.
- The board should regularly assess compliance with these policies to ensure that conduct towards stakeholders complies with the code of ethics and the law and is within broadly accepted social, environmental, and ethical norms – generally subject to the interests of shareholders.
- Public sector entities should report at least annually to inform the public of their activities and performance, including on how they have served the interests of their stakeholders.

11.4.3 NZX Corporate Governance Best Practice Code (NZX Code)

The New Zealand Stock Exchange (NZX) updated its corporate governance code in 2017 following a year-and-a-half review process, with the changes coming into force in October 2017.[174] The new NZX Code aligns with the tiered approach followed by the 2014 ASX *CG Principles and Recommendations* and also with the FMA Guidelines, discussed above. Significantly, Principle 9, relating to stakeholders, is omitted, although the requirements of Principle 9 have been included in the other eight Principles. The new NZX Code reflects changes in focus since 2003, now focusing on environmental, social and governance (ESG) reporting, reporting on board diversity, workplace health and safety risk management, and director and CEO remuneration reporting requirements.

Along with the improved alignment, the NZX Code also gives issuers flexibility to tailor their corporate governance practices to the needs of their company (or other entity).

In line with the ASX *CG Principles and Recommendations*, the drafters of the new NZX Code adopted a three-tiered approach:

- the top tier sets out eight principles closely based on the FMA's 2014 Principles (discussed above);
- the second tier contains recommendations that apply on a 'comply or explain' basis: the requirement for an explanation is new; and
- the third tier contains commentary and additional optional guidance on suggested good practice.

---

173   Ibid. 38.
174   See <https://nzx.com/files/static/cms-documents//NZX%20-%20Corporate%20-%20Governance%20-%20Code%20-%202017.pdf>.

In addition to the NZX Code, the mandatory corporate governance provisions set out in the NZX Listing Rules continue to apply.

The NZX Code sets out eight principles:

- Code of ethical behaviour: Directors should set high standards of ethical behaviour, model this behaviour and hold management accountable for those standards being followed throughout the organisation.
- Board composition and performance: To ensure an effective board, there should be a balance of independence, skills, knowledge, experience and perspectives.
- Board committees: The board should use committees where this will enhance its effectiveness in key areas, while still maintaining board responsibility.
- Reporting and disclosure: The board should demand integrity in financial and non-financial reporting and in the timeliness and balance of corporate disclosures.
- Remuneration: The remuneration of directors and executives should be transparent, fair and reasonable.
- Risk management: Directors should have a sound understanding of the material risks faced by the issuer and how to manage them. The board should regularly verify that the issuer has appropriate processes to identify and manage potential and material risks.
- Auditors: The board should ensure the quality and independence of the external audit process.
- Shareholder rights and relations: The board should respect the rights of shareholders and foster relationships with shareholders that encourage them to engage with the issuer.

The new NZX Code suggests that: 'An issuer should provide non-financial disclosure at least annually, including considering material exposure to environmental, economic and social sustainability risks and other key risks. It should explain how it plans to manage those risks and how operational or non-financial targets are measured.'[175] The NZX recommends that issuers explain how they intend to manage enviromental, social and governance (ESG) factors, that they report against a recognised international framework such as the Global Reporting Initiative, and that they describe how the business is performing against its strategic objectives.

11.4.4 New Zealand Corporate Governance Forum (NZCGF) Guidelines (Forum Guidelines)

The Forum Guidelines build on the FMA Guidelines, with the focus in many ways on shareholders: on how information is presented to them, and on consideration and protection of their interests. Reporting should help shareholders understand a company's strategic objectives, and should report on ESG considerations specific to the company.[176] Additional ethical standards relate to a review of whistleblowing arrangements, a policy on the company's political engagement, and on employee and director trading in company securities.[177] They

---

175   Ibid. Recommendation 4.3.
176   Forum Guidelines 7.
177   Ibid. 3.

also recommend disclosure of policy and practices on related party transactions.[178] For diversity, a policy with measurable objectives is recommended, as is its disclosure, including reports on progress.[179] Directors may not be independent if they have been employed in the past three years, or have been a director of a related company.[180] The Guidelines recommend a majority and the chair of committees be independent,[181] and that boards should foster a risk culture where financial strategic and ESG risks are considered.[182]

11.4.5 Institute of Directors' Code of Practice for Directors (IOD Code)

The IOD Code recommends monitoring and control of performance through reporting that provides shareholders with an assessment of the company's performance and position in a form that shareholders can readily understand.[183] As well as a code of conduct, directors should lead a culture of high ethical standards.[184] Boards should be balanced, with a mix of skills, knowledge and experience.[185] Listed companies should have a majority of non-executive directors and at least two independent directors and the CEO should not also be the chair.[186] Audit committees should be made up of independent directors with the chair of the board not the chair of the audit committee and should meet with external auditors at least once a year.[187] Remuneration committees should also be comprised of independent directors.[188] Risk management plans, including systems of internal control within the company, should be created and monitored.[189]

The IOD also supports boards reporting on ESG matters and on workplace health and safety performance.[190] Remuneration should be fair and transparent, and set to attract, motivate and retain the best people possible, with incentives aligned with strategy and performance, and with fees reviewed annually and disclosed in the annual report.[191] Auditors should maintain communication with audit committees, meeting with them at least once a year and with auditors able to attend and speak at meetings.[192]

Remuneration is considered from the perspective of shareholders, and it is recommended that remuneration policy is aligned with the long-term objectives of the company and that performance measures do not incentivise inappropriate risks.[193]

---

178   Ibid.
179   Ibid. 5.
180   Ibid.
181   Ibid. 6.
182   Ibid. 9.
183   IOD Code [3.16].
184   Ibid. [3.1].
185   Ibid. [3.6].
186   Ibid. [3.7].
187   Ibid. [3.12].
188   Ibid. [3.13].
189   Ibid. [3.5].
190   Caird et al., 'Corporate Governance Codes Compared' 10.
191   IOD Code [3.13].
192   Ibid. [3.11] and [3.12].
193   Ibid. [3.13] and [3.15].

11.4.6 The *Companies Act 1993* (NZ)

The first objective of the *Companies Act 1993*, set out in its long title, is:

> ... to reaffirm the value of the company as a means of achieving economic and social benefits through the aggregation of capital for productive purposes, the spreading of economic risk, and the taking of business risks ...

Section 131 of the Companies Act puts a subjective duty of good faith on directors. There is a separate statutory duty to use powers for a proper purpose (s 133), duties and processes around conflicts of interest (sections 139 to 144) and on directors dealing in shares (sections 148 and 149). Under New Zealand company law there is also a positive obligation on directors not to trade recklessly (s 135), and an obligation not to allow the company to enter into obligations that it will not be able to perform (s 136). Although explicitly not owed to creditors, these duties primarily protect the interests of creditors.[194] There is also a statutory duty of care (s 137) and a duty to comply with the Act and the constitution (s 134).

Opinion is divided on whether the statutory duties set out in the Companies Act attempt to, or in fact succeed in, codifying the common law duties. At the very least, the pre-existing case law remains relevant in understanding the origins of the rules and in assisting in interpreting them. Perhaps the statement of Heath J in *Benton v Priore*, that sections 131–138 of the Act 'should be seen as a restatement of basic duties [developed by the common law] in an endeavour to promote accessibility to the law', represents the predominant view.[195]

11.5 Canada

11.5.1 Overview

In an increasingly globalised world economy, competition is intense and good corporate governance can make a difference to how Canadian companies are viewed. There are benefits to being recognised as a country where excellence in corporate governance has a high priority; these benefits accrue to individual Canadian companies when operating abroad, as well as to the entire Canadian capital market as viewed by international investors.[196]

Broadly speaking, in common with the general approach to corporate governance in the UK and Australia, Canada also places great emphasis on guidelines rather than prescriptive rules.[197] There is, to some degree, a basic level of congruence in the principles governing the corporate governance framework in international jurisdictions. In particular, there are similar

---

194   *Companies Act 1993* (NZ) s 169(3) provides that the duties are owed to the company and not to shareholders. In the leading case, *Nicholson v Permakraft (NZ) Ltd* [1985] 1 NZLR 242 (CA), it was held that in a situation of doubtful solvency, directors owe a duty to consider the interests of the creditors.

195   *Benton v Priore* [2003] 1 NZLR 564 (HC) at [46], followed in *Sojourner v Robb* [2006] 3 NZLR 808 (HC) at [100].

196   *Beyond Compliance: Building a Governance Culture – Final Report Joint Committee on Corporate Governance* (November 2001) 7 (sponsored by the Canadian Institute of Chartered Accountants, the Canadian Venture Exchange, Toronto Stock Exchange and chaired by Guylaine Saucier).

197   Exceptions to this general categorisation arise, however, when the impact of the rules-based approach under SOX on Canadian corporate governance is considered. The Canadian response to SOX is dealt with later in this chapter.

themes in Canada, Australia and the UK on the guidelines relating to, *inter alia*, board composition, the establishment of independent audit, nominating and compensation committees, and the operation of the disclosure regime of corporate governance practices (the 'comply or explain' system).

11.5.2 Regulatory environment

In focusing on the Canadian securities regulatory framework, it is worth noting that Canada is the only developed country that does not have a national securities regulator.[198] Each Canadian province (of which there are 10) and territory (of which there are three) has its own securities regulator responsible for administering the province's or territory's Securities Act and formulating its own set of rules and regulations. The difficulties and concerns arising from this patchwork approach are captured in the report issued to the Canadian Government by the Expert Panel on Securities Regulation in Canada:[199]

> The Expert Panel heard repeated . . . concerns about the cost and confusion caused by our fragmented system of thirteen separate securities regulators . . . While the terminology has differed over the years – single, common, Canadian, national, or federal – the conclusion of virtually every study [over the years] has been the same: Canadians are ill-served by such a balkanized system . . . The lack of a national Canadian securities regulator also raises wider concerns about systemic risk, as there is no national entity accountable for the stability of our national capital markets.

The Expert Panel viewed Canada's fragmented system as a serious shortcoming, and recommended the establishment of a single securities regulator administering a single Securities Act for Canada.[200] The report and draft Securities Act make a number of recommendations to improve securities regulation and investor protection. These include:

- establishing a single, comprehensive system to measure the performance of securities regulation in Canada to promote greater accountability;
- establishing the Canadian Securities Commission to administer a single Securities Act for Canada;
- advancing a principles-based approach to securities regulation;
- promoting fairness in the adjudication of regulatory matters by establishing an independent adjudicative tribunal; and
- establishing an investor panel and an investor compensation fund to better serve the needs of investors.

---

198   *Final Report and Recommendations: Creating an Advantage in Global Capital Markets* (12 January 2009) Chair's Foreword.

199   Ibid. For earlier reports warning of similar dangers and advocating a single national securities regulator in Canada, see Wise Person's Committee to Review the Structure of Securities Regulation in Canada, *It's Time* (December 2003) <www.wise-averties.ca/reports/WPC%20Final.pdf>; Crawford Panel on a Single Canadian Securities Regulator, *Blueprint for a Canadian Securities Commission* (June 2006).

200   This criticism was made despite the existence of 'passport', a regulatory system designed to aid the harmonisation of laws, and which provides market participants with streamlined access to Canada's capital markets. Although a major step forward, the passport system has been criticised as being limited in application and too slow, cumbersome and expensive. See *Final Report and Recommendations* (12 January 2009) Chair's Foreword.

The philosophical approach to securities regulation adopted by the Expert Panel is captured in the following extract from the report:[201]

> We recommend Canadian securities regulators should focus less on process and more on outcomes; relying more on articulating principles than on multiplying rules. We believe that regulation should be grounded in guidance and rules on a bedrock of well-formulated principles. This will help reduce unnecessary compliance costs, improve regulatory outcomes, and give Canada a competitive edge.

In 2010, the Canadian Government prepared a draft bill for a Federal Securities Act and sought an advisory opinion on its constitutionality from the Supreme Court of Canada. Any chance of a unified national securities regulation system was scuttled when the Supreme Court held that the proposed Act did not fall within the general trade and commerce power under the *Constitution Act 1867* and thus was unconstitutional.[202] The Supreme Court held that the reform would be an improper 'wholesale takeover of the regulation of the securities industry'[203] and that it would trespass into the provincial sphere of decision-making. Provinces that opposed the proposed Securities Act (Alberta, Québec, Manitoba, New Brunswick and other interveners) welcomed the decision. However, the Supreme Court did note that, looking forward, a cooperative solution which respects the federalism principle upon which Canada's constitutional framework rests will be required.[204]

The Canadian Securities Administrators (CSA) continues its mission: to achieve harmonisation of the 13 separate securities regime. The CSA is an umbrella organisation representing all 13 Canadian securities regulators and provides a coordinating function to maintain confidence in, and protect the integrity of, the market.[205]

In the wake of the passage of SOX in 2002 in the US, the Canadian securities and corporate governance landscape has changed. Canada was not immune to failures in corporate governance and also had its share of financial scandals, such as Nortel, Livent and Cinar Corporation.[206] The combination of internal failures and pressure from the US to implement reforms, due to the existence of the Multi-Jurisdiction Disclosure System that allows Canadian issuers to list in US markets, resulted in significant debate and eventual action on the part of Canadian securities regulators to implement corporate governance reforms.[207] The CSA adopted and

---

201   Ibid.
202   *Reference re Securities Act* [2011] 3 SCR 837.
203   Ibid. at [128].
204   Ibid. at [132]–[133]. Subsequent to this case, in September 2013, the Federal Government announced that it had reached an agreement in principle with the provinces of Ontario and British Columbia that would see the creation of a Cooperative Capital Markets Regulator (CCMR). Although not yet operational, appointments have been made to this regulatory body. See <http://ccmr-ocrmc.ca/capital-markets-regulatory-authority-executive-management-team-announced/> (January 2017); <http://ccmr-ocrmc.ca/chief-regulator-named-capital-markets-regulatory-authority/> (November 2016).
205   For an examination of Canadian securities regulation, see Task Force to Modernise Securities Regulation in Canada, *Canada Steps Up* (2006) <www.tfmsl.ca>.
206   Stephanie Ben-Ishai, 'Sarbanes-Oxley five years Later: A Canadian perspective' (2008) 39 *Loyola University Chicago Law Journal* 469, 476.
207   Ibid.

modified certain aspects of SOX, which has ensured that the Canadian securities regulatory environment remains closely aligned in principle with that in the US.[208]

The key instruments and policies that impact on Canadian corporate governance practices are:

- National Instrument 58–101: Disclosure of Corporate Governance Practices;
- National Instrument 51–102: Continuous Disclosure Obligations;
- National Instrument 52–109: Certification of Disclosure in Issuers' Annual and Interim Filings (CEO and CFO Certifications);[209]
- National Instrument 52–110: Audit Committees;[210]
- Companion Policy 52–110CP: Audit Committees;
- National Instrument 52–108: Auditor Oversight;[211]
- National Policy 51–201: Disclosure Standards; and
- National Policy 58–201: Corporate Governance Guidelines.

On 30 June 2005, the CSA introduced a key policy document, National Policy 58–201: Corporate Governance Guidelines, which was recommended as a guide to best practice for issuers to follow. It was envisaged that National Policy 58–201 would be replaced over time. Initiatives aimed to review and improve the current corporate governance regime,[212] however, have been shelved.[213] The CSA concluded, in November 2009, that it was not an appropriate time to recommend significant changes to Canada's corporate governance regime.[214]

----

208 Susan Jenah, 'Commentary on a blueprint for cross-border access to US investors: A new international framework' (2007) 48 *Harvard International Law Journal* 78. For a critique of the Canadian approach to regulatory policy initiatives, see Ronald Davis, 'Fox in S-Ox North, a question of fit: The adoption of United States market solutions in Canada' (2004) 33 *Stetson Law Review* 955. For a brief comparison of the Canadian and US regulatory schemes, see Ben-Ishai, 'Sarbanes-Oxley five years later: A Canadian perspective' (2008) 481.

209 This instrument covers the certification requirements of s 302 of SOX. It requires each CEO and CFO of an issuer company to file a separate annual certificate stating that he or she has reviewed annual filing, has no knowledge of any material misrepresentation, and that he or she is responsible for establishing and maintaining disclosure controls and procedures and internal control over financial reporting for the issuer.

210 This instrument covers, with some modification, the independent audit committee requirements of s 302 of SOX. Unlike the US position, Canadian audit committees are not required to have a financial expert – however, similar to the position in the US, each member must be financially literate.

211 This instrument is influenced by ss 101–105 of SOX, which deal with the audit requirements of public companies. In 2014, the CSA repealed and replaced NI 52–108: Auditor Oversight. See further <www.osc.gov.on.ca/documents/en/Securities-Category5/rule_20140717_52-108_-repeal-replacement-auditor oversight.pdf>.

212 See CSA Staff Notice 58–304, *Review of NI 58–1–1 Disclosure of Corporate Governance Practices and NP 58–201 Corporate Governance Guidelines* (28 September 2007) <www.osc.gov.on.ca/documents/en/Securities-Category5/csa_20070928_58-304_review-58-101.pdf>.

213 See CSA Staff Notice 58–305, *Status Report on the Proposed Changes to the Corporate Governance Regime* (13 November 2009) <www.osc.gov.on.ca/documents/en/Securities-Category5/csa_20091113_58-305-gov-regime.pdf>. In December 2008, the CSA published, for comment, proposed changes to the corporate governance regime entitled 'Proposed Repeal and Replacement of National Policy 58–21, *Corporate Governance Guidelines*, National Instrument 58–1–1 *Disclosure of Corporate Governance Practices*, and National Instrument 52–110 and Companion Policy 52–110CP *Audit Committees*.

214 Ibid.

11.5.3 National Policy 58–201: Corporate governance guidelines

The national policy sets out non-prescriptive corporate governance guidelines with the following purposes, as stated in the preamble:

- achieve a balance between providing protection to investors and fostering fair and efficient capital markets and confidence in capital markets;
- be sensitive to the realities of the greater numbers of small companies and controlled companies in the Canadian corporate landscape;
- take into account the impact of corporate governance developments in the U.S. and around the world; and
- recognize that corporate governance is evolving.

The current governance policy applies to all reporting issuers (both corporate and non-corporate entities) other than investment funds. The following are relevant (edited) extracts from the National Policy 58–201: Corporate Governance Guidelines:

Composition of the Board

3.1   The board should have a majority of independent directors.

3.2   The chair of the board should be an independent director. Where this is not appropriate, an independent director should be appointed to act as "lead director". However, either an independent chair or an independent lead director should act as the effective leader of the board and ensure that the board's agenda will enable it to successfully carry out its duties.

Meetings of Independent Directors

3.3   The independent directors should hold regularly scheduled meetings at which non-independent directors and members of management are not in attendance.

Board Mandate

3.4   The board should adopt a written mandate in which it explicitly acknowledges responsibility for the stewardship of the issuer, including responsibility for Rules and Policies.

Position Descriptions

3.5   The board should develop clear position descriptions for the chair of the board and the chair of each board committee. In addition, the board, together with the CEO, should develop clear position description for the CEO, which includes delineating management's responsibilities. The board should also develop or approve the corporate goals and objectives that the CEO is responsible for meeting.

Orientation and Continuing Education

3.6   The board should ensure that all new directors receive a comprehensive orientation.

3.7   The board should provide continuing education opportunities for all directors, so that individuals may maintain or enhance their skills and abilities as directors, as well as to ensure their knowledge and understanding of the issuer's business remains current.

Code of Business Conduct and Ethics

3.8   The board should adopt a written code of business conduct and ethics (a code). The code should be applicable to directors, officers and employees of the issuer. The code should constitute written standards that are reasonably designed to promote integrity and to deter wrongdoing. In particular, it should address the following issues:

(a)   conflicts of interest, including transactions and agreements in respect of which a director or executive officer has a material interest; . . .

3.9   The board should be responsible for monitoring compliance with the code.

Nomination of Directors

3.10   The board should appoint a nominating committee composed entirely of independent directors.

3.11   The nominating committee should have a written charter that clearly establishes the committee's purpose, responsibilities, member qualifications, member appointment and removal, structure and operations (including any authority to delegate to individual members and subcommittees), and manner of reporting to the board.

3.12   Prior to nominating or appointing individuals as directors, the board should adopt a process involving the following steps:

(A)   Consider what competencies and skills the board, as a whole, should possess. In doing so, the board should recognize that the particular competencies and skills required for one issuer may not be the same as those required for another; . . .

Compensation

3.15   The board should appoint a compensation committee composed entirely of independent directors.

3.16   The compensation committee should have a written charter that establishes the committee's purpose, responsibilities, member qualifications, member appointment and removal, structure and operations.

3.17   The compensation committee should be responsible for:

(a)   reviewing and approving corporate goals and objectives relevant to CEO compensation, evaluating the CEO's performance in light of those corporate goals and objectives, and determining (or making recommendations to the board with respect to) the CEO's compensation level based on this evaluation;

(b)   making recommendations to the board with respect to non-CEO officer and director compensation, incentive-compensation plans and equity-based plans; and

(c)   reviewing executive compensation disclosures before the issuer publicly discloses this information.

Regular Board Assessments

3.18   The board, its committees and each individual director should be regularly assessed regarding his, her or its effectiveness and contribution.

Originally, the national policy did not fully address the issue of board diversity. The Ontario Securities Commission (OSC) led the push towards greater disclosure in this area and proposed amendments regarding disclosure of the number of women on boards and in senior management.[215] The OSC favoured a 'comply or explain' model to promote diversity, including gender diversity, on corporate boards. The amendments, in effect from December 2014, are set out in the National Instrument 58–101: Disclosure of Corporate Governance Practice. It addresses policies regarding the representation of women on the board (Manitoba, New Brunswick, Newfoundland and Labrador, Northwest Territories, Nova Scotia, Nunavut, Ontario, Québec and Saskatchewan only) – and recommends that the following matters be addressed:[216]

(a) Disclose whether the issuer has adopted a written policy relating to the identification and nomination of women directors. If the issuer has not adopted such a policy, disclose why it has not done so.

(b) If an issuer has adopted a policy referred to in (a), disclose the following in respect of the policy:

(i) a short summary of its objectives and key provisions,

(ii) the measures taken to ensure that the policy has been effectively implemented,

(iii) annual and cumulative progress by the issuer in achieving the objectives of the policy, and

(iv) whether and, if so, how the board or its nominating committee measures the effectiveness of the policy.

11.5.4 National Instrument 58–101: Disclosure of corporate governance practices

Currently, this instrument requires a reporting issuer (other than an investment fund) to include in its information circular, annual information form or equivalent document disclosure regarding its corporate governance practices: issuers must disclose whether their practices are consistent with those recommended under National Policy 58–201: Corporate Governance Guidelines. This approach is consistent with the 'comply or explain' disclosure regime in other jurisdictions, such as Australia and the UK.[217]

11.5.5 National Instrument 52–110 and Companion Policy 52–110CP: Audit committees[218]

As a response to major corporate fraud and misconduct in the US, Canada reformed the audit function to enhance the quality of the audit process by adopting the following measures:

---

215 On 18 December 2013, the OSC delivered OSC Report 58–402 Report to Minister of Finance and Minister Responsible for Women's Issues – *Disclosure Requirements Regarding Women on Boards and in Senior Management*. See further <www.osc.gov.on.ca/en/NewsEvents_nr_20140116_osc-amd-wob.htm>.

216 See further <www.osc.gov.on.ca/documents/en/Securities-Category5/csa_20141014_58-101_noa-national-instrument.pdf>.

217 Since 1995, companies listed on the TSX have been required to disclose on an annual basis a 'Statement of Corporate Governance Practices'. Although the TSX guidelines (set out in the TSX Company Manual) were not prescriptive, they were predicated on the 'comply or explain' disclosure regime. For examples of disclosure of Canadian corporate governance practices, see disclosure documents of public companies at <www.sedar.com>.

218 See <www.osc.gov.on.ca/documents/en/Securities-Category5/rule_20101210_52-110_unofficial-consolidated.pdf> 7–8.

- establishing the Canadian Public Accountability Board (CPAB), which parallels the creation of the Public Company Accounting Oversight Board (PCAOB), seen as the centrepiece of SOX;
- creating an Auditing and Assurance Standards Oversight Council (AASOC);
- promulgating new auditor independence standards; and
- passing a national instrument on auditor oversight.

In line with international trends, which have concentrated attention on audit committees fulfilling their oversight responsibilities with respect to the integrity of financial statements and reporting,[219] Canada has also focused on the expanded role of audit committees. This national instrument, similarly to s 301 of SOX, requires every reporting issuer (unless exempted) to have an audit committee, composed of independent directors, responsible for the oversight of the external auditor and for reviewing the company's financial statements. The National Instrument establishes requirements for the responsibilities, composition and authority of audit committees.[220] The companion policy provides information regarding the interpretation and application of the instrument.

In the case of a non-venture issuer, an audit committee must be composed of a minimum of three directors who must be, subject to limited exceptions, independent and financially literate.[221] For purposes of the instrument, a director is financially literate if he or she has the ability to read and understand a set of financial statements that present a breadth and level of complexity of accounting issues that is reasonably comparable to the breadth and complexity of the issues that can reasonably be expected to be raised by the issuer's financial statements.[222] Furthermore, issuers must disclose the education and experience of each audit committee member that is relevant to the carrying out of his or her responsibilities as an audit committee member.[223]

The definition of 'independent director', which is also applicable to the corporate governance guidelines discussed earlier, is contained in National Instrument 52–110 and is determined with reference to the following specific 'bright-line' tests:

- an individual who is, or with the prior three-year period has been, an employee or executive officer of the issuer;
- an individual whose immediate family member is, or within the prior three-year period has been, an executive officer of the issuer;
- an individual who is, or has been, or has an immediate family member who is, or has been, a partner or employee of a current or former internal or external auditor of the issuer, or

219   See, for example, *Report and Recommendations of the Blue Ribbon Committee on Improving the Effectiveness of Corporate Audit Committees* (New York Stock Exchange [NYSE] and National Association of Securities Dealers, 1999).
220   The instrument applies to a reporting issuer other than an investment fund, an issuer of asset-backed securities, a designated foreign issuer or an SEC foreign issuer.
221   National Instrument 52–110 Part 3.2 <www.osc.gov.on.ca/documents/en/Securities-Category5/rule_20101210_52-110_unofficial-consolidated.pdf>.
222   Ibid. Part 4.1 of Companion Policy 52–110CP.
223   Ibid. Part 4.2 of Companion Policy 52–110CP.

personally worked on the issuer's audit within the past three years as a partner or employee of that audit firm;

- an individual who is, or has been, or whose immediate family member is, or has been within the past three years, an executive officer of an entity if any of the issuer's current executive officers serve or served at the same time on that entity's compensation committee;
- an individual who received, or whose immediate family member who is employed as an executive officer of the issuer received, more than $75 000 in direct compensation from the issuer during any 12-month period within the past three years; and
- for purposes of this definition, an 'issuer' includes any parent or subsidiary entity.

The definition above is extended for audit committee composition purposes.

The responsibilities of the audit committee are set out in Part 2.3 of National Instrument 52–110, which states:

(1) An audit committee must have a written charter that sets out its mandate and responsibilities.

(2) An audit committee must recommend to the board of directors
   (a) the external auditor to be nominated . . .; and
   (b) the compensation of the external auditor.

(3) An audit committee must be directly responsible for overseeing the work of the external auditor engaged for the purpose of preparing or issuing an auditor's report or performing another audit, or attest services for the issuer, including the resolution of disagreements between management and the external auditor regarding financial reporting.

(4) An audit committee must pre-approve all non-audit services to be provided to the issuer or its subsidiary entities by the issuer's external auditor.

(5) An audit committee must review the issuer's financial statements, MD&A and annual and interim profit or loss press releases before the issuer publicly discloses this information.

(6) An audit committee must be satisfied that adequate procedures are in place for the review of the issuer's public disclosure of financial information extracted or derived from the issuer's financial statements . . . and must, periodically, assess the adequacy of those procedures.

(7) An audit committee must establish procedures for:
   (a) the receipt, retention and treatment of complaints received by the issuer regarding accounting, internal accounting controls, or auditing matters; and
   (b) the confidential, anonymous submission by employees of the issuer of concerns regarding questionable accounting or auditing matters.

(8) An audit committee must review and approve the issuer's hiring policies regarding partners, employees and former partners or employees of the present or former external auditor of the issuer.[224]

224   Ibid. Parts 7–8.

11.5.6 Future directions

The following section highlights some of the key concerns expressed about the future direction of corporate governance in Canada. A common concern of various commentators[225] is the tendency for Canadian corporate and securities law reform to move in lockstep with that of the US despite considerable differences between the Canadian capital markets and those in the US. The key major difference is that most US companies are widely held; in Canada, half of the top firms have controlling shareholders (wealthy families, other firms, or large financial institutions).[226] Those controlling shareholders usually dominate the board, giving rise to governance problems, as controlling shareholders are either unsophisticated or wield control without owning very many shares through control-magnifying devices such as super-voting shares and pyramiding.[227] Randall Morck and Bernard Yeung note that much empirical research links these problems to weak performance.[228] In their view, the 2005 corporate governance reforms in Canada are ill-suited, for the following reasons:

> Canadian corporate governance laws, regulations and best practices must attend to controlling-(shareholder) interests versus public-shareholder disputes in firms with controlling shareholders, and to shareholder-manager disputes in firms without them. This requires a fundamentally broader focus than in the United States and the United Kingdom, where controlling shareholders are relatively rare and good governance is mainly about preventing or solving shareholder-manager disputes.[229]

The following questions posited by a Canadian commentator illustrate the fierce debate about the future direction of Canadian corporate governance reform:

- Should Canada harmonise its securities laws with SOX?
- Since Canada has traditionally employed a principles-based model of corporate governance, is it necessary for Canada now to shift its corporate governance culture and adopt a rules-based model in order to harmonise with SOX?
- Given that Canada does not have a federal securities regulator like the US's SEC, can Canada even achieve domestic harmonisation, let alone external harmonisation with SOX?[230]

---

225   See, for example, Sukanya Pillay, 'Forcing Canada's hand? The effect of the Sarbanes-Oxley Act on Canadian corporate governance reform' (2004) 30 *Manitoba Law Journal* 285; Davis, 'Fox in S-Ox North, a question of fit: The adoption of United States market solutions in Canada' (2004) 990; Paul D Paton, 'Rethinking the role of the auditor: Resolving the audit/tax services debate' (2006) 32(1) *Queen's Law Journal*; Edward Waitzer, 'Paradigm flaws: An agenda for corporate governance reform' (2007) *Banking & Finance Law Review* 405; Stephen Sibold, 'Assessing Canada's regulatory response to the *Sarbanes-Oxley Act of 2002*: Lessons for Canadian policy makers' (2008–09) 46 *Alberta Law Review* 769.

226   Randall Morck and Bernard Yeung, 'Research Study: Some Obstacles to Good Corporate Governance in Canada and How to Overcome Them', commissioned by the Task Force to Modernise Securities Legislation in Canada, *Canada Steps Up* (18 August 2006) 293–300.

227   Ibid.

228   Ibid. 295.

229   Ibid. 296. For similar concerns, see Janis Sarra, 'The corporation as symphony: Are shareholders first violin or second fiddle?' (2003) 36 *University of British Columbia Law Review* 403, who notes that corporate law reforms shift oversight power to large investors and their ability to influence corporate governance.

230   Pillay, 'Forcing Canada's hand?' (2004).

An unanswered question, posed by Ronald Davis,[231] is whether the importation of the SOX regulatory requirements will adversely affect the culture of Canada's corporations by encouraging the abandonment of a 'culture of compliance' and the replacing of it with a loophole-conscious, rules-based culture. Answering this question merits empirical research into corporate governance practices. It is noted, with some irony, by one commentator[232] that the recent calls to roll back s 404 of SOX (dealing with internal controls) due to the high cost of compliance (in particular for smaller public companies)[233] suggests that the US may be moving in the Canadian direction.

The contemplated change in philosophy, from a set of recommended governance practices to the principles-based approach in National Policy 58–201, would bring with it opportunities and risks[234] for those at the coal-face who are familiar with the current governance culture.

11.6 South Africa

11.6.1 Introduction

In South Africa corporate governance became particularly prominent with the publication of the first King Report (generally known as King I), named after Professor Mervyn King SC. King I was inspired by the UK Cadbury Report (1992) and was released in 1994.[235] The second King Report (King II) came out in 2002[236] and the third King Report (King III), *The King Code of Governance for South Africa 2009*, in 2009.[237] During 2015 it was announced that King III will be updated and that King IV should be effective by the middle of 2017.[238] A draft was released on 15 March 2016 and public comments were due by 15 May 2016. On 1 November 2016 the

---

231   Davis, 'Fox in S-Ox North, a question of fit: The adoption of United States market solutions in Canada' (2004) 990.

232   Ben-Ishai, 'Sarbanes-Oxley five years later: A Canadian perspective' (2008) 490.

233   'SEC Votes to Propose Interpretive Guidance for Management to Improve Sarbanes-Oxley 404 Implementation', SEC Press release (13 December 2006) <www.sec.gov/news/press/2006/2006-206.htm>; 'SEC Approves New Guidance for Compliance with Section 404 of Sarbanes-Oxley', SEC Press release (23 May 2007) <www.sec.gov/news/press/2007/2007-101.htm>; and see John W White, *SEC's Proposed Interpretive Guidance to Management for Section 404 of Sarbanes-Oxley Act*, SEC Press release (23 May 2007).

234   For a comprehensive discussion of the costs and benefits of rules and principle-based regulatory systems, see Cristie Ford, 'Principles-Based Securities Regulation' (Expert Panel on Securities Regulation, 2008). For critique of the use of such labels, see Lawrence Cunningham, 'A prescription to retire the rhetoric of "principle-based systems" in corporate law, securities regulation, and accounting' (2007) 60 *Vanderbilt Law Review* 1411.

235   *The King Report on Corporate Governance* (Institute of Directors in Southern Africa [IoDSA], 1994).

236   *King Report on Corporate Governance for South Africa – 2002* (King Report (2002)) (IoDSA, 2002).

237   *The King Code of Governance for South Africa 2009* (the Code) and the *King Report of Governance in South Africa 2009* (together, King Report (2009)) <http://african.ipapercms.dk/IOD/KINGIII/kingiiireport/>. These two documents are together referred to as the King Report (2009), although they are separate documents. The Institute of Directors in Southern Africa (the IoDSA) also issued Practice Notes on the King Report (2009). The King Report (2002) (King II), replacing King I, was applicable to South African enterprises until the end of February 2010, after which the King Report (2009) (King III) became effective. See <www.iodsa.co.za>. On the King Report (2002), see Anneli Loubser, 'Does the King II Report solve anything?' (2002) 3 *Juta's Business Law* 135.

238   On King IV see <http://www.iodsa.co.za/?page=KingIV>. King IV was developed by building on King III. The drafting of King IV was led by the King III lead (Ansie Ramalho).

final Report was launched.[239] Disclosure under King IV is effective for the financial years starting on or after 1 April 2017, but immediate transition is encouraged. King IV replaces King III in its entirety. The Institute of Directors of Southern Africa (IoDSA) indicated that King IV will build on the content of King III.

In South Africa, it has been maintained, for several years, that corporate governance revolves around sustainability, leadership and corporate citizenship.[240] With these values in mind we will provide a brief overview of the South African corporate governance best practices embedded in King IV. Where relevant, reference will also be made to King III. We will also highlight some of the important governance provisions that are now regulated in the South African *Companies Act 71 of 2008* (2008 Companies Act).[241] In South Africa, directors' duties and principles of good governance are regulated by legislation and the common law.[242] Important recommendations are also contained in codes of best practice. Of specific significance is the fact that corporate social responsibility (CSR) is now, for the first time, dealt with in legislation. This will also be discussed.

In South Africa several indexes and matrixes have been designed to indicate whether or not companies adhere to good corporate governance principles. During 2008 the Centre for Corporate Governance in Africa was formed by the South African Public Investment Corporation (PIC)[243] to develop a Corporate Governance Rating Matrix to be applied to listed South African corporations. The matrix measures corporate governance levels of the top 100 Johannesburg Stock Exchange (JSE) listed companies.[244] It has 16 categories: board, individual directors, executive management, remuneration, shareholder treatment, auditing and accounting, disclosure and reporting, corporate behaviour, corporate culture, sustainability reporting, UN Global Compact, human rights, transformation, workplace health and safety, corporate responsibility, and environmental reporting.[245]

The JSE *Listing Requirements* also impose a duty on all listed companies to report on social, health, environmental and ethical performance, and the efficiency of risk management and internal control, and to disclose the degree of compliance with King III.[246] In addition to requiring listed companies to comply with King III, the JSE launched a Socially Responsible Investment Index (SRI Index) in May 2004.[247] In this Index the JSE measured the 'triple-bottom line' performance of the FTSE/JSE All Share Index.[248] The SRI Index was replaced at the end of

---

239   See <www.iodsa.co.za/page/KingIVReport>.
240   King Report (2009) 9. Under King IV the relevant governance outcomes are ethical culture, good
        performance, effective control and legitimacy (King IV 20).
241   See R32 in *GG 34239* of 26 April 2011 for the final Act and its Regulations. See <www.saflii.org/za/legis/
        consol_act/ca2008107/> for the most recent version of the 2008 Companies Act.
242   For corporate governance in the NGO sector see J Geldenhuys, 'Corporate governance and NGOs' in
        I Esser and MK Havenga (eds), *Corporate Governance Annual Review 2012* (LexisNexis, 2012) Ch 5.
243   See <www.pic.gov.za/>. PIC is one of the largest investment managers in Africa.
244   For the Johannesburg Stock Exchange see <www.jse.co.za/Home.aspx>.
245   See <www.usb.ac.za/governance/Pages/pic-corporate-governance-rating-matrix.aspx> and <www
        .fanews.co.za/article/people-and-companies/12/news/1163/new-matrix-launched-to-measure-
        corporate-governance-levels-in-sa/7792>.
246   See *Listings Requirement* 3.84, dealing with corporate governance requirements.
247   For the SRI Index see <www.jse.co.za/About-Us/SRI/Criteria.aspx>.
248   See <www.jse.co.za/sri/index.htm>. See <www.jse.co.za/content/
        JSEIndexConstituentsandWeightingsItems/2014SRIIndexConstituentsbestperformers.pdf>.

2015: the FTSE ESG (Environment, Social and Governance) Ratings are now used to select the constituents of the FTSE/JSE Responsible Investment (RI) Index.[249]

11.6.2 The King III (2009) and IV (2016) Reports

The King III Report applies to all entities, regardless of the manner and form of incorporation or establishment, and whether they are in the public, private or non-profit sectors.[250] The Report operates on an 'apply or explain' basis, but it will be seen below that King IV operates on an 'apply and explain' basis. This is similar to the 'comply and explain' basis that King II operated on. The King III committee found the word 'apply' more appropriate than 'comply'.[251]

King IV, on the other hand, has been drafted to be more accessible to organisations and entities. Most listed companies were generally applying King III.[252] Other organisations, such as non-profit organisations, private companies and entities in the public sector, experienced challenges in interpreting and adapting King III to their particular circumstances.[253]

It was submitted, by the IoDSA, that a mere update of King III was not sufficient to deal with global developments and emerging issues. The principles of King IV reflect the aspirations of the journey towards good corporate governance.[254] Mindless compliance and a quantitative approach is not the aim. The objectives of King IV are framed as the promotion of good governance as integral to running a business which should deliver benefits that include an ethical culture and the enhancement of performance, reputation and legitimacy. King IV frames corporate governance as a holistic set of arrangements that must be implemented in an integrated manner. It is not merely about structure and process, but about ethical concise-ness and behaviour.[255]

The main aim of King IV can thus be summarised as mindful compliance, adding value across the board. Corporate governance is defined as:

---

249   *JSE FTSE/JSE Responsible Investment Index Series* (October 2015) and <www.jse.co.za> Products and Services – FTSE/JSE Responsible Investment Index Series.

250   See King III, Introduction and Background in the Code para 13.

251   Ibid. para 3.

252   On the application of King III see N Waweru, 'Determinants of quality corporate governance in Sub-Saharan Africa' (2014) 29 *Managerial Auditing Journal* 455–85: Waweru conducted a study during 2014 to examine the factors influencing the quality of corporate governance in South Africa and Kenya. See IoDSA, *IoDSA Perceptions and Practice of King III in South African Companies* (March 2013). See Irene-marié Esser, 'Corporate governance: Soft law regulation and disclosure – the cases of the United Kingdom and South Africa' in Jean J du Plessis and C Low (eds), *Corporate Governance Codes for the 21st Century* (Springer, 2017) on compliance with *King III*. Finally, see Jansen van Vuuren and J Schulschenk, 'Perceptions and practice of King III in South African Companies' (University of Pretoria and IoDSA, March 2013) and J Solomon and W Maroun, 'Integrated reporting: The influence of King III on social, ethical and environmental reporting' (2012) *Association of Chartered Certified Accountants (ACCA)*.

253   Broader terms such as 'governing body', 'organisations' and 'those charged with governance duties' are now used in King IV.

254   King IV 36.

255   King IV part 2, 22.

> ... the exercise of ethical and effective leadership[256] by the governing body towards the achievement of the following governance outcomes: Ethical culture, Good performance, Effective control, Legitimacy.[257]

This is done by way of governance outcomes, principles and practices.[258] King IV is, like its predecessors, a set of voluntary principles and practices.[259] Part 5.1 deals with leadership, ethics and corporate citizenship.[260] Part 5.2 deals with strategy, performance and reporting.[261] Part 5.3 deals with governing structures and delegation.[262] Part 5.4[263] concerns governance function areas, with Principle 11 requiring that the governing body should govern risk in a way that supports the organisation in setting and achieving its strategic objectives. Part 5.5 deals with stakeholder relationships.[264]

The main difference between King III and King IV is its application and scope. King IV uses the 'apply and explain' (King III used 'apply or explain') approach, and is based on 17 Principles, with practices which are linked to governance outcomes. The broad application of King IV – the view is that all organisations should be able to follow the principles and strive to achieve the governance outcomes – is thus really the main difference. The sector supplements, providing practices developed for specific sectors, are new.[265] With regard to the contents, there are not many differences. A number of issues are, however, addressed in King IV to bring it into line with international developments. For example, integrated thinking has been introduced in King III but it has evolved substantially through the work of the International Integrated Reporting Council (IIRC).[266] King IV is now in line with these international practices.[267] King IV also provides new recommendations on audit committees and auditor independence, which are in line with the 4 December 2015 rule of the South African Independent Regulatory Board for Auditors.[268] In response to the 2008 Companies Act, whose provisions on the social and ethics committee have been in place for some time now, the new code expands on the role of this committee.[269]

---

256 Ethical leadership is exemplified by integrity, competence, responsibility, accountability, fairness and transparency. Effective leadership is results-driven. It is about achieving strategic objectives and positive outcomes. Ethical and effective leadership should complement and reinforce each other.
257 King IV part 2, 36.
258 Ibid. para 3.
259 King IV 35.
260 Ibid. 43–6.
261 Ibid. 47–8.
262 Ibid. 49–60.
263 Ibid. 61–70.
264 Ibid. 71–3.
265 Ibid. part 6.
266 See <http://integratedreporting.org/the-iirc-2/>.
267 See <http://integratedreporting.org/>.
268 See <www.irba.co.za/>. In terms of this rule it is mandatory to disclose in the auditor's report the number of years for which the audit firm has been the auditor of the organisation. See King IV part 5.3, principle 8, paras 51–59.
269 Ibid. paras 68–70.

11.6.3 The *Companies Act 71 of 2008*

Many of the recommendations of King III (and thus King IV) are now embedded in the 2008 Companies Act. This is explained in detail by Anneli Loubser.[270]

It is not the purpose of this discussion to deal with the 2008 Companies Act in detail, but merely to give a few examples of some of the recommendations of King III and now King IV that are legislated. These are important because they were not dealt with in the South African *Companies Act 61 of 1973*.

Corporate citizenship is once again emphasised in King IV,[271] and it is stated that support for the idea of corporate citizenship is also found in legislation, as certain companies must establish a social and ethics committee.[272] A unique aspect of the South African legislation is that s 72 of the 2008 Companies Act introduces a *compulsory* social and ethics committee for all state-owned and listed companies, as well as other companies with a 'public interest score'[273] of more than 500.[274] The number of employees and the turnover are some of the factors that will determine whether or not a company is obliged to have such a committee. It is worth noting that it is the company – in other words the shareholders – and not the board, that must appoint this committee.

A minimum of three directors or prescribed officers must serve on a company's social and ethics committee. One of them must not, at least for the previous three financial years, have been involved in the day-to-day management of the company's business.[275]

The social and ethics committee has the following function: to monitor the company's activities, having regard to any relevant legislation, other legal requirements or prevailing codes of best practice, in matters concerning social and economic development, including the company's position regarding the goals and purposes as envisaged in, for example, the G20/OECD *Principles* and the *Global Compact Principles*. It also maintains records of sponsorships, consumer relationships and labour and employment. The committee should report annually to the shareholders at the company's annual general meeting on the matters within its mandate.[276]

---

270   See A Loubser, 'The King Reports on corporate governance' in Esser and Havenga (eds), *Corporate Governance Annual Review 2012* (2012) 20ff. This is based on King III, but will be very similar in King IV. The differences are more in application and scope.

271   See also King III Ch 1.

272   King IV 25.

273   The 'public interest score' is calculated at the end of a financial year, and is the sum of a number of things, including the average number of employees, the turnover of the company and the nature and extent of the company's activities during that financial year. It is used to determine whether a company must comply with enhanced accountability requirements based on its social and economic impact. See Regulation 26(2) of the 2008 Companies Act; Natania Locke, 'Enhanced Accountability' in Esser and Havenga (eds), *Corporate Governance Annual Review 2012* (2012) 88; and, generally, <www.business-rescue.co.za/regulations/Regulation-26-2-public-interest-score.php#.U5pG-BA4KBg>; <www.saipa.co.za/sites/saipa.co.za/files/How%20to%20calculate%20the%20PIS.pdf>.

274   See 2008 Companies Act s 72(4) and Regulations 43 and 26(2). See HJ Kloppers, 'Driving Corporate Social Responsibility (CSR) through the Companies Act: An overview of the role of the social and ethics committee' (2013) 16 *Potchefstroomse Elektroniese Regsblad (PER)* 166 for an overview of the social and ethics committee.

275   Regulation 43(4). See Natasha Bouwman, 'Are we moving to a two-tier board structure?' (April 2010) *Without Prejudice* 14.

276   Regulation 43(5).

Second, in King III, the ultimate responsibility for good corporate governance rested with the board of directors.[277] Section 66(1) of the 2008 Companies Act now also states that the business and affairs of the company must be managed by and be under the direction of the board. The Act now partially codifies the duties of directors, in sections 75 and 76.[278] The business judgment rule is also codified, in s 76(4).[279]

Third, board committees are now also dealt with in the 2008 Companies Act.[280] Persons who are not directors can form part of a board committee. These persons are subject to the same duties and responsibilities as directors, but they cannot vote on any matter to be decided by the committee.[281] This is contrary to the recommendation in King III. Principle 2.23 of King III relates to board committees, and states that the board should delegate certain functions to well-structured committees, but without abdicating its own responsibilities. Reference is specifically made to an audit committee, a risk committee and a remuneration committee. King IV deals with board committees in Principle 8, where it is stated that the board should ensure that its arrangements for delegation promote independent judgment, and assist with balance of power and the effective discharge of its duties. King IV specifically clarifies the objectives of these delegation arrangements. They include the promotion of independent judgment, to assist with balance of power and to assist with the effective discharge of its duties by the governing body.

Lastly, Principles 5.1–5.7, in King III Chapter 5, deal with the governance of information technology. This is dealt with under Principle 12 of King IV, where it is recommended that the governing body should govern technology and information in a way that supports the organisation's setting and achieving its strategic objectives. Many provisions in the Act now allow or compel the use of technology. Section 63(2), for example, allows shareholder meetings to be held electronically.

11.6.4 Corporate social responsibility (CSR) and South African company law[282]

CSR issues enjoy more prominence in the 2008 Companies Act than in any previous company legislation in South Africa. Section 7(d) confirms that one of the purposes of the new Act is to reaffirm the concept of the company as a means of achieving economic and social benefit.[283]

---

277   King III Chapter 2, Principles 2.1–2.5, dealing with the board as focal point for corporate governance and Principles 2.6–2.14, dealing with the board and directors and, specifically, their responsibilities in respect of certain issues. This is dealt with in King IV Principle 6.

278   On the codification of directors' duties, see N Bouwman, 'An appraisal of the modification of the director's duty of care and skill' (2009) 4 *South African Mercantile Law Journal* 509 and MM Botha, 'The role and duties of directors in the promotion of corporate governance: A South African perspective' (2009) 30 *Obiter* 702.

279   See, on this rule, M Havenga, 'The business judgment rule – Should we follow the Australian example?' (2000) 1 *South African Mercantile Law Journal* 25 and S Lombard, 'Importation of the statutory business judgment rule into South African company law: Yes or no?' (2005) 68 *Journal of Contemporary Roman Dutch Law* 614.

280   2008 Companies Act s 72.

281   Ibid. s 72(2).

282   See I Esser, 'Corporate Social Responsibility: A company law perspective' (2011) 23 *South African Mercantile Law Journal* 317.

283   Section 5(1) of the 2008 Companies Act states that the Act must be interpreted in such a way as to give best effect to the purposes listed in s 7.

Stakeholder protection is addressed in s 76(3)(b). Section 72(4) provides for the establishment of a social and ethics committee. Several sections afford protection to stakeholders.

Section 76(3)(a) and (b) of the 2008 Companies Act provides as follows:

> A director of a company, when acting in that capacity, must exercise the powers and perform the functions of director (a) in good faith and for a proper purpose; (b) *in the best interests of the company* ... (emphasis added)

When considering s 76(3)(b), it is unclear whether directors should consider the interests of stakeholders, as suggested in the stakeholder-inclusive approach, or should act as determined by the enlightened shareholder value approach. In the inclusive approach directors must consider the interests of various stakeholders on a case-by-case basis, but in the end the decision must be in the best interests of the company, even if it is to the detriment of the shareholders.[284]

The King III Report paid specific attention to CSR issues in Chapter 1, which deals with ethical leadership and corporate citizenship, in Chapter 8, which deals with stakeholder relationships, and in Chapter 9, which deals with integrated reporting and disclosure.

The stakeholder approach advocated by King IV is that:

> directors owe their fiduciary duties to the company and to the company alone as the company is a separate legal entity from the moment it is registered until it is deregistered ... The company is represented by several interests and these include the interests of shareholders, employees, consumers, the community and the environment. Thus, requiring of directors to act in good faith in the interest of 'the company' cannot nowadays mean anything other than a blend of all these interests, but first and foremost they must act in the best interest of the company as a separate legal entity... An interest that may be primary at one particular point of time in the company's existence, may well become secondary at a later stage.[285]

Integrated sustainability performance and integrated reporting are integral parts of King III. Integrated sustainability reporting relates to a holistic representation of a company's performance in terms of its finances and sustainability.[286] In terms of King IV, in the context of reporting, it is important to take the international integrated reporting framework[287] into account. Integrated reporting is an outcome of integrated thinking. It is argued that this has

---

284   See *Swart v Beagles Run Investments 25 (Pty) Ltd* (2011) (5) SA 422 (GNP) on how the court balances the interests of shareholders and creditors in the context of business rescue proceedings.

285   This approach is taken from: Irene-marié Esser and Jean du Plessis, 'The stakeholder debate and directors' fiduciary duties' (2007) 19 *South African Mercantile Law Journal* 346. See also I Esser and PA Delport, 'Shareholder protection philosophy in terms of the Companies Act 71 of 2008' (2016) 79 *Journal of Contemporary Roman Dutch Law* 1–29.

286   King III Principle 9.1.

287   See <http://integratedreporting.org/resource/international-ir-framework/>. The International Integrated Reporting Council (IIRC) is a global coalition of regulators, investors, companies, standard setters, the accounting profession and NGOs. Together, this coalition shares the view that communication about value creation should be the next step in the evolution of corporate reporting. The International Framework has been developed to meet this need and provide a foundation for the future. See King IV part 5.2, on integrated reporting.

to be part of the actual report and that a mere practice note will not be sufficient to address this. Organisational ethics did not receive a lot of attention in King III, but is addressed in King IV. Ethics should go further than mere internal ethics: it also has an impact on society and corporate citizenship and this is now incorporated, bringing King IV into line with international practices.[288]

11.6.5 Conclusions on South Africa

South Africa has an extensive and detailed corporate governance framework. King III (and now King IV) provides ample guidance on corporate governance issues and how company directors should act. Many of these recommendations, especially on CSR and directors' duties, are also embedded in the 2008 Companies Act.

In a South African case, the court tested directors' conduct against King II.[289] The court found that if not complying with the principles embedded in King II (the report applicable at that stage), directors may be in breach of their duty of care and skill, and that this may even be extended to breaches of their fiduciary duties. In the 2008 Companies Act, directors' duties are codified, and any person who contravenes any provision of that Act may be liable to any other person for any loss or damage suffered by that person as a result of the contravention. Directors may therefore be held accountable under the 2008 Companies Act for not complying with King III or King IV. It may be asked whether this does not go too far.[290]

In short, South Africa has a good and extensive corporate governance framework. However, the question remains whether the South African society and South African companies reflect the values, ethics and good governance principles embedded in the legislation, codes of best practice and case law.[291]

11.7 India
11.7.1 Introduction

This chapter provides an overview of the regulatory framework for corporate governance in India, followed by a contextual account of the development of the *Companies Act 2013*, and the Securities and Exchange Board of India (SEBI) Listing Obligation and Disclosure

---

288   See <http://integratedreporting.org/>.
289   *Stilfontein Minister of Water Affairs and Forestry* v *Stilfontein Gold Mining Co. Ltd* (2006) 5 SA 333 (W).
        See, on this case, Stephanie Luiz and Zuene Taljaard, 'Mass resignation of the board and social
        responsibility of the company: *Minister of Water Affairs and Forestry v Stilfontein Gold Mining Co. Ltd*'
        (2009) 21 *South African Mercantile Law Journal* 420.
290   See Irene-marié Esser and Piet Delport, 'The duty of care, skill and diligence: The King Report and the
        2008 Companies Act' (2011) 74 *Journal of Contemporary Roman Dutch Law* 449.
291   See the Failed States Index of the Fund for Peace – <http://global.fundforpeace.org/> – where South
        Africa is ranked 156/178 countries <http://fsi.fundforpeace.org/2016-southafrica>. Social, political and
        economic indicators are used to determine if a state is at an 'alert' phase or sustainable. South Africa is on
        'warning' level. See also the Corruption Perceptions Index 2013: <www.transparency.org/cpi2013/
        results>. South Africa has been ranked 72 out of 175 countries, with a 42% rating (with 0 as highly
        corrupt and 100 as very clean). See also Loubser, 'The King Reports on corporate governance' in Esser
        and Havenga (eds), *Corporate Governance Annual Review 2012* (2012) 61 on South Africa's corporate
        governance framework and its impact on society and South African companies.

Requirement Regulation 2015 and the impetus for governance reform, particularly in the aftermath of the mammoth failure of Satyam Computers (2009) and the Global Financial Crisis. The contextual account assists in understanding the historical, cultural, social and economic factors that have helped shape governance practices in India.[292]

11.7.2 Regulatory framework for corporate governance[293]

The Indian statutory framework has been influenced by the international best practices of corporate governance. Broadly, the corporate governance mechanism for companies in India is located in the following enactments/regulations/guidelines/listing agreement:

1. The *Companies Act 2013*, *inter alia*, contains provisions relating to board constitution, board meetings, board processes, independent directors, general meetings, audit committees, related party transactions, and disclosure requirements in financial statements.

India is the only country in the world with codified corporate social responsibility (CSR) obligations.[294] The Companies Act requires specified companies to spend at least 2 per cent of the average net profits made during the three immediately preceding financial years on prescribed CSR activities. This provision operates on a 'comply or explain' basis, and the board of directors must provide an explanation in the directors' report if the company does not spend the requisite amount on CSR. This requirement is applicable to companies which have:

- a net worth of at least INR 5 billion during any financial year;
- a turnover of at least INR 10 billion during any financial year; or
- a net profit of at least INR 50 million during any financial year.

Every company which fulfils the above threshold requirements must set up a corporate social responsibility committee, formulate a CSR policy and make recommendations on CSR to the board.

There is a mandatory requirement to report the details of the CSR policy and the implementation of the CSR initiatives taken by a company during a financial year.[295]

A company can engage in a broad category of CSR activities, including eradication of poverty, promotion of education, promotion of gender equality and environmental sustainability. The CSR activities must be performed within India and are not permitted to be for the exclusive benefit of the company's employees or their family members.

---

292 See Tirthankar Roy and Anand V Swamy, *Law and the Economy in Colonial India* (University of Chicago Press, 2016); Nayan Mitra and René Schmidpeter (eds), *Corporate Social Responsibility in India* (Springer, 2017).

293 The content on the regulatory framework is drawn largely from the following sources: Vaish Associates Advocates <www.mondaq.com/india/x/456460/Shareholders/Corporate+Governance+Framework+In+India> (8 January 2016) and the chapter on India in Koustri Gosh and Bhusan Jatania, *International Comparative Legal Guide to Corporate Governance* (2016) <https://iclg.com/practice-areas/corporate-governance/corporate-governance-2016/india>.

294 See further Bhaskar Chatterjee and Nayan Mitra 'CSR Implementation: How It Is Done in India' and 'The Why, What and How of the CSR Mandate: The India Story' in Mitra and Schmidpeter (eds), *Corporate Social Responsibility in India* (2017).

295 For an empirical and analytical study during the pre-mandate and mandate onset period, see Sumona Gosh, 'Reporting of CSR Activities in India: Are We Still at a Nascent Stage Even After the Legal Mandate?' in Mitra and Schmidpeter (eds), *Corporate Social Responsibility in India* (2017).

2. Securities and Exchange Board of India (SEBI) Guidelines: SEBI is a regulatory authority having jurisdiction over listed companies. It issues regulations, rules and guidelines to companies to ensure the protection of investors.

3. Accounting Standards issued by the Institute of Chartered Accountants of India (ICAI): ICAI is an autonomous body which issues accounting standards that operate as guidelines for disclosure of financial information. Section 129 of the *Companies Act 2013*, *inter alia*, provides that financial statements shall give a true and fair view of the state of affairs of the company or companies, and comply with the accounting standards notified in s 133 of the Companies Act.

4. Secretarial Standards issued by the Institute of Company Secretaries of India (ICSI): ICSI is an autonomous body which issues secretarial standards in terms of the provisions of the Companies Act. So far, the ICSI has issued Secretarial Standards on 'Meetings of the Board of Directors' (SS-1) and on 'General Meetings' (SS-2). These Secretarial Standards came into force on 1 July 2015. Section 118(10) of the *Companies Act 2013* provides that *every company* (other than a one-person company) shall observe Secretarial Standards specified by the ICSI with respect to general and board meetings.

11.7.3 Background to the *Companies Act 2013*

The British transplanted English company law in 1850. The objective was to facilitate British trade and commerce in the country through the incorporation of registered companies. The Act underwent several changes and, in 1930, a consolidated and updated Companies Act was introduced. It was amended in 1934 and lasted until 1955. The Act introduced certain provisions[296] relating to company management which were a departure from the British principles of company law.[297] The Indian Parliament introduced the *Companies Act 1956*, with the primary objective of strengthening the devastated post-colonial economy. The Act was amended 30 times to accommodate policy changes relating to company administration, and was repealed by Act No. 18 of 2013 (*Companies Act 2013*). The introduction of the New Economy Policy (NEP) in 1991 by the Central (Federal) Government was the catalyst for the 2013 Act. NEP represented a decisive shift, from centralised bureaucratic control to a liberalised market economy. Under the post-independent economic regime, government (of different layers) became the largest equity holder.

---

296   Detailed provisions were introduced relating to 'Managing Agencies'. In the late 1890s companies used to appoint Managing Agencies to carry out the day-to-day management. These Managing Agencies were mainly British firms. The Amendment Act of 1936 formalised the appointment of 'Managing Agencies' by incorporating a chapter with defined Agency responsibilities. The system was abolished after 1970. See, generally, Bhabha Committee 'Report on Company Law Committee' (1952) <http://reports.mca.gov.in/Reports/22-Bhabha%20committee%20report%20on%20Company%20law%20committee,%201952.pdf>; 'Shastri Committee Report on Company Act Amendment, 1957' (Ministry of Finance, Government of India, 1957) <http://reports.mca.gov.in/Reports/21-Shastri%20committee%20report%20on%20Company%20act%20amendment,%201957.pdf>; 'Working Group on Company Law Administration, 1968 (Mazumdar Committee Report)' (Administrative Reform Commission, 1968) <http://reports.mca.gov.in/Reports/28-Mazumdar%20committee%20report%20working%20group%20on%20company%20law%20Administration,%201968.pdf>; 'Symposium on New Company Law, 1957' 22 <http://reports.mca.gov.in/Reports/33-Symposium%20on%20new%20Company%20Law,%201957.pdf>.

297   See Umakanth Varottil, 'The evolution of corporate law in post-colonial India: From transplant to autochthony' (2016) 31 *American University International Law Review* 253.

Prior to the 2013 Act and the NEP, industrial sectors were classified[298] as public or private, and the majority were not open for private investment. The NEP attempted to declassify a large number of the industrial sectors (mainly manufacturing sectors) and open them up for private and foreign direct investment. This is popularly known as the 'end of License Raj'. With this change in economic philosophy, investment from the private sector escalated over time, which re-energised the demand for capital market and related institutional reforms. Business associations and conglomerates lobbied for the introduction of international standards in investor protection and management decision-making.

The government established a capital market regulator, the Securities and Exchange Board of India (SEBI). SEBI was entrusted with several responsibilities, including 'to protect the interests of investors in securities and to promote the development of, and to regulate, the securities market'.[299]

To develop the capital market and promote transparency, predictability and openness in the market, SEBI proposed several institutional reforms and adopted a series of guidelines, rules, and regulations. The primary objectives of the reforms were to protect the market from initial distortions, and to allow further diversity in the economy. Companies, mainly private equity companies, emerged as the preferred business vehicle for major commercial and business activities in the post-reform period (that is, after 1990).

11.7.4 Development of Corporate Governance Code and Clause 49 in the Listing Agreement

The Confederation of Indian Industries (CII), a leading business association, led a major initiative to introduce a code of corporate governance. In 1998 a committee was set up, under the leadership of a noted industrialist,[300] to develop a voluntary code of corporate governance. The code, which drew heavily on the Anglo-American model of corporate governance, was titled 'Desirable Corporate Governance: A Code'.[301] Many industrial houses and companies welcomed this move.[302]

Following the CII initiative, SEBI constituted a committee, under Kumar Mangalam Birla,[303] to develop a standard of good corporate governance for public listed companies (PLCs). The committee made several recommendations, including regarding the composition and functions of audit committees and remuneration committees, the composition of the board of directors[304] and the appointment of independent directors, and the board's role in risk management. The committee observed that the board had responsibilities to stakeholder well-being.[305]

---

298   Industries were classified under the *Industries (Development and Regulation) Act, 1952*.
299   See Preamble of the Act, *Securities and Exchange Board of India Act 1992* 1.
300   Rahul Bajaj, former Chairman of Bajaj Group.
301   'Desirable Corporate Governance: A Code (CII Code)' (Confederation of Indian Industries, April 1998) 1 <www.nfcgindia.org/desirable_corporate_governance_cii.pdf>.
302   For critical appraisal, see Umakanth Varottil, 'A cautionary tale of the transplant effect on Indian corporate governance' (2009) 21 *National Law School of India Review* 1.
303   Chairman of Aditya Birla Group, one of big industrial houses in India.
304   In common with the Anglo-American model, India has a single-tier board system.
305   'Report of the Committee Appointed by the SEBI on Corporate Governance (Kumarmanglam Birla Committee)' (SEBI, 2000) 1 <www.sebi.gov.in/commreport/corpgov.html> (popularly known as Kumarmagalam Birla Committee Report).

SEBI adopted the recommendation and inserted a clause (clause 49)[306] on corporate governance compliance[307] for PLCs in Listing Agreements.[308] Clause 49 required a PLC to create a dedicated section on corporate governance in its Annual Report.[309] Key features of clause 49 included the need for disclosure of the following matters: ownership structure, the composition of the board, the ratio of executive to non-executive directors, the qualifications of directors, the number of board meetings, the composition and functions of the audit committee, and the CEO/CFO's certification of the company's financial result. The primary objectives of clause 49 are to protect the interest of investors, and to strive for the equitable treatment of all stakeholders.

Under clause 49, PLCs are required to submit a quarterly compliance report to the stock exchange within 15 days of their quarterly financial reporting. The report is to be submitted by either the compliance officer or the CEO of the company after obtaining the approval of the board. Stock exchanges can obtain information from companies under eight sub-classes: Board of Directors; Audit Committee; Shareholders/Investor Grievance Committee; Remuneration of Directors; Board Procedures; Management; Shareholders; and Report on Corporate Governance. Stock exchanges are required to set up independent groups to monitor compliance with the corporate governance provisions of Listing Agreements, and are required submit a consolidated compliance report to SEBI within 30 days of each quarter end.[310]

SEBI has observed that though compliance with clause 49 is largely satisfactory, the quality of the analysis of financial statements and of corporate governance disclosure lacks uniformity. SEBI has stressed that compliance with the corporate governance code should be of substance, and not merely of form.

International corporate collapses, such as Enron and WordCom in the US, prompted SEBI to set up a committee in 2003, under the chairmanship of Narayana Murthy,[311] to review existing corporate governance practices and suggest measures to improve compliance. The Murthy Committee produced a report which focused on the role and structure of the board, the involvement of independent directors, the role of board subcommittees and companies' disclosure practices.[312] As a result of the Murthy Committee report,[313] clause 49 was amended and updated.

---

306   In February, 2000, clause 49 was added in the Listing Agreement by SEBI.

307   The report of the committee was adopted by SEBI in its meeting on 25 January 2000.

308   A Listing Agreement is entered into between a registered stock exchange (in India) and each PLC. The minimum standard of content of a Listing Agreement is prescribed by SEBI under the *Security Contract Regulation Act 1956*.

309   Under the *Companies Act 2013*, every company should prepare an Annual Report for a general meeting of the shareholders.

310   See SEBI's Circular No. SMD/Policy/CIR-03/2001 (22 January 2001).

311   He is the promoter and chairman of Infosys Ltd, an IT service-providing company. The company is known for its strong corporate governance compliance culture. The committee submitted the report on 8 February 2003.

312   'Report of SEBI Committee on Corporate Governance (Narayana Murthy Committee)' (Business, Security and Exchange Board of India, 8 February 2003) 43 <www.sebi.gov.in/commreport/corpgov.pdf>.

313   Adopted by SEBI on August 2003. This led to wide protests and representations from industry. The committee revisited their recommendations and a new recommendations was put up on the SEBI website for public comment on 15 December 2003. On 29 October 2004 SEBI announced the revision of clause 49, which was effective from the end of financial year 2004–05.

The amended clause 49 requires companies to provide specific corporate disclosures relating to independent directors,[314] whistleblower policy, performance evaluation of non-executive directors, mandatory training of non-executive directors, related party transactions, accounting treatment, reasons for deviations from accounting standards, risk management procedures, proceeds of various kinds of share issues, remuneration of directors, management discussions, plus a section regarding general business conditions and outlook, and details of committee members and new directors.[315] The amended clause 49 further stipulated that non-executive members should comprise at least half of the board of directors.

SEBI implemented clause 49 of the Listing Agreement in a phased manner. On 31 March 2001 it was made applicable to all the companies in the BSE 200 and S&P CNX indices[316] and all newly listed companies. The application of the clause extended to companies with a paid-up capital of Rs.100 million, or with a net worth of Rs.250 million at any time in last five years (dated from 31 March 2002). On 31 March 2003, the clause was extended to other listed companies with a paid-up capital of over Rs.30 million.[317] By 1 January 2006, clause 49 applied to all PLCs. Further amendments were made to clause 49 in 2014, clarifying its contents on related party transactions and on board composition and powers, to align it with the new *Companies Act 2013*. A company's failure to comply with clause 49 can result in delisting, and in financial penalties.

11.7.5 Statutory provisions

The Department of Company Affairs,[318] under the Ministry of Finance and Company Affairs, appointed a high-powered committee (popularly known as the Naresh Chandra Committee) in August 2002 to examine various governance issues.[319] The committee made a large number of recommendations on several issues, including financial and non-financial disclosure, independent auditing and the board responsibility to monitor management closely. The report strongly emphasised the need for the improvement of audit practices. It prescribed grounds for disqualifying the auditor, the types of other non-audit services the auditor should be prohibited from performing, the compulsory rotation of audit partners etc.[320] These recommendations led

---

314   The committee laid down the qualifications of an independent director, a first in Indian corporate governance.

315   Madan Bhasin and A Manama, 'Corporate governance disclosure practices in India: An empirical study' (2008) 5 <www.wbiconpro.com/103.Bhasin.pdf>; Rajesh Chakrabarti, William Megginson and Pradeep K Yadav, 'Corporate governance in India' (2008) 20(1) *Journal of Applied Corporate Finance* 59, 64.

316   Ibid. 64.

317   'Report of SEBI Committee on Corporate Governance (Narayana Murthy Committee)' (2003) 4.

318   The Department of Company Affairs, under the Ministry of Finance, was designated a separate Ministry in 2004. Later it was renamed the Ministry of Corporate Affairs and detached from the Ministry of Finance. The Ministry of Corporate Affairs administered the *Companies Act 1956* (a federal law), other allied Acts and rules and regulations thereunder. Though SEBI is an independent market regulator, for administrative purpose it reports to the Ministry of Corporate Affairs.

319   The Committee submitted the report in December 2002.

320   'Report of the Committee on Corporate Audit and Governance (Naresh Chandra Committee)' (August 2002).

to amendments to the *Companies Act 1956*[321] that added specific provisions on corporate governance. The provisions related to 'accounting standards,' 'the appointment of auditors' (the gatekeepers), and 'audit committees of the board'. The Act detailed the function and composition of the audit committee and prescribed that members should be financially literate and independent. These changes were applicable to all companies: public listed, unlisted and private companies.

In 2004, JJ Irani (a board member of Tata Sons) was appointed as chairman of a committee set up by Ministry of Corporate Affairs to revamp and redraft the Companies Act in line with the NEP (and on the recommendation of the Naresh Chandra Committee). The mandate of the Irani Committee was to offer advice on the New Companies Bill. Based on the Committee's recommendations, the Ministry introduced the Companies Bill 2008. The Bill failed, due to the dissolution of the 14th Lok Sabha (lower house of parliament).

Mandatory and voluntary corporate governance practices in India developed in parallel, under clause 49 and other ancillary clauses of the Listing Agreement[322] and statutory provisions of the *Companies Act 1956* (now the *Companies Act 2013*). The Listing Agreement is administered by SEBI and the Companies Act is administered by the Ministry of Corporate Affairs (MCA). Regulators in India did not adopt 'comply or explain principles', unlike other jurisdictions. Companies needed to comply with mandatory and statutory provisions under the Listing Agreement and Companies Act respectively. However, the voluntary provisions of the Listing Agreement were left to companies to report on a case-by-case basis.

11.7.6 Impact of Satyam

January 2009 was significant from a corporate governance development perspective due to the collapse of Satyam Computer Services Ltd, one of the largest IT companies in India. The failure of corporate governance in Satyam centred on three issues. First, accounting fraud – fabricated accounts had been presented by the company for years; second, related party transactions – promoters of Satyam computers were personally interested; third, the failure of the independent directors to effectively monitor the company.

The Satyam scam shook the Indian corporate world and prompted CII[323], the National Association of Software and Service Companies (NASSCOM)[324] and the Institute of Company Secretaries of India (ICSI)[325] to set up expert committees to recommend corporate governance

---

321   The Companies (Amendment) Bill 2003.
322   SEBI is empowered to administer the Listing Agreement under s 21 (Condition for Listing) of the *Security Contract Regulation Act 1956*.
323   CII appointed Sri Naresh Chandra as the head of Task Force Committee, and they submitted the report on November 2009: 'Report of the CII Task Force on Corporate Governance Chaired by (Sri Naresh Chandra)' (Business, Confederation of Indian Industries, November 2009) 1 <www.mca.gov.in/Ministry/latestnews/Draft_Report_NareshChandra_CII.pdf>.
324   NASSCOM appointed the committee under the chairmanship of NR Narayana Murthy: 'NASSCOM Corporate Governance Report' (27 April 2010) <http://survey.nasscom.in/sites/default/files/upload/66719/Corporate_Governance_Report.pdf>.
325   'ICSI Recommendations to Strengthen Corporate Governance Framework' (Institute of Company Secretaries of India, 2009) <www.mca.gov.in/Ministry/latestnews/ICSI_Recommendations_Book_8dec2009.pdf>.

reforms in response to the Satyam experience. The collective recommendation of the committees was to enlarge the role of independent directors;[326] to incorporate/constitute various mandatory subcommittees of boards which would be chaired by the independent directors; to endure that the chairman of the board would be an independent director; to evolve mechanisms to assess the performance of individual directors and the board subcommittees; and to reform the appointment procedure for internal and external auditors. The committees emphasised that every related party transaction should be critically examined by the board and subject to any measures necessary to protect the independence of the directors. The recommendations also advocated that corporate governance orientation should shift towards stakeholders.

In late 2009, the Ministry of Corporate Affairs issued 'Voluntary Guidelines for Corporate Governance' based on the recommendations of the committees. The guidelines recognised that corporate governance 'may go well beyond the law and that there are inherent limitations in enforcing many aspects of corporate governance through legislative and regulatory means'.[327] The guidelines were for all private and public companies. Companies were to adopt the guidelines in their day-to-day operations. In cases of partial adoption, companies had to disclose the reasons for non-adoption to their shareholders. The guidelines did not replace any existing Regulations; they were in addition to the existing framework.

Important features of the Voluntary Guidelines included the appointment of independent directors, the remuneration of directors, the responsibilities of the board, the audit committee of the board, the auditors, the secretarial audit and the institutionalisation of whistleblower mechanisms. The guidelines set out the following process. A company would need to issue a formal letter of appointment to non-executive directors and independent directors. The appointment letter would specify terms of appointment, the expectations of the board and fiduciary duties, along with accompanying liabilities, provision for directors' insurance, the code of business ethics, a list of activities directors should not indulge in, and the remuneration or sitting fees, stock options etc. It proposed to limit the board membership of the individual director and formalised the nomination committee of the board. The independent directors' qualifications would need to indicate positive attributes such as integrity, experience and expertise, foresight and an ability to read and understand financial statements. The tenure of independent directors would not exceed five years. Independent directors would be provided with the option and freedom to interact with the company's management to enable them to perform their functions effectively.

Remuneration policy for a member of the board and the key management person would be laid down clearly and disclosed in the public domain. The remuneration would be reasonable and sufficient to attract, retain and motivate quality directors. The remuneration package would be performance driven for the executive director and designed to align their interests with those of shareholders. The remuneration of non-executive directors, including

---

326   For a critical analysis of independence requirements, see Luke Nottage and Fady Aou, 'Independent director requirements in Australia and the Asian region' (2016) 32 *Company and Securities Law Journal (C&SLJ)* 631.

327   'Corporate Governance Voluntary Guidelines 2009' (Ministry of Corporate Affairs, 2009) 1, 9 <www.mca.gov.in/Ministry/latestnews/CG_Voluntary_Guidelines_2009_24dec2009.pdf>.

independent directors, would be divided into three basic categories: fixed component,[328] variable components, and additional variable payments. Additionally, for independent directors, sitting fees would depend upon the criteria of net worth and turnover of the company.

The company would ensure that directors were inducted into the board through formal orientation about their role, responsibilities and liabilities. Apart from this, the board would adopt a suitable method to enhance the skill of directors from time to time. The board would introduce a critical risk management framework across the company and review it every six months. The audit committee would have independent backup, support and other resources from the company and have access to all information contained in the records of the company. Companies would also provide the necessary support to obtain professional advice to members of the audit committee to help them understand/analyse the financial situation of the company. In order to maintain the independence of the auditor, the audit firm would be rotated periodically. The board would institutionalise a whistleblower mechanism so that employees could report concerns about unethical behaviour, suspected fraud, and/or violation of the company's code of conduct or ethics policy.

11.7.7 *Companies Act 2013*

The Companies Bill 2008 was reintroduced in the Parliament as the Companies Bill 2009. The MCA received numerous suggestions for amendments from the various stakeholders. The Lok Sabha referred the bill to the Parliamentary Standing Committee on Finance (PSCF). The Standing Committee on Finance held several consultations with various stakeholders and suggested a number of amendments. The MCA decided to withdraw the Companies Bill 2009 and introduce a fresh bill after incorporating the recommendation of Standing Committee. At the end of 2011, the MCA re-introduced Companies Bill 2011.

The Companies Bill 2011 was passed by the Indian Parliament (both Lok Sabha [Lower House] and Rajya Sabha [Upper House]) in 2013, thereby repealing the *Companies Act 1956*. The Act legislates extensively on corporate governance provisions[329] relating to directors and boards, auditors and auditing standards. Board composition and functions are also dealt with under the Act.

A maximum number of members for any board is fifteen directors.[330] PLCs are required to have independent directors making up at least one third of the board.[331] The Act defines who is an independent director,[332] and the appointment procedure of the independent director is

---

328 'Fixed Component: This should be relatively low, so as to align Non-Executive Directors (NEDs) to a greater share of variable pay. These should not be more than one third of the total remuneration package. Variable Component: Based on attendance of board and committee meetings (at least 75% of all meetings should be an eligibility precondition). Additional Variable Payment(s) for being: The Chairman of the board, especially if he/she is non-executive chairman, the Chairman of the audit committee and/or other committees, member of board committees': 'Corporate Governance Voluntary Guidelines 2009'.
329 Most of the issues mentioned in the 'Voluntary Guidelines for Corporate Governance 2009' were legislated under the *Companies Act 2013*.
330 *Companies Act 2013* s 149(1)(b) <www.mca.gov.in/Ministry/pdf/CompaniesAct2013.pdf>.
331 Ibid. s 149(4).
332 Ibid. s 149(6).

specified in Schedule IV.[333] An independent director cannot be appointed for more than five consecutive years.[334]

The Act addresses gender diversity and provides for the mandatory appointment of women directors for classes of companies.[335] Directors are required to make disclosures in the event of changes of their interest in respect of the company.[336] All related party transactions are to be scrutinised by the board.[337] The composition and responsibilities of board subcommittees – audit committee,[338] nomination committee,[339] remuneration committee,[340] stakeholder relations committee[341] and the Corporate Social Responsibility committee[342] – are addressed. The duties of directors are enumerated: he/she should act in good faith in order to promote the objects of the company for the benefit of its members as a whole, in the best interests of the company's employees, shareholders and the community, and for the protection of the environment.[343]

Significant changes have been introduced relating to audit and accounting standards. The listed companies belonging to a class or classes notified by MCA shall not reappoint any individual as an auditor for more than one term of five consecutive years, and as an audit firm for more than two terms of five consecutive years.[344] The Act lays down the rules on eligibility, qualification, and disqualification of auditors. An audit firm shall not be engaged unless it is a Limited Liability Partnership (LLP) and unless the partner of an LLP is not a former employee the company. Also, he/she personally or his/her relative or partner shall not hold any securities or interest in the company or its subsidiary or its holding or associate company, or a subsidiary of such holding company.[345] The auditor, as part of the report, needs to mention the state of the company's internal financial control system and how effectively such control is operating.[346] The auditor also needs to certify if any director has failed to discharge his/her financial responsibilities (which disqualifies him/her from continuing as a director).[347] The Act has been substantially amended by the Companies

---

333   Ibid.
334   Ibid. s 149(10).
335   Ibid. s 142(2) proviso.
336   Ibid. s 184.
337   Ibid. s 188.
338   Ibid. s 177.
339   Ibid. s 178.
340   Ibid.
341   Ibid. s 178(6).
342   Ibid. s 135: 'Every company having net worth of rupees five hundred crore or more, or turnover of rupees one thousand crore or more or a net profit of five crore or more during any financial year shall constitute a Corporate Social Responsibility Committee of the Board consisting of three or more directors, out of which at least one director shall be an independent director.' India also introduced mandatory Corporate Social Responsibility spending requirements for certain classes of companies through the *Companies Act 2013* (see Section 11.7.2).
343   *Companies Act 2013* s 166(2); NYSE, *Section 303A: Corporate Governance Standards* (31 December 2009) s 303A.11.
344   *Companies Act 2013* s 139(2).
345   Ibid. s 139(2).
346   Ibid. s 143(3)(i).
347   Ibid. s 143(3)(g). Auditors need to certify if any company has not filed financial statements or annual returns or has failed to repay the deposits and interest or debentures accepted by the company during the tenure of the director in question.

(Amendment) Bill 2016,[348] on the recommendation of 'Report of The Companies Law Committee'.[349] The amended Act strengthens the compliance and procedure on several issues, including financial reporting. For example, a financial statement of a company shall include the consolidated financial statement of its subsidiary and associate companies. Every listed company having a subsidiary shall place the separate audited account in respect of its subsidiary/ies on the website. The policy on evaluation of director performance shall also be put on the website of the company.

11.7.8 Reforms brought by SEBI

Based on the 'Consultative paper on review of Corporate Governance norms in India' introduced by SEBI in 2013, significant reforms were made in the area of corporate disclosure by PLCs.[350] The approach taken in the paper was based on the local problems faced by shareholders and Indian companies. Instead of amending clause 49 through notification, SEBI framed SEBI (Listing Obligation and Disclosure Requirement) Regulation 2015,[351] which has emerged as a comprehensive Corporate Governance Code for PLCs. Regulation 2015 is also aligned with the corporate governance requirements under the *Companies Act 2013*.

The corporate governance compliance requirement under Regulation 2015 has enhanced timely disclosures relating to company promoters and shareholder holdings, boards and their functions, risk management and the protection of stakeholders. The board has also been entrusted with the responsibility of overseeing the governance practices of the subsidiaries. The audit committee of the holding company needs to assess the financial condition and the risk management status of the subsidiaries. Regulation 2015 has made a board risk management subcommittee mandatory.

11.7.9 Conclusions on India

Following the spectacular collapse of Satyam Computers and the Global Financial Crisis, Indian business and regulators have been active in focusing on making governance principles and rules compatible with international standards, taking account of the local variances. Over the years, corporate governance compliance has become more mature and businesses are generally adopting governance practice in the true sense of its spirit, rather than as a mere formality. For example, ICSI has instructed all its members who are designated as company secretary (under the *Companies Act 2013*) to maximise governance compliance and to foster the development of a governance culture within their organisation. To that end, they have also

---

348   The Companies (Amendment) Bill 2016.

349   'Report of The Companies Law Committee' (Ministry of Company Affairs, Government of India, February 2016) 1 <www.mca.gov.in/Ministry/pdf/Report_Companies_Law_Committee_01022016.pdf>.

350   'Consultative Paper on Review of Corporate Governance Norms in India' (SEBI, 7 January 2013) 1 <www.sebi.gov.in/cms/sebi_data/attachdocs/1357290354602.pdf>.

351   'The regulations start by providing broad principles for periodic disclosures by listed entities and also have incorporated the principles of Corporate Governance. These principles underline specific requirements prescribed under different chapters of the Regulations': SEBI, *SEBI Listing Obligations and Disclosure Requirements Regulations 2015* <www.sebi.gov.in/sebiweb/home/detail/31894/yes/PRSEBI-Listing-Obligations-and-Disclosure-Requirements-Regulations-2015-Listing-Regulations>.

standardised many internal governance practices.[352] The challenge ahead is to assess whether the legal transplants, such as the requirements for independent directors, will translate into effective governance mechanisms in India.[353]

11.8 Conclusion

There were considerable developments in the area of corporate governance in all the jurisdictions discussed in this chapter. Although signs of convergence of corporate governance models were identified, it is far from certain that all corporate governance systems will converge. Cultural differences and other factors noted in this chapter will almost certainly ensure that there will always be differences in the systems adopted by different countries, irrespective of globalisation generally. An interesting illustration of this is the strong divergence that occurred between the US and the UK with the adoption of SOX and the Dodd-Frank Act – they have put the two jurisdictions on different corporate governance paths, with a self-regulatory aspiration still dominant in the UK, and a far more prescriptive and regulatory model in the US. However, as was pointed out, President Donald Trump indicated that the SOX and the Dodd-Frank Acts will come under the spotlight, with the aim being to make compliance with them less burdensome. Also, the differences between models relying on the principle of 'comply and explain' or 'comply or else' or 'apply or explain', also commented on in Chapter 3, illustrate that variety in approaches to corporate governance will probably remain for the foreseeable future.

---

352   The secretarial standard on board meetings was issued by ICSI: *Companies Act 2013* s 118(10). The standard was approved by MCA and published in the Gazette of India on 23 April 2015. The standard is applicable to all companies incorporated under the Act except one-person companies (OPCs). 'Secretarial Standard on Meetings of The Board of Directors' <www.icsi.edu/docs/Website/SS-1% 20Final.pdf>.

353   See further Vikramaditya S Khanna and Umakanth Varottil, 'Board Independence in India: From Form to Function?' in Harald Baum, Souichirou Kozuka, Luke R Nottage and Dan W Puchniak (eds), *Independent Directors in Asia: A Historical, Contextual and Comparative Approach* (CUP, 2017).

12

CORPORATE GOVERNANCE IN THE EU, THE G20/OECD *PRINCIPLES OF CORPORATE GOVERNANCE*, AND CORPORATE GOVERNANCE IN GERMANY, JAPAN, CHINA AND INDONESIA

Nothing so concentrates the mind as an urgent and complex problem.

Frederick G Hilmer, *Strictly Boardroom: Improving Governance to Enhance Company Performance* (Hilmer Report (1993)) 1

12.1 Introduction

In Chapter 11 we discussed corporate governance in the US, the UK, New Zealand, Canada, South Africa and India. They are some of the major traditional Anglo-American corporate governance jurisdictions. There are among them some fundamental differences in approach.

In this chapter the focus is on corporate governance developments in countries where the two-tier board system is used. The number of EU member states with different corporate law systems makes corporate governance harmonisation quite difficult, but also leads to very interesting and dynamic discussion within the EU. The OECD *Principles* cover board structures. Germany has a two-tier board structure with employee representatives forming part of the supervisory board. Elements of the German corporate governance model influenced the original Japanese corporate governance model, but Anglo-American influence emerged after World War II. China has a unique corporate governance model because Chinese corporations were traditionally state-owned and many major corporations are still either state-owned or state-controlled. Nevertheless, elements of both the German model and the Anglo-American model, especially as far as independent, non-executive directors for listed companies are concerned, have influenced the Chinese corporate governance model. Indonesia also has a two-tier board model, originally based on the Dutch model, but is now developing its own corporate governance principles based on international best practices. Indonesia is of course important for Australia, because of its close proximity and the potential for expanding economic and commercial ties between the countries,[1] especially in light of the extensive ongoing negotiations regarding the Indonesia-Australia Comprehensive Economic Partnership (IA-CEPA).[2]

12.2 European Union (EU)[3]
12.2.1 Enhancing corporate governance

The European Commission (EC) represents the interests of the EU as a whole. It proposes new legislation to the European Parliament and the Council of the European Union, and it ensures that EU law is correctly applied by member countries.[4] The EC specifically aims at the

---

1   Indonesia has a population of 237.6 million according to the 2010 census and in 2015 was estimated to be 255.4 million <https://en.wikipedia.org/wiki/Demographics_of_Indonesia>. Australia's population was about 24.5 million on 16 April 2017 based on the estimated resident population at 30 September 2016 <www.abs.gov.au/ausstats/abs%40.nsf/94713ad445ff1425ca25682000192af2/1647509ef7e25faaca2568a900154b63?OpenDocument>.

2   See <http://dfat.gov.au/trade/agreements/iacepa/pages/indonesia-australia-comprehensive-economic-partnership-agreement.aspx>.

3   This section is partly based on Jean J du Plessis and Ingo Saenger, 'Corporate Governance in the EU, the OECD Principles of Corporate Governance and Corporate Governance in Selected Other Jurisdictions' in Jean J du Plessis et al., *German Corporate Governance in International and European Context* (Springer Verlag, 3rd edn, 2017) Part 11.2.

4   See <http://ec.europa.eu/atwork/index_en.htm>.

harmonisation of the rules relating to company law and corporate governance, and to account-ing and auditing. Ultimately the aim is to create a single market for financial services and products. Some of the most significant objectives of the EU in the fields of company law and corporate governance are: providing equivalent protection for shareholders and other parties concerned with companies; ensuring freedom of establishment for companies throughout the EU; fostering efficiency and competitiveness of business; promoting cross-border cooperation between companies in different member states; and stimulating discussion among member states on the modernisation of company law and corporate governance.[5]

In its 2003 Action Plan, *Modernising Company Law and Enhancing Corporate Governance in the European Union – A Plan to Move Forward*,[6] the EC defined its main objectives as: (1) to strengthen shareholders' rights, and (2) to protect employees, creditors and other parties companies deal with. In 2010, the 2003 European Company Law Action Plan was 'revisited' in a publication that included some excellent papers taking stock of what had happened from 2003 to 2010.[7] Considerable further progress has been made with the implementation of some of the identified areas for reform and harmonisation. As the EC explains in a further Action Plan, released in December 2012:[8]

> A large number of initiatives announced in the 2003 Action Plan have been adopted. In particular rules on corporate governance statements have been introduced in the Accounting Directive, [and] a Directive on the exercise of shareholders' rights and the Tenth Company Law Directive on Cross-border Mergers have been adopted. Moreover, the Commission adopted two Recommendations regarding the role of independent non-executive directors and remuneration. Besides, the Second Company Law Directive on formation of public limited liability companies and the maintenance and alteration of their capital and the Third and Sixth Company Law Directive on mergers and divisions have been simplified. Nevertheless, new developments have taken place since that require in the Commission's view further action.

The key elements of the 2012 Action Plan were summarised as follows:[9]

1. Increasing the level of transparency between companies and their shareholders in order to improve corporate governance. This will include in particular:

---

5   See <http://ec.europa.eu/internal_market/company/index_en.htm>.

6   COM (2003) 284. European Parliament resolution on that topic: OJ C 104 E 30 April 2004, 0714. See generally Klaus J Hopt, 'European Company Law and Corporate Governance: Where Does the Action Plan of the European Commission Lead?' in Klaus J Hopt, Eddy Wymeersch, Hideki Kanda and Harald Baum (eds), *Corporate Governance in Context: Corporations, States, and Markets in Europe, Japan, and the US* (Oxford University Press [OUP], 2005) 119; Klaus J Hopt, 'Die internationalen europarechtlichen Rahmenbedingungen der Corporate Governance' in Peter Hommelhoff, Klaus J Hopt and Axel von Werder (eds), *Handbuch Corporate Governance: Leitung und Überwachung börsennotierter Unternehmen in der Rechts- und Wirtschaftspraxis* (Otto Schmidt Verlag, 2nd edn, 2009) 51–7.

7   Koen Geen and Klaus J Hopt, *The European Company Law Action Plan Revisited* (Leuven University Press, 2010).

8   EC, *Action Plan: European Company Law and Corporate Governance – A Modern Legal Framework for More Engaged Shareholder and Sustainable Companies*, COM (2012) 740 (12 December 2012) <http://eur-lex.europa.eu/LexUriServ/LexUriServ.do?uri=CELEX:52012DC0740:EN:NOT> / <http://eur-lex.europa.eu/LexUriServ/LexUriServ.do?uri=COM:2012:0740:FIN:EN:PDF>.

9   EC, 'Commission Plans to Modernise European Company Law and Corporate Governance', Press Release (12 December 2012) <http://europa.eu/rapid/press-release_IP-12-1340_en.html>.

- Increasing companies' **transparency** as regards their board diversity and risk management policies;
- Improving corporate governance reporting;
- Better identification of shareholders by issuers;
- Strengthening transparency rules for institutional investors on their voting and engagement policies.

2. Initiatives aimed at encouraging and facilitating **long-term shareholder engagement**, such as:
   - More transparency on remuneration policies and individual remuneration of directors, as well as a shareholders' right to vote on remuneration policy and the remuneration report;
   - Better shareholders' oversight on related party transactions, i.e. dealings between the company and its directors or controlling shareholders;
   - Creating appropriate operational rules for proxy advisors (i.e. firms providing services to shareholders, notably voting advice), especially as regards transparency and conflicts of interests;
   - Clarification of the 'acting in concert' concept to make shareholder cooperation on corporate governance issues easier;
   - Investigating whether employee share ownership can be encouraged.

3. Initiatives in the field of **company law** to support European businesses and encourage their growth and competitiveness:
   - Further investigation on a possible initiative on the cross-border transfer of seats for companies;
   - Facilitating cross-border mergers;
   - Clear EU rules for cross-border divisions;
   - Follow-up of the European Private Company statute proposal (IP/08/ 1003) with a view to enhancing cross-border opportunities for SMEs;
   - An information campaign on the European Company/European Cooperative Society Statute;
   - Targeted measures on groups of companies, i.e. recognition of the concept of the interest of the group and more transparency regarding the group structure.

In addition, the Action Plan foresees merging all major company law directives into a single instrument. This would make EU company law more accessible and comprehensible and reduce the risk of future inconsistencies.

12.2.2 The European Corporate Governance Forum (ECGF)

This Forum was reasonably active from 2005 to 2011, but activities ceased by the end of 2011[10] because of new guidelines on expert groups set by the EU.[11] It is, however,

---

10   See <http://ec.europa.eu/internal_market/company/ecgforum/index_en.htm>.
11   Minutes of the Meeting held on 9 June 2011, circulated on 1 August 2011 <http://ec.europa.eu/internal_market/company/docs/ecgforum/minutes-20110801_en.pdf>.

worthwhile to mention the ECGF as its activities included some significant initiatives. The ECGF was comprised of representatives from member states, European regulators (for example, CESR/ESMA), investors and issuers, other market participants and academics. The working program of the Forum (2008–11) included: '(1) Empty voting and transparency of investors' positions,[12] (2) Cross-border voting and application of CG (corporate governance) codes in cross-border situations (double listings etc),[13] (3) Impact of hedge funds, private equity and sovereign wealth funds on CG.' Working groups dealt with minority shareholder protection and corporate governance infrastructure. It is noteworthy to give some background on how and why the ECGF was established and then to focus on some of its initiatives.

The ECGF was formed because the Final Winter Report (November 2002) recommended that a structure should be set up to coordinate member states' efforts to improve their corporate governance systems.[14] Following this recommendation, the EC made it a priority in its 2003 Action Plan to encourage the coordination and convergence of national codes through regular high-level meetings of a then still to be established ECGF. The ECGF was formed in October 2004.[15] The EC specified that the Forum, to be chaired by the Commission, should meet two or three times a year.[16] The ECGF consisted of 15 senior experts from various professions.

The ECGF held its first meeting in January 2005. A core aim was to evaluate the effectiveness of monitoring and enforcement systems that the member states had put in place.[17] In November 2009 the EU published an external study (conducted by the RiskMetrics Group) that provided a basis for the ECGF's work on this subject.[18]

This study, *Study on Monitoring and Enforcement Practices in Corporate Governance in the Member States*, is interesting not only because of its scope, but also because it reveals some interesting facts about corporate governance developments and trends in the EU.[19]

There were some sensitive issues involved in the composition and general aims of the ECGF, especially the excluding of trade union representatives from 2008 and the primary focus on convergence of corporate governance practices in the EU based on a shareholder value model of corporate governance, with employee interests seen as a matter of corporate social

---

12   ECGF Statement (20 February 2010) <http://ec.europa.eu/internal_market/company/docs/ecgforum/ecgf_empty_voting_en.pdf>.

13   ECGF Statement (23 March 2009) <http://ec.europa.eu/internal_market/company/docs/ecgforum/ecgf-crossborder_en.pdf>.

14   *Final Report of the High Level Group of Company Law Experts on a Modern Regulatory Framework for Company Law in Europe* (Final Winter Report) 12, Item III.16 <www.ecgi.org/publications/winter.htm>.

15   'Corporate governance: Commission creates European Forum to promote convergence in Europe', Press release (IP/04/1241 (18 October 2004) <http://europa.eu/rapid/press-release_IP-04-1241_en.htm?locale=en>.

16   EC, 'The EU Single Market, European Corporate Governance Forum' <http://ec.europa.eu/internal_market/company/ecgforum/index_en.htm>.

17   Ibid.

18   DG Internal Market, *Study on Monitoring and Enforcement Practices in Corporate Governance in the Member States*, EC (23 September 2009) <http://ec.europa.eu/internal_market/company/docs/ecgforum/studies/comply-or-explain-090923_en.pdf>.

19   Ibid. 9 and 11.

responsibility (CSR).[20] However, all in all the ECGF was a valuable initiative striving for company law and corporate governed harmonisation in the EU.

12.2.3 The EU single market

For EU companies in general, the EU is also attempting to establish a 'strong and successful single market', one 'which refocuses on citizens and regains their trust'.[21] In its Green Paper, *The EU Corporate Governance Framework*, released on 5 April 2011, the EU addresses three subjects 'which are at the heart of good corporate governance':

1. The board of directors – High-performing, effective boards are needed to challenge executive management. This means that boards need non-executive members with diverse views, skills and appropriate professional experience.

    Such members must also be willing to invest sufficient time in the work of the board. The role of chairman of the board is particularly important, as are the board's responsibilities for risk management.

2. Shareholders – The corporate governance framework is built on the assumption that shareholders engage with companies and hold the management to account for its performance. However, there is evidence that the majority of shareholders are passive and are often only focused on short-term profits. It therefore seems useful to consider whether more shareholders can be encouraged to take an interest in sustainable returns and longer-term performance, and how to encourage them to be more active on corporate governance issues. Moreover, in different shareholding structures there are other issues, such as minority protection.

3. 'Comply or explain' – How to apply this approach, which underpins the EU corporate governance framework. Evidence indicates[22] that the informative quality of explanations published by companies departing from the corporate governance code's recommendation is – in the majority of the cases – not satisfactory and that in many member states there is insufficient monitoring of the application of the codes. It is therefore appropriate to consider how to improve this situation.[23]

These areas are broad and there are some fundamentally different approaches among EU members. This means there are no easy solutions, and harmonisation and convergence in the EU will continue to be challenging. However, if one focuses on how widely the principle of 'comply or explain' is used in the EU, there are clear signs of some convergence.[24]

---

20   Andrew Johnston, *EC Regulation of Corporate Governance* (Cambridge University Press [CUP], 2009) 355–6.
21   EC, *Green Paper: The EU Corporate Governance Framework, 5.4.2011* (COM, 2011) 164, 2 <http://ec.europa.eu/internal_market/company/docs/modern/com2011-164_en.pdf>.
22   'Study on Monitoring and Enforcement Practices in Corporate Governance in the Member States' <http://ec.europa.eu/internal_market/company/docs/ecgforum/studies/comply-or-explain-090923_en.pdf>.
23   Ibid. 3.
24   See Janet Dine and Marios Koutsias, *The Nature of Corporate Governance: The Significance of National Cultural Identity* (Edward Elgar, 2013).

12.2.4 The significance of continued EU corporate governance harmonisation

The EU is still focusing[25] on ensuring a comprehensive and strong strategy that boosts the competitiveness of Europe's businesses in global markets. A comprehensive review of the situation in view of the Global Financial Crisis was presented in 'Report of the Reflection Group on the Future of EU Company Law' (the Report) in April 2011.[26] On corporate governance, the Report states that the 'member states display a multitude of highly sophisticated corporate governance systems that regulate the distribution of powers within a company and the organisational structures that constitute the company'.[27]

These systems reflect 'a careful balancing of interests'. This shows what any expert in legal comparison knows: 'this diversity far transcends the simple dichotomy of a one-tier/two-tier system and goes beyond the legal discipline of company law', because a governance system often 'interacts with and relies on other parts of the national law of that jurisdiction and reflects different historical and societal events and interests'.[28] This multiplicity should be preserved. However, the Report goes on to say that the Global Financial Crisis has shown 'that there is no room for complacency'. Harmonisation is required in order to guarantee the necessary transparency with respect to governance structures.[29] The key elements of the EC's 2012 Action Plan (summarised above) provide strong evidence that there is a considerable drive for further modernisation and harmonisation of corporate law and corporate governance in the EU.

12.2.5 Recent harmonisation initiatives legalised through EU Directives

In April 2014, the EC submitted a proposal to amend both the European Shareholders' Rights Directive (2007/36/EC) as regards the encouragement of long-term shareholder engagement, and the European Accounting Directive (2013/34/EU), as both concern elements of the corporate governance statement.[30] The amendments implement the Action Plan on Corporate Governance[31] and primarily intend to safeguard a stronger influence of shareholders on the remuneration of management board members ('say on pay') and promote corporate governance within European listed companies.

The amendment of the European Accounting Directive (2013/34/EU) was adopted by Directive 2014/95/EU at the end of 2014 and had to be transposed into national law by

---

25   View before the Global Financial Crisis: EC Directorate General for Internal Market and Services (ed.), *Consultation and Hearing on Future Priorities for the Action Plan on Modernising Company Law and Enhancing Corporate Governance in the European Union* (2006) 9.2.3.

26   'Report of the Reflection Group on the Future of EU Company Law' (5 April 2011) <http://ec.europa.eu/internal_market/company/docs/modern/reflectiongroup_report_en.pdf>. See also 3–4, on the members who do not represent particular institutions or member states, and the work of the Reflection Group.

27   Ibid. 10(1.3).

28   Ibid. 11(1.3).

29   Ibid.

30   See <http://eur-lex.europa.eu/legal-content/EN/TXT/?uri=COM:2014:213:FIN>.

31   See <http://eur-lex.europa.eu/legal-content/EN/ALL/?uri=CELEX:52012DC0740>.

6 December 2016.[32] Though it was expected to be adopted in 2015,[33] the Shareholders' Rights Directive (2007/36/EC) was delayed because of amendments, which led to an altered version of the original draft.[34] Subsequently, the Parliament entered into negotiations with the Council and the Commission regarding the final wording of the amendments. While these European processes continued, the Governmental Commission on the German Corporate Governance Code widely criticised the European amendments because they may limit the dual system, and because they may lead to insufficient protection against predatory shareholders.[35] Regardless of this, the Shareholders' Rights Directive (2007/36/EC) was adopted on 3 March 2017.[36]

As has been pointed out elsewhere,[37] the EC made a further recommendation regarding the quality of corporate governance reporting (2014/208/EU), which should contribute to the establishment of increased transparency ('comply or explain').[38] It can be expected that all these measures will lead to a further harmonisation of the corporate governance system in Europe.

At the end of 2014, the entire approach to voluntary disclosure of and reporting on non-financial matters was transformed in the EU. This took place through the adoption of Directive 2014/95/EU of the European Parliament and the Council on 22 October 2014. This Directive deserves more attention, but only a very basic overview can be provided here.

Directive 2014/95/EU amends Directive 2013/34/EU (Disclosure of non-financial and diversity information by certain large undertakings and groups). The Explanatory Preamble to Directive 2014/95/EU explains that since 2011 the EC has aimed to harmonise the level of transparency regarding social and environmental information provided by undertakings in all sectors among EU members. Since then there has been a particular focus in the EU on Corporate Social Responsibility (CSR), and on a model that would promote accountability, transparency, responsible business behaviour and sustainable growth. This aims to support

---

32 See <http://ec.europa.eu/finance/company-reporting/non-financial_reporting/index_en.htm#news>.
33 Christoph H Seibt, 'Richtlinienvorschlag zur Weiterentwicklung des europäischen Corporate Governance-Rahmens' (2014) 34 *Der Betrieb (DB)* 1910.
34 See <www.europarl.europa.eu/sides/getDoc.do?pubRef=-//EP//NONSGML+TA+P8-TA-2015-0257+0 +DOC+PDF+V0//EN> for the European Parliament's amended version.
35 Statement of the Governmental Commission from 1 February 2015, 1–2 <www.dcgk.de/de/ kommission/die-kommission-im-dialog/deteilansicht/kodex-kommission-kritisiert-ueberbordende-buerokratie-bei-eu-corporate-governance-empfehlungen-und-richtlinien-ohne-angemessenen.html? file=files/dcgk/usercontent/de/download/Stellungnahmen/2015-01-30%20Stellungnahme% 20Regierungskommission%20zur%20Aktionaersrechterichtlinie.pdf>.
36 See <www.consilium.europa.eu/en/press/press-releases/2017/04/03-shareholder-rights-eu-companies/>.
37 The following paragraphs have been extracted, with permission of the *Companies and Securities Law Journal (C&SLJ)*, from Jean J du Plessis, 'Disclosure of non-financial information: A powerful corporate governance tool' (2016) 34 *C&SLJ* 69, 72–3.
38 2014/208/EU, L 109 (12 April 2014).The recommendation is an implementation of the Action Plan Corporate Governance as well: <http://eur-lex.europa.eu/legal-content/EN/TXT/?uri= CELEX:32014H0208>; see also the statement by the Government Commission on the German Corporate Governance Code <www.dcgk.de/de/kommission/die-kommission-im-dialog/deteilansicht/kodex-kommission-kritisiert-ueberbordende-buerokratie-bei-eu-corporate-governance-empfehlungen-und-richtlinien-ohne-angemessenen.html?file=files/dcgk/usercontent/de/download/Stellungnahmen/2015-01-30%20Stellungnahme%20Regierungskommission%20zur%20Aktionaersrechterichtlinie.pdf>; and Axel von Werder, 'EU-Empfehlung für das Corporate Governance Reporting: Zehn Thesen zur Kodexpublizität' (2015) 15 *Der Betrieb (DB)* 847.

society's interests and achieve a sustainable and inclusive recovery of the EUs economies. The ultimate aim is explained well in Paragraph (3) of the Explanatory Preamble to Directives 2014/95/EU:

> The European Parliament acknowledged the importance of businesses divulging information on sustainability such as social and environmental factors, with a view to identifying sustainability risks and increasing investor and consumer trust. Indeed, disclosure of non-financial information is vital for managing change towards a sustainable global economy by combining long-term profitability with social justice and environmental protection.

The legislation that EU member states are expected to adopt should be highly flexible, with minimum requirements, so as not to make it too burdensome, and will only apply to large undertakings and groups, exempting small and medium size companies (SMEs).[39] The legislation limited the mandatory reporting requirements to:

> [P]ublic-interest entities and to those public-interest entities which are parent undertakings of a large group, in each case having an average number of employees in excess of 500, in the case of a group on a consolidated basis.[40]

The legal requirement is for these undertakings to prepare a non-financial statement (or a consolidated non-financial statement for groups) containing information relating to at least environmental matters, social and employee-related matters, respect for human rights, anti-corruption and bribery matters.

There is an expectation that non-financial statements should include a description of the policies, outcomes and risks related to those matters, and should be part of the management report of the undertaking concerned. The non-financial statement should also include information on the due diligence processes implemented by the undertaking, also regarding, where relevant and proportionate, its supply and subcontracting chains, in order to identify, prevent and mitigate existing and potential adverse impacts. There is provision for exempting undertakings from preparing the non-financial statement, but only 'when a separate report corresponding to the same financial year and covering the same content is provided'.[41]

The fact that the disclosure of and reporting on these matters can be quite onerous becomes clear in paragraph (7) of the Explanatory Preamble to Directive 2014/95/EU. As far as environmental matters are concerned the following must be disclosed or reported:

> Details of the current and foreseeable impacts of the undertaking's operations on the environment, and, as appropriate, on health and safety, the use of renewable and/or non-renewable energy, greenhouse gas emissions, water use and air pollution.[42]

As far as social and employee-related matters are concerned the following must be disclosed or reported:

---

39   Explanatory Preamble to Directive 2014/95/EU paragraph (14).
40   Implemented by way of Directive 2013/34/EU Arts 19a and 29a.
41   Explanatory Preamble to Directive 2014/95/EU, paragraph (6).
42   Ibid. paragraph (7).

The information provided in the statement may concern the actions taken to ensure gender equality, implementation of fundamental conventions of the International Labour Organization, working conditions, social dialogue, respect for the right of workers to be informed and consulted, respect for trade union rights, health and safety at work and the dialogue with local communities, and/or the actions taken to ensure the protection and the development of those communities.[43]

As far as human rights, anti-corruption and bribery are concerned it is suggested that the non-financial statement could include:

Information on the prevention of human rights abuses and/or on instruments in place to fight corruption and bribery.[44]

The legislation that member states are expected to prepare was supposed to be in force by 6 December 2016 and the non-financial statement was supposed to be prepared for the financial year starting on 1 January 2017. It is not difficult to predict that all undertakings that know they will be affected by this will be busy planning to ensure that they are prepared for the implementation even before specific legislation has been adopted in their particular member state. In order to facilitate the transition, the EC offers workshops, and also intends to publish 'non-binding guidelines on methodology for reporting'.[45]

12.2.6 Reflection

What actual progress with company law harmonisation and the convergence of corporate governance model in the EU has been made will probably be judged differently by analysts. However, there are some who are starting to refer prominently to European Company Law.[46] Also, it is excellent that a commentator such as Andrew Johnston,[47] in a solid analysis of the EC regulation of corporate governance, concludes in a positive way, by referring to 'the genius of EC corporate governance regulation', drawing an analogy from Roberta Romano's book, *The Genius of American Corporate Law*.[48] It may well be that the UK's exiting the EU (Brexit) may cause some confusion and uncertainty, but the EU harmonisation process will not be derailed by this. The UK law had considerable influence on EU law and the law of EU member states (take, for example, the widely used nowadays UK 'comply or explain' approach), and there are numerous examples of the UK law being affected by EU Directives. There is strength in numbers, and it might just be that the UK will re-enter the EU in time.[49]

---

43   Ibid.
44   Ibid.
45   <http://ec.europa.eu/finance/company-reporting/non-financial_reporting/index_en.htm#news>.
46   See Simon Kempny, *Coordination and Creation: Two Aspects of European Company Law* (Saarbrücker Verlag für Rechtswissenschaften, 2010).
47   Andrew Johnston, *EC Regulation of Corporate Governance* (CUP, 2009) 359.
48   Roberta Romano, *The Genius of American Corporate Law* (AEI Press, 1993). See generally Klaus J Hopt, 'Comparative Company Law' in Mathias Reimann and Reinhard Zimmermann (eds), *Comparative Law* (OUP, 2006) 1174–8.
49   See Jean-Claude Juncker, 'UK will Rejoin European Union some day, says EU Commission chief – video', *The Guardian*, 11 March 2017 <www.theguardian.com/world/video/2017/mar/10/uk-will-rejoin-european-union-some-day-says-eu-commission-chief-video>.

12.3 G20/OECD *Principles of Corporate Governance*

12.3.1 Background

The Organisation for Economic Co-operation and Development (OECD) is a group of 35 member countries that share a mission to promote policies that will improve the economic and social well-being of people around the world. It shares expertise and exchanges views with more than 100 other countries, non-government organisations and civil societies. The OECD aims to:[50]

- support sustainable economic growth;
- boost employment;
- raise living standards;
- maintain financial stability;
- assist other countries' economic development; and
- contribute to growth in world trade.

One of the OECD's early projects was to develop a set of principles of corporate governance. The first such set was completed in 1999 under the title *OECD Principles of Corporate Governance*.[51] These principles provided minimum requirements for best practice and were not aimed at promoting a single corporate governance model for all OECD countries, but rather at promulgating principles that could be applied in all OECD and non-OECD countries. In April 2004 the OECD countries approved the 2004 *OECD Principles of Corporate Governance*.[52] These principles confirmed several sound corporate governance practices already identified and explained in the 1999 Principles, but also contained some refinement in light of the corporate scandals of the late 1990s and early 2000s. The Global Financial Crisis reinforced the need for continual review and improvement of the Principles.[53] The OECD has conducted peer reviews of various aspects of the Principles, including the role of institutional investors (2011), related-party transactions (2012) and board member nominations and elections (2013).[54]

In early 2014 the OECD conducted a review of its *Principles of Corporate Governance*, in order to ensure the 'continuing high quality, relevance and usefulness of the *Principles*, taking into account recent developments in the corporate sector and capital markets'.[55] The G20 countries were invited to participate on an equal footing. Experts from relevant international

---

50   See 'About OECD' <www.oecd.org/pages/0,3417,en_36734052_36734103_1_1_1_1_1,00.html>.
51   OECD, *Principles of Corporate Governance* (1999).
52   OECD, *Principles of Corporate Governance* (2004) <www.oecd.org/document/49/0,3343, en_2649_ 34813_31530865_1_1_1_1,00.html>.
53   See further OECD, *Corporate Governance and the Financial Crisis* <www.oecd.org/daf/ca/ corporategovernanceandthefinancialcrisis.htm>.
54   See the peer review papers <www.oecd.org/daf/ca/2014-review-oecd-, corporate-governance- principles.htm>.
55   OECD, *2014 Review of the OECD Principles of Corporate Governance* <www.oecd.org/daf/ca/2014- review-oecd-corporate-governance-principles.htm>.

organisations, notably the Basel Committee on Banking Supervision, the Financial Stability Board and the World Bank Group, also participated actively in the review.[56]

This led to the implementation of the current document, known as the G20/OECD *Principles of Corporate Governance*, in recognition of the fact that today policy-makers and regulators are faced with adapting corporate governance frameworks to rapid changes in both the corporate and the financial landscape. Examples of such challenges, as noted by the OECD,[57] include the increasing complexity of the investment chain, the changing role of stock exchanges and the emergence of new investors, investment strategies and trading practices.

12.3.2 Broad aims and application

The OECD *Principles* aim to help governments in their efforts to evaluate and improve the legal, institutional and regulatory framework for corporate governance, and to provide guidance and suggestions for stock exchanges, investors, corporations and other parties that have a role in the process of developing good corporate governance. One of the unique aspects of the OECD *Principles* is that they operate across borders and without preference for any particular corporate law system or board structure[58] – they focus, in the true sense of the word, on 'the principles of corporate governance'. Thus an open-minded approach to corporate governance is adopted:[59]

> Corporate governance involves a set of relationships between a company's management, its board, its shareholders and other stakeholders. Corporate governance also provides the structure through which the objectives of the company are set, and the means of attaining those objectives and monitoring performance are determined.
>
> The Principles do not intend to prejudice or second-guess the business judgment of individual market participants, board members and company officials. What works in one company or for one group of investors may not necessarily be generally applicable to all of business or of systemic economic importance.

12.3.3 Structure

The document containing the OECD *Principles* sets out six core principles with annotations that are intended to help readers understand their rationale. The annotations also provide descriptions of dominant trends and offer alternative implementation methods and examples that may be useful in making the principles operational. The *Principles* cover the following areas:

I.   Ensuring the basis for an effective corporate governance framework;

II.   The rights and equitable treatment of shareholders and key ownership functions;

III.   Institutional investors, stock markets, and other intermediaries;

IV.   The role of stakeholders in corporate governance;

---

56   G20/OECD, *Principles of Corporate Governance* (2015) 4.
57   <www.oecd.org/corporate/principles-corporate-governance.htm>.
58   G20/OECD, *Principles of Corporate Governance* (2015) 10.
59   Ibid. 9.

V.   Disclosure and transparency; and

VI.   The responsibilities of the board.

Each of the sections is headed by a single principle, followed by a number of sub-principles. In this discussion we focus only on the principles not dealt with specifically in any other chapter of this book, namely those in Parts I and V.

12.3.4 Ensuring the basis for an effective corporate governance framework

The basic principle is expressed as follows:[60]

> The corporate governance framework should promote transparent and fair markets, and the efficient allocation of resources. It should be consistent with the rule of law and support effective supervision and enforcement.

Six specific sub-principles that aim to ensure the implementation of this principle are mentioned:

A.   The corporate governance framework should be developed with a view to its impact on overall economic performance, market integrity and the incentives it creates for market participants and the promotion of transparent and well-functioning markets.

B.   The legal and regulatory requirements that affect corporate governance practices should be consistent with the rule of law, transparent and enforceable.

C.   The division of responsibilities among different authorities should be clearly articulated and designed to serve the public interest.

D.   Stock market regulation should support effective corporate governance.

E.   Supervisory, regulatory and enforcement authorities should have the authority, integrity and resources to fulfil their duties in a professional and objective manner. Moreover, their rulings should be timely, transparent and fully explained.

F.   Cross-border co-operation should be enhanced, including through bilateral and multilateral arrangements for exchange of information.

Many of the aspects discussed in this part of the G20/OECD *Principles of Corporate Governance* have already been mentioned in Chapter 3 under the heading 'Board structures'. As was discussed in Chapter 5, the G20/OECD *Principles* emphasise the point that a corporate governance framework typically comprises legislation, regulation, self-regulatory arrangements, voluntary commitments and business practices that are the result of a country's specific circumstances, history and tradition. The costs and benefits of laws and regulations should be considered carefully before they are enacted and implemented, to guard against over-regulation or the enactment of unenforceable laws. Any corporate governance model should support entrepreneurship.[61]

---

60   Ibid. 13.
61   Ibid.

The document stresses that the regulatory and legal environment within which corporations operate is of key importance to overall economic outcomes. A corporate governance model is typically influenced by several legal arrangements, such as company law, securities regulation, accounting and auditing standards, insolvency law, contract law, labour law and tax law. These laws all require effective enforcement.[62] Many corporate governance systems involve overlapping public and private enforcement mechanisms. The allocation of responsibilities for supervision, implementation and enforcement among authorities, and the overlap between public and private enforcement, should be clearly defined so that the competencies of complementary bodies and agencies are respected and used most effectively. If this is not done, overlaps can occur or, even worse, 'regulatory vacuums' can be created.[63]

12.3.5 Disclosure and transparency

The basic principle is expressed as follows:

> The corporate governance framework should ensure that timely and accurate disclosure is made on all material matters regarding the corporation, including the financial situation, performance, ownership, and governance of the company.[64]

Five specific ways of ensuring the implementation of this principle are listed:

    A. Disclosure should include, but not be limited to, material information on:
        1. The financial and operating results of the company.
        2. Company objectives and non-financial information.
        3. Major share ownership, including beneficial owners, and voting rights.
        4. Remuneration of members of the board and key executives.
        5. Information about board members, including their qualifications, the selection process, other company directorships and whether they are regarded as independent by the board.
        6. Related party transactions.
        7. Foreseeable risk factors.
        8. Issues regarding employees and other stakeholders.
        9. Governance structures and policies, including the content of any corporate governance code or policy and the process by which it is implemented.
    B. Information should be prepared and disclosed in accordance with high-quality standards of accounting and financial and non-financial reporting.
    C. An annual audit should be conducted by an independent, competent and qualified auditor in accordance with high-quality auditing standards in order to provide an external and objective assurance to the board and shareholders that the financial statements fairly represent the financial position and performance of the company in all material respects.

---

62   The enforcement of corporate governance principles is discussed in OECD, *Supervision and Enforcement in Corporate Governance* (2013) <www.oecd.org/daf/ca/ SupervisionandEnforcementinCorporateGovernance2013.pdf>.
63   Ibid. 29–31.
64   G20/OECD, *Principles of Corporate Governance* (2015) 37.

D.   External auditors should be accountable to the shareholders, and owe a duty to the company to exercise due professional care in the conduct of the audit.

E.   Channels for disseminating information should provide for equal, timely and cost-efficient access to relevant information by users.

The G20/OECD *Principles* note that most OECD countries already have in place both mandatory and voluntary disclosure arrangements. The main advantages of a strong disclosure regime are that it promotes transparency, ensures effective monitoring of companies and is central to shareholders' ability to exercise their ownership rights on an informed basis. Disclosure is also a powerful tool with which to influence the behaviour of companies and protect investors.[65] The advantages of an effective disclosure regime are summarised neatly as follows:

> A strong disclosure regime can help to attract capital and maintain confidence in the capital markets. By contrast, weak disclosure and non-transparent practices can contribute to unethical behaviour and to a loss of market integrity at great cost, not just to the company and its shareholders but also to the economy as a whole ... Insufficient or unclear information may hamper the ability of the markets to function, increase the cost of capital and result in a poor allocation of resources.[66]

It is, however, important that disclosure requirements should not place unreasonable administrative or cost burdens on enterprises or require companies to disclose information that may endanger their competitive position. The principle adopted in most OECD countries to ensure that the right kind of information is disclosed is the principle of 'materiality': 'material information can be defined as information whose omission or misstatement could influence the economic decisions taken by users of information'.[67]

12.3.6 Conclusions on G20/OECD *Principles*

As was pointed out, one of the unique aspects of the G20/OECD *Principles* is that they operate across borders and without preference for any particular corporate law system or board structure. It is, therefore, of particular importance to adopt the principles most appropriate for a specific country. They also provide some of the most convincing arguments for the importance of good corporate governance and how adhering to good corporate governance adds value to a corporation.

12.4 Germany[68]

12.4.1 Background to the corporate governance debate

The German corporate governance debate is particularly interesting and relevant, as German corporations law makes a two-tier board system (supervisory board and management board)

---

65   Ibid. 37.

66   Ibid. 38.

67   Ibid. 37.

68   For a more comprehensive discussion of the German corporate law and governance models, see Jean J du Plessis et al., *German Corporate Governance in International and European Context* (Springer, 2017). This part is based on Chs 5 and 6 of that book.

compulsory for all public corporations and for private companies that have more than 500 employees. In the past, the German two-tier system has been criticised for: the ineffectiveness of its supervisory boards generally; the practical difficulty in distinguishing between the managerial and supervisory functions of the management board and the supervisory board; the practical difficulties associated with the relationship between the supervisory and management boards; the defects in the composition of supervisory boards; and, in particular, employee participation at supervisory board level.[69] Many of the original criticisms of the German board system have been addressed since the middle of the 1990s.

The German corporate governance debate, and in particular the debate on the functions of the supervisory board, was for many years considered of academic interest only.[70] This perception has changed significantly since the mid-1990s. The supervisory board has been a focus of attention for the German Government; it formed the central theme of several seminars and symposiums; German industry committed itself to finding solutions; trade unions made recommendations; and eminent German academics participated keenly in the debate.[71]

The debate was closely linked with the relatively difficult economic conditions experienced in Germany during the middle and late 1990s,[72] and in particular with the difficulties experienced in the German iron and steel industry.[73] Difficulties in some of the large German industries, such as the coal and iron industries, were blamed on the failure and neglect of management and those overseeing the business of large corporations, particularly supervisory boards.[74] The Global Financial Crisis took a particular toll on the German economy, which has always been heavily dependent on the export of expensive and sophisticated commodities such as luxury cars; during a financial crisis, purchases of luxury items are cut first.[75] However, Germany was able to recover from the Global Financial Crisis and the European financial crises faster than most other countries in the world – and, in particular, countries that are part of the European Union (EU). That recovery is attributed, to a large extent, to the effective functioning of labour relations in Germany, including its system of codetermination:[76] employee participation at supervisory board level (see Section 12.4.3 below).

---

69   See Detlev F Vagts, 'Reforming the "modern" corporation: Perspectives from the German' (1966) 80 *Harvard Law Review* 76–8 and 87–9; Mark J Roe, 'Some differences in corporate structure in Germany, Japan, and the United States' (1993) 102 *Yale Law Journal* 1927, 1995–7; Jean J du Plessis, 'Corporate governance: Reflections on the German two-tier system' (1996) *Journal of South African Law* 41–4; Jean J du Plessis, 'Corporate Governance: Some Reflections on the South African Law and the German Two-tier Board System' in Fiona Macmillan Patfield (ed.), *Perspectives on Company Law: 2* (Kluwer Law, 1997) 139–43.

70   Marcus Lutter, 'Defizite für eine effiziente Aufsichtsratstätigkeit und gesetzliche Möglichkeiten der Verbesserung' (1995) 159 *Zeitschrift für das gesamte Handelsrecht und Wirtschaftsrecht* 288–9.

71   See Jean J du Plessis, 'Reflections on some recent crporate governance reforms in Germany: A transformation of the German *Aktienrecht?*' (2003) 8 *Deakin Law Review* 384–5.

72   This fact has been mentioned by quite a few chairmen of management boards in their yearly reports – see Klein-Gunnewyk (Chairman's Statement: PWA AG) 1994.06.24. See also Carsten P Claussen, 'Aktienrechts-reform 1997' (1996) 41 *Die Aktiengesellschaft (Zeitschrift)* 481.

73   Marcus Lutter, 'Deutsche Corporate Governance Kodex' in *Reform des Aktienrechts, der Rechnungslegung und der Prüfung* (Schäffer-Poeschel Verlag, 2003) 68, 69.

74   Claussen, 'Aktienrechts-reform 1997' (1996).

75   See generally Anatole Kaletsky, 'Europe Needs Rescue Act from Germany', *The Australian*, 19 May 2009, 21; 'Thomas Cook Up for Grabs After Retailer Folds', *The Australian*, 11 June 2009, 20.

76   Jean J du Plessis et al., *German Corporate Governance in International and European Context* (Springer, 2012) 151, 174–5, 191, 196, 199 and 269–80.

The official reaction to the corporate governance debate of the middle 1990s came in November 1996, with a Ministerial Draft Bill dealing with issues relating to more transparency in corporations and the powers of control of the various organs of public corporations[77] – generally known as the *Aktienrechtsreform 1997*.[78] The 1997 Draft Bill dealt with several fundamental areas: the duties, responsibilities and liabilities of members of supervisory boards; proxies; financial statements and disclosure; votes by the banks on behalf of shareholders; and financial instruments and capital markets.[79] This Draft Bill was widely discussed in 1997,[80] and several amendments were made before it became law in May 1998.[81]

The proposed changes were described by some as comprehensive and akin to the reform of German corporations law in the 1960s.[82] Others were more sceptical, and described the changes as no more than cosmetic,[83] or done piecemeal instead of by way of a comprehensive review of the corporations law.[84] Some of the more fundamental questions asked during the reform process were how German corporations law could be modified to ensure the improvement of the state of businesses in Germany and how to create more jobs.[85] Other items, such as the role and functions of the management board and the general meeting, and removing some unnecessary bureaucratic provisions, were later mentioned as items on the long-term reform agenda of German corporations law;[86] these items have been debated actively in Germany in recent years.

It was realised at an early stage of the debate that most of the changes in the Draft Bill could be achieved without statutory changes[87] – in other words, through voluntary or self-imposed good corporate governance practices. Some commentators warned specifically against the dangers of over-regulation by the legislature.[88]

Following the changes in 1998, a government commission, chaired by Theodor Baums, was appointed by the German Chancellor on 29 May 2000.[89] The Baums Commission made 150 recommendations in its report, released on 10 July 2001.[90]

---

77   *Referentenentwurf eines Gesetzes für Kontrolle und Transparenz im Unternehmensbereich (KonTraG)* – Dokumentation (Special Edition, 1997) *Die Aktiengesellschaft* (AG) 7.
78   Heinz-Dieter Assmann, 'AG-Sonderheft: Die Aktienrechtsreform 1997', *Die Aktiengesellschaft (Zeitschrift)* (Special Edition, 1997) 3.
79   See Michael Adams, *Die Aktiengesellschaft (Zeitschrift)* (Special Edition, 1997) 9 ff for a comprehensive discussion of the issues dealt with in the Draft Bill.
80   Ibid.
81   *Gesetz zur Kontrolle und Transparenz im Unternehmensbereich (KonTraG)* – Bundesgesetzblatt Teil I (BGBI. I., 1998) 786 ff.
82   Claussen, 'Aktienrechts-reform 1997' (1996) 494.
83   Ekkehard Wenger, *Die Aktiengesellschaft (Zeitschrift)* (Special Edition, 1997) 57.
84   Ulrich Seibert, 'Aktienrechtsreform in Permanenz?' (2002) 45 *Die Aktiengesellschaft (Zeitschrift)* 417. However, at 419–20 the author explains that such piecemeal reform was necessary as there was simply not enough time to wait for comprehensive corporate law reform.
85   Claussen, 'Aktienrechts-reform 1997' (1996).
86   Seibert, 'Aktienrechtsreform in Permanenz?' (2002) 419.
87   Conrad Berger, *Die Kosten der Aufsichtsratstätigkeit in der Aktiengesellschaft* (Peter Lang, 2000) 10.
88   Claussen, 'Aktienrechts-reform 1997' (1996) 487.
89   'Corporate Governance – Unternehmensführung – Unternehmenskontrolle – Modernisierung des Aktienrechts', Press release (3 August 2001) 3 <http://www.bundesregierung.de/Nachrichten/-,433/Pressemitteilungen.htm> (for a copy of the press release, contact Jean du Plessis).
90   Ibid.

The recommendations dealt with the introduction of a corporate governance code for listed German corporations; intensifying the control over directing the business of the corporation by increasing the powers of supervisory boards; improving the rights of shareholders; improving protections for investors; improving provisions for the disclosure of information; improving accounting standards and financial reporting; and the use of modern information and communication technology.[91] For current purposes the focus will be on the first two aspects.[92]

12.4.2 The German Corporate Governance Code (GCGC)[93]

12.4.2.1 Background to adoption

In Germany, the introduction of a code of good corporate governance practices was always seen in the context of the broader definition of corporate governance. The approach to such a definition was a realistic one, with two aspects being highlighted: first, that corporate governance cannot ignore the stakeholder debate; and second, that the concept of corporate governance encompasses more than just the creation of legal structures for decision-making and supervising a corporation. It was, furthermore, realised that because of the peculiarities of German corporations law, in particular the prescriptive nature of the German Corporations Act (*Aktiengesetz* (*AktG*)) regarding a two-tier board, no international code would fit the German situation perfectly. In the EU context, the vast differences between the OECD *Principles of Corporate Governance* and the UK Corporate Governance Code served as a clear illustration of this.

Soon after the release of the Baums Commission report it was made known that a group of experts would be appointed to draft a code of best practice for Germany that would apply to all listed German corporations, and that the code should follow the 'comply or explain' principle adopted in the UK. This task was given to the German Corporate Governance Commission under the chairmanship of Gerhard Cromme (the Cromme Commission), who was appointed in September 2001.

Although there were some private initiatives to introduce a code of best practice for Germany in 2000, the official German Code was only adopted on 26 February 2002. Since 2005, the Code has been amended and adjusted slightly in June of each year.[94] Several of the amendments have been influenced by international developments, and after the publication of several corporate governance reports based on conferences held under the auspices of the Cromme Committee. The papers of these conferences were published in German and in

---

91   Ibid. 3–8.
92   As far as the supervisory board in particular is concerned, see the comprehensive and excellent article by Jan Lieder, 'The German supervisory board on its way to professionalism' (2010) 11 *German Law Journal* 115 *et seq*. For some of the more general issues dealing with the German corporate governance model, see Christel Lane, 'Changes in Corporate Governance of German Corporations: Convergence to the Anglo-American Model?' in Thomas Clarke and Jean-Francois Chanlat (eds), *European Corporate Governance* (Routledge, 2009) 157.
93   This section is partly based on extracts from the following two articles – Du Plessis, 'Reflections on some recent corporate governance reforms in Germany' (2003); and Jean J du Plessis, 'The German two-tier board and the German Corporate Governance Code' (2004) 15 *European Business Law Review* 1139 *et seq*.
94   See <www.ecgi.org/codes/all_codes.php>.

English.[95] The current Code is dated 13 May 2013.[96] The Code adopts the two basic principles referred to above: that in essence it would apply only to listed corporations and that it would not be mandatory, but that listed corporations must explain if they did not follow certain specific recommendations of the Code (the 'comply or explain' principle). It should be noted that there was originally a reference to the principle of 'comply *or disclose*', but that has changed over time, to 'comply *or explain*'.[97] The reason for this is that in 2006 the EU Commission issued Directive 2006/46/EC,[98] introducing the 'comply or explain' principle into European law.[99] This has been accepted in Germany through the Modernisation of Accounting Laws Act (BilMoG), and German commentators started to point out that 'comply or explain' is the appropriate way to refer to this principle.[100]

What distinguishes Germany[101] from most other systems where voluntary corporate governance models have been adopted is that the *AktG* was amended on 19 July 2002 by inserting a new s 161 in order to give this arrangement statutory backing.[102] Section 161[103] basically imposes a statutory duty on the supervisory boards and management boards of all listed German companies to 'annually'[104] make a declaration of compliance. This declaration must state whether they complied or will comply with the German Corporate Governance Code (hereafter GCGC or the German Code) as published electronically[105] from time to time by a

95   See, for instance, Gerhard Cromme (ed.), *Corporate Governance Report 2006: Vorträge und Diskussionen der 5. Konferenz Deutscher Corporate Governance Kodex* (Schäffer-Poeschel Verlag, 2006); Gerhard Cromme (ed.), *Corporate Governance Report 2007: Vorträge und Diskussionen der 6. Konferenz Deutscher Corporate Governance Kodex* (Schäffer-Poeschel Verlag, 2007); Gerhard Cromme (ed.), *Corporate Governance Report 2008: Vorträge und Diskussionen der 8. Konferenz Deutscher Corporate Governance Kodex* (Schäffer-Poeschel Verlag, 2008).
96   Government Commission, *German Corporate Governance Code* (2013) <www.dcgk.de/en/code.html>.
97   *Bericht der Regierungskommission Deutscher Corporate Governance Kodex an die Bundesregierung* (November 2010) 11, para 1.1.4 <www.corporate-governance-code.de/ger/download/16122010/Governance_Bericht_Nov_2010.pdf>.
98   Directive 2006/46/EC of the European Parliament and of the Council (14 June 2006).
99   DG Internal Market, *Study on Monitoring and Enforcement Practices in Corporate Governance in the member states*, EU Commission (23 September 2009) 11 and 12 <http://ec.europa.eu/internal_market/company/docs/ecgforum/studies/comply-or-explain-090923_en.pdf>.
100   Hendrik-Michael Ringleb, Thomas Kremer, Marcus Lutter and Axel von Werder, *Kommentar zum Deutschen Corporate Governance Kodex* (Verlag CH Beck, 4th edn, 2010) 22–3, para 20, fn 55 and 33, para 47.
101   See further Du Plessis et al., *German Corporate Governance in International and European Context* (2012) 33–6.
102   *Gesetz zur weiteren Reform des Aktien- und Bilanzrechts, zu Transparenz und Publizität (Transparenz- und Publizitätsgesetz)* – Bundesgesetzblatt Teil I (BGBl.I, 2002) 2681 *et seq*. See generally Klaus J Hopt, 'Die internationalen europarechtlichen Rahmenbedingungen der Corporate Governance' in Hommelhoff, Hopt and von Werder (eds), *Handbuch Corporate Governance* (2009) 40 *et seq*.
103   For a more comprehensive discussion of s 161, see Du Plessis and Saenger, 'Corporate Governance in the EU, the OECD Principles of Corporate Governance and Corporate Governance in Selected Other Jurisdictions' in Du Plessis et al., *German Corporate Governance in International and European Context* (2017) Part 2.6.2.
104   There is no certainty as to what is meant by the word 'annually' (*jährlich*) in s 161 of the *AktG* – see Joachim Rosengarten, 'Die "jährliche" Abgabe der Entsprechenserklärung nach §161 AktG' (2009) 30 *Zeitschrift für Wirtschaftrecht (ZIP)* 1837.
105   Elektronischer Bundesanzeiger (<www.ebundesanzeiger.de>). This does not, however, make the code a statute – see Christoph H Seibt, 'Deutscher Corporate Governance Kodex: Antworten auf Zweifelsfragen der Praxis' (2003) 48 *Die Aktiengesellschaft (AG)* 470.

Standing Commission, the *Regierungskommission Corporate Governance* (Government's Corporate Governance Commission). In addition, they must explain why they have not complied or will not comply with the recommendations (the 'comply or explain' provisions) of the GCGC.[106] The declaration of compliance and disclosure of the reasons for non-compliance must also be made available to the shareholders at all times. This basic duty under s 161 of the *AktG* is confirmed by Article 3.10 of the GCGC. Here it is called the 'Corporate Governance Report', which is part of the company's Annual Report. The declarations of compliance of companies listed on the DAX 30 are all available on the German Government's Corporate Governance Commission webpage.[107] The declaration of compliance should not be confused with the 'Corporate Governance Statement' under s 289a of the German *Handelsgesetzbuch* (*HGB*).[108]

It was also recognised that a voluntary corporate governance model has the advantage of being able to respond quickly and effectively to the changing needs of business – something that cannot be achieved if corporate governance practices are formalised through legislation. Klaus J Hopt describes the basic aims of a first-class corporate governance code as brevity, certainty, allowance for individualisation and flexibility,[109] and it seems that most of these aims are achieved by the German Code.

12.4.2.2 Structure and explanatory nature of the Code

The Code has seven parts. The first part, the Foreword, explains the purpose of the Code and how its provisions should be interpreted. Part 2 deals with shareholders and the general meeting; Part 3 with the relationship between the management board and the supervisory board; Part 4 with the management board; Part 5 with the supervisory board; Part 6 with information that should be disclosed to ensure transparency; and Part 7 with aspects such as financial reporting, audits and financial statements.

The Foreword explains that there are basically two types of provisions in the Code.[110] The first type is identifiable by the use of the word 'shall' (*soll*). These provisions contain the core

---

106 See Theodor Baums (ed.), *Bericht der Regierungskommission Corporate Governance* (Baums Report) (Otto Schmidt Verlag, 2001) 59–60 paras 16–17 for the background to this approach. See also Marcus Lutter, 'Die Erklärung zum Corporate Governance Kodex gemäß §161 AktG' (2002) 166 *Zeitschrift für das gesamte Handelsrecht und Wirtschaftsrecht (ZHR)* 525–6; Martin Peltzer, *Handlungsbedarf in Sachen Baums Report 2001: Bericht der Regierungskommission Corporate Governance: Unternehmensführung – Unternehmenskontrolle – Modernisierung des Aktienrechts* (reproduced by Baums) (Otto Schmidt Verlag, 2001) 594–5; Hans-Christoph Hirt, 'Germany: The GCGC: Co-determination and Corporate Governance Reforms' (2002) 23 *Company Lawyer* 350; Thomas Strieder and Andreas Kuhn, 'Die Offenlegung der jährlichen Entsprechenserklärung zum Deutschen Corporate Kodex sowie die zukünftigen Änderungen durch das EHUG' (2006) 59 *DB* 2247 *et seq*.
107 See <http://www.corporate-governance-code.de/eng/entsprechenserklaerung/index.html#ms>.
108 Gregor Bachmann, 'Die Erklärung zur Unternehmensführung (Corporate Governance Statement)' (2010) 31 *ZIP* 1526, but see 1521 for alternative views.
109 Klaus J Hopt, 'Unternehmensführung, Unternehmenskontrolle, Modernisierung des Aktienrechts – Zum Bericht der Regierungskommission Corporate Governance' in *Corporate Governance: Gemeinschaftssymposion der Zeitschriften (ZHR/ZGR)* (Verlag Recht und Wirtschaft GmbH, 2002) 27, 49–51.
110 See generally Ingo Saenger, *Gesellschaftsrecht* (Verlag Franz Vahlen, 3rd ed, 2015) 268 para 523; Klaus Ruhnke, 'Prüfung der Einhaltung des Deutschen Corporate Governance Kodex durch den Abschlussprüfer' (2003) 48 *AG* 371–2.

recommendations of the Code and are the provisions to which the principle of 'comply or explain' will apply. The second type of provision is identifiable by the words 'should' (*sollte*). These provisions are considered to be good corporate governance principles, although not really the core ones. Corporations are encouraged to follow them, but no disclosure is required if they do not follow them.[111]

All remaining provisions in the Code that are not identifiable by any one of the words used above are considered to be provisions summarising or restating the existing legal requirements under German corporations law.[112] However, as will be seen from the discussion below, the exact legal nature of the Code is really controversial: *sehr strittig*, as one commentator puts it.[113] Problems may occur in particular if there are interpretive differences between the summarised or restated provisions of the GCGC and the actual legislation. These provisions are, especially for those without a specialised legal knowledge of German corporations law, useful as they provide one of the most basic and simple explanations of the principles of the German two-tier board system and the relationship among the various corporate organs.[114] Almost half of the provisions of the Code do indeed fall into the category of summarised or restated legal principles.[115]

It should be noted that the changes to the GCGC since its adoption in 2002 have been significant, but based on the principle that the Code should be changed as little as possible and only insofar as it is really essential (*so wenig wie möglich und so viel wie nötig*).[116]

12.4.2.3 Some noteworthy provisions of the Code[117]

At the heart of the Code is the improvement of the supervisory and overseeing functions of the supervisory board.[118] Thus the Code explains in some detail the relationship between the supervisory board and the management board, as well as the respective roles and functions of both.[119] Part 2 and Part 3 of the GCGC primarily summarise or restate the current law. There is also a fair bit of explanation of the existing law in Part 4, which deals with the management board.

---

111 See generally Gerd Krieger, 'Corporate Governance und Corporate Governance Kodex in Deutschland' (2012) 41 *ZGR* 202, 205–6.

112 Ibid. 206–8.

113 Michael Kort, 'Corporate Governance-Fragen der Größe und Zusammensetzung des Aufsichtsrats bei AG, GmbH und SE' (2008) 53 *AG* 137. See also Frank Wooldridge and Matthias Pannier, 'The German Corporate Governance Code: Status and Development' [2005] *EBLR* 225, 228–9.

114 See also Peter Ulmer, 'Der Deutsche Corporate Governance Kodex – ein neues Regulierungsinstrument für börsennotierte Aktiengesellschaften' (2002) 166 *ZHR* 153.

115 Marcus Lutter, 'Deutscher Corporate Governance Kodex' in Dietrich Dörner, Dieter Menold, Norbert Pfitzer and Peter Oser (eds), *Reform des Aktienrechts, der Rechnungslegung und der Prüfung* (Schäffer-Poeschel Verlag, 2nd ed, 2003) 73.

116 *Bericht der Regierungskommission Deutscher Corporate Governance Kodex an die Bundesregierung* (November 2010) 5 <www.corporate-governance-code.de/ger/download/16122010/Governance_Bericht_Nov_2010.pdf>.

117 This part is based on Du Plessis and Saenger, 'Corporate Governance in the EU, the OECD Principles of Corporate Governance and Corporate Governance in Selected Other Jurisdictions' in Du Plessis et al., *German Corporate Governance in International and European Context* (2017) Part 2.6.5.

118 Government Commission, *German Corporate Governance Code* (GCGC) (2013) Parts 3 and 5 <www.dcgk.de/en/code.html>.

119 Ibid. Parts 3–5.

A few 'comply or explain' provisions that are particularly interesting are dealt with briefly:

- The supervisory board shall specify the management board's information and reporting duties in greater detail.[120]

- The management board and supervisory board shall report each year on the enterprise's corporate governance in the annual report (Corporate Governance Report) and publish this report in connection with the statement on Corporate Governance.[121]

- The company shall keep previous declarations of compliance with the GCGC under s 161 of the *AktG* for viewing on its website for a period of five years.[122]

- The management board shall comprise several persons and have a Chairperson or Spokesman.[123]

- Terms of reference shall regulate the allocation of areas of responsibility and the cooperation of the management board.[124]

- By-Laws need to be adopted to delineate the functions of the management board.[125] It is required of the By-Laws to allocate duties among individual members of the management board. In addition, these By-Laws need to indicate which matters were reserved for the management board as a whole and which resolutions of the management board would require unanimous assent and which resolutions would require a majority vote.

- It is expected that the contracts of appointment of management board members must include a cap on the amount paid to management board members as severance payments where their employment is terminated before the end of their appointed terms of office and without cause.[126] The cap expected is no more than two years of compensation and that should not exceed the amount of the remaining term of office. In addition, payments promised in the event of premature termination due to a change of control should not exceed 150 per cent of the severance payment cap.[127]

- The chairman of the supervisory board shall outline the salient points of the compensation system and any changes thereto to the general meeting.[128]

- In terms of s 107(3) of the *AktG* the supervisory board is empowered to appoint committees, consisting of supervisory board members, to assist it with the preparation for its meetings and resolutions or to assist it in monitoring the execution of its resolutions. Supplementing this power, the GCGC provides that the supervisory board shall form specialised committees 'with sufficient expertise',[129] but apart from two such committees that are specifically mentioned, there is no indication in the GCGC which committees there

---

120   Ibid. Art 3.4 (3rd para).
121   Ibid. Art 3.10 (1st sentence).
122   Ibid. Art 3.10 (last sentence).
123   Ibid. Art 4.2.1 (1st sentence).
124   Ibid. Art 4.2.1 (2nd sentence).
125   Ibid. Art 4.2.1 (2nd sentence).
126   Ibid. Art 4.2.3 (4th para).
127   Ibid. Art 4.2.3 (5th para).
128   Ibid. Art 4.2.3 (6th para).
129   Ibid. Art 5.3.1.

should be. An audit committee[130] and a nomination committee[131] shall be appointed by the supervisory board. It is a 'comply or explain' provision that the chair of the audit committee shall have specialist knowledge and experience in the application of accounting principles and internal control processes.[132] Other committees are only mentioned in passing, for instance 'the body dealing with management board contracts'.[133] It must be noted that since 2009, it is an expectation that the full supervisory board determines the total compensation of the individual management board members and the supervisory board shall determine and regularly review the management board compensation system.[134] Since about 2005 about 20 per cent of companies with employee participation in supervisory boards increased the size of their supervisory boards slightly to improve efficiency and, in particular, to enable supervisory boards to establish more committees (consisting of supervisory board members) to assist the supervisory board with its task of overseeing and supervising the management board.[135]

• The total compensation of each member of the management board is to be disclosed by name, divided into fixed and variable compensation.[136] Disclosure shall be made in a compensation report which, as part of the Corporate Governance Report, describes the compensation system of management board members in a generally understandable way.[137] Furthermore, the compensation report shall also include information on the specific matters mentioned in Art 4.2.5 (3rd para).

• All members of the management board shall disclose conflicts of interest to the supervisory board without delay and inform the other members of the management board thereof.[138] In addition, all material transactions where management board members have an interest shall require the approval of the supervisory board.[139]

• Members of the management board shall only take on sideline activities, especially supervisory board mandates outside the enterprise, with the approval of the supervisory board.[140]

• The supervisory board, in consultation with the management board, shall ensure that there is long-term succession planning for management board members.[141]

• The chair of the supervisory board shall regularly maintain contact with the management board – in particular, with the chair or spokesperson of the management board, and consult with him or her on strategy, planning business development, risk situation, risk management and compliance of the enterprise.[142]

---

130   Ibid. Art 5.3.2.
131   Ibid. Art 5.3.3.
132   Ibid. Art 5.3.2 (2nd sentence).
133   Ibid. Art 4.2.2.
134   Ibid. Art 4.2.2 (1st sentence).
135   See Elmar Gerum, *Das deutsche Corporate Governance-System* (Schäffer-Poeschel Verlag, 2007) 207–8 and 425.
136   GCGC Art 4.2.4 (1st sentence).
137   Ibid. Art 4.2.5 (1st para).
138   Ibid. Art 4.3.4 (1st sentence).
139   Ibid. Art 4.3.4 (last sentence).
140   Ibid. Art 4.3.5.
141   Ibid. Art 5.1.2 (1st para, 3rd sentence).
142   Ibid. Art 5.2 (3rd para, 1st sentence).

- Article 4.1.5 (2nd sentence) now provides that the management board shall lay down targets for increasing the share of women on the two management levels below the management board. In a footnote it is explained that the initial targets should have been determined by 30 September 2015 at the latest. In addition, the initial deadlines to be determined for achievement of the target must not extend beyond 30 June 2017.[143] This provision basically reflects s 76(4) *AktG*. The fact that neither the Code nor the law provides a legally binding minimum quota for management boards and the upper management levels but only requires companies to set target quotas (contrary to the situation for supervisory boards), seems to be an incentive for some companies to simply set the target quota to 0 per cent.[144] Corporations justify this by referring to their need for extensive 'entrepreneurial freedom' and for members to be chosen according to their qualifications and expertise only. This behaviour is clearly not following the spirit of the law, but since no sanction for abusive behaviour in this regard is provided, it remains to be seen if public pressure will suffice to encourage good conduct. But if the company knows beforehand that it won't comply with this provision – either because a target quota won't be set or because this won't happen within the time limit or because the quota won't be reached within the time limit – it has to indicate this in its annual declaration of compliance

12.4.3 Employee participation at supervisory board level – codetermination[145]

Any discussion of the German corporate governance system would be incomplete without at least a brief mention of one of its outstanding features, a feature which has captured the imagination of those who view the German corporate governance model from abroad.[146] This is, of course, the German system of employee participation at supervisory board level – or codetermination, as it is more commonly known. This is a theme that regularly pops up in the EU context, often with direct or indirect reference to German corporations law and corporate governance model. It was, indeed, because of conflicting views on the two-tier board and employee participation in the supervisory board that the Draft Fifth Directive has had such a

---

143   Reference is made to the Law on Equal Participation of Men and Women in Private-Sector and Public-Sector Management Positions, *EG-AktG* (Introductory Law of the German Stock Corporation Act) s 25(1), *German Federal Gazette* I (2015), 642, 656. For details, see, for example, Claudia Junker and Jan Schmidt-Pfitzner, 'Quoten und Zielgrößen für Frauen (und Männer) in Führungspositionen' (2015) 24 *Neue Zeitschrift für Gesellschaftsrecht (NZG)* 929 *et seq*; Gerhard Röder and Christian Arnold, 'Zielvorgaben zur Förderung des Frauenanteils in Führungspositionen' (2015) 21 *Neue Zeitschrift für Arbeitsrecht (NZA)* 1281 *et seq*.

144   See, for example, Thyssen Krupp's and Commerzbank's statements on diversity and their target quota <www.thyssenkrupp.com/en/nachhaltigkeit/diversity.html>; <www.commerzbank.de/de/hauptnavigation/karriere/arbeiten_bei_der_commerzbank/diversity___/frauen_2/gesetz_gleichberechtigte_teilhabe.html>.

145   For a more comprehensive discussion of employee participation at supervisory board level, see Du Plessis et al., *German Corporate Governance in International and European Context* (2017) Ch 5.

146   See Margaret M Blair and Mark J Roe (eds), *Employees and Corporate Governance* (Brookings Institution, 1999); and sources quoted in Du Plessis, 'Reflections on some recent Corporate governance reforms in Germany' (2003) 381–2.

stormy history and has, with the UK leaving the EU, no chance of being implemented,[147] although that had already been predicted.[148] Paul Rose explains the opposing approaches succinctly:

> The German co-determination system and the UK shareholder primacy model represent contrasting poles on an EU governance continuum. Given the deep structural and cultural differences that exist between EU member states, convergence will entail significant expense. Convergence costs may include not only regulatory structure costs – the costs required to develop a new regulatory regime or alter an existing regime – but also cultural costs.[149]

Codetermination by employees at supervisory board level has recently also been the focus of renewed attention in Germany, after a relatively long period during which it was simply accepted as part of the German corporate governance model. This reflection was triggered because of several cases in the European Court of Justice.[150] It should also be noted that when Theresa May replaced David Cameron as the UK Prime Minister, she expressed a keen interest in getting employees on UK boards,[151] although it was later reported that she had changed her view on this issue.[152]

Germany has a long legislative history of support for industrial democracy. While this was initially reflected in the creation of elected worker committees and worker councils, which gave employees a voice on the shop floor, later legislation introduced employee representation at supervisory board level. The main impetus for supervisory codetermination by employees actually came from the determination of British occupation authorities and German trade unionists to ensure that the nation would never again fall into dictatorial situations like the Third Reich.[153] The specific method invented was to make it compulsory for employees to hold up to half of the seats on supervisory boards. As the supervisory board appoints the management board, there is an assumption that labour and management have a role to play in looking after the interests of the enterprise, so the system was called 'codetermination'. This was supposed to ensure that the very strict class distinction that had existed in Germany would

---

147 See Jean J du Plessis and J Dine, 'The fate of the Draft Fifth Directive on company law: Accommodation instead of harmonisation' [1997] *The Journal of Business Law* 25–7.

148 Du Plessis et al., *Principles of Contemporary Corporate Governance* (CUP, 2015) 428, fn 104.

149 Paul Rose, 'EU company law convergence possibilities after CENTROS' (2001) 11 *Transnational Law and Contemporary Problems* 121, 133. See also Jonathan Charkham, *Keeping Better Company* (OUP, 2nd edn, 2005) 28–9.

150 See Otto Sandrock and Jean J du Plessis, 'The German corporate governance model in the wake of company law harmonisation in the European Union' (2005) 26 *Company Lawyer* 88.

151 Stephanie Baker, 'Theresa May's plan to put workers on boards is borrowed from Germany and France', *The Independent*, 12 July 2016 <www.independent.co.uk/news/business/news/theresa-may-board-corporate-plan-germany-france-productivity-economics-a7132221.html>.

152 See Chrisopher Williams, 'Theresa May Backtrack on Putting Workers on Company Boards', *The Telegraph*, 16 November 2016 <www.telegraph.co.uk/business/2016/11/21/theresa-may-backtracks-on-putting-workers-on-company-boards/>; Jessica Elgot, 'UK government defends apparent U-turn over workers on boards', *The Guardian*, 29 November 2016 <www.theguardian.com/business/2016/nov/29/government-defends-apparent-u-turn-over-workers-on-boards#img-1>.

153 Brian Robinson, 'Worker Participation: Trends in West Germany' in Mark Anstey (ed.), *Worker Participation* (Juta, 1990) 49.

not emerge again.[154] The government of the day campaigned for a one-third employee representative regime, but the trade unions got their way after a strike in the mining, iron, coal and steel industries and full parity codetermination was introduced.[155]

The system of electing the employee representatives is a very complicated one. Furthermore, the number of employees who are appointed to the supervisory board varies from industry to industry; it also depends on the size of the corporation. However, there are basically only three forms of employee participation:[156]

1. For certain types of corporations it is required that one-third of the supervisory board must be appointed by the employees or their representatives and two-thirds by the general meeting or in accordance with provisions in the articles of incorporation or comparable documents (*die Satzung, der Gesellschaftsvertrag* or *das Statut*).

2. For other types of corporations half of the members are appointed by the employees (or their representatives), the other half by the shareholders, and then one neutral member has to be appointed by the two groups together – this is called parity codetermination, as the power balance does not rest with either of the constituents.

3. For a final group of corporations an equal number of representatives are appointed by the employees (or their representatives) and the shareholders. In addition, for the corporations falling under this system, the chairperson (with a casting vote) must be elected from the group of persons appointed by the general meeting, while the employee representatives must include at least one person from 'the leading personnel' (managers and executive employees). This is called quasi-parity codetermination, as the power balance is tilted towards the shareholder representatives.

In the early 2000s employee participation at supervisory board level came under severe criticism, as illustrated by several articles in leading law review journals – including an editorial by an eminent academic, Peter Ulmer, in one of the leading academic commercial and business law journals[157] and two articles in perhaps the leading corporate law journal in Germany.[158] Moreover, other legal scholars and managers experienced in codetermination

---

154   Hellmut Wißmann, 'Das Montan-Mitbestimmungsänderungsgesetz: Neuer Schritt zur Sicherung der Montan-Mitbestimmung' (1982) *Neue Juristische Wochenschrift (Zeitschrift)* 423.

155   Ibid. See further, on 'full parity codetermination', Du Plessis et al., *German Corporate Governance in International and European Context* (2017) Parts 4.2 and 5.2.3.2.

156   Ibid. Part 4.2 and footnotes accompanying the text.

157   Peter Ulmer, 'Editorial: Paritätische Arbeitnehmermitbestimmung im Aufsichtsrat von Großunternehmen – noch zeitgemäß?' (2002) 166 *Zeitschrift für das gesamte Handels-und Wirtschaftsrecht* 271. See also Peter Ulmer, 'Der Deutsche Corporate Governance Kodex – ein neues Regulierungsinstrument für börsennotierte Aktiengesellschaften' (2002) 166 *Zeitschrift für das gesamte Handels-und Wirtschaftsrecht* 150, 180–1.

158   Martin Veit and Joachim Wichert, 'Unternehmerische Mitbestimmung bei europäischen Kapitalgesellschaften mit Verwaltungssitz in Deutschland nach "Überseering" und "Inspire Art"' (2004) 49 *Die Aktiengesellschaft (Zeitschrift)* 14, 17–18; Otto Sandrock, 'Gehören die deutschen Regelungen über die Mitbestimmung auf Unternehmensebene wirklich zum deutschen ordre public?' (2004) 49 *Die Aktiengesellschaft (Zeitschrift)* 57 *et seq.* See also Sandrock and Du Plessis, 'The German corporate governance model in the wake of company law harmonisation in the European Union' (2005) 88 ff; Jean J du Plessis and Otto Sandrock, 'The rise and the fall of supervisory codetermination in Germany?' (2005) 16 *International Company and Commercial Law Review* 67 ff.

matters have published work pointing to several shortcomings of parity codetermination during the past few years.[159]

Despite this, members of management and shareholder representatives generally have been reluctant to openly challenge the legitimacy and usefulness of parity codetermination, seeking to avoid confrontations with the powerful German trade unions – confrontations that could also provoke strikes. Further, for fear of losing general elections at the level of either federal German unions or the important federal industrial states, most of the political parties have not lent any support to modifications, even the most moderate ones. The German system of codetermination has therefore been characterised as a taboo area,[160] or as a 'dinosaur model'.[161] It is only during the past few years that some voices from management and political parties have been willing, in this respect, to 'call a spade a spade'.

The Global Financial Crisis seems to have changed perceptions and opinions slightly. It is quite remarkable that foreign businessmen who[162] until recently just could not comprehend the concept of codetermination, and were astounded by the complex and extensive German rules regarding codetermination, now seem to be beginning to understand that these codetermination rules are embedded in a comprehensive system of mostly friendly labour relations – relations which have helped Germany recover fast and thoroughly from the Global Financial Crisis and the European financial crisis that followed. That recovery is attributed – to a large extent – to the labour relations system, including the system of codetermination.[163]

It is very unlikely that Germany will move away from a two-tier board system, not only because of path dependency, but also because the advantage of such a board system is widely recognised. The most controversial aspect of the system is still employee participation at supervisory board level. Although it is too soon to draw any definite conclusions, it is clear that the topic of codetermination has once again become a subject for lively debate in Germany, and it will be difficult to keep codetermination off the political agenda.[164] It is, however, also to be

159   Otto Sandrock, 'Die Schrumpfung der Überlagerungstheorie' (2003) 102 *Zeitschrift für Vergleichende Rechtswissenschaft* 447, 490–3; Sandrock and Du Plessis, 'The German corporate governance model in the wake of company law harmonisation in the European Union' (2005) 88 ff; Du Plessis and Sandrock, 'The rise and the fall of supervisory codetermination in Germany?' (2005) 67 ff.

160   Expression used by Maximilian Schiessl, 'Leitungs und Kontrollstrukturen im internationalen Wettbewerb – Dualistisches System und Mitbestimmung auf dem Prüfstand' (2003) 167 *Zeitschrift für das gesamte Handels-und Wirtschaftsrecht* 235, 237.

161   Expression used by Theodor Baums, according to a note in the *Frankfurter Allgemeine Zeitung* (nation-wide German daily newspaper), 27 June 2003.

162   Du Plessis et al., *German Corporate Governance in International and European Context* (2017) Part 6.8.

163   Ibid. 151, 174–5, 191, 196, 199 and 269–80.

164   See in particular Ulmer, 'Editorial: Paritätische Arbeitnehmermitbestimmung im Aufsichtsrat von Großunternehmen – noch zeitgemäß?' (2002) 272. See also Ulmer, 'Der Deutsche Corporate Governance Kodex' (2002) 180–1 and Klaus J Hopt, 'Unternehmensführung, Unternehmenskontrolle, Modernisierung des Aktienrechts – Zum Bericht der Regierungskommission Corporate Governance' in *Corporate Governance: Gemeinschaftssymposion der Zeitschriften (ZHR/ZGR)* (Verlag Recht und Wirtschaft GmbH, 2002) 42–6 and 66–7.

expected that German trade unions, in particular, will not easily accept any changes to the codetermination model that have the potential to erode their power base in any way.[165]

12.4.4 The German board structure

If we use Bob Tricker's 'governance circle' and 'managerial pyramid', as explained in Chapter 3, the typical German two-tier board structure will look like Figure 12.1.

Figure 12.1   German two-tier board structure

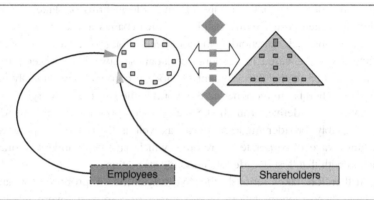

12.4.5 Conclusions on Germany

There have been considerable developments in the areas of corporate law and corporate governance in Germany over recent years. The first wave of developments focused on the role and effectiveness of supervisory boards. Since the adoption of the German Corporate Governance Code (GCGC) in February 2002, the focus has been on promoting good corporate governance practices through the Code. This has enabled the German corporate governance model to remain relevant and to reflect international best corporate governance practices.

Codetermination, or employee participation at supervisory board level, is still one of the most controversial and most debated issues in Germany. Some German commentators have expressed critical views of it and there are powerful market forces putting strains on the system. It is not difficult to predict that globalisation and internationalisation, where the financial markets of all countries become more and more accessible, will lead to further pressure. With the Global Financial Crisis still fresh in the minds of all entrepreneurs, it will be difficult for German entrepreneurs to continue to cling to a governance model that is viewed with scepticism by many entrepreneurs from other countries. The more options investors have to move their money around internationally, the more pressure there will be on German corporations law and corporate governance models to become more flexible if they want to remain competitive and to ensure that the German economy attracts more international investment.

---

165   See Otto Sandrock, 'German and International Perspectives on the German Model of Codetermination', 2013 Inaugural ICGL Forum, Muenster, Germany <www.icgl.org.au/abstracts/professor-otto-sandrock/>.

12.5 Japan

12.5.1 Introduction

Corporate law and practice in Japan have long attracted considerable attention among foreign commentators, and an extensive literature in Western languages.[166] Much of the commentary increasingly refers to 'corporate governance', reflecting the emergence of this broader term worldwide since the 1980s (outlined in Chapter 1) and indeed generating another neologism in the Japanese language: *koporeto gabanansu*.[167] But contemporary corporate law analyses and discussions focused on Japan have long tended to adopt a broader perspective. This reflects an awareness of the pervasive but typically informal role in firms of stakeholders other than shareholders, especially core 'lifelong' employees, 'main banks' and *keiretsu* corporate groups.

Before examining such stakeholders in more detail, alongside an account of corporate law topics conventionally covered in accounts of Japanese law, this chapter presents a brief historical introduction to the development of modern corporate law, initially based mainly on German law, when Japan reopened to the world in the late 19th century.[168] Corporate and securities law elements derived from the US were superimposed during the Allied Occupation (1945–51). Arguably, broader Anglo-American as well as EU law developments have influenced the 'third wave' of corporate law reforms, which have been underway since the 1990s, in conjunction with that 'lost decade' of economic stagnation.

This part therefore takes seriously the 'five ways forward' proposed for navigating and assessing often diverse interpretations of contemporary corporate governance in Japan (and indeed elsewhere).[169] Particularly when considering the 'convergence' debate (outlined in Chapter 1), we need always to be attentive to:

1. timing, or the historical periods selected for analysis (with longer time spans often suggesting that major transformations are underway);

2. both 'black-letter law' or the 'law in books' (which also tends to emphasise change) and socioeconomic context or the 'law in action' (tending to emphasise continuities);

3. multiple points of comparison (comparing just two legal systems is risky, as this often results in assessments of either great differences or great commonalities and hence convergence);

4. normative preferences (even when commentators – inevitably influenced by their own backgrounds or eras – profess to have none); and

5. processes of law creation and enforcement, not just outcomes (even when legal rules or their impact in practice appear to display limited change, the processes by which

166   Harald Baum, Luke Nottage, Joel Rheuben and Markus Thier, *Japanese Business Law in Western Languages: An Annotated Selective Bibliography* (William Hein & Son, 2nd edn, 2013) 282–327.

167   See, for example, *TSE-Listed Companies White Paper on Corporate Governance*, published biannually <www.tse.or.jp/english/listing/cg/>.

168   For a succinct overview of Japanese legal history and institutions, see Masaki Abe and Luke Nottage, 'Japanese Law' in Jan Smits (ed.), *Encyclopedia of Comparative Law* (Edward Elgar, 2nd edn, 2012) 462–79; an earlier version is available at <www.asianlii.org/jp/other/JPLRes/2008/1.html>.

169   Luke Nottage, 'Perspectives and Approaches: A Framework for Comparing Japanese Corporate Governance' in Luke Nottage et al. (eds), *Corporate Governance in the 21st Century: Japan's Gradual Transformation* (Edward Elgar, 2008) 41–51. For an overview focused more on the statutory framework, see Bruce Aronson, Souichirou Kozuka and Luke Nottage, 'Corporate Legislation in Japan' in Parissa Haghirian (ed.), *Routledge Handbook of Japanese Business and Management* (Routledge, 2016) 103–13.

this occurred may have been very different from past experience – in turn creating a greater possibility of more far-reaching changes in future iterations).

12.5.2 Historical transformations in Japanese corporate law and practice

The importance of politics to corporate law and practice has long been evident in modern Japan. When Japan reopened fully to the world in 1868, after two and a half centuries of almost complete isolation under Tokugawa rule, it had to agree to 'unequal treaties' with the US and European imperial powers. A precondition to renegotiation was the establishment of a modern legal system, and the Meiji Government decided to enact comprehensive codes along European lines, including a commercial code containing corporate law provisions to support both smaller enterprises and large-scale industrialisation.[170]

After law reform initiatives significantly influenced by English and then French law, the more German law-inspired Commercial Code of 1899 was enacted, including 1884 legislation on stock companies. Key terms such as *sokai* (general shareholders' meeting), *torishimariyaku* (directors) and *kansayaku* (statutory auditors)[171] were introduced. A comprehensive reform to the Code was made in 1938, again largely based on Germany's *Stock Corporation Act of 1937*, with both countries attempting to address the emerging separation of ownership and control. At the same time, Japan belatedly enacted separate legislation for a private limited liability company (*yugen kaisha* or YK), similar to the *GmbH* already found in the German Code of 1897. By the end of World War II, there were nearly half as many YKs as KKs, although many closely held companies persisted in incorporating as KKs.

The US-led occupation brought securities regulation and anti-monopoly law, and significant reforms to the Commercial Code, all based this time on US law. The Code amendments first aimed to redistribute corporate powers. The *sokai*'s jurisdiction was limited to matters set in law or articles of incorporation, ushering in the institution of the board of directors to collectively hold and exercise powers and managerial functions.

The four decades from the Occupation through to the collapse of Japan's bubble economy in 1990 witnessed the emergence of a new hybrid corporate governance regime, intertwined with other economic institutions of the era. One central pillar was the 'main bank', the largest lender as well as a principal shareholder (although each bank's holding was subject to a statutory 5 per cent cap). Main banks provided diverse financing, monitoring (usually before but sometimes after lending, if borrowers got into difficulty), and information and management support. Cross-shareholding was a second feature, with about two-thirds of listed company shares held by 'stable' shareholders in the early 1990s. The epitome were the *keiretsu*, 'historically derived clusters of affiliated firms held together by stable cross-share ownership, interlocking directorates, extensive product market exchanges, and other linkages that

---

170   The following summary, through to the early 1990s, is based on the detailed analysis of corporate law reforms in full economic and political context provided by Harald Baum and Eiji Takahashi, 'Commercial and Corporate Law in Japan: Legal and Economic Developments after 1868' in Wilhelm Röhl (ed.), *History of Law in Japan since 1868* (Brill, 2005) 330.

171   The ongoing evolution of *kansayaku* roles and impact, especially in recent years, remains relatively under-researched: see Bruce Aronson, 'Japanese corporate governance reform: A comparative perspective' (2015) 11 *Hastings Business Law Journal* 85, 98–102.

enhance group identity and facilitate information exchange'.[172] Six major post-war 'horizontal' *keiretsu* were centred on main banks (for example, Mitsubishi); 'vertical' *keiretsu* brought together groups of production and investment chains (for example, Hitachi).

A third significant practice in larger firms (and an ideal for many others) was 'lifetime employment', whereby workers implicitly traded initially below-market wages for continuous employment and above-market wages in the second half of their career. Fourth, government–business relations involved considerable 'administrative guidance' (informal enforcement of regulatory objectives), with bureaucrats – and the long-reigning Liberal Democratic Party (LDP) – promoting consensus-based policy-making through repeated informal contacts with firms and industry associations. The first three features, in particular, reduced the need for the active board monitoring function promoted by Occupation reformers and, indeed, for the disciplinary effect of hostile takeovers.

This system was never universal or completely stable, and it began to fray in the 1980s, when larger firms turned increasingly from bank to shareholder finance. Bigger challenges came from the collapse of asset prices in 1990 and Japan's consequent 'lost decade' of economic stagnation, which included failures of major financial institutions and 'Big Bang' deregulation of financial markets from 1997.[173] Its direct consequence was the reduction of cross-shareholdings, first motivated by banks improving their balance sheets, then accelerated by new controls over banks holding other companies' assets. Aggregate listed shares held by 'insider shareholders' (banks, insurers and other non-financial business corporations), which may be approximated to cross-held shares, decreased from the peak of 61.8 per cent in 1986 to 31.2 per cent in 2012. Most of the shares that insider shareholders released were picked up by 'outside shareholders' – individuals, foreigners and trust banks (collectively holding 65.9 per cent of all shares in 2012).[174] The shift, however, occurred unevenly among listed companies: it was more conspicuous in large, globally well-known companies than in smaller, domestically focused companies. The former firms therefore gradually faced pressures from outside shareholders, in particular foreign and institutional investors, demanding more disciplined corporate governance. This pressure came not only from foreign investors. The Japan Pension Fund Association (PFA) also encouraged developments towards the monitoring model by publishing principles calling for greater independence; other calls came from individual investors in Japan and (especially) abroad.[175]

The apparent failure to restore a vibrant economy, and the changes in shareholding structure, drove domestic policy-making elites to embark on major reforms to commercial regulation generally, and corporate law in particular. Their main objectives, long sought also by Anglo-American investors and governments, included greater flexibility in corporate law

---

172   See Curtis J Milhaupt and Mark D West, *Economic Organizations and Corporate Governance in Japan* (OUP, 2004) 14.

173   See Tetsuro Toya, *The Political Economy of the Japanese Financial Big Bang* (OUP, 2006).

174   Gen Goto, 'Legally "strong" shareholders of Japan' (2014) 3 *Michigan Business & Entrepreneurial Law Review* 125.

175   Though less adversarial than its well-known US counterpart, CalPERS, the PFA gradually gained significance as the promoter of better corporate governance after the turn of the century. See Bruce Aronson, 'A Japanese CalPERS or a new model for institutional investor activism? Japan's Pension Fund Association and the emergence of shareholder activism in Japan' (2011) 7 *NYU Journal of Law & Business* 571. Eguchi foresees larger engagement of institutional investors in Japan after the dissolution of cross-shareholdings, bringing Japan closer to the UK in the future: Takaai Eguchi, 'Management–shareholder Relations in Japan: What's Next After Cross-Shareholdings?' in Zenichi Shishido (ed.), *Enterprise Law: Contracts, Markets and Laws in the US and Japan* (Edward Elgar, 2014) 191–204.

rules – moving away from the German tradition of detailed mandatory provisions – and greater focus on the interests of shareholders vis-à-vis other stakeholders (such as core employees, trading partners and main banks).[176] The amendments were first made in a piecemeal manner and then consolidated into the Companies Act, enacted in 2005, followed by amendments in 2014. In parallel with finalising the 2014 amendments, a roundtable of stakeholders started deliberations on the Corporate Governance Code, which was published in 2015 and has been adopted and implemented by all five stock exchanges in Japan since June of that year.[177] The Corporate Governance Code does not impose any mandatory regulations but merely requires listed companies to 'comply or explain', thus allowing a company to derogate as long as it gives reasons. Still, in several important respects, the Corporate Governance Code introduces more radical corporate governance changes than the Companies Act.[178]

Overall, therefore, Japan has experienced three major waves in the development of corporate law, linked to similar shifts in other fields of legislation, at roughly half-century intervals. The Meiji-era Commercial Code around the turn of the 20th century was followed by US-inspired (even 'US-imposed') reforms during the post-war Occupation, then the much more wide-ranging reforms from around the turn of the 21st century. Even in terms of formal legislative changes, the trajectory has not been one of straightforward 'Americanisation', and the overall position now is also very different from US law, as evidenced by the persistence of the statutory auditor governance structure.[179] Also evident are some influences from – or at least parallels with – aspects of English law, epitomised recently in listing requirements, but also a tendency in takeover regulation to give priority to decisions of shareholders over those of directors. The impact of German law, filtered sometimes now through EU law, remains important. Japan's complex corporate law landscape is also matched by persistently distinctive features of contemporary corporate governance practice, even though this, too, is undergoing gradual transformation.

12.5.3 Japanese corporate forms and internal governance mechanisms

12.5.3.1 Overview

By 2005, there were about 1.5 million YK companies and 2.5 million KK companies, but of the latter, 86.7 per cent had capital of less than 20 million yen. Most of these small companies were

---

176   See further, for example, the summary Appendix in Nottage et al. (eds), *Corporate Governance in the 21st Century: Japan's Gradual Transformation* (2008) 13–20, based on the detailed descriptions in Tomotaka Fujita, 'Modernising Japanese corporate law: Ongoing corporate law reform in Japan' (2004) 16 *Singapore Academy of Law Journal* 321; the summary Table 11.1 (and accompanying text) in Hiroshi Oda, *Japanese Law* (OUP, 3rd edn, 2009) 219; and more theoretically Curtis J Milhaupt, 'A Lost Decade for Japanese Corporate Governance Reform?: What's Changed, What Hasn't, and Why' in Magnus Blomstrom and Sumner LaCroix (eds), *Institutional Change in Japan* (Routledge, 2006) 97.

177   *Japan's Corporate Governance Code [Final Proposal]* (5 March 2015) <www.fsa.go.jp/en/refer/councils/corporategovernance/20150306-1.html>.

178   On the 2014 amendments and the Code, see Gen Goto, Manabu Matsunaka and Souichirou Kozuka, 'Japan's Gradual Reception of Independent Directors: An Empirical and Political-Economic Analysis' in Harald Baum et al. (eds), *Independent Directors in Asia* (CUP, 2107).

179   Cf R Daniel Kelemen and Eric C Sibbitt, 'The Americanization of Japanese Law' (2002) 23 *University of Pennsylvania Journal of International Economic Law* 269 (focusing, however, on securities law and product liability in Japan).

not among the fewer than 4000 listed companies, and instead restricted share transferability through articles of association.[180] This growing gap between the 'law in books' and the 'law in action' had led to problems, such as minority shareholder 'squeeze-outs' and other features characteristic of family-run businesses that were subject to no relief provisions. Yet legislation drafted by a study group in 1986 was not adopted.[181]

In 2005, the new Companies Act abolished YK companies altogether, subsuming them into the KK form, rather than forcing the smaller KK companies to adopt provisions like those that existed for larger companies. The Companies Act also provided multiple options within the KK rubric, including simplified governance structures very suitable for smaller companies, as part of a broader shift away from narrow mandatory rules and towards greater choice for business-people. The *Companies Act of 2005* restricts governance options according to whether or not the company is 'large' and/or 'public' (meaning that transferability of *any* class of shares is unrestricted – to be a *listed* public company, by contrast, *all* shares be fully transferable). The law's somewhat complex rules can be interpreted to provide for these four KK subcategories:[182]

(i) For non-public and non-large companies: the most practicable structure is likely to involve just one or several directors (but no requirement for a board). Shareholders seeking to add a governance mechanism likely to appeal to banks might also add a statutory auditor (but who may be restricted through the articles of association to assessing accounting matters, not the legality of directors' actions).

(ii) For non-public but large companies: all possible structures require accounting audit-ors (CPAs). It may involve statutory auditors (with or without full powers).

(iii) For public but not large companies: a board of directors is mandatory. The most practicable structure is likely to involve a board of directors plus one statutory auditor.

(iv) For public and large companies: there are three options. One is the 'company with nominations and other committees' (*shimei iinkaitô setchi kaisha*). The second is 'a company with a board of statutory auditors' (*kansayakukai setchi kaisha*). The third is the company with an 'audit and supervisory committee' (*kansatô iinkai setchi kaisha*). All of these three structures require one or more accounting auditors.

It remains to be seen whether this much-expanded menu of options that businesspeople can select from for smaller companies will lead courts to become even more reluctant to police 'oppression'[183] of shareholders, on the theory that they – or their legal advisers – should have chosen a more sophisticated form to improve governance from the outset. This issue is complicated because some forms of 'oppression', such as share issuance, raise issues covered

---

180 Oda, *Japanese Law* (2009) 221–3 (comparing also the numbers of differently capitalised companies in the forms provided now under the Companies Act).

181 Zenichi Shishido, 'Problems of the closely held corporation: A comparative study of the Japanese and American legal systems and a critique of the Japanese tentative draft on close corporations' (1990) 38 *American Journal of Comparative Law* 337.

182 Keiko Hashimoto et al., 'Corporations' in Gerald McAlinn (ed.), *Japanese Business Law* (Kluwer, 2007) 102–5.

183 See Chapter 10 (Section 10.3) for the Australian remedy.

by provisions that are also creating problems – and court precedents in takeover disputes involving large listed companies. Yet Japanese courts may make allowance for the fact that the government has enacted the new Companies Act with a considerable element of 'policy push' (trying to channel behaviour), rather than the more usual 'demand-pull' approach, whereby legislation tends to reflect emerging practices. They may also take into account the fact that smaller businesses still lack access to sophisticated legal advice, despite the parallel effort to reform the legal profession and justice system more generally.[184]

12.5.3.2 The board of directors and choice in governance structures

For public companies in Japan, the focus of corporate governance reform during the last two decades has been the board of directors. The legislative amendment in 2002 created the option of substituting a (more Anglo-American) 'company with committees' for the (German) statutory auditor board structure.[185] This 'elective corporate governance reform' partly reflected a compromise among Japan's major corporate law reform institutions.[186] The amendments of 2014 further allowed, as a third option, a 'company with audit committee'.

In fact, some corporate practice preceded the legislative reform. In 1996, Sony decreased the number of board members from 38 to 10, while creating the status of 'senior officers' (*shikko yakuin*) for the senior employees who used to be junior members of the board of directors. Apparently the aim was to adopt the monitoring model of corporate governance, under which the board of directors concentrated on the monitoring of the officers instead of engaging itself in management. Downsizing the board of directors became the trend in the following years. Among the companies listed in the First Section of the Tokyo Stock Exchange (TSE), companies with 20 or more board members decreased from 92 in 2002 to 31 in 2007, with the mean board size decreasing from 10.9 to 9.4 and the largest board size declining from 49 to 30 during the same period. Meanwhile, companies appointing senior officers burgeoned from 461 (31 per cent of all First Section TSE firms) to 992 (58 per cent).[187]

It was against this background that the 2002 law reform introduced a 'company with nomination and other committees' (which was then called 'company with committees') as an option. If the company chooses this structure, the board of directors establishes three

---

184 Tomoyo Matsui, 'Corporate Governance and Closely-held Companies in Japan: The Untold Story' in Nottage et al. (eds), *Corporate Governance in the 21st Century: Japan's Gradual Transformation* (2008) 108, applying the distinction between the two approaches developed by Zenichi Shishido, 'The Turnaround of 1997: Changes in Japanese Corporate Law and Governance' in Masahiko Aoki et al. (eds), *Corporate Governance in Japan: Institutional Change and Organizational Diversity* (OUP, 2007) 310. In other areas, such as contract law, Japanese case law has developed a more flexible (German rather than French) approach to protecting the weaker party in a long-term relationship. See (with further references) Souichirou Kozuka and Luke Nottage, 'Policy and Politics in Contract Law Reform in Japan', Research Paper No. 13/86, Sydney Law School (2013) <http://ssrn.com/abstract=2360343>.

185 Dan W Puchniak, 'The 2002 reform of the management of large corporations in Japan: A race to somewhere?' (2003) 5 *Australian Journal of Asian Law* 42.

186 Ronald Gilson and Curtis Milhaupt, 'Choice as regulatory reform: The case of Japanese corporate governance' (2005) 53 *American Journal of Comparative Law* 353–4; Luke R Nottage and Leon Wolff, 'Corporate Governance and Law Reform in Japan: From the Lost Decade to the End of History?' in Rene Haak and Markus Pudelko (eds), *Japanese Management: In Search of a New Balance between Continuity and Change* (Palgrave Macmillan, 2005) 133.

187 Konari Uchida, 'Does corporate board downsizing increase shareholder value? Evidence from Japan' (2011) 20 *International Review of Economics and Finance* 562.

committees (nomination committee, audit committee and remuneration committee: Companies Act, Article 404), each having three or more members with the outside directors occupying the majority (Article 400). No statutory auditor is appointed. The board of directors in this type of a company can abstain from executive decisions (though it is not required to do so) and delegate them to the executive officers (*shikkoyaku*) (Article 416).[188] Such a company with committees is clearly designed to implement the monitoring model.

Within a few years of its introduction, this structure proved to be extremely unpopular. As of January 2017, only 69 firms among 3541 companies listed on the Tokyo and Osaka Stock Exchanges have opted for this structure.[189] These have included the Nomura financial holding company, together with 13 privately held subsidiaries, plus Hitachi, with 21 affiliates. These two major corporate groups are not traditional bank-centred *keiretsu*, and many of the other adopting firms diverge from conventional patterns of Japanese industrial organisation (Orix, for example) and/or have high foreign ownership (Sony, for example).

A qualitative study in 2006 concluded that the system had the potential to generate stronger and more transparent corporate governance, and had been perceived in this way, but the empirical reality had not met these expectations.[190] Similarly, Kenichi Osugi argues that many Japanese companies have been hesitant in turning to the idea of the monitoring board (from the traditional decision-making board), perhaps because the latter is intertwined with the culture of 'company community'.[191]

The legislature also introduced an option for a 'company with audit committee' (*kansatô iinkai setchi kaisha*) into the 2014 amendments to the Companies Act. Unlike in a 'company with nomination and other committees', this new (optional) type of company is required to have only the audit and supervisory committee dominated by the outside directors. In other words, nomination of the top management and the assessment of the managers' performance through determination of their remuneration can remain in the hands of (board) insiders. Still, because outsiders are members of the board of directors and not statutory auditors, they can cooperate with other board members to dismiss an executive director when necessary. This third optional structure has proven much more popular, attracting 689 companies already as of January 2017.[192] The legislature seems to have adopted the 'hybrid approach' that Aronson

---

188   *Shikkoyaku* must be distinguished from *shikko yakuin*. The former is a position required by the
       Companies Act for a company with committees (and open to shareholder derivative action, for example,
       similarly to board directors). *Shikko yakuin* is merely a status given by the company and, as a regulatory
       matter, is a senior employee protected as such by labour law.
189   See the database of Japan Exchange Group <www.jpx.co.jp/english/listing/cg-search/index.html>.
190   Peter Lawley, 'Panacea or Placebo? An Empirical Analysis of the Effect of the Japanese Committee
       System Corporate Governance Law Reform' in Nottage et al. (eds), *Corporate Governance in the 21st
       Century: Japan's Gradual Transformation* (2008) 154.
191   Kenichi Osugi, 'Stagnant Japan? – Why Outside (Independent) Directors have been Rare in Japanese
       Companies' in Shishido (ed.), *Enterprise Law: Contracts, Markets and Laws in the US and Japan* (2014).
       Compare also, on the 'community firm', J Buchanan et al., *Hedge Fund Activism in Japan* (CUP, 2012).
       Pointing to cultural and institutional elements limiting transformations to Japanese corporate governance
       more generally, see Caslav Pejovic, 'Japanese corporate governance: Behind legal norms' (2011) 29
       Penn State International Law Review 483.
192   See the database of Japan Exchange Group <www.jpx.co.jp/english/listing/cg-search/index.html>.

argued for before the amendments.[193] However, in a broader context considering other concurrent reforms, a shift towards the monitoring model may now be irreversible.

First, the 2014 amendments modified the definition of 'outside' director or auditor to exclude managers and employees of parent and sibling companies, while stopping short of excluding other 'grey' outsiders such as employees of the firm's main bank. Second, the amendments required listed companies with statutory auditors to disclose, at the shareholders' general meeting, the reasons for choosing not to appoint outside directors (unless they have, voluntarily, appointed one or more outside directors). The 2015 Corporate Governance Code declared that the board must 'promote sustainable corporate growth and the increase of corporate value over the mid- to long-term' and that the roles of the board include 'effective oversight of directors and the management from an independent and objective standpoint' (General Principle 4). The Code consequently urges listed companies to appoint at least two independent directors (or explain why not). It even goes so far as to suggest appointing at least one-third independent directors in view of the industry, company size, business characteristics, organisational structure and other circumstances, and lays down a roadmap for doing so (Principle 4.8). The reference to 'independent' and not 'outside' director is intentional, apparently excluding the 'grey' outsiders (unlike the amended Companies Act), although the Code refrains from defining independence and instead requires each company to establish and disclose criteria (Principle 4.9). The issue of independent directors and the underlying idea of the 'monitoring model' for the board is a typical example of 'gradual transformation' in Japanese corporate governance, produced by the interactions among corporate practice, self-regulation and formal law-making.

12.5.3.3 Directors' duties and derivative actions

Article 355 of the Companies Act, which the Supreme Court of Japan has held as merely clarifying and restating the duty of care provided in Article 254(3) (now Article 330), which incorporated – following German law – the high standard set out in the Civil Code (*zen kan chui gimu*),[194] requires directors to obey all laws, articles of association and resolutions of general shareholders' meetings. The Supreme Court (7 July 2000) has ruled that 'laws' should be interpreted broadly. The Daiwa Bank judgment (Osaka District Court, 20 February 2000) held that it extended to relevant foreign law, namely US law, which had been breached by a locally hired New York employee, causing huge losses to the bank and its shareholders. The judgment also held that the board must establish a system for internal control, with non-executive directors obliged to monitor its effectiveness. (The system of internal control was later codified in the Financial Products and Exchange Act, colloquially known as J-SOX regulation, in effect since 2008.)[195]

---

193   Bruce Aronson, 'The Olympus scandal and corporate governance reform: Can Japan find a middle ground between the board monitoring model and management model?' (2012) 30 *Pacific Basin Law Journal* 93.

194   Towa Niimura, 'Case No. 31' in Moritz Bälz et al. (eds), *Business Law in Japan – Cases and Comments* (Kluwer, 2012) 331.

195   Zenichi Shishido and Sadakazu Osaki, 'Reverse Engineering SOX versus J-SOX: A Lesson in Legislative Policy' in Shishido (ed.), *Enterprise Law: Contracts, Markets and Laws in the US and Japan* (2014) 349–66.

The emergence of derivative suits in Japan since the 1990s has been even more striking, enlivening and interacting with these directors' duties. The issue was highlighted by the 80 billion yen awarded at first instance in the Daiwa Bank case, although a 250-million yen settlement was reached during the appeal.[196] The US-style derivative suit mechanism, though introduced in the 1950 reform, had long been dormant. Shareholder plaintiffs typically had to pay lawyers an up-front fee, and even if successful, remained liable for further 'success fees' beyond what the court might find 'reasonable'. Regarding court costs, they also faced the 'loser pays' rule that is standard in civil litigation in Japan and, most importantly, had to pay significant amounts upon filing; these were based on the amount claimed. Courts liberally construed a provision, modelled on Californian law, allowing defendants to seek security for costs if it was credible that the suit was brought in bad faith, and could also invoke the 'abuse of rights' doctrine. Only plaintiffs holding at least 10 per cent of shares (3 per cent after 1993) could access company financial information, through rights to examine its books or (only upon showing cause) to appoint an inspector.

Suits burgeoned after the Code was amended in mid-1993, primarily to fix the court filing fee at the flat rate of 8200 yen by deeming derivative actions to be non-property claims (now Article 847(6) of the Companies Act).[197] Yet some statistical analysis of suits filed between 1993 and 1999 found very low success rates and quite limited settlements for plaintiffs, as well as negligible indirect benefits reflected in share price 'event studies' – not unlike findings from the US. Curtis Milhaupt and Mark West therefore conclude that suits persist primarily because of various financial advantages to Japanese lawyers. But they also acknowledge some influence from (a) non-monetary motives for some plaintiffs, (b) piggybacking on information disclosure ensuing from white-collar crime prosecutions, (c) proliferating professional indemnity insurance (although settlements remain few and low), and (d) new-generation *sokaiya*.[198] In contrast, subsequent empirical analysis presents persuasive evidence against the 'rational attorney' explanation, and instead emphasises non-monetary motives and various heuristics as driving these lawsuits.[199]

Tomotaka Fujita identifies other empirical work suggesting that the 1993 reform may have enhanced the monitoring of misbehaving managers, but ultimately finds the evidence ambiguous, particularly as other major changes in the management liability regime

---

196   See generally Bruce Aronson, 'Reconsidering the importance of law in Japanese corporate governance: Evidence from the Daiwa Bank shareholder derivative case' (2003) 36 *Cornell International Law Journal* 11.

197   Derivative suits pending in District and High Courts rose from 86 by the end of 1993 to around 200 in 1997: Tomotaka Fujita, 'Transformation of the Management Liability Regime in Japan in the Wake of the 1993 Revision' in Hideki Kanda et al. (eds), *Transforming Corporate Governance in East Asia* (Routledge, 2008) 17.

198   Milhaupt and West, *Economic Organizations and Corporate Governance in Japan* (2004) 22–37. For more on the (arguably diminishing) roles of *sokaiya* as well as Japanese organised crime more generally see Fujita, 'Transformation of the Management Liability Regime in Japan in the Wake of the 1993 Revision' in Kanda et al. (eds), *Transforming Corporate Governance in East Asia* (2008) 109–78; and Matt Nichol, 'Japanese corporate governance and the market for corporate information disclosure: What is the role of private rights enforcement?' (2013) 27 *Australian Journal of Corporate Law* 262.

199   Masafumi Nakahigashi and Dan Puchniak, 'Land of Rising Derivative Action: Revisiting Irrationality to Understand Japan's Unreluctant Shareholder Litigant' in Dan Puchniak et al. (eds), *The Derivative Action in Asia* (CUP, 2012) 128.

followed.[200] One set of changes, originally introduced in 2001 by the reform to the Commercial Code, focused on procedural rules in derivative actions themselves, elaborating a procedure by which the company could intervene and assist director defendants. In particular, the statutory auditor(s) (in a company with nomination and other committees, a member of the audit committee; in a company with audit and supervisory committees, a member of the audit and supervisory committee) must decide within 60 days of a request from shareholders whether or not to sue, and provide written reasons for not suing (see Articles 386(2), 399–7(1) and 408(1) read together with 847(3) of the Companies Act).

Such changes in procedural rules tie into another set of developments: transformations in the substantive law on directors' duties. In particular, a Japanese version of the 'business judgment rule' has become more prominent since the late 1980s. Japanese courts do check that the substance of directors' decisions was not markedly inappropriate or not based on detailed fact findings, even if they find no problems with the decision-making or information-gathering processes in general. But increasingly, judgments begin by expressly referring to the rule and proclaiming limited scope for reviewing substantive business judgments, before examining and ruling on the facts. Finally, the Supreme Court affirmed the rule in its judgment of 15 July 2010, by denying the liability of directors with regard to restructuring of the corporate group after finding that the procedure for decision-making involved nothing inappropriate and that the decision itself was not grossly unreasonable.[201] In addition, the Companies Act now applies negligence-based rather than strict liability regarding illegal distributions or self-dealing.

Fujita concludes that the 1993 change to the filing fee issue and the rapid growth of derivative suits pose problems for path-dependence theory (including his own earlier work with Hideki Kanda), which had predicted change only where complementarities with other rules had been weak, or where strong complementarities could be overturned through comprehensive reforms in extraordinary political circumstances. He now suggests that where strong complementarities do exist and persist, narrow reform will lead to further changes to the overall system – like the more recent sets of changes to Japan's management liability regime.[202]

Interestingly, the legislature took a step further in 2014. The amended Companies Act allowed shareholders of the parent company to pursue liability of the subsidiary's director if the parent company owns all the outstanding shares of the subsidiary (which means that there is no minority shareholder who might raise a derivative suit) and the book value of the subsidiary exceeds 20 per cent of the parent company's total assets. This 'multi-layered derivative suit' could, if only to a limited extent, enlarge directors' liability exposure. Overall,

---

200   Fujita, 'Transformation of the Management Liability Regime in Japan in the Wake of the 1993 Revision' in Kanda et al. (eds), *Transforming Corporate Governance in East Asia* (2008) 15.

201   Puchniak and Nakahigashi, 'Case No. 21' in Bälz et al. (eds), *Business Law in Japan – Cases and Comments* (2012) 215. Mitsuhiro Kamiya and Tokutaka Ito, 'Corporate Governance at the Coalface: Comparing Japan's Complex Case Law on Hostile Takeovers and Defensive Measures' in Nottage et al. (eds), *Corporate Governance in the 21st Century* (2008) 178; Luke Nottage et al., 'Introduction' in Nottage et al. (eds), *Corporate Governance in the 21st Century* (2008) 1; Luke Nottage, *The Politics of Japan's New Takeover Guidelines*, East Asia Forum (31 August 2008) <www.eastasiaforum.org/2008/08/31/the-politics-of-japans-new-takeovers-guidelines>.

202   Fujita, 'Transformation of the Management Liability Regime in Japan in the Wake of the 1993 Revision' in Kanda et al. (eds), *Transforming Corporate Governance in East Asia* (2008) 15.

therefore, Japan's 'gradual transformation' seems not to be straightforward: instead it shifts backwards and forwards.

12.5.4 Shareholder versus bank finance

12.5.4.1 Overview

Greater choice of governance form and enhanced minority shareholder protections such as derivative suit mechanisms were aimed at expanding capital-raising from shareholders. This consolidated a trend that had accelerated since the 1980s, as companies turned to bond and share markets. It also acknowledged the growing role of foreign investors, holding around 20 per cent of TSE-listed shares by the early 2000s, compared to just 4 per cent in 1990. Shareholder finance also became crucial as banks accumulated huge, non-performing loan portfolios and a credit crunch persisted throughout Japan's 'lost decade' and into the early 2000s. Relatedly, corporate law was liberalised to allow directors to issue share purchase warrants with a call option (share options, or *shinkabu yoyaku-ken*: Article 236(1)(7)). It provides management with flexibility to raise capital from equity market investors.

12.5.4.2 Takeover regulation

Hostile takeovers had been very rare in post-war Japan due to other means of monitoring incumbent managers: *keiretsu* or broader cross-shareholding relationships, main banks, stable core employees and informal relationships with the economic ministries. However, Milhaupt and Pistor argue that these and other economic institutions came under prolonged stress from the 1990s on, leading to great controversy surrounding the February 2005 bid aimed at a Fuji Television subsidiary (NBS) by internet firm Livedoor. Led by maverick entrepreneur Horie, the bid pitted the new against the old. It also arose in the context of growing concern about increased foreign investment in Japan, facilitated by new entrants to deregulated financial markets – illustrated by Lehman Brothers' financing of Horie's bid.[203]

When the target's board issued *shinkabu yoyaku-ken* warrants to Fuji that would dilute this stake, Livedoor invoked a provision in the 2001 Code amendments that allowed injunctions if such warrants were 'substantially unfair'. All three levels of the courts enjoined NBS in March 2005, extending earlier case law that had interpreted the issuance of actual shares (to 'white knights' or the like) as not unfair if its 'primary purpose' was to raise capital rather than entrench the management against hostile bidders.[204] But the courts recognised exceptions for specified 'abusive motives' by the bidder that would clearly harm other shareholder interests (such as 'greenmail' or 'scorched earth' policies), provided the measures were proportionate.[205]

---

203   Curtis Milhaupt and Katharina Pistor, *Law & Capitalism* (University of Chicago Press, 2008). Livedoor also aggressively used the legal framework, circumventing tender-offer rules through a securities law loophole. For a detailed analysis, see Tomotaka Fujita, 'The takeover regulation in Japan: Peculiar developments in the mandatory offer rule' (2011) 3 *UT (University of Tokyo) Soft Law Review* 24.

204   For details on that case law, based on Code Article 280–10 (effectively restated in Article 210 of the Companies Act), see Tomotaka Fujita, 'Case No. 29' in Bälz et al. (eds), *Business Law in Japan – Cases and Comments* (2012) 313. See also Souichirou Kozuka, 'Recent developments in takeover law: Changes in business practices meet decade-old rule' (2006) 22 *Journal of Japanese Law* 5.

205   Milhaupt and Pistor, *Law & Capitalism* (2008) 90–8.

Milhaupt and Pistor join other commentators in highlighting strong parallels with Delaware case law on similar 'poison pills' decided in the 1980s. The influence of US law is even more apparent in the first report of METI's Corporate Value Study Group, established in September 2004 to clarify whether and how Japan's new legislative provisions could be used to provide defensive measures against takeovers. The report was released on 27 May 2005, with significant additions to the Summary Outline (published on 7 March, shortly before the first Livedoor judgment). But one professor who served on that Group instead points out that the (non-binding but influential) guidelines agreed between METI and Ministry of Justice (MoJ), also on 27 May:

> had virtually no trace of Delaware rules and developed native legal thoughts instead. In the beginning, the Guidelines indicated three fundamental principles:
>
> 1. adoption, activation, and abolition of the defensive plan shall be made for maintaining or improving corporate value and eventually shareholders' collective interests;
> 2. a defensive plan shall disclose its purpose, contents, etc. when it is adopted and be dependent on the rational will of shareholders; and
> 3. a defensive plan shall be allowed only when it is necessary and proper to prevent [inadequate] takeovers. (brackets in original)[206]

Subsequently, the guidelines issued various legal structures for rights plans and the legal procedures for adopting them. The guidelines did not mention what constituted an appropriate standard that would help adjudicate a target board's activation of a defensive plan during a control contest. This was probably because the authority to interpret statutes is vested only with the judiciary. Compared to the Delaware rules, the METI Report – and to a larger extent the guidelines – laid greater emphasis on shareholders' power to adopt and/or abolish a defensive plan.

This 'emphasis on shareholders' power' was developed in the controversial Supreme Court ruling in the 2007 Bulldog Sauce case. It replaced approval of the shareholders with a determination that the bidder would harm the shareholders' collective interests if it successfully acquired control of the target company.[207] The Corporate Value Study Group published another report the following year, attempting a modest rollback by pointing to the possibility that excessive emphasis on shareholders' approval would encourage inefficient (re-)building of cross-shareholding.[208]

---

206 Osugi, 'Transplanting Poison Pills in Foreign Soil' in Kanda et al. (eds), *Transforming Corporate Governance in East Asia* (2008) 39. Oda, *Japanese Law* (2009) 265 also notes parallels to German law's 'balance of powers doctrine' in the context of the primary purpose rule.

207 See also Buchanan et al., *Hedge Fund Activism in Japan* (2012); Hiroshi Oda, 'Case No. 30' in Bälz et al. (eds), *Business Law in Japan – Cases and Comments* (2012) 323; Kamiya and Ito, 'Corporate Governance at the Coalface: Comparing Japan's Complex Case Law on Hostile Takeovers and Defensive Measures' in Nottage et al. (eds), *Corporate Governance in the 21st Century: Japan's Gradual Transformation* (2008) 178–96. Milhaupt argues that such emphasis on shareholders' power has given Japanese directors incentives to re-establish ties with stable shareholders (i.e. rebuild cross-shareholdings) rather than introduce independent directors. See Curtis Milhaupt, 'Takeover Law and Managerial Incentives in the United States and Japan' in Shishido (ed.), *Enterprise Law: Contracts, Markets and Laws in the US and Japan* (2014) 177–90.

208 See Hideki Kanda, 'Takeover defenses and the role of law in Japan' (2010) 2 *UT Soft Law Review* 2. The English translation of the 2008 Report is in the same issue at 91.

The METI/MoJ guidelines' framework has also affected the 'advance warning' poison pills that many listed companies jumped at after the Livedoor judgment.[209] These generally require the bidder to present an acquisition plan and other information, and to give the target shareholders time to assess the bid and decide whether or not to have directors seek out 'white knights'. They usually also provide for directors to deploy defensive tactics such as share warranty issuance, discriminating against a non-compliant bidder. Such schemes were mostly set up with shareholder approval and were accompanied by some type of independent committee to advise the directors, although the final say for triggering the activation of the pill was reserved for the board. Such an independent committee is expected to judge whether or not the bidder is abusive and the bid will be detrimental to corporate value. These features were adopted pursuant to the TSE's strong suggestions that listed companies should take into account (1) transparency, (2) the effect of their actions on secondary markets and (3) shareholder rights. John Armour et al. therefore consider that the 'TSE's listing rules and policy statements have become the de facto mandatory rules governing takeover defenses for Japanese listed companies.'[210]

In 2007, Kanda had already observed that, regarding defensive measures against takeovers, 'the scope of permitted discretion of a target board seems much narrower in Japan than in the US'.[211] Indeed, the Japanese rules seem more consistent with many substantive rules under Anglo-Australian law. There are even some parallels between the emergence of guidelines and the way Takeovers Panels in the UK and Australia issue guidance notes for market participants and observers. One difference between these panels and the system in Japan is that these panels (more informal in the UK than Australia) also issue the binding rulings in takeover disputes – not regular courts. Another is that poison pills per se – as opposed to other measures that can also impede takeovers – are effectively outlawed altogether in Australia and the UK through a combination of panel decisions, listing rules and directors' fiduciary duties.[212]

Thus Japan continues to develop its own hybrid regime.[213] As Milhaupt and Pistor point out, taking Delaware law as a major starting point, rather than the UK's City Code on Takeovers and Mergers (the Code)[214] requirements for 'strict neutrality' from target managers and hence shareholder approval of defensive measures, promised a system more protective of those

---

209 Gaku Ishiwata et al., 'Japanese legal structure for corporate acquisition: Analyses and prospects (panel discussion)' (2010) 2 *UT Soft Law Review* 44–9.

210 John Armour et al., 'The evolution of hostile takeover regimes in developed and emerging markets: An analytical framework' (2011) 52 *Harvard International Law Journal* 219. See also Hideki Kanda, 'What Shapes Corporate Law in Japan?' in Kanda et al. (eds), *Transforming Corporate Governance in East Asia* (2008) 63–6.

211 Hideki Kanda, 'Hostile Takeovers, Defenses and the Role of Law: A Japanese Perspective' (Draft Paper, 10 July 2007) 9 <www.kdi.re.kr/upload/8213/2-2.pdf>.

212 Luke Nottage, 'Perspectives and Approaches: A Framework for Comparing Japanese Corporate Governance' in Nottage et al. (eds), *Corporate Governance in the 21st Century* (2008) 21 (referring especially to the respective studies of Emma Armson and Jennifer Hill).

213 Puchniak and Nakahigashi also argue that the Japanese rules are not identical with either the UK rules or US (Delaware) law: Dan W Puchniak and Masafumi Nakahigashi, 'The Enigma of Hostile Takeovers in Japan: Bidder Beware', NUS Law Working Paper No. 2016/008 (2016) <https://papers.ssrn.com/sol3/papers.cfm?abstract_id=2830286>.

214 See <www.thetakeoverpanel.org.uk/wp-content/uploads/2008/11/code.pdf>.

managers and thus more politically acceptable. It also offered a new business opportunity to US law firms and financial advisers, as well as elite Japanese lawyers who have increasingly had US law training.[215]

Partly due to the Global Financial Crisis that began a year after the Supreme Court's ruling in the Bulldog Sauce case (see above),[216] the takeover rush in Japan waned as quickly as it had developed. No significant case over a hostile takeover has subsequently been brought before Japan's highest court. Reflecting the perception that the threat of being targeted by a hostile bidder is lessening, the number of companies adopting defensive measures started to gradually decline from 2009. The requirement in the 2015 Corporate Governance Code not to adopt a defensive measure to entrench incumbent management (Principle 1.5) will further discourage listed companies from maintaining such a measure. As of January 2017, of the 3541 companies listed on Tokyo and Osaka Stock Exchanges, only 445 are equipped with a defensive measure.[217]

Still, Dan Puchniak may be overstating his case for *de minimus* change and impact in objecting to those who have already proclaimed a more drastic reconfiguration.[218] The concept of corporate value, whatever that means,[219] has now been widely accepted among blue-chip companies; the TSE even inaugurated in 2012 an 'award for improving corporate value'. A gradual transformation therefore seems underway in this field as well.

As noted, mergers and acquisitions burgeoned after the late 1990s, and now include a considerable proportion involving foreign acquirers.[220] Although the confrontational activities of some hedge funds failed to gain strong support in Japan, they reinforced the gradual changes that Japanese companies were already going through. Less confrontational shareholder activism also achieved more success, indicating a move 'in the direction of a model of engagement based on dialogue and possibly partnership between active shareholders and the boards of targets'.[221]

---

215   Milhaupt and Pistor, *Law & Capitalism* (2008) 99–100. They also remark that at least one-third of the (original) Corporate Value Study Group's members had extensive exposure to Delaware corporate law. However, unlike in Delaware, the relationship between the judiciary and the non-judiciary rulemaking bodies (the Corporate Value Study Group at METI) has been more 'symbiotic' in Japan. See Armour et al., 'The Evolution of Hostile Takeover Regimes in Developed and Emerging Markets' (2011) 264. See also Stephen Givens, 'Looking through the wrong end of the telescope: The Japanese judicial response to Steel Partners, Murakami, and more' (2011) 88 *Washington University Law Review* 1571.

216   See also generally Buchanan et al., *Hedge Fund Activism in Japan* (2012).

217   See the database of Japan Exchange Group <www.jpx.co.jp/english/listing/cg-search/index.html>.

218   Dan Puchniak, 'Delusions of hostility: The marginal role of hostile takeovers in Japanese corporate governance remains unchanged' (2009) 28 *Journal of Japanese Law* 89.

219   The term is often used ambiguously. See Etsuro Kuronuma, 'Corporate Director's Liabilities Towards Shareholders' in Harald Baum (ed.), *Germany and Japan: A Legal Dialogue Between Two Economies* (Carl Heymanns, 2012) 52–3.

220   The takeovers story also needs to be read in the context of other evidence that managers are placing greater weight on shareholder interests: see even the recent work by Ronald Dore and more cited in Nottage, 'Perspectives and Approaches' in Nottage et al. (eds), *Corporate Governance in the 21st Century* (2008) 21.

221   Buchanan et al., *Hedge Fund Activism in Japan* (2012) 304–10. Also arguing that a market for corporate control in a 'hybrid Americanised version' has emerged in Japan, see Enrico Colcera, *The Market for Corporate Control in Japan* (Springer, 2007).

12.5.4.3 New firms in the IPO market

Those affected by corporate law in Japan have not been just large public companies. Beginning in the early 2000s, after the changes in industrial structure during the 'lost decade', the government (especially METI) has attempted to facilitate the creation of new venture businesses. The securities exchanges created new markets for initial public offerings (IPOs) by young businesses, such as the TSE's MOTHERS. The *Companies Act of 2005* also then emphasised the scope for negotiations between a venture business and investors or financiers. The requirement of minimum paid-in capital was abolished and permitted classes of share were diversified.[222] Now, under Articles 107 and 108 of the Act, there may be classes with different rights regarding, for example:

- distribution of surplus or residual assets;
- rights of a shareholder to require companies to acquire the shares ('shares with a put option');
- rights of the company to acquire the shares ('shares with a call option', with the acquisition price payable in other classes of shares, bonds etc);
- a veto for the class regarding certain corporate actions ('golden shares'); and
- rights of a class to appoint directors or auditors (except for public companies and 'Companies with Committees': Article 347).

Such diversity enables, in particular, closely held newer firms and joint ventures to reflect negotiations between investors and management.

Japan's 'venture boom' arrived soon after these new provisions were enacted. Some of the new businesses grew to be leading forces of the Japanese economy, such as one online business company (DeNA) which was established in 1999, made an IPO in 2005 and purchased a baseball team in 2011. However, others failed to continue growing after making their IPOs and started to consider capital restructuring. That often raised conflicts between controlling shareholders aligned with the managers (often the founders of the company) and the minority shareholders that purchased the shares after the IPO.

Conflict typically becomes apparent when managers decide to go private and launch management buyouts (MBOs) (often with private equity financing, at least before the Global Financial Crisis). While the data shows that MBOs on average generate higher premiums for shareholders than other takeover bids, jurists have been quick to point out that managers in these situations have an incentive to take actions diminishing the market price. On 13 December 2006, amendments to the securities law required bidders to disclose any written evaluation from third parties that had influenced the tender-offer price. METI 'Guidelines on Increasing Corporate Value and Ensuring Regulatory Compliance in the Context of MBOs', released in September 2007 under the chairmanship of the ubiquitous Professor Kanda, also emphasised the need for an appropriate price (for example, through longer tender-offer periods or avoiding 'no shop' agreements between the bidders and the company). They further recommended means for promoting fairness in the target company's processes for evaluating the

---

222   Matsui, 'Corporate Governance and Closely-held Companies in Japan: The Untold Story' in Nottage et al. (eds), *Corporate Governance in the 21st Century* (2008) 108.

offer, including obtaining independent advice about the process and reports from third parties about price.[223] The Guidelines appear to have influenced the concurring opinion of Justice Tahara in the Supreme Court's judgment in the *Rex Holdings* minority squeeze-out case (29 May 2009), as both emphasise transparency and appropriate valuation.[224]

The 2014 Companies Act amendments aim to enhance transparency in the process of acquiring the entire class of shares by the decision of the qualified majority, which is the device used (and often abused) in the second stage of MBOs to squeeze out the minority shareholders. The amendments also add shareholder injunctions as a remedy against an abusive call of the entire class of shares. They also envisage a short-form procedure for squeeze-outs, with sufficient disclosure and remedies of injunction and annulment by the court. The legislature apparently hopes that the new procedure will be utilised for decent cash-outs, rather than the oft-abused call of the entire share class.

The second type of oppression, apart from squeeze-outs, that the failing venture business typically engages in vis-à-vis its minority shareholders is to issue a large number of new shares to a third party that has privately negotiated with the incumbent management. The post-war Commercial Code gave large discretionary powers to the directors in the issuing of new shares; absent a contest over control, management enjoyed full freedom as long as the issuance price was not unfairly low (which is unlikely to be the case in a young venture failing to grow). The 2014 amendments note that a change in the controlling shareholder, even involving agreement with the incumbent managers, will affect the minority shareholders. It requires approval of the shareholders' general meeting by qualified majority, if the voting rights that the new controlling shareholder will end up with would be more than double the total amount of outstanding voting rights (including the voting rights on the newly issued shares). The 2015 Corporate Governance Code echoes this by requiring that 'capital policy that results in the change of control or in significant dilution', such as share offerings and management buy-outs, should be examined in terms of both necessity and procedures, and be accompanied by sufficient explanation to shareholders (Principle 1.6).

12.5.4.4 Main banks

Central to post-war bank finance in Japan has been the 'main bank', the primary lender and provider of many other services to a firm. A firm would disclose information extensively to its main bank, usually assisted by the bank becoming a major shareholder (albeit subject to a 5 per cent statutory limit), and with retiring bank officials often becoming its senior finance officers. If the borrower nonetheless got into difficulties, the main bank would try to tide it over or restructure it through new loans or refinancing, guaranteeing other firm debts or sending officials to assist as managers or directors. However, this constituted an *implicit* promise to

---

223   Soichiro Fujiwara and Masanori Tsujikawa, 'New Procedures for Fair MBO', *International Financial Law Review* (2008) <www.iflr.com/Article/1984140/News>.

224   Squeeze-outs for cash became possible under the new Companies Act, but subject to court appraisal if the price is unfair. The Supreme Court upheld the Tokyo High Court's judgment (of 12 September 2008) that the offer price should be around 120% of the six-month average market price before the tender offer. See Maki Saito, 'Case No. 28' in Bälz et al. (eds), *Business Law in Japan – Cases and Comments* (2012) 299. More generally, on the remedies for minority shareholders in MBO situations, see Wataru Tanaka, 'Going private and the role of courts: A comparison of Delaware and Japan' (2011) 3 *UT Soft Law Review* 12.

attempt a rescue instead of a reliance on often higher-priority security interests. It depended on main banks being able to take a long-term view of the relationship, which would include possibilities for more extensive profits on other business provided to the firm. Main bank rescue, and its role as an important monitoring mechanism for corporate governance of firms in Japan, also relied on borrowers retaining quite extensive intangible value (beyond the book value of assets). Another premise was an informal relationship between the main bank and the government, promising long-term advantages (for example, more approvals for new branches) if main banks supported economic stability by informally supporting firms with desirable long-term prospects.[225]

Logically, the system is challenged by deregulation of financial markets, particularly since the 1990s, and a general shift towards more arm's-length relationships, including the government now occasionally allowing banks to fail, and a more accessible formal bankruptcy law regime.[226] But it is still worth debating the precise impact of these changes, now and in the foreseeable future, on main banks. Experienced Tokyo practitioners have argued, for example, that 'in the last 10 years this main bank system has seriously declined'.[227] On the other hand, although large firms continued to lessen ties with banks in favour of bond issuance over the 1990s, smaller listed firms continued borrowing, and firms already carrying high levels of bank debt relied on main banks for a growing proportion of their debt. Empirical studies suggest that the banking crisis did not result in a credit crunch, at least among firms with strong growth opportunities, while:

> debt did play a disciplinary role in the 1990s, but a high concentration of loans with the main bank tended to delay the corporate restructuring. This suggests that banks facing financial distress engaged in soft-budgeting and followed an 'evergreen' policy of rolling over loans.[228]

A more recent empirical study based on a commercial database (covering nearly 400,000 listed and non-listed companies) also reports that companies with only one main bank and heavily reliant on borrowing from that main bank have lower cash holdings than companies that have no or two or more main banks and are less reliant on bank borrowing.[229] Another study based on the same database points out that concentration on main banks is larger with regard to

---

225   Paul Sheard, 'Main Banks and the Governance of Financial Distress' in Masahiko Aoki and Hugh Patrick (eds), *The Japanese Main Bank System* (OUP, 1994) 142.

226   See generally Kent Anderson et al., 'Insolvency Law' in Luke Nottage (ed.) *CCH Japan Business Law Guide: Looseleaf* (CCH Asia, 2009).

227   Robert Grondine and Brian Strawn, 'Corporate and Project Finance' in McAlinn (ed.), *Japanese Business Law* (2007) 519.

228   Gregory Jackson and Hideaki Miyajima, 'Introduction: The Diversity and Change of Corporate Governance in Japan' in Aoki et al. (eds), *Corporate Governance in Japan: Institutional Change and Organizational Diversity* (2007) 1, 18–19, summarising Yasuhiro Arikawa and Hideaki Miyajima, 'Relationship Banking in Post-Bubble Japan: Coexistence of Soft- and Hard-Budget Constraints' (ibid. 51) and referring to Masahiko Aoki, *Towards a Comparative Institutional Analysis* (MIT Press, 2001). See also Noriyuki Yanagawa, 'The Rise of Bank-Related Corporate Revival Funds' in Aoki et al. (eds), *Corporate Governance in Japan: Institutional Change and Organizational Diversity* (2007) 205.

229   Kazuo Ogawa, 'What do Cash Holdings Tell us About Bank-Firm Relationship? A Case Study of Japanese Firms' in Tsutomu Watanabe et al. (eds), *The Economics of Interfirm Networks* (Springer, 2015) 215–35.

settlement (time deposit) than financing (borrowing).[230] The current role of main banks seems to be more focused on liquidity than on financing.

Puchniak therefore seems to overstate the position when he suggests that 'the main bank system dramatically increased its influence over the Japanese economy throughout the lost decade'.[231] But he convincingly shows how evergreening and perverse lending (to more poorly performing borrowers, usually with no interest-rate premium) were facilitated particularly through main banks, and thanks to a new informal government policy regime aimed at supporting the banking system overall. That analysis certainly undercuts Yoshiro Miwa and Mark Ramseyer, who assert that market forces and arm's-length enforceable rules are all that matter in the Japanese economy, thus rendering the main bank system another pernicious 'myth' about Japanese corporate governance.[232]

The continued but arguably diminished existence of the main bank system is also consistent with a broader revival of cross-shareholding and stable shareholding in recent years, also involving banks. But that is also now viewed with greater scepticism, as evidenced by the Corporate Governance Code's requirement to disclose the company's cross-shareholdings policy (Principle 1.4). Overall, therefore, it does seem that:

> corporate finance in Japan is increasingly characterized by the co-existence of two different, and in ways competing logics – a pattern rather similar to Germany or Italy ... While the main bank system has not disappeared, it has been institutionally displaced and its scope limited to a more specific niche segment of firms than in the past.[233]

While the main bank may be capable of monitoring the management of the company, some of the other creditors lack capacity to monitor and therefore have to resort to legal measures. Trade creditors or non-bank lenders of a small 'mom-and-pop' company often utilise a provision on directors' liability for damages that the third party incurs if the director acted intentionally or with gross negligence (Article 429) to collect its claim from the director, by arguing that the company was managed recklessly. The duty of non-executive (often nominal) directors to monitor the managing director has been useful in such litigation.[234] The doctrine of

---

230 Arito Ono et al., 'A New Look at Bank-Firm Relationships and the Use of Collateral in Japan: Evidence from Teikoku Databank Data' in Watanabe et al. (eds), *The Economics of Interfirm Networks* (2015) 191–214.

231 Dan W Puchniak, 'Perverse Rescue in the Lost Decade: Main Banks in the Post-Bubble Era' in Nottage et al. (eds), *Corporate Governance in the 21st Century* (2008) 106.

232 See, for example, Yoshiro Miwa and J Mark Ramseyer, *The Fable of the Keiretsu: Urban Legends of the Japanese Economy* (University of Chicago Press, 2006); see also Curtis J Milhaupt, 'On the (fleeting) existence of the main bank system and other Japanese economic institutions' (2002) 27 *Law and Social Inquiry* 425 and the further critiques by Dan Puchniak, 'A skeptic's guide to Miwa and Ramseyer's: "The Fable of the Keiretsu"' (2007) 24 *Journal of Japanese Law* 230 as well as Craig Freedman and Luke Nottage, *You say tomato, I say tomahto, let's call the whole thing off* (Centre for Japanese Economic Studies, Macquarie University, Sydney, 2006).

233 Jackson and Miyajima, 'Introduction: The Diversity and Change of Corporate Governance in Japan' in Aoki et al. (eds), *Corporate Governance in Japan: Institutional Change and Organizational Diversity* (2007) 19.

234 Shishido, 'Problems of the closely held corporation' (1990) 347–8. Other than trade creditors, the provision can be used by the victims of mass torts (in consumer fraud, for example) or, as in a recent case (Osaka High Court, 25 May 2011, upheld on appeal), by an employee overworked to death due to inappropriate labour management.

'piercing the corporate veil', adopted by the Supreme Court in 1969, is also useful for similar types of creditors.[235] As company split-ups have become a popular tool for addressing impartial satisfaction of some of the creditors, the legislature in 2014 allowed the creditor of the parent company to hold the subsidiary liable (to the extent of the value of the asset transferred) if the latter was created fraudulently by a company split. These developments again show that the interaction of the judiciary and the legislature generates gradual but irreversible transformation. It also hints at an uncultivated but interesting subject for researchers into Japanese law: the law on the protection of corporate creditors.[236]

12.5.5 Core employees

Significant 'displacement' is also evident in Japan's lifelong employment system, although the transformation is arguably even more gradual. The implicit promise of a job for life – combined with related practices such as seniority-based wages and promotions, cooperative industrial relations, entry-level hiring followed by job rotations (and hence generalist or firm-specific skills training), and a relatively weak external labour market – have long been identified as a further key monitoring mechanism distinguishing post-war corporate governance in Japan. Indeed, Puchniak argues that career management incentivised by lifelong employment was essential to efficient main bank monitoring, making the system the most important element for trust in the market and hence the expansion (and dispersion) of shareholdings in post-war Japan.[237] Yet there has been a range of new strategies since the 1990s:

> [P]romoting 'shareholder value' may provoke a number of conflicts with employees around the issues of corporate disclosure, business portfolios, equity-oriented perform-ance targets and the use of performance-oriented pay, such as stock options. Shareholder value creates pressure for more market responsiveness in employment through reducing excess employment, divesting from less profitable businesses and decentralizing bargain-ing to match wages with productivity.[238]

Nonetheless, the *ideal* of the lifelong employment system has always been more important than its reality. By the 1990s, lifelong employment already applied:

> to less than 10 percent of all corporate entities, barely 20 percent of all workers, and only 8 percent of working women. Even if lifelong employment *were* dying, this is hardly a strong basis [from which] to project major shifts in Japan's corporate governance system or capitalist configuration. Nor, given the enormous powers management have to command

---

235   See, for example, the judgment translated in Yukio Yanagida et al. (eds), *Law and Investment in Japan: Cases and Material* (Harvard University Press, 2000) 336–41.

236   For a preliminary study of trade creditors, see Hirofumi Uchida et al., *Interfirm Relationships and Trade Credit in Japan* (Springer, 2015).

237   Dan Puchniak, 'In the Company We Trust: Japanese Lifetime Employment Redefines Why Law Matters' (manuscript available on request from the National University of Singapore, Faculty of Law). See also Toru Kitagawa 'Complementarity among the Abusive Dismissal Rule, Company Community Norms, and an Illiquid External Labor Market' in Shishido (ed), *Enterprise Law: Contracts, Markets and Laws in the US and Japan* (2014) 70–80.

238   Jackson and Miyajima, 'Introduction: The Diversity and Change of Corporate Governance in Japan' in Aoki et al. (eds), *Corporate Governance in Japan* (2007) 24–5.

labour even for core workers, is lifelong employment the radical departure from at-will employment that is said to define more liberal market economies.[239]

In predicting the employment system's likely future influence, moreover, Leon Wolff stresses the importance of determining its main causes. A cultural theory seems implausible in light of the limited reach of lifelong employment in practice. The neo-classical market theory sketched by Miwa and Ramseyer asserts that the system survives only due to strict restraints on dismissals developed quite creatively by Japanese courts, but that development occurred *after* the system emerged, which was soon after World War II. The 'institutional complementarities' theory emphasised by Aoki and others struggles to explain how those institutions arose, why they became associated with (seemingly endogenous) economic stagnation over the 1990s, and other dark sides to the lifelong employment system (for example, for women).[240]

For example, data from the late 1990s mostly show only small or statistically insignificant shifts towards more market-oriented human resource management (HRM) practices, as predicted by a model emphasising complementarities with more readily observed transformations in corporate finance.[241] Data from 2003 indicate that such practices – especially major shifts towards completely or partly merit-based pay – are not significantly impacted by foreign ownership, but are impacted by more outside board executives or by managerial stock options becoming a form of remuneration.[242] Overall, 'changes in corporate governance have affected the role of employees but, in fact, some elements of Japanese-style HRM may be compatible with a wider range of corporate governance institutions than suggested by some theories of complementarity'.[243]

The best explanation for the lifelong employment system therefore appears to be that it was a political decision: a post-war agreement among at least some major interest groups established a 'flexicurity' mode of regulation – balancing security of tenure with extensive flexibility in the working conditions that managers can impose. Tensions are apparent within this mode of regulation, but until it becomes subject to a new political settlement, the main trend is an intensification of flexicurity for a diminishing core group.[244] In 2003 the legislature confirmed the overarching 'abuse of rights' doctrine (Article 16 of the Labour Contract Act). Employment security for women has been promoted through amendments to the Equal Employment Opportunity Law (1997 and 2006) and the Child Care and Family Care Leave Law (2004), while whistleblowers gained protection through a new statute in 2004. In exchange, since the late 1990s flexibility has been enhanced to allow managers to (re)direct labour even more

---

239   Leon Wolff, 'The Death of Lifelong Employment in Japan?' in Nottage et al. (eds), *Corporate Governance in the 21st Century* (2008) 53, 60.

240   Ibid. 61–4.

241   Masahiro Abe and Takeo Hoshi, 'Corporate Finance and Human Resource Management in Japan' in Aoki et al. (eds), *Corporate Governance in Japan* (2007) 257.

242   Gregory Jackson, 'Employment Adjustment and Distributional Conflict in Japanese Firms' in Aoki et al. (eds), *Corporate Governance in Japan* (2007) 282. From a more qualitative case-study perspective, however, see George Olcott, *Conflict and Change: Foreign Ownership and the Japanese Firm* (CUP, 2009).

243   Jackson and Miyajima, 'Introduction: The Diversity and Change of Corporate Governance in Japan' in Aoki et al. (eds), *Corporate Governance in Japan* (2007) 26.

244   Wolff, 'The Death of Lifelong Employment in Japan?' in Nottage et al. (eds), *Corporate Governance in the 21st Century* (2008) 53, 74.

efficiently, including lifting the prohibition on holding companies and amendments facilitating corporate spinoffs and the outsourcing of labour.[245]

It remains to be seen how Japan will respond to the present tensions in the lifelong employment system. The current Abe administration appears to seek greater flexibility in the labour market, which will result in further displacement (or even 'exhaustion'[246]) of the system in favour of HRM practices that are more focused on the external labour market, and to encourage women and other marginalised workforces to take greater responsibility at the same time. However (in)significant the lifelong employment system used to be, it is indisputable that the system is changing – once again, gradually.

12.5.6 Conclusions on Japan

This brief introduction to two still-important and quite distinctive monitoring mechanisms in Japanese corporate governance – the lifelong employment system and main banks – has reminded us that government policy and the vicissitudes of politics are as important as economics and the broader social or cultural context in explaining and predicting trajectories. This is particularly evident from the Company Law Reform Act passed on 20 June 2014. Nonetheless, a gradual transformation seems to be underway even along these two dimensions, in parallel with more significant changes in the relationship between shareholders and directors or managers.

Among those who have examined Japanese corporate governance from the 1970s, some (such as Haley) still emphasise continuities – especially in relation to employment relationships – and indeed tend to acclaim such features of Japan's more coordinated market economy. A very few revisionists (notably Ramseyer) instead now proclaim Japan to be already a liberal market economy, just like the US, and that it has been so for many decades. A much younger generation of foreign commentators who have tracked developments since the late 1990s (such as Kelemen and Sibbitt) tend to perceive drastic shifts towards 'Americanisation' and LMEs. But some (especially Puchniak) now see very little significant change, though they are impressed by, for example, the renewed economic growth enjoyed by Japan over 2002–07 – albeit belatedly, at low rates, and thanks to considerable pump-priming.

A third group (including Kozuka, Nottage, Wolff and Anderson as well as Deakin, Whittaker and their co-researchers, and Milhaupt especially over recent years) have tracked aspects

---

245   Ibid. 75–8. See also Luke Nottage and Leon Wolff, 'Corporate Governance and Law Reform in Japan: From the Lost Decade to the End of History?' in Rene Haak and Markus Pudelko (eds), *Japanese Management: In Search of a New Balance between Continuity and Change* (Palgrave Macmillan, 2005) 133. However, whistleblower protection can serve to promote broader shareholder interests or the interests of consumers – more prominent than outside stakeholders these days – rather than conventional insiders.

246   Wolff, 'The Death of Lifelong Employment in Japan?' in Nottage et al. (eds), *Corporate Governance in the 21st Century* (2008) 53 agrees with Nottage, 'Perspectives and Approaches: A Framework for Comparing Japanese Corporate Governance' (ibid. 21) that 'exhaustion' (the slow withering away of lifelong employment) may be the closest description from among the five modes of 'gradual transformation' proposed by Wolfgang Streeck and Kathleen Ann Thelen, 'Introduction' in Wolfgang Streeck and Kathleen Ann Thelen (eds), *Beyond Continuity: Institutional Change in Advanced Political Economies* (OUP, 2005) 1, although 'displacement' (the emergence of hitherto subordinate institutions and norms) is also a possible description given the declining core of lifelong employees.

of Japanese corporate governance from the 1980s and tend to see significant but gradual transformations. They see growing diversification – of processes generating law and policy (especially over the last decade), of comparative law borrowings or adaptations, and of corporate practices and norms – as a key feature. This growing and admittedly sometimes messy diversity,[247] especially in organisational forms, may itself be evidence of a move from coordinated market economy-type institutions (demanding high levels of mutual investment in relationship-specific assets) towards liberal market economy-type institutions.[248] But Japan's experience confirms some indications from other jurisdictions that such changes do not necessarily occur at the same rates along all dimensions – and the political aspects reinforce the possibility of such complexity, even of some 'reverse course'. Evidence from two surveys (in 2003) indicates considerable support even among managers for employees being as important as shareholders and for a stakeholder model of corporate governance more generally.[249] Japan, therefore, continues to offer a fascinating reference point in comparative corporate governance debates.

12.6 China

12.6.1 Introduction

Corporate law and corporate governance in China have been influenced by a variety of factors: the traditional dominance of the state-owned sector and the continuing ideological commitment by policy-makers to the 'socialist market economy'; the decision by the government to attract foreign capital by encouraging the establishment of foreign investment companies (that is, incorporated joint ventures with Chinese and foreign investment and wholly foreign-owned companies which are established under and subject to specialist Chinese foreign investment laws) in China and subsequent decisions to encourage the growth of a corporatised private sector in order to develop the Chinese economy; and the use of the stockmarkets, in China and overseas, to capitalise and expand first state-owned and then private Chinese companies.

The development of corporate governance in China is an ongoing process, in the course of which Chinese decision-makers have adopted and adjusted ideas from a wide range of legal systems in order to construct a corporate and securities legal system that will be appropriate and effective in China. Corporate governance is an issue for Chinese entities of all kinds. It became an issue for foreign and domestic investors in listed companies inside and outside

---

247   See the critique of Japan's current diversity in generating rules for 'Cross-Border M&A', by Kenichi Osugi and Yoshihisa Hayakawa in their 'Keynote Report' for Toshiyuki Kono et al., '*Koko ga Hen da yo – Nihon-Ho* [Is Japanese law a strange law?]' (2009) 28 *Journal of Japanese Law* 242–3. For a more positive appraisal of hybridisation more generally in contemporary Japanese corporate governance, see Simon Deakin and D Hugh Whittaker (eds), *Corporate Governance and Managerial Reform in Japan* (OUP, 2009).

248   Mari Sako, 'Organizational Diversity and Institutional Change: Evidence from Financial and Labor Markets in Japan', in Aoki et al. (eds), *Corporate Governance in Japan* (2007) 399; and more generally Jackson and Miyajima, 'Introduction: The Diversity and Change of Corporate Governance in Japan' in Aoki et al. (eds), *Corporate Governance in Japan* (2007) 1. Cf, for example, Sanford M Jacoby, *The Embedded Corporation: Corporate Governance and Employment Relations in Japan and the United States* (Princeton University Press, 2005).

249   Wolff, 'The Death of Lifelong Employment in Japan?' in Nottage et al. (eds), *Corporate Governance in the 21st Century* (2008) 53, 70.

China because of government-backed efforts by state-owned enterprises to raise money on Chinese and international markets while still maintaining control over the listed entity. Indeed, the controlling shareholder (generally state-owned) diverting assets and business advantages from its listed subsidiaries continues to be a major issue in Chinese corporate governance. Corporate governance issues are also raised by the need to provide adequate protection both for investors in listed companies and for shareholders in the fast-growing private sector. It is also an issue for the state-owned sector: the Chinese Government has stated its commitment to the principle of corporate social responsibility (CSR) and better standards of corporate governance and internal controls for state-owned enterprises and their subsidiaries.[250]

A varied system of controls and controllers has been developed in China to deal with these different types of entities and issues. Although principles of corporate governance imposed on listed companies have attracted much of the scholarly attention devoted to corporate governance in China, and are obviously important indicators of how Chinese regulators approach the various issues, it is important not to overlook other Chinese companies and corporate entities, the regulation of which also causes concern for investors, other stakeholders and regulators.

This part starts by examining the legislative structure in China, particularly as it relates to corporate governance. It looks briefly at the different kinds of corporate entity in China and the different issues which they present, and examines the regulatory structure relating to corporate governance. It then considers the main issues for corporate governance in China, the varying methods that have been used to resolve these issues and the consequent development of corporate governance principles and rules, and concludes with a brief discussion of the efficacy of these methods and likely future developments.

12.6.2 Government and legislation

The National People's Congress (NPC) is the premier law-making authority in China. Only the NPC (and its Standing Committee when the NPC itself is not in session) can make laws (*falü*),[251] and the Constitution, as implemented by the Law on Legislation,[252] makes clear that the right to legislate on important issues such as criminal law, deprivation of a citizen's right to liberty, civil institutions and fundamental economic systems (including tax, customs, finance and trade) belongs solely to the NPC or its Standing Committee. Thus the principal items of legislation in the corporate area – the Company Law, the Securities Law,[253] the Securities

---

250   National People's Congress, *Company Law of the People's Republic of China* (2005, amended 2003, 2005, and 2013, effective 1 March 2014) (Company Law) Art 5: 'When engaging in business activities, a company must abide by laws and administrative regulations, observe social morals and business ethics, act in good faith, accept supervision by the government and the public, and bear social responsibilities'; Ministry of Finance, China Securities Regulatory Commission, National Audit Office and China Insurance Regulatory Commission, *Basic Internal Control Norms for Enterprises* (2008); State-Owned Assets Supervision and Administration Commission of the State Council (SASAC), *Interim Measures for Administration of Overseas State-owned Property Rights of Central Enterprises* (2011) Art 3.
251   National People's Congress, *Constitution of the People's Republic of China* (1982, amended 1988, 1993, 1999 and 2004) Art 62.
252   Standing Committee of the National People's Congress, *Law on Legislation of the People's Republic of China* (2000) (Law on Legislation) Art 8.
253   National People's Congress, *Securities Law of the People's Republic of China* (1998, amended 2004, 2005 and 2013) (Securities Law).

Investment Fund Law[254] and the Criminal Law[255] – were all passed by the NPC or its Standing Committee. The State Council, the highest level of executive authority in China, under the Premier, may issue administration regulations (*xingzheng guiding*) on important matters.[256] These often include detailed implementing regulations fleshing out areas in the laws which are vague or which are felt to need further elaboration. This extends to the Securities Law and the Company Law, under which the State Council retains a wide range of authority, including the power to issue regulations relating to such matters as independent directors for listed companies and the classes of shares which a company may issue.[257]

China is not a federal system. Thus although provincial, municipal and other lower-level governments have the power to issue rules and decrees, the provinces and other governments do not have distinct areas of responsibility which belong specifically to them. They do have the power to issue implementing legislation and legislation on 'local matters'.[258] The central government has maintained strict control over companies and securities law and regulation in China and local legislation has been permitted only to have limited impact in these areas.[259] Although Shenzhen and Shanghai introduced experimental corporate law regimes in the early 1990s in order to underpin their budding stockmarkets,[260] these rules were replaced in their entirety by the Company Law and the national corporate law regime in 1993.

The various ministries, administrations and other bodies under the State Council can also issue rules, decrees and other instruments with legislative impact.[261] The State Administration for Industry and Commerce (the SAIC) is the company registration body,[262] and its rules and activities have some impact on corporate issues such as governance. The State-owned Assets Supervision and Administration Commission of the State Council (SASAC) is responsible for centrally administered state-owned enterprises and plays a regulatory, legislative and supervisory role in relation to those enterprises.[263] Similar state-owned assets administrations play a role in relation to locally administered state-owned enterprises. The primary regulator for listed companies is the China Securities Regulatory Commission (CSRC), another body under the State Council.[264] The CSRC is a prolific issuer of rules and documents in the securities area and

---

254   Standing Committee of the National People's Congress, *Law on Securities Investment Funds* (2003, amended 2012).

255   National People's Congress, *Criminal Law of the People's Republic of China* (1997, amended 1990, 2001 (twice), 2002, 2005, 2006, 2009 and 2011).

256   Law on Legislation Ch 3.

257   Company Law Arts 122 and 131 (123 and 132). The 2014 amendments have changed the numbering of articles in the Company Law from Art 29. All references are therefore to the new numbers, with the previous numbers (which are often cross-referenced in other pieces of legislation and in the academic literature) in parentheses.

258   Law on Legislation Ch 4.

259   Standing Committee of the National People's Congress, *Law on Administrative Licensing of the People's Republic of China* (2003) Art 15, for example, makes very clear that local authorities may not impose pre-qualification or other requirements on entities seeking to incorporate under the Company Law.

260   See Vivienne Bath, 'Introducing the Limited Company' (1993) 1–2 *China Business Review* 50–4.

261   Law on Legislation Art 71.

262   See <www.saic.gov.cn>.

263   See <www.sasac.gov.cn>.

264   The primary activities of the CSRC are described in China Securities Regulatory Commission, *CSRC Annual Report 2012* (English version) <www.csrc.gov.cn/pub/csrc_en/about/annual/201307/P020130716403852654782.pdf>.

has been the major force in regulating for and implementing a comprehensive corporate governance system in China.[265] In the corporate governance area, a significant step recognising the importance of corporate governance standards was taken with the issuing in 2001 of the *Code of Corporate Governance for Listed Companies in China*,[266] which was followed by the *Guidelines on Introducing the Independent Director System in Listed Companies*.[267] The importance of corporate governance was reiterated by the CSRC in 2005[268] and again in 2007 with the issuing of the *Notice on Matters concerning Carrying out a Special Campaign to Strengthen the Corporate Governance of Listed Companies*,[269] followed in 2008 by the jointly issued *Basic Internal Control Norms for Enterprises*.[270] The CSRC has also issued a number of regulations on important corporate governance issues such as rights of shareholders of public companies[271] and requirements for public disclosure of information.[272] Most recently, in order to regularise the financing of medium and small enterprises, the CSRC has issued rules to regulate the activities of non-listed public companies which also deal with questions of corporate governance.[273]

The China Insurance Regulatory Commission has primary responsibility for insurance companies, and the China Banking Regulatory Commission, under the People's Bank of China, has primary responsibility for banks and financial institutions. These two commissions thus have regulatory responsibility in relation to the structure and activities of insurance and financial companies.[274] The Supreme People's Court and the Supreme People's Procuratorate also issue opinions, interpretations and regulations on the application of particular laws or the handling of particular matters by the courts, which can have significant practical effects on litigation.[275] The Listing Rules and other requirements of stock exchanges on which the securities of Chinese companies are listed and traded, both inside and outside China, also have a major impact on corporate governance and the behaviour of listed companies.

---

265   Nicholas Howson, 'Quack corporate governance as traditional Chinese medicine – The Securities Regulation cannibalization of China's Corporate Law and a State Regulator's battle against party state political economic power' (2014) 2 *Seattle University Law Review* 667–716 <http://ssrn.com/abstract= 2279264>.

266   CSRC, *Code of Corporate Governance for Listed Companies in China* (2001).

267   CSRC, *Guidelines on Introducing the Independent Director System in Listed Companies* (2001).

268   State Council, *Circular on Approving and Forwarding the Opinions of the China Securities Regulatory Commission on Improving the Quality of Listed Companies* (2005).

269   CSRC, *Notice on Matters Concerning Carrying Out a Special Campaign to Strengthen the Corporate Governance of Listed Companies* (2007).

270   Ministry of Finance, China Securities Regulatory Commission, National Audit Office and China Insurance Regulatory Commission, *Basic Internal Control Norms for Enterprises* (2008).

271   For example, CSRC, *Several Regulations concerning Reinforcement of Protection of Public Shareholders' Rights and Interests* (2004); CSRC, *Rules on Shareholders' Meetings of Listed Companies* (2006).

272   CSRC, *Measures on Administration of Information Disclosure of Listed Companies* (2007).

273   CSRC, *Measures for the Supervision and Administration of Non-listed Public Companies* (2013). Art 1 defines a non-listed public company as a joint stock company which has more than 200 shareholders after the transfer or issues of shares where shares are publicly sold to the general public.

274   See, for example, People's Bank of China, *Guidelines on Corporate Governance of Commercial Banks* (2013, replacing previous legislation on this subject); CSRC, *Guidelines on Corporate Governance of Financing Guarantee Companies* (2010); China Insurance Regulatory Commission, *Administrative Measures for Controlling Shareholders of Insurance Companies* (2012).

275   See Wallace Wen-Yeu Wang and Jian-Lin Chan, 'Reforming China's securities civil actions: Lessons from PSLRA reform in the US and government-sanctioned non-profit enforcement in Taiwan' (2008) 21 *Columbia Journal of Asian Law* 115.

Although the Communist Party plays a 'leadership' role under the Preamble to the Constitution and is given no formal legislative role, it has a continuing and highly significant role in administration, implementation of policies and policy-making itself. Article 19 of the Company Law provides for the establishment of a party organisation in each company set up under the law.[276] This influence may extend to the issuing of influential policy documents but also operates through less obvious and less formal means. Government officials derive power from their positions in the Communist Party, and the official government hierarchy may not therefore provide an accurate indication of where power actually lies.[277] In the corporate governance context, the fact that there may be a dual organisation within the entity, or that important decisions about managers and management are actually made by the Party organisation rather than the board of directors, has the potential to affect the effectiveness of measures taken (based on the structures set out in the Company Law) to improve internal management structures and activities.[278]

12.6.3 Corporate entities

There are three main categories of companies and corporate entities in China: state-owned enterprises and companies, foreign investment enterprises, and privately owned companies.

12.6.3.1 State-owned enterprises

Until the introduction of foreign investment enterprises in 1979, the Chinese economy was dominated by state-owned enterprises, which were under the control of various parts of government and administered as a part of government rather than as autonomous corporate entities.[279] The dominance of the state-owned enterprise in the economy was not, however, accompanied by an equivalent level of efficiency or productivity.[280] The 1980s and 1990s saw a concerted effort by government to reform state-owned enterprises by a combination of means, including reorganisation, mergers and takeovers, and privatisation.

An important step in terms of the formalisation of the structure of state-owned enterprises was the promulgation of the 1988 *Law on Industrial Enterprises owned by the Whole People*.[281]

---

276   See also Sonja Opper and Sylvia Schwaag-Serger, 'Institutional analysis of legal change: The case of corporate governance in China' (2008) 26 *Washington University Journal of Law & Policy* 245, 253, 261.

277   For a more detailed discussion, see Nicholas Howson, 'China's Restructured Commercial Banks: *Nomenklatura* Accountability Serving Corporate Governance Reform?' in Min Zhu, Jinqing Cai and Martha Avery (eds), *China's Emerging Financial Markets: Challenges and Global Impact* (John Wiley & Sons (Asia), 2009) Ch 8.

278   Yihong Zhang, 'Party's long shadow: The party's control and influence over the corporate governance of Chinese listed companies' (2012) 23(10) *International Company and Commercial Law Review (ICCLR)* 323.

279   Chao Xi, *Corporate Governance and Legal Reform in China* (Wildy, Simmonds and Hill Publishing, 2009) 6 *et seq*.

280   Wallace Wen-Yeu Wang, 'Reforming state enterprises in China: The case for redefining enterprise operating rights' (1992) 6 *Journal of Chinese Law* 92.

281   National People's Congress, *Law of the People's Republic of China on Industrial Enterprises owned by the Whole People* (1988, amended 2009). See also Xi, *Corporate Governance and Legal Reform in China* (2009) 6–35, for a description of the historical development of management and structure of state-owned enterprises.

This Law gave substantial power to the factory director, who was appointed by the relevant level of government or elected by the workers,[282] acted as the legal representative of the enterprise[283] and assumed overall responsibility for the work of the enterprise.[284] He (or she) acted as the chief executive officer of the enterprise with the assistance of a management committee chaired by the factory manager and composed of employee representatives and 'leading persons' in charge of parts of the enterprise (Article 47). There was no board of directors or shareholder structure required in the Law even though the *Chinese-Foreign Equity Joint Venture Law*,[285] which required a board of directors and a chairman, had been in effect since 1979. The role of the relevant local government in relation to the enterprise was to formulate policies, coordinate relationships with other enterprises, provide information, protect state assets and improve public facilities (Article 56). The Communist Party was guaranteed a role in the enterprise: to supervise the implementation of the guiding principles of the Party.[286]

This was succeeded by a policy requiring the corporatisation of state-owned enterprises.[287] Thus the Company Law contains a chapter[288] which deals specifically with wholly state-owned companies. In addition, many listed companies have substantial amounts of state ownership. There are still, however, a number of kinds of state-owned enterprises in existence, the corporate organisation of which varies depending on the history of the entity. An examination of the list of centrally controlled state-owned enterprises administered by the SASAC, for example, shows that many of these, although considered to be companies with limited liability, have not been converted into corporations complying with the Company Law.[289] The SASAC is focused on corporate governance issues.

The fundamental principles relating to the management and governance of state-owned enterprises are reflected in the Enterprise State Assets Law, which states that the relevant entity of the state should act as the investor in state-owned enterprises 'in accordance with the separation of government from enterprises, the separation of public administrative functions from the functions of state-owned asset investors and respecting the lawful and independent operation of enterprises'.[290] The Enterprise State Assets Law also requires that state-owned enterprises both accept social responsibilities and establish corporate governance systems.[291] Although the number of state-owned enterprises in China has been reduced since 1979 by a concerted policy of privatisations, planned bankruptcies and consolidations, the state-owned sector continues to be strong. Government policy is to continue state dominance of ownership

---

282   *Law on Industrial Enterprises owned by the Whole People* (1988) Art 44.
283   Ibid. Art 45.
284   Ibid. Art 7.
285   National People's Congress, *Law of the People's Republic of China on Chinese-Foreign Equity Joint Ventures* (1979, amended 1990 and 2001).
286   Ibid. Art 8.
287   Cindy Schipani and Junhai Liu, 'Corporate governance in China: Then and now' (2002) 1(1) *Columbia Business Law Review* 22–8.
288   Company Law Arts 65–71.
289   See list of central enterprises on SASAC website <www.sasac.gov.cn/n1180/n1226/n2425/index.html>.
290   National People's Congress, *Enterprise State-owned Assets Law of the People's Republic of China* (2008) Art 6.
291   Ibid. Art 17.

and control in certain sectors[292] and to protect 'state assets' generally. The challenge for regulators and companies alike is maintaining the separation of the roles of managers, investors and regulators in entities which are essentially guaranteed a dominant place in the market, and improving the corporate governance regimes within companies which do not have a diverse group of shareholders monitoring the performance of the company and the behaviour of its executives.

12.6.3.2 Foreign investment enterprises

Modern corporate law in China dates from 1979, with the promulgation of the Chinese-Foreign Equity Joint Venture Law. This was followed in 1986 by the Wholly Foreign Owned Enterprise Law[293] and subsequently by the Cooperative (or Contractual) Joint Venture Law.[294] These three laws and their associated implementing regulations, notices, decrees and other subordinate legislation still define the shape of foreign investment enterprises, which generally take the form of Chinese legal persons with limited liability, issuing registered capital rather than shares.[295] It was not until the promulgation of the *General Principles of Civil Law* in 1986,[296] however, that there was a serious attempt to provide a definition of the concept of legal personality. The 1993 Company Law applied to foreign investment enterprises in a limited fashion. After the promulgation of the amendments to the Company Law in 2005 a concerted attempt was made by the government department in charge of company registration, the SAIC, to bring foreign investment enterprises into line with wholly Chinese-owned companies and to apply the corporate structure rules (such as the requirement to have a supervisory board) set out in the Company Law to foreign investment enterprises.[297] The foreign investment laws and regulations set out only basic rules relating to corporate management structures, and do not contain detailed provisions relating to corporate governance. The investors can, however, impose corporate governance standards themselves through their constituent documents or company policies and codes. The structure of joint venture companies in particular does not fit neatly into the management structure contemplated by the Company Law, since joint ventures are not required to have meetings of shareholders. Instead, directors are appointed by the parties and can only be removed by the party that appointed them.[298] An advantage offered by the joint venture structure, however, is that the joint venture contract sets out in considerable detail what the relationship between the investors is and how it should operate. The minority

---

292   General Office of the State Council, State-Owned Assets Supervision and Administration Commission of the State Council, *Circular of the General Office of the State Council concerning Transfer of the Opinions of the SASAC on Guidance for Promotion of Adjustment of State-owned Assets and Restructuring of State-owned Enterprises* (2006).

293   National People's Congress, *Law of the People's Republic on Foreign Capital Enterprises* (1986, amended 2000) 12.6.3.3 The private sector and companies under the Company Law.

294   National People's Congress, *Law of the People's Republic of China on Chinese-Foreign Cooperative Joint Ventures* (1988, amended 2000).

295   See, however, State Council, *Measures for the Administration of the Establishment of Partnership Enterprises in the Territory of China by Foreign Enterprises or Individuals* (2009).

296   National People's Congress, *General Principles of Civil Law* (1986, amended 2009) Ch 3.

297   See Vivienne Bath, 'The Company Law and Foreign Investment Enterprises in China – Parallel systems of Chinese-Foreign regulation' (2007) 30 *University of New South Wales (UNSW) Law Journal* 774.

298   Equity Joint Venture Law Art 6.

party in a joint venture therefore has considerable scope, when it negotiates the joint venture contract, to incorporate the protections it considers necessary.

12.6.3.3 The private sector and companies under the Company Law

Non-state-owned entities may take a variety of forms. Although they are generally referred to in this chapter as private entities, they may include investment from a range of investors, including state-owned entities, government interests, private investors and domestic companies owned by foreigners. They may be established under a range of different items of legislation, particularly the Company Law but also the Enterprise Partnership Law and the Sole Proprietorship Enterprise Law.[299] The range of business structures can be seen in the catalogue attached to the *Provisions on Categorising Enterprise Registration*, which lists of types of entity that can be registered with the State Administration for Industry and Commerce. These include various kinds of foreign investment entities – entities with investment from foreign countries (including, for this purpose, investment from Hong Kong, Macao or Taiwan), limited liability companies, joint stock (or share) companies, partnerships, and private entities.[300] Although this discussion focuses on listed and unlisted companies set up under the Company Law, a review of recent Chinese regulation indicates that authorities are aware of the importance of strong corporate governance generally.[301]

Companies set up under the Company Law can be privately owned, partly privately owned or wholly state-owned and can take the form of either limited liability companies or companies which are listed on a Chinese stock exchange or outside China. The number and value of both private and listed companies have grown considerably. In 1990, there were eight listed companies on the Shanghai Stock Exchange with a total market capitalisation of RMB 123.4 billion. In 2012, there were 954 listed companies, with a total market capitalisation of RMB 15.9 trillion.[302] Xinhua, China's state press agency, attributes a 15.8 per cent increase in the number of privately owned enterprises in 2006 to the amendments to the Company Law, which facilitated the establishment of small private companies.[303]

The Company Law was passed in 1993 and was followed by the Securities Law in 1998. Both laws were significantly amended in 2005 in order to provide a higher degree of protection to shareholders, particularly minority shareholders. In addition, a substantial number of regulations, notices, decrees and codes of conduct have also been issued, largely by the State Council and the CSRC, in order to improve the system and the standards of corporate governance in Chinese companies. These apply mainly to listed companies, although the Basic Internal Control Norms for Enterprises are also aimed at large and medium-size unlisted enterprises.

---

299 National People's Congress, *Enterprise Partnership Law of the People's Republic of China* (1997, amended 2006); Standing Committee of the National People's Congress, *Sole Proprietorship Enterprise Law* (1999); State Council, *Regulations on Individual Businesses* (2011).

300 National Bureau of Statistics; State Administration of Industry and Commerce (2011).

301 See, for example, Ministry of Commerce, *Notice on the Pilot Launch of Commercial Factoring* (2012), which requires, among other things, that the investor in a commercial factoring company have a sound corporate governance structure and internal risk control system (Art 2(2)).

302 Shanghai Stock Exchange, *Fact Book 2013* <http://english.sse.com.cn/aboutsse/publications/factbook/c/factbook_us2013.pdf>.

303 Xinhua, 'New Corporate Law Drives Growth of China's Private Sector in 2006' (2007) <http://english.peopledaily.com.cn/200704/24/eng20070424_369117.html>.

The Company Law provides for a three-tier structure of management: a shareholders' meeting, a board of directors and a supervisory board. The role and functions of these three levels of management are prescribed in some detail in the Company Law itself. Each company must have Articles of Association, and some leeway is provided in the Company Law for the Articles to modify the relationship between the shareholders. The main difference between a limited liability company and a joint stock company (or company limited by shares) is that a limited liability company has registered capital (that is, a specified sum of capital which may be paid in cash and/or in kind) and a joint stock company has shares. Only joint stock companies can be listed – a limited liability company or other entity must be converted into a joint stock company if the shareholders wish to conduct a public offering.[304] Most features of the management and corporate governance regime for the two types of companies, as set out in the Company Law, are, however, identical.

The vast majority of foreign investment enterprises with legal personality are limited liability companies. Corporatised state-owned companies are either limited liability companies or, if listed, joint stock companies. There are, however, some differences between the form of these companies and a standard limited liability company under the Company Law. A joint venture, as noted above, does not have a shareholders' meeting; a private company with only one shareholder does not hold a shareholders' meeting but makes decisions by written memorandum (Article 61 (62)). A wholly state-owned company with one investor effectively does not hold shareholders' meetings either, and may delegate a large amount of its authority to the board of directors, although the consent of the relevant government authority acting as investor is required for certain actions.[305]

Generally, however, the shareholders' meeting is the organ of authority of a company (Articles 36 (37) and 98 (99)) and has, at least in theory, power over most of the major management issues of a company, including the ability to approve business plans and budgets, elect and remove directors and supervisors, approve dividend distribution plans, review and approve reports of the board of directors and the supervisory board, change the corporate plan of the company and so on (Articles 37 (38) and 99 (100)).[306] Decisions of the shareholders are generally taken by a majority vote, with the exception of decisions on amendments to the Articles of Association, changes to the registered capital and decisions on merger, division, dissolution or change of the corporate form of the company, for which a two-thirds vote of the shareholders is required (Articles 43 (44) and 103 (104)). In theory, Chinese companies issue only one class of shares. In practice, there have been many types of shares: state shares (held by the state); legal person shares (often held by legal persons in which the state had a controlling interest); employee shares; A shares (listed on Chinese exchanges and available for sale only to Chinese investors, with some exceptions); B shares (listed on Chinese exchanges and traded in foreign exchange); H shares (traded on the Hong Kong Stock

---

304   Company Law Arts 9, 95 (96).

305   Ibid. Art 66 (67).

306   See Charles Zhen Qu, 'The representative power of the shareholders' general meeting under Chinese law' (2008) 17 *Pacific Rim Law & Policy Journal* 300–2. See also Sandra Kister, 'China's share-structure reform: An opportunity to move beyond practical solutions to practical problems' (2007) 45 *Columbia Journal of Transnational Law* 312.

Exchange) and so on.[307] In 2013, the State Council announced the pilot launch of preference shares.[308] With the exception of preference shares, voting rights of shareholders are, in principle, equal (Articles 48 (49) and 103 (104)).

The board of directors is elected by the shareholders and acts as the overall management organ of the company. It is responsible for developing the budget and plans presented to the shareholders, establishing management structure and appointing and dismissing the managers, convening shareholders' meetings and so on (Articles 46 (47) and 108 (109)).

The supervisory board (or supervisor, in the case of a small company) has essentially a monitoring role. The supervisors who make up the board should include employee representatives as well as supervisors elected by the shareholders (Articles 51 (52) and 117 (118)). The supervisory board is responsible for examining the financial affairs of the company, supervising the activities of the directors and requiring them to rectify wrongful actions – and, if necessary, instituting litigation to protect the shareholders (Articles 53 (54) and 118 (119)).

In addition to these three tiers, a limited liability company, a wholly state-owned company and a joint stock company should each have a manager whose powers are also specified in the Company Law (although subject to the provisions of the Articles of Association), including responsibility for operations and production and internal management (Articles 49 (50), 68 (69) and 113 (114)).

The two main Chinese stockmarkets are the Shanghai Stock Exchange and the Shenzhen Stock Exchange.[309] Shares of some Chinese companies are also listed outside China, principally on the Stock Exchange of Hong Kong.

12.6.4 Corporate governance – issues and resolutions

The main problem relating to Chinese listed companies arises from the number of companies which are listed, but have one principal or controlling shareholder – often the Chinese state in one form or another. Chinese government policy originally promoted the idea of listing on the basis that it would be a useful way of raising additional capital from outside shareholders without giving away significant amounts of control. Companies could not initially list at all without obtaining government approval, and this approval was given to state-owned enterprises which were in need of new capital, rather than to companies with a strong commercial track record and which could attract enthusiastic investors.[310] Investors' enthusiasm for Chinese shares has, however, been reduced somewhat by a series of major scandals, in China and in Hong Kong, relating primarily to the problem of 'tunnelling' – that is, the use by the controlling shareholder of its position to divert cash, assets and business advantages from the listed company to itself – but also relating to fraud, false accounts, faulty disclosure, insider

---

307   Chenxia Shi, 'Protecting investors in China through multiple regulatory mechanisms and effective enforcement' (2007) 24 *Arizona Journal of International and Comparative Law* 455–6.

308   State Council, *Guiding Opinions on the Pilot Launch of Preference Shares* (2013).

309   The CSRC has also established a 'New Third Board' (the NEEQ National Equities Exchange and Quotations) for the transfer of shares of unlisted public companies. China Securities Regulatory Commission, *CSRC Annual Report 2012*, English version, 2 <www.csrc.gov.cn/pub/csrc_en/about/annual/201307/P020130716403852654782.pdf>. See also Appendix 3 to the Report for a list of self-regulatory bodies, including exchanges.

310   Xi, *Corporate Governance and Legal Reform in China* (2009) 42–51.

trading and other forms of market manipulation.[311] Implementing a decision made by the 18th Third Plenary Session of the 18th Central Committee of the Communist Party of China,[312] the CSRC has initiated a program relating to initial public offerings (IPOs) which aims to reform the IPO process by increasing the market orientation of IPOs, particularly pricing, strengthening the duties of good faith of issuers, and controlling shareholders and other relevant parties by, among other things, strengthening undertakings and improving transparency.[313]

Chao Xi[314] comments that the two major problems in corporate governance can be summarised as conflicts between the owners of a company and the managers, who may misuse their power to disadvantage the shareholders, and conflict caused by the majority shareholder or shareholders misusing their position to the disadvantage of the minority shareholders. As noted above, in China, it is the second of these – that is, the domination of listed companies by state-owned enterprises – which has been the main problem. China is not, however, free from issues related to management capture. Insider trading and market manipulation were specifically addressed in the 2006 amendments to the Criminal Law, and the 2005 revisions to the Securities Law provided for the establishment of a special fund to protect investors in such circumstances.[315]

The Chinese legislature and regulators (including the stock exchanges) have attempted to deal with issues around corporate governance by a variety of means, including mandating and encouraging the adoption of internal management and governance mechanisms, direct intervention in relation to particular corporate governance issues, public sanctions and education, and administrative and criminal penalties. Although the focus has been on listed companies, private (including foreign) and state-owned companies have also been included in this comprehensive effort to establish a functional corporate governance regime. The following section summarises the methods which have been adopted to deal with corporate governance issues, and the ways in which attempts have been made to enforce them.

12.6.5 Controlling the board of directors and the managers – the supervisory board

As discussed above, Chinese companies under the Company Law have three organisational bodies, with roles and responsibilities allocated under the Company Law. Legislators and regulators have looked at regulating all three levels, as well as the senior managers of companies, in order to improve standards of corporate governance. Article 146 (147) of the

311 Examples include Guangdong Kelon Electrical Holdings Co. (executives accused of fraud and inflating profits, a scandal in which Deloitte also became the subject of an investigation). See Ran Zhang, 'Deloitte faces double trouble in China', *China Daily* (2006) <www.chinadaily.com.cn/bizchina/2006-03/31/content_556998.htm>. See also Hongming Cheng, 'Insider trading in China: The case for the Chinese Securities Regulatory Commission' (2008) 15 *Journal of Financial Crime* 165.
312 Central Committee of the Communist Party of China, *Decision on Several Major Issues on Comprehensively Deepening Reforms* (2013).
313 CSRC, *Opinions on Further Promoting the Reform of the System of Initial Public Offerings* (2013) Art 2. The expression '*chengxin yiwu*' is often translated as 'fiduciary duty', a phrase which carries implications which are not necessarily reflected in Chinese law and practice.
314 Xi, *Corporate Governance and Legal Reform in China* (2009) 51–2.
315 CSRC, *Circular concerning Deepening Study of Criminal Law Amendment (6) by Listed Companies* (2006); Securities Law Art 116.

Company Law (discussed below), which sets out the basic criteria relating to appointment, therefore applies to directors, supervisors and senior managers. Senior managers are defined as the general manager, deputy or vice managers, the financial manager, the secretary of the board of directors (in the case of a listed company) and any other officer specified in the company's Articles of Association (Art 216(1) 217(1)).

The 1993 Company Law envisaged that the supervisory board would play a monitoring and supervisory role in a Chinese company. The supervisory board, which is composed of representatives elected by the shareholders and employee representatives,[316] would investigate the financial affairs of the company, supervise acts of the directors and managers and, if any acts breach laws, regulations or the Articles of Association, or are harmful to the company, order rectification of those acts. The Company Law did not, however, give the supervisory board any power to obtain information or to enforce their decisions.[317]

Under Articles 52 (53) and 53 (54) of the Company Law as amended in 2005, supervisors were given more power – they could investigate the company's financial affairs, supervise the directors and officers and recommend their removal, require a misbehaving officer or director to 'rectify' their misbehaviour, propose that shareholders' meetings be convened and convene them themselves if the directors fail to do so, and initiate litigation against directors for breach of duty if requested to do so by at least 1 per cent of the shareholders. However, supervisors do not have the power to initiate litigation on their own, based on what is in other jurisdictions called the statutory derivative action. In order to fulfil their obligations, supervisors can attend board meetings as non-voting members and conduct investigations (including by hiring outside accounting firms) into the affairs of the company (Article 54 (55)), with all costs and expenses to be paid by the company (Article 56 (57)).

Supervisors are subject to the same requirements as directors and officers of the company in relation to qualification to act as a director (discussed below), and are also required to comply with the law, administrative regulations and the Articles of Association and to compensate the company for any losses due to their failure to do so (Articles 147 (148) and 149 (150)). They may not take bribes or otherwise take advantage of their position and are subject to duties of loyalty (or faithfulness [*zhongshi*]) and diligence in relation to the company (Article 147 (148)), on the same basis as the directors and officers. These terms are not defined, but some assistance in determining their scope can be obtained from the content of the relevant Articles (discussed below).

The 2005 amendments did not change the basic method by which supervisors are selected; nor did they impose any obligation that supervisors be independent of the company or, in particular, of the controlling shareholder (if there is one).[318] There are, however, requirements

---

316   Company Law (as issued in 1993) Arts 52 and 54; Arts 117 and 118. Under the current version of the Company Law, there must be at least three supervisors, except in the case of a small limited liability company. An 'appropriate' number of the supervisors, constituting at least one-third of the total number, as specified in the Articles of Association, must be 'democratically' elected by the employees (Art 52 (53)) and, in the case of a company limited by shares, democratically elected through a general meeting of employee representatives or of employees (Art 117 (118)). In the case of a wholly state-owned company, there must be at least five supervisors, with at least one-third elected by the employees in a general meeting of the employees (Art 70 (71)).

317   Xi, *Corporate Governance and Legal Reform in China* (2009) 151–6.

318   Ibid. 178, on issues of independence of the supervisory board.

in Article 52 (53) and 117 (118) that at least one-third of the supervisors be democratically elected representatives of the workers.[319] In addition, supervisors of joint stock companies, like directors, may be elected on a cumulative voting system (Article 105 (106)) if the company's Articles of Association so provide. If implemented, this provision would give minority shareholders the opportunity to elect supervisors in a number proportionate to their total voting power.[320] Nevertheless, the lack of any requirement that the supervisors be independent is likely to mean that the supervisory board will continue to be a relatively ineffective check upon the powers of the board of directors. Indeed, in relation to listed companies, although the role of the supervisory board continues to be included by regulators as an essential part of a coherent corporate governance regime,[321] more emphasis has been put on improving the board of directors itself than in turning the supervisory board into an effective monitoring and control mechanism. This contrasts with the two-tier structure in Germany, where the supervisory board plays an active role, including appointing and removing, on sufficiently compelling grounds, members of the management board.[322]

Unlisted companies are not required to have independent directors under the Company Law. Monitoring of these companies, therefore, still relies on the supervisory structure, which is required for foreign investment enterprises established from the beginning of 2006,[323] as well as for wholly state-owned companies.[324]

12.6.6 Increasing the duties of directors

The 2005 amendments to the Company Law significantly expanded the duties of directors, supervisors and officers of the company and, for the first time, gave shareholders a direct remedy in relation to breaches of duties by these officers. The 1993 Company Law allowed for the confiscation of unlawful proceeds, punishment of a guilty director or officer by the company or, in extreme cases, criminal prosecution (Articles 214 and 215). It also provided that a director, supervisor or manager who causes loss to the company as a result of breaching

---

319   See Chao Xi, 'In search of an effective monitoring board model: Board reforms and the political economy of Corporate Law in China' (2006) 22 *Connecticut Journal of International Law* 1, 21–2.

320   Art 105 (106) defines cumulative voting as a mechanism whereby each share carries with it one vote for each position of director (or supervisor), with the shareholder having the right to cast all such votes for one person. Voting for employee representatives is regulated by Art 117 (118). See, for example, the proxy form for the 2014 Extraordinary General Meeting of Hisense Kelon Electrical Holdings Company Limited at <www.kelon.com/investor/general/Notice/201311/P020131121687615759224.pdf>, which provides for cumulative voting for the shareholder representatives on the supervisory board of the company.

321   For example, see CSRC, *Notice on Matters concerning Carrying Out a Special Campaign to Strengthen the Corporate Governance of Listed Companies* (2007) Annex.

322   See Jean J du Plessis et al., *German Corporate Governance in International and European Context* (Springer Verlag, 2nd edn, 2012) 22–4 and 145.

323   State Administration for Industry and Commerce, Ministry of Commerce, General Administration of Customs, State Administration of Foreign Exchange, *Opinion on Several Issues on the Application of Laws on the Administration of the Examination and Approval and the Registration of Foreign-Funded Companies* (2006) Art 18. See also Bath, 'The Company Law and Foreign Investment Enterprises in China' (2007).

324   Company Law Art 71. See, however, SASAC, *Rules for Central Enterprises to Support and Cooperate with the Boards of Supervisors in State-owned Enterprises in Contemporaneous Supervision (for Trial Implementation)* (2009).

the Company Law or the company's Articles of Association should compensate the company (Article 63). The weakness in these provisions was that there was no clarification of the way in which the 'company' as an entity should impose punishment on its erring officers, or enforce its claim for compensation. In a case where the director or manager involved in defrauding the company was not acting alone, or was collaborating with a majority shareholder, the minority shareholders did not have adequate remedies under the Company Law to take the appropriate action.

The Company Law now, in Chapter 6, sets out much more concrete provisions relating to the duty of directors, supervisors and officers, and the ways in which action can be taken against infringing parties. Article 146 (147) follows the previous law in setting out the qualifications for directors, supervisors and senior managers. Generally, a person may not serve in such a position, and his or her election to such a position is invalid, if he or she:

- has no or limited capacity for civil acts;[325]
- has a criminal conviction for a crime of dishonesty such as corruption and no more than five years has elapsed since his or her sentence ended;
- held a position within the last three years as director, factory director or manager of an enterprise liquidated in a bankruptcy for which he or she was personally responsible, or of an enterprise which had its business licence revoked for a violation of law for which he or she was responsible; or
- is a person with a comparatively large amount of personal debts which are due but unsettled.[326]

The Company Law does not otherwise provide for the concept of a person being disqualified to serve as a director. It does, however, provide that directors, supervisors and senior officers all have duties to the company in which they serve. These duties are the same for both limited liability companies and joint stock companies. Article 147 (148) requires that directors, supervisors and senior managers comply with the laws, administrative regulations and Articles of Association of the company, and provides that they have in addition duties of fidelity and diligence to the company.[327]

Although the concept of the duties of fidelity (also translated as 'loyalty' or 'good faith') and diligence (*zhongshi yiwu he qinmian yiwu*) are often construed as fiduciary duties, the Chinese system is a civil law system and it is not at all clear that equitable concepts relating to fiduciaries can be imported into these expressions.[328] The law does not attempt to define the exact scope of these duties, although Article 148 (149) sets out a list of actions in which directors are not permitted to engage, ending with the expression 'other acts in breach of his duty of fidelity to the company', and may therefore be construed as setting out a list of actions

---

325   *General Principles of Civil Law.*
326   Note that the Enterprise Bankruptcy Law does not deal with personal bankruptcies. National People's Congress, *Enterprise Bankruptcy Law of the People's Republic of China* (2006).
327   By contrast, Art 33 of the Code of Corporate Governance provides that directors shall 'faithfully, honestly and diligently perform their duties in the best interests of the company and all the shareholders'.
328   See comments on the borrowed concept of 'fiduciary' duties by Donald C Clarke, 'Lost in Translation? Corporate Legal Transplants in China', GWU Law School Public Law Research Paper No. 213 (2006) <https://papers.ssrn.com/abstract=913784>.

which are in breach of the duty of fidelity. These acts focus on financial misbehaviour and revealing business secrets, and include:

- encroaching on the property of the company (Article 147 (148));
- misappropriating funds of the company; depositing company funds in a personal account; lending the funds of the company or providing security over company property for the benefit of a third person without the consent of the shareholders or directors;[329]
- entering into a contract with the company in violation of the Articles of Association of the company or without the consent of the shareholders;
- taking for his or her personal benefit commercial opportunities that belong to the company; and
- taking secret commissions or disclosing the secrets of the company without authorisation.

As a result, it is not clear whether the scope of the duty extends beyond financial misfeasance to, for example, such acts as causing the company to trade while insolvent, or beyond the company to the shareholders themselves. Article 152 (153) gives the shareholders the right to bring action against directors, supervisors or officers who harm the interests of shareholders in violation of the law, administrative regulations or the provisions of Articles of Association. It is not clear, however, how and to what extent this concept of harm to the shareholders extends beyond the more clearly spelled out concept of harm to the company itself.

A major development in the 2005 amendments was the creation of a regime where direct court action can be taken against infringing officers by the supervisors (at the behest of the shareholders) or by the shareholders themselves. Article 149 (150) provides that a director, supervisor or senior manager who violates 'provisions of laws, administrative regulations or the articles of association of the company in the execution of company duties and thereby causes losses to the company' will be liable to pay compensation. Under Article 151 (152), in such a case, shareholders holding at least 1 per cent of the voting rights in the company may require the supervisors – or, if the action complained of was an act of the supervisors, the directors – to take action, and if they fail to do so, the shareholders may take court action themselves 'for the interests of the company'. A shareholder who is directly affected by such a breach may take action in his or her own name under Article 152 (153). The Supreme People's Court, in its Second Interpretation on the Company Law, has extended the right of shareholders to bring a suit under Article 151 (152) to the right to institute an action against members of the liquidation group when the company is in liquidation (Article 23).[330]

Articles 151 (152) and 152 (153) have, not surprisingly, attracted a considerable amount of academic attention, due to their similarity to the Western concept of a derivative action,[331] although the sparse content of the provision has raised a number of significant questions about its practical implications. It should noted that this provision applies to limited liability companies as well as to joint stock companies and therefore offers opportunities to oppressed

---

329   Company Law Art 16 provides that the grant of security for a third-party debt must be authorised by either the board or the shareholders as set out in the Articles of Association.

330   Supreme People's Court, *Provisions of the Supreme People's Court on Some Issues about the Application of the Company Law of the People's Republic of China (II)* (2008) Art 23.

331   Hui Huang, 'The statutory derivative action in China: Critical analysis and recommendations for reform' (2007) 4 *Berkeley Business Law Journal* 227.

minorities in private companies, as well as to shareholders in listed companies.[332] Issues relating to this provision are discussed in more detail below.

12.6.7 Independent directors

The Code of Governance for Listed Companies in China, issued by the CSRC in 2001, provided that listed companies should introduce independent directors to the board (Article 49). This was followed later that year by the *Guidelines for Introducing the Independent Director System in Listed Companies*,[333] which required that by 2003 at least one-third of the directors on the board of a listed company should be independent (Article 1). More than half of the membership of remuneration, audit, nomination and other committees should also be independent, if the listed company has such committees (Article 5(4)). Under the Guidelines, an independent director must have substantial professional work experience (Article 2) and cannot be related to officers of the company or its subsidiaries, shareholders holding 1 per cent or more of the shares of the company or certain shareholders of subsidiaries or persons providing professional services to or holding office in organisations providing services. An independent director cannot be removed without cause unless he or she ceases to be independent (Article 4(5)), and if he or she resigns, he or she must provide an explanation for the resignation to the shareholders and creditors of the company (Article 4(6)). The independent directors are given specific rights and functions, including the right to engage an agency to provide an independent consulting report on major transactions submitted to the director, and to propose that meetings of the shareholders or directors be convened. In the case of a listed company where a management buy-out is proposed, at least one-half of the board of directors must be independent directors, and two-thirds of the independent directors must approve the buy-out proposal before it is submitted to the non-affiliated shareholders of the company for approval.[334] The importance of ensuring that the independent directors are able to carry out their functions of independent review was reiterated by the CSRC in 2007,[335] when it made it clear that a company should review whether or not independent directors had fulfilled their duty of overseeing the operations of the company; whether or not the performance of their functions had been affected by the actions of the principal shareholder; and whether or not an independent director had been improperly removed from office (Annex 2(1)).

---

332   Interestingly, one reported case under Art 152 (153) involves the Chinese party of a Chinese-foreign joint venture taking action against the manager appointed by the foreign party. See Sino-Link Consulting, 'The First Case on Foreign Shareholder Representative Litigation in China' (no date) <www.sinolinkconsulting.com/rizh/html/?774.html>. Huang notes that it is easier for shareholders in a limited liability company to obtain standing to sue under the Company Law (see Huang, 'The statutory derivative action in China' (2007) 236).

333   CSRC, *Guidelines on Introducing the Independent Director System in Listed Companies* (2001).

334   CSRC, *Measures for the Administration on Acquisition of Listed Companies* (2006, amended 2008 and 2012) Art 51. Arts 216(4) and 217(4) of the Company Law provide a broad definition of 'affiliation': the relationship between a controlling shareholder, actual controller, director, supervisor or senior manager of a company with an enterprise under his or her direct or indirect control, and any other relationship that may lead to the transfer of interests in the company.

335   CSRC, *Notice on the Matters concerning Carrying Out a Special Campaign to Strengthen the Corporate Governance of Listed Companies* (2007).

There are a number of stated purposes in requiring a company to have independent directors,[336] including to represent smaller shareholders, to monitor related-party transactions, to act as an independent consultant and adviser and to serve the public interest on the board. Both the desirability of these functions and the extent to which the independent directors serve these purposes can be disputed. Questions have been raised as to the competence and experience of the persons selected as independent directors, and as to their ability to act effectively and independently, and the willingness of the board and its managers to utilise independent directors effectively. The selection of independent directors still seems to be dominated by the majority shareholders through their control of the board of directors and the supervisory board.[337] Studies suggest that the majority of independent directors have tended to be academics and government officials rather than experienced business men and women. In addition, with some exceptions, the independent directors have not fulfilled the expectation that they would be active – and, if necessary, controversial – members of the board of directors. As a result, some commentators have concluded that the effect of independent directors on the performance of listed companies is minimal.[338] The significance of the independent director in the Chinese corporate governance scheme continues to be underlined, however, in recent legislation.[339]

12.6.8 Committees

The Code of Corporate Governance (Articles 52 to 58) provides that the board of directors of a listed company could establish a number of specialist board committees – a corporate strategy committee, an audit committee, a nomination committee, a remuneration and appraisal committee and other special committees.[340] Pursuant to the Guidelines on Independent Directors (Article 5(4)), if such committees are established, independent directors must form more than half of their members. The 2005 Opinions of the China Securities Regulatory Commission on Improving the Quality of Listed Companies[341] provides that a listed company should establish an audit committee and a remuneration and assessment committee, and this is reiterated in the 2007 CSRC *Notice on Matters concerning Carrying Out a Special Campaign to Strengthen the Corporate Governance of Listed Companies*.[342] The *Guidelines for the Application of Internal Control in Enterprises No. 1 – Organisational Structure*[343] provides that

336   See discussion in Donald C Clarke, 'The independent director in Chinese corporate governance' (2006) 31 *Delaware Journal of Corporate Law* 169 *et seq.*
337   Jie Yuan, 'Formal convergence or substantial divergence? Evidence from adoption of the independent director system in China' (2007) 9 *Asian-Pacific Law and Policy Journal* 71.
338   Ibid.
339   See, for example, China Insurance Regulatory Commission, *Administrative Measures for Controlling Shareholders of Insurance Companies* (2012) Art 24; CSRC, *Guidelines on Governing Securities Companies* (2012).
340   This chapter does not discuss the requirements of stock exchanges outside China which may require Chinese companies listed there to establish audit and other committees.
341   See State Council, *Circular of the State Council on Approving and Forwarding the Opinions of the China Securities Regulatory Commission on Improving the Quality of Listed Companies* (2005) Annex, Item 3.
342   CSRC, *Notice on Matters concerning Carrying Out a Special Campaign to Strengthen the Corporate Governance of Listed Companies* (2007).
343   Ministry of Finance (2010).

companies subject to the standard may set up a strategy committee, audit committee, nomination committee, remuneration committee, appraisal committee and other special committees.

Studies on the top 100 Chinese listed companies in 2009 and 2012 suggest that major listed companies in China have made substantial improvements in the establishment of board committees, particularly audit committees. [344]

12.6.9 Controlling shareholders and protection for minority shareholders under the Company Law

The major issue for Chinese listed companies has been the role of the major or controlling shareholder, which is generally, although not always, a Chinese state-owned enterprise.[345] As a consequence, the regulatory authorities, the stock exchanges and the legislature have all focused on the role of the controlling or majority shareholder. The issue of abuse of power by the majority shareholder is not, however, confined to listed companies, and the 2005 amendments to the Company Law placed considerable emphasis on protecting the position of minority shareholders in limited liability companies as well. Thus the Company Law sets out not only provisions of general application but provisions which are specifically designed to provide protection for shareholders in limited liability companies.

Article 21 of the Company Law applies to all companies and forbids controlling shareholders, de facto controlling persons, directors and senior managers of a company from using 'their affiliation' with another enterprise which they control to harm the interests of the company. The concept of affiliation includes a relationship which may lead to the transfer of shares in the company (Article 216 (217)).[346] If they do use their affiliation in such a manner, they are liable to compensate the company. The Second Interpretation of the Company Law[347] (Article 23) places obligations on controlling shareholders or de facto controllers of listed companies in relation to failures to act properly in the liquidation process.

A 'controlling shareholder' is generally a person with 50 per cent of the voting rights, but also includes a person with a substantial interest (Article 216 (217)). A 'de facto controlling person' is defined quite broadly as a person capable of controlling the company through agreements or some other means (Article 216 (217)).

Under Article 20, any shareholder of the company which abuses its 'shareholder rights' to 'harm the interests of the company or other shareholders' is liable to pay compensation to the company or the other shareholders. If it 'abuses the independent status of the company legal person and the limited liability of shareholders' to evade debts and seriously harm the interests

---

344 Centre for Corporate Governance, Chinese Academy of Social Sciences, Centre for Research on Assessment of Leaders, China National School of Administration & Protiviti Consulting, *Corporate Governance Assessment; Summary Report on the Top 100 Chinese Listed Companies for 2009* (2010) <www.complianceweek.com/s/documents/GovAssessChinese.pdf>; Protiviti, *Corporate Governance Assessment on the Top 100 Chinese Listed Companies for 2012* (2013) 19–20 <www .protiviti.com.au/China-en/Documents/CN-en-2012-Corporate-Governance-Survey-Report.pdf>.

345 Protiviti, *Corporate Governance Assessment on the Top 100 Chinese Listed Companies for 2012* (2013) 10.

346 Art 216(4) (217(4)) provides that there is no affiliation between two state-owned enterprises merely by virtue of the fact that the state controls both enterprises.

347 Supreme People's Court, *Provisions of the Supreme People's Court on Some Issues about the Application of the Company Law of the People's Republic of China (II)* (2008).

of the creditors of the company, it may also be jointly liable with the company to the creditors. It seems, however, that together with Article 63 (64), which provides creditors with a remedy where the sole shareholder of a single shareholder company intermingles his or her assets with company assets, an important purpose of this provision is the protection of creditors, not just other shareholders or the company itself. Some clarification in relation to this Article has been provided by the People's Supreme Court Guiding Case 15,[348] where the court held that several affiliated companies which had commingled personnel, business and assets with a third affiliate had thereby lost their independent personalities and were jointly and severally liable for the affiliate's debts.

The Company Law also provides several other protections for shareholders. Article 22 allows a shareholder the right to go to court to ask for a declaration of invalidity where a shareholders' or board resolution or voting procedure contravenes the Articles of Association or the law. Article 74 (75) gives a dissenting shareholder in a limited liability company the right to require the company to buy it out in certain limited circumstances: when there has been no distribution of dividends for five years, the company is about to merge or transfer major property, or the other shareholders vote to extend the term of a company (with a limited operating period). Article 74 (75) is vague on the mechanism and procedures for the buy-out. It does, however, provide an enforcement mechanism, since if the company and the dissenting shareholder do not agree on a price within 60 days of the date of the shareholders' resolution, the shareholder has a 30-day period within which it may institute proceedings in a People's Court. It is not clear what the court will do in order to resolve the dispute.

Article 182 (183) applies to both limited liability companies and joint stock companies. It gives shareholders holding 10 per cent of the voting rights of a company the right to petition the court for dissolution of the company where 'there are serious difficulties in the operation and management of the company and the continued existence will cause major losses to the rights and interests of the shareholders, and they cannot be resolved through other means'. The Second Interpretation of the Company Law fleshes out this provision and clarifies that it will apply in circumstances in which the operation or management of the company is dysfunctional: that is, when the company has been unable to hold a shareholders' meeting for two years, or it has not been possible to form a quorum for two years, or there is a long-standing dispute between the directors which the shareholders cannot resolve, or there are other major difficulties in the company's operation or management causing material losses to the interests of the shareholders (Article 1). It is not necessary to show that the company itself has sustained significant losses.[349]

In addition to these specific provisions, the institution of the supervisory board and the requirement for a listed company to have independent directors are also intended to have

---

348 Adjudication Committee of the Supreme People's Court, *XCMG Construction Machinery Co Ltd v Chengdu Chuanjiao Industry and Trade Co Ltd et al., A Sale and Purchase Contract Dispute*, Guiding Case No 15 (2013), English translation and commentary at Stanford Law School China Guiding Cases Project <http://cgc.law.stanford.edu/wp-content/uploads/2013/12/CGCP-English-Guiding-Case-15.pdf>.

349 Adjudication Committee of the Supreme People's Court, *LIN Fangqing v Changshu Kailai Industry Co Ltd and DAI Xiaoming, A Corporate Dissolution Dispute*, Guiding Case No 8 (2012), English translation and commentary at Stanford Law School China Guiding Cases Project <http://cgc.law.stanford.edu/wp-content/uploads/2013/04/CGCP-English-Guiding-Case-8.pdf>.

some impact on the controlling shareholder issue. The requirement in the Code of Corporate Governance that a company with a controlling shareholder which holds more than 30 per cent of the equity should institute a system of cumulative voting,[350] as well as the provision in Article 105 (106) of the Company Law that a listed company may institute cumulative voting for directors and supervisors, are designed to ensure that minority shareholders have representation on the board of the company and the supervisory board.

The major issue has, however, been the listing of companies which were converted or created from state-owned enterprises and in which the majority shareholder is the state. The Code of Corporate Governance sets out the basic requirement that the corporate governance structure of a listed company 'shall ensure equal treatment toward all shareholders, especially minority shareholders' (Article 2). Article 21 provides that the controlling shareholder must not interfere with the company's decisions or business activities or impair the interests of the company or the other shareholders. Article 27 provides that a controlling shareholder must not engage in the same or a similar business as the listed company and that a controlling shareholder must adopt measures to avoid competition with the listed company.

The stock exchanges have also included provisions in their listing rules to deal with the conflicts of interest which arise when a listed company has a controlling shareholder or de facto controller.[351] For example, the Shanghai Stock Exchange Rules require a lock-up for shares of a controlling shareholder for a set period after listing.[352] They also control transfers of shares by the controlling shareholder or de facto controller of the company.[353] Other detailed requirements deal with the disclosure and handling of related-party transactions, including preventing a related director from voting on the transaction in a board meeting and preventing related shareholders from voting in a shareholders' meeting. Similarly, disclosure must be made of guarantees granted to related parties.[354] Subsequent regulations, particularly the 2010 *Guidelines on the Behavior of Controlling Shareholders and De Facto Controllers of Companies Listed on the Shanghai Stock Exchange*, place responsibility on the controlling shareholders in relation to sound governance and information disclosure.[355]

A more comprehensive solution to the controlling shareholder issue, at least in relation to state-owned shares, would be for the state to cease holding majority interests in major listed companies.[356] In this respect, the decision by the State Council in 2004[357] to end the distortions in the market caused by the distinction between tradable and non-tradable shares has resulted

---

350   Code of Corporate Governance Art 31.
351   The definition of these terms follows the Company Law, although 'control' is defined in more detail. Shanghai Stock Exchange, Shanghai Stock Exchange Listing Rules (2008, amended 2012), Art 18.1.
352   Shanghai Stock Exchange Listing Rules Art 5.1.5 (36 month lock-up).
353   Ibid. Ch 9.
354   Ibid. Ch 10.
355   Shanghai Stock Exchange (2010) particularly Chs 2 and 3.
356   See, for example, recommendation by Xiao Geng, Xiuke Yang and Anna Janus, 'State-owned Enterprises in China, Reform Dynamics and Impacts' in Ross Garnaut, Ligang Song and Wing Thye Woo (eds), *China's New Place in a World in Crisis* (ANU ePress, 2009) Ch 9, recommending the reduction of state ownership to less than 30%.
357   State Council, *Nine Opinions on Expediting Reform and Development of Capital Markets* (2004). See Sandra Kister, 'China's share-structure reform: An opportunity to move beyond practical solutions to practical problems' (2007) 45 *Columbia Journal of Transnational Law* 312.

in the reduction of the stakes held by controlling shareholders. In practice, however, the state continues to hold major interests in many large listed companies.[358]

12.6.10 Disclosure requirements

Chinese legislators and regulators have recognised that access to up-to-date reliable information is essential for shareholders of all kinds. Thus the Company Law and the Securities Law provide for the disclosure of information – to shareholders in the case of the Company Law and to the public (and hence investors) in the case of the Securities Law.

The 2005 amendments to the Company Law expanded the ability of the shareholders to obtain access to corporate information. Article 33 (34) gives shareholders in limited liability companies rights to see the Articles of Association, minutes of shareholder meetings and supervisors' meetings, resolutions of the directors and the financial and accounting reports of the company, as well as the right to see the account books (under some conditions). Article 97 (98) gives shareholders in joint stock companies the right to examine the Articles of Association of the company, the register of shareholders, counterfoils (or stubs) of corporate bonds, minutes of shareholders' general meetings, minutes of the meetings of the board of directors, minutes of the meetings of the supervisory board, and financial and accounting reports, as well as the right to offer suggestions in relation to or inquire about the operation of the company. Under Article 124 (125), the secretary of a joint stock company is required to handle the provision of information as required under the Company Law.

The Securities Law requires ongoing disclosure of information to the public (Chapter 3). All such information must be authentic, accurate and complete (Article 63). Chapter 3 also requires annual reports, half-yearly reports and the disclosure of major events that may affect the trading price of a listed company's shares (Article 62), including changes in business scope, major investments or asset purchases, major contracts, the incurring of or failure to pay major debts, major losses, major changes in circumstances, change in the Chairman, change in one-third or more of the directors or the manager, major changes in shareholdings (by shareholders holding 5 per cent or more of the company's shares), changes in capital or an application for bankruptcy, major litigation, criminal investigation of the company or its officers and so on. Failure to disclose information, or to disclose it accurately, may result in the imposition by the CSRC of a fine and an order to correct the information, on the issuer, a person responsible for disclosure and a controlling shareholder or de facto controller who is responsible for the omission or provision of incorrect information (Article 193). These requirements are fleshed out in the 2007 *Measures on Administration of Information Disclosure of Listed Companies*[359] and the stock exchange rules, and further emphasised in the 2013 *Measures of the Shanghai Stock Exchange for Appraisal of the Information Disclosure Work of Listed Companies (for Trial Implementation)*. The 2013 *Opinions of the China Securities Regulatory Commission on Further Promoting the Reform of the System of Initial Public Offerings* places responsibility firmly on the issuer in relation to true, complete and accurate disclosure.

---

358 Protiviti, *Corporate Governance Assessment on the Top 100 Chinese Listed Companies for 2012* (2013) 10.

359 CSRC, *Measures on Administration of Information Disclosure of Listed Companies* (2007).

12.6.11 Imposing additional requirements on the sponsors of public offerings

Another way in which the CSRC has attempted to deal with the question of corporate governance is to impose additional obligations on the sponsors of a listing. The 2008 *Measures for the Administration of the Sponsorship of the Offering and Listing of Securities*[360] replaced and strengthened the previous legislation.[361] The Measures require issuers to engage a qualified securities company to act as its sponsor for a public offering or offering of new shares or bonds (Article 2). A securities company proposing to act as a sponsor must be approved by the CSRC (Article 3). In order to qualify, the company must submit, among other things, evidence of its own corporate governance and internal control systems (Article 10). The sponsor's duties include conducting a full investigation of the issuer (Article 24); providing guidance and training to the issuer and its directors, supervisors, senior managers and shareholders holding more than 5 per cent of the shares (Article 25); and satisfying itself that the issuer complies with laws, administrative regulations and CSRC provisions before it sponsors the offering (Article 28).

The sponsor is also responsible for post-IPO guidance for at least two years (Articles 35 and 36), during which its responsibilities include the implementation of internal control systems in the issuer, including a system guarding against the controlling shareholder, de facto controller or other affiliated persons appropriating the issuer's resources. If the sponsor subsequently believes that the issuer may have violated laws or committed another 'improper act', it must procure an explanation and a rectification and, if the matter is serious, report it to the CSRC and stock exchange (Article 57). The sponsor and its officers may be subject to penalties ranging from an order to rectify, warnings, being declared 'persona non grata', administrative penalties or criminal penalties, to suspension from qualification to act as a sponsor (Articles 66 and 67 *et seq*). In 2012, the CSRC issued the *Opinions on Further Strengthening the Regulation over the Sponsor Business*, which requires sponsors to strengthen management and risk control, and to improve the quality of services the sponsors provide.

12.6.12 Higher standards of accounting and internal control – *Basic Norms for Internal Control of Enterprises*

Efforts have also been made to improve the accounting standards of listed companies, by requiring independent audits and by moving, from the beginning of 2007, towards the adoption of standards that are closer to international standards.[362] The CSRC has been engaged in a process of supervising the annual reports of listed companies to review compliance with

---

360   CSRC, *Measures for the Administration of the Sponsorship of the Offering and Listing of Securities* (2008, amended 2009).

361   CSRC, *Tentative Measures for the Sponsorship System for Issue and Listing of Securities* (2001); CSRC, *Measures for the Provision of Guidance for Initial Public Offerings of Shares* (2001).

362   See Noelle Trifiro, 'China's financial reporting standards: Will corporate governance induce compliance in listed companies?' (2007) 16 *Tulane Journal of International and Comparative Law* 271.

the new accounting standards.[363] In addition, a much more comprehensive effort is underway to improve all forms of internal control of Chinese enterprises. The 2008 *Basic Norms for Internal Control of Enterprises* (Norms),[364] implemented by the *Guidelines for Evaluation of Internal Control of Enterprises*[365] and numerous other specific guidelines, are directed at large and medium-sized Chinese enterprises (Norms, Article 2). They encompass controls over the 'internal environment' of an enterprise (including corporate governance, audit policy, human resources, social responsibility and legal education), risk assessment, internal control, information and internal supervision. The Norms were initially applicable to companies listed in China and abroad, and at the beginning of 2012 were extended to all companies listed on the main boards of the Shanghai and Shenzhen Stock Exchanges.[366] Small and medium-sized enterprises are encouraged to adopt the standards. The effect on internal regulation and related corporate governance remains difficult to assess. A report on the impact of corporate governance in 2012 on the top 100 listed companies suggested that implementation had been slower than was hoped. In particular, companies have been slow to establish corporate governance principles, foster a culture of compliance and develop anti-fraud and whistleblowing systems.[367] The increase in the number of companies obliged to comply with the Norms should result in an improvement in compliance.

12.6.13 Direct intervention – the case of dividends

The multifaceted approach to regulation outlined above focuses on general principles of corporate governance, with a strong emphasis on the implementation of adequate internal control and governance systems. The question of how best to enforce these requirements, however, continues to present difficulties. An interesting example of the issues presented by the many methods of regulation and enforcement relates to the declaration of dividends, which has long been an issue for shareholders, and which has apparently not been resolved by compelling Chinese companies to adopt better internal systems of management or governance.

Many Chinese companies have historically been reluctant to pay dividends. The Company Law does not address this issue, since although the shareholders have the power to approve the plan for distribution of profits, it is the responsibility of the directors to formulate the plan in the first place (Articles 37 (38) and 46 (47)). The Company Law recognises that this can be an issue in the case of a limited liability company by giving the dissenting shareholder a right to be bought out where a profitable company has not distributed profits for five years (Article 74 (75)). Shareholders in a joint stock company do not have a similar right under the Company Law.

---

363   See, for example, CSRC, 'Answers by Principal of CSRC Accounting Department to Questions by Correspondent on Supervision over Listed Companies' Annual Reports of 2008' (2009), English version <www.csrc.gov.cn/pub/csrc_en/newsfacts/release/200908/t20090822_121162.htm>.
364   Ministry of Finance, CSRC, National Audit Office and China Insurance Regulatory Commission (2008).
365   Ministry of Finance (2010).
366   Eunice Ku, 'China's Internal Control Audit and Regulatory Framework', *China Briefing* (2012) <www.china-briefing.com/news/2012/03/09/chinas-internal-control-and-audit-regulatory-framework.html>.
367   Protiviti, *Corporate Governance Assessment on the Top 100 Chinese Listed Companies for 2012* (2013) 14.

The Chinese Academy of Social Science report on corporate governance in the top 100 Chinese listed companies in 2008[368] noted that only about 10 per cent of Chinese listed companies paid dividends regularly. In 2008 only 13 of the top 100 listed companies paid dividends at all, and of those only two paid more than 10 per cent of their profits in the form of dividends – well below world-market norms. In response, the CSRC has imposed a number of additional requirements on listed companies to compel them to declare and pay dividends. These include requiring listed firms that apply to make a new share issue to have paid out dividends in cash equal to not less than 30 per cent of distributable profits over the previous three years and requiring companies to disclose in their annual report their profit distribution plan, with an explanation for any decision not to distribute dividends.[369]

A CSRC notice in 2012 directed at listed companies emphasised the importance of dividend policy and in January 2013 the Shanghai Stock Exchange attempted to enforce the payment of a minimum amount of dividends (30 per cent of net profits) by requiring the provision of reasons and providing fast track treatment for those companies that complied.[370] Notwithstanding these provisions, it appears that although remuneration for directors, supervisors and officers has increased, dividend payments have not.[371] A similar issue in relation to unlisted state-owned enterprises was dealt with in 2007 by the Implementing Regulations on the Management of Income and Receipts from the State-owned Assets of Central Enterprises,[372] which required the centrally controlled state-owned enterprises to pay a specified percentage of their profits. The need to address this issue directly strongly suggests that the efforts made in the Company Law and by the CSRC and the stock exchanges to promote corporate governance through a variety of efforts are having only mixed success.

12.6.14 Enforcement

A major issue in relation to corporate governance in China is the question of enforcement – whose responsibility it is and should be, how effective it is and how enthusiastically breaches of relevant legislation are pursued. There is a variety of remedies for breaches of corporate governance requirements and a variety of entities which have responsibility for enforcement. Penalties may range from warnings, reprimands, public criticisms and bans to the imposition of fines and administrative penalties and criminal prosecution. Civil remedies may be sought by aggrieved shareholders through the courts under the Company Law and the Securities Law.

---

368   Centre for Corporate Governance, Chinese Academy of Social Sciences, Centre for Research on Assessment of Leaders, China National School of Administration & Protiviti Consulting, *Corporate Governance Assessment; Summary Report on the Top 100 Chinese Listed Companies for 2009* (2010).

369   CSRC, *The Decisions on Amending Some Provisions on Cash Dividends by Listed Companies* (7 October 2008, effective 9 October 2008); see also Bi Xiaoning, 'State firms urged to do more dividend spread', *China Daily*, 2 July 2009 <www.chinadaily.com.cn/bizchina/2009-07/02/content_8345700.htm>.

370   CSRC, *Notice on Further Implementing Issues concerning Cash Dividends of Listed Companies* (2012); Shanghai Stock Exchange, *Guidelines on the Distribution of Cash Dividends by Listed Companies* (2013).

371   Protiviti, *Corporate Governance Assessment on the Top 100 Chinese Listed Companies for 2012* (2013) 22–3; Josh Noble, 'China's companies spurn notice to pay 30% dividends', *Financial Times* (2013) <www.ft.com/cms/s/0/a1a0338c-bdd9-11e2-890a-00144feab7de.html#axzz2t9o5hpNO>.

372   Ministry of Finance and State-owned Assets Supervision and Administration Commission of the State Council, *Interim Measures for the Administration of Collection of Proceeds of State-Owned Capital from Central Enterprises* (2007).

Cases involving state-owned and other enterprises may involve action by the SASAC or an equivalent state-owned asset administration, and where they involve Communist Party members and government interests, it can be expected that the Communist Party and other parts of government will become involved in investigation and the ultimate determination of cases.[373]

12.6.15 Consequences of breach

The Chinese system has traditionally not relied on shareholders or the courts to enforce systems of corporate governance. Indeed, historically the legislature and the courts have been generally reluctant to encourage shareholder litigation – against listed companies in particular.[374] The amendments to the Company Law in 2005 opened up various possibilities in relation to shareholder litigation, although, as discussed above, the legislation expresses a preference for action to be taken by the directors or supervisors of a company rather than by the shareholders.

The shareholders are, however, empowered to sue directors or officers for actions contrary to law or the Articles of Association which harm the interests of shareholders under Article 152 (153). Under Article 22, a shareholder may institute litigation to have declared void a resolution or action of the company where the procedure or method of voting contravenes laws, regulations or the Articles of Association of the company, although the court can require the shareholder to provide security for the action.[375] The prominence given to corporate cases involving shareholder issues in the newly issued *Guiding Cases of the Supreme People's Court* suggests that the court is now taking an interest in the enforcement of rights under the Company Law. A suit brought recently by a former trader in the First Beijing Intermediate Court against the CSRC, appealing against a penalty, also suggests that the role of the courts in securities disputes is growing.[376]

The concept of enforcing shareholder rights through litigation by shareholders in listed companies is often attractive to Western commentators, who see in the provisions of Articles 151 (152) and 152 (153) of the Company Law[377] an opportunity for the development of

---

373   See also Cheng, 'Insider trading in China: The case for the Chinese Securities Regulatory Commission' (2008).

374   Wang and Chan, 'Reforming China's securities civil actions' (2008). See also Marlon Layton, 'Is private securities litigation essential for the development of China's stock markets?' (2008) 83 *New York University Law Review* 1948.

375   Adjudication Committee of the Supreme People's Court, *LI Jianjun v Shanghai Jiapower Environment Protection Science and Technology Co Ltd, A Corporate Resolution Revocation Dispute*, Guiding Case No 10 (2012), English translation and commentary at Stanford Law School China Guiding Cases Project <http://cgc.law.stanford.edu/wp-content/uploads/2013/04/CGCP-English-Guiding-Case-10.pdf>, makes clear that the court looks only at the content of the resolution and the procedures, not the truth of the underlying facts.

376   Caixin.com, 'Ex-Everbright Trader Sues CSRC over Punishment' (2014) <http://finance.caixin.com/2014-02-14/100638698.html>. Securities Law Art 235 gives a concerned party the right to appeal against a decision of the CSRC or other administrative body by way of either administrative review or litigation.

377   See also the Securities Law. Art 47 gives shareholders the right to institute a suit in their own name in the interests of the company if a director, officer or major shareholder breaches the six month lock-up on the sale of shares and the directors fail to take action to confiscate the proceeds.

shareholder activism.[378] In the period 2001 to 2003, the Supreme People's Court severely restricted the ability of shareholders to bring actions (limiting the types of cases that could be brought and requiring that the CSRC should first have made a determination on corporate wrongdoing before the shareholders could seek compensation).[379] A circular issued by the Supreme People's Court and other regulatory and judicial bodies in 2008 acknowledged the right of shareholders to seek compensation from the courts, but focused on investigation and punishment of illegal securities action by regulatory authorities rather than on the question of compensation of victims.[380] There is nonetheless an increasing number of cases brought by shareholders on corporate governance grounds, suggesting that the role of the courts in enforcement will grow.[381]

A major way in which China deals with cases of corporate malfeasance of various kinds is through the criminal law system, although it is questionable whether the emphasis on criminal prosecutions rather than civil actions provides an adequate remedy to the shareholders. The Criminal law is a basic tool in dealing with securities and companies in China. In particular, the Criminal Law includes detailed provisions imposing penalties of up to 10 years for serious cases of insider trading (Article 180), three years for false or misleading disclosure of financial information (Article 161) and three to seven years for market manipulation by a director, supervisor, officer or controlling supervisor causing serious harm to a listed company (Article 169), as well as other crimes of management malfeasance by such a person, and five to ten years for serious cases of market manipulation (Article 182). The 2008 Supreme People's Court Circular referred to above focuses on transfer of stocks to the public without approval; issuing securities without approval; and unlawful operation of securities businesses as matters of the greatest concern. A 2012 Interpretation deals with the definition of 'insider trading' for the purposes of Article 180.[382]

The CSRC is primarily responsible for pursuing these cases, in conjunction with other bodies such as the procuratorate and the public security bureau, although its ability to do so effectively is arguably limited not only by resources but by the difficulties placed in the way of Chinese regulators in pursuing government officials and businessmen with strong connections to government.[383] The CSRC can investigate and issue administrative sanctions[384] (including orders for rectification, confiscation of illegal proceeds and fines) and impose a ban on persons or organisations from entering the securities market. For example, according to its 2008 report,[385] 107 new cases were registered in 2008, involving insider trading (34 cases), market

---

378   See Jiong Deng, 'Building an investor-friendly shareholder derivative lawsuit system in China' (2005) 46 *Harvard International Law Journal* 347.
379   Layton, 'Is private securities litigation essential for the development of China's stock markets?' (2008).
380   Supreme People's Court, Supreme People's Procuratorate, Ministry of Public Security and CSRC, *Circular on the Relevant Issues on the Suppression of Illegal Securities Activities* (2008). Art 6 provides that victims of securities crimes should seek compensation through criminal procedures for recovery; victims of general legal violations can seek compensation as set out in the *Civil Procedure Law*.
381   See, for example, Wei-Qi Cheng, 'Protection of minority shareholders after the new company law: 26 case studies' (2010) 52 *International Journal of Law and Management* 283.
382   Supreme People's Court and the Supreme People's Procuratorate, *Interpretation regarding Certain Issues Related to Specific Application of Laws in Handling Criminal Cases Involving Insider Trading and Divulgation of Inside Information* (2012).
383   See Cheng, 'Insider trading in China: the case for the Chinese Securities Regulatory Commission' (2008).
384   Securities Law Art 179.
385   CSRC, *Annual Report 2008* 34–6.

manipulation (12 cases), fraudulent disclosure (15 cases), illegal investment advice (19 cases) and other misconduct (27 cases). In the course of the year, the CSRC closed 130 cases, placed 157 under informal investigation, transferred 210 to public security authorities, and imposed 77 administrative penalties or market entry bans. RMB320 million was confiscated (of which RMB250 million was actually collected or frozen).[386] The courts pronounced judgments in approximately 20 cases of illegal securities activities. The stock exchanges also have powers in relation to listed companies, including the ability to suspend trading and issue other sanctions in the form of suspension, delisting and other warnings or sanctions. However, as noted above, the stock exchanges are essentially still subordinate to the CSRC, even though they are notionally independent.

It is, of course, difficult to make an accurate assessment from these statistics of how effective securities enforcement is in China, and opinions vary widely.[387] It has been argued that reputational sanctions such as public criticisms issued by the stock exchanges are effective in encouraging listed companies to improve their standards of corporate governance, due to the impact on the share price and on such matters as access to financing.[388] It is also important to look at the significance of the greatly increased availability of information on the internet in China, through government websites, blogs, and the reporting of business and economic issues, as a result of which information on the stockmarkets and the behaviour of companies and their executives is published more rapidly and read more widely.[389]

Finally, the role of publicity, education and training should not be underestimated. The existence of regular studies and surveys of corporate governance of Chinese companies puts pressure on listed companies to implement corporate governance systems. Websites of listed companies include information on their corporate governance systems. Continued emphasis on corporate governance in the form of regulations and notices from all relevant regulatory authorities also places continuing pressure on companies to improve their systems of internal management and control.

12.6.16 Conclusions on China

Legislative and regulatory authorities in China have made, and continue to make, extensive efforts to formulate and implement a comprehensive system of corporate governance. There continue to be a number of difficult issues, however. These include questions of clarity and

386   By way of comparison, the Australian Securities and Investments Commission 2008–09 reported the completion of 39 criminal cases, 35 civil proceedings and the recovery of A$14.5 million and the freezing of A$13.8 million in assets (a total of approximately RMB176 million). See ASIC, 'Publications, ASIC Annual Reports' 16 *et seq* <http://asic.gov.au>.

387   See Peng Sun and Yi Zhang, 'Is there penalty for crime? Corporate scandal and management turnover in China' (2006) <http://papers.ssrn.com/sol3/papers.cfm?abstract_id=891096>, casting doubt on the effectiveness on punishment of managers in Chinese companies; Donald Clarke, 'Law without order in Chinese corporate governance institutions' (2010) 30(1) *Northwestern Journal of International Law & Business* 131 argues that both state and non-state institutions are surprisingly ineffective in their contributions to corporate governance.

388   Benjamin Liebman, 'Reputational sanctions in China's securities market' (2008) 108 *Columbia Law Review* 945.

389   See also comments in Colin Hawes and Thomas Chiu, 'Flogging a dead horse? Why Western-style corporate governance reform will fail in China and what should be done instead' (2006) 20 *Australian Journal of Corporate Law* 25–54.

internal consistency (the conflicting role of the supervisory board and the independent directors is a good example), the continuing issue of controlling shareholders in Chinese listed companies, and the involvement of multiple enforcement authorities, primarily the CSRC, the stock exchanges, the public security bureau, police and the procuratorate (in relation to criminal prosecutions) and the courts (in relation to private enforcement actions). In particular, the close relationship between the state and its instrumentalities and corporate entities in China continues to cause difficulties in establishing and in enforcing the system which has been established.

Suggestions as to the best way in which to resolve these issues and create a workable and comprehensible system range from privatisation,[390] encouraging private enforcement,[391] following the Taiwanese example by establishing a government-sanctioned non-profit organisation to support shareholder litigation,[392] and providing additional resources to the CSRC to strengthen its enforcement efforts,[393] to changing the entire approach to corporate governance and focusing instead on increasing public scrutiny, executive qualifications and business ethics.[394]

The Chinese Government will not, it is clear, resolve the issue of state control of major companies by simply engaging in massive privatisation programs. Government policy is that state-owned enterprises will continue to be participants in the marketplace for some time to come, despite the structural reforms which have resulted in state shares becoming tradable and therefore theoretically disposable. Private enforcement through the court system is improving but still problematic as a method of enforcing accountability on major enterprises. For shareholders in small, privately held companies, in the absence of a regulator with an interest in minority rights in small companies, stronger and more active courts, willing and able to enforce the rights granted to shareholders under the Company Law, are vital. Two studies on derivative suits indicate that shareholders in limited liability companies are becoming much more active in seeking – and often obtaining – redress through the court system.[395] However, until the courts are prepared to accept and deal with major and complex securities cases in ways which may be generally unpopular with major companies, private litigation is unlikely to have a major impact on the wider market for tradable shares. It is also questionable whether reputational sanctions and a focus on business ethics alone, without the strong threat of investigation, sanction or prosecution, would be more effective than the current system, which combines all of these methods.

Overall, convincing company management that good corporate governance is good for the company and for their own future must be a major element in corporate governance implementation and reform. Improving the resources available to the CSRC, allowing CSRC

---

390   Xiao Geng, Xiuke Yang and Anna Janus, 'State-owned Enterprises in China, Reform Dynamics and Impacts' in Garnaut, Song and Woo (eds), *China's New Place in a World in Crisis* (2009) Ch 9, 169.
391   Huang, 'The statutory derivative action in China' (2007) 227.
392   Wang and Chan, 'Reforming China's securities civil actions' (2008).
393   Cheng, 'Insider trading in China: The case for the Chinese Securities Regulatory Commission' (2008).
394   Hua Cai, 'Bonding, law enforcement and corporate governance in China' (2007) 13 *Stanford Journal of Law, Business & Finance* 82.
395   Nicholas Howson and Donald Clarke, 'Pathway to Minority Shareholder Protection: Derivative Actions in the People's Republic of China' (2012) <http://ssrn.com/abstract=1968732>; Hui Huang, 'Shareholder derivative litigation in China: Empirical findings and comparative analysis' (2012) 27 *Banking and Finance Law Review* 619.

regulators greater independence in aggressively and publicly enforcing securities laws against offenders and giving the stock exchanges more power to deal with offences and offenders are essential.

The experiences of securities and financial markets worldwide during the Global Financial Crisis have made it abundantly clear that there are no simple answers to the issue of corporate governance. Despite the recurring problems in the system and the shortcomings in such corporate structures as the supervisory board and the independent director system, the multifaceted approach taken by legislators, regulators and company management in China has resulted in considerable progress in persuading Chinese companies of the importance of a stronger corporate governance regime. The stresses in the system due to the continuing role of state-owned enterprises in the economy and the market, the influence of government and Party in the judicial and enforcement system and the competitiveness of the markets, however, mean that the implementation of a strong corporate governance system will continue to present challenges.

12.7 Indonesia

12.7.1 Introduction

The history of Indonesia's corporate governance is closely linked to the South Asian financial crisis of the late 1990s, which started in Thailand and spread to the Philippines, Indonesia, Malaysia and South Korea.[396] To resolve the crisis, the Indonesian Government needed financial assistance. The International Monetary Fund came to offer a conditional loan – Indonesia had to meet certain requirements in return for the loan. One of the requirements was to improve the corporate governance system.[397]

In 2011, a new state agency was formally introduced in Indonesia through Law No. 21 of 2011 on Financial Services Authority (*Otoritas Jasa Keuangan* or OJK). Under the law, the role of Indonesia's Central Bank in regulating and supervising financial activities in the banking sector was transferred to OJK. The new state agency came into operation on 3 December 2013. In addition to this role, OJK carries out regulatory and supervisory duties over financial services in capital markets and non-bank financial industries sectors. Thus OJK plays a significant role in realising corporate governance in Indonesia.

This part looks at the implementation of corporate governance principles in three categories of business in Indonesia: banking, state-owned enterprises (SOEs), and insurance and reinsurance companies. It is organised as follows: Section 12.7.2 relates to the national code of corporate governance; Section 12.7.3 examines the Indonesian two-tier board model; Section 12.7.4 discusses the implementation of corporate governance in the three different sectors; Section 12.7.5 focuses on some core corporate governance features; and in Section 12.7.6 a few conclusions are drawn.

---

396 Jeremy J Kingsley, 'Transplantation: Is this what the doctor ordered and are the blood types compatible? The application of interdisciplinary research to law reform in the developing world – a case study of corporate governance in Indonesia' (2004) 21 *Arizona Journal of International & Comparative Law* 501.

397 Dudi M Kurniawan and Nur Indriantoro, 'Corporate Governance in Indonesia' (2000), Paper delivered at the Second Asian Roundtable on Corporate Governance, 21 March 2008, 9 <www.oecd.org/dataoecd/6/62/1931154.pdf>.

12.7.2 The national code of corporate governance[398]

The Indonesian Government, through the Coordinating Ministry for Economy, Finance and Industry, created the National Committee on Corporate Governance (NCCG) in 1999. The committee had two main duties: to codify corporate governance principles and to develop an institutional framework to implement the code.[399] In March 2000 the committee successfully established the Code for Good Corporate Governance.[400]

In 2004 the government changed the NCCG to the National Committee on Governance (NCG), which included the Public Governance Sub-committee and Corporate Governance Sub-committee.[401] In 2006 the NCG reviewed the Code for Good Corporate Governance under the title Indonesia's Code of Good Corporate Governance.[402] The code consists of eight parts:

1. the basis for an effective corporate governance framework in Indonesia;

2. the principles of good corporate governance;

3. business ethics and code of conduct;

4. company organs;

5 the rights and roles of shareholders;

6. the rights and roles of other stakeholders;

7. implementation of the code; and

8. general guidelines for good corporate governance.

This Code, which sets out the basic principles of good corporate governance in Indonesia, applies to all companies regardless of their type or size and sets the minimum standard of corporate governance in Indonesia. The code-makers put forward particular companies as 'champions': listed companies, SOEs, province and region-owned companies, companies that raise and manage public funds, companies with products or services that are widely used by the public, and companies with extensive influence on the environment.

12.7.3 The Indonesian two-tier board model[403]

Indonesia uses a two-tier board model. It was initially adopted under the Dutch Commercial Code of 1847. As a colony of The Netherlands, Indonesia had to follow colonial laws, including company law.[404] This law was further formalised in 1995 following the enactment of Law No. 1

---

398   The following discussion draws largely from Miko Kamal, 'Corporate governance and state-owned enterprises: A study of Indonesia's Code of Corporate Governance' (2010) 5 *Journal of International Commercial Law and Technology* 19.

399   The Decree of the Coordinator Minister of the Economic, Finance and Industry No. 1/M. EKUIN/08/1999 (9 August 1999).

400   See William E Daniel, 'Corporate governance in Indonesian listed companies – a problem of legal transplant' (2003) 15 *Bond Law Review* 360.

401   NCG, 'Indonesia's Code of Good Corporate Governance' (2006) <www.bapepam.go.id/pasar_modal/publikasi_pm/info_pm/Indonesia%20Code%20of%20GCG%202006.pdf>.

402   Ibid.

403   This part extracts largely from Miko Kamal, 'The Indonesian Company Law: Does it support good corporate governance?' (2009) 6 *Macquarie Journal of Business Law* 19.

404   Benny Simon Tabalujan, *Indonesian Company Law: A Translation and Commentary* (Sweet & Maxwell, 1997) 12; Benny Simon Tabalujan, 'Corporate governance of Indonesian banks: The legal & business context' (2001) 13 *Australian Journal of Corporate Law* 3.

of 1995 on limited liability companies.[405] In Law No. 40 of 2007, the legislation regulating Indonesia's two-tier board model replaced Law No. 1 of 1995.

The main feature of the two-tier board model is the clear demarcation between management functions and supervisory functions. Under this model (as in the other civil law countries) there are three legal entities in a company: the general meeting of shareholders (GMS), the executive management (*direksi*) and the board of commissioners (*dewan komisaris*), comparable to a supervisory board.[406]

12.7.3.1 The general meeting of shareholders (GMS)

The general meeting of shareholders (GMS) is the company organ that has residual powers: Article 1 paragraph 4 of Law No. 40 of 2007 states that the GMS is 'the Company organ which has powers which are not delegated to *direksi* and *dewan komisaris* within the limits stipulated in this law and/or the company's Articles of Association'. As the primary company organ, the GMS has authority to make decisions relating to the organisational structure of a company (that is, creating and changing the company's by-laws, conducting mergers, creating spin-off companies, liquidating the company's assets, etc), in addition to deciding the rights and obligations of shareholders, issuing new shares and sharing/utilising the company's returns.[407] In practice, through a GMS, a shareholder can compel either the *direksi* or the *dewan komisaris* to provide information about the company as long as it relates to the GMS's agenda and is not against the interests of the corporation.[408]

There are annual GMSs and extraordinary GMSs.[409] The annual GMS must be held no later than six months after the end of a fiscal year;[410] the extraordinary GMS can be held at any time, as needed by the corporation.[411]

The convening of a GMS, both annual and extraordinary, is generally initiated by the *direksi*.[412] However, the *dewan komisaris* could convene a general meeting if the *direksi* is unwilling to do so.[413] Furthermore, if the *direksi* or the *dewan komisaris* does not call a GMS within the time period referred to in Article 79 paragraph (5) and paragraph (7), shareholders can approach a district court to call a GMS.[414]

The most strategic task of a GMS is that of appointing and dismissing both the *direksi* and the *dewan komisaris*. As the primary company organ, it is in a position to elect and remove members of both the *direksi* and the *dewan komisaris*.[415] The GMS can dismiss a member of

---

405   In Indonesia the limited liability company is called as Perseroan Terbatas (PT), which is similar to the naamloze vennotschap (NV) in The Netherlands; see Benny Simon Tabalujan, 'The new Indonesian Company Law' (1996) 17 *University of Pennsylvania Journal of International Economic Law* 885.

406   Jean J du Plessis, 'Corporate governance: Reflections on the German two-tier board system' (1996) 20 *Journal of South African Law* 21; Grit Tügler, 'The Anglo-American Board of Directors and the German Supervisory Board – Marionettes in a puppet theatre of corporate governance or efficient controlling devices?' (2000) 12 *Bond Law Review* 233.

407   Fred BG Tumbuan, 'Tugas dan Wewenang Organ Perseroan Terbatas Menurut Undang-undang tentang Perseroan Terbatas UU No 40/2007' (2007) 10 <www.governance-indonesia.com/index.php>.

408   Law No. 40 of 2007 Art 75 para 2.

409   Ibid. Art 78 para 1.

410   Ibid. Art 78 para 2.

411   Ibid. Art 78 para 4.

412   Ibid. Art 79 paras 1, 3 and 4.

413   Ibid. Art 79 para 6 letters a and b.

414   Ibid. Art 80 para 1.

415   Ibid. Art 94 para 1 and Art 119.

the *direksi* at any time by mentioning specific reasons:[416] in other words, for good cause. Specific reasons for a member of the *direksi* being dismissed include, for example, that his or her deliberate conduct caused the company to incur losses.[417]

12.7.3.2 The *direksi*[418]

Article 1 paragraph 5 of Law No. 40 of 2007 provides:

> The Board of Directors means the organ of the Company that has the authority and full responsibility to manage the Company for the interest of the Company, in accordance with the purposes and objectives of the Company as well as to represent the Company, either in or out the court in accordance with the provisions of the Articles of Association.

Thus, every member of the *direksi* is personally liable if he or she has committed a wrongdoing or is negligent in performing his or her duties.[419]

As far as the number of members of the *direksi* is concerned, the law states that the *direksi* must consist of at least one member.[420] However, a corporation that has the mobilisation of public funds as part of its business, or is a public corporation, is obliged to have a *direksi* of at least two members.[421] In practice, members of the *direksi* are appointed by the general GMS[422] for a specific term with the possibility of being re-elected.[423] The *direksi*'s election mechanism – nomination, election, substitution and dismissal – is regulated by each company's own Articles of Association.[424]

12.7.3.3 The *dewan komisaris*

The definition of the *dewan komisaris* is set out in Article 1 paragraph 3 of Law No. 40 of 2007: it is the corporate organ that has duties to generally, and specifically, supervise and advise the *direksi* in accordance with the company's Articles of Association. In effect, the *dewan komisaris* is responsible for making sure the *direksi* is conducting the company's business properly, but it is not involved in the day-to-day activities of the company. In other words, it fulfils a supervisory or governing role.

A *dewan komisaris*, consisting of at least one member, is compulsory for all companies.[425] A *dewan komisaris* that has more than one member is called a board of commissioners. This type of *dewan komisaris* acts and makes decisions collectively, and the members cannot act independently.[426] As with the provisions applying to the *direksi*, large companies – that is, companies whose business includes the mobilisation of public funds or issuing an acknowledgment of debt, or public companies – must have a *dewan komisaris* of at least two members.[427]

---

416   Ibid. Art 105 para 1.
417   Ibid. Elucidation of Art 105 para 1.
418   Commonly translated as the 'board of directors', but it can also be translated as 'executive management'.
419   Law No. 40 of 2007 Art 97 para 3.
420   Ibid. Art 92 para 3.
421   Ibid. Art 92 para 4.
422   Ibid. Art 94 para 3.
423   Ibid.
424   Ibid. Art 94 para 4.
425   Ibid. Art 108 para 3.
426   Ibid. Art 108 para 4.
427   Ibid. Art 108 para 5.

So that the *dewan komisaris* can exercise its duties appropriately, the law obliges every member of the *dewan direksi*:

> with good faith, prudent and full of responsibility to perform his supervisory duty and provide advices to the Board of Directors ... for the interest of the Company and ... in accordance with the purpose and objective of the Company.[428]

And just as for the members of the *direksi*, under this law every member of the *dewan komisaris* is also fully personally liable if he or she is at fault or is negligent in performing his or her duties.

The law provides some particular roles for the *dewan komisaris*. According to Article 64 paragraph 1, it should be written in the Articles of Association of a corporation that one of the roles of the *dewan komisaris* is to receive the annual business plan of the corporation from the *direksi*.[429] Also, the *dewan komisaris* may have the capacity to approve the annual business plan of the corporation.[430] However, if the Articles of Association stipulate that a GMS should approve the annual business plan, the *dewan komisaris* has responsibility for analysing the annual business plan.[431] The *dewan komisaris* must also analyse[432] and sign the Annual Report.[433] The *dewan komisaris* is, furthermore, responsible for approving the interim dividends of the company proposed by the *direksi*.[434]

The nomination, election, substitution and dismissal of the *direksi* are ultimately a responsibility of the GMS. However, the law empowers the *dewan komisaris* to suspend the *direksi* for good cause: specific reasons must be provided.[435] In addition to the aforementioned roles, a company may specify in its Articles of Association that power has been granted to the *dewan komisaris* to give written approval or assistance to the *direksi* in undertaking particular legal acts.[436] In addition to this, again based on the Articles of Association, the *dewan komisaris* may undertake managing the company in specific situations for specific periods of time.[437] Lastly, a *dewan komisaris* has the power to approve a merger or takeover of another company.

12.7.4 Corporate governance 'champions'

There are three types of companies that are seen as 'champions' for implementing and adhering to good corporate governance principles in Indonesia: banking companies, state-owned enterprises and insurance companies.

12.7.4.1 Banking companies

In the banking sector, the implementation of corporate governance formally started in 2006 when Indonesia's Central Bank issued Regulation No. 8/4/PBI/2006 on the Implementation of

---

428   Ibid. Art 114 para 2.
429   Ibid. Art 64 para 2.
430   Ibid.
431   Ibid. Art 64 para 3.
432   Ibid. Art 66 para 1.
433   Ibid. Art 67 para 1.
434   Ibid. Art 72 para 4.
435   Ibid. Art 106 para 1.
436   Ibid. Art 117 para 1.
437   Ibid. Art 118 para 1.

Good Corporate Governance, which was then revised through the Bank of Indonesia's Regulation No. 8/14/PBI/2006. In 2016, this regulation was replaced by OJK Regulation No. 55/POJK.03/2016 on the Implementation of Good Corporate Governance for General Banks. Another regulation on that matter is OJK Regulation No. 18/POJK.03/2016 on the Application of Risk Management for General Banks. On 29 April 2013, the Central Bank sent a formal letter to all the banks, directing that every bank should apply the principles of good corporate governance. In 2009, the Central Bank also developed a corporate governance regime for Islamic banks and Islamic business units by way of Regulation No. 11/33/PBI/2009. Transparency, accountability, responsibility, independence and fairness are the five basic principles of corporate governance.[438] These are compulsory for all banks,[439] and administrative sanctions can be imposed on any bank not applying these principles. As stated in OJK Regulation No. 55/POJK.03//2016, the administrative sanctions include a warning letter, the downgrading the rating of governance factors, the suspending business activities, the dismissing of members of the bank's *direksi* and/or members of *dewan komisaris* and the appointment temporary members of *direksi* and/or members of *dewan komisaris* until a general meeting of shareholders appoints permanent successors to members of *direksi* and/or of *dewan komisaris* with the final approval of OJK, and/or including the names of members of the company organs, employees and bank shareholders who have not passed the 'fit and proper person' test.[440]

12.7.4.2 State-owned enterprises

The implementation of corporate governance in Indonesian SOEs was formally first established through the Decree of Minister for State-owned Enterprises No. KEP-117/ MBU/2002 on the Implementation of Good Corporate Governance Practice in the State-owned Enterprises. It was then revised by the Decree of Minister for State-owned Enterprises No. KEP-01/MBU/2011 and partly revised again by the Decree of Minister for State-owned Enterprises No. KEP-09/MBU/2012.[441] According to the Decree, SOEs are obliged to consistently apply the concept of corporate governance and/or establish corporate governance as their operational basis.[442] Consequently, corporate governance principles apply to all Indonesian SOEs regardless of their size or form, but there is in fact no effective sanction that can be imposed if good corporate governance principles are not adhered to, or are disobeyed, by SOEs.[443]

12.7.4.3 Insurance companies

In 2009, the NCG established a code of corporate governance for insurance and reinsurance companies. The code consists of the following nine chapters: the creation of conducive conditions for the implementation of good corporate governance; principles of good corporate

---

438   Bank of Indonesia Regulation No. 8/4/PBI/2006 and Regulation No. 11/33/PBI/2009 Art 1 para 10 and Art 2 para 6.

439   Bank of Indonesia Regulation No. 8/4/PBI/2006 Art 2 and Regulation No. 11/33/PBI/2009 Art 2.

440   OJK Regulation No. 55/POJK/03/2016 Art 71.

441   The Decree of Minister for State-owned Enterprises No. KEP-09/MBU/2012 only revised one paragraph of the Decree of the Minister of State-owned Enterprises No. KEP-01/MBU/2011, namely Art 12, para 10.

442   The Decree of the Minister for State-owned Enterprises No. KEP-01/MBU/2011 Art 2, para 1.

443   Miko Kamal, 'Good Corporate Governance dan Pengadilan [Good Corporate Governance and Court]' (4 September 2004) *Republika*.

governance; business ethics and code of conduct; company organs; shareholders; stakeholders; good business practices; statement on the implementation of good corporate governance; and practical guidelines for the implementation of good corporate governance. In addition to the NCG's code, in 2012 the Minister for Finance issued the Decree of Minister for Finance No. 152/PMK.010/2012 on Good Corporate Governance for insurance companies. The Decree requires every insurance company to implement good corporate governance,[444] and includes three sanctions that can be imposed: formal warnings; restrictions on business activities; and revocation of business permits.[445] OJK formally started to regulate and supervise insurance companies in 2014 when it issued Regulation No. 2/POJK.05/2014 on Good Corporate Governance for Insurance Companies. It was then revised through OJK Regulation No. 73/POJK.05/2016.

12.7.5 Some core features of the Indonesian corporate governance model

The core features of corporate governance in Indonesia are independent commissioners; a *direksi* that is independent of controlling shareholders and has experience in risk management; the supporting committees of the *dewan komisaris*; internal and external auditors; and risk management. In addition, for a company that applies Islamic principles in its business activities, a Sharia supervisory board must be established regardless of the business sector in which the business is involved.

12.7.5.1 Independent commissioner/s

In the banking sector, OJK Regulation No. 55/POJK.03/2006 Article 24 paragraph 2 provides that at least 50 per cent of the members of the *dewan komisaris* must be independent. In the SOE sector at least 20 per cent of the members of the *dewan komisaris* must be independent.[446] For insurance and reinsurance companies, Article 18 paragraphs 2 of the Decree of Minister for Finance No. 152/PMK.010/2012 provide that at least one member of *dewan komisaris* should be independent. Besides, Article 19 paragraph 2 of OJK Regulation No. 73/POJK.05/2016 states that at least half of the numbers of the *dewan komisaris* of an insurance or reinsurance company should be independent. A member of the *dewan komisaris* is considered to be independent when he or she does not have any financial relationship, management relationship, stock ownership relationship, and/or family relationship with another member of the *dewan komisaris*, with a member of the *direksi* and/or a controlling shareholder or with a bank, all of which could affect their ability to act independently.[447]

The banking sector has additional requirements: former members of the *direksi* or executive officers of a bank, or parties who have other relationships with the bank that could affect their ability to act independently, will *not* be considered to be independent commissioners

---

444   The Decree of Minister for Finance No. 152/PMK.010/2012 Art 4.
445   Ibid. Art 75.
446   The Decree of the Minister for State-owned Enterprises No. KEP-01/MBU/2011 Art 13, para 1.
447   OJK Regulation No. 55/POJK.03/2016 Art 1 para 4 and the Decree of the Minister for State-owned Enterprises No. KEP-01/MBU/2011 Art 13, para 3.

unless a year (for conventional commercial banks[448]) or six months (for Islamic banks[449]) has passed since they stopped being members of the bank's *direksi*.

12.7.5.2 The supporting committees of the *dewan komisaris*

In the banking sector, OJK requires three committees to give assistance to the *dewan komisaris*. The three committees are an audit committee, a risk monitoring committee and a remuneration and nomination committee.[450] The audit committee members must include an independent commissioner to serve as the chairman of the committee, an independent person who has expertise in finance or accounting, and an independent person who has expertise in the field of law or banking.[451] The Central Bank also states that only a person who has expertise in the field of Islamic banking can be a member of an audit committee for Islamic banks.[452] Moreover, for Islamic banks, members of the *direksi* are not allowed to be members of the bank's audit committee. The Central Bank recommended that, for all banks, the majority of the *dewan komisaris* who serve as members of the audit committee should also be independent commissioners.[453]

The risk monitoring committee must include at least one independent commissioner, who serves as the chairman of the committee, and an independent person who has expertise in financial matters related to conventional banks.[454] Islamic banks must also include an independent party who has expertise in the field of Islamic banking and risk management as a member of the committee.[455] In addition, Article 34 paragraph 4 of Bank of Indonesia Regulation No. 11/33/PBI/2009 states that Islamic banks' *direksi* members are prohibited from being members of the risk monitoring committee. It also provides that the majority of commissioners who are members of the risk monitoring committee should be independent.[456]

As far as the remuneration and nomination committee is concerned, OJK requires each bank to appoint its independent commissioner as a chairman of the committee. The other members of the committee include other commissioners, the bank's executive officer in charge of human resources or an employee representative.[457] As with an Islamic bank's risk monitoring committee (mentioned above), the members of the *direksi* are prohibited from being members of the remuneration and nomination committee, and the majority of commissioners who are members of the remuneration and nomination committee must be independent.[458]

An SOE is obliged to establish a secretariat to the *dewan komisaris*, the audit committee and other committees so that the *dewan komisaris* is able to fulfil its functions properly and efficiently.[459] Other committees include, but are not limited to, the risk management

---

448   OJK Regulation No. 55/POJK.03/2016 Art 24 para 3.
449   Bank of Indonesia Regulation No. 11/33/PBI/2009 Art 5 para 1.
450   OJK Regulation No. 55/POJK.03/2016 Art 34 para 1.
451   Ibid. Art 41 paras 1 and 2.
452   Bank of Indonesia Regulation No. 11/33/PBI/2009 Art 36 para 1.
453   Ibid. Art 36 para 4.
454   OJK Regulation No. 55/POJK.03/2016 Art 42 para 1.
455   Bank of Indonesia Regulation No. 11/33/PBI/2009, Art 34 para 1.
456   Ibid. Art 34 para 4.
457   OJK Regulation No. 55/POJK.03/2016, Art 44 paras 1 and 2.
458   Bank of Indonesia Regulation No. 11/33/PBI/2009 Art 35.
459   The Decree of Minister for State-owned Enterprises No. PER – 01/MBU/2011 Art 18 para 1.

monitoring committee, the nomination and remuneration committee, and the business development committee.[460]

The authors of the code of corporate governance for insurance and insurance companies recommend that insurance and reinsurance companies establish the following *dewan komisaris* supporting committees: an audit committee; a nomination and remuneration committee; a risk management committee; and a corporate governance policy committee.[461] In addition, the Decree of Minister for Finance No. 152/ PMK.010/2012 requires insurance and reinsurance companies to establish both an audit committee and a risk management committee,[462] and to consider forming a nomination and remuneration committee, and a committee of corporate governance policies.[463]

12.7.5.3 Internal and external auditors

The issue of internal and external auditors is also pivotal for corporate governance in the banking sector in Indonesia. OJK requires every bank to have an effective internal audit function that is independent from the bank's operational unit.[464]

In the Islamic banking sub-sector, the Central Bank affirms that the implementation of the banks' internal functions must be supported by a sufficient number of personnel competent in the field of Islamic banking: that is, at least one person who has knowledge and/or understanding of Islamic banking operations.[465] Every Islamic bank is also required to appoint a public accountant and a registered public accounting firm as external auditors to audit the bank's financial statements. These appointments must be approved by the bank's GMS.[466]

External auditors are also important in SOEs. The Decree states that an SOE has an obligation to use the services of an external auditor that has been selected by the GMS from a group of candidates proposed by the board of commissioners.[467] The appointed external auditors must be free from the influence of board of commissioners, the *direksi* and other SOE stakeholders.[468]

The presence of an external auditor is also compulsory in insurance and reinsurance companies. The GMS must elect the external auditor from three candidates proposed by the *dewan komisaris* on the advice of the audit committee.[469]

12.7.5.4 Risk management

Risk management is an important internal mechanism in the banking sector. Therefore, OJK requires every bank to effectively implement a risk management mechanism that is tailored to the bank's objectives, business policies, size, complexity and ability. The requirements and

460   Ibid. para 2.
461   National Committee on Governance, *Pedoman Good Governance Perusahaan Ausransi dan Perusahaan Reasuransi Indonesia* (2009) 21–2.
462   The Decree of Minister for Finance No. 152/PMK.010/2012 Art 23 para 1.
463   Ibid. para 5.
464   OJK Regulation No. 55/POJK.03/2016 Art 54 paras 1 and 2.
465   Bank of Indonesia Regulation No. 11/33/PBI/2009 Art 53 para 3.
466   Ibid. Art 54 paras 1 and 2.
467   The Decree of Minister for State-owned Enterprises No. PER – 01/MBU/2011 Art 31 para 1.
468   Ibid. Art 13 para 4.
469   The Decree of Minister for Finance No. 152/PMK.010/2012 Art 49 para 1.

procedures are set out in OJK Regulation No. 18/POJK.03/2016, on Implementation of Risk Management for Commercial Banks.[470]

Risk management is also considered very important in the management of SOEs. The Decree recommends that the *direksi*, in any decision-making, should consider the business risks.[471] A risk management program is expected to be an integral part of the corporate governance program. The Decree states that the risk management program can be implemented either by forming a separate unit under the board of directors, or by giving assignments to existing units which have a risk management function.[472]

Finally, for insurance and reinsurance companies, the NCG's code of good corporate governance and OJK Regulation No. 73/POJK.05/2016 state that *direksi* shall establish and implement a risk management system that covers all aspects of the company's activities.[473]

12.7.5.5 Business ethics and anti-corruption

Business ethics and anti-corruption programs are serious issues in Indonesian SOEs. As stated in Article 40 paragraph 1 of the Decree of Minister for State-owned Enterprises No. PER – 01/MBU/2011, members of the *direksi* and the *dewan komisaris* are prohibited from giving or offering or accepting, directly or indirectly, anything of value to or from a customer or a government official in order to influence or reward them for what they have done or what they expect them to do in the future. The Decree also requires the *direksi* to sign an integrity statement for any business transactions that need approval from the *dewan komisaris* and/or a GMS. Apart from that, the Decree also instructs members of the *direksi*, the *dewan komisaris* and SOE officers appointed by the *direksi* to report their assets as stipulated in relevant legislation.[474]

Giving and receiving gifts is also one of the important governance issues in the insurance and reinsurance sector. It is clear from the code and OJK Regulation No. 73/POJK.05/2016 that all members of the *dewan komisaris* and the *direksi*, and all employees, are prohibited from giving or offering something, either directly or indirectly, to anyone who can influence their decisions in running the company.[475] Also, they are banned from receiving something from any business person or government official that can compromise their discretion in making independent business decisions.[476]

In terms of donations, the code asserts that donations by a company or giving a company's assets to any political party or one or more candidates for the legislature and executive should only be carried out in accordance with legislation.[477] However, a company can still make a legitimate donation to a charity according to its wishes.[478]

---

470   OJK Regulation No. 55/POJK.03/2016 Art 56.
471   The Decree of Minister for State-owned Enterprises No. PER – 01/MBU/2011 Art 25 para 1.
472   Ibid. para 2.
473   National Committee on Governance, *Pedoman Good Corporate Governance Perusahaan Asuransi dan Perusahaan Reasuransi Indonesia* (2009) 25.
474   The Decree of Minister for State-owned Enterprises No. PER – 01/MBU/2011 Art 41 paras 1 and 2.
475   National Committee on Governance, *Pedoman Good Corporate Governance Perusahaan Asuransi dan Perusahaan Reasuransi Indonesia* (2009) 14.
476   Ibid.
477   Ibid.
478   Ibid.

Moreover, to ensure that the rules about giving and receiving gifts are transparent, the code requires that each member of the *dewan komisaris* and the *direksi* make an annual statement, stating that he or she will not give something and/or receive something that can affect his or her decisions.[479]

12.7.5.6 Sharia supervisory board

In the Islamic banking sector, the Central Bank requires every bank to establish a Sharia supervisory board for a maximum term equal to the term of members of the *direksi* or the *dewan komisaris*.[480] The Central Bank also requires Islamic banks to consider the remuneration and nomination committee's recommendation for the proposed appointment and/or dismissal of a Sharia supervisory board.[481] There is no requirement for the members of the Sharia supervisory board to be independent of the shareholders or other company organs. The main duties of the Sharia supervisory board are to provide oversight and advice to the *direksi* in regard to how the executive conforms to Islamic principles in its business activities.[482]

Insurance and reinsurance companies that run a business based on Sharia principles are also obliged to establish a Sharia supervisory board in addition to a *dewan komisaris*.[483] The Sharia supervisory board for an insurance or reinsurance company must consist of one or more Sharia experts appointed by the company's GMS on the recommendation of the National Sharia Council.[484]

12.7.5.7 Some additional requirements for members of *direksis*

OJK Regulation No. 55/POJK.03/2016 states that the president of the *direksi* of a commercial bank shall be totally independent of the bank's controlling shareholders.[485] This provision also applies to Islamic banks.[486] However, there is no legislation that requires the *direksi* to be independent of the bank's controlling shareholders in either SOEs or the insurance sectors.

Apart from that, in insurance and reinsurance companies, Article 6 of the Decree of Minister for Finance No. 152/PMK.010/2012 requires that at least half of the members of the *direksi* should be persons who have knowledge and experience in risk management in the company's business field. Also, all the members of *direksi* are required to reside in Indonesia.[487]

12.7.6 Conclusion on Indonesia

This section has covered the implementation of corporate governance in three sectors: banking, state-owned enterprises, and insurance and reinsurance companies. The main focus

---

479   Ibid.
480   Bank of Indonesia's Regulation No. 11/33/PBI/2009 Art 45 para 2.
481   Ibid. para 1.
482   Ibid. Art 47 para 1.
483   National Committee on Governance, *Pedoman Good Corporate Governance Perusahaan Asuransi dan Perusahaan Reasuransi Indonesia* (2009) 23.
484   Ibid.
485   OJK Regulation No. 55/POJK.03/2016, Art 5.
486   Bank of Indonesia Regulation No. 11/33/PBI/2009, Art 18.
487   The Decree of Minister for Finance No. 152/PMK.010/2012, Art 7.

has been on the national code of corporate governance and the Indonesian two-tier board model, which includes the *direksi* and the *dewan komisaris*. The role and functions of the general meeting of shareholders (GMS) has also been explained briefly. Some core features of corporate governance in Indonesia have also been dealt with. They include: independence of some commissioners; some additional requirements for members of *direksis*; the supporting committee of the *dewan komisaris*; internal and external auditors; risk management; and the Sharia supervisory board. Also, it has been explained briefly that OJK is a new government agency that has the role of implementing principles of corporate governance in banking and insurance sectors.

It will be clear that there are some features that distinguish the Indonesian corporate governance model from most other corporate governance models discussed in this book. However, as in other jurisdictions, the importance of contemporary principles of good corporate governance is appreciated in Indonesia and serious attempts are made to adhere to good corporate governance practices.

12.8 Conclusion

In this chapter we have discussed some of the developments in corporate governance in the EU and we have given an overview of the OECD *Principles of Corporate Governance* as they guide both unitary and two-tier board structures in various jurisdictions. These principles apply internationally and are based on international best practice, irrespective of the company law model followed.

The German corporate governance system is unique because of the very specific and rather rigid requirements applying to public companies and large proprietary companies. They must have a two-tier board system (management board and supervisory board) and there must be employee representatives on the supervisory board, although the number varies from industry to industry and also depends on the type of company. The introduction of the German Corporate Governance Code (GCGC) in 2001 added a new dimension to German law by setting up a 'comply or explain' system for listed companies. Contemporary international best practice in corporate governance has been identified and promoted for listed companies through the GCGC, which has been updated and refined annually since 2005. The issue of employee participation at supervisory board level, or codetermination, is still one of the most controversial issues facing German corporate law and corporate governance.

As far as Japan is concerned, corporate law and practice have long attracted considerable attention from foreign commentators. Much of the commentary increasingly refers to 'corporate governance', reflecting the emergence of this broader term worldwide since the 1980s (outlined in Chapter 1). Contemporary corporate law analyses and discussions focused on Japan have long tended to adopt a broader perspective regarding stakeholders. This reflects an awareness of the pervasive but typically informal role of stakeholders other than shareholders, especially core 'lifelong' employees, 'main banks' and '*keiretsu*' corporate groups, in firms. The two important and quite distinctive monitoring mechanisms in Japanese corporate governance also remind us that government policy and the vicissitudes of politics are as important as economics and the broader social or cultural context in explaining and predicting trajectories.

This is particularly evident from the amendments to the Companies Act passed in June 2014. Gradual transformation seems to be underway at the same time as more significant changes in the relationship between shareholders and directors or managers.

Corporate law and corporate governance in China have been influenced by a variety of factors: the traditional dominance of the state-owned sector and the continuing ideological commitment by policy-makers to the 'socialist market economy'; the decision by the government to attract foreign capital by encouraging the establishment of foreign-invested companies; and, more recently, the rapid growth of the Chinese private sector. The amendment of the Company Law and the Securities Law in 2005, together with the introduction by the China Securities Regulatory Commission of corporate governance requirements, are highlights in corporate law and corporate governance developments in China. These developments include the introduction of minority shareholder rights, elements of the German two-tier board system designed to give the supervisory board the ability to monitor the actions of the board of directors, and the introduction of outside or independent directors, from the Anglo-American corporate governance model, in order to deal with the controlling shareholder issue.

Legislative and regulatory authorities in China have made extensive efforts to formulate and implement an adequate system of corporate governance. The Chinese courts are also playing a greater role in the area of shareholder rights. There continue to be a number of difficult issues, however, in relation to corporate governance in China. These include questions of clarity and internal consistency in the corporate governance system (of which the conflicting role of the supervisory board and the independent directors is a good example), the involvement of multiple enforcement authorities, primarily the China Securities Regulatory Commission, the stock exchanges, the public security bureau, police and procuratorate (in relation to criminal prosecutions) and the courts (in relation to private enforcement actions), and issues with effective enforcement. The multifaceted approach taken by legislators, regulators and company management in China has resulted in considerable progress in persuading Chinese companies of the importance of a stronger corporate governance regime. Nevertheless, convincing company management that good corporate governance is good for the company and for their own future remains a major challenge to corporate governance implementation and reform in China. Improving the resources available for enforcement is also very important. It was also observed that the continuing stresses in the Chinese corporate system – due to the continuing role of state-owned enterprises in the economy and the market, the influence of the government and the Communist Party in the judicial and enforcement system, and the competitiveness of the markets – indicate that the implementation of a strong corporate governance system in China will continue to present challenges. There seems little doubt that Corporate Social Responsibility (CSR) is creeping higher on the agenda of corporate law and corporate governance reforms in China and this is being observed with considerable interest by the rest of the world – the practical realities of change will be monitored very closely.

In Indonesia, corporate governance became particularly prominent after the South Asian financial crisis of the latter half of 1997. In order to obtain financial assistance from the International Monetary Fund, Indonesia was required to improve its corporate governance system. A National Committee on Corporate Governance (NCCG) was created and refined over time. The Indonesian corporate governance model is based on a two-tier board system, influenced by the Dutch Commercial Code of 1847. However, it has been modernised over time. Currently it is primarily Law No. 40 of 2007 that contains the demarcation of the functions of the general meeting of shareholders (GMS), the *direksi* (board of directors) and the *dewan komisaris* (board of commissioners).

PART

4

SHAREHOLDER ACTIVISM
AND BUSINESS ETHICS

13

SHAREHOLDER ACTIVISM

One of the hidden 'assets' in many companies is top management: get rid of them and the value goes up. What's going on in companies these days is absurd. It's like a corporate welfare state. We're supporting managements who produce nothing. No, it's really worse than that. Not only are we paying these drones not to produce, but we're paying them to muck up the works.

Carl Icahn, activist investor

An activist argues that a corporation would be more valuable if it changed its business strategy, but is not prepared to buy the company or to even commit to hold its stock for any particular period of time.

Leo Strine, Chancellor, Delaware Court of Chancery

The only thing I know is that from chaos comes opportunity.

Daniel Loeb, Third Point (activist hedge fund)

13.1 Introduction

Australia has a long tradition of shareholder activism. What has changed in recent years is the nature of the shareholders who are taking activist positions.[1] Large public corporations in Australia have long been criticised by individual activist shareholders such as retired school-teacher Jack Tilburn, who has attended over 500 annual general meetings (AGMs) over the past 25 years,[2] and Australian Shareholder Association and high-profile media commentator Stephen Mayne. In recent years, however, it is more common to speak of activist hedge funds, activist sovereign wealth funds (such as Australia's Future Fund) and activist fund managers (such as Allan Gray).

Institutional investors have always exercised some measure of influence with the management of large public corporations,[3] but recent developments in shareholder activism have brought these manoeuvres into the public spotlight.[4] Australia's corporate landscape has featured a range of high-profile boardroom battles with activist investors, including fund managers advocating the break-up of interlocked listed companies Brickworks and Washington H. Soul Pattinson, the Future Fund putting pressure on Telstra, and a consortium of institutional investors advocating change at Qantas. In recent times Australia has seen a rise in US-style activism tactics with public criticism of existing board members and overall

---

1   For a review of recent shareholder activism activities see Activist Insight and Arnold Bloch Leibler, 'Shareholder activisim in Australia' (2016) <www.abl.com.au>.

2   Jack Tilburn calls himself the 'corporate terminator' and has published a book on 'do it yourself corporate governance'.

3   For a discussion of the past reticent attitude of institutional investors towards taking activist stances see Geoff Stapledon, 'Disincentives to activism by institutional investors in listed Australian companies' (1996) 18 *Sydney Law Review* 152.

4   For a cross-disciplinary review of the literature on shareholder activism see Maria Goranova and Lori Ryan, 'Shareholder activism: A multidisciplinary review' (2014) 40(5) *Journal of Management* 1230 <https://papers.ssrn.com/abstract=2384280>.

denouncement of management strategy being played out through both traditional and social media.[5]

Australia is by no means alone in experiencing rising shareholder activism. A range of large and high-profile international hedge funds,[6] pension funds[7] and other collective investment vehicles have built a business out of taking small positions in public companies in order to advocate change that will, in their view, improve returns. The US has had the most high profile and sustained tradition of shareholder activism,[8] but numerous examples can also be found in England and, in more recent times, in countries with block-holder corporate governance systems, such as Japan, South Korea, Italy, France and Germany.[9]

It should be noted that the improved returns do not necessarily mean improved long-term returns to shareholders or indeed improved returns to all shareholders.

Several of the developments in corporate law and corporate governance have contributed to rising shareholder activism in Australia. First, Australian institutional investors have warmly embraced participation in shareholder class actions. Large-scale shareholder class actions began in Australia with the GIO (a large public insurance company) class action in the late 1990s which resulted in a settlement of close to A$100 million. This was followed by a plethora of shareholder class actions against some of the largest public companies in Australia, including Telstra (Australia's largest telco), Aristocrat (the world's largest gaming machine manufacturer), Multi-plex (a large construction company), Downer EDI (a large construction and manufacturing company) and NAB (one of Australia's big four banks). Shareholder class actions will be discussed at Section 13.7.2. Second, changes to the rules relating to director elections at annual general meetings (AGMs) – allowing for a spill motion where more than 25 per cent of the voting shareholders vote against the company's remuneration report in two consecutive years[10] – have led to high-profile activist positions being taken by large investment funds such as Perpetual. The two strikes rule has also emboldened proxy advisers such as Ownership Matters, CGI Glass Lewis, ISS Proxy and ACSI, who use their reports and recommendations for institutional investors to drive governance changes at large listed companies, sometimes recommending voting against remuneration reports in order to push for change on other matters.

This chapter will explore the nature and scope of shareholder activism in Australia (including reference to international developments) and its implications for corporate governance.

---

5   See, for example, the campaigns against Bellamy's and against Quintis in early 2017.
6   The Children's Investment Fund Management LLP (based in the UK) and Carl Icahn Capital Management LP (based in the US) are two of the most high profile activist hedge funds. See further Marcel Kahan and Edward Rock, 'Hedge funds in corporate governance and corporate control' (2007) 3 *Corporate Governance Law Review* 134; John Coffee and Darius Palia, 'The wolf at the door: The impact of hedge fund activism on corporate governance' (2016) 41 *Journal of Corporation Law* 545.
7   The California Public Employees' Retirement System (CalPERS) has been an activist pension fund for several decades.
8   See further Jay Eisenhofer and Michael Barry, *Shareholder Activism Handbook* (Aspen Publishers, Looseleaf – latest issue); Stuart Gillan and Laura Starks, 'The evolution of shareholder activism in the United States' (2007) 19 *Journal of Applied Corporate Finance* 55.
9   A search of the respected journal *Corporate Governance: An International Review* reveals numerous studies on the effects of shareholder activism in dozens of both developed and developing countries.
10   See *Corporations Act 2001* (Cth) s 250U and the Productivity Commission Inquiry Report, 'Executive Remuneration in Australia', Report No. 49, Final Enquiry Report (December 2009).

13.2 What is shareholder activism?

Shareholder activism refers to attempts by one or more shareholders to influence the management of a particular company.[11] The goals of shareholder activism are to effect some form of management and/or strategic change in the company. This may involve pressuring existing managers to resign or pressuring the company to accept new candidates for the board. It is common for shareholder activists to pursue representation on the board, or at least to pursue having certain directors removed from the board as a consequence of alleged underperformance.

Activism may also involve persuading companies to change their operational plans – refraining from pursuing a particular transaction or adopting a certain corporate strategy, for example. Activist shareholders may also pursue personal agendas such as pressuring the company to adopt particular environmental policies or approaches to human rights and/or labour practices.[12]

Shareholder activism may be seen as one part of a broader debate concerning shareholder engagement and shareholder empowerment.[13] There have long been concerns raised about the low level of shareholder participation in shareholders' (or members, as the Corporations Act calls them) meetings and the high level of disengagement of shareholders with their companies. In Australia, this has led to a wide-ranging review of the AGM and shareholder engagement, undertaken by the Corporations and Markets Advisory Committee (CAMAC) since 2011, but with CAMAC's abolition the project (now transferred to Treasury) seems to have stalled.[14]

The AGM as it currently stands is one of the most useful tools for shareholder activists, as they can use question time to ask challenging questions of the board and the CEO. Particularly for large publicly listed companies, this can be a very useful tool in gaining publicity for the activist's agenda. This is the approach favoured by individual shareholder activists such as Mayne, and to representatives of retail investors such as the Australian Shareholders' Association. Larger institutional shareholder activists may rely more on meetings with company management and on proxy advisory firms as a more forceful method of furthering their agenda, although high-profile proxy fights involving Westfield and UniSuper and Soul Pattison and Perpetual suggest that that may be changing, and that institutional investors are not hesitant to out themselves on a public platform to drive their change agenda.

---

11   See European Corporate Governance Institute <www.ecgi.org/activism/>.
12   See, for example, Kirsten Anderson and Ian Ramsay, 'From the picket line to the board room: Union shareholder activism in Australia' (2006) 24 *Company and Securities Law Journal* 279; Shelley Bielefeld, 'Directors' duties to the company and minority shareholder environmental activism' (2004) 23 *Company and Securities Law Journal* 28; Susan Shearing, 'Raising the boardroom temperature? Climate change and shareholder activism in Australia' (2012) 29 *Environmental and Planning Law Journal* 479.
13   For a comparative study of shareholder empowerment and shareholder activism see Jennifer Hill, 'The rising tension between shareholder and director power in the common law world' (2010) 18 *Corporate Governance: An International Review* 344.
14   See further CAMAC, *The AGM and shareholder engagement*, Discussion Paper (December 2012) <www.camac.gov.au>.

13.3 What attracts shareholder activism?

Shareholder activists usually act against companies that they see as underperforming or under-utilising their assets, with the aim of benefiting investors. Another incentive to act has been underperformance at the board level, such as an apparent failure by a board to take responsibility for poor performance or misconduct by executives below board level – the Bellamy's proxy contest was a good recent example of this.

Another common target for shareholder activists is allegations of mishandled conflicts of interest and related-party dealings. Lastly, but most commonly, remuneration packages of senior executives and board members will often give rise to activism. The widespread industry benchmarking of executive remuneration makes it easy for activist investors to target companies whose remuneration programs are inconsistent with peer companies or are otherwise not believed to be justified based on the performance of management. Proxy advisory firms typically provide detailed reports on remuneration practices and how industry benchmarks stack up against individual company practices.

13.4 Does shareholder activism add value?

There is a large number of case studies that have examined the performance of companies following the intervention of activist investors, but the evidence is inconclusive, with numerous studies showing improved returns and other studies showing little or no improvement.[15] Shareholder activism does seem to affect management behaviour, with firms targeted by shareholder activitism more likely than other firms to change their CEO.[16] It is also widely believed that shareholder activism provides value to the activist investor.[17] Indeed there is a growing number of hedge funds and individual institutional funds whose primary investment strategy is to take an activist stance against what they perceive to be underperforming companies.

13.5 Characteristics of shareholder activism

Shareholder activists use a range of private and public strategies to influence company management. It is difficult to gauge the level of private influence that activist shareholders have over particular companies, as such conduct occurs behind closed doors. Public companies, and other disclosing entities, in Australia are required to comply with continuous disclosure laws,[18] which limit the ability of management to give market-sensitive information to individual shareholders without also disclosing the same information to the market. However, this does not mean that company management cannot engage in private discussions with investors and their advisers, provided they do not disclose confidential and market-sensitive information.

---

15   Goranova and Ryan, 'Shareholder activism: A multidisciplinary review' (2014).
16   Ibid. For a review of both financial and non-financial outcomes of investor activism in the US see Gillan and Starks, 'The evolution of shareholder activism in the United States' (2007).
17   See Ronald Gilson and Jeffrey Gordon, 'The agency costs of agency capitalism: Activist investors and the revaluation of governance rights' (2013) 113 *Columbia Law Review* 863.
18   *Corporations Act 2001* (Cth) Pt 6CA.

The most common tactic of shareholder activists is to publicise their interactions with the target company, particularly by disclosing correspondence where the activists lay out the problems with the company and their demands for corporate governance change. High-profile activists may then further push their message by engaging in media activity to highlight their arguments for change. Well-known activist investors such as American Carl Icahn are regularly interviewed in the press. It is also becoming common for activist investors to use online media tools to further their arguments, using social media and blog sites to spread their message as widely as possible.

Activist institutional shareholders who want to pressure company management are likely to want a substantial stake in the company to use as a leverage point. In large public companies it may be expensive for an activist investor to purchase enough shares to build up a substantial stake in the company. Purchasing large parcels of shares in a publicly listed company will usually generate market rumours and suspicions of potential takeover activity that will drive the price of the shares up. Activist institutional investors are increasingly using derivatives[19] to assist with their portfolio purchases. It is possible to use equity swaps, which may be entered into with a number of investment counterparties (usually investment banks), to obtain millions of dollars' worth of shares within a relatively short period, without showing up on the company's register of members. This has been used in activist campaigns against Bellamy's and Echo Entertainment.

Under Australian law a substantial shareholder is required to disclose movements in their shareholdings of more than 1 per cent.[20] A substantial shareholder is one with a relevant interest of 5 per cent or more of the voting shares in a company.[21] However, the holder of an equity swap that is not physically settled will not fall within these provisions even though it may be relatively easy for the holder of the swap to request that the swap counterparty unwind the swap and settle by selling the shares to the holder. The practice of using derivatives to mask actual positions of control and influence in public companies has been the subject of extensive scholarly debate, particularly in the US, where Professor Henry Hu and Professor Bernard Black have undertaken a deep vein of scholarship on the issue.[22]

Another common technique used by activist fund managers is to 'move in packs'. While not necessarily coordinating their activities so as to render themselves formally associated, it is common for multiple hedge funds to work simultaneously to put increased pressure on target management. They may be joined in such efforts by other institutional investors and private equity investors. Given the often dramatic effect of shareholder activism on the short-term

---

19   Derivatives are financial instruments which involve an obligation to pay money or to deliver a product sometime in the future, but where the value of the contract is referenced to something else, typically a commodity price or an interest rate, or an index rate. Futures, options, currency and interest rate swaps are the most common forms of derivatives: see further *Corporations Act 2001* (Cth) s 761D; Alastair Hudson, *Law of Financial Derivatives* (Sweet & Maxwell, 5th edn, 2012).

20   *Corporations Act 2001* (Cth) s 671B.

21   Ibid. s 9.

22   See, for example, Henry Hu and Bernard Black, 'Hedge funds, insiders, and the decoupling of economic and voting ownership: Empty voting and hidden (morphable) ownership' (2007) 13 *Journal of Corporate Finance* 343; Henry Hu and Bernard Black, 'The new vote buying: Empty voting and hidden (morphable) ownership' (2006) 79 *Southern California Law Review* 811.

share price of a public company, it is common for multiple activist funds to 'pile into a stock'[23] while it is under the spotlight of a public governance campaign.

Activist institutional investors may use their substantial holdings to requisition members' meetings, to distribute material to investors, to propose resolutions to members and ultimately to seek the replacement of incumbent directors or to vote against the remuneration report. Individual activist investors are usually not able to achieve the passage of resolutions at members' meetings due to their relatively small holdings in the company.

13.6 Internal activism

13.6.1 Overview

Shareholder activism may involve a number of actions taken within the company, usually actions that may only be taken by members. These will be regulated by the company's constitution and any subsidiary by-laws or board/committee charters as well as by the *Corporations Act 2001* (Cth) and by the listing rules of the licensed financial market if the company has its securities listed for public trading.

13.6.2 Obtaining information

The first element of shareholder activism is to obtain relevant information about what the company is doing or proposing to do or not do. Shareholders have a range of information rights, including access to periodic reports (Part 2M of the Act), and to notices of members' meetings.[24] However, much of this information will already be available because most target companies in shareholder activism cases are disclosing entities, so they are required to keep the financial market informed of material information on an immediate and ongoing basis.

Shareholders may request access to information that is not generally available, such as the company's register of members, and copies of such registers, provided that the use of the information is permissible under the Corporations Act.[25] Members may also seek access to books that are required to be kept by the company.[26]

13.6.3 Convening members' meetings

Members with at least 5 per cent of the votes in a members' meeting may convene a members' meeting under *Corporations Act 2001* (Cth) s 249D. This will involve them paying for the meeting themselves, but they will also control the conduct of the meeting (within the terms of the constitution). A more common occurrence is for members with at least 5 per cent of the votes to require the company to convene a members' meeting (also s 249D). In these instances

---

23   This refers to multiple fund managers purchasing securities in the company in the expectation that they can benefit from the rising price of the securities or can benefit from price volatility in the securities (usually combined with hedging arrangements such as using derivatives to protect themselves from too much volatility, and thus risk).

24   *Corporations Act 2001* (Cth) s 249J.

25   Ibid. ss 173, 177.

26   This ability is not restricted to members only: *Corporations Act 2001* (Cth) s 1300.

the company will control the conduct of the meeting, but the members can force the company to convene a meeting only if the purpose of the meeting is within the power of the meeting to determine, such as the removal and appointment of directors. If a meeting requisition is made for an improper purpose it may be ignored by the directors.[27]

13.6.4 Distributing information to members

Members with at least 5 per cent of the votes may require the company to put resolutions to the next members' meeting (s 249N) and may require the company to distribute information to members for the next meeting (s 249P).[28] There are limitations on how long the information may be and it must not be defamatory. Members may also obtain a copy of the share register in order to contact members about an upcoming meeting, although this would be at their own expense (sections 173 and 177).

13.6.5 Voting at members' meetings

One of the basic components of an ordinary share in an Australian company is the right to vote on a resolution at a members' meeting (s 250E – a replaceable rule). For activist shareholders this may be used to vote for changes in the composition of the board of directors, but even large shareholders are unlikely to have enough votes to successfully undertake this without the support of numerous other large shareholders, and usually one or more widely used proxy advisers.

Proxy advisers are firms that assist institutional investors with voting on resolutions that are put to members' meetings, typically AGMs. Where an individual owns shares in a small number of companies it may not be too onerous to participate in voting either in person or by proxy. But an institutional fund manager may own shares in dozens or even hundreds of companies, most of which will have their AGMs around the same time each year. This makes it difficult for the institutional shareholder to properly evaluate each proposal for each company, leading them to rely on proxy advisers, who can give them (for a fee) an informed view about how to vote. In Australia there are a number of proxy advisers, from large-scale international operations such as ISS Proxy and CGI Glass Lewis, to local firms such as the Australian Council of Superannuation Investors and Ownership Matters. Proxy advisers have come under a great deal of scrutiny and criticism, particularly from the boards of major corporations, because of their power and influence over the institutional shareholders who control the majority of shares in most publicly listed companies. There have been calls for regulation of proxy advisers, particularly in the US, but Australia has resisted that trend.[29] There are two areas where reform has occurred: first, fund managers are now required to disclose their use of

---

27   *NRMA Ltd v Parker* (1986) 6 NSWLR 517.

28   *Australasian Centre for Corporate Responsibility v Commonwealth Bank of Australia* (2016) 113 ACSR 600. See further, Jason Harris, 'Barbarians at the gate' (2016) 34 *Companies and Securities Law Journal (C&SLJ)* 151.

29   For a summary see Egan Associates, 'The Influence of Proxy Advisors' <https://eganassociates .com.au/influence-of-proxy-advisers/>. See further Lars Klohn and Philip Schwarz, 'The regulation of proxy advisors' (2013) 8 *Capital Markets Law* 90; Holger Fleischer, 'Proxy advisors in Europe: Reform proposals and regulatory strategies' (2012) 9 *European Company Law* 12;

proxy advisory services, and second, companies are required to formulate voting policies which are given to proxy advisers and disclosed to fund members. [30]

13.7 Court action
13.7.1 Individual actions

There is a variety of individual court actions that can assist with a shareholder activist agenda. The obvious disadvantages of individual court actions are that the activist must meet the cost of the action, which can be high, and court actions often involve months, if not years, of work. For activist institutional investors (as opposed to hedge funds or private equity funds) there is also the reputational risk involved in litigation: it may jeopardise relationships with current or future clients. Many, perhaps most, institutional investors (such as insurance companies and pension funds) do not want to be seen to be picking fights with major corporates and potential future clients. However, for well-funded activists who are not concerned about the reputational risk, the goal may not be a final court order but rather the company management accepting their agenda. Sometimes the threat of expensive litigation can bring the parties together to negotiate a resolution of the dispute.

An activist's complaint that the company has issued shares improperly gives rise to an equitable right to seek a court order rescinding the share issue.[31]

Activist shareholders may also take advantage of a range of statutory rights of action, assuming that it could be argued that the conduct by the company or by the directors or executives is in breach of the *Corporations Act 2001* (Cth). These include:

- minority oppression (s 232);
- applying for a statutory injunction (s 1324); and
- seeking compensation for breach of a financial services civil penalty provisions (s 1317HA).

Each of these statutory rights was explained in Chapter 10.

Where the conduct that the activist is targeting is a breach of a right held by the company, the activist shareholder may apply for a statutory derivative action under Part 2F.1A to enforce the company's rights. This may involve suing the directors or officers on behalf of the company or seeking to enforce a right that the company has against a third party. However, a statutory derivative action is unlikely to be frequently used because it is expensive – and the applicant bears the cost – and there is no guarantee that the court will order the company to indemnify them even if they win. Furthermore, a shareholder activist with a long-running dispute against the company may face difficulties satisfying the good faith requirement under s 237(2)(b) when applying for leave to commence the proceedings. Statutory derivative actions were discussed in detail in Chapter 10.

If the conduct of the company is in breach of the company's constitution, the activist shareholder may seek to enforce the contractual nature of the constitution (s 140). This too is

30   See Financial Services Council, *Standard 13 Voting Policy, Voting Record and Disclosure* (2013), which applies to all Financial Services Council members (this includes most of the largest fund managers in Australia) and took effect from 1 July 2014.
31   *Residues Treatment & Trading Co Ltd v Southern Resources Ltd (No 4)* (1988) 14 ACLR 569.

unlikely to be a major avenue for court action because the activist agenda will usually involve more than mere compliance with the company's constitution.

It is also possible that an activist investor may take action for alleged disclosure contraventions by the company, particularly where underperformance or undisclosed fraud is at issue. The Corporations Act contains a prohibition on misleading or deceptive conduct in relation to financial products (shares and debentures), as well as a positive obligation to disclose material information (for disclosing entities).[32] However, there have been very few cases of individual enforcement action for disclosure breaches against publicly listed companies. In recent times it is more likely that an activist investor would participate in a shareholder class action.

13.7.2 Class actions

It is possible for shareholder activists to become involved in a shareholder class action against a target company. Shareholder class actions are large-scale forms of litigation, often involving thousands of investors, which means they are always highly publicised. The publicity and large amounts of damages claimed can mean that they will drive institutional change inside the target company. However, activist investors are likely to pursue other means to push their agenda given the length of time – usually several years – that class actions take. Nonetheless, they are clearly one of many techniques that can be used to force corporate governance change.

Shareholder class actions have been on the rise in Australia since the settlement of the GIO class action in the late 1990s.[33] A class action is a form of group litigation, the aim of which is to stop multiple parallel proceedings, which would waste court time and resources. Group proceedings have long been part of court procedure, but class actions allow a lead plaintiff to represent the class members, who thereby maintain anonymity and assume little risk in participating in the action.

Several states have a specific class action procedure, but the most commonly used procedure is the one in Part IVA of the *Federal Court of Australia Act 1976* (Cth). That procedure involves seven or more plaintiffs with claims against the same defendant, where the claims arise out of substantially the same facts and give rise to common legal issues.[34] The plaintiff lawyers need to define the scope of the class, which for shareholder class actions will usually involve setting a time period within which a potential class member bought, sold or held shares in the company. It is possible for class members to opt out of the class within a certain timeframe and undertake their own individual case if they wish. If the court determines that there is not a sufficient similarity between the claims the class action may be directed to proceed as individual cases; this will usually make most of the proceedings too expensive to

---

32   *Corporations Act 2001* (Cth) ss 674 (continuous disclosure) and 1041H (misleading or deceptive conduct). For the definition of 'disclosing entity', 'listed disclosing entity' and 'unlisted disclosing entity', see *Corporations Act 2001* (Cth) ss 111AC, 111AL(1) and 111AL(2). See further Jason Harris and Suzanne Webbey, 'Personal liability for corporate disclosure problems' (2011) 29 *C&SLJ* 463.

33   See Michael Legg, 'Shareholder class actions in Australia – the perfect storm?' (2008) 31 *University of New South Wales (UNSW) Law Journal* 669. See also Damien Grave and Helen Mould (eds), *25 Years of Class Actions in Australia: 1992–2017* (Ross Parsons Centre of Commercial, Corporate and Taxation Law, 2017).

34   *Federal Court of Australia Act 1976* (Cth) s 33C.

run. The advantage of class actions is that they allow for the consolidation of the proceedings into one case that will be claiming a sufficiently large amount of compensation to pay for the substantial costs involved and award compensation to class members.

Most class actions, and indeed all shareholder class actions, are funded not by the representative plaintiff but by litigation funders. These are independent bodies, usually companies, that provide funding for a range of conduct relevant for litigation, such as initial investigations, briefing legal counsel, commissioning expert reports, and then funding the case (assuming the matter actually reaches a courtroom before being settled). Litigation funders also usually make funds available to pay for adverse costs orders if the litigation fails. Litigation funders do not, however, run the litigation: that is done by the plaintiff lawyers on behalf of the class members. The funders will be regularly briefed on the progress of the litigation and will be consulted on major decisions. Funders have contractual rights to withdraw their funding in certain situations; this will mean the collapse of the case unless another funder can be found.

In Australia, litigation funding has traditionally been limited to financial assistance to liquidators, with the courts recognising an exception to the torts of maintenance and champerty (which arise for benefiting and encouraging litigation). These torts have been abolished in many jurisdictions, but concerns lingered about whether litigation funding was an abuse of process. These concerns were swept aside by the case of *Campbell's Cash and Carry Pty Ltd v Fostif Pty Ltd*,[35] in which the High Court held that litigation funding was not an abuse of process. Since that time litigation funding has become increasingly popular, so popular that there is a publicly listed company whose sole business is litigation funding: Bentham IMF Ltd (formerly IMF (Australia) Ltd). This company has a market capitalisation of over A$300 million and made a net profit of A$13 million in 2012–13. Bentham IMF has exported its business to several overseas countries, including the US and England, and is the largest litigation funder in Australia. Bentham IMF also holds an Australian Financial Services Licence (AFSL), which allows it to operate managed investment schemes. Funding of litigation could potentially be seen as a 'managed investment scheme'. However, ASIC has issued an order ('class order relief') making it clear that an AFSL is currently not required for others that are involved, or would be interested in getting involved, in litigation funding. Requiring all litigation funding companies to have an AFSL would be likely to reduce competition and further entrench the dominant position that Bentham IMF has in the market.

The most common ground used in shareholder class actions is an alleged failure to comply with continuous disclosure laws and/or misleading or deceptive conduct.[36] Following changes to the Corporations Act in 2010, it is not possible for a shareholder class action to claim compensation from a company that is in liquidation or voluntary administration unless all non-shareholder creditors have been paid in full.[37]

Once the class action is commenced it is a judicially managed process. The parties cannot terminate the action, including by settlement, without the permission of the court.[38] Class actions are usually brought in the hope of obtaining a favourable settlement. There have been no shareholder class actions in Australia that have reached final judgment. Given the large

---

35   (2006) 229 CLR 386.
36   See further Peter Cashman, *Class Action Law and Practice* (Federation Press, 2007) Ch 8.
37   *Corporations Act 2001* (Cth) s 563A.
38   *Federal Court of Australia Act 1976* (Cth) s 33V.

claims and large numbers of class members involved, the settlements can be substantial, with several actions being settled for more than A$100 million, the largest being the Centro class actions, which settled for A$200 million in 2012. Market-based causation was given limited recognition in a recent first instance decision, albeit in a long-running insolvency matter that pre-dated the 2010 amendments.[39] It remains to be seen what effect this will have on securities class actions generally.

Although shareholder class actions have been criticised for being expensive and complex and opening the door to frivolous claims, they are growing in number and have been embraced by institutional investors. They have been recognised as having a valuable role in complementing public enforcement by the Australian Securities and Investments Commission (ASIC).[40]

13.8 Case studies

CARL ICAHN

Carl Icahn is perhaps the most famous activist investor in the world.[41] He has operated a number of enterprises over the years, including a securities firm (Icahn & Co.), a hedge fund (Icahn Capital LP) and a diversified holding company with interests across a range of business lines (Icahn Enterprises LP). Icahn built a fearsome reputation as a corporate raider in the 1980s: his actions included the hostile takeover and eventual breakup of TWA (Trans World Airlines). In recent years Icahn has become a shareholder activist and advocate for corporate governance reform rather than merely a corporate raider. He has advocated corporate governance and business operations reforms in large public companies such as Yahoo (advocating the resignation of CEO Jerry Yang and the merger with Microsoft), Dell Computer (opposing the privatisation proposed by CEO Michael Dell) and eBay (advocating the spin-off of PayPal).[42]

In recent times Icahn has made a high-profile and sustained attack on Apple, arguing that Apple is the most over-capitalised company in history. Apple has over US$150 billion in cash reserves, which has provoked widespread public criticism from the investment community. Activist hedge fund Greenlight Capital called for Apple to issue preference shares as a way of returning some of the excess capital to investors; this led Apple to announce a buyback and dividend program that would involve more than US$100 billion over several years. Icahn then became involved by buying up over US$4 billion worth of Apple shares, and advocated loudly that Apple should both increase and accelerate its buyback program. This action included a meeting with the Apple CEO and a pending proxy fight at an Apple

39   *Re HIH Insurance Ltd (in liq)* (2016) 113 ACSR 318.
40   See further Michael Legg, 'ASIC'S Nod to Class Actions May Backfire', *The Australian*, 12 April 2012.
41   See 'Anything You Can Do, Icahn Do Better', *The Economist*, 15 February 2014, 55.
42   For an empirical study of the Icahn effect on public companies see Vinod Venkiteshwaran, Subramanian Iyer and Ramesh Rao, 'Is Carl Icahn good for long-term shareholders? A case study in shareholder activism' (2010) 22 *Journal of Applied Corporate Finance* 45.

shareholders' meeting. Apple responded to this by increasing its public buyback program and Icahn dropped his proxy proposal.

One major feature of Icahn's shareholder activism is the highly public nature of his battles with company management. Icahn has set up a Twitter feed and his tweets about companies often have an effect on the company's share price. He has also established a shareholder activist website, writes opinion pieces in newspapers and magazines and has previously issued a regular corporate governance report (The Icahn Report). As corporate governance expert Robert Monks said, Icahn has made 'it clear to the greediest people in the world that you can make a lot of money out of activism'.[43]

DANIEL LOEB AND THIRD POINT LLC

Daniel Loeb's Third Point LLC owned just over 5 per cent of shares in Yahoo, which it disclosed to the market at the same time as seeking the appointment of four directors to the Yahoo board and the removal of several incumbent directors. The company's CEO, Jerry Yang, set up a conference call between Third Point and senior management. The call was cut short by Yahoo management, and Third Point then engaged in a prolonged public debate about the performance of Yahoo management and the future value of the company. During this time both the Yahoo CEO and Chairman resigned from the company. Third Point publicly criticised the qualifications and appropriateness of the new CEO, Scott Thompson, and he resigned 10 days later. On the same day Loeb and two Third Point associates were appointed to the Yahoo board. In the 14 months during which Third Point had three board members on the board of Yahoo, the value of the company's share price increased from US $15 per share to more than US$28 per share. Third Point announced that Yahoo was buying back two-thirds of its shares in the company for a profit – to Third Point – in excess of US$500 million. The three Third Point board members then also resigned from the Yahoo board.

The high-profile success that Daniel Loeb and his Third Point hedge fund had with Yahoo has been followed up with similar activities by Third Point involving Sotheby's (requesting board seats and calling for the CEO/Chairman to resign), Sony (calling for the spin-off of the company's ailing entertainment division) and Dow Chemical (calling for the spin-off of a subsidiary). Third Point conducts its corporate governance battles with public companies in a highly public manner, publishing correspondence with company management online. These letters from Daniel Loeb have typically led to large increases in the target company's share prices, of 5 per cent or more in the short term.

---

43   'Anything You Can Do, Icahn Do Better', *The Economist*, 15 February 2014, 55.

MARK CARNEGIE

Mark Carnegie has had a long and successful career, both in Australia and internationally, as a corporate adviser. After selling his corporate advisory firm Carnegie, Wylie & Co. to Lazard he established MH Carnegie & Co. as an investment house and asset management business. In recent years Carnegie has taken on the role of shareholder activist by being involved in corporate governance battles with major public companies such as Qantas and Brickworks/Washington H Soul Pattinson. Each of these contests has involved large consortiums of investors and extensive public criticism of incumbent management. For Qantas, Carnegie teamed up with former Qantas CEO Geoff Dixon, former Qantas CFO Peter Gregg, Harvey Norman executives Gerry Harvey and Katie Price and advertising and media entrepreneur John Singleton to purchase just under 2 per cent of the shares in Qantas. The group then released public plans to pressure Qantas management to dump CEO Alan Joyce, to revise the tie-up with Emirates Airlines and to spin off the company's frequent flyer program. However, these plans did not attract further institutional investor support and the group later sold its Qantas shares.

Carnegie teamed up with fund manager Perpetual in 2013 to pressure the listed companies Brickworks and Washington H Soul Pattinson to unwind a decades-long (and complex) cross-shareholding arrangement that effectively prevents either company from being taken over. The group also criticised the role of executive Chair Robert Millner in both companies. The proposal was a complex one that was to be put to the members' meetings of each company. If approved, it would lead to a series of asset disposals and returns of capital to shareholders in both companies. At the time of writing the companies had rejected the proposals and recommended that shareholders also reject them, but Carnegie and his associates had properly requisitioned a members' meeting to consider the proposals, which failed. Their court challenge also failed: *RBC Investor Services Australia Nominees Pty Ltd v Brickworks Ltd* [2017] FCA 756.

In addition to the use of publicity, Carnegie has also used other techniques adopted by hedge funds – namely derivatives – to obtain large share parcels, or the potential to obtain large share parcels, and thus build up his position in target companies. This is a tactic that James Packer also used in his corporate governance attack on Echo Entertainment (a large gaming and casino operator) in 2013.

Carnegie is certainly not alone as a major shareholder activist in Australia. In recent times wealthy businesspeople such as Kerry Stokes, James Packer, Gina Rinehart and Jan Cameron have also used activist tactics to gain influence over the corporate strategy of major public companies without launching a full takeover. Stokes took a major (but not controlling) position in West Australian Newspapers, used this to secure board seats and eventually merged the business into his broader media and industrial empire. Packer undertook a highly public and personal attack on Echo Entertainment, which resulted in widespread management change. Rinehart purchased a major stake in Fairfax (a large media company) and used this to pressure management on operational matters, although she was unsuccessful in obtaining board representation. Cameron took a public activist stance in late 2016/early 2017 by criticising the board of Bellamy's Organic (which makes baby food). This was done using an opaque offshore trust to hold shares (called the 'Black Prince Trust') which held a large shareholding in Bellamy's and voted together with Ms Cameron, who held shares and swaps over shares. Over several months leading up to a shareholder meeting Ms Cameron engaged in a bitter public attack on the company's management and their handling of distribution issues in China. This resulted in several directors losing their board positions, replaced by candidates supported by Ms Cameron. The Bellamy's CEO and Chair both resigned from the company.

13.9 Conclusion

Shareholder activism has been a hot topic of debate in recent years. A number of high-profile businesspeople have fashioned themselves as shareholder activists after discovering that control and influence over a company, even a large public company, can be achieved without the need for a full takeover. While activism has its critics, who highlight that profit motives, rather than a desire for corporate governance change, underpin the majority of activist agendas, there is no doubt that shareholder activism works and is here to stay.[44]

44 See further OECD, 'The Role of Institutional Investors in Promoting Good Corporate Governance' (2011) <www.oecd.org/corporate/ca/corporategovernanceprinciples/theroleofinstitutionalinvestors inpromotinggoodcorporategovernance.htm>.

14

BUSINESS ETHICS AND CORPORATE GOVERNANCE

Companies have proved enormously powerful not just because they improve productivity, but also because they possess most of the legal rights of a human being, without the attendant disadvantages of biology: they are not condemned to die of old age and they can create progeny pretty much at will.

John Micklethwait and Adrian Wooldridge, *The Company: A Short History of a Revolutionary Idea* (Modern Library, 2005) xv.

The greatest trade scandal in Australian history started over lunch. Domenic Hogan was there, which was as much a surprise to him as to anyone. To look at Hogan is not to think: well, here is an international man of mystery. Here is a player in a grand plot to funnel hundreds of millions of dollars to Saddam Hussein's brutal regime ... No. On the contrary, to look at Hogan is to think: now here's an ordinary guy.

Caroline Overington, *Kickback: Inside the Australian Wheat Board Scandal* (Allen & Unwin, 2007) 2

14.1 Introduction

One only has to scan the daily newspaper or follow a newsfeed to find plentiful examples of corporations being criticised for unethical conduct. It would take little more time to find businesses or business leaders who have suffered significant reputational damage, enforcement actions or damages claims. Since the 1970s, a considerable academic and practical literature has developed that considers and explores the field of business ethics, drawing on theory, practice and empirical data. Subjects that consider business ethics have become standard within university business courses.[1] There can be no doubt that the conduct of corporations attracts considerable public interest. For a corporation, the consequences of perceived unethical activity can be profound: they include significant penalties for breaches that amount to regulatory infringements.[2] It can also lead to calls for enhanced regulation and broader scrutiny of corporate activity.[3] In this context the management of a corporation's ethical climate and conduct is increasingly seen as critical to its success, and a matter with which the senior management and the board should be deeply concerned. No book on corporate governance would, therefore, be complete without canvassing this topic.

Despite this considerable focus, it is not easy to navigate the complexities of the way organisations can, do and should manage business ethics. To traverse this area successfully it is

1   Henk van Luijk, 'Business Ethics: Cases, Codes and Institutions' in Wim Dubbink, Luc van Liedekerke and Henk van Luijk (eds), *European Business Ethics Casebook: The Morality of Corporate Decision Making* (Springer, 2011) 3.
2   Jill Treanor, 'Barclays bank reaches $100m US settlement over Libor rigging scandal', *The Guardian*, online edition, 9 August 2016; David J Lynch, 'VW admits guilt and pays $4.3bn emissions scandal penalty', *Financial Times*, 12 January 2017; Danielle Ivory and Bill Vlasic, '$900 Million Penalty for G.M.'s Deadly Defect Leaves Many Cold', *New York Times*, 17 September 2015.
3   Justin O'Brien, 'Normal science and paradigmatic shifts: Political and regulatory strategies to develop investor protection in the aftermath of crisis' (2012) 52(s1) *Accounting and Finance* 217, 224.

critical to understand how ethical problems arise. The strategies for their management can then be tailored to respond to these pressure points. It is also vital that those governing corporations be intimately connected to the ethics of their organisation. Without scrutiny, thoughtful responses and commitment from those leading the organisation, the risk of poor outcomes is considerable. Steven Brenner points out that 'all organizations have ethics programs' even if, as he asserts, 'most do not know they do'.[4] In fact, whatever they are, 'processes of governance and regulation imply particular sets of ethical values and norms'.[5] This chapter considers how the external regulatory settings, and processes of governance within corporations, can affect ethical conduct.

Before going any further, a note of caution. The discipline of ethics and the applied area of business ethics are complex, contested and important. While this chapter, and the others in this volume, consider and explain the ethical dimensions of corporate governance, by necessity they can only introduce some key concepts and ways of thinking about business ethics. They cannot provide the fullness of a deep consideration of the philosophical roots of ethical theory,[6] nor a comprehensive picture of business ethics theory and practice. Our aim is to be introductory.

It is also pertinent to note that business ethics is related to concepts of corporate social responsibility, and corporate responsibility, as discussed in Chapters 1 and 3. Rosamund Thomas explains that:

> Corporate Social Responsibility (CSR) differs from Business Ethics insofar as it concentrates principally on the social, environmental, and human rights concerns of business companies, more than their moral leadership. However, in practice, CSR and Business Ethics are frequently entwined in the company's Mission Statement or Code of Ethics.[7]

As this points out there is a practical link between these areas. CSR and corporate responsibility relate to the way the corporation exercises its power, in particular its effects on external constituencies. Business ethics is relevant to this but operates across all corporate activities, including CSR. It is the platform that underlies all corporate activity.

With those matters in mind, this chapter opens with a brief discussion of the nature of business ethics, its significance for corporations and the ethical dimensions of a corporation's stakeholder relationships. The next section is focused on the causes of ethical problems: bad apples, bad cases and bad barrels. In order to examine these it presents the theory related to each before drawing on three case studies: the HIH failure, the LIBOR case and the GM ignition switch. The extent to which we attempt to encourage ethical conduct is discussed in the following section. In particular, that section examines corporate accountability, individual accountability and organisation-level approaches that seek to shape the ethical conduct of corporations. The final section is devoted to some concluding remarks.

---

4   Steven N Brenner, 'Ethics programs and their dimensions' (1992) 11 *Journal of Business Ethics* 391, 391.
5   Glenn Morgan, 'Governance and Regulation: An Institutionalist Approach to Ethics and Organizations' in Martin Parker (ed.), *Ethics and Organizations* (Sage, 1998) 197, 229.
6   For an accessible account of ethical theory see Noel Preston, *Understanding Ethics* (Federation Press, 3rd ed, 2007).
7   Rosamund M Thomas, *Business Ethics and Corporate Social Responsibility* (Ethics International Press, 2015) 83.

14.2 The case for business ethics

In order to understand the significance and complexities of business ethics, this section explores the concept of business ethics and its relationship to the way corporations operate, mediating between the interests of, and obligations to, various stakeholder groups.

14.2.1 The significance of the modern corporation

It is difficult to overestimate the reach and significance of the modern corporation in our daily lives, and in the progress of our economies. The products and services provided by corporations touch us in myriad ways every moment of our lives. Corporations often employ us, we use corporate vehicles to preserve and enhance our personal wealth, we rely on corporations for housing, transport, healthcare, entertainment and nutrition. We are avid consumers of the goods and services created by corporations across the globe. The pervasive nature of the corporation, and its ability to influence our lives at the personal and societal level, makes it a powerful actor in enhancing or undermining social and individual welfare.[8] We are all vulnerable to negative impacts when corporations act unethically. Accordingly, it might be expected that we take an interest in the extent to which corporations 'do the right thing'.

While the corporation is predominantly a source of progress and prosperity, there are certainly numerous instances where corporations have been conducted in ways that harmed others. Famous examples include the Ford Pinto case, the Bhopal disaster, the Exxon Valdez oil spill and the Enron collapse. In this chapter, three case studies of unethical conduct will be examined.

Each of these examples provides concrete evidence about why we want corporations to act ethically. The impact of the corporate activity was profound, rippling out from each corporation to affect many beyond. Following these events, individual and corporate decision-making was scrutinised and in some cases significant penalties were visited on the corporations and some individuals.[9] In each case the conduct flowed from a decision or, more likely, a number of decisions or non-decisions. In these cases, the person or persons concerned either failed to see the ethical issue or made the wrong call. In some cases the ethical problems were deep-seated within structures, policies and processes, making ethical decision-making more difficult, or making the ethical dimensions of particular issues harder to spot.

14.2.2 What are business ethics?

Defining business ethics has been likened to 'nailing jello to a wall'.[10] Nonetheless it is possible to capture at least a working definition using the general concept of ethics. The study of ethics

---

8   Christine Parker, *Open Corporation: Effective Self-Regulation and Democracy* (Cambridge University Press [CUP], 2002) 2.

9   See, for example, Mike Spector and Mike Colias, 'VW Cops $3.7bn Fine For Emissions Rigging', *The Australian*, 13 March 2017.

10   Phillip V Lewis, 'Defining "business ethics": Like nailing jello to a wall' (1985) 4 *Journal of Business Ethics* 377, 382.

can be focused on a singular question: what does it mean to be 'right, fair, just or good'?[11] According to Christine Parker and Adrian Evans:

> Ethics is concerned with deciding what is the good or right thing to do – right or wrong action, and with the moral evaluation of our own and others' character and actions – what does it mean to be a good person? In deciding what to do and how to be, ethics requires that we look for coherent reasons for our actions and character that show why it is right or wrong.[12]

Logically then, business ethics provides a focus on the right thing to do in the context of business endeavour.

Part of the definitional difficulty associated with defining business ethics can be attributed to the fact that it has 'macro' and 'micro' aspects. As Noel Preston explains:

> At the micro level we may be concerned to identify virtues which make a good business person, for example, diligence and service; this level also includes the ethics of intra-organisational relationships, matters of employee well-being for instance, or respectful treatment of customers. The macro level refers to the moral duties of a company with respect to the rest of society. It implies leadership in business characterised by the virtue of civic responsibility.[13]

It is possible, however, to craft a definition that is capable of accommodating both of these perspectives, though it will necessarily be somewhat abstract. Phillip Lewis, after reviewing contemporary definitions in textbooks and articles, settled on the following: '"business ethics" is moral rules, standards, codes, or principles which provide guidelines for right and truthful behavior in specific situations'.[14] Such a definition can encompass both the micro and the macro aspects.

Drawing on this discussion, and turning to corporate governance, the question then becomes what is the right, good, fair and just approach for those leading corporations to take? At the macro level, as we can see from the discussion above, there is no doubt that the value choices made by those who lead corporations can have significant impact. At the micro level the rules, standards, codes, norms or principles that guide activity within a particular corporation can also affect those within and those outside the corporation in profound ways. Ultimately corporate boards are responsible for both of these aspects of the corporation's ethics. As Philip Styles and Bernard Taylor point out:

> Boards ... set the ethical tone with regard to their monitoring and accountability roles. What is expected of management, both by way of performance and behaviour, is ultimately the responsibility of directors. The board is thus recognized as crucial in the process of developing an ethical framework, implicit or explicit, for the formulation of strategy and policy, monitoring management and ensuring accountability.[15]

---

11   Noel Preston, *Understanding Ethics* (Federation Press, 3rd ed, 2007) 16.
12   Christine Parker and Adrian Evans, *Inside Lawyers' Ethics* (CUP, 2007) 2.
13   Preston, *Understanding Ethics* (2007) 171.
14   Lewis, 'Defining "business ethics": Like nailing jello to a wall' (1985) 382.
15   Philip Styles and Bernard Taylor, *Boards at Work* (Oxford University Press [OUP], 2002) 39 (citations omitted).

Turning first to the macro level, in the 1960s and 1970s the concerns about corporate activity prompted a public debate about how we should think about the ethics of corporate enterprise in the wider sense. This debate was not new. Professors Berle and Dodd canvassed similar issues several decades earlier.[16] However, the debate provides a useful starting point to understanding the ethics of corporations. The debate was championed on one side by Milton Friedman, the US economist, whose essay 'The Social Responsibility of Business is to Increase its Profits'[17] is still cited as representing a conservative view of the ethics of corporations.[18]

In that essay Friedman sought to clarify, and debunk, those who 'declaim that business is not concerned "merely" with profit but also with promoting desirable "social" ends'.[19] His argument is that the corporation itself could not have responsibilities, as it is purely an artificial construct, and therefore the more accurate articulation of the position is that individuals, such as corporate executives, have social responsibilities in their professional roles. He then asserts that the responsibility of these individuals must be to achieve the aims of the owners of the business, and that this is, most commonly, to generate profits. He argued that any allegiance by corporate executives to 'social goals', where they derogate from their primary profit-making function, would not only undermine the executives' devotion to the interests of the shareholders, but also mean that an executive 'self-selected or appointed directly or indirectly by stockholders ... is to be simultaneously legislator, executive and jurist'.[20] For Friedman, there are two legitimate checks on conduct. First, corporate executives should conform to the 'basic rules of society, both those embodied in the law and those embodied in ethical custom'. The 'invisible hand' of the market provides the second limit. In his view any external interventions or expectations beyond these are counterproductive.[21]

The contrary argument sees corporations as having a social role that goes beyond their economic impact.[22] This argument is formulated in various ways. Some suggest that as corporations are given significant benefits, such as separate perpetual legal existence and limited liability, they should then be expected to 'pay' for those advantages by prioritising social good, or at least considering the social impact of their activities.[23] Another strand of the argument is focused on ensuring that corporations are 'managed so that individuals are treated as "ends"

---

16   Adolf A Berle Jr, 'Corporate powers as powers in trust' (1931) 44 *Harvard Law Review* 1049;
       E Merrick Dodd, 'For whom are the corporate managers trustees?' (1932) 45 *Harvard Law Review* 1145.
       See also John CC Macintosh, 'The issues, effects and consequences of the Berle–Dodd debate,
       1931–1932' (1999) 24 *Accounting, Organizations and Society* 139.

17   Milton Friedman, 'The Social Responsibility of Business is to Increase its Profits', *The New York Times*
       Magazine, 13 September 1970.

18   James Arnt Aune, 'How to Read Milton Friedman: Corporate Social Responsibility and Today's
       Capitalisms' in S May, G Cheney and J Roper (eds), *The Debate over Corporate Social Responsibility*
       (OUP, 2007) 207–8; Thomas Mulligan, 'A critique of Milton Friedman's essay "The Social Responsibility
       of Business is to Increase its Profits"' (1986) 5 *Journal of Business Ethics* 265, 265.

19   Friedman, 'The Social Responsibility of Business is to Increase its Profits', 13 September 1970.

20   Ibid.

21   Ibid; Helen Anderson, 'The theory of the corporation and its tortious liability to creditors' (2004) 16
       Australian Journal of Corporate Law 1, 3; Kent Greenfield, *The Failure of Corporate Law* (University of
       Chicago Press, 2008) 31 (summing up the argument that any legal intervention in corporate governance
       should be minimal due to its private law nature).

22   David Millon, 'Communitarians, contractarians, and the crisis in corporate law' (1993) 50(4) *Washington*
       and Lee Law Review 1373, 1379.

23   Peter Nobel, 'Social responsibility of corporations' (1999) 84 *Cornell Law Review* 1255, 1257.

instead of as "means".[24] A further point made is that market mechanisms cannot necessarily appropriately compensate for the costs visited on others by corporate activity,[25] and that both government intervention and internal ethical governance arrangements are required to reduce the costs imposed by corporations on external constituencies.

Nor is this debate consigned to history. The furore about donations by Australian corporations that occurred in the wake of the Boxing Day tsunami in 2004 canvassed exactly these issues.[26] It also came to the fore when the James Hardie group of companies moved its parent company offshore and made insufficient provision for current and future liabilities arising from the manufacture and sales of asbestos by a number of its subsidiaries.[27] In 2017, an open letter to the Prime Minister signed by a number of Australian corporate leaders advocating legalisation of same-sex marriage sparked both approbation, on the basis that they were championing an issue relevant to their businesses, and critique, on the basis that they were improperly intervening on a moral issue.[28]

In essence, both perspectives agree that certain aspects of ethical conduct are unproblematic. That is, conduct that advances the interests of shareholders, while also benefiting other stakeholders, is clearly acceptable. This could include conduct that enhances the corporate brand, increases employee, shareholder and consumer motivation and loyalty and avoids negative publicity and/or regulatory sanctions. These rationales, on their face, provide significant latitude and support for those governing corporations to develop and support ethical conduct. As Peter Henley explains, 'The current law is capable of supporting a broad range of philanthropic and "socially responsible" activities and "sustainable" business practices.'[29] In 2006, a Commonwealth Parliamentary Joint Committee on Corporations and Financial Services reached a similar conclusion. It took the view that 'the Corporations Act permits directors to have regard for the interests of stakeholders other than shareholders'.[30]

We have dealt with various corporate law theories and the importance of an all-inclusive approach in detail in Chapters 1 and 2, but it is important to be reminded of the importance of stakeholders, as emphasised by the G20/OECD *Principles of Corporate Governance*:

> Corporations should recognise that the contributions of stakeholders constitute a valuable resource for building competitive and profitable companies. It is, therefore, in the long-term interest of corporations to foster wealth-creating co-operation among stakeholders.[31]

---

24   Timothy L Fort, 'The corporation as mediating institution: An efficacious synthesis of stakeholder theory and corporate constituency statutes' (1997) 73(1) *Notre Dame Law Review* 173, 196.

25   Millon, 'Communitarians, contractarians, and the crisis in corporate law' (1993) 1383.

26   Peter Henley, 'Were corporate tsunami donations made legally? Directors and corporate social responsibilities' (2005) 30(4) *Alternative Law Journal* 154, 158.

27   See the case study in Chapter 2.

28   Rachel Baxendale and Dennis Shanahan, 'Sparks fly as chiefs tell Turnbull "marriage equality good for business"', *The Australian*, online edition, 16 March 2017.

29   Henley, 'Were corporate tsunami donations made legally? Directors and corporate social responsibilities' (2005) 154.

30   Parliamentary Joint Committee on Corporations and Financial Services, 'Corporate responsibility: Managing risk and creating value' (2006) xiv.

31   G20/OECD, *Principles of Corporate Governance* (2015) 34.

More difficult questions arise where an ethical dilemma seems to lead to a decision that does not seem to advance, or even undermines, shareholder interests, perhaps in order to prioritise another stakeholder group. It is then going be up to corporate management to disclose and justify their decision or actions in a way that is satisfactory to the shareholders, assuming the shareholder primacy model still underpins our corporate law model,[32] and the board. The board would also have a role in monitoring management actions of this kind and ensuring that they are in the best interests of the company. And shareholders have mechanisms (which may or may not be effective) that enable them to discipline the directors if they fail.

While the debate above seems to assume that ethical decision-making is a clean deliberative process, leading to ethical failure or success, in reality ethical failures are complex and not always deliberate. Ethical failures can arise when the relevant actors fail to see and understand the ethical dimensions of particular decisions, policy settings or practices. Such failures can also flow when there is recognition of an ethical aspect to a particular part of business but a failure to act, or an action that is problematic. Failures can be predicated by decisions taken decades before, or the previous day. The dilemmas can be derived from external forces or entirely generated within the corporation. They can flow from one event or from a series of events over days, months, even years. In order to understand this complexity, the next step is to understand better how ethical problems emerge.

14.3 The causes of ethical problems

In their meta-analysis, Jennifer Kish-Gephart, David Harrison and Linda Klebe Treviño argue that the causes of unethical conduct in workplaces can be grouped into three categories.[33] First are 'bad apples' – individuals who engage in unethical behaviour. 'Bad cases' are the second group. These occur where the activity is such that it is difficult to identify the ethical dimensions, or the effect of the decision is seen as remote, unlikely or minor. Finally, 'bad barrels' are those organisational settings that encourage or allow unethical conduct. While these three categories provide a useful way to think about problematic conduct, of course, as the case studies below indicate, there is potential for the categories to overlap and reinforce each other in complex ways. There may well be elements of each category present in any one event. Nonetheless they provide a useful starting point for thinking about ethical risks and opportunities within the corporate governance sphere. Each is considered more fully below.

14.3.1 Bad apples

It is common to see 'bad apples' as key contributors to ethical problems. This descriptor seeks to explain ethical problems by reference to particular individuals or individual characteristics. It is a familiar approach. The Australian Securities Exchange's (ASX) *CG Principles and Recommendations* asserts that 'Good corporate governance depends on the personal integrity

---

32   See Jean J du Plessis, 'Shareholder primacy and other stakeholder interests' (2016) 34 *Company and Securities Law Review (C&SLJ)* 238, 241.

33   Jennifer J Kish-Gephart, David A Harrison and Linda Klebe Treviño, 'Bad apples, bad cases, and bad barrels: Meta-analytic evidence about sources of unethical decisions at work' (2010) 95 *Journal of Applied Psychology* 1, 2.

of those on boards and in management.'[34] In the wake of corporate scandal or collapse the significance of various individuals often becomes a focus of discussion. For example, the role and actions of Ray Williams and Rodney Adler in the collapse of the HIH insurance group were heavily criticised in the press and in the Royal Commission, and ultimately led to significant jail terms. In the wake of the Enron collapse, Fastow, the CFO, Skilling, the CEO, and Lay, the chairman, were prosecuted, and Fastow and Skilling were jailed.[35] In the LIBOR case study below some of the sentencing remarks seem to fit with 'bad apple' status being attributed to Jay Merchant. The judge finds that '[t]he evidence of the way in which manipulation of the rate began in earnest after you arrived in New York was compelling' and 'It was under your leadership on the desk that the requests to the LIBOR submitters really took off'.[36]

The foundation of the 'bad apple' explanation lies in the understanding that each corporation acts through the agency of the individuals within it. It recognises that 'in order to conduct business or do anything at all, corporations must always have accomplices, since without people to run them, corporations are mere legal constructs – ideas, not things'.[37] When ethical problems emerge, it is often possible to trace those back to people within the organisation whose actions – or failures to act – are seen as having contributed to the problem. It is also consistent with the view that ethical or unethical conduct is a matter of personal, rather than collective, responsibility. In contrast, attributing ethical problems to bad cases and bad barrels shifts the focus to the corporation and its activities as a factor in the genesis and management of ethical issues. Having said that, there is clearly a role for those involved in the governance of a corporation in identifying and managing individuals who may be predisposed to ethically problematic conduct. And bad apples, particularly where they are in positions of influence and power, can have a significant impact on the way organisations see and manage ethical activity, hence potentially contributing to bad cases and barrels.

14.3.1.1 A case study of the HIH collapse

We have discussed the HIH case from a legal point of view and as far as the liability of directors were concerned – see Chapter 9 Section 9.3.2. The case is, however, also significant as far as ethical lessons are concerned. HIH had its origins in an insurance agency started by Ray Williams and Michael Payne in 1968, MW Payne Liability Agencies Pty Ltd.[38] Its descendent, CE Heath Underwriting Agencies, was listed on the ASX in 1992.[39] Once listed, the company engaged in a rapid expansion, with a series of mergers and acquisitions both within Australia and overseas.[40] By 2001, the year of its collapse, the corporation, then known as HIH, was a

34   ASX, *CG Principles and Recommendations* (3rd ed, 2014) 19.
35   Lay died after his conviction and prior to serving a sentence: Kristen Hays and Anna Driver, 'Former Enron CEO Skilling's sentence cut to 14 years', Reuters Online, 21 June 2013 <www.reuters.com/article/us-enron-skilling-idUSBRE95K12520130621>.
36   *R v Peter Johnson, Jonathan Mathew, Jay Vijay Merchant and Alex Pabon*, Sentencing remarks of HHJ Anthony Leonard QC, Southwark Crown Court, 8 July 2016.
37   Sean F Griffith, 'Afterword and comment: Towards an ethical duty to market investors' (2003) 35 *Connecticut Law Review* 1223, 1252.
38   Report of the HIH Royal Commission (Owen Report), *The Failure of HIH Insurance* (Commonwealth of Australia, 2003) Vol. 1, 3.1.
39   Ibid. 54.
40   Farid Varess, '"The buck will stop at the board"? An examination of directors' (and other) duties in light of the HIH collapse' (2002) 16 *Commercial Law Quarterly* 12, 13.

major player in the Australian insurance market. It held thousands of 'professional liability, public indemnity, home warranty and travel insurance policies'.[41]

The HIH collapse has the dubious honour of being Australia's largest corporate failure.[42] Ultimately the corporation was revealed to have debts of at least A$5.3 billion.[43] The subsequent Royal Commission identified the cause of the HIH failure as insufficient attention having been paid to the financial health of the corporation. In particular, there were inadequate systems and processes in place for the proper review of business practices and outcomes.[44] As a result, ongoing poor risk management led to insufficient premiums being charged and inadequate provision being made for claims. Fundamental problems with the bread and butter business of HIH were compounded by decisions to buy into several failing businesses, without due diligence. These transactions were entered into without a full appreciation of their complexities, and the ultimate effect that they might have on the viability of HIH. For example, the Allianz joint venture, entered into in September 2000, had the effect of requiring HIH to hand over its most profitable lines to Allianz. The agreement required payment into trust of a lump sum of $500 million, to be followed by a requirement to contribute the insurance premiums for these lines to the trust until an actuarial analysis justified their quarterly distribution. By this time HIH was so chronically short of funds that the purchase price from Allianz of $200 million had to be paid into the trust to satisfy the lump sum obligation. Then the delay associated with the actuarial report and distribution caused the cash flow crisis that hastened the end. The Royal Commission found that the 'trust provisions and their potential adverse effect on cash flow were either completely overlooked or not properly appreciated'.[45] In addition, a number of overseas ventures were spectacularly unsuccessful, draining the group of much-needed funds.

A number of commentators have noted that HIH's failure can be traced to the corporation's rapid transition from a small private company through to Australia's second-largest insurer.[46] Despite the tumult of the transition from private to public company, and the many suitors and substantial shareholders who at one stage or another had a finger in the HIH pie, one man, its CEO, Ray Williams, dominated HIH. This dominance had two aspects that were particularly problematic. First, he treated HIH's assets as his own.[47] Second, he surrounded himself with

---

41   Owen Report, *The Failure of HIH Insurance* (2003) Vol. 1, xiv.

42   Jean J du Plessis, 'Reverberations after the HIH and other recent Australian corporate collapses: The role of ASIC' (2003) 15 *Australian Journal of Corporate Law* 1, 1; Phillip Lipton, 'The demise of HIH: Corporate governance lessons' (2003) 55 *Keeping Good Companies* 273.

43   Tina Mak, Hemant Deo and Kathie Cooper, 'Australia's major corporate collapse: Health International Holdings (HIH) Insurance "May the force be with you"' (2005) 2 *Journal of American Academy of Business* 104.

44   Owen Report, *The Failure of HIH Insurance* (2003) Vol. 1, xvii.

45   Ibid. xxvi.

46   Kamel Mellahi, 'The dynamics of boards of directors in failing organizations' (2005) 38 *Long Range Planning* 261; Owen Report, *The Failure of HIH Insurance* (2003) Vol. 1, xxvi–ii; note also that this criticism was made by Blake Dawson Waldron in a due diligence report in 1995, some six years before the collapse.

47   Williams' philanthropy was well known. HIH shareholders unknowingly bankrolled much of this: see HIH Royal Commission Report, vol. 3, 310; Andrew Main, *Other People's Money: The Complete Story of the Extraordinary Collapse of HIH* (HarperCollins, 2005) 227. When questioned at the Royal Commission on the payment by HIH of more than $38,000 for airfares for Mrs Williams in the year prior to the collapse, Williams was unrepentant.

people he trusted, but who were deferential to his views.[48] This meant that HIH had a senior management team with insufficient experience and expertise:

> No one rivalled him in terms of authority or influence. Even as his business judgment faltered in the second half of the 1990s he remained unchallenged. No one else in senior management was equipped to grasp what was happening and to bring about a change of direction for the group.[49]

This deference meant that the proposals of Williams and the affairs of HIH were not subject to the 'countervailing effect of close review, debate and questioning'.[50] Even the board was not immune to Williams' preference for loyalty over rigour, with longtime associates being shoe-horned into non-executive board roles. The board and its committees operated as rubber stamps of management decisions.

It was the practice of the HIH audit committee to meet before or after the main board meeting. The proximity to the board meeting, as well as a standing invitation to all members of the board to attend the audit committee meetings, meant that the committee operated as 'little more than an extension of the board'.[51] This had a number of consequences in terms of its effectiveness. It was potentially constrained in the time available to it to examine the necessarily complex issues arising from HIH's position. This issue was mentioned by a director, Head, in a detailed letter of complaint[52] to the company chairman, Geoffrey Cohen. Head's view was that the board was not being given sufficient information to enable it to make an informed contribution to the governance of the company. In the same month Justin Gardener, another HIH director,[53] had also approached the CEO, Ray Williams, with a list of matters for discussion.[54] The list reveals that Gardener was troubled by the lack of involvement of the board in the strategic direction of the company. Despite an apparent dismissal of these concerns,[55] Williams called a meeting of non-executive directors on 1 June 1999, when the other concerned director was away. Gardener explained his disquiet and Williams asked the directors present whether they were satisfied with HIH's governance arrangements:

---

48   The executive directors were all close associates of Williams. Fodera had been head-hunted from Arthur Andersen to take up a position as Chief Financial Officer. Sturesteps and Cassidy had been working alongside Williams since 1969 and 1972 respectively. Wein had been retained after the Swiss insurer Winterthur sold its majority shareholding in HIH.
49   Owen Report, *The Failure of HIH Insurance* (2003) Vol. 1, xxvii.
50   Ibid. xxvii.
51   Ibid. Vol. 3, 279.
52   The text of the Head's letter is reproduced in Owen Report, *The Failure of HIH Insurance* (2003) Vol. 3, 267–8. It cites a number of concerns about management not using the board effectively.
53   Despite the claims of HIH, analysis reveals that in fact Gardener's independence was compromised by his past association with the corporate auditor: Owen Report, *The Failure of HIH Insurance* (2003) Vol. 3, 261.
54   Ibid. 267: 'Gardener prepared an analysis of matters for discussion with Williams. The analysis covered the desired mindset of the board; matters to be reviewed with management including HIH's vision, purpose and strategy; oversight of management performance; and accountability' (citations omitted).
55   Gardener later described the meeting: 'Ray was very polite and said, "Well, thank you. But you don't have to worry about these things. You know, that's really the concern of management." And he, you know, metaphorically patted me on the head and sort of sent me on my way: 'Odds on to Fail', *ABC Four Corners*, 2 July 2001 (10 March 2009).

Ray asked, um, asked the um, er ... the board members whether they felt the board was operating satisfactorily – in response to my comment – and they all said, yes, they thought it was. I was somewhat nonplussed. I-I-I thought probably, er, Ray doesn't like, er, criticism. Er, and, um, he wanted to just make sure that, um, there was only one person that was being, being critical of him.[56]

Williams later asserted that Gardener had indicated that he was satisfied with the information provided in advance of the next board meeting.[57] No further action was taken in response to these concerns.[58]

One further incident provides an example of the way Williams discouraged free dialogue. Following an audit committee meeting where the auditors had signalled that HIH was facing serious difficulties, Alan Davies, then the HIH auditor, asked Head and Gardener to lunch. At the lunch a number of concerns that the auditors had were discussed. Williams appeared upset when he discovered that the meeting had occurred without his sanction or presence.[59] The end result for Davies was that Williams asked Arthur Andersen to remove him from the audit. Arthur Andersen duly complied.[60] It seems that the CEO felt it was inappropriate for the audit committee members to fulfil what would normally be seen as the standard role of an audit committee: that is, to meet with the auditor without management being present. This series of events had the potential to chill the free communication between the auditors and the non-executive directors.

14.3.1.2 Managing bad apples

The HIH case indicates the way an individual can influence the culture of a corporation. Kamel Mellahi argues that the board was passive and accepting of management dominance in the period before 1998. After 1998 'the CEO and management took deliberate steps to prevent the board from observing the warning signals'.[61] The formal complaints of Head and Gardener provided the CEO with an opportunity to 'employ a number of political techniques to overcome board opposition, such as distortion, reduction of communication with the board, and threats of punishment'.[62] By these means it was made clear to all the board members that their role was to follow management's lead.

The analysis of Kish-Gephart, Harrison and Treviño identifies four factors that are correlated with the unethical conduct of individuals.[63] First, there are those who are obedient to the ethical directives of others or who are motivated only to avoid punishment. Second are those who are motivated by self-interest. The third group do not appreciate the link between their actions and outcomes. Finally, there are those who are moral relativists: that is, they are not convinced that there are moral absolutes but rather believe that ethical principles change according to the circumstances. In each case these traits are likely to contribute to ethical

---

56   Ibid.
57   Owen Report, *The Failure of HIH Insurance* (2003) Vol. 3, 269.
58   Ibid.
59   Main, *Other People's Money* (2005) 231; Owen Report, *The Failure of HIH Insurance* (2003) Vol. 3, 91.
60   Main, *Other People's Money* (2005) 231–3;
61   Mellahi, 'The dynamics of boards of directors in failing organizations' (2005) 271.
62   Ibid. 275.
63   Kish-Gephart, Harrison and Treviño, 'Bad apples, bad cases, and bad barrels' (2010) 18.

problems. From a corporate governance perspective, recruitment policy could be a useful way to reduce the likelihood that bad apples, and hence ethical problems, become part of the corporation. The ability of bad apples to influence others can be particularly problematic, and profoundly so where the bad apple is in a position of influence. The data suggest that there is a case for acting decisively where a bad apple emerges. This is important from the perspective of removing the bad apple and because the appearance of tolerating a bad apple can create a bad barrel.

14.3.2 Bad cases

Bad cases are those where the nature of the issue is such that it inhibits ethical action. Writing in 1991, Thomas Jones posited that the characteristics of the issue can affect its moral intensity and hence influence whether or not individuals respond ethically.[64] He identified six elements that could make ethical decisions less likely. First, he argued that the *magnitude of the consequences* is significant.[65] In contemplating an action or inaction, individuals will consider the extent to which their act affects others. The greater the number of persons negatively affected, and the more acute the harm done to those persons, the more likely it is that the individual will act ethically. The second factor is *social consensus*.[66] Where there is broad agreement that a particular action is wrong it is harder to rationalise taking that course. This would suggest that unethical activity that is also illegal is more likely to be avoided. Third, Jones considers the *probability of the effect* important.[67] So an act that is more likely than not to cause harm will be given greater ethical weight than one where the probability of the harm occurring is small. The *temporal immediacy* of the effect is the fourth factor identified by James as influencing the ethical choices of individuals.[68] Where an act would take years to cause harm it is less likely to be taken seriously. This might be a factor with harm from asbestos exposure, which can take up to 40 years to emerge, or tobacco consumption, which again tends not to emerge for many years. Fifth, *proximity* highlights the 'feeling of nearness (social, cultural, psychological, or physical) that the moral agent has for victims (beneficiaries) of the evil (beneficial) act in question' as a factor that increases moral intensity.[69] The final factor is *concentration of effect*.[70] An act that causes slight harm to many people will have less importance in the mind of an actor than one that causes profound harm to fewer people.

14.3.2.1 A case study of the LIBOR scandal

In the LIBOR scandal, the incentives to act unethically were considerable. LIBOR is the trimmed averaged interest rate used as the basis for a benchmark interest rate that is referenced

---

64   Thomas M Jones, 'Ethical decision making by individuals in organizations: An issue-contingent model' (1991) 16(2) *Academy of Management* 366.
65   Ibid. 374–5.
66   Ibid. 375.
67   Ibid. 375–6.
68   Ibid. 376.
69   Ibid. 376–7.
70   Ibid. 377–8.

in financial transactions worth more than $300 trillion.[71] The benchmark is determined by reference to a self-report from 18 banks that make up a panel.[72] Each panel member responds to the question: 'At what rate could you borrow funds, were you to do so by asking for and then accepting inter-bank offers in a reasonable market size just prior to 11 am?'[73] The response is an estimate, with no requirements for any evidence or actual transaction to support it.[74] The responses are then trimmed, with the top 25 per cent and bottom 25 per cent being discarded and the remaining responses averaged.[75] At the time of the manipulations the bank submissions were made publicly available contemporaneously.[76]

This system can be seen as a bad case. First, the banks were both setting the benchmark and trading using the benchmark. This created an incentive to manipulate the rate to benefit the banks' trading arms. In relation to the manipulation by Barclays Bank, Professor Bainbridge notes:

> Because of the large amounts of financial contracts referencing LIBOR and the leverage inherent in the use of options and other derivatives, even very small changes in the LIBOR rate could earn a bank's trading desk significant profits. Evidence was emerging that Barclays derivatives traders pushed the bank employees who reported its LIBOR quote to provide high or low estimates depending on which would produce higher profits.[77]

In the sentencing remarks for four Barclays' employees who took part in the activity, the judge noted that while there was no substantial bonus resting on the outcome of the manipulation, it was motivated by the fact that 'retaining your job or being promoted to the next level at the bank did depend on making a profit on your book, something which was under daily scrutiny at the bank'.[78]

The second incentive arose in the wake of the 2008 Global Financial Crisis when it became critically important to some banks not to reveal their precarious financial position, which was reflected in their inability to secure funds at low rates. This created an incentive to register a higher rate than that which was genuinely available to the bank. It has been suggested that submitters were directed to present an inflated response by senior managers and also that the Bank of England gave an 'implicit nod' to this approach.[79] This indicates that there was little evident social consensus that the conduct was unethical.

This example provides almost a perfect storm of incentives, pressures and practices that encouraged unethical conduct: the apparent low risk of detection, the ease of implementation, the 'everyone's doing it' factor as banks joined forces to enable the manipulation, the fact that the harm caused was distant and not immediately obvious to the perpetrators, the sense of

---

71   UK Treasury, Wheatley Review of LIBOR, Final Report (2012) 7.

72   The current panel composition and policy on the panel composition are available at <www.theice.com/iba/libor>. At the time of the impugned conduct the panel was made up of 16 banks.

73   <www.theice.com/publicdocs/IBA_LIBOR_FAQ.pdf>.

74   Stephen M Bainbridge, 'Reforming LIBOR: Wheatley versus the alternatives' (2013) 9 *New York University Journal of Law and Business* 789, 796.

75   <www.theice.com/publicdocs/IBA_LIBOR_FAQ.pdf>.

76   Bainbridge, 'Reforming LIBOR: Wheatley versus the alternatives' (2013) 797.

77   Ibid. 800–1 (citations omitted).

78   *R v Peter Johnson, Jonathan Mathew, Jay Vijay Merchant and Alex Pabon*, Sentencing remarks of HHJ Anthony Leonard QC, Southwark Crown Court, 8 July 2016.

79   Bainbridge, 'Reforming LIBOR: Wheatley versus the alternatives' (2013) 801 (citations omitted).

sanction from both those higher in the organisation and those outside it and the strong incentives to act dishonestly. As such it represents a 'bad case'.

14.3.2.2 Managing bad cases

From a corporate governance perspective this case study suggests that the board should be alert to the potential for certain activities to lead to unethical conduct. One way to address this is by strengthening the narrative associated with the potential harm. Kish-Gephart, Harrison and Treviño argue that 'unethical behavior may be reduced if employees learn to associate potential unethical behavior with severe, well-defined harm (magnitude of consequences) to a familiar or recognizable victim similar to the actor (proximity)'.[80] In addition, the way incentives work could have a downward or upward spiral effect by encouraging either ethical or unethical conduct where there is a bad case. Policy settings, such as incentives and codes of conduct, as well as actions of the leadership team and narratives that encourage ethical conduct are all likely to play a significant role in shaping the consensus around acceptable and unacceptable conduct.

14.3.3 Bad barrels

The theory of the bad barrel is based on the idea that an organisation can significantly affect the ethical conduct of the individuals within it, in either positive or negative ways. A number of aspects of the organisation have been implicated in this process: the presence of organisational chaos, the lack of appropriate 'tone' at the top, the lack of a code of conduct, or more compellingly, the lack of a code of conduct that matters, the presence of an ethic of self-interest, a gulf between policy and practice, a 'siloed' approach, a lack of accountability and incentives to act unethically. More subtly, Fiona Haines argues that:

> Organizations, or more specifically organizational culture, may influence individual action
> in an unobtrusive and indirect manner by manipulating premises and providing norma-
> tive frameworks, rather than [by] any authoritarian control from above.[81]

It is possible that the way processes are organised could make it more difficult to identify and respond to ethical problems or that a focus on one corporate aim could drown out others. In the latter case, for example, a focus on efficiency might downgrade customer service below appropriate levels. As noted by Marianne Jennings and Lawrence Trautman, 'Psychologically, humans respond to the pressures and pain in the present, not the future and non-quantifiable costs that accompany poor risk decisions.'[82]

14.3.3.1 A case study of the GM ignition switch

The third example of corporate misconduct is provided by an ignition switch installed in a number of car models, especially the Chevrolet Cobalt, manufactured by the US-based conglomerate General Motors from 2002 to 2007. The ignition switch was approved for installation

---

80   Kish-Gephart, Harrison and Treviño, 'Bad apples, bad cases, and bad barrels' (2010) 20.

81   Fiona Haines, *Corporate Regulation: Beyond Punish or Persuade* (Clarendon Press, 1997) 93.

82   Marianne Jennings and Lawrence J Trautman, 'Ethical culture and legal liability: The GM switch crisis and lessons in governance' (2016) 22 *Boston University Journal of Science and Technology Law* 187, 207.

despite the fact that it did not meet the company's own specifications.[83] In particular, it had a lower torque than was specified, which meant that it could easily toggle from 'Run' to 'Accessory'.[84] This could be caused by uneven road surfaces, driver movement (such as a 'slight graze'[85] of the key), the weight of other items on the key ring (such as additional keys or accessories), or some event that jolted the car (such as running off the road prior to an accident). The effect of the car being switched to 'Accessory' mode was that it then had a 'moving stall'.[86] Once this occurred the driver had reduced ability to control the vehicle and the airbags would not deploy.[87]

Despite complaints about the switch being communicated to GM as early as September 2003, a number of legal claims, and damning media and police reports, no decision to recall the affected vehicles was made until 7 February 2014. In the meantime, at least 124 fatalities and 275 injuries that have since been linked to the defective ignition switch had occurred.[88] Even once the recall was initiated it was incomplete, with several further recalls affecting other GM lines having to be made. The most recent recall related to the switch was announced on 1 January 2015.[89] The costs of the recalls have been estimated at $2.7 billion as at October 2014.[90] GM has also paid out extraordinary sums, estimated to be around $2 billion, in civil and criminal penalties.[91]

This story begins as an engineering failure. The design engineer approved the ignition switch in full knowledge that it did not meet the company's own specifications.[92] According to the Valukas Report, in 2006 he then made it more difficult to identify the problem by modifying the part without changing its part number.[93] This cured the airbag issue and led later investigators to conclude – incorrectly – that the ignition switch could not have been responsible, as later cars with apparently the same switch did not have the defect.[94] A second critical error occurred because the problem with the switch was badged as one of customer convenience rather than a safety issue when the engineers failed to recognise that the switch problems would lead to non-deployment of the airbag.[95] This led to a lack of urgency about its resolution.

---

83   Anton R Valukas, 'Report to Board of Directors of General Motors Company Regarding Ignition Switch Recalls' (Valukas Report) (2014) 51. This report is written by a lawyer at an external law firm, Jenner & Block LLP, and was commissioned by the board in order to establish 'what happened, why it happened, and what GM should do to ensure it never happens again'. The report was designed also to focus on the extent of knowledge of senior executives and the board: Valukas Report 12. The investigation underlying the report was exhaustive: Valukas Report 12–15.

84   Ibid. 1.

85   As described by a GM employee in 2004: Valukas Report 62.

86   Ibid. 1.

87   Ibid.

88   Reuters, 'G.M. Settles 2 Cases Claiming Faulty Ignition Switches', *New York Times*, 5 September 2016.

89   David Shepardson, 'Recall Woes Follow GM Into New Year', *The Detroit News*, 1 January 2015.

90   Linda Sandler, 'GM Nine-Month Recall Costs Total $2.7 Billion on Repairs', Bloomberg Business, 27 October 2014 <www.bloomberg.com/news/articles/2014-10-27/gm-nine-month-recall-costs-total-2-7-billion-on-repairs>.

91   Ibid.

92   Valukas Report 50.

93   Ibid. 100. But also see Bill Vlasic, 'A Fatally Flawed Switch, and a Burdened G.M. Engineer', *New York Times*, 13 November 2014.

94   Valukas Report 50.

95   Valukas Report 2–3.

Information available to GM employees that could have rung alarm bells included:

- GM's own Technical Services Bulletins, issued in December 2005 and October 2006, warning of 'Inadvertent Turning of Key Cylinder, Loss of Electrical System';[96]
- a report from Trooper Young, Wisconsin State Patrol, correctly identifying that in a fatal crash the 'two front airbags did not deploy ... the ignition switch had somehow been turned from the run position to the accessory position prior to the collision';[97]
- media interest in ignition switch problems and non-deployments in May and June 2005[98] and November 2006;[99]
- a number of fatality cases involving non-deployment evaluated for settlement or otherwise brought to GM's attention in 2006 (5), in 2007 (3), in 2008 (2), in 2009 (2), in 2010 (1), in 2011(1); and
- warnings from the external counsel in fatality cases that punitive damages were a possibility due to the airbag's 'malfunction' (twice in 2010 and once in 2011).[100]

Despite these red flags, no GM employee took the problem seriously enough to take it to higher ranks, or even take effective steps to ensure that it was thoroughly investigated.[101] Nor did the board or senior management take effective steps to ensure that they would be made aware of problems such as these. Extraordinarily, the CEO and General Counsel only became aware of the issue in December 2013 and were not aware of the details of the problem until after the recall in January 2014.[102] The board too, while they received a number of high-level reports on various aspects of vehicle performance, were not briefed on the ignition switch until February 2014.[103]

Below board level, employees were negotiating a highly complex environment under extreme pressure as financial woes meant that GM was under existential threat. One effect of this was that cost became a primary focus.[104] The Valukas Report relates:

> Repeated throughout the interview process we heard from GM personnel two somewhat different directives 'when safety is at issue, cost is irrelevant' and 'cost is everything'.[105]

It is worth examining how those two messages collided.

Once the ignition switch issue was labelled as a 'customer convenience' issue, rather than a matter related to safety, cost became a paramount concern.[106]

---

96 Ibid. 114–5. There is no evidence that the Legal Department was aware of these Bulletins until 2012: Valukas Report 124.
97 Ibid. 117: the Report was saved in the Legal Department's electronic files but apparently not accessed by the lawyers.
98 Ibid. 7.
99 Ibid. 114.
100 Ibid. 140, 148.
101 Ibid. 4–11.
102 Ibid. 227.
103 Ibid. 244.
104 Paul L Walker, William G Shenkir and Thomas L Barton, 'Establish a risk challenge culture: All organizations must thoroughly examine their current operating environment and question how and how well they are prepared to face any kind of potential threat or disaster' (2015) 96(10) *Strategic Finance* 22, 27.
105 Valukas Report 249.
106 Ibid. 251.

The Valukas Report cites four cultural factors that inhibited a rapid identification of the problem and an appropriate response. First, there was a 'resistance to raising issues'. Employees described management attitudes and approaches that inhibited the identification of problems and, further, even if they were identified, the labelling of problems as safety matters. This included training staff to avoid clear language in written communication. So employees were faced with instructions to swap clear language for more equivocal terms: 'problem = issue, condition, matter'.[107] There was a belief that taking notes at important safety meetings was contrary to legal advice.[108]

The second cultural issue was a lack of accountability. The Report refers to the 'GM salute', where a person crosses their arms and points to others, indicating that accountability for something rests elsewhere, and the 'GM nod' where everyone agrees to a course of action at a meeting and then promptly leaves the room with no plan or sense of responsibility for implementation.[109]

The third issue was the failure to share information. While sufficient information about the problem was known to GM employees, no one person or work team held the information. This fragmentation and lack of communication between groups meant that even when individuals sought to investigate the issue they were unable to draw the information together and understand the big picture.

Finally, even when information about the problem was gathered, employees had an allegiance to determining a 'root cause' and solution before taking any steps of resolution. This commitment became a further cause of delay for years.[110] Inevitably, further lives would have been lost during this period.

14.3.3.2 Managing bad barrels

This example animates a number of aspects of the bad barrel theory. While there is no general sense that the individuals are corrupt or dishonest, collectively not one of the many employees who touched this matter identified or responded effectively and promptly to it. It is also notable that this is not the first ethical crisis of this type that has beset GM. Jennings and Tautman describe this as part of 'GM's history of problem cars'.[111] In fact, despite these previous experiences, wrestling with this problem was made more difficult by the way the organisation worked. Hurdles included the cost focus, discouragement of frank discussion, fragmentation, and lack of accountability. Most telling, however, was the way that the information flow about the issue to the board and senior management was entirely ineffective. While it is clear that, for an extended period, information about the issue was fragmented and incomplete, before the initiation of the recall that information crystallised. Yet the information is only conveyed to the CEO and General Counsel shortly before, and the board after, the recall.

There is a range of factors that contribute to the conduct of GM in this case. The cultural issues point out the importance of managing culture carefully. This is not an easy process. Key

---

107   Ibid. 254.
108   Ibid.
109   Ibid. 255.
110   Ibid. 258.
111   Jennings and Trautman. 'Ethical culture and legal liability: The GM switch crisis and lessons in governance' (2016) 192.

contributors to culture will be the ethics program – made up of the ethical policies and practices that are understood and accepted throughout the corporation, including, but not limited to, the code of conduct and the tone set by the board and senior management. Another aspect is the extent to which both the structures and culture inhibited the flow of critical information. Finally, incentives were created to cut costs, and these overshadowed the message of 'safety first'.

14.4 Mechanisms that regulate business ethics

As the preceding section illustrates, there is a range of ways in which unethical conduct can emerge. As noted above, the root causes of ethical problems can be attributed to individuals (bad apples), particular transactions (bad cases) or the corporation itself (bad barrels). There are also various ways that it can be addressed and discouraged. The law has long been accustomed to regulating individuals using a variety of mechanisms, including education, incentives, personal liability and criminal law. However, given that unethical conduct is not just a consequence of individual conduct, simply regulating individuals is insufficient. Corporations are an important part of the picture. The following discussion is focused on ways corporations can be regulated so as to discourage unethical conduct.

14.4.1 Legal consequences

Friedman argued that 'the basic rules of the society, both those embodied in law and those embodied in ethical custom' provide an appropriate check on corporate activity.[112] In fact according to his analysis these 'basic' rules and the markets are the only legitimate mechanisms for controlling corporate activity. The view that the corporation should abide by the general law is widely, though not universally, accepted. Interestingly, there is a line of argument in the US, underpinned by sacrosanct following of the shareholder primacy theory, that directors and management only have a duty to comply with the law where the consequent penalty to the shareholders exceeds the benefit.[113] This would not be the position in Australia, where directors and officers can breach their duty of care if the corporation under their direction fails to comply with the law.[114] Directors or 'high managerial' agents could also potentially breach the *Criminal Code Act 1995* (Cth) if they 'intentionally, knowingly or recklessly carried out the relevant conduct, or expressly, tacitly or impliedly authorised or permitted' an offence under the Criminal Code,[115] or the corporation's culture 'directed, encouraged, tolerated or led to non-compliance with the relevant provision'.[116] The Code defines corporate culture as:

---

112   Friedman, 'The Social Responsibility of Business is to Increase its Profits', 13 September 1970.
113   Frank H Easterbrook and Daniel R Fischel, 'The proper role of a target's management in responding to a tender offer' (1981) 94(6) *Harvard Law Review* 1161, 1192–4. See also Kent Greenfield, *The Failure of Corporate Law* (University of Chicago Press, 2008) 73–4.
114   See, for example, *Corporations Act 2001* (Cth) s 180.
115   *Criminal Code Act 1995* (Cth) s 12.3(2)(a) and (b).
116   Ibid. s 12.3(2)(c).

an attitude, policy, rule, course of conduct or practice existing within the body corporate generally or in the part of the body corporate in which the relevant activities take place.[117]

In addition, persons, including professional advisers, can be subject to accessorial liability under s 79 of the *Corporations Act 2001* (Cth) where they 'aided, abetted, counselled or procured', induced or were 'knowingly involved in' a contravention of the Corporations Act.[118] This regulation, therefore, attempts to address the possibility of bad apples, bad cases and bad barrels.

It will not always be the case that unethical conduct is also illegal. However, ethical breaches that also breach the law may have particularly profound implications. Where unethical conduct is also illegal there is a possibility that the corporation might be subjected to some form of legal consequence. For example, the corporation may be subjected to criminal or civil penalties, there could be harm to the company's reputation, and employees and officers may be subjected to sanctions.[119]

The legal risk associated with illegal conduct has focused attention on legal compliance as a key governance function. The G20/OECD *Principles of Corporate Governance* states that a key function of the board is:

> ensuring the integrity of the corporation's accounting and financial reporting systems, including the independent audit, and that appropriate systems of control are in place, in particular, systems for risk management, financial and operational control, and *compliance with the law and relevant standards*. (emphasis added)[120]

The ASX *CG Principles and Recommendations* is less forthright, but relevantly advises that 'Acting ethically and responsibly goes well beyond mere compliance with legal obligations', and recommends that each entity 'establish a sound risk management framework'.[121]

14.4.2 Market mechanisms

In theory the market should provide a powerful check on the unethical conduct of companies where investors are wary of regulatory fallout or of the potential for shares to diminish in value as a consequence of the misconduct. That is, investors should react negatively to shares that have an underlying unreported revenue problem, like that evident in the HIH scenario, or as Enron used special purpose vehicles deceptively to shore up their share price. Those investors should sell their shares, causing the share price to drop and thereby making the company an attractive prospect for takeovers and bringing the reign of management to an end. Should it operate effectively, the market for corporate control and the market for management could provide significant checks. This could therefore place pressure on both the corporation as a whole, and the individuals within it, to do the 'right thing', thus addressing both bad apple and bad barrel possibilities.

117   Ibid. s 12.3(6).
118   See, for example, *Australian Securities and Investments Commission v Somerville* (2009) 77 NSWLR 110.
119   For further discussion of the existing possibilities, see Senate Economic References Committee, '"Lifting the fear and suppressing the greed": Penalties for white-collar crime and corporate and financial misconduct in Australia' (2017) Ch 2.
120   G20/OECD, *Principles of Corporate Governance* (2015) 49.
121   ASX, *CG Principles and Recommendations* (2014) 19, 28.

As Kent Greenfield explains:

> Perhaps the most important market protection for shareholders is the large and relatively efficient capital market, which rapidly incorporates information about a company into the prices for that firm's securities. If corporate management pursues actions that harm investors, the price of the firm's securities will fall in the capital market. The efficient market also allows investors to sell their interest in firms whenever they hear that managers are failing to maximize profits. The liquidity of the security means that existing shareholders can dispose of their security before they suffer significant harm because of the managers' actions. Potential shareholders are protected as well, since (unless there is fraud) the price of a firm's security will more or less reflect the management's diligence in maximizing returns to shareholders. If management is inefficient, the share price will likely be less than what it would be under efficient management. This will make a takeover of the company cheaper and more likely. Because takeovers usually result in a change in management, a manager who wants to keep her job will work to maintain a high share price.[122]

There are, however, considerable hurdles that can prevent these mechanisms from operating in the way described above. First, the information that could signal to investors that the corporation is compromised may not be publicly available, or sufficiently accessible. Even where the disclosure system is working, where fraud is involved, considerable efforts may be made to conceal the fraudulent activity from scrutiny. Disclosure is also a noisy system, so while critical information may well be disclosed, there is no guarantee that it will be noticed and or acted on in any systematic way. Second, the kind of conduct that might prompt investor action is only a portion of the possible unethical conduct in which corporations could engage. Some unethical conduct may appear to be, at least in the short term, in the interests of shareholders. Accordingly, conduct that promotes or appears to promote shareholder wealth in unethical or illegal ways, such as the LIBOR activity or the ignition switch, may not be subject to disclosure, but also may not, even if revealed, prompt shareholder exit.

14.4.3 Disclosure

Disclosure, as a regulatory technique, had its birth alongside incorporation legislation itself, featuring in the 'first general incorporation act', the *Joint Stock Companies Act 1844* (UK).[123] It gained further momentum in the reforms introduced in the US in the wake of the Depression.[124] Then, as now, its aims were to:

> improve the functioning of the securities markets by providing to investors the information they needed to evaluate the merits of a potential investment. Moreover, although this goal was distinctly secondary, it was also recognized that disclosure would help to deter fraud and self dealing.[125]

---

122   Greenfield, *The Failure of Corporate Law* (2008) 49.
123   Paul Redmond, *Company and Securities Law: Commentary and Materials* (Lawbook, 5th ed, 2009) 38.
124   Securities Act of 1933 and the Securities Exchange Act of 1934.
125   Russell B Stevenson, *Corporations and Information: Secrecy, Access and Disclosure* (Johns Hopkins University Press, 1980) 80.

Over time, a third aim became evident as disclosure requirements were widened beyond matters related to the proper functioning of the securities market. That is, disclosure was used for 'influencing a wide range of corporate primary behavior that has only the most tenuous connection with the securities market'.[126] In Australia, it remains a key strategy for discouraging unethical conduct, exposing corporate activity to scrutiny and addressing the information asymmetry of investors and creditors. The use of disclosure to shape ethical outcomes is also an approach that is taken transnationally. The G20/OECD *Principles of Corporate Governance* states:

> In addition to their commercial objectives, companies are encouraged to disclose policies and performance relating to business ethics, the environment and, where material to the company, social issues, human rights and other public policy commitments. Such information may be important for certain investors and other users of information to better evaluate the relationship between companies and the communities in which they operate and the steps that companies have taken to implement their objectives.[127]

This suggests that social and ethical disclosure extending beyond financial matters could be relevant to investor choices. This could then encourage companies to act ethically in order to attract investor funds.

All corporations are subject to disclosure requirements, with listed companies subject to the most extensive obligations. These requirements are rationalised as the corollary of limited liability. As stated by RP Austin and IM Ramsay, 'Proper financial record keeping and public disclosure of financial information are normally justified as the price to be paid for the privilege of limited liability.'[128] The effectiveness of the disclosure regime is often questioned. For creditors to absorb financial disclosure requires commitment and investment of time. This is only likely to occur in the case of large creditors, who arguably could bargain for the access to the information in any event or protect themselves through security arrangements.[129] Disclosure is more likely to be of moment for investors, but even then the density of the information provided and the marginal commitment of many investors constitute considerable hurdles.

Nevertheless, the commitment to disclosure has been evident in Australia since the 1970s[130] and it was substantially reinforced in the period following the excesses of the 1980s, by the *Corporate Law Reform Act 1994* (Cth). Under the Corporations Act all companies must provide basic information to the corporate regulator, including the details of their officeholders and their registered office.[131] Large proprietary companies and public companies must provide a financial report,[132] a directors' report[133] and an auditor report[134] each financial year. Specific disclosure requirements are triggered should a corporation embark on

---

126   Ibid. 82.
127   G20/OECD, *Principles of Corporate Governance* (2015) 38–9.
128   RP Austin and IM Ramsay, *Ford, Austin and Ramsay's Principles of Corporations Law* (LexisNexis, 16th ed, 2015) 774; see also Redmond, *Company and Securities Law: Commentary and Materials* (2009) 38.
129   Austin and Ramsay, *Ford, Austin and Ramsay's Principles of Corporations Law* (2015) 775.
130   Ibid.
131   *Corporations Act 2001* (Cth) ss 201L, 142, 146.
132   Ibid. s 292.
133   Ibid. s 299.
134   Ibid. ss 301, 307A, 308(a) and (b).

fundraising or in connection with a takeover. Additionally, the continuous disclosure regime applies to listed companies (disclosing entities[135]). Under this framework listed companies are required (by s 674 and the Listing Rules) to disclose to the ASX immediately any information of which they are, or become, aware that a reasonable person might expect to have a material effect on the price or value of the entity's securities.[136] Carve-outs contained in Listing Rule 3.1A indicate that disclosure is not required where it would be a breach of law to disclose the information or the information is related to an incomplete proposal, matters of supposition, insufficiently definite, generated for internal management or is a trade secret, provided also that it is confidential and a reasonable person would not expect it to be disclosed.[137]

The consequences of a failure to disclose can be profound. Disclosure regulation generally relies on compelling a proper process for disclosure. That is, provided the discloser can establish that they adhered to a proper process in determining the information to be disclosed, they will have satisfied their obligations, even if the information turns out to be inaccurate.[138] Generally, persons involved in a contravention of the disclosure regime will contravene a civil penalty provision, and also commit a criminal offence.[139] For directors and officers, a failure to comply with any of the disclosure requirements could also be a breach of their duty of care and diligence under s 180 and the equivalent common law duty.[140] Again this seems to cover the bad apple and bad barrel options.

14.4.4 Gatekeepers

A number of scholars have considered the role that professional experts, or 'gatekeepers', play in preventing unethical conduct by corporations. Gatekeeper theory suggests that professionals, such as lawyers, securities analysts, auditors, credit ratings agencies, and investment bankers,[141] who sign off or provide necessary consent to corporate activity, thereby vouch for the legitimacy of their client's activity. According to the theory, should the gatekeeper detect fraudulent or unethical conduct, they are incentivised to intervene to prevent such conduct, or to refuse to act, in order to protect their reputation. No single client is worth risking a hard-won reputation lost by colluding or consenting to unethical or illegal conduct.

John Coffee Jr defines a corporate gatekeeper as:

> an agent who acts as a reputational intermediary to assure investors as to the quality of the 'signal' sent by the corporate issuer. The reputational intermediary does so by lending or 'pledging' its reputational capital to the corporation, thus enabling investors or the market to rely on the corporation's own disclosures or assurances where they otherwise might not.[142]

135   A listed disclosing entity is one that is listed and has issued 'enhanced disclosure securities'. This includes securities that are permitted to be traded on a prescribed financial market: *Corporations Act 2001* (Cth) ss 111AD, 111AE, 111AL and 111AM.
136   ASX Listing Rule 3.1.
137   ASX Listing Rule 3.1A.
138   Leif Gamertsfelder, *Corporate Information and the Law* (LexisNexis, 2013) 102.
139   *Corporations Act 2001* (Cth) ss 674(2), 1317E(1) and 1311(1).
140   See, for example, *Australian Securities and Investments Commission v Healey* (2011) 196 FCR 291.
141   John C Coffee Jr, *Gatekeepers: The Professions and Corporate Governance* (OUP, 2006) 1.
142   Ibid. 2.

According to this definition, the gatekeeper has an incentive to identify and prevent wrongdoing because its later revelation has the potential to harm his or her reputation. Reinier Kraakman first proposed that 'gatekeepers' could provide a check on corporate activity in the 1980s. He saw gatekeepers as supplementing the regulation that discourages corporations and their managements from misconduct. The central aspect of this concept is a duty imposed 'on private "gatekeepers" to prevent misconduct by withholding support'.[143]

While gatekeeper activity holds some promise as a way of monitoring and responding to corporate misconduct, it is by no means a comprehensive solution. The focus on reputation and its protection as the key motivator for effective gatekeeper action has been challenged as insufficient, and increased gatekeeper liability has been proposed as a means of providing further incentives for gatekeeper action.[144] The other aspect of the definition is that it identifies the gatekeeper's remit as related to the 'corporation's own disclosures or assurances'. Coffee also states that the gatekeeper provides 'certification or verification services' to investors.[145] The focus is, therefore, on a narrow band of activity where the gatekeeper's reputation is on the line or where a transaction requires gatekeeper consent or cooperation. That is, where there is public verification of corporate activity by a gatekeeper. This means that the reputation of the gatekeeper is only called into question in certain types of transactions. If the theory were to apply to matters beyond these transactions, the gatekeeper would have to be sensitive to reputational damage in these contexts. That is, the gatekeeper would have to be incentivised to decline to act or to offer resistance where corporate activity was unethical beyond the financial arena.

Moreover, the continued existence of corporate fraud suggests that gatekeeper failure is a problem. In his masterly analysis of the excesses of the Australian corporations in the 1980s, Trevor Sykes colourfully describes the way the 'professions prostituted themselves – with the odd notable exception – to the bold riders'.[146] As Roger Crampton highlights, 'compliant lawyers as well as greedy executives, lazy directors and malleable accountants are necessary for large corporate frauds to come to life and persist long enough to cause major harm'.[147] Coffee attributes these failures to four factors. First, agency problems within gatekeeper firms that make acquiescence with the client make sense to individuals or teams; second, market failures that mean gatekeepers are not operating in sufficiently competitive markets; third, a decline in the value of gatekeeper reputation; and, finally, reduced litigation.[148] Reflecting on the failure of gatekeepers before the Enron failure, Sean Griffith noted that the 'responsibility of lawyers for the current crisis may arise from tensions in their dual role as gatekeepers and

---

143   Reinier H Kraakman, 'Gatekeepers: The anatomy of a third-party enforcement strategy' (1986) 2(1) *Journal of Law, Economics, and Organization* 53, 54.

144   See, for example, Frank Partnoy, 'Strict liability for gatekeepers: A reply to Professor Coffee' (2004) 84 *Boston University Law Review* 365; John C Coffee Jr, 'Gatekeeper failure and reform: The challenge of fashioning relevant reforms' (2004) 84 *Boston University Law Review* 301.

145   Coffee, *Gatekeepers: The Professions and Corporate Governance* (2006) 2.

146   Trevor Sykes, *The Bold Riders behind Australia's Corporate Collapses* (Allen & Unwin, 2nd ed, 1996) 575.

147   Roger C Crampton, 'Enron and the corporate lawyer: A primer on legal and ethical issues' (2002) 58 *The Business Lawyer* 143, 144.

148   Coffee, *Gatekeepers: The Professions and Corporate Governance* (2006) 6.

transaction engineers'. Their roles as 'authors' of corporate transactions may weaken their structural independence, as they are asked to sit in judgment on their own work.[149]

Despite the potential for gatekeeper failure, and the fact that gatekeepers will not be relevant in all areas of corporate endeavour, the role of the gatekeeper is an important one in the context of ethical conduct. Gatekeepers such as lawyers and accountants are committed to professional codes of ethics.[150] They are in a privileged position in that they can have information about problem transactions in advance, at a point when the course of action can be changed. In the boardroom, the prevalence of independent board members may mean that gatekeepers are particularly important as board advisers.[151] In addition, gatekeepers can provide a regulatory option that does not rely on state regulators, thus extending the regulatory reach in a context where resources are tight and remit is broad.

14.4.5 Whistleblowers

Whistleblowing is influentially defined as the 'disclosure by organization members (former and current) of illegal, immoral and illegitimate practices under the control of their employers to persons or organizations that may be able to effect action'.[152] The support and protection of whistleblowers has garnered significant regulatory attention in recent decades. This was founded in the post-war focus on the power and rights of the individual,[153] but is now anchored in the potential for whistleblowers to extend the regulatory ability of the state to respond to negative conduct. According to Ashley Savage and Richard Hyde, 'Modern governance relies on decentred regulatory networks, and these networks involve whistleblowers.'[154]

In the corporate sphere, the G20/OECD *Principles of Corporate Governance* endorses the significance of whistleblowing. It recommends that the responsibility for encouraging whistleblowing should rest with the board:

> In fulfilling its control oversight responsibilities it is important for the board to encourage the reporting of unethical/unlawful behaviour without fear of retribution. The existence of a company code of ethics should aid this process, which should be underpinned by legal protection for the individuals concerned. A contact point for employees who wish to report concerns about unethical or illegal behaviour that might also compromise the integrity of financial statements should be offered by the audit committee or by an ethics committee or equivalent body.[155]

In Australia, the ASX Corporate Governance Council recommends that listed companies have a Code of Conduct to '[i]dentify the measures the organisation follows to encourage the reporting

---

149   Griffith, 'Afterword and comment: Towards an ethical duty to market investors' (2003) 1225.
150   See, for example, Law Society of South Australia, *Australian Solicitors Conduct Rules* (2014).
151   Coffee, *Gatekeepers: The Professions and Corporate Governance* (2006) 7–8.
152   J Near and Marcia P Miceli, 'Organizational dissidence: The case of whistle-Blowing' (1985) 4(1) *Journal of Business Ethics* 4.
153   Robert Vaughn, *The Successes and Failures of Whistleblowing Laws* (Edward Elgar, 2012); see also Ashley Savage and Richard Hyde, 'The response to whistleblowing by regulators: A practical perspective' (2015) 35(3) *Legal Studies* 408, 409–10.
154   Savage and Hyde, 'The response to whistleblowing by regulators' (2015) 408.
155   G20/OECD, *Principles of Corporate Governance* (2015) 49.

of unlawful or unethical behaviour' and 'include a reference to how the organisation protects "whistleblowers" who report violations in good faith'.[156] Companies themselves are increasingly appreciating the risk management potential associated with formalising channels for, and protection of, whistleblowers.[157]

The key elements of the whistleblowing process are that there is a disclosure by an insider with special knowledge of wrongdoing to a party capable of intervention. The kind of wrongdoing that is contemplated is drawn broadly, to include conduct beyond, but encompassing, illegal conduct. AJ Brown has suggested defining whistleblowers to include those with a 'special relationship such as to mean that their disclosure comes "from within"'.[158] In addition to current employees and officers, this would include former employees and contractors. From a regulatory perspective, these parties have the potential to address the informational disadvantage of the regulator by providing inside knowledge, while the regulator can provide the heft necessary to respond to the wrongdoing.

While the legislative recognition of the significance of whistleblowers in Australia has a way to go, it has gained some momentum in both the corporate and the public sector. For the public sector, the enactment of the *Public Interest Disclosure Act 2013* (Cth) was a significant milestone. This Act drew on the similarly named UK legislation to provide protection for public servants making certain disclosures.[159] In addition, each state has enacted some whistleblowing legislation.[160]

The Corporations Act offers some protection for whistleblowers in sections 1317AA–AE. These provisions only protect officers, employees, those with contracts for the supply of goods or services to the company, or those employed by a person who has a supply contract.[161] The Part 9.4AAA formula potentially excludes those who have reason to interact with the company without a formal contractual relationship or office with the company. Those who self-protect by moving on to a new position before whistleblowing will not be covered. Those who discover wrongdoing while employed by, or contracted with, related companies would also be vulnerable to sanction if they disclose.

The nature of the wrongdoing is also significant. Protection is extended to the whistleblower who has reasonable grounds to suspect a breach of the Corporations Act and the ASIC Act, or an attempt, incitement or conspiracy to breach the law. This can be contrasted with the protection provided by the *Public Interest Disclosure Act 2013* (Cth) definition of 'disclosable conduct', which has been described as 'broad to the point of all-encompassing'.[162] Similarly, the *Banking Act 1959* (Cth) provides a more inclusive regime, stating that disclosure of

156   ASX, *CG Principles and Recommendations* (2014) 20.
157   Janine Pascoe and Michelle Welsh, 'Whistleblowing, ethics and corporate culture: Theory and practice in Australia' (2011) 40 *Common Law World Review* 144, 147.
158   AJ Brown, 'Restoring sunshine to the Sunshine State: Priorities for whistleblowing law reform in Queensland' (2009) 18(3) *Griffith Law Review* 666, 684.
159   *Public Interest Disclosure Act 1998* (UK).
160   Terry Morehead Dworkin and AJ Brown, 'The money or the media? Lessons from contrasting developments in US and Australian whistleblowing laws' (2013) 11 *Seattle Journal for Social Justice* 653, 691–3.
161   *Corporations Act 2001* (Cth) s 1317AA(1)(a).
162   AJ Brown, 'Towards "ideal" whistleblowing legislation? Some lessons from recent Australian experience' (2013) 2 *E-Journal of International and Comparative Labour Studies* 4, 13.

possible misconduct or an improper state of affairs and a belief that the information could assist the recipient in the performance of their duties is enough.[163]

The Corporations Act regime requires that the whistleblower act in good faith.[164] The aim of this limitation appears to be to discourage false or misleading disclosures. However, such disclosures would seemingly already be discouraged by provisions that require the whistleblower to have 'reasonable grounds to suspect'[165] and the criminal offence that might be committed if a person knowingly provided false or misleading information to ASIC.[166] The whistleblower must also provide his or her name in advance of the information.[167] This assists investigation of the wrongdoing, but also has the potential to exclude a poorly advised whistleblower providing information in good faith about what appears to be a 'technicality'. The process embraced by the Corporations Act is to require that the disclosure be made to ASIC, the directors or senior officers within the corporation, and the auditor or a member of the audit team.[168] Should the whistleblower be able to meet these requirements, they will gain immunity from civil and criminal prosecution,[169] protection from victimisation[170] and the right to seek compensation if victimisation occurs.[171]

Australia's private whistleblower protections have been scrutinised and found wanting in a review of whistleblower laws across the G20.[172] The recommendations for Australia include extending the definition of 'whistleblower', and strengthening protections. The whistleblower provisions in the Corporations Act are currently under review, with a Treasury consultation paper released on 16 December 2016. Areas highlighted for consultation include the definition of 'whistleblower' and the kinds of disclosures that qualify for protection, the value of the good faith limitation, anonymous disclosures, the parties to whom disclosures may be made, protection arrangements and financial rewards.[173] Dana Gold has argued, in the US context, that creating:

> A comprehensive legal scheme that protects all private employees who blow the whistle on any violation of law or policy and that required employers to investigate and resolve the concerns raised by whistleblowers would radically alter the troubling status quo. Responsibility for corporate legal compliance would shift, both culturally and legally, from the backs of vulnerable employees with literally everything to lose to the corporations themselves.[174]

---

163   *Banking Act 1959* (Cth) s 52A(2)(c).
164   *Corporations Act 2001* (Cth) s 1317AA(1)(e).
165   Ibid. s 1317AA(1)(d).
166   *Criminal Code Act 1995* (Cth) s 137.1.
167   *Corporations Act 2001* (Cth) s 1317AA(1)(d), cf *Public Interest Disclosure Act 2013* (Cth) s 28(2).
168   *Corporations Act 2001* (Cth) s 1317AA(1)(b).
169   Ibid. s 1317AB.
170   Ibid. s 1317AC.
171   Ibid. s 1317AD.
172   Simon Wolfe, Mark Worth, Suelette Dreyfus and AJ Brown, *Whistleblower Protection Laws in G20 Countries: Priorities for Action* (Melbourne University, Griffith University, Blueprint for Free Speech, Transparency International Australia, 2014).
173   Department of the Treasury, *Review of Tax and Corporate Whistleblower Protections in Australia*, Consultation Paper, 16 December 2016. The consultation period concluded on 10 February 2017.
174   Dana L Gold, 'Whistleblowers: The Critical Link in Accountability' in Stephen Tully (ed.), *Research Handbook on Corporate Legal Responsibility* (Edward Elgar, 2005) 267.

While there appears to be a commitment to reform of current arrangements, there is clearly some distance to go before Australia embraces such an approach.[175]

14.5 Organisation-level approaches

In addition to the mechanisms for discouraging unethical conduct by corporations discussed above, elements within corporations will have profound effects on the way those interacting with, or working within, corporations see, understand and respond to ethical problems.

14.5.1 Leadership

Edgar H Schein sees leadership as critical to any organisation's culture.[176] He argues that there are 'six primary embedding mechanisms' that a leader can use to influence an organisation's culture: attention, reaction to crises, allocation of resources, role modelling, rewards and status, and criteria for selection and dismissal.[177] Bob Garratt also focuses on leadership, with a particular emphasis on the role of the board. He notes:

> It is the board's job to ensure sufficient numbers of members [of the organization] are pointing in the same direction, committed to a common purpose, with similar values and behaviours, so that the organization can function effectively and efficiently.[178]

Ronald R Sims and Johannes Brinkmann argue that 'issues that capture the attention of the leader (i.e. what is criticized, praised or asked about) will also capture the attention of the greater organization and will become the focus of the employees'. In the GM case study a management focus on costs dominated the professed commitment to safety.[179] In Enron the focus was on the bottom line.[180]

Similarly, the reaction of leadership to a crisis can be a powerful indicator of ethical values.[181] In HIH, the reaction of Williams to the challenge posed by the discussions between the auditor and some directors and the relaying of concerns by directors indicated a level of intolerance of constructive dissent. Relatedly, the modelling of ethical conduct by leadership can be significant to those observing it. The seeming acquiescence by leadership to the LIBOR manipulation, including by the Bank of England, provided a powerful example to more junior employees: 'Employees often emulate leaders' behavior and look to the leaders for cues to appropriate behavior'.[182] So at Enron, when the CEO 'bragged about Enron's sophisticated controls but undermined them at every turn',[183] it encouraged others to do the same.

---

175   For a discussion of some recent international and Australian developments regarding whistleblowing, see Jim Apollo Mathiopoulos, Katrina Hogan and Jean J du Plessis, 'Whistleblowing reforms: A critical analysis of the current law and the new "bells and whistles" proposed' (2017) 35(3) C&SLJ.
176   Edgar H Schein, *Organizational Culture and Leadership* (Jossey-Bass, 4th ed, 2010) 219.
177   Ibid.; see also Ronald R Sims and Johannes Brinkmann, 'Enron ethics (or: culture matters more than codes)' (2003) 45(3) *Journal of Business Ethics* 243.
178   Bob Garratt, *The Fish Rots from the Head: The Crisis in Our Boardrooms: Developing the Crucial Skills of the Competent Director* (Profile, 2003) xxix.
179   Valukas Report 249.
180   Sims and Brinkmann, 'Enron ethics (or: culture matters more than codes)' (2003) 247.
181   Ibid. 247.
182   Ibid. 247.
183   Bethany McLean and Peter Elkind, *The Smartest Guys in the Room: The Amazing Rise and Scandalous Fall of Enron* (Portfolio, 2004) 114.

The allocation of resources, rewards and punishments and the criteria for selection and dismissal are also critical: 'Reward systems can ... become unfair and, therefore, increase the likelihood of unethical conduct by tending to politicise the compensation and promotion system.'[184] For example, the significance of LIBOR manipulation for promotion indicated to employees that rule-breaking was accepted. In Enron, the 'rank and yank' performance review system placed employees in the bottom 15 per cent under extreme pressure to perform, while also rewarding those who broke the rules to get ahead.[185]

14.5.2 Corporate culture

Corporate culture is attracting considerable attention. Speaking in 2016, Greg Medcraft, the chairman of the Australian Securities and Investments Commission, defined corporate culture as 'a set of shared values and assumptions within an organisation. It reflects the underlying 'mindset of an organisation', the 'unwritten rules'.[186] For ASIC, the significance of culture is that:

> poor culture can be a driver of poor conduct – and we regulate conduct. Bad conduct can flourish, proliferate and may even be rewarded in a poor culture. A good culture, on the other hand, can help uncover and inhibit bad conduct and reward and encourage good conduct.[187]

This emphasis from the Australian regulator is not unusual. Corporate culture has become the 'focus of attention in the business media and is a topic of discussion in corporate board rooms'.[188] This focus is also backed by empirical study. So, for example, Muel Kaptein found that 'the ethical culture of work groups has a negative relationship with the frequency of observed unethical behavior within work groups'.[189] In his study:

> Six of the eight dimensions of ethical culture that were tested had a negative relationship with observed unethical behavior. These dimensions are: ethical role modeling of management, ethical role modeling of supervisors, capability to behave ethically, commitment to behave ethically, openness to discuss ethical issues, and reinforcement of ethical behavior.[190]

For some scholars concerned with ethical conduct in particular, the weight is given to the 'ethical climate ... [as] one component of the organizational culture'.[191] In this literature a

---

184   Lynne Dallas, 'Enron and Ethical Corporate Climates' in Nancy Rapoport, Jeffrey Van Neil and Bala Dharan (eds), *Enron and Other Corporate Fiascos: The Corporate Scandal Reader* (Foundation Press, 2nd ed, 2009) 158.
185   Duane Windsor, 'Business Ethics at the Crooked E' in Rapoport, Neil and Dharan (eds), *Enron and Other Corporate Fiascos: The Corporate Scandal Reader* (2009) 139.
186   Greg Medcraft, 'The Importance of Corporate Culture in Improving Governance and Compliance', Speech, Challenger Legal and Corporate Affairs team offsite, Sydney (28 July 2016).
187   Ibid.
188   Jerome Want, *Corporate Culture: Illuminating the Black Hole* (St Martin's Press, 2006) 3.
189   Muel Kaptein, 'Understanding unethical behavior by unraveling ethical culture' (2011) 64(6) *Human Relations* 843, 858.
190   Ibid. 843.
191   Bahram Soltani, 'The anatomy of corporate fraud: A comparative analysis of high profile American and European corporate scandals' (2014) 120 *Journal of Business Ethics* 251, 254.

distinction is drawn between ethical culture and ethical climate. For example, Muel Kaptein explains that 'ethical climate is substantive in that it pertains to the content of ethical and unethical behavior, whereas ethical culture is procedural in that it pertains to the conditions for ethical and unethical behavior'.[192] Lynne Dallas describes 'climate' as 'the ethical meaning attached by employees to organizational policies, practices and procedures'.[193] It is certainly plausible that culture, including as it does norms of conduct, written and unwritten rules and expectations, will be correlated with the attitudes that make up the ethical climate within a corporation. That is, a culture that creates the conditions for ethical conduct is likely to have values and perceptions consistent with that and vice versa.

Reflecting on the bad apples, cases and barrels discussion above, it is plausible that culture could have a positive or negative impact on all three. Haines, in her work exploring worker deaths, draws a contrast between two types of culture. She finds that 'At the core of each culture was the understanding of how to achieve "success" as an organization.'[194] She describes the 'virtuous' culture and 'blinkered' culture in a safety context by explaining how a virtuous culture was able to combine safety concerns with business priorities whereas the blinkered culture saw them as oppositional.[195] As Dallas explains, 'the corporation itself creates a social environment that can increase or decrease the likelihood of ethical decision-making'.[196]

14.5.3 Codes of conduct

In 2017, the CEO of QBE, a large Australian insurance company, reportedly took a $550,000 pay cut for breaching the company's executive code of conduct by failing to advise the board of a personal relationship with a company employee immediately.[197] Corporate codes of conduct, such as the one that proved so costly for the QBE chief executive, have become common elements of the ethical infrastructure of large corporations. Moreover, beyond the individual corporation, there are a variety of supra-corporate and sector codes that seek to shape corporate conduct in positive ways.[198] The G20/OECD *Principles of Corporate Governance* recommends that 'Companies are also well advised to establish and ensure the effectiveness of internal controls, ethics, and compliance programmes or measures to comply with applicable laws, regulations, and standards.'[199] Corporate codes of conduct have also been given regulatory impetus through a variety of regulatory instruments in a number of jurisdictions.[200] Nonetheless, there remain significant questions about their effectiveness. The

192   Kaptein, 'Understanding unethical behavior by unraveling ethical culture' (2011) 846.
193   Lynne Dallas, 'Enron and Ethical Corporate Climates' in Rapoport, Neil and Dharan (eds), *Enron and Other Corporate Fiascos: The Corporate Scandal Reader* (2009) 157–8.
194   Fiona Haines, *Corporate Regulation: Beyond Punish or Persuade* (Clarendon Press, 1997) 99.
195   Ibid. 97–9.
196   Dallas, 'Enron and Ethical Corporate Climates' in Rapoport, Neil and Dharan (eds), *Enron and Other Corporate Fiascos: The Corporate Scandal Reader* (2009) 155.
197   Christine Lacey, 'QBE CEO John Neal takes $550,000 pay cut over 'personal decisions'", *The Australian*, 27 February 2017.
198   See, for example, the Ethical Trading Initiative, Base Code <www.ethicaltrade.org/resources/eti-base-code>; UN Global Compact, 'The Global Compact: Nine Principles' <www.unglobalcompact .org/system/attachments/7618/original/Zenith.pdf?1282019232>.
199   G20/OECD, *Principles of Corporate Governance* (2015) 50.
200   See, for example, *Sarbanes-Oxley Act of 2002* (US) s 406; ASX, *CG Principles and Recommendations* (2014) Recommendation 3.1; US Federal Sentencing Guidelines for Organizations.

example of Enron is often cited as indicating that the presence of a lengthy and detailed code of conduct does not necessarily mean that ethical conduct is observed.[201] More persuasively, a meta-analysis of empirical studies fails to shore up the case for the effectiveness of these codes.[202]

Joshua Newberg defines corporate codes of conduct as follows:

> The typical CCOE of a large public company is a hybrid that combines some general statements of the firm's commitment to broadly expressed normative formulations of principled business conduct – such as acting with 'integrity', or adherence to 'the highest ethical standards' – with a number of specific pronouncements or rules addressing discrete areas of unlawful and/or unethical conduct.[203]

Codes have both an internal and external aspect. As Josef Wieland explains, 'When firms design an explicit code of ethics, they are attempting to transform moral ambiguity in their environment into organizational self-commitment by rules and values.'[204] They can provide a framework for existing employees, and can be used to explain corporate expectations to new employees.[205] As such they can be used to manage bad apple conduct, as well as having a more general application. They can reduce the risk of organisational chaos and enhance the likelihood that a large organisation will work consistently even where it is geographically separated. They can also signal to outsiders the organisation's commitment to ethical conduct.

The challenge for the code of conduct approach is that simply writing a code is insufficient. Michael Deck notes that 'of the 90% of companies that have codes, only 28% do any training'.[206] Following his empirical study, Kaptein advised that corporations should 'adopt at least eight components in the following sequence: a code; training and communication; accountability policies; monitoring and auditing; investigation and corrective policies; an ethics office(r); ethics report line; and incentive policies'.[207] Dallas highlights the:

> mission statement and code of ethics, the criteria for business decisions, the words and actions of leaders, the handling of conflicts of interest, the reward system, the guidance provided to employees concerning dealing with ethical issues, and the monitoring system.[208]

201   Joshua A Newberg, 'Corporate codes of ethics, mandatory disclosure, and the market for ethical conduct' (2005) 29 *Vermont Law Review* 253, 265.
202   Patrick M Erwin, 'Corporate codes of conduct: The effects of code content and quality on ethical performance' (2011) 99 *Journal of Business Ethics* 535, 536.
203   Newberg, 'Corporate codes of ethics, mandatory disclosure, and the market for ethical conduct' (2005) 258 (citations omitted).
204   Josef Wieland, 'The ethics of governance' (2001) 11(1) *Business Ethics Quarterly* 73, 81 (citations omitted).
205   Lutz Preuss, 'Codes of conduct in organisational context: From cascade to lattice-work of codes' (2010) 94 *Journal of Business Ethics* 471, 473.
206   Michael C Deck, 'Corporate Codes and Ethics Programs' in Laura P Hartman (ed.), *Perspectives in Business Ethics* (McGraw-Hill Irwin, 3rd ed, 2005) 250.
207   Muel Kaptein, 'The effectiveness of ethics programs: The role of scope, composition, and sequence' (2015) 132 *Journal of Business Ethics* 415, 429.
208   Dallas, 'Enron and Ethical Corporate Climates' in Rapoport, Neil and Dharan (eds), *Enron and Other Corporate Fiascos: The Corporate Scandal Reader* (2009) 139.

As this indicates, the code is only part of the picture. Codes of conduct are required by the general corporate governance codes of many countries, normally applying to listed companies and based on the 'comply or explain' principle. This 'soft law' approach has come under scrutiny in recent times,[209] but whether a more robust 'hard law' approach to the ethical conduct of corporations will be adopted is difficult to predict, as it is so difficult to define 'business ethics' (see Section 14.2.2 above). And legislation for 'corporate culture' is controversial too (see Section 14.5.2 above).

14.5.4 Structures

There is a connection between the way a corporation is structured and its culture. In the GM and the HIH case studies, structures appear to have significantly affected the way the corporations responded to their challenges. In GM, for example, the way information flowed was curtailed by the fragmentation of responsibilities across various committees and senior management were structurally distant from the information, concerns and efforts of employees. In HIH the structure of the audit committee and its relationship with the board, CEO and the external auditor inhibited its effectiveness.

At the board level, 'the first and primary obligation of a board should be to ensure that its structure and operation are of the highest standards for integrity'.[210] The importance of board structure is recognised in corporate governance codes. So, for example, the ASX *CG Principles and Recommendations* recommends that all corporations have audit, nomination and compensation committees. It also outlines the preferred membership of these committees and their areas of responsibility.

The issue of fragmentation of responsibility and information is more complex, but clearly has a structural aspect to it. The G20/OECD *Principles of Corporate Governance* entrusts the board with 'ensuring the integrity of the essential reporting and monitoring systems' and states that this 'will require the board to set and enforce clear lines of responsibility and accountability throughout the organisation'.[211]

14.5.5 Complaints handling

As was noted in the whistleblowing discussion above, there is an increased interest in the potential for whistleblowers to contribute to the risk management of corporations by alerting senior management and the board to problems and concerns. The way an organisation responds to complaints and concerns is a powerful indicator of their ethical culture. For example, the response of HIH to the concerns raised by directors indicated to others the likely reception of any complaints. Such conduct can only inhibit the free flow of information to those who have the power to address risks. The importance of having proper complaints management is emphasised in several key regulatory instruments.

---

209 See Jean J du Plessis and Chee Keong Low (eds), *Corporate Governance Codes for the 21st Century – International Perspectives and Critical Analyses* (Springer Verlag, 2017) <www.springer.com/br/book/9783319518671>.

210 Dawn-Marie Driscoll, 'Ethics and corporate governance: Lessons learned from a financial services model' (2001) 11(1) *Business Ethics Quarterly* 145.

211 G20/OECD, *Principles of Corporate Governance* (2015) 49.

The G20/OECD *Principles of Corporate Governance*, for example, highlights the need to provide avenues for complaints from employees and those external to the company to be made. It recommends that regulation be created to encourage boards to take this in hand:

> It is ... to the advantage of the company and its shareholders to establish procedures and safe-harbours for complaints by employees, either personally or through their representative bodies, and others outside the company, concerning illegal and unethical behaviour. The board should be encouraged by laws and or principles to protect these individuals and representative bodies and to give them confidential direct access to someone independent on the board, often a member of an audit or an ethics committee.[212]

The ASX *CG Principles and Recommendations* offers a gentle nudge in this direction, recommending that the corporation's Code of Conduct:

> identify the measures the organisation follows to encourage the reporting of unlawful or unethical behaviour. This might include a reference to how the organisation protects 'whistleblowers' who report violations in good faith.[213]

14.6 Conclusion

This chapter has explored the nature and significance of business ethics within the context of corporate governance. While difficult to define, business ethics can be seen at a macro level, with regard to the role of corporations in society, as well as at a micro level, in the way corporations operate. In order to unpack this further this chapter has used bad apples, bad cases and bad barrels as devices to explore the way ethical problems can arise, and analysed these with reference to three case studies: the HIH collapse, the LIBOR scandal and the GM ignition switch problem. These case studies reveal the complex interactions that preceded the relevant events. In each case it is possible to attribute the outcomes to a mix of structures, policies, shared understandings and practices that together make up the ethics of the organisation.

In order to 'reduce unethical behavior, management first needs to understand and unravel the existing ethical culture'.[214] This will involve scrutiny of the way external regulation affects the corporation, as well as understanding internal processes, policies, narratives and practices that inhibit or encourage ethical action. External influences including general law, market activity, disclosure, gatekeeper activity and whistleblower regulation are all considered to be mechanisms that may change the way corporations respond to ethical matters. Internally, those leading corporations have a profound effect on the way those within the corporation see and respond to ethical dilemmas. The culture of the organisation, incorporating structures, policies and practices, will also be highly influential.

There can be no doubt that the interaction of business ethics with corporate governance poses many challenges. However it also presents great opportunities. According to Tony Watson:

---

212   Ibid. 35.
213   ASX, *CG Principles and Recommendations* (2014) 20.
214   Kaptein, 'Understanding unethical behavior by unraveling ethical culture' (2011) 863.

Moralities are social constructions – guidelines for human action which people acting socially have devised to handle the problems of their existence in a contingent world. What we might try to do, therefore, as the inhabitants of organizations … is to come fully to terms with the extent of our interdependencies and set out to create a good world.[215]

While this points out the agency of those working within organisations, it is also evident that a similar challenge is posed to policy-makers, regulators, gatekeepers and community members.

---

215   Tony Watson, 'Ethical Codes and Moral Communities; the Gunlaw Temptation, the Simon Solution and the David Dilemma' in Martin Parker (ed.), *Ethics and Organizations* (Sage, 1998) 238, 267.

INDEX

Printed in the United States
by Baker & Taylor Publisher Services